Can You Hear My Pain Now? Making Pastoral Theology Relevant in a Modern World

Can You Hear My Pain Now? Making Pastoral Theology Relevant in a Modern World

Foreword by Dr. Gerald R. McDermott
Jordan-Trexler Professor of Religion, Roanoke College
Distinguished Senior Fellow, Baylor Institute for Studies of Religion
Research Associate, Jonathan Edwards Centre,
University of the Free State, South Africa

Introduction by Dr. Michael G. Maness
Managing Editor, *Testamentum Imperium*

Kevaughn Mattis
Founder and Director, *Testamentum Imperium*

www.PreciousHeart.net/ti

WIPF & STOCK · Eugene, Oregon

CAN YOU HEAR MY PAIN NOW?
Making Pastoral Theology Relevant in the Modern World

Copyright © 2022 Wipf and Stock Publishers. All rights reserved. Except for brief quotations in critical publications or reviews, no part of this book may be reproduced in any manner without prior written permission from the publisher. Write: Permissions, Wipf and Stock Publishers, 199 W. 8th Ave., Suite 3, Eugene, OR 97401.

Wipf & Stock
An Imprint of Wipf and Stock Publishers
199 W. 8th Ave., Suite 3
Eugene, OR 97401

www.wipfandstock.com

PAPERBACK ISBN: 978-1-6667-9849-4
HARDCOVER ISBN: 978-1-6667-9848-7
EBOOK ISBN: 978-1-6667-9847-0

We dedicate this book to all those souls who hurt
and to those who help the hurting soul,
all to the glory of God.

Blessed be the God and Father of our Lord Jesus Christ,
the Father of mercies and God of all comfort,
who comforts us in all our affliction,
so that we may be able to comfort those
who are in any affliction, with the comfort with
which we ourselves are comforted by God.

2 Corinthians 1:3–5, ESV

Contents

Contents vii
Foreword by Professor Gerald R. McDermott ix
Introduction by Rev. Dr. Michael G. Maness xi
Part One: Problem of Pastoral Theology 1
1. Can Pastoral Care Successfully Merge Secular Disciplines with
   Biblical Theology?
   Rev. Dr. Vasileios Thermos 2
2. Is Pastoral Theology Still Relevant in an Age of Modern Psychology?
   Dr. Taunya Marie Tinsley and Rev. Dr. Joan Prentice 13
3. A Correction of Pastoral Care that Overlooks the Most Vulnerable
   Dr. Nontando Hadebe 41
4. Religious Belief, Conflict, and Violence: Theological Basis in 1 John
   for Being Passionate and Loving Those who Disagree with Us
   Dr. Caroline G. Seed 55
5. "They Shall Not Inherit the Kingdom of God"—Is the Bible's Language of
   Judgment and Sin too Condemnatory to Patiently Deal with Human Sins?
   An Evangelical Protestant Perspective
   Rev. Daniel Funke and Dr. Tomas Bokedal 73
6. "They Shall Not Inherit the Kingdom of God"—Is the Bible's Language of
   Judgment and Sin too Condemnatory to Patiently Deal with Human Sins?
   An Anglican Perspective
   Rev. Dr. Matthias Grebe 91
7. "They Shall Not Inherit the Kingdom of God"—Is the Bible's Language of
   Judgment and Sin too Condemnatory to Patiently Deal with Human Sins?
   A Modernist Perspective
   Rev. Dr. John Michael Kiboi 113
8. Does the Roman Catholic Church's Language of Sin Make Pastoral Care of
   Victims too Difficult?
   Fr. Dr. Daniel Ude Asue 133
9. Is the Roman Catholic Theology of Sin too Judgmental?
   Professor Robert Fastiggi 149
10. Was Jesus' Language of Judgment and Sin too Condemnatory for him to Deal
    Graciously with Human Sin?—A Reflection from the Matthew's Gospel
    Professor Wayne Baxter 161
Part Two: Pastoral Theology in Human Need 171
11. Addressing Spiritual Lethargy: A Biblical, Theological, and
    Homiletical Approach
    Dr. Rock M. LaGioia 172
12. Midwifing Model of Pastoral Care with Addicted Persons
    Rev. Dr. Myrna Thurmond-Malone 181
13. Practical Theology/Spirituality and Fostering Healthy Human Relationships
    in the Workplace
    Rev. Dr. Hundzukani Portia Khosa-Nkatine 195

14. "Women Don't Like Nice Guys"—Dating, Attraction, and Christian Values: Teaching Our Young People How to Fall in Love
    Dr. Walter S. Chung and Dr. Stephanie Chung 203
15. Judgmental Attitudes and Their Impact on Our Pastoral Effectiveness
    Kevaughn Mattis 215
16. Ethics of Judging between Truth and Love when the Absolutely Right Choice Is Elusive
    Rev. Dr. Michael G. Maness 231
17. The Church as Alternative Community: A South African Perspective
    Professor Godfrey Harold 253
18. Church and State in Ethiopia: Contribution of the Lutheran Understanding of the Community of Grace
    Dr. Samuel Yonas Deressa 265

Part Three: Pastoral Theology in Human Suffering 283

19. When Sickness Heals: Pastoral Reflection on Finding Meaning in Suffering
    Dr. Dana Costin-Stelian and Dr. Siroj Sorajjakool 284
20. Finding (or Missing) God and Meaning in Suffering
    Dr. Erhard S. Gerstenberger 299
21. Ecclesiology and Theodicy: Bonhoeffer's *Sanctorum Communio* as Response to Human Suffering
    Dr. Maury Jackson 317
22. The God of All Comfort: Karl Barth and Hope in Suffering
    Rev. Dr. Nathan D. Hieb 339
23. Disability and Suffering?—Pastoral and Practical Theological Considerations
    Dr. Amos Yong 361
24. What Kind of Response Can Pastoral Theology Give in the Midst of Suffering?
    Dr. HyeRan Kim-Cragg 379

Bibliography 393
Indices 431
    Persons Referenced 431
    Scriptures & Semi-sacred... 436
    General 439
Other Books by Maness 443
Other Books from *Testamentum Imperium* 444

Foreword
Professor Gerald R. McDermott
Anglican Chair of Divinity, Director of the Institute of Anglican Studies Beeson Divinity School, Sanford University, Birmingham, Alabama; Distinguished Senior Fellow, Baylor Institute for Studies of Religion [1]

When he saw the crowds, he was moved with pity for them, because they were harassed and helpless, like sheep without a shepherd. Matt 9:36

Remember that at one time you were without Messiah, alienated from the commonwealth of Israel and strangers to the covenants of promise, without hope and without God in this world. Eph 2:12

Pastoral theology is an attempt by leaders in God's Church to be like Jesus, the great shepherd of the sheep. The word "pastoral" comes from the Latin and Old French and means a shepherd who leads his flocks to places where they can eat.

Jesus saw that the crowds were afflicted from without (harassed) and tormented from within (helpless). So is the worldwide Body of Christ

---

[1] Prof. McDermott teaches in the areas of history and doctrine, world religions, Anglican studies, and Jonathan Edwards. Before Beeson, he was the Jordan-Trexler Professor of Religion at Roanoke College. An Anglican priest, he is the teaching pastor at Christ the King Anglican Church, Hoover, Alabama. He is married to Jean, and they have three sons and twelve grandchildren. He has written 20 books, including *Do Christians, Muslims, and Jews Worship the Same God?: Four Views* (Zondervan, 2019; 240 pp.); *Everyday Glory: The Revelation of God in All of Reality* (Baker Academic, 2018; 224 pp.); *Israel Matters: Why Christians Must Think Differently about the People and the Land* (Brazos Press, 2017; 192 pp.); *Famous Stutterers: Twelve Inspiring People Who Achieved Great Things while Struggling with an Impediment* (Cascade, 2016; 121 pp.); editor and contributor, *The New Christian Zionism: Fresh Perspectives on Israel and the Land* (IVP Academic, 2016; 353 pp.); with Ron Story, *The Other Jonathan Edwards: Selected Writings on Society, Love, and Justice* (University of Massachusetts Press, 2015; 168 pp.); with Harold Netland, *A Trinitarian Theology of Religions: An Evangelical Proposal* (Oxford University Press, 2014; 428 pp.); with Michael McClymond, *The Theology of Jonathan Edwards* (Oxford University Press, 2012; 784 pp.; which won *Christianity Today*'s 2013 award for Top Book in Theology/Ethics); *The Oxford Handbook of Evangelical Theology* (Oxford University Press, 2010; 554 pp.); *Jonathan Edwards Confronts the Gods: Christian Theology, Enlightenment Religion, and Non-Christian Faiths* (Oxford University Press, 2000; 258 pp.); *Can Evangelicals Learn from Non-Christian Religions? Jesus, Revelation and the Religions* (InterVarsity Press, 2000; 235 pp.); *Seeing God: Jonathan Edwards and Spiritual Discernment* (Regent College Publishing, 2000; 262 pp.), and with William A. Fintel, M.D., *Cancer: A Medical and Theological Guide for Patients and Their Families* (Baker Books, 2004; 351 pp.). Plus he has made many contributions to books and written many articles, including articles in *Bibliotheca Sacra*, *Journal of Markets and Morality*, *Christianity Today*, *Journal of the Evangelical Theological Society*, *Theology Today*, *First Things*, *Journal of Religious Ethics*, and *The New England Quarterly*. See GMcDermo@samford.edu.

today. More and more it is persecuted by enemies who want to destroy it, even in the global North where until recently it was the principal bulwark of civilization. It is attacked from within by two great heresies. The first is against the doctrine of creation, which holds that marriage is the union of man and woman. The second is against the doctrine of salvation, which holds that Jesus Messiah (Christ) offers salvation from eternal suffering apart from God, and that this eternal suffering is real.

In this dark world where many are alienated and without God and hope, pastoral theology offers both God and hope. Orthodox pastoral theology knows that Jesus responded to harassed sheep by providing both healing and teaching (Matt 9:35). Orthodox pastoral theologians know that the Church must appeal to both mind and heart, for neither intellectualism nor sentimentalism satisfies. It knows that it is not enough for people to find God's forgiveness (justification) without also pursuing holiness (sanctification). It recognizes that Lone Ranger Christianity (me and Jesus) is a perversion of the gospel and risks losing the true Jesus. It uses the great wealth of the historic Church to bring enlightenment and healing to sick and benighted souls. It points people toward not only the Word but also the Sacraments of the church. There they will find true community with genuine healing and restoration.

This book will help provide the healing which this world and Church so desperately need. May the Triune God use this volume to help pastors ministering to God's sheep.

Prof. Gerald R. McDermott
Beeson Divinity School
Sanford University

Introduction
Rev. Dr. Michael G. Maness
Managing Editor, *Testamentum Imperium*[2]

What an honor to work with so many fine-hearted scholars.

QR Codes have been placed at each article to allow a reader to scan with their phone or iPad and access the links therein, and likewise for the bibliography.

When a soul hurts, the person looks to God. Herein, the articles were chosen by Kevaughn Mattis, founder of *Testamentum Imperium*, to look at the theology of pastoral care from a host of experts from a variety of disciplines. As you will see, all have extensive experience in their fields, each 20, 30, 40 years, and some with more.

In many ways, all have given their lives to pastoral care theology. From Greece to Detroit, Michigan; Canada; Limuru, Kenya; Riverdale, Georgia; South Africa; Marburg, Germany; Pasadena, California; Gboko, Nigeria—and more—herein experts from all over the world represent hundreds of years of pastoral care for the soul.

Senior academics and researchers mingle with senior clinical practitioners. The institutions represented speak volumes: Medical School of Athens University as well as the Theological School of Athens University; Waynesburg University, Pennsylvania; Ephesus Project, Pennsylvania; University of South Africa; Presbyterian University of East Africa, Kenya; North-West University, South Africa; King's College and University of Aberdeen, Scotland; Evangelisch-Theologische Fakultät Rheinische Friedrich-Wilhelms-Universität, Germany; St. Paul's University, Kenya; Catholic Diocese of Gboko, Nigeria; Sacred Heart Major Seminary, Michigan; Heritage College and Seminary, Canada; Grace Theological Seminary, Indiana; MHT Family Life Center, Georgia; University of

---

[2] Maness earned his DMin from New Orleans Baptist Theological Seminary; his MDiv from Southwestern Baptist Theological Seminary, Fort Worth; and his BA from the Criswell Center for Biblical Studies, Dallas. He is the author of nine books and over 100 articles, including *How We Saved Texas Prison Chaplaincy 2011—Immeasurable Value of Volunteers and Their Chaplains* (AuthorHouse, 2015; 414 pp., www.PreciousHeart.net/Saved). He is a retired senior clinical chaplain from the Texas Department of Criminal Justice (20 years). His web domain www.PreciousHeart.net hosts his books and links to over 100k sites to resources over the world and hosts perhaps the largest collection of papers and data on prison chaplaincy in the world and the most for Texas. He has been managing editor and publisher of *Testamentum Imperium* for most of its publication history, www.PreciousHeart.net/ti. See Maness' fuller vita under his article below in chapter 16, "Ethics of Judging between Truth and Love when the Absolutely Right Choice Is Elusive."

Pretoria, South Africa; South African Military Health Services; Eastern University, Pennsylvania; Cairn University, Pennsylvania; Texas Department of Criminal Justice; Cape Town Baptist Seminary, South Africa; Concordia University, Minnesota; Loma Linda University, California; University of Bucharest, Romania; Romanian Academy of Science; Charter Hospice, California; Asia Pacific International University, Thailand; Seventh-day Adventist Theological Seminary of Andrews University, Michigan; University of Marburg, Germany; H.M.S. Richards Divinity School and La Sierra University, California; Alliance Theological Seminary, New York; Fuller Theological Seminary, California; and St. Andrew's College, Canada.

Pastoral care and its theology get a gentle boost from some of the best in the business of caring for the soul, referencing over 900 persons from just over 1,000 sources. I found jewels in all the articles. Many of their references revealed more intriguing sources that further transfixed me, and I bought several. Look at the massive bibliography. In the process of editing, I annotated a few references to highlight the pathfinders' magnificent work.

Because each speaks powerfully, uniquely, and artfully, one cannot truly rank the articles. That said, and personally, Dr. Amos Yong's article on disability caught me off-guard and shocked me. He introduced me—and we hope to help spread the news—to a new and amazingly helpful term: the "temporarily able-bodied"! My goodness, I cannot remember when such an innocent and innocuous term confronted me so powerfully. Though slightly aware of the discrimination, I had little idea of the work being done on disability, the continued fight to end discrimination, the continuing struggle to increase dignity in service, and, indeed, on a "theology of disability."[3] And the resources unfurled there seemed unparalleled.

The perspectives of Greek Orthodox Dr. Vasileios Thermos and Roman Catholic Dr. Robert Fastiggi enlighten and manifest the experience they bring to bear. Professor Godfrey Harold on South Africa and Dr. Samuel Yonas Deressa on Ethiopia bring us powerful testaments. I could go on and on.

Dr. Myrna Thurmond-Malone's midwifing model of pastoral care provided to me another unique metaphor, and from my years of counseling prisoners, I could see her heart and the depth into which she walked with the souls blessed by the light of her guidance.

Each uniquely trained and tried author contributes universal insights into the grace of our great God in Christ and challenges pastors throughout the

---

[3] In reading this article, the 2007 movie, *Music Within*, kept coming to mind, a comedy-drama based on the true story of Richard Pimentel who lost his hearing in Vietnam, befriends a wheelchair-bound man with cerebral palsy, and becomes an activist/catalyst for the 1990 Americans with Disabilities Act.

Christian world to kindly consider the heart of the afflicted. The finely hewn stones herein can be used by anyone in the ministry to sharpen their serve.

Kevaughn Mattis began *Testamentum Imperium—An International Theological Journal* in 2005 with a vision to gather scholarly dialogue from a multitude of disciplines on the security of the Christian believer, our "Great Testament," which in Latin is *Testamentum Imperium.* Our first publication came in 2009, titled *Perspectives on Eternal Security* with the thirteen articles from the 60 published in the 2007 journal.[4] It has been my honor to aid and publish the works of these fine scholars from many of the best universities, seminaries, and fields of ministry all around the world. They highlight the relevance and need of pastoral care today and shine a great light.

We offer this collection with a prayer that the principles and deep insights will open new avenues of sensitivity to the hearts and souls of those in travail and aid those who are called by God to serve.

Rev. Dr. Michael G. Maness
Managing Editor, *Testamentum Imperium*
Retired Senior Clinical Chaplain
Texas Department of Criminal Justice

---

[4] See www.PrciousHeart.net/TI/2007.

Part One:
Problem of Pastoral Theology

1. Can Pastoral Care Successfully Merge Secular Disciplines with Biblical Theology?
   Rev. Dr. Vasileios Thermos 2
2. Is Pastoral Theology Still Relevant in an Age of Modern Psychology?
   Dr. Taunya Marie Tinsley and Rev. Dr. Joan Prentice 13
3. A Correction of Pastoral Care that Overlooks the Most Vulnerable
   Dr. Nontando Hadebe 41
4. Religious Belief, Conflict, and Violence: Theological Basis in 1 John for Being Passionate and Loving Those who Disagree with Us
   Dr. Caroline G. Seed 55
5. "They Shall Not Inherit the Kingdom of God"—Is the Bible's Language of Judgment and Sin too Condemnatory to Patiently Deal with Human Sins?
   An Evangelical Protestant Perspective
   Rev. Daniel Funke and Dr. Tomas Bokedal 73
6. "They Shall Not Inherit the Kingdom of God"—Is the Bible's Language of Judgment and Sin too Condemnatory to Patiently Deal with Human Sins?
   An Anglican Perspective
   Rev. Dr. Matthias Grebe 91
7. "They Shall Not Inherit the Kingdom of God"—Is the Bible's Language of Judgment and Sin too Condemnatory to Patiently Deal with Human Sins?
   A Modernist Perspective
   Rev. Dr. John Michael Kiboi 113
8. Does the Roman Catholic Church's Language of Sin Make Pastoral Care of Victims too Difficult?
   Fr. Dr. Daniel Ude Asue 133
9. Is the Roman Catholic Theology of Sin too Judgmental?
   Professor Robert Fastiggi 149
10. Was Jesus' Language of Judgment and Sin too Condemnatory for him to Deal Graciously with Human Sin?—A Reflection from the Matthew's Gospel
    Professor Wayne Baxter 161

1.
Can Pastoral Care Successfully Merge Secular Disciplines with Biblical Theology?

Rev. Dr. Vasileios Thermos
Professor of Pastoral Theology and Psychology
University Ecclesiastical Academy in Athens
Editor, *Psyches Dromoi: Ways of the Soul* [5]

Introduction: Pastoral Care and Psychology in Ancient Themes 2
A. Pastoral Care Encountering Psychological Processes... 4
B. Pastoral Care Permeated with Psychology Plus God... 4
C. Pastoral Care in Theology vs. Epistemology... 6
D. Pastoral Care Rich Patristic Theology... 7
E. Pastoral Care Rich Patristic Theology 9
Conclusion—Disciplines Aid Pastoral Care's End in Christ.................................. 10

All biblical excerpts are quoted from *The Oxford New Annotated Bible, New Revised Standard Version* (New York: Oxford University Press, 1991).

Introduction: Pastoral Care and Psychology in Ancient Themes

The Bible was composed many centuries ago in a premodern spatiotemporal context, whereas secular disciplines have emerged comparatively recently and still grow in the middle of a technological

---

[5] Thermos was born in Lefkada, Greece, and earned a MD from the Medical School of Athens University and a PhD from the Theological School of the Athens University. He is a practicing psychiatrist for Children and Adolescents in Athens, Greece, and an ordained priest for the Greek Orthodox Church. He has been a Visiting Scholar at Harvard Divinity School, Harvard School of Arts and Humanities, Boston College, Andover Newton Theological School, and a Visiting Research Scholar at the Institute for Medical Humanities of the University of Texas. He has been engaged in training programs for clergy in Greece, Cyprus, and the USA, and has written numerous books and articles in Greek, some translated into English, French, Russian, Romanian, Bulgarian, Serbian, and Spanish. His books in English include *Sexual Orientation and Gender Identity: Answers and ... People* (Athens: En Plo, 2019; this is an abridged version of a 700-page book in Greek: *Attraction and Passion: An Interdisciplinary Approach of Homosexuality*), trans. from Greek by Vasileios Tsangalos (Alhamba, CA: Sebastion Press, 2019); *Psychology in the Service of the Church* (Alhambra: Sebastian Press, 2017; 166 pp.); *Thirst for Love and Truth: Encounters of Orthodox Theology and Psychological Science* (Montreal: Alexander Press, 2010; 80 pp.); and *In Search of the Person: According to Gregory of Palamas* (Montreal: Alexander Press, 2002). He is the editor of the Greek journal *Psyches Dromoi* (Ways of the Soul), published every six months on the relationships between theology/religion and psychiatry/psychology (first issue in May 2011). In 2004, Peter Kazaku did a master thesis on Thermos' work for the Theological School of Balamand University, Lebanon, which resulted in *Orthodoxy and Psychoanalysis: Dirge or Polychronion to the Centuries-Old Tradition?* (New York: Peter Lang, 2013; 147 pp.). In 2018 his essay "The Paradox of Mental Health Care and Spirituality: The Culture of Extreme Individualism as a Mediator" was awarded the prize for the category "Culture, Care, and Spirituality" by the Jean-Marc Fischer Foundation in Switzerland which highlights contributions to the fields of human, social and theological sciences. See bibliography for two links. Contact: thermosv@otenet.gr.

culture characterized by rationalism and other mentalities impressively different from the ancient mind. However, Scripture and its theology have been for decades in a continuous dialogue with modernity and the secular disciplines that sprang out of it, a dialogue with a variety of outcomes.

Pastoral care can definitely benefit from sociological research, economic theory, biological knowledge, and medical technology progress. In this essay I will focus on psychology, the topic on which I have much specific experience. Among all secular disciplines that keep encountering biblical theology, psychology definitely prevails, which I find reasonable given that human beings and the way they function have always been a key subject of scientific curiosity. Besides, it is the domain of the human psyche that triggers the most exciting discussions between ancient and contemporary perspectives, to the degree that they sometimes become competitive, as both parts vindicate the truth.

From the very beginning psychology manifested its importance as one reads about the first temptation (Gen 3: 1–6). What is at stake here is not the teasing taste of a particular fruit, but the perennial issue of *narcissism*. Fantasy completes the image: "You will be like gods."

A pervasive psychological issue appears in the first sentences of the Bible. Narcissistic fantasies are so common that they make up a big part of our everyday life, both individually and collectively. They often form the basis of interpersonal behaviors and distort ecclesiastical life. People may not fantasize that they are gods or that they will be (after all, this would make a serious psychiatric delusion), nevertheless they frequently behave *as if* they are close to a divine power or infallibility or invulnerability.

Pastoral care encounters remarkable problems when facing narcissism. Some people divorce their spouses because of a lack of humility, others get sick because they adopt an unhealthy lifestyle permeated with ambition and greediness, and we certainly should not omit those who are reluctant or reactive to any pastoral advice because they supposedly know better. What all narcissistic problems share in common is the implicit illusion that one actually does not need God or that one merely uses Him for one's own goals.

Pastoral care also deals with the social problems of *poverty* and *marginalization*; here we must recall the parables of the two rich men (Luke 12:16–21 and 16:19–31). Pastors struggle with both, the narcissism of wealthy people who sometimes consider themselves Christians, and the pain of the poor who suffer from the formers' indifference. Use of money is the most crucial field in our society of wild capitalism where narcissism becomes the central motivation. At the other side of the gap, depression or resentment may trouble the lives of the deprived ones who deserve our pastoral care too.

A. Pastoral Care Encountering Psychological Processes

Amplifying further with the first temptation in the Garden of Eden, we come upon another core issue of psychological theory, especially of the psychoanalytic kind. These are the *ego mechanisms of defense*, among which *repression* and *projection* dominate. "The woman whom you gave to be with me, she gave me fruit from the tree and I ate" and "The serpent tricked me and I ate" (Gen 3:8–13). To be more precise, *splitting* between a totally good and a totally bad person paved the road, only to find repression and projection cooperating in an admirable way with the purpose of offering the subject a relief from *guilt*. These mechanisms are unconscious, omnipresent, and quite popular; pastoral care comes upon them literally every day in all types of human relationships and is called to overcome them if it is to be effective.

Later, God institutionalized a ritual of projection (Lev 16:7–26), obviously not to sanction mechanisms of defense but to depict vividly what was going to happen with Christ's sacrifice. As the entire O.T. is implemented and justified in the N.T., the scapegoating ritual, rather than accepting projection, reveals its pervasive nature and emphasizes that with Christ, scapegoating is needless, even sinful. We do not need scapegoats anymore; it is Christ Who undertook the burden of guilt so that we are enabled to face our own guilt without fear and to repent for our sins.

But the practice of scapegoating keeps arising within interpersonal relationships as if the merciful Christ was not incarnate, thus motivating pastors to convince people to abandon this dysfunctional practice.

In general, pastoral care includes various aspects of handling guilt. Sometimes the pastor has to help resolve conflicts, because no one accepts responsibility and blames the "bad other" for causing the trouble. Other conditions subject to pastoral care pertain to behaviors which stem out of an anxious effort to avoid or repress guilt; they may include anger, complaints, workaholism, or other manic defenses and substance abuse. The list has no end.

Besides, some people are subject to self-victimization in the form of self-scapegoating or yield to pathological guilt and fall into depression. And for sure we should not forget spiritual guidance and growth, with repentance being a central point, which makes a core part of pastoral care.

B. Pastoral Care Permeated with Psychology Plus God

This issue of spiritual life is excellently described in 2 Samuel 12:1–13 and Matthew 18:23–35. The combination of repression and projection (by David and the servant in the respective passages) shows very eloquently how unconscious psychological processes affect seriously both our spiritual lives and our interpersonal relationships. It is true to argue that numerous individuals, family, and group problems that are the recipients of pastoral care, and are likewise generated by a failure to handle guilt in a constructive way.

Shifting now to a different kind of psychological issue, I revisit Saint Paul's dictum: "Fathers, do not provoke your children, or they may lose heart" (Col 3:21). In this short commandment the dynamics of repression of anger or aggression is considered, namely as a means to produce a *disheartening* or a *depression*. The Greek original reads ἀθυμία, which means *low mood*. It is reasonable: for if even nowadays when provoked by their father many children would not dare to express their anger or aggression to their fathers, we can hardly imagine what the conditions were 20 centuries ago!

How is pastoral care involved in this context? Pastoring families often involves dealing with silent yet angry children. This includes coercive or explosive adult children who have spent years being depressed or in passive-aggressive resistance. Pastors handling anger and aggression with pastoral care never have an easy task, and the psychological hint of this verse partially explains why. We should not omit here the dire contexts in which those provoking and inducing anger or aggression have been and could be symbolic "fathers" figures of power such as leaders and pastors. The dynamics in the ecclesiastical groups and organizations can be quite exhaustive and destructive, requiring much of pastoral care.

I will finish this indicative list of biblical excerpts with the famous description of Romans 7:15–25, where the inner conflict is vividly expressed. Inner conflicts, a quite familiar human condition, provides us with dilemmas, anxieties, doubts, pressure, regrets, etc. This passage does not refer to common everyday conflicts (which are not trivial in themselves), but this passage focuses upon those conflicts which pertain to faith and virtue. A pastor has to reply to hard questions in order to encourage or to discourage choices, to support spiritual lives, to facilitate spiritual warfare, and to help the Christian discern behaviors that are impulsive or self-made "solutions" of existential conflicts. Listening is hard work. Pastors try to facilitate the liberation of souls from meaningless conflicts as well as hazardous conflicts.

Generalizing here, I would dare to say that our inner psychic divisions, when externalized, become the causes of great social conflicts and fragmentation, a field in which pastoral care is called to intervene in the form of social activism and social change.

In general, the spiritual and the psychological elements are mutually intertwined. Pastoral care deals with most of the situations in human life, regardless if it appears as secular or spiritual, because secular or spiritual elements may be disguised as the other one. Who fully knows the heart? So psychology permeates almost every theological truth expressed in the Bible, with the only exception being the Triadological and Christological doctrines, for—obviously—God cannot be examined by mere human psychology.

C. Pastoral Care in Theology vs. Epistemology

So far so good—the reader has my positive answer to the title question: yes, pastoral care *can* successfully merge the secular disciplines with biblical theology.

Let us further explore some corollary theological and epistemological issues. From the history of the Church we have learned that heresies emerge out of people reading the same Bible. This is quite impressive: how could people read the same Gospels and Epistles and some of them believe that Christ was only God, whereas others imply that He was only a man? How is it possible that, studying the same Scripture, some concluded that the Holy Spirit is God and others that He is not? Ancient Christians used to read the same O.T.: yet how and why did some end up requiring circumcision for the Gentiles and others did not?

Examples like these show that implications derived from the Bible are always mediated by interpretation. The reader is not merely internalizing what they are reading; instead, one interprets constantly in a certain way, even at times when one has no idea they may be doing that.

I consider the same valid for the question posed at the title of my chapter. What exactly is "Biblical Theology"? Which Biblical Theology should we have in mind in attempting to reply to such an interesting question? Biblical Theology is not actually something completely settled and therefore treasured, waiting to be quoted; rather, it is a product of continuous interpretation.

On the particular issue of the contribution of secular sciences, we come upon a vertiginous range throughout Christianity. At one hand, conservatives and fundamentalists tend to consider Biblical Theology as a body of truth shaped in a definite form, and many of those view that "definite form" should not be contaminated by secular science because secular science is a product of a godless modernity. For many of the most "conservative," pastoral care is basically condensed to teaching the Bible, implying that if someone merely applies the divine commandments they would be cured and not find themselves in conditions requiring pastoral care. So, on this particular issue, they almost reject psychology wholly and manufacture what they call "biblical counseling"; the strictest of them have coined the term "psycho-heresy," a construct which threatens the purity of what they perceive as Biblical Theology.

While not all the conservative fundamentalists reject all of psychology, those that do reject all the good psychology that does not conflict with biblical precepts are led astray and away from very good natural revelations to be had in the "psychology" of the person, just as we've seen in the rest of God's creation.

At the other extreme of the spectrum, one finds liberal churches that have completely surrendered to psychology, which has been seen, sadly, as a kind of upgrade to their basic biblical tools, and not a mere accessory. They are willing to apply all available psychological knowledge to pastoral care, even to counter the Bible, yet one can legitimately wonder whether this "care" is "pastoral" anymore. In several cases, pastors behave more as counselors, and the ecclesiastical life is more organized around a variety of ministries which boast of being very inclusive. Unfortunately, one can hardly discover theological concepts or the best spiritual elements of the Christian message in the middle of this anthropocentric activism.

While worldwide Christianity is quite nuanced, I chose the two extremes in order to show how much the key to answering the title question lies within the spirit of the particular Christian and on how they interpret the Scripture. Is the Church perceived as a sect that should be isolated from the world? Then the answer to the title is an angry negative. Is the Church perceived as an organization whose gospel message can be watered down by the "triumph of the therapeutic"? Then the answer is "No!" Is the Church an organization led by God who ordained the natural laws, the sciences, and the wonders of psychological truths that help define the *Imago Dei* of "humankind"? Then the answer is enthusiastically positive.

Where can I position myself in this extremely divergent and multicolored spectrum? Judging from the first part, the reader may presume that I am standing somehow at the middle. Without denying it, I would like to further explain my attitude.

D. Pastoral Care Rich Patristic Theology

In the Christian tradition to which I belong, the Fathers of the Church are considered respectable figures and occupy a remarkable space of interpretive work. For us, the Bible is not the exclusive source of truth. Exegesis in the Orthodox Church is continuously active, yet it neither perceives a 20-century gap (as if the Holy Spirit was present only during the Scripture's authors' times) nor attributes the same validity to anyone attempting to articulate Biblical Theology. The fundamental criterion is *sanctity*: to the degree that the interpreter has been (or is being) sanctified, namely spiritually transformed, so that their Biblical Theology becomes perspicacious and reliable. People actively engaged in the process of their spiritual transformation contribute to the enrichment of Biblical Theology.

Thus Patristic Theology (this is the name under which the theology of the Fathers is known) has been a huge and ongoing body that evidences their effort to derive theology out of the Bible. Needless to say, they do not agree in everything; their concept of tradition is not a copy-and-paste one. Yet this does not create a big problem, because theology has plenty of space for divergent interpretations which serve as portions of the marvelous mosaic of truth. Human complexities demand multifaceted arrays of theological contents and pastoral techniques.

Have the Fathers made use of the secular disciplines like psychology? The question makes no sense, because during their premodern time very little science existed as we know it today. They used the terminology that was not as scientific as today. So how can we guess about their attitude?

Two aspects of their behavior help. First, the Church Fathers accepted the healthy parts of philosophy, which were not only prevalent but also an officially acknowledged branch of thought. They accepted "philosophy" critically of course, but they were bold enough to respect its achievements, its truths, and did not demand it to merge into theology. Second, they recruited any psychological intuition they could. Even though psychology as a discipline was a long way off, looking back at their writings, they were heavily invested with psychological processes.

Augustine's *Confessions* (c. AD 397) has become a classic and even exquisite case study. The Patristic works are full of psychological remarks, most of them still useful for pastoral care today.

- **Saint Gregory the Theologian** (AD 329–390) writes that usually it is men who legislate, so that is why the laws favor men against women.
- **Saint Basil the Great** (AD c. 329–379) makes a crucial distinction between our real selves and things around us or belonging to us or attributes of us. Such a distinction sounds so timely in an era of alienation through reductionism to wealth and fame.
- **Saint John Chrysostom** (AD c. 349–407) advises the teacher not to scorn pupils in public, because by doing so they are humiliated and thus the corrective words cannot reach their hearts.
- **Saint John Climacus of Sinai** (AD c. 579–649) in his famous "Ladder" warns that chastity sometimes is accompanied by a latent bitterness.
- **Saint Gregory Palamas** (1296–1359) defends affects and desires while he considers fake a spirituality that is based primarily on the intellect.

The above list is quite short because its intention is to show that the 20-century old Christian tradition has not hesitated to recruit products of human thought and experience (later known as psychology) if they can serve salvation. At premodern times those products lacked any autonomous scientific existence as they have today. But nowadays the patristic principles of pastoral care can be described and classified through the contemporary tools of secular disciplines, especially psychology.

E. Pastoral Care Rich Patristic Theology

An additional point to consider is the word "merge" in the title:

> Are Biblical Theology and secular disciplines
> really meant to merge?

When a merger takes place, a new entity is created. Two companies merge into a new brand. Two streets merge, and another one appears in a new name. Should no merger happen, there would be no new name. Instead, with a merger, we have the disappearance of the old and the assimilation of the two into one entity.

What is the new entity between a Biblical Theology and Psychology? Let me recall: if such an entity existed, little to none of the two domains could be discerned inside the new entity. That is, the new creature would consist of neither "Biblical Theology" nor "Psychology," but such would form a new street mixing new forms.

To my knowledge, I am not aware of such a mixture yet that functions as a new entity. Instead, I know of hybrids such as:

1. Pastoral Counseling, counseling informed by pastoral theology;
2. Pastoral Psychotherapy, therapy inspired by pastoral concerns;
3. Sacrament of Confession, enriched by a pastor's psychological knowledge and training.

These genres are not a result of a true merger; rather, they are distinct entities in which a dialectical *coexistence* unfolds, thus enhancing their fruits. I am not even sure that the widely used term *integration* of theology and psychology is epistemologically correct. Obviously, it does not indicate a merger, and, in a way, the term *integration* may undermine both the integrity of each component and their mutual interaction.

This issue reminds us of the Chalcedonian doctrine (AD 451). When the 4th Ecumenical Council articulated the ecclesiastical credo about the person of Christ, they spoke about "two natures, divine and human, existing indivisibly and unconfusedly." This double condition in which the two natures are simultaneously not separated and not merged warrants the *integrity* of either nature, as well as their salvific cooperation. From that point on, the Chalcedonian doctrine has become the archetype of any synergistic relationship between God and human beings.

As sciences are products of human beings, the same principle applies here. Biblical Theology as a work of and about divine revelation, and psychology about human endeavor, are both called to coexist synergistically, without altering or reducing each other. This is somehow difficult to capture. The human mind tends to perceive unilateral conditions more easily than those which make space for both entities, and that is why the extremes of fundamentalism and ecclesiastical secularism are more popular. Simply put, indivisible and unconfused coexistence is part of the mystery that surrounds our entire life—the *Mystery of Incarnation*.

Conclusion—Disciplines Aid Pastoral Care's End in Christ

Biblical Theology and the secular disciplines, particularly psychology, can and must encounter each other and let themselves be affected by each other. This is my stance, consistent with the fact that I have dedicated my entire life to this project. Contemporary perplexing subjects need much psychological knowledge in order to be thoroughly served in pastoral care. After all, what are the secular disciplines if not updated forms of the human effort to describe the reality of the world? In the case of psychology, it systematically articulates all the available empirical experience of what it means to be human, in terms of intellect, emotions, desire, unconscious, memory, imagination, behavior, etc. Who would find a reason to object to such a synchronization of the descriptions if the content of the ecclesiastical message remains intact?

Indeed, the core of the Scripture in the good news of the renovating power of Christ's Cross and Resurrection remains and will continue to be our hope and the meaning of life. These are what should prevail and lead during this encounter.

This is the right moment to consider another word of the title:

What does "successfully" mean?

By what measure is that success assessed? Having said all the above, I would dare to imply that, if pastoral care is defined as merely an (ecclesiastical) intervention to a variety of problematic human conditions, then its effectiveness in terms of assessable results becomes one measure of success. Furthermore, if pastoral care is conceived as the sum of practical ways for announcing and making manifest Christ's anthropic presence and power and mercy through psychological support in the varieties of human troubles, then success becomes something that takes place deep in the heart and is difficult to estimate.

Without this latter option, we are to experience various forms of sophisticated care carried out by persons wearing a collar and vestments (a care called pastoral), while wondering why Christianity keeps losing its nerve and potential in the West. To me charismatic movements, including healing ones, are not the answer to the devastating crises in Christianity, because (a) they are primarily immanent and utilitarian, seeking for soothing and inventing emotions; and (b) they seem to ignore the redemptive and transformational theology that the Bible contains.

To regain balance, we need also to embed a spiritual perspective into pastoral care: a pastor's mission cannot be reduced to counseling the divorced, the sick, or the youth. Pastoral care is an indispensable part of his calling, yet secularization remains an insidious danger if priority is not given to live the mystery of theology in the practice of our real lives. Secular disciplines are neither to be expelled nor idealized, but invited to serve this mystery, according to Saint Paul's saying: "We take every thought captive to obey Christ" (2 Cor 10:5). The Bible has the answer once more.

2.
Is Pastoral Theology Still Relevant in an Age of Modern Psychology?

Dr. Taunya Marie Tinsley
Owner of Transitions Counseling Service LLC, Paoli, PA
Rev. Dr. Joan Prentice
Prentice is Director of The Ephesus Project[6]

Introduction	13
A. Is Pastoral Theology Still Relevant in the Age of Modern Psychology?	14
B. Literature Review	16
1. Pastoral Theology	16
2. Pastoral/Spiritual Care	20
3. Psychology	22
4. Pastoral Counseling	24
C. The Marriage of Pastoral Theology, Pastoral Counseling, Spiritual Care, and Psychology in the 21st Century	26
D. Case Study	28
1. Conceptualization	28
2. Pastoral Theologian	29
3. Pastoral/Spiritual Care	30
4. Psychologist (or other licensed clinical mental health professionals)	32
5. Pastoral Counselors	33
E. Ethical Issues and Considerations	34
F. Recommendations for Training and Professional Practice	37
Conclusion	38

Introduction

This article discusses the relevancy of pastoral theology in an age of modern psychology. Today, people searching for relevance and meaning in life find themselves in a matrix of developing and increasingly complex worlds of technological and scientific information. In such an information-

---

[6] Tinsley earned her PhD from Duquesne University, Pittsburgh, PA, and her DMin from United Theological Seminary in Dayton, Ohio. She holds a NCC and LPC. She has been an associate professor in counseling at University of Pennsylvania; director of Graduate Programs in Counseling, Waynesburg University, Pennsylvania; and director of the Graduate School of Counseling, Missio Seminary, Philadelphia. She remains director of the Mount Ararat Counseling Center at Mount Ararat Baptist Church, Pittsburgh. She has worked with the National Football Foundation, the National Football League, and the Pittsburgh Steelers in a variety of counseling certification programs. She has served as the North Atlantic Regional Representative for the Association for Multicultural Counseling and Development, as president of the Pennsylvania College Counseling Association, and as president of the Pennsylvania Counseling Association. See ttinsley@transitionsaalp.com and www.Transitionsaalp.com.

Prentice earned her DMin and MDiv from Pittsburgh Theological Seminary, and she is now a board member of PTS. She is also staff pastor for new members at Mount Ararat Baptist Church, Pittsburgh. See drjbpephesus@gmail.com and http://theephesusproject.org.

saturated time, persons are challenged to live healthy holistic lives discerning meaning and purpose within that matrix of ideas and ideals. Human beings and human nature are consistent in their search for the ultimate meaning of life (Utazi, 2012). The article clarifies the inquiry and defines the disciplines of pastoral theology and psychology. While both disciplines help people find meaning in life and with their search for solutions to life's challenges and questions, pastoral theology and psychology are two distinct disciplines aimed at different outcomes.

Pastoral theology came to be more therapeutic, rather than pastorally grounded in the nature of God for soteriological, eschatological, ecclesiastical purposes which inspire reconciliation to God, self, others, and ultimate healing. By discussing historical developments and insights, identity of social and cultural shifts, the authors show how these factors influence the practice and defining roles and trends of pastoral theology and modern psychology. These are inclusive of pastoral and spiritual care and pastoral counseling and are designed to assist with finding solutions to the existential concerns of individuals, family groups, and communities. Finally, the exploration of competencies and ethical requirements of the disciplines and individual practitioners are discussed and support the integrity of each discipline sustained by the expertise each professional brings to their respective disciplines.

A. Is Pastoral Theology Still Relevant in the Age of Modern Psychology?

Despite the fact that today we live in an age of rapid development of science and high technological achievements, vast communication abilities, and economic growth, people are still searching for the ultimate meaning of life (Utazi, 2012). However, there still exists in our world existential situations as well as developmental and situational crises, all of which create situations of suffering and injustices that neither science, technology, nor reason can provide full solutions (Utazi, 2012). Though there are many diverse strategies that may assist to address those issues, pastoral theology has been employed to provide meaning and care in the midst of difficulties and crisis situations toward the formation of a communal identity.

The distinctive character of pastoral theology as a discipline is its attempt to understand the ministerial role from the lived experiences of people. Pastoral theology is not an abstract understanding of God detached from the tapestries and fibers of life's experiences. Pastoral theology is a living and organic theology that shapes and informs everyday experience (Utazi, 2012).

Pastoral theology is that field of theological knowledge and inquiry which brings the shepherding perspective to bear upon all the operations and functions of the church and the minister, and then it draws conclusions of a theological order from reflection on these observations. It is an operation-centered or function-centered theology, which begins with a situation of suffering and need. It attends to theological questions raised by the practice of care in response to that need, and it brings theological and as well as contemporary knowledge into this question in order to deliver "care" in response to a need (Hiltner, 1958). The particulars of caring for suffering congregational bodies are central to this application of Hiltner's understanding of pastoral theology (1958).

Oden (1983, p. xii) reports that pastoral theology as a unifying discipline was flourishing a century ago and remained robust until the beginning of the 20th century, yet it has largely faded into such hazy memory that none of its best representations are still in print. Throughout the 20th century, there have been attempts for revisioning pastoral theology (Graham, 2006, p. 845). The shift to view pastoral theology through the lens of postmodern thought stems from the transition from modernity to postmodernity (Graham, 2006, p. 846). It was Oden's hope in 1983 to "hammer out a rudimentary pastoral theology half as well as any of a dozen that were available a century ago" (p. xii).

Today, pastoral theology is now experiencing a shift of paradigms from modernity to postmodernity (Graham, 2006). This is evident in the following statements:

> The present state of pastoral theology is a strong and vigorous one. Its range of interests has been widening since it got off to a new start in the years following Vatican II. Its subject took on a new life and meaning and the response became prolific. Its importance is substantial to such demands as sustaining and giving support to the weak, comforting and understating people in crises. Pastoral theology in the person of the minister also guides and helps people to find solutions to various problems and life's questions, healing and aiding them to find wellness; and reconciling people to restore relationships (Utazi, 2012, p. 9).

Thus, the practice of pastoral care has been central to the disciplinary identity of pastoral theology (Graham, 2006).

Psychology is the discipline that guides and helps people to find existential meaning and solutions to various problems and to life's ultimate questions. Historically, psychology has been described as having "a long past but only a short history" (Hermann Ebbinghaus, as cited in Pastorino and Doyle-Portillo, 2012). Although psychology did not formally become a science until the 1870s, people have always been interested in explaining behavior (Pastorino and Doyle-Portillo, 2012, p. 7):

> The roots of psychology can be traced to philosophy and medicine in ancient Egypt, Greece, India, and Rome. Philosophers debated whether the mind, or the thinking part of a human, could be studied scientifically; they discussed the nature of the mind and where it was located.

Because of the mind's association with the body, much of what we consider psychology today was traditionally a part of the field of medicine (Pastorino and Doyle-Portillo, 2012). Sigmund Freud studied medicine that focused on neurology and disorders of the nervous system as he formulated the psychoanalytic approach to human behavior, and he is probably the most influential and well-known figure in psychology's formation (Pastorino and Doyle-Portillo, 2012; Plante, 2008). Other than a few classical studies, many early psychologists had never shown an interest in religion (Collins, 1977).

Although, pastoral theology and psychology are two distinct disciplines aimed at different outcomes, pastoral theology is equated by historical practice and is overly influenced by psychological theory and practice (Oden, 1983; Murphy, 2012). In the counseling sense (i.e., pastoral/spiritual care and pastoral counseling), the religious truth becomes the framer and interpreter, and not strictly the clinical considerations. The pastor utilizes pastoral theology, which can have similarities with psychology, but the primary source for the pastor is scripture and not the therapeutic and clinical frameworks (W. H. Curtis, personal communication, October 28, 2016). Within pastoral theology, there are levels of care and counseling that include pastoral/spiritual care and pastoral (or biblical/Christian) counseling.

So, to answer the question of whether pastoral theology is still relevant in the age of modern psychology—the answer is unequivocally, "Yes"!

While a lot more can and has been said about pastoral theology's relevance in the age of modern psychology, the authors want to provide enough information for the reader to see how wise it is to see that pastoral theology certainly remains relevant. Herein, the authors have several goals in mind, including increasing the awareness of the cultural, individual, and role differences within pastoral theology, pastoral and spiritual care, pastoral counseling and psychology, and how to consider these disciplines when working with individuals, families, groups, and the community.[7]

B. Literature Review
1. Pastoral Theology

It has been said that pastoral theology is not easily *defined*, but rather *described*, which allows for a fluid and open approach to a theology that has roots in the experiences contained within and outside of its distinct boundaries (Utazi, 2012). Despite the diversity of definitions and

---

[7] For the purpose of this article, the term "psychologists" will be used interchangeably with other licensed clinical mental health counseling professionals.

descriptions of pastoral theology, there is a consensus on the terms themselves and of the knowledge gained by systematic study.

Pastoral theology is designed to assist the Christian minister in applying the truths of the gospel to the heart and lives of individuals (Murphy, 2013). "It is 'theology' because it has chiefly to do with the things of God and his word" (Murphy, 2013, p. 1). It is "pastoral" because it treats of these divine things in that aspect of them which pertains to the pastor, and it is practical because it relates to the work of the pastor who is appointed to influence individuals by applying them to the teachings of the Holy Scriptures (Murphy, 2013). "The term 'pastoral' is derived from the Latin word 'Pastor' meaning shepherd, and it thus suggests the work of a shepherd in relation to the priestly pastoral ministry and the care giving to his sheep" (Utazi, 2012, p. 2). Pastoral theology is the science of the care of souls (Drum, 1912/2016; Utazi, 2012). Although an extensive historical overview of pastoral theology is beyond the scope of this manuscript, a brief summary will be provided to assist with understanding the science behind the name and concepts of pastoral theology.

Pastoral theology is a branch of theology that cannot be neglected because of its fundamental relevance and importance to both the church and to society. It bridges the relationship between the church and society (Utazi, 2012). Pastoral theology begins where the other theological sciences leaves off, taking the results of them all and making these results effective for the salvation of souls through the pastoral ministry that has been established by Christ (Drum, 1912/2016). One school of thought states that pastoral theology is a branch of practical theology, a practical science or ministry, with particular attention given to the systematic definition of the pastoral office and its function (Drum, 1912/2016; Oden, 1983).

All branches of theology, whether theoretical or practical, are purposed to "let us [who minister] be regarded as servants of Christ and stewards of the mysteries of God [that He chooses to reveal]" (1 Cor 4:1 AMP). This branch of theology, pastoral theology, presupposes other various branches of theology and is distinguishable, yet inseparable, from exegesis, historical and systematic theology, ecclesiastical history, the sacraments, homiletics, apologetic, dogmatic, ethics, ascetical, liturgics, and psychology of religion (Drum, 1912/2016; Murphy, 2013; Oden, 1983). Although pastoral theology integrates insights from all these disciplines, it is and therefore should be viewed as a distinctive discipline designed to provide care for the individual through personal experiences and make meaningful contributions to the development of human beings without neglecting their salvation (Oden, 1983; Utazi, 2012). Additionally, pastoral theology should be viewed as a preparation that increases knowledge, skills, and the sacred art of bringing souls to Christ and training them for the glory of God (Murphy, 2013).

Like other branches of theology, pastoral theology has its roots in the Holy Scriptures and in the traditions of the church; these are pastoral theology's first sources. In other words, the *science* of pastoral theology is as old as the church itself as reflected in the many diverse instructions and special directions for the guidance given to the disciples by Jesus (Matt 10; Mark 6:1–13; Luke 9:1–6) and given by Paul in the pastoral letters of Timothy (1 Tim 4:12–16; 2 Tim 2:22–25) and Titus for the care of souls (Drum, 1912/2016; Murphy, 2013). The instructions given by Jesus and Paul, as well as tradition and the Holy Scriptures, portray the ideal priest, teacher, and pastor; those instructions provide us with God's ideas and ideal for the church.

Care of Souls

(Drum, 1912/2016; Utazi, 2012). Additionally, these scriptural passages and instructions support pastoral theology as an important and vital branch of study demanding special preparation and training, including the rules and the art of bringing the gospel to the hearts and lives of individuals, families, and groups (Murphy, 2013).

As we continue to peruse the history of pastoral theology, we find that there was not a separated and systematized science of pastoral theology until the Counter-Reformation (Drum, 1912/2016). The Counter-Reformation, or Catholic Reformation, focused on four major elements including an ecclesiastical reconfiguration, religious orders, and spiritual movements designed to provide proper training for clergy (Cunningham et al., 2016). Prior to the reformation period, there were concerns about pastoral duties, including the care of souls, which were being neglected. The result was the development of the treatment of the care of souls as a science in itself (Drum, 1912/2016).

During the eighteenth and nineteenth centuries, the science of pastoral theology continued to gain momentum. Specific pastoral duties were applied practically to the proper care of souls including that of the teacher, servants of Christ, those entrusted with the mysteries God has revealed (1 Cor 4:1), and of the shepherd (i.e., pastor) (Drum, 1912/2016). In addition, throughout the past century, there have been other definitions and descriptions of pastoral theology for the practice of the care of souls as follows:

1. Pastoral theology teaches the priest his part in this work of Catholic and Christian tradition of revealed truth.
2. Pastoral theology teaches the practical bearing of the laws of God and the Church, and teaches the means of grace within these laws as well as

teaches the hindrances upon the daily life of the priest, alone and in touch with his people.
3. Pastoral theology applies Canon law to the care of souls (Drum, 1912/2016, para. 2).
4. Pastoral theology is attentive to the knowledge of God witnessed to in the Scripture, mediated through tradition, reflected upon by systematic reasoning, and embodied in personal and social experiences.
5. Pastoral theology seeks to give clear definition to the tasks of ministry and to enable its improved practice. Because it is a pastoral discipline, pastoral theology seeks to join the theoretical with the practical. It is theoretical insofar as it seeks to develop a consistent theory of ministry, accountable to Scripture and to tradition, and be experientially sound and internally self-consistent. It is also a practical discipline for it is concerned with implementing concrete pastoral tasks rather than merely defining them. Its proximate goal is an improved theory of ministry. Its longer ranged goal is the improved practice of ministry (Oden, 1983, p. x).
6. Pastoral theology is a systematic process through which people are led to God. People have different needs and reasons by which they are drawn to God. This significantly proves the need for a pastoral guide who can minister to them, making present or mediating to them the world of God in their concrete life situation. This is the specific task of the practitioner of pastoral theology (Utazi, 2012, p. 6).

Through the many descriptions, the bottom line is that pastoral theology has been observed to provide meaning in the midst of difficulties and practical help in crisis situations toward the forming of a communal identity; it is a living and organic theology that shapes and informs everyday experience (Utazi, 2012). The everyday experience and the circumstances of the times must be studied effectively in constructing a relevant contemporary system of pastoral theology. The principles of the gospel are the same; these cannot be changed or improved. The word of God must be the chief and authoritative arbiter of the rules that are to guide the Christian minister. But humans change, as well as cultural contexts, and obstacles to truth are ever rising up (Murphy, 2013). Pastoral theology addresses the difficulties of individuals, families, and the larger societal issues that contribute to the Christian's growth in faith, and it aims to seek out the best way possible to render service to those who need God, whether it is in administration, preaching, teaching, worship, singing, praying, counseling, spiritual life, or sacramental life (Utazi, 2012).

The duties that are directed towards the salvation and caring of souls that have been conveniently divided into those of the teacher, of the minister of sacred mysteries, and of the shepherd (Drum, 1912/2016). Blackburn (1999) states that many pastors divide their work as pastors into three main areas: (a) leadership/administration, (b) preaching/teaching, and (c) pastoral care/pastoral counseling. The three areas of the pastoral minister overlap and are intertwined. The goal is to minister as Jesus did, as the Lord is the chief shepherd of the Christian community and the ultimate model of ministry (Utazi, 2012). Christ is the model for pastoral care and Care of Souls.

The present state of pastoral theology is a strong and vigorous one. Its range of interests expanded following the Second Vatican Ecumenical Council (Graham, 2006; Murphy, 2013; Oden, 1983; Utazi, 2012). In the person of the minister, pastoral theology guides and helps people find solutions to various problems and life's ultimate questions, aids in healing a variety of brokenness, facilitates wholeness and wellness, and reconciles relationships (Graham, 2006; Utazi, 2012).

Additionally, germane to pastoral theology today is the emerging thought of the postmodern situation and cultural condition. One of the unique characteristics of pastoral theology and pastoral care's relevancy is that it is now a practice of care *in community* as well as *in the market place*. The new openness to spiritual and human needs within the context of a new paradigm of pastoral theology and care is emerging. The remainder of this literature review will now focus on the roles and responsibilities of those ministers who engage in pastoral/spiritual care and pastoral counseling as well as focus on the roles and responsibilities of psychologists and other licensed clinical mental health counseling professionals.

2. Pastoral/Spiritual Care

As stated earlier, within pastoral theology there are levels of care and counseling that include pastoral/spiritual care that has always been of special importance in the Christian community (Oden, 1987; Chadwick et al., 2016). Pastoral care has had a long history within Christianity and the early church. Although there is no lengthy reference to the specific duties and role of the pastor within the Bible, it does associate it with teaching (Eph 4:11–12) and involves shepherding the flock (Psalm 23; 78:52 and 53a; 1 Pet 5:1–4), a task of pastoral care:

> Shepherding involves protection, tending to needs, strengthening the weak, encouragement, feeding the flock, making provision, shielding, refreshing, restoring, leading by example to move people on their pursuit of holiness, comforting, and guiding (Rowden, 2009, p. 227).

Additionally, in the short letters of 1 and 2 Timothy as well as Titus, Paul wrote specifically instructing pastors on how to care for people in the church (Murphy, 2013; Petersen, 2007).

One of the most important contributions to pastoral care after the N.T. was by an early church father, Pope Gregory I, known as St. Gregory the Great (Chadwick et al., 2016). Gregory was actively concerned with the work of priests and wrote one of his most famous and influential writings, *Liber Regulae Pastoralis*, known commonly as the "Pastoral Care," or the

"Pastoral Rule" following his investiture as pope in 590 (*Christianity Today*, 2008; Gregory I the Great, 590/1994; Halsall, 1998). This instructional book was written to outline the role, duties, and obligations of clergy, and it was presented to new bishops upon their ordination and included the following definition of pastoral care:

Pastoral care is the ministry of care and counseling provided by pastors, chaplains, and other religious leaders to members of their church or congregation, or to persons of all faiths and none within institutional settings. This can range anywhere from home visitation to formal counseling provided by pastors who are licensed to offer counseling services. This is also frequently referred to as "spiritual care" (Gregory I the Great, 590/1994).

Drawing on various classical authors, another theologian, Thomas Oden, equates pastoral care to that of a medical doctor stating: "As the physician cares for the body, so the pastoral leader cares for the soul" (Johnston, 2016; Oden, 1987). He further describes pastoral care as that:

> branch of Christian theology that deals with the care of persons by pastors. It is pastoral because it pertains to the offices, tasks and duties of the pastor. It is care because it has charge of, and is deliberately attentive to, the spiritual growth and destiny of persons. Pastoral care is analogous to a physician's care of the body. Since that particular sphere over which one exercises care is the psyche ... pastoral care is also appropriately called the care of the souls. (Oden, 1987, p. 5)

In classical Christian terms, the soul is defined as the "unitive center of the inner powers" of persons. The pastoral counselor is responsible for the inner life of persons to help them through the crisis of emotional conflict and interpersonal pain toward growth in responsiveness toward God (Oden, 1983).

Pastoral care in the 20th century has been defined as "a person-centered, holistic approach to care that complements the care offered by other helping disciplines while paying particular attention to spiritual care. The focus of pastoral care is upon the healing, guiding, supporting, reconciling, nurturing, liberating, and empowering of people in whatever situation they find themselves" (Rumbold, n.d.). Pastoral care refers to the total range of help offered not only by pastors, but also elders, deacons, spiritual leaders, and other members of the congregation to those they seek to serve (Benner, 2003). Whereas, spiritual care "can be a dimension of any discipline, when a practitioner provides holistic care, that includes the spiritual dimension" (Pastoral Care Council of the ACT, 2016).

Spiritual support is an essential aspect of pastoral care that offers emotional support and spiritual care by helping people connect with their own inner and community resources (Pastoral Care Council of the ACT,

2016). Spiritual support "consists of a range of activities in which people cooperatively interact with God and with the spiritual order deriving from God's personality and action" (Dallas Willard as cited in McMinn, 1996, p. 11). In addition to pastoral care, pastoral leaders and practitioners must understand spirituality and the process of spiritual formation in emotional healing (McMinn, 1996). Spiritual training is experiential and often private. It includes prayer and devotional reflection, in church sanctuaries where Christian communities worship, as well as in quiet intimate disciplines of fasting and solitude (McMinn, 1996).

Blackburn (1997) refers to pastoral care as hospital visits, telephone calls expressing concern or reassurance, and informal brief conversations about the needs in people's lives. Within pastoral care, psychological and theological perspectives are integrated in the practice of the Christian counselor (Graham, 2006). Although there is an adoption of secular therapies within the pastoral care that creates a tension between sacred and secular sources of pastoral care and is a clear sign of modernity, religious worldviews continue to dominate and persevere, and even revive the pastoral care movement (Graham, 2006).

> Pastoral care has always attempted to respond to the totality of human needs in every age in consonance with the words of Jesus Christ, "I was hungry and you gave me food, I was thirsty and you gave me drink, I was a stranger and you welcomed me, I was naked and you clothed me, I was sick and you visited me, I was in prison and you came to me." (Chadwick et al., 2016; Matt 25:35–36)

The ultimate goal of the modern pastoral care movement has been one of personal wholeness and well-being with the individual viewed as one possessing an innate orientation towards self-actualization (Graham, 2006).

The pastor can profit from the "anthropological" worldviews of social and behavioral sciences (Lester, 1995). The significant contributions that social and behavioral sciences have made to anthropology and the theology of personhood and human personality should not be diminished. Social learning theories, cognitive theories, behavior theories, systems theories, and other psychological theories have done much to speak to the present situations of persons from the offerings of the social and behavioral sciences (Lester, 1995).

3. Psychology

Pastoral and spiritual care as defined and described in this manuscript is rooted in word, sacrament, sacred scriptures, in prayer, in proclamation, and in the care of the soul (Brushwyler, Fancher, Geoly, Matthews, and Stone, 1999). Pastoral and spiritual care does not have it origins in various evidenced-based, scientifically grounded theoretical approaches or schools of psychotherapeutic modalities (Brushwyler et al., 1999). Although there are many similarities between pastors and psychologists, who both guide and help people to find existential meaning and solutions to various problems and life's questions, psychologists [or other licensed clinical mental health counseling professionals] provide both short-term and longer-term, formal, intimate conversations that may be preventative in nature or interventions within a variety of settings (Gladding and Newsome, 2010; Hiltner, 1949; Johnston, 2016; Oates, 1974). Psychologists and other professionals may be concerned about pathology, the lifespan of human development, the social development while implementing evidenced-based practices, and the treatment of those seeking productive lives and healthy life-stage transitions (Gladding and Newsome, 2010).

Psychology has been defined as the scientific study of behavior and mental processes that focuses on empirical evidence and critical thinking and consists of four goals:

1. Describes Behavior, tells "what" occurred,
2. Explain Behavior, tells "why" a behavior or mental process occurred,
3. Predicts Behavior, identifies conditions under which a future behavior or mental process is likely to occur, and
4. Change Behavior, applies psychological knowledge to prevent unwanted behavior or to bring about desired goals. Carpenter and Huffman, 2010.

The American Psychological Association (APA) defines psychology as:

> a diverse discipline, grounded in science, but with nearly boundless applications in everyday life. Some psychologists do basic research, developing theories and testing them through carefully honed research methods involving observation, experimentation, and analysis. Other psychologists apply the discipline's scientific knowledge to help people, organizations and communities function better. (2016, para. 4)

Psychologists and others study both normal and abnormal functioning, treat patients with mental and emotional problems, and encourage behaviors that build emotional resilience and wellness (American Psychological Association, 2016).

Approaching behavior, mental processes, and mental health holistically is not new as this considers the mental, physical, emotional, environment, and spiritual factors (i.e., the whole person) (Gladding and Newsome, 2010). Over the course of the 20th century, there have been many psychologists who have focused on the spiritual dimension of human wholeness including Carl Jung, Abraham Maslow, William James, Karl Menninger, and M. Scott Peck (American Association of Pastoral Counselors [AAPC], 2016). Today, in the age of modern psychology, psychologists and others are recognizing the link and correlation between mind, body, and soul—including religion, spirituality, and health—and working together with other health care professionals as well as pastors, clergy, pastoral counselors, and spiritual care givers to provide whole-person care to individuals, families, groups, and the community (APA, 2016; Carpenter and Huffman, 2010; McMinn, 1996; Pastorino and Doyle-Portillo, 2012). In fact, APA, the American Counseling Association (ACA), and the National Association of Social Workers (NASW) have included codes of ethics that state the importance of understanding the diverse cultural backgrounds including religion and spirituality (ACA, 2014; APA, 2010; NASW, 2008). Thus, as Arthur Caliandro, Senior Minister Emeritus, Marble Collegiate Church in New York City states, "It only makes sense that religion and psychology, each of which is concerned with the fullness of the human experience should be recognized as partners, because they function as partners within the human psyche" (AAPC, 2016).

4. Pastoral Counseling

Pastoral leaders have traditionally sought to provide biblically-based solutions that are oriented toward mission, anchored in scripture, centered on Christ and the Gospel, dependent upon the Holy Spirit and prayer, and directed toward sanctification for those in trouble (AAPC, 2016; Johnston, 2016). Additionally, pastoral leaders "have listened intently to personal problems for centuries and have developed religious counseling responses to those who suffer from mental and emotional illness and relational difficulties" (AAPC, 2016, para. 1). During the past century, a diversity of definitions of this kind of counseling had been set forth by pastors. Hiltner (1949, p. 80) described pastoral counseling as a process and "the attempt by a pastor to help a parishioner help himself, granted that certain conditions are present." According to Hiltner, the aims of pastoral counseling are the

> same as those of the Church itself, bringing people to Christ and the Christian fellowship, aiding them to acknowledge and repent of sin and to accept God's freely offered salvation, helping them to live with themselves and their fellow men in brotherhood and love, enabling them to act with faith and confidence instead of the previous doubt and anxiety, bring peace where discord reigned before. (Hiltner, 1949, p. 19)

For Hiltner, the role of the pastor is that of a shepherd who assists their sheep with theological understanding, healing arts, sciences, and social work (Ogden, n.d.).

Oates (1974, p. 56) stated that "pastoral counseling may be said to be a systematic effort to apply inductive, clinical, and scientific method to the accepted function of the minister as he confers with persons about their personal problems and life destiny." Oates (1982) further defined pastoral counseling as the multiple interviews and counseling conducted by a pastor, teacher, or chaplain: i.e., a generalist. According to Oates (1974, p. 78; 1982), the pastoral counselor is a contemporary theologian at work with "the living human documents" of suffering people who reach out for care or to whom the pastoral counselor can extend care. The pastoral counselor is a person who is on speaking terms with God and has taken the time and the energy to discipline himself or herself in the body of data that describes humankind's dealings with God throughout history. Pastoral counseling has also been identified as times when an appointment with a church member who asks for help, guidance, or perspective on an issue or problem that they are facing (Blackburn, 1997).

These traditional forms of pastoral counseling continue to help many individuals. However, it has been recognized that many cases require specialized professional counseling for effective treatment and healing (AAPC, 2016). And the above pastoral care scholars would also say that part of the competence of the pastor is to be able to identify when a referral to a trained psychological professional is needed.

The American Association of Pastoral Counselors (2016, para. 2) reported that "the intimate link between spiritual and emotional well-being began to receive serious attention by religious leaders in the early 1900s when they developed innovative educational programs and disciplined training that recognized the historical connection between faith and mental health." A brief historical sketch of Clinical Pastoral Education (CPE) shows that:

> In 1923, William S. Keller, M.D. brought a group of theological students to his home in Cincinnati for the summer. He sent them out in pairs to study and work in hospitals, social agencies, and welfare institutions. In 1925, the Rev. Anton T. Boisen who, after recovering from a severe mental illness, studied all that was then known about clinical pastoral training and became chaplain of the Worcester, Massachusetts, State Hospital, brought a group of theological students to study at the hospital. There were differences between these two movements [approaches], but both men believed that the way to learn to help was to try helping under supervision. (Hiltner, 1956, p. 114)

Furthermore, beginning in the 1930s, the integration of religion and psychology for psychotherapeutic purposes began in several contexts (AAPC, 2016). First, the collaboration of renowned minister Norman Vincent Peale and psychiatrist Smiley Blanton resulted in the American Foundation of Religion and Psychiatry, now known as the Blanton-Peale Institute and Counseling Center located in New York (AAPC, 2016; Blanton-Peale Institute and Counseling Center, 2016; Menz, 2003). Additionally, there was a collaboration between clergy and psychoanalytic psychiatrists including Helen Flanders Dunbar, who was one of the four seminary students who trained at Worcester State Hospital with Anton Boisen (AAPC, 2016; Vande Kemp, 2001). Finally, in the decades that followed, pastoral counseling continued to mature and find a place in the mental health community (Menz, 2003).

More recently, pastoral counseling has experienced a shift of paradigms that evolved during the latter half of the 20th century which is epitomized by the separation of pastoral counseling from the worshiping community and its absorption into a medicinal model of healing and clinical care (Graham, 2006). Pastoral counseling or psychotherapy that reflects modernist commitments refers to a specialized and controlled therapy done by exception rather than the rule of the pastorate (Oates, 1982; Graham, 2006). Menz (2003, p. 7) states, "The term pastoral counselor is not a reference to pastors who counsel, but a reference to a specialized discipline for those who have been trained in theology and credentialed in psychotherapy."

The American Association of Pastoral Counselors (AAPC) (2016) defines pastoral counseling as

> a unique form of counseling which uses spiritual resources as well as psychological understanding for healing and growth. Certified pastoral counselors are licensed mental health professionals who have also had in-depth religious and theological education and training. Clinical services are non-sectarian and respect the spiritual commitments, theological perspectives and religious traditions of those who seek assistance without imposing counselor beliefs onto the client.

From these perspectives, pastoral counselors (i.e., specialists) are thoroughly educated in both religious/theological training and psychotherapy and are licensed mental health professionals, making it a highly disciplined subspecialty of ministry (AAPC, 2016; McMinn, 1996; Menz, 2003; Oates, 1982).

Thus, in 1963, AAPC was founded, and it represents and sets professional standards for over 1,500 pastoral counselors. Its mission is to provide spiritually informed and integrated counseling, collaborative community-based services, training and education in order to enhance the well-being of individuals, families and communities (AAPC, 2016). Today, a pastoral counselor assists individuals in crisis, helping those are looking for personal growth and attending to the person's spirituality, theology, and faith tradition. At the same time, counselors provide guidance, aid skills, facilitate longer-term relationships, and provide the information needed to promote wholeness. They do all this within the context and support a person who needs to make changes to live life more fully. Those affiliated with AAPC account for three million hours of treatment annually (AAPC, 2016; McMinn, 1996).

C. The Marriage of Pastoral Theology, Pastoral Counseling, Spiritual Care, and Psychology in the 21st Century

The following case study illustrates a congregant/client who presents themselves to a pastor, pastoral/spiritual care provider, psychologist, or pastoral counselor seeking assistance in times of a developmental, existential, and situational crisis. The responses from each type of helping professional discussed here will include specific points to consider. This case study is designed to assist with recognizing that pastors do not need to do all of the counseling. As Johnston (2016, p. 4) states,

> There may be significant differences in training, gifting, and competence. In cases of real difficulty, it will be wise to refer the counselee to someone who has sufficient expertise in understanding a problem. Of course, the pastors will still remain involved, but they are also ensuring that folk are receiving the level of care that they require. Counseling is certainly a pastoral activity that can be appropriately delegated.

On the subject of pastoral theology, pastoral care, and counseling:

> The postmodern perspectives portray the self as a subject-in-relation, whose identity is forged within the complex interplay of economic, cultural and political facts. Contemporary pastoral/practical theology is gradually revising.... The subject of care is shifting from that of a self-actualized individual for whom care functions primarily at times of crisis towards one of a person in need of nurture and support as she or he negotiates a complexity of moral and theological challenge in a rapidly-changing economic and social context (Pattison as cited in Graham, p. 858).

The human being is understood as a complex being that functions on two levels, the soul or mind, to which the body is subject. For the well-being of the person, the soul and body, or flesh and spirit must operate in harmony. Peace entails a harmony of sorts and agreement with self and with God. Disease (dis-ease) results when we are not in agreement or harmony with God, with self, and with others.

Pastoral counseling and modern psychology are not mutually exclusive of each another. There is a synergy to be realized when the difference as well as the importance of each area of expertise brings healing and comfort into lives of persons in need of healing—emotional, spiritual, and psychological. It is important to discern the need and identify which area of expertise is called for. "The pastoral counselor brings a specific historical identity as a counselor which enables the pastor to bring a fresh consciousness and unique contribution to the general field of counseling" (Oates, 1992, p. 293).

Wayne E. Oates uses the term God-in-relation-to-persons to identify the distinctive character of pastoral counseling, and it must be informed by philosophy, ethics, anthropology, psychology, medicine (psychiatry), and social work (Chapman, 1992). This suggests the "need for interprofessional collaboration rather than mere cooperation or amateurish competition" (Chapman, 1992, p. 295). Pastoral and spiritual care and modern psychology and counseling do not exist exclusive of each other. The role of the pastor in pastoral/spiritual counseling is to bring healing or comfort by the skillful use of theological reflection, biblical interpretation, and spiritual discernment that brings the reality of God or "God as reality" into the situation for which the person is seeking help.

D. Case Study

Larry Jones is a 40-year-old African American male. He is single with two daughters, ages 5 and 17, and has custody. Larry finished college with a degree in secondary education. As a student-athlete, he won a Division II scholarship to play basketball for four years at a historically Black university (HBCU). Larry admits that during his second semester at college he began feeling depressed but never sought counseling, due to the stigmas of being an African American male seeking counseling and an athlete seeking counseling. He is the youngest of five children with four sisters and a brother. Larry lives in the city with his 65-year-old mother due to financial problems. Larry is currently employed as a teacher at a Christian charter school with no illegal history and no alcohol or drug use. As a church member, he volunteers with several ministries. Larry's presenting issues from his perspective are that he needs assistance with making good decisions, managing his anger, and assistance with how to be a better Christian. He admits to making spur-of-the-moment unhealthy decisions and is feeling empty since the death of his father last year. And his girlfriend of two years ended their relationship three months ago. Larry admits to being very angry lately especially at his daughters' mothers (two different mothers of his two daughters) who are seeking full parental custody of their daughters due to Larry's financial situation (Tinsley, 2013).

1. Conceptualization

Larry is struggling with economic, social, and relationship issues that are affecting him emotionally, psychologically, and spiritually. Feelings of emptiness, anger, sadness, grief and loss, and anxiety are concerns that need to be addressed. Larry admits that he has a tendency towards depression. Larry's anger is getting worse as evidenced in the anger directed towards his daughter. Poor decision making is another presenting issue of major concern. Larry is feeling the need to connect with his Christian/spiritual roots perceiving it as another broken relationship that needs to be restored. There is a need for reconciliation and healing as these presenting behaviors and concerns are evidence of both spiritual and psychological trauma.

The integration of the following interventions of pastoral theology, pastor/spiritual care, psychological support, and pastoral counseling could be offered to Larry for integrative healing, emotional resilience and wellness, healthy life-stage transitions, and reconciliation and restoration of relationships with self and with others.

For the purpose of this case study, only the most salient treatment plans will be discussed for each professional.

2. Pastoral Theologian

As a pastoral theologian, the response to Larry would be framed through a theologically reflective and interpretive lens. The knowledge of the nature and action of God in the context of the human experience is essential. This provides the pastoral theologian with a foundation for his or her work with Larry. Because the pastor is first a theologian, the method of the pastor to guide, nurture, protect, and care for the individual is grounded in the nature and knowledge of God and the Scriptures. A biblical interpretation and a theological anthropology guides the pastor's work with a soteriological, eschatological, and ecclesiastical goal. The focus is not simply the healing of the mind and relative behaviors, but to give attention to the spiritual complexities of the person addressing their relationship with God, self, and others, understanding the human-self as God's creation, the Scriptures as the revealed will of God.

The first observation reveals a sadness that may be related to a depressive disorder. The pastoral theologian's knowledge of behaviors connected to depression may inform the necessity of additional integrative intervention of a professional psychologist or another licensed clinical mental health professional. However, other concerns dominate, too, like the grief and loss from the death of Larry's father, the broken relationship with his girlfriend, the anger toward his daughters and their mother. And these seem to be getting progressively worse. These are emotions that need assessment. From the perspective of the pastor, the underlying spiritual issues that could be contributing factors to Larry's situation need to be identified and addressed.

The redeeming factor for the pastoral theologian in Larry's case is that a relationship and knowledge of God is a part of his experience; he is connected to the church community. Larry feels the need to be a better Christian, and that is the entry point for the pastoral theologian's work with him. The theologian understands that Larry's emotional struggles have a spiritual component that influences his behaviors and choices. The pastor brings to bear on Larry's situation a clearly theological reflection.

The Genesis narrative of the fall of Adam and Eve provides a foundation for understanding humanity's journey from innocence toward a responsibility for sin. The Fall reveals the violation of the divine relationship that resulted in destructive consequences for the individual and society. Paul Tillich posits that there are three dimensions of estrangements as a result of sin. "Sin is estrangement from other persons in self-centeredness and lovelessness; from our true selves in pursuing fragmented and inauthentic goals; and it is estrangement from God, the ground of our being" (Barbour, 2002, p. 51). Thus, sin is identified as a self-centeredness and turning away from God, an ultimate state of brokenness and disconnect which is relational. The subsequent disconnect in relatedness to God, self, others represents the emotional and behavioral dilemmas that many face and to which pastoral counselors are called to minister. This disconnect renders us vulnerable to relational, spiritual, and emotional dysfunction. Subsequently, Larry's situation may stem from the fact that he needs to repair his relationship with God in order for him to relate better to his own self and to be reconciled to others and find healing.

Larry needs to meet with the pastor privately for a few sessions to work through the issues. The pastor will help Larry understand his brokenness and struggles in the light of biblical and theological insights. The pastor helps Larry's interpret and reinterpret his behaviors from a self-in-relation with God and then with others.

The Gospel then becomes the message for Larry to understand the atoning sacrifice of Christ, the grace of reconciliation provided in Christ, and the Spirit's presence to empower him to live into the truth of the God's word and ultimately his own truth and purpose. The pastor might help Larry understand the Gospel as a living and viable reality that exists in the person of Christ and that the Scriptures point to the living, relational Christ (John 5:38–40). Larry's healing comes through reconciliation and agreement with the written word and with the Living Word in Christ.

This pastor's role with Larry would encompass helping Larry listen and build a relationship with God through prayer, meditation, spiritual practices and disciplines that together build him up in his most holy faith (Jude 1:20–21 NIV). The pastor would also recommend that Larry seek pastoral counseling with someone who the pastor . This may assist with a smooth transition between the two professionals which may assist to decrease Larry's stigmas of seeking counseling.

3. Pastoral/Spiritual Care

The pastor (or elder, deacon, spiritual leader or other members of the congregation) will reach out and provide Larry with a ministry of compassion that includes encouragement and support that stems from the love of God (Benner, 2003). The pastoral care provided is, as Benner (2003, p. 19) states, "the gift of Christian love and nurture from one who attempts to mediate the gracious presence of God to another who desires, to one degree or another, to live life in the reality of that divine presence."

The ministry of care provided by pastors [or other members of the congregation] will also require an understanding of spiritual formation (McMinn, 1996). "Those who yearn for God and take the spiritual life most seriously always experience periods of spiritual darkness and loneliness; it is part of the spiritual quest for Christians" (McMinn, 1996, p. 11). During this time, the ministry of care is concerned about the welfare of others and encourages reaching out in fellowship and relationships with one another (Benner, 2003).

Help for Larry as a member of the church provides care from a contextual, communal perspective. Healing and comfort can be found in the midst of the community. Consider Hebrews 10:24–25 (AMP) which reads,

> And let us consider [thoughtfully] how we may encourage one another to love and to do good deeds, not forsaking our meeting together [as believers for worship and instruction], as is the habit of some, but encouraging one another; and all the more [faithfully] as you see the day [of Christ's return] approaching.

Larry needs to be in a supportive community where he is being encouraged and uplifted by the people of faith within his church. It is also within this context that the embodied love of Christ and the Gospel can deepen his love of God, self and others. This can provide a context to temper his anger as the love of Christ is received and embodied for himself and then others. Larry's anger may stem from a self-anger, lamenting his lived experience due to bad decisions and choices made. Larry's relationships with others can be healed and his ability to function in a healthy manner may be discovered within a loving community that provides support in an encouraging and supportive environment. It is the community of the congregation, that itself becomes pastoral in its ministry to Larry.

The Scriptures are God-breathed, "and is useful for teaching, rebuking, correcting and training in righteousness, so that the servant of God may be thoroughly equipped for every good work" (2 Tim 3:16–17 NIV). Thus, it is advisable for Larry to attend Bible study or a Bible study group or cell group. Bible study in the context of the community provides a communal context for developing helping relationships, learning, and interpreting biblical principles for life application. There are specific teachings in scripture that can attend to Larry's financial habits, anger, and relationship issues.

Larry should be directed to attend prayer sessions. Prayer that fosters communal sharing on a more intimate level of spirituality may help Larry to focus attention not only on himself and his concerns but on the concerns of others. The biblical principle of reciprocity (e.g., Matt 5:7, Matt 6:33, Matt 6:38; 2 Cor 9:6, 8, and 11; Gal 6:7–10), has the potential to effect spiritual edification. Furthermore, pastoral care realized through the worship experience and the preached Word must not be underestimated as a context for pastoral/spiritual care. The pastor/preacher's homiletic can be a source of teaching where the word of God is encountered for transformation and change. Notwithstanding, pastoral and spiritual care takes place in the context of the congregation, utilizing the various ministries in the church and gifting of people within the congregation. Because much of Larry's difficulties are identified as relational in nature, this context for his care is advisable.

4. Psychologist (or other licensed clinical mental health professional)

Prior to developing a culturally appropriate intervention and treatment plan for Larry, a psychologist will conduct a thorough psychosocial assessment, "a systematic procedure for collecting information that is used to make inferences or decisions about the characteristics of a person" while beginning to develop a cross-cultural therapeutic relationship (Drummond and Jones, 2010). The assessment is designed for screening, identification, diagnosis and intervention planning purposes. Additionally, the assessment is designed to assess Larry's mental and emotional health and to develop an understanding of Larry's role within his family and his community. Furthermore, the psychologist may integrate the FICA Spiritual Assessment. The acronym FICA can help structure questions in taking a spiritual history (i.e., Faith, belief, meaning; Importance; Community; and Address/Action in Care) (Puchalski and Romer, 2000).

The approach that a psychologist may take with Larry depends on their theoretical orientation to counseling and mental health and their competency level of training with theology and/or spiritual, ethical and religious values in counseling. A psychologist who focuses on pathology and diagnosis, may refer Larry to a psychiatrist for antidepressant medication to be prescribed, and may recommend therapy. This reflects an approach that might be taken by many psychologists who have no religious training or experiences (McMinn, 1996). A psychologist who integrates spiritual and Christian interventions into the previous description may have some theological understanding or understanding of the competencies for addressing spiritual and religious issues in counseling (McMinn, 1996).

Based on the conceptualization of Larry and the assessments, the psychologist will continue strengthening a therapeutic alliance with Larry due to his stigmas toward seeking counseling. Additionally, the psychologist will develop a culturally appropriate intervention and treatment plan that would include goals for decreasing Larry's level of depression/depressive symptoms utilizing evidence-based theoretical approaches such as cognitive behavioral therapy. Moreover, the psychologist will assist Larry with progressing through the stages of grief and loss (i.e., shock/denial/isolation, anger, depression, bargaining and acceptance) and tasks of mourning (i.e., accepting the loss, experience the pain and emotions of grief, adjusting to the new environment without the deceased or significant loss and finding an enduring connection with the deceased and significant loss in the midst of embarking on a new life) due to the loss of his father and the ending of his relationship with his girlfriend of two years [and possibly the loss of his athletic identity] (Kübler-Ross, 1969;

Tinsley, 2008; Worden, 2009). The grief and loss that Larry is experiencing may be the trigger for his intense anger and poor, unhealthy decision making. Furthermore, the psychologist will also assist Larry with developing effective coping strategies and skills that may assist him with managing his emotions, stressors, and relationships with his mother, his daughters, and his daughters' mothers.

While working with Larry, the psychologist, with Larry's consent, may want to include Larry's church community as part of the intervention and treatment plan. Collaboratively, the psychologist and Larry could determine how his church could serve as a support for him during his existential crises and counseling process. Larry's prognosis is excellent as long as he and the psychologist continue their collaborative therapeutic alliance and Larry stays committed and motivated with the counseling process. Future issues that Larry may want to consider addressing in counseling is his athletic identity, racial/cultural identity as well as his identity as a single parent. Increasing Larry's understanding of who he is and who he can be can assist with Larry's awareness of self, increase both his self-esteem and self-efficacy as well as can assist with strengthening his relationships with others.

5. Pastoral Counselors

The pastoral counselor will integrate the role and responsibilities of the psychologist as previously discussed. However, only those psychologists and licensed clinical mental health professionals who are aware of, and trained in, psychological symptoms, theological principles, and spiritual formation will be able to discern the best treatment for Larry (McMinn, 1996; Menz, 2003). Thus, the pastoral counselor will also integrate biblical-based solutions that are oriented toward mission, anchored in scripture, centered on Christ and the Gospel, and dependent upon the Holy Spirit and prayer (AAPC, 2016; Johnston, 2016). The pastoral counselor will utilize spiritual resources as well as psychological understanding for healing and growth (AAPC, 2016).

In addition to the intervention and treatment plan developed previously by the psychologist, the pastoral counselor will assist Larry with restoring and reconciling his relationship with God, with himself and with others, including his daughters, his daughters' mothers, and his mother. As a result of Adam and Eve's sin, all mankind was affected as well. Adam and Eve's selfish and sinful attitude ruined God's perfect design and what God created for human beings to enjoy. The problems caused by sin and rooted in the same decisions as Eve's (i.e., selfishness, disobedience and conflict) only worsened throughout history. Mankind, still challenged with living in the structure of God's plan, rejects ultimate freedom within God's structure and laws and chooses instead to live enslaved to their own rules and structures.

Sin continues to permeate Creation infecting relationships, culture, politics, work, and play to name a few, resulting in brokenness, destruction and death which for some has become normalized because of the lack of awareness of God's perfect plan (McCown and Gin, 2003).

The pastoral counselor will assist Larry with understanding that through redemption in Jesus Christ, he has become a member of His kingdom where God's perfect structured has been restored and broken relationships with God, self, others and Creation has been made whole again through the transformation of the heart (McCown and Gin, 2003). The pastoral counselor would provide Scripture passages (e.g., 2 Cor 5:15–17, Rom 6:4, John 13:34–35, Col 2:9–10) that provides support of these restored relationships (Tinsley, 2016).

These Scriptures are not offered with the expectation that this would set Larry's thinking straight about God. Rather, the scripture readings are intended to point him toward God and to help him see how he differed from the God of his experiences (Benner, 2003). In God's original perfect plan for Creation, he gave human beings, including Larry, the privilege and responsibility of cultivating and developing relationships. With the restoration of Creation to right relationships and the redemption of hearts through Jesus Christ, Larry can now work to restore his relationships to God's intended purpose (Tinsley, 2016). At this point, much of the work of the pastoral counselor is that of an educative or didactic quality to assist Larry with becoming "a better Christian" (Benner, 2003).

Once Larry begins to understand the salvific role of Jesus Christ, the pastoral counselor will continue encouraging Larry to explore further the spiritual aspects of his presenting issues and engage in an exploration of his spiritual and religious functioning across his lifespan as well as an exploration of his family of origin and his relationships (Benner, 2003). The goal is to begin making connections between Larry's relationships with himself as well as with others and God while developing a good working alliance. Additionally, the pastoral counselor wants to provide a safe space for Larry to explore and express his feelings while modeling unconditional positive regard and acceptance that is a reflection of God's acceptance. This modeling behavior may hopefully assist Larry with learning to accept himself which in turn will strengthen his communication and decision-making skills as well as assist with managing his emotions (Benner, 2003).

E. Ethical Issues and Considerations

Ethical and legal issues as well as professional challenges surround pastors, professionals who engage in pastoral/spiritual care, pastoral counselors and psychologists every day. Psychologists and other licensed clinical mental health counseling professionals must be attentive to the ethical behavior, standards and responsibility to which they aspire (AAPC,

ACA, 2014; APA, 2010, NASW, 2008). Those who are members of a professional counseling organization such as AAPC, APA, ACA, NASW are already accountable to the ethical codes of that organization. "However, all pastors who counsel whether they have such memberships or not, need to be familiar with the ethical framework of counseling" (Benner, 2003, p. 147).

Although pastors have codes of conduct to guide their activities, they are religious in origin based on religious beliefs and canonical or ecclesiastical law (Benner, 2003; Brushwyler et al, 1999). Pastoral codes may be more generalized in nature than professional counseling organizations' codes of ethics with the exceptions of rules and laws regarding sexual misconduct (Brushwyler et. al., 1999). Because the potential for the abuse of power in the therapeutic relationship has become a matter of concern in recent years, and is an emerging issue in pastoral theology as well, a discussion of ethics is warranted and central (Blackburn, 1999; Graham, 2006).

While training in counseling can assist pastors to work more effectively with their congregations, their calling is a very distinct discipline of pastoral theology (Brushwyler et al, 1999; Murphy, 2013). Pastoral theology is primarily concerned with the things of God and his word and is designed to assist the Christian minister in applying the truths of the gospel to the heart and lives of individuals (Murphy, 2013). As Eugene Peterson (1989) states, "the definition that pastors start out with, given to us in our ordination, is that pastoral work is a ministry of word and sacrament" (p. 22).

Although Blackburn (1999), and Brushwyler (et al.) suggest that pastors may need to return to their distinct ancient calling and embrace their unique, set-apart ministry, it is the authors' belief that some pastors are already returning to their distinct ancient/classical calling within a new cultural situation that is calling forth pastoral ministry to be relevant to a contemporary ethos. It is a new and emerging paradigm of pastoral ministry as reflected:

> In 1993, Patton coined the phrase "Paradigm shift" to describe a dramatic turning in the practice of pastoral care [calling it a "healing art"]. Patton pointed out that pastoral care was focusing more and more on social and cultural concerns, moving from a "clinical pastoral paradigm" to one that Patton named "communal-contextual." (Hunter, 2001, para. 1)

For those pastors who already engage, or are planning to engage, in the practice of pastoral/spiritual care or pastoral counseling, there are some guidelines that are important to consider. Benner (2003, p. 148) provides five guidelines that serve as a framework for ethical practice for pastors and those ministers who engage in pastoral care and counseling:

1. **Protect the rights of those you counsel.** As part of your informed consent, be clear about the work undertaken together and your level of expertise, the right and freedom from any form of manipulation, coercion, harassment or discrimination, and the right to protection of confidentiality and privacy.
2. **Avoid dual role relationships.** "Dual-role relationships are those relationships in which a pastor provides formal counseling to someone while also maintaining a different relationship with that same person" (Cappa, 1999, p. 833). Avoid counseling someone with whom you have a close friendship, business or work relationships, or any other type of ongoing interaction. Such people should be referred to someone else in your network of psychologists or other licensed clinical mental health counselors, especially persons with chronic or more serious mental and emotional health issues (Blackburn, 1999; Brushwyler et al, 1999). As Johnston (2016) states, referring is not a failure of pastoral leadership but an expression of loving and wise leadership.
3. **Avoid romantic or sexual intimacies.** While this is assumed, it is an immensely important and pervasive issue. Additionally, "in the area of sexuality, the pastor must be careful not to seek, directly or indirectly, information that is not germane to the issue at hand. Seeking information for sexual titillation is inappropriate, unfair, and counterproductive" (Blackburn, 1999, p. 7).
4. **Be aware of your limitations.** Practice within the boundaries of professional and personal competence of pastoral theology, pastoral/spiritual care, pastoral counseling or psychology [clinical mental health counseling]. As a pastor in a counseling session, you are seeking to be faithful to the Lord and to your calling as you listen and address a person who is seeking help (Blackburn, 1999). If you practice as a licensed professional or psychologist, the law will treat you as one (Brushwyler et al., 1999).
5. **Remain in relationships of personal accountability.** The ethical practice of pastoral/spiritual care and pastoral counseling is best achieved and maintained within a context of close accountability, rather than just familiarity with standards and guidelines, beginning with the church and faith community. Accountability can also be achieved through ongoing consultation and supervision with other experienced pastors, counselors and psychologists.

Because many congregants come to pastors for counseling with certain expectations that may be unrealistic, and many pastors have neither sufficient training nor gifting to shepherd someone through complex situations of suffering, injustices, and mental/emotional struggles, it may behoove a pastor to lead well and navigate wisely through these difficulties (Johnston, 2016). Furthermore, another important consideration:

> is that of the pastor being clear when counseling is occurring and when it is not. That is, counseling is best performed in a formal setting, within an office and at specific times, and this must be communicated to the counselees prior to initiating the service. Additionally, it is important for pastors to know their own limitations in helping people. Well-meaning pastors often overextend themselves with people's issues that are far in excess of their expertise, leading to more harm than good. These limitations can best be addressed through such things as peer supervision or professional supervision within the helping community. It is also important that pastors have the foresight to predict possible role conflicts to their counselees, discussing such things as future contact in non-counseling settings and how that might be handled. (Cappa, 1999, p. 834).

To practice ethically, it is important that pastors focus on their calling and embrace their unique, set-apart ministry of pastoral theology and shepherding and to acknowledge their limitations as it relates to their role and responsibilities of pastoral/spiritual care and pastoral counseling. Additionally, to practice ethically, it will be beneficial for pastors to explore some of the ethical dimensions of counseling. Finally, being able to foresee possible ethical challenges and dilemmas can enhance the effectiveness and well-being of both the pastor and those who come for help (Cappa, 1999).

F. Recommendations for Training and Professional Practice

The authors recommend that pastors, clergy and pastoral counselors begin to include the value of professional counseling in the pedagogy of the congregation. Believing there to be a natural suspicion on the part of most congregants to professional counseling, one of the challenges is aiding members to see the spiritual connection between spiritual crisis counseling and professional counseling (Richardson and June, 2006). Pastors, in large measure, are including therapy in sermonic presentation on a regular basis. Strong support for the marriage of spiritual counseling and professional counseling would be created with strong pastoral support included in sermonic presentation. Most congregants value what is shared from the pulpit and fear what is silent from the pulpit or not strongly supported (Tinsley and Curtis, 2009).

Theology, divinity and ministerial training programs may also benefit from learning the intervention techniques and language necessary to maintain both the integrity of the counseling process and the counselors' sincere desire to see a congregant live whole and healthy. In addition, theology, divinity and ministerial programs may benefit from letting the language of faith and the languages of psychology and counseling converse until a commonality of languages is created (Tinsley and Curtis, 2009). It may behoove psychologists to develop relationships with pastors and ministers as a way of understanding church members' issues and concerns and communicating more effectively with religious and spiritual clients (Spriggs and Sloter, 2003).

Finally, the authors recommend that professional counselors collaborate with local universities, community agencies, and professional private practices to bring a variety of mental health services into one community facility such as a church (Tinsley and Curtis, 2009). Establishing ties with pastors of churches, [psychologists and other licensed mental health professionals] would create a referral network and complementary resources for clients (Richardson and June, 2006). Additionally, psychologists with specific training in religion and spiritual counseling can offer a valuable service to the mental health and religious communities by providing specific spiritual counseling competencies and mental health outreach programs that may better meet the needs of culturally diverse populations (Constantine, Lewis, Conner, Sanchez, 2000; Getz, Kirk, and Driscoll, 1999; Spriggs and Sloter, 2003).

Conclusion

In conclusion, the question of whether pastoral theology is still relevant in the age of modern psychology, the answer is unequivocally yes. The discussion has been presented by providing insights and research that define, describe, and inform the understanding and practice of pastoral theology and psychology in our contemporary context of lived experiences. Thus, "What happens in the church is related to political and social trends in the world at large" (Heitink, 1999, p. 62.). Our parishioners and those who come to us seeking help and healing often find themselves trying to maneuver through life caught in a maze of challenges and experiences of pain, suffering, joys and sorrows as well as emotional and spiritual quandaries. They live in the context of a social reality that influences the lived experience of being human in the world as they seek healing while finding purpose and meaning in life. People enter through the doors of our churches from a world that has not been kind and, in some cases, hostile, seeking understanding, help and healing. These are among the existential issues that we as helpers and "healers" are called to address and the people we are called to serve.

Today, pastoral theology and modern psychology exist in what is described as a spiritual openness towards holistic ways of knowing that embraces the affective, intuitive, and the cognitive (Grenz, 1996). The ethos of our contemporary context embraces an understanding of persons as embedded in a wider realm of reality. Thus, this is the context in which the pastor and professional counselor and psychologist must provide care and counsel. The strength of what is brought to bear on lives from the pastoral and psychological perspectives and practices must not be diminished or devalued in what each brings to a world and culture of brokenness, pain and suffering where individual lives are challenged to live well, whole and healed. The complexity of design of the human being existing as body, soul, and spirit, necessitates disciplines that are equipped with the competency to perform effectively in each area of such human complexity. The pastoral counselor, pastoral/spiritual counselor, and the licensed clinical mental health professional must be knowledgeable of the psychological and spiritual reality of the human being, working within their particular area and level of expertise.

This chapter concludes that pastoral theology is still relevant in an age of modern psychology. While there are general competencies relative to each discipline, such as human, cultural, philosophical, and technological understanding, the synergy and strength is found in maintaining the integrity of each discipline. In other words, they remain distinctly what they are in definition and practice yet able to integrate the diversities of each discipline for more complete and sustained outcomes in the lives of people in need.

3.
A Correction of Pastoral Care that Overlooks the Most Vulnerable

Dr. Nontando Hadebe
Lecturer, St. Augustine College
Johannesburg, South Africa[8]

Introduction 41
A. Liberation Theologies: Voices of Vulnerable and Marginalized 43
   1. Latin American Liberation Theologies 44
   2. Feminist/Womanist Liberation Theologies 44
   3. African Liberation Theologies 45
   4. LGTBIQ Challenges in Liberation Theologies 46
B. Pastoral Care, Injustice and Taboo Subjects 47
C. Two Case Studies from Southern Africa: HIV, AIDS, Violence Against LGTBIQ 48
   1. Southern Africa HIV/AIDS Case Study 48
   2. Violence Against LGTBIQ Case Study 51
Conclusion 52

Introduction

Despite the integration of social justice principles that prioritize the liberation of vulnerable groups in the mission of both Catholic and Protestant churches, there seem to be inconsistencies in the application of

---

[8] Hadebe earned her ThD from St. Augustine College, Johannesburg, South Africa, and her ThM and BT from the University of KwaZulu/Natal, South Africa. She was Fulbright Scholar in residence at Emmanuel College, Boston, MA, and an International Fellow at the Jesuit School of Theology, Berkley, CA. She is a member of the Circle of Concerned African Women Theologians and the Theological Colloquium on Church, Religion and Society in Africa's Women's Caucus comprosed of catholic women theologians in Africa. She has written several articles and book chapters, including "Commodification, Decolonisation and Theological Education in Africa: Renewed Challenges for African Theologians," *HTS Teologiese Studies/Theological Studies* 73, no. 3 (2017); "The Cry of the Earth Is the Cry of Women: Ecofeminisms in Critical Dialogue with Laudato Si," *Grace and Truth* 42, no. 2 (2017); "Moving in Circles. A Sankofa-Kairos Theology of Inclusivity and Accountability Rooted in Trinitarian Theology as a Resource for Restoring the Liberation Legacy of the Circle of Concerned African Women Theologians," *Verbum et Ecclesia* 37, no. 2 (2016); "Not in Our Name without Us: The Intervention of Catholic Women Speak at the Synod of Bishops on the Family: A Case Study of a Global Resistance Movement by Catholic Women," *HTS Teologiese Studies/Theological Studies* 72, no. 1 (2016); "Whose Life Matters? Violence Against Lesbians and the Politis of Life in the Church," in *Visions and Vocations, The Catholic Women Speak Network*, ed. Tina Beattie and D. Culberston (Mahwah, NJ: Paulist Press, 2018); "Toward an Ubuntu Trinitarian Prophetic Theology: A Social Critique of Blindness to the Other," in *Living With(Out) Borders: Catholic Theological Ethics in the World Church and the Migration of Peoples*, ed. Agnes Brazal and Maria Theresa Davila (Maryknoll: Orbis Books, 2016; 260 pp.); "HIV and AIDS in Southern Africa Gender Inequality and Human Rights: A Prophetic Trinitarian Anthropology," chapter 19, in *Dignity, Freedom and Grace: Christian Perspective on HIV, AIDS and Human Rights*, ed. Gilliam Paterson and Callie Long (Geneva: WCC, 2016; 168 pp.). See www.StAugustine.ac.za and noehadebe@gmail.com.

these ideals to the pastoral care of groups that have a history of marginalization within these churches. The experiences of these groups are associated with taboo subjects that further alienate them resulting in a lack of access to pastoral care in some cases. In Southern Africa these challenges are compounded by the intersection of culture and colonialism. Two case studies of the experiences of the most vulnerable from this region will be discussed: namely, Persons Living with HIV and AIDS; and the experiences of sexual minorities, particularly of lesbians. It will be argued that their experiences of exclusion from pastoral care presents a disjuncture between the ideals of social justice and the practice of pastoral care, and that disjuncture imposes an ethical imperative for the correction of pastoral care that overlooks the most vulnerable.

The social and political policies that make for starving children, battered women, and the evils of rising fascism remain in place as people learn through prayer to find the tranquility to live with corrupt political and social structures instead of channeling their distress and anger and anxiety into energy for constructive change (Jantzen 1994, p. 201).

The social teachings of both Catholic and Protestant churches would argue against the above statement because their mission is to confront unjust social systems that oppress the most vulnerable groups in society. Catholic social teaching for example includes several principles such as a preferential option for the poor, solidarity, subsidiarity and justice as foundational to the mission of the Catholic Church in the world. In his encyclical on the environment entitled *Laudato Si*, Pope Francis reiterated these principles in his argument that the exploitation of the environment cannot be separated from the exploitation of the poor:

> Today, however, we have to realize that a true ecological approach *always* becomes a social approach; it must integrate questions of justice in debates on the environment so as to hear *both the cry of the earth and the cry of the poor.* (LS 49 [italics mine])

Similarly, the World Council of Churches defines one of its goals as "service by serving human need, breaking down barriers between people, seeking justice and peace, and upholding the integrity of creation."[9] Hence the inclusion of social justice into the mission of churches should be evident

---

[9] World Council of Churches "brings together churches, denominations and church fellowships in more than 110 countries and territories throughout the world, representing over 500 million Christians and including most of the world's Orthodox churches, scores of Anglican, Baptist, Lutheran, Methodist and Reformed churches, as well as many United and Independent churches. While the bulk of the WCC's founding churches were European and North American, today most member churches are in Africa, Asia, the Caribbean, Latin America, the Middle East, and the Pacific. There are now 348 member churches." See www.oikoumene.org/en/about-us.

in the practice of pastoral care that engages in the struggle for justice for all vulnerable groups.

However, the practice of pastoral care in western Christianity, which has been "exported" to the rest of the world, has primarily been individual centered and acontextual. This form of pastoral care is critiqued as one that is detached from its own stated-mission context and supportive of the status quo. Marginalized groups have not been passive and have challenged the theological basis of this model of pastoral care through liberation theologies that integrate their experiences of oppression from systemic injustice. In addressing their lived experiences, marginalized groups have had to confront taboo subjects such as domestic violence, gender inequality, rape, sexuality, abuse of power, masculinities, sex work, sexual minorities, and sexual diversity.

These issues are further compounded in the Southern African context by culture and colonialism. The two case studies regarding HIV/AIDS and violence against sexual minorities (particularly lesbians) illustrate how their experiences of taboo and exclusion from pastoral care impose an ethical imperative for the correction of pastoral care that moves toward a more inclusive care, especially of the most vulnerable.

The rest of the article will discuss these issues in an overview of how the liberation theologies try to address the challenges for the correction of overlooking the most vulnerable toward that of a pastoral care model that includes the most vulnerable.

A. Liberation Theologies: Voices of Vulnerable and Marginalized

Liberation theologies have been extensively discussed. The focus of this section is on the common features of and some examples of diversity in liberation theologies as background for an analysis of pastoral care. Schüssler Fiorenza (1991) defines the common features as follows:

> In a broad sense, the term *liberation theology* refers to any theological movement that criticizes a specific form of oppression and views liberation as integral to the theological task. Feminist theologies, African American theologies and certain Asian theologies are major types of liberation theology (1991, p. 62).

Liberation theologies emerge from experiences of oppressed groups in relation to systemic injustices that pursue material and spiritual liberation. They challenge the universal claims and acontextual nature of western theologies. Though not monolithic, each of the varied liberation theologies reflect the particular experiences of oppressed groups. In their multiplicity they share similar methodology and commitments. Three examples of liberation theologies will be discussed namely: Latin American, Feminist, and African.

1. Latin American Liberation Theologies

Latin American liberation theologies challenged the middle-class bias and exclusion of the poor in western theologies. Gutiérrez explains the differences between these two theologies as follows:

> In Latin America and Caribbean, the challenge comes not in the first instance from the non-believer, but from the 'non persons', those who are recognised as people by the existing social order; the poor, the exploited, those systematically and legally deprived of their status as human beings, those who barely realise what it is to be a human being. The 'non-person' questions not so much our religious universe but above all our economic, social, political and cultural order, calling for a transformation of the very foundations of a dehumanizing society. (2007, p. 28)

The unjust economic and political systems that oppress the poor as well as the theologies that ignore the plight of the poor are confronted in Latin American liberation theologies. Pastoral care in this context responds to the immediate needs of the poor and actively engages in the struggle for social justice.

2. Feminist/Womanist Liberation Theologies

Similarly, feminist theologians challenge androcentrism, sexism, and patriarchy in church and society that perpetuates and justifies the marginalization of women. Rosemary Ruether defines feminist theology as follows:

> Feminist theology takes feminist critique and reconstruction of gender paradigms into the theological realm. They question patterns of theology that justify male dominance and female subordination such as exclusive male language for God, the view that males are more like God than females, that only males can represent God as leaders in church and society, or that women are created by God to be subordinate to males and thus sin by rejecting this subordination (2002, p. 3).

African American and Hispanic women theologians have added their distinctive voices to feminist theologies. Both have rejected the term feminism and named their theologies "womanist" and *"mujerista"* respectively. African American womanist theology integrated race and class in their gender analysis as a response to the racism of white Christian feminists and the sexism of black male theologies. Thomas defines womanist theology as "a critical reflection upon black women's place in the world that God has created and takes seriously black women's experience as human beings who are made in the image of God" (2004, p. 38). Similarly, Hispanic women's *mujerista* theology established their particular experiences of oppression as a minority group in the USA. *Mujerista* theology challenges "oppressive structures that refuse to allow us to be full members of society while preserving our distinctiveness as Hispanic women" (Isasi-Diaz, 1994, p. 88).

Outside the USA, Latin American, Asian, and African women added their unique experiences to feminist theology. Elina Vuola from Latin America describes the praxis of *vida cotidiana* that is "everyday life" in public and private as one of the key contributions to Latin American feminist theologies and also forms a critique to liberation theology's "'ideological slipping' which left out sexist and machista elements in society, church and theology" (2002, p. 148). Vuola contends that at the center of Latin American feminist liberation theology is "life, human integrity, justice and liberation of all women" (2002, p. 148). Like their African counterparts, Asian women theologies focus on culture.

Kowk Pui-Lan and Musimbi Kanyoro emphasize the centrality of culture in both contexts. Pui-Lan states that,

> Culture has become a site of struggle as people who have experienced colonialism, slavery, or exploitation and genocide reclaim their cultural identity and their sense of who they are after a long history of oppression. Women in these marginalized communities have to negotiate their cultural identities in multiple and complex ways taking into consideration gender, class, race and other differences. Feminist theology must pay attention to diversity of culture and social contexts. (2002, p. 23)

3. African Liberation Theologies

Not only is culture central in Asian women's theologies as a source of oppression and liberation, but culture is similarly central in African women theologians as explained by Kanyoro,

> All questions regarding the welfare and status of women in Africa are explained within the framework of culture, e.g. women cannot inherit land or own property because it is no culturally 'right' whether the subject is politics, economics, religion or social issues, none of these are safe from the sharp eyes of culture. (2002, p. 23)

The central role of culture and liberation found in African theologies are responses to multiple challenges from western theologies including the vilification of African cultures; racism, colonialism, and apartheid; post-independence oppression; gender as already discussed; and emerging Lesbian, Gay, Transgender, Bisexual, Intersex, and Queer (LGTBIQ) theological discourses. African theologies are diverse and not monolithic.

The emergence of African theology has been characterized by two different emphases on inculturation and liberation. Simon Maimela describes the differences between inculturation and black theologies as follows,

> Inculturation is characterized by an attempt to marry Christianity with the African worldview so that Christianity could speak with an African idiom and

accent, and the liberation approach developed in the 1970s gave birth to black theology in South Africa which emphasized struggle for socio-economic and political liberation from white racial domination. (1991, p. 2)

These two streams represent the context of the development of African theologies as protest movements for the liberation of Africans from colonialism and apartheid. However, many scholars argue against the dichotomy between culture and liberation seeing these two streams as complementary.

According to Bujo an inculturation theology without liberation is as deficient as a liberation theology without inculturation. He argues as follows,

> In fact, it is true that a purely culturally-centered theology is neither Christian nor African, nor simply human, it is no less true that a theology unilaterally based on social and economic issues without a cultural background goes very much against the dignity of the human person. (2003, p. 2)

4. LGTBIQ Challenges in Liberation Theologies

The emerging theological discourse on LGTBIQ presents new challenges to African theologies from groups that are experiencing oppression from culture, governments, and religion. The two dominant discourses are that LGTBIQ identities are "unAfrican" and "unChristian." The unAfrican argument is based on the belief that LGTBIQ persons did not exist in pre-colonial Africa and are a by-product of colonialism and western influences: "In this argument, precolonial African culture was unitary and strictly heterosexual, and homosexuality and gender diversity are decadent, neocolonial Western imports" (Gunda, 2017, p. 22).

Similarly the "unChristian" argument is based on the interpretation of certain biblical texts that are believed to be against LGTBIQ persons: "The Sodom narrative (Gen 19), the Levitical laws on sexual purity (Lev 18 and 20) and certain Pauline texts (Rom 1, 1 Cor 6, 1 Tim 1) are read as evidence of the Bible's unequivocal opposition to homosexuality" (Gunda, 2017, p. 21).

In the Roman Catholic Church, homosexuality is described as "contrary to natural law" and "intrinsically disordered" (Catechism 2357.[10] However, there is also opposition to the violation and discrimination of LGTBIQ persons: "We would like before all else to reaffirm that every person, regardless of sexual orientation, ought to be respected in his or her dignity and treated with consideration" (Pope Francis, 2016, p. 190).

The foregoing discussions on liberation theologies from oppressed groups provide tools and resources for comprehensive pastoral care that can

---

[10] Catechism of the Roman Catholic Church, www.vatican.va/archive/ENG0015/_P85.HTM.

adequately respond in liberating ways to the personal, social and spiritual challenges of vulnerable groups.

B. Pastoral Care, Injustice and Taboo Subjects

There are different definitions of pastoral care, three of which will be discussed. The first is from Lynch who describes pastoral care in the Catholic Tradition:

> Pastoral care has often been described as a 'cure of souls' ministry of healing in the broad sense. The term denotes a concern for the emotional, moral and spiritual dimensions within the life of the individual. (Lynch, 2005, p. 10)

This model is individual centered and describes the care activities undertaken by a priest in relation to individual parishioners.

The second definition is from Lartey (1997) who synthesizes a range of definitions from prominent scholars from around the world including Clinebell (USA), Wimberley (African American), and Masamba ma Mampolo (Africa) in his broad-based definition of pastoral care:

> Pastoral care consists of helping activities, participated in by people who recognise a transcendent dimension to human life, which, by the use of verbal or non-verbal, direct or indirect, literal or symbolic modes of communication, aim at preventing, relieving or facilitating persons coping with anxieties. Pastoral care seeks to foster people's growth as full human beings together with the development of ecologically and socio-political holistic communities in which all persons may live humane lives. (1997, pp. 30–31)

The last definition is a method used in communal pastoral care in the contexts of injustice, namely, the "See, Judge, Act" approved by Pope John XXIII in his encyclical letter *Mater et Magistra* (1961) for use in local parishes. The three-stage process starts with "Seeing" which includes a thorough analysis of the context so that the systems of injustice are named and made visible for all to understand. The second stage is "Judge" in a process of discernment through the study of scripture in relation to the information provided from the "Seeing" process. The last stage of "Acting" is the practical action in response to "Seeing" and "Judging." This cycle is repeated as a way of refining and deepening the process.

The foregoing definitions and descriptions of pastoral care correspond to the three cycles in the history of pastoral care described by Patton which are: classical, clinical, and community-contextual. The classical "universalizes understanding of human problems and expresses them in exclusively religious terms" (1993, p. 39); the clinical paradigm "interprets human problems psychologically and makes the males of the dominant culture be recognized as normative" (1993, p. 39); and the communal contextual paradigm "insists that there are multiple contexts to be taken into account. In fact, a central part of the ministry of pastoral care today is discerning the contexts most relevant for understanding a pastoral situation" (1993, p. 40).

The communal contextual paradigm has been influenced by liberation theologies including feminist and womanist theologies. In an article entitled "Three Decades of Women Writing for our Lives," Grieder, Johnson, and Leslie summarized seven areas of focus namely: 1) *Ekklesia* and its ministry, 2) marginalized people and taboo topics, 3) female experience, 4) theological education, 5) soulfulness, 6) violence, and 7) systems of care (1999, p. 23). One of the key themes from these seven areas is the "othering" of marginalized groups, including women, and the classifying their experiences under the rubric of that which is "taboo." As part of their resistance, feminist and womanist scholars have written about taboo subjects such as sexual violence; intersections between race, class and gender; adolescent girls; divorce and remarriage, sexual desire and expression; infertility; stillbirth and miscarriage and political oppression (Grieder, Johnson and Leslie, 1999, p. 32). The liberative aspect of their struggle is that "attention to margins and taboos decenters dominant paradigms, reveals differentials in the misuse of social power and thus enables prompt response where justice ministries are urgently needed" (1999, p. 29).

C. Two Case Studies from Southern Africa: HIV and AIDS and Violence Against LGTBIQ

1. Southern Africa HIV/AIDS Case Study

Southern Africa continues to the be an epicenter of HIV and AIDS with high infection rates among marginalized groups which include young women, men who have sex with men, injecting drug users, and sex workers (UNAIDS, 2016). The drivers of the epidemic are gender inequality and gender-based violence which includes violence against LGTBIQ. The brutal practice of "corrective rape" of black lesbians represents one of the most extreme acts of violence against LGTBIQ.

In this context, Christianity is implicated in the experiences of marginalization and exclusion by these two groups. HIV and AIDS were first detected in the USA in 1981 among gay communities. The relationship between HIV and gay communities led to the belief by many Christians that HIV and AIDS were a punishment from God against homosexuality. HIV and AIDS were associated with homosexuality, sexual immorality, sin, punishment, and God's judgement in dialogues and writings of many western Christians.

Similar theological responses were also common in Africa where HIV was transmitted primarily through heterosexual sex and associated with marginalized groups like commercial sex workers and the practice of multiple partners. The negative impact of judgmental theology was acknowledged in a confession made by church leaders in Africa at the *Global Consultation on the Ecumenical Response to the Challenge of HIV/AIDS* in Nairobi, Kenya (25–28 November 2001):

> As the pandemic has unfolded, it has exposed fault lines that reach to the heart of our theology, our ethics, our liturgy and our practice of ministry. Today, churches are being obliged to acknowledge that we have—however unwittingly—contributed both actively and passively to the spread of the virus.... Our tendency to exclude others, our interpretation of the scriptures and our theology of sin have all combined to promote the stigmatization, exclusion and suffering of people with HIV or AIDS. This has undermined the effectiveness of care, education and prevention efforts and inflict additional suffering on those already affected by the HIV. Given the extreme urgency of the situation, and the conviction that the churches do have a distinctive role to play in the response to the pandemic, what is needed is a rethinking of our mission, and the transformation of our structures and ways of working.[11]

The confession clearly outlined the key "fault lines" in theological responses, including judgmental attitudes and the difficulty of addressing sexual issues and stigma. Yet in that very confession, there was also a commitment by church leaders to redefine their role and mission in the context of HIV and AIDS.

As an outcome of a more compassionate theology, churches are currently responsible for a significant number of projects responding to the humanitarian aspect of HIV such as orphan care, hospices, counselling, and education. There has been a substantial increase in theological discourse on all aspects of HIV and AIDS.

However, one of the weaknesses of focusing mostly on compassionate needs is that the root causes of HIV and AIDS have tended to be marginalized, resulting in a limited understanding of HIV and AIDS. This is illustrated in two related researches carried out in 2004 and 2005 on ministers, lay persons, women's groups, and people living with HIV and AIDS. The first by the Pietermaritzburg Agency for Christian Social Action (PACSA) was entitled *Research Report: Churches and HIV/AIDS: Exploring how local churches are integrating HIV/AIDS in the life and ministries of the church and how those most directly affected experience these*, and it found that,

> Church leaders had adequate knowledge about HIV/AIDS though most of this focuses on biological facts and does not adequately take into account the social complexities surrounding the pandemic and how they impact on individuals. This factual knowledge has in many cases not led to a transformation of attitudes, and many church leaders hold judgmental opinions about the main

---

[11] WCC 2001: www.wcc-coe.org.

way people become infected (63%) and why God is allowing the pandemic (70%). These attitudes tend to apportion blame to individuals for their HIV+ status, assuming that they become infected through their own promiscuity. (Gennrich et al., 2004, pp. 4–5)

There seems to be a correlation between how transmission of HIV is understood and the theological responses. If as shown in this research HIV transmission is linked to sexual behavior, particularly "promiscuity" without an understanding of the wider social factors that influence sexual behavior, then the theological response will tend to be moralistic and judgmental.

These findings were confirmed by the research done in 2005 by Kwazulu-Natal Church AIDS Network (KZNCAN) entitled *Churches and HIV/AIDS A Research on KwaZulu-Natal Christian Council (KZNCC)*. Researchers concluded that:

> Judgmental attitudes like the church's contextualization that *immoral lifestyles* are the root causes of HIV/AIDS repeated throughout the study. Biased attitudes towards homosexuals were evident when well over half the members of women's groups and ministers thought that homosexuals *always* transmit HIV. Hence, the church's contextualization of HIV/AIDS centers around sexual behavior. (2005, p. 33)

This conclusion is partially based on findings that 97% of ministers and 83% of women's groups agreed that leading immoral lifestyles was the foundation for the spread of HIV/AIDS, and therefore abstinence from sex before marriage was the only effective preventative measure against HIV infection (2005, p. 21).

Thus, the reduction of HIV and AIDS to immorality assumes an agency and ignores social factors such as gender inequality that compromise the capacity of women to exercise power over their sexuality as described in the following quotation from UNAIDS,

> In many places, HIV-prevention efforts do not take into account the gender and other inequalities that shape people's behaviours and limit their choices. Many HIV strategies assume an idealized world in which everyone is equal and free to make empowered choices, and can opt to abstain from sex, stay faithful to one's partner or use condoms consistently. In reality, women and girls face a range of HIV-related risk factors and vulnerabilities that men and boys do not—many of which are embedded in the social relations and economic realities of their societies. These factors are not easily dislodged or altered, but until they are, efforts to contain and reverse the AIDS epidemic are unlikely to achieve sustained success. (2004, pp. 3–4)

According to the UNAIDS 2016 report, young girls continue to constitute the most vulnerable group infected with HIV in sub-Saharan Africa,

> In sub-Saharan Africa, adolescent girls and young women accounted for 25% of new HIV infections among adults, and women accounted for 56% of new HIV infections among adults. Harmful gender norms and inequalities, insufficient

access to education and sexual and reproductive health services, poverty, food insecurity and violence, are at the root of the increased HIV risk of young women and adolescent girls. (UNAIDS 2016, p. 8).[12]

There is a great need in western Christian pastoral care to understand its role of judgment that ignores the social pressure and injustices forced upon the most vulnerable; these pressures are quite beyond the ability of the vulnerable to escape.

Other marginalized groups vulnerable to HIV infection include many groups: "Key populations at increased risk of HIV infection include sex workers, people who inject drugs, transgender people, prisoners and gay men and other men who have sex with men" (UNAIDS, 2016, p. 9). Significant underlying reasons for vulnerability are that they are "pushed to the fringes of society by stigma and the criminalization of same-sex relationships, drug use and, sex work" (UNAIDS, 2016, p. 10). Marginalization creates vulnerability to HIV infection which constitutes a violation of rights, the most basic of which is the right to life.

2. Violence Against LGTBIQ Case Study

A particularly horrid case of violence against LGTBIQ includes "corrective rape" of lesbians, of which the following describes the brutal detail.

> The partially clothed body of Eudy Simelane, former star of South Africa's acclaimed Banyana Banyana national female football squad, was found in a creek in a park in Kwa Thema, on the outskirts of Johannesburg. Simelane had been gang-raped and brutally beaten before being stabbed 25 times in the face, chest and legs. As well as being one of South Africa's best-known female footballers, Simelane was a voracious equality rights campaigner and one of the first women to live openly as a lesbian in Kwa Thema.[13]

The "corrective rape of lesbians" is a practice believed by perpetrators who are mostly heterosexual men to be a means of transforming lesbians into "real African women." "Lesbians are raped in ways intended to be punitive, or 'corrective' or 'curative,' because they undermine monolithic notions of masculinity and heterosexuality and refuse men's proposals and advances" (Swarr, 2012, p. 962). Corrective rape is driven by multiple intersecting factors including culture, religion, colonialism, and apartheid as explained in the following quotation:

---

[12] UNAIDS Global Aids Update, 2016. See https://www.unaids.org/sites/default/files/media_asset/global-AIDS-update-2016_en.pdf.

[13] Annie Kelly, "Raped and Killed for Being a Lesbian: South Africa Ignores Corrective Attacks," *The Guardian* (12 March 2009), accessed 11 October 2015. Banyana Banyana is the nickname for the South Africa national women's football team. See www.theguardian.com/world/2009/mar/12/eudy-simelane-corrective-rape-south-africa.

In sum, deep-rooted patriarchy, a history of state-based discrimination and violence, negligible risk of arrest or prosecution for sexual violence, and cultural and religious intolerance of homosexuality form the severe animosity towards homosexuality and other minority sexual orientations that results in widespread corrective rape. (Brown, 2012, p. 54)

In a context of the above discourses, religious judgmentalism that label LGTBIQ as "unAfrican" and "unChristian" perpetuates the vilification and so the challenge for pastoral care is to address these systemic, deeply ingrained beliefs as part of its ministry to LGTBIQ.

In their article entitled "When Faith Does Violence, re-imagining engagement between churches and LGTBIQ groups on homophobia in Africa," West, Kaoma, and Van der Walt argue for the "epistemological privilege" of LGTBIQ as the interlocutors of theologies of resistance:

Liberation theologies have made such a commitment the starting point of the doing of theology. The epistemological privileging of particular marginalized experience is what characterizes liberation theologies. (2017, p. 9)

They also propose a minimum pastoral care response to LGTBIQ that needs to be practiced by all churches irrespective of their theological views.

By constructing theological resources that facilitate and enable a minimal pastoral response that is life-affirming and dignity-granting for queer Christians our churches will have some minimal capacity for theological change. Fortunately, Jesus reminds us in the parable of the mustard seed that the beginnings of redemptive faith need only be small (Mark 4:30-32). (West, Kaoma, and Van der Walt, 2017, p. 31)

The experiences of marginalization described in these two cases serve to highlight the necessity of a comprehensive theology and practice of pastoral care that extends to all vulnerable groups without exception. Many of the root causes of vulnerability are in unjust social, cultural, and religious practices and beliefs which need to be deconstructed and reconstructed so that pastoral care can truly be an expression of the ideals of society embedded in the mission of churches.

Conclusion

This chapter attempted to respond to the challenges of exclusion of the most vulnerable groups from adequate and comprehensive pastoral care, and that despite the fact that the social teachings of Catholic and Protestant churches claim to be based on a fundamental commitment to the poor, the marginalized, and the vulnerable. The disjuncture often occurs because of the surfacing of highly contested and controversial taboo themes which stigmatize and alienate marginalized groups. Yet these issues are unavoidable and provide opportunities for contextually mediated knowledge as evidenced in liberation theologies that critique, transform, and act on the basis of the experiences of vulnerable groups merging the ideals of justice, human dignity, and common good that underlie Christianity and offer new avenues and horizons for pastoral care that is inclusive of all persons. Therefore, these issues behoove the church to try to correct its shortcomings and develop a quality of pastoral care that brings the best of the church to the most vulnerable.

4.
Religious Belief, Conflict, and Violence: Theological Basis in 1 John for Being Passionate and Loving Those who Disagree with Us

Dr. Caroline G. Seed
Theological Education Consultant for
Postgraduate Studies, George Whitefield College
South Africa[14]

Introduction	55
A. Theological Center of 1 John	57
1. A Midrash Pesher on Genesis 1–4	57
Table 1: Proposed Macro Chiastic Structure of 1 John	59
2. The Cain and Abel Motif	59
B. Religious Belief, Conflict, and Violence	62
1. Origins in Genesis 4	62
2. Conflict in the Johannine Fellowship	63
C. Being Passionate about What We Believe	65
1. The Concreteness of Belief	65
2. The Correctness of Belief	66
D. Being Passionate about Loving Those Who Disagree with Us	67
1. The Root of Disagreement	68
2. The Nature of God	68
3. The Morality of Belief	69
Conclusion	71

Introduction

The theological basis in 1 John for being passionate about what we believe and being passionate about loving those who disagree with us lies in the missional heart of God. Using the Cain and Abel motif from Genesis 4:1–16, the author of 1 John weaves a Midrash Pesher to give a prophetic

---

[14] Seed earned her PhD from the Greenwich School of Theology, UK, through the North-West University, Potchefstroom campus, South Africa, and was awarded the Robert Grainger Beckett Prize for Academic Excellence. Prior to Whitefield, she was senior lecturer, North-West University/Greenwich School of Theology, supervising Masters and PhD students; senior lecturer in theology, Presbyterian University of East Africa, Kikuyu; director of academic affairs, then principal, School of Mission, Carlile College, Nairobi, Kenya; and academic dean for Kigali Anglican Theological College, Rwanda. She has written several articles including, "Monotheism, Messianism and Children of Israel: Reception of the Gospel of John among the Isawa of Northern Nigeria and the Qiang of Western China, 1913-1935," *International Bulletin of Mission Research* (September 2019; first given as a research paper to the 2nd Annual Research Conference of the Presbyterian University of East Africa, 2016); and "'Translatability and Non-Translatability,' Bible, Qur'an and Land in northern Nigeria, 1913-1915," conference paper given at the inaugural conference of The Sanneh Institute, Accra, Ghana, February 26-28, 2020. She is writing a commentary on 1 John for Islamic contexts for Langham Literature with a completion date of December 2021. See cgseed@outlook.com, cseed@gwc.ac.za, and Caroline.Seed@nwu.ac.za.

explanation of the eschatological fulfilment of the ancient Jewish "protohistory" in the life of the beleaguered Johannine fellowship. The fellowship is to emulate the righteous Abel, who worshipped God with a pure heart. They are to hold firm to the gospel teaching regarding God and his incarnate Son, Jesus Christ, because it is the essence of eternal life. They are to eschew those who oppose them violently and walk in the ways of Cain. However, because they live in *koinōnia* with the triune God, they must also reflect his character of self-giving love. Their reaction to religious conflict and violence perpetrated against them is not to return like for like, but to love their neighbors (both inside and outside the fellowship) and to reach out to them in missional zeal through proclamation and prayer.

1 John is often seen to present a moral dilemma for Christians, who are commanded to "love one another" (2:10; 3:11; 4:7, 21) and yet, at the same time, to hold a "consistently hateful attitude towards their opponents ... the Antichrists" (2:22; 4:3).[15] The author is seen to limit love to the fellowship circle of the Christian community, thereby implying a rejection of those, now outside, who hold different beliefs.[16] It would seem, therefore, that hatred and religious conflict are the inevitable consequence of the stark polarization in the epistle between those who are in the light and those who walk in the darkness (1:5–7). Yet, the often-overlooked missional nature of 1 John belies this interpretation.[17] The purpose of the proclamation of the gospel (1:3) is not to exclude those who disagree with the apostolic teaching, but to bring them into life and fellowship through repentance and belief (1:9; 2:2; 5:16). Indeed, the purpose of writing (5:13) is both that they "may believe in the name of the Son of God" (an initial drawing into fellowship) and that they may know that they "have eternal life" (an assurance of continuance in the fellowship).[18] There may be conflict and even violence over opposing religious beliefs, but this is not an ethical ideal to which the Johannine fellowship should aspire. They are to hold firmly to the truth, while seeking through faithful proclamation (1:3) and fervent prayer (5:16) to bring those who oppose them into the fellowship of eternal life.

---

[15] Tom Thatcher, "Cain the Jew the Antichrist: Collective Memory and the Johannine Ethic of Loving and Hating," in *Rethinking the Ethics of John: "Implicit Ethics" in the Johannine Writings, Contexts and Norms of N.T. Ethics*, vol. III, ed. Jan G. van der Watt and Ruben Zimmerman (Heidelberg: Mohr Siebeck, 2012), 350.

[16] As this article has no space to engage with the substantial debate regarding the authorship of 1 John, it uses "the author" to indicate authorship.

[17] Caroline G. Seed, "The Missional Nature of Divine-human Communion: T. F. Torrance and the Chinese Church" (PhD thesis, Potchefstroom, ZA: North-West University, 2016), 106–114.

[18] All Bible references in this article are taken from the English Standard Version (ESV), 2011.

A. Theological Center of 1 John

The author uses the Jewish history of Cain and Abel (Gen 4:1–16) to situate the current conflict in the O.T. historical-theological tradition. The role of O.T. scripture in 1 John has been widely debated. Carson holds that the only allusion is the Cain and Abel narrative in 1 John 3:12.[19] Lieu, on the other hand, argues that the O.T. underlies the entire Jewish worldview of the epistle.[20] Both positions are, in fact, correct, but with reservations. The only specific scriptural allusion is to Genesis 4, and there is scriptural underpinning in the broad sense throughout the epistle, but this is secondary to the narrative of Cain and Abel that forms the structural and theological center. To read 1 John this way, is to propose an alternative to traditional interpretations of the epistle.[21] Instead, 1 John is understood in the context in which it was composed during the period of Second Temple Jewish hermeneutics.[22]

1. A Midrash Pesher on Genesis 1–4

Anthony Royle proposes that the author uses Genesis 1–4 as Midrash Pesher applied eschatologically to the contemporary situation found in the Johannine fellowship.[23] Midrash Pesher in eschatological fulfillment was a common exegetical technique in use during the Second Temple period. Jewish scholar Jacob Neusner describes this type of prophetic Midrash as the process by which "the exegete will read Scripture as an account of things that are happening or are going to happen," so that the Scripture portion exegeted serves as a prophetic reading of contemporary events.[24] The historical life of Israel would therefore be seen to prefigure contemporary events and to act as a guide for to the unfolding of events in the near future.[25] Royle maintains that 1 John has Genesis 1–4 in view, and this is no doubt true because Genesis 4 presupposes Genesis 1–3. However, when

---

[19] D. A. Carson, "1–3 John," in *Commentary on the N.T. Use of the O.T.*, ed. G. K. Beale and D. A. Carson (Grand Rapids: Baker Academic, 2007), 1063–1067.

[20] Judith M. Lieu, "What Was from the Beginning: Scripture and Tradition in the Johannine Epistles," *N.T. Studies* 39, no. 3 (July 1993): 461.

[21] See, for example, Judith M. Lieu, *The Theology of the Johannine Epistles* (Cambridge: Cambridge University Press, 1991): 31–71.

[22] Anthony Royle, "1 John as Midrash Pesher on Genesis 1–4: Eschatology, Typology, Structure and Early Christian Polemics," conference paper presented at the *British N.T. Society Conference* at the University of Manchester, 6 September 2014.

[23] Royle, "1 John as Midrash Pesher." In this article, the word "fellowship" translates the Johannine usage of *koinónia* (1 John 1: 3, 7), rather than *ekklesia* (church), to designate the community of believers. The popular use of the "Johannine community" has been avoided because of its association with Raymond Brown's theories regarding the authorship, dating and purpose of the epistle.

[24] Jacob Neusner, *What is Midrash?* (Eugene: Wipf and Stock, 1987), 1, 7.

[25] Neusner, *What is Midrash?*, 53.

1 John is read as Midrash Pesher specifically on the Genesis 4 account of Cain and Abel, applied in eschatological fulfillment to the situation facing the Johannine fellowship, then its intention to address the issue of current religious conflict through the Genesis account of Cain and Abel becomes apparent.

To make sense of the current conflict over religious belief that has split the visible Johannine fellowship (Gen 2:19), the author appeals to the Jewish collective memory of the first instance of religious conflict in Genesis 4 (3:11–15). Tom Thatcher proposes that the narrative serves to categorize individuals into those who are of Cain (of the devil) and those who are of Abel (of God, of Christ).[26] The Cain and Abel motif (3:12) is placed in the center of the structural chiasm so that it dominates the interpretation. Those who are like Abel hold passionately to the truth and live in love and obedience. Those who are like Cain demonstrate opposite behavior. Yet, the Abelites are called to reflect the love that is the essence of the character of God their Father (4:16). They are not to hate their brothers (4:19–21). Instead, like the apostles, they are to proclaim the truth passionately, with the missional purpose of bringing those who are outside, into the fellowship of the truth (1:3, 7).

Proving that 3:12 is the center of the epistle is not, however, a simple task. The structure of 1 John has long been a matter of debate. Köstenberger notes that opinion varies widely from the complete lack of coherence to intricately balanced composition.[27] Van Staden, for example, applies Hebrew parallelism and concludes that the epistle consists of three sections organized in chiasm with introductions and transitions linking them.[28] The problem with Van Staden's schema is that it is based on a reading of 1 John as an apologetic document to refute opponents' claims about the Gospel of John.[29] It does not, therefore, allow the text to speak for itself. A more intrinsic approach is needed.

In his work on the rhetoric of 1 Corinthians, Middle East scholar Kenneth Bailey demonstrates that typical Jewish prophetic rhetorical structure uses parallelism in the micro as well as the macro structures[30] He shows that the rhetorical structures of Isaiah's prophetic oracles are often

---

[26] Thatcher, *Cain the Jew*, 354.

[27] Andreas Köstenberger, *A Theology of John's Gospel and Letters: The Word, the Christ, the Son of God* (Grand Rapids: Zondervan, 2009), 171.

[28] P. J. Van Staden, "The Debate on the Structure of 1 John," *HTS Teologiese Studies/Theological Studies* 47 (April, 1991): 487–502.

[29] Van Staden, "Debate ... 1 John," 498.

[30] Kenneth Bailey, *Paul through Mediterranean Eyes: Cultural Studies in 1 Corinthians* (Downers Grove: IVP, 2011), 34–52.

reflected in Paul's writings. If it were possible to postulate that the same Hebrew prophetic rhetorical traditions have been used in the composition of 1 John, then we may expect to find evidence of Hebrew parallelism in the macro and micro structures of this epistle too. If the text of 1 John is read intrinsically as a chiasm of theological concepts, then there is no need for the introductions and transitions suggested by Van Staden. 1 John forms a macro chiasm with the Cain and Abel motif at the center. This is reflected in the proposed schema below.[31]

Table 1: Proposed Macro Chiastic Structure of 1 John

> A. 1: 1 –2:6 Fellowship
>   B. 2: 7– 11 New Commandment
>   C. 2: 12–14 Testimony
>   D. 2: 15–17 Overcoming the World
>   E. 2: 18– 27 The Last Hour
>   F. 2: 28–3:10 Practicing Righteousness
>   **G. 3:11–15 Cain and Abel (Gen 4).**
> F^1. 3: 16–24 Practicing Righteousness
> E^1. 4: 1–21 The Last Hour
> D^1. 5: 1–5 Overcoming the World
> C^1. 5: 6–15 Testimony
> B^1. 5: 16–17 New Commandment
> A^1. 5: 18–21 Fellowship

The careful balance between the first and second sections of the chiasm relates the theological themes of the epistle to the central narrative. The core conflict between Cain and Abel is over the way they "practice righteousness" (F–F1). This conflict should be interpreted eschatologically as the inevitable conflict of the "last hour" (E–E1). The issue is the victory over the world by the Lord Jesus Christ (D–D1), to which both the experience of the disciples and the blood, water, and Spirit bear testimony (C–C1). The essence is the new commandment to love one another (B–B1), which arises from the nature of faith as entry into and maintenance of fellowship with the triune God, as opposed to Cain's alternative, which is, in reality, fellowship with idols (A–A1).

2. The Cain and Abel Motif

The Cain and Abel allusion at the center of 1 John, therefore, provides an O.T. framework through which to interpret the pain of rejection experienced

---

[31] This schema does not reflect the micro chiasms within the macro chiasm.

by the Johannine fellowship. This came because of the opposition of those who had split the group and left the church (2:19). Wenham maintains that the events of Genesis 2:4–4:26 are "protohistorical," in that they narrate events concerning real historical figures, whose actions have an influence on all humanity, but that they are also "paradigmatic" as they stand as a warning against types of behavior that humans might fall into if they disobey God.[32] The author of 1 John intends that the fledgling church should understand the contemporary conflict within its fellowship in terms of the "protohistorical" Cain and Abel narrative that forms an interpretative motif through the epistle.

The Cain and Abel pericope (Gen 4:1–16) is part of the first cycle of "generations," introduced in Genesis 2:4. This genealogy of creation encompasses the disobedience of God's first creatures, the entry of sin into the world, and the curse leading to the expulsion of Adam and Eve from the Garden of Eden. This is followed by examples of the multiplication of the sin of Adam and Eve in their progeny, Cain and Lamech, and the corresponding multiplication of grace in the righteous progeny, Abel and Seth. When Eve gives birth to Cain outside the Garden of God's presence, she believes that the son she has given birth to is the "seed of the woman" who will "bruise the head of the serpent" and reverse the effects of the curse (Gen 3:15; 4:1).[33] However, subsequent events will prove her wrong. The births of Cain and his younger brother Abel will not reverse the effects of sin and curse, but rather enhance them through the conflict over religious worship that plays out in their lives (Gen 4:8–12). At the same time, the history of the gracious intervention of the Lord in the lives of the righteous is seen in the life of the Lord's appointed (Strong's H7896, *shith*) righteous brother, Seth (Gen 4:25–26). Thus, the primordial family history begins a pattern of sin, conflict, and the gracious intervention of the Lord that will be repeated down the generations of the nations of the earth.

The foundational Genesis 1–4 pattern serves as a motif for understanding religious conflict through the ages.[34] God creates the world "very good" (Gen 1:31), but Satan tempts those made "in [God's] own image" (Gen 1:27) to rebel and so to fall into sin and judgment. The full effects of sin are seen in the lives of their sons, Cain and Abel. Cain continues to rebel against the Lord, leading to the murder of his righteous brother (Heb 11:4).

---

[32] Gordon J. Wenham, *Genesis 1–15. Word Biblical Commentary*, 1 (Waco: Word, 1987), 117.

[33] Walter C. Kaiser Jnr, *Mission in the O.T.: Israel as a Light to the Nations*. (Grand Rapids: Baker Books, 2000), 16. The Hebrew words are ambiguous. Kaiser interprets Eve's statement in the light of the "promise plan" of God to deliver humanity from the effects of sin and death.

[34] Ida Glaser with Hannah Kay, *Thinking Biblically About Islam* (Carlisle: Langham Global Library, Kindle edition, 2016), location 832.

The "blood of Abel," the righteous one, continues to cry out to the Lord for justice (Gen 4:10). A pattern is set. Righteousness and evil dwell side by side in the post-Fall world. Within the first family, there are those who "walk in the ways of the Lord" and those who choose the path that leads to destruction. Those who walk the path of sin persecute those, who by grace, walk the life of faith as Abel did (see Gen 21:8–12).

The paradigmatic nature of the Cain and Abel narrative in establishing a pattern of contrast between the righteous and the wicked can be illustrated by the use of the motif in the Jewish writings. *Targum Pseudo-Jonathan,* a fifth century B.C. Aramaic translation, locates the problem of Cain's evil nature in his conception by an angel.[35] The *Genesis Rabbah*, a fifth century B.C. Midrash on the Torah, on the other hand, places the blame for Cain's conception in Eve's connivance with Satan in tempting Adam to sexual arousal.[36] In the early Christian period, Philo of Alexandria (c. 20 B.C. to 5 A.D.) interprets the conflict between the two brothers in terms of their contrasting loves: the sin of self-love as opposed to the love of God. Cain's self-love is indicative of the sin of idolatry, while Abel's love of the Lord is indicative of humility and good.[37] In the same period, Josephus contrasts the righteousness of Abel with the evil of Cain and the *Apocalypse of Abraham* 24:5 comments that Cain acted lawlessly under the influence of Satan.

Given the paradigmatic nature of the Cain and Abel motif in Jewish thought at the time of the composition of the epistle, it may not be unreasonable to suggest that is the foundation text for a prophetic Midrash on the interpretation of unfolding apocalyptic events in the early church. Yarbrough notes that the allusion to the Cain and Abel narrative in 1 John is more restrained than the extra-biblical material but suggests that it is in harmony with what is implied.[38] The final exhortation, "Little children, keep yourself from idols" (5:21), may express something of Philo's opinion that the self-love of Cain was tantamount to idolatry. However, in 1 John, it is not the conception of Cain that is at the heart of the exegesis, but the contrasting religious practices of the brothers. As Waltke observes, the root of the conflict paradigm initiated by Cain and Abel is religious.[39]

---

[35] *The Targum of Palestine, commonly entitled the Targum of Jonathan ben Uzziel on the Book of Genesis*, available from http://targum.info/pj/pjgen1-6.htm; accessed 9 May, 2017.

[36] Robert C. Gregg, *Shared Stories, Rival Tellings; Early Encounters of Jews, Christians and Muslims* (Oxford: Oxford University Press, Kindle edition, 2015), 602.

[37] Gregg, *Shared Stories*, 827.

[38] John Yarbrough, *1–3 John* (Grand Rapids: Baker), 198.

[39] Bruce Waltke, *An O.T. Theology: An Exegetical, Canonical and Thematic Approach* (Grand Rapids: Zondervan, 2007), 270.

B. Religious Belief, Conflict, and Violence
1. Origins in Genesis 4

In the post-Fall world of Genesis 4, evil has become a reality. The Lord tells Cain, "Sin is crouching at your door. Its desire is for you, but you must rule over it" (Gen 4:7). The sin of Adam and Eve has marred the relationship with the Creator. No longer does the first family live in secure knowledge of an uninterrupted relationship with God. Sin is personified as a demon waiting at the door to pounce on its victims.[40] Glaser points out that this does not mean that people have no knowledge of God.[41] Genesis 4 records a religious act of reaching out to the Lord by bringing offerings to him in sacrifice. The core issue is the Lord's reaction to the sacrifice (Gen 4:4). The Lord has "regard for Abel and his offering", but for Cain and his offering, the Lord has "no regard". The Hebrew root *shaah* (Strong's H8519) means to "gaze with interest". Thus, the Lord looks with favor on Abel (implying the blessing of restored relationship) and does not consider Cain's religious act (implying that Cain continues in broken relationship and sin).

The surprise in this section is not that Cain's offering does not please the Lord, but that Abel's offering does.[42] Somehow, the broken relationship has been restored through Abel's actions. Commentators have speculated on the difference in the Lord's reaction to the religious acts of the brothers.[43] The Genesis 4 passage does not give an answer. Instead, the narrative moves to set the scene for the entry of the crouching sin into Cain's heart. Cain is "very angry", the Hebrew root *charah* meaning to "burn with anger" (Strong's H2734). His "face falls", meaning he is displeased with the Lord and turns his face away. Rebellion, the chief characteristic of sin, has entered his heart. The Lord upbraids Cain, telling him that if he "does well", he will be accepted. The term *yatab* used in Gen 4:7 implies doing that which is ethically correct (Strong's H3190). The reason for the failure of Cain's grain offering to find favor with the Lord lies in the attitude of Cain's heart.

However, Cain shows no propensity to listen to the Lord or to repent of the sin that has entered his heart. He plots against his brother and murders him. The word used for "killed" in v.8 is *harag*, implying ruthless, personally motivated violence (Strong's H2026). When the Lord calls Cain to account, Cain multiplies sin by lying about his knowledge of his brother's

---

[40] Wenham, *Genesis*, 104.

[41] Glaser, *Thinking Biblically*, 857.

[42] Glaser, 857.

[43] Wenham, *Genesis*, 104.

whereabouts (Gen 4:9), so that it is the innocent blood that "cries to the Lord from the ground" (Gen 4:10). Cain has failed to do what is right. His original unethical worship has now been compounded by lying and murder. He has no concern for the glory of God.[44] When rebuked, instead of repenting and turning to the Lord, he turns away. His heart is not right with God.

Thus, when the author of 1 John speaks of Cain, he says that he was "of the evil one" and that his "deeds were evil" (3:12). The implication is that Cain follows his parents into the sin of listening to Satan. The root of Satan's rebellion against the Lord is to tempt people to relate to God on their own terms, rather than to come to him on his terms. Cain's actions of rebellion, murder and lying were of Satan and thus, of essence, evil. It is here that the root of religious conflict and violence is found. Cain's deeds were evil and so his offering to the Lord was not accepted. All the Lord required of Cain, was a change of heart. Instead, Cain pursued religious hatred to the point of violent premeditated murder. When the author of 1 John looks at the contemporary situation in the fellowship, he sees two groups of people who resemble Cain and Abel and interprets the current situation through the paradigmatic primordial narrative.

2. Conflict in the Johannine Fellowship

A question that has vexed commentators has been the nature of the opponents to the Johannine fellowship. In 2:19, we learn that they are a group of people who were once part of the fellowship, but have now left, causing distress in the process. Theories relating to the expulsion of the Johannine community from the synagogue for their faith in Jesus the Messiah and the subsequent writing of John's Gospel as an apologetic document have been widely disputed in recent times.[45] This study, therefore, considers the internal evidence of the epistle that there has been a schism: the dissenters have withdrawn, the fellowship has been shaken by the experience and the dissenters still pose a danger to the believers.

The question under consideration is the nature of the conflict in the fellowship because the core unity of the fellowship is at stake. The nature of this unity, stated clearly in the prologue (1:3), is both human and divine. It has horizontal and vertical dimensions that involve both *koinōnia* with the leaders (the eye-witness apostles) and *koinōnia* with the Father and the Son. The entire fellowship should operate in perfect unity with God in Christ, as a body of like-minded believers who live in truth, love, and righteousness

---

[44] S. McKnight, "Cain," in *Dictionary of the O.T., Pentateuch*, ed. Desmond Alexander and David Baker (Downers Grove: IVP, 2003): 108.

[45] Köstenberger, *Theology*, 51–53.

(3:7b). The challenges posed to the fellowship by the dissenters threaten to destroy the *koinōnia* through conflict and division. Using Stott's three basic "tests" as a guide, the problems facing the fellowship can be examined in three categories, using the internal evidence of the text.[46]

Firstly, the dissenters show evidence of stirring up doctrinal conflict with the fellowship. They claim to be made perfect, perhaps by a special anointing of the Spirit (2:27), and so deny the reality of sin (1:8, 10). Therefore, they deny the necessity of the atoning sacrifice of the Son (2:2). In denying the work of the Son, they "deny that Jesus is the Christ" (2:22). In 4:2–3, they show themselves to be the "antichrist" because they do not confess that Jesus is the Christ, the one sent from God. Their belief system is diametrically opposed to the open confession of the fellowship that, "our *koinōnia* is with the Father and with his Son, Jesus Christ" (1:3). Thus, it appears that the primary conflict is on the level of theological assent. They do not believe the truth.

Secondly, the lives of the dissenters display moral/ethical problems. They claim to have *koinōnia* with the Father, as the rest of the fellowship does, but they do not show evidence of this in their lives. Claiming to "walk in the light," their behavior shows that they are walking in the "darkness" (1:6). This can be seen by their inability to keep God's commandments (2:3). Their ethical behavior displays the antithesis of their theological claims. Instead of being sinless, they "keep on sinning" and "make a practice of sinning" (3:4–7). The author of 1 John, therefore, interprets their behavior as being "of the devil" because "the devil has been sinning from the beginning" (3:8). As those who are evil, they "love the things of the world" (2:15) and show that they are "from the world" and not "from God" (4:5). Their religious practice denies their claims. They cannot be born of God because they are under the influence of the evil one (5:18).

Thirdly, the dissenters bring social problems into the fellowship. They do not love the believers ("brothers") and therefore, by inference, hate them (2:9; 4:20). Painter states that the use of the Cain and Abel motif in 3:12 to illustrate the polarity between the believers and dissenters could imply that they had taken violent action against the believers in the same way that Cain acted violently against Abel.[47] Although this cannot be proved from the text, the Epistle of James accuses the Jewish churches to which it is addressed of fights, quarrels, and murder (Jas 4:1–2). It is possible that religious conflict and violence had also occurred in the Johannine fellowship.

---

[46] J. R. W. Stott, *The Epistles of John*, Tyndale Commentary Series (Grand Rapids: Eerdmans, 1960), 55.

[47] John Painter, *1, 2, and 3 John* (Sacra Pagina. Collegeville: The Liturgical Press, 2002), 238.

The result of the violent conflict is schism (2:19). The dissenters have "gone out from us" because they are "not of us." The dissenters are not part of the true *koinōnia* that holds the fellowship in perfect unity with one another and with God in Christ. False theology leads the dissenters to inappropriate ethics, resulting in violent antisocial behavior. That antisocial behavior, understood eschatologically, is the behavior of the antichrist (2:22). There are only two ways to live: in Christ or in Satan. This is the witness of the ancient Hebrew Scriptures concerning the lot of the righteous Abel and the way of the evil Cain (Heb 11:4). It corresponds with the way of faith (5:10) or the way of idolatry (5:21), being "from God" or "in the power of the evil one" (5:18). The polarity is stark. Either people are in fellowship with the Father and the Son and are righteous like Abel, or they are in fellowship with idols and Satan and are unrighteous like Cain. The distressing situation in the Johannine fellowship can therefore be explained as eschatological fulfillment of the motifs of Genesis 4.

C. Being Passionate about What We Believe

The key to remaining in the fellowship and not being derailed by the deception of dissenters is holding onto the message that the Johannine fellowship had heard "from the beginning." In 1:1–4, the author roots this belief firmly in the historicity of the incarnation, so that there is concrete content to the message. The message is grounded in historical fact and they are to hold on to it passionately in its absoluteness. There is no negotiation on the truth. Whatever is not truth, is a lie and lies are the work of the evil one (3:8). Thus, conflict cannot be avoided by means of negotiating a middle position between truth and falsehood. The Johannine fellowship is to hold passionately to what it has received and is not to accept compromise in any form.

1. The Concreteness of Belief

In 1 John, the "children of God" (5:2) are those who hear the witness to the incarnation proclaimed by the apostles and are brought into fellowship with the Father and the Son (1:3). The basis for their entry into the fellowship is their reception of the proclaimed word regarding the person of the Son (1:1–4). The epistle begins in an enigmatic way, introducing the eternal Deity objectively using the neuter pronoun Ό (that). *"That* which was from the beginning" (1:1) suggests the divine Being in his eternal existence, an allusion that would be readily understood by an audience familiar with John 1:1 and Genesis 1:1.[48] At this point, there is no explicit reference to the *logos* or to the Christ. The reader is expected to understand

---

[48] I. Howard Marshall, *The Epistles of John* (Grand Rapids: Eerdmans, 1978), 100.

that the gospel message is located in the person of the Creator God, who reveals the identity of the pre-existent Son to the believers.

There is a multi-sensory approach to the Johannine witness in 1:1–3. The remote Being, who was present at the beginning, became a tangible human being who could be perceived with the senses, that is, someone who was "heard," "seen," "looked on," and "touched" (1:1). This speaks of the reality of the entry of the eternal creator God into the human space-time continuum by means of the incarnation. The One who was intrinsically "life" was revealed through the incarnation, and those who knew him bear witness to what they have "seen and heard" (1:2–3). The purpose of their witness is to bring those who hear and accept their testimony concerning the revelation of the eternal *logos*, the "word of life" (1:1), into fellowship with God the Father and the Son, Jesus Christ (1:3). The revelation of the identity of the eternal *logos* in the person of Jesus Christ therefore has a missional purpose. It proclaims the truth about the reality of the coming of the Christ (the Messiah), so that those who hear it believe and enter the fellowship of the triune God. The outcome of this fellowship, in Johannine terms, is "complete joy" of unity with the Father and with one another (1:4).

The truth about Jesus the Christ is, therefore, not some myth or religious tale. Throughout 1 John there are witnesses to the reality of the incarnation. The prologue speaks of the eye-witness record of the apostles (1:1–3). In 2:12–14, the children, fathers and young men bear witness to the reality of the incarnation through their experiential knowledge of God. In 2:27, the anointing that the believers have received from the Spirit teaches them the truth about the Son.[49] In 5:6–9, the water of Christ's baptism, the blood of the cross and the Spirit who knows the mind of God all bear witness to the truth.[50] The believer therefore has the confidence to approach the throne of grace at the hour of need (5:14–15). That confidence is based in faith in a real, historical person.

2. The Correctness of Belief

The historicity of the incarnation means that there is an objectivity to belief. The reality is found in the death of Christ on the cross on our behalf, alluded to throughout the epistle. The blood of Jesus "cleanses us from all unrighteousness" (1:7); Christ is the atoning sacrifice (*hilasmos,* Strong's G2434) for our sins and the "sins of the whole world" (2:2); Christ "laid down his life for us" (3:16); "God sent his only Son into the world ... to be the propitiation for our sins" (4:9–10); "the Father has sent his Son to be the

---

[49] Marshall, *The Epistles of John*, 162.

[50] David Jackman, *The Message of John's Letters*, The Bible Speaks Today (Leicester: IVP, 1992), 148–149.

savior of the world" (4:14). All these references are to the work of Jesus Christ in his sacrificial death upon the cross on behalf of sinners. This was accomplished both in his humanity, on our behalf and in his divinity as the sinless One who was with God "at the beginning." Therefore, there is no room for negotiation on the substance of belief. It is necessary to confess that "Jesus has come in the flesh" (4:2). This is not just an intellectual assent. To confess that "Jesus is the Christ" is to "have the Father" (2:22–23) or to be in fellowship with the Father. To have the Father is to be "born of God" (5:1).

The importance of the substance of faith is apparent in the discussion on the dissenters in 2:18–25. The problem is that they have rejected the absoluteness of the historicity of faith. They deny that Jesus is the Christ, and therefore they deny the triune God (the "Father and the Son" 2:22). In denying the triune God, they have placed themselves outside the *koinōnia* of the Father and the Son (1:3) and have moved themselves outside the fellowship of Christ's followers by willful apostasy.[51] Their rejection of Jesus as the Christ, therefore, numbers them in the ranks of the antichrist (2:18). The believers are not to follow them. They have been "anointed by the Holy One," a reference to the Spirit of Jesus, whom they know intellectually and relationally to be the Christ (2:20).[52]

There is no room for doubt about the substance of faith. The historical concreteness of the events of the incarnation, death, and resurrection of Jesus Christ make this impossible. The Johannine fellowship is to stand passionately on what they know to be true and not to compromise their belief to accommodate those who preach otherwise. In terms of the Cain and Abel motif that dominates the epistle, it is the substance of belief that differentiates those who walk in the path of the righteous Abel from those whose deeds are evil like Cain. As the contrast between them is starkly polarized, what should the attitude of the righteous be towards those who are of different religious opinion to themselves?

D. Being Passionate about Loving Those Who Disagree with Us

The use of the Cain and Abel motif suggests a strongly polarity between those who hold an orthodox position regarding the person and work of Jesus Christ and those who dissent. While they are to hold tenaciously to the truth, their attitude towards the dissenters is not to replicate the violence perpetrated on them. They are not to hate or to murder like Cain (3:12).

---

[51] John Yarbrough, *1–3 John, Baker Exegetical Commentary* (Grand Rapids: Baker Academic, 2008), 146.

[52] Painter, *1–3 John*, 198–199.

Rather, they are to reflect the character of God, who loves the sinner (4:19), and who sent his Son to lay down his life for them (3:16).

1. The Root of Disagreement

The root of the conflict lies in the doctrinal position of the two groups regarding the person and work of Jesus Christ. In the N.T., the writer of the book of Hebrews interprets the Cain and Abel narrative in terms of the faith of Abel and comments that Abel, though he died, still speaks through his example of faith (Heb 11:4). Jackman, commenting on 1 John 5:6–12, adds faith as a fourth dimension to the three witnesses of water, blood, and Spirit.[53] He observes that the external assent of knowledge must be accompanied by the inner witness of the transformed life that Johannine literature speaks of as being "in Christ" or "abiding in him" (2:24–26).

It is abiding in the fellowship of the Son and the Father by faith, through dependence on the cleansing blood of Christ for forgiveness of sin, that enables the believer to live a life of righteousness and love. On the other hand, those who do not "abide in Christ" dwell in the world and are conformed to it with all its passions and desires (2:15–17; 4:5). The essential difference between the two lies in the object of faith. Those who believe in the Son of God live by faith and produce fruit that is acceptable to God. Those who reject Christ are guilty of idolatry (5:21). For Yarbrough, the root of the conflict in the Johannine fellowship lies in the refusal of those who are on the outside of the family of God, to recognize those who are within.[54] The question is, how are those who are rejected to respond to their tormentors?

2. The Nature of God

The essence of *koinōnia* is the participation of the believer in the divine life (*theosis*).[55] The character of the believer must therefore reflect the nature of the Creator, which the epistle presents essentially as self-giving love (4:9). The ground and the source for love is found in God and not in the will of the believer, because God is the ultimate source of love.[56] Through the epistle, the concept of love is always on the horizon. The new commandment (2:7–10) demands love of the brother as proof of a life lived in the light. The love of the Father is given to his children and is reflected in their lives through provision of material needs (3:17). Love is the essential characteristic of God and therefore is essentially evident in the life of the

---

[53] Jackman, *Letters*, 152–156.

[54] Yarbrough, *1–3 John*, 176.

[55] Cornelis Bennema, "Moral Transformation in the Johannine Writings," *In die Skriflig/In Luce Verbi* 51, no. 3 (January 2017): accessed May 8, 2017. See www.Academia.edu/30826704/.

[56] Painter, *1–3 John*, 268.

believer. However, the love of God is qualified. It is related to his holiness (1:5). God loves the world so much that he gives his only Son to restore it to holiness. It is the cross of Jesus that is the supreme demonstration of the nature of the love of God (4:9).[57] This sets a precedent for the type of love self-sacrificing love demanded of his followers (3:19).

3. The Morality of Belief

Bennema further lists the moral attributes of God as life, light, and truth.[58] These qualities are intrinsic to his Being. To come into relationship with him is to have eternal life (1:7), which necessitates walking in the "light" and living in the truth. Being in relationship with God through Christ therefore has moral implications, chief of which is love.

It can be argued that throughout the epistle believers are only told to love their brothers, therefore there is no obligation on them to love their enemies. Thompson speaks of the inevitable dualisms created in the epistle by the use of the Cain and Abel motif with its stark "love" and "hate" polarities.[59] She asks why there is no suggestion of mending the split and answers her own question negatively: we do not know what measures the fellowship has already taken to bring the dissenters back; and by the time the letter is written, the split is a *fait accompli*, the "absolute, dualistic terms" are set. However, arguments from silence are not convincing. There is evidence in the epistle that the teaching of the Gospels, in which the disciples are commanded to "love their enemies" and to "do good to those who oppose them" (Matt 5:43–38), is assumed, despite the apparent love/hate polarities. I John is intensely theological. The fellowship is to emulate the character of God with whom they are in *koinōnia*. God sent his only Son into the world to provide forgiveness for sin and restoration to fellowship. They are likewise to be mission minded.

In 5:16–17, the believers are told to pray for those who commit sin not leading to death so that they are restored to life.[60] The word used for the sinner is "brother," but Stott comments that the word used here cannot speak only of those within the fellowship, because they already "have life."[61] The fellowship is instructed to pray so that God will grant the sinner eternal life

---

[57] Marshall, *Epistles*, 214.

[58] C. Bennema, "Moral Transformation…," 3.

[59] Marianne Meye Thompson, *1–3 John*, IVP N.T. Commentary (Leicester: IVP, 1992), 105.

[60] Stott, *Epistles*, 186. Stott lists "sins leading to death" as: 1) specific sins of the Mosaic law, 2) apostasy, 3) blasphemy against the Holy Spirit.

[61] Judith M. Lieu, *I, II and III John: A Commentary* (Louisville, Westminster John Knox Press, 2008), 225. Lieu maintains that it is only the believers who are in view here because the general outlook of the Epistle makes it unlikely that it concerns outsiders. This, despite acknowledging the evangelistic tenor of the rest of the Scriptures.

with the assumption that the sinner is in a position of eternal spiritual death.[62] Therefore, "brother" in 5:16 must mean those in the wider sense who are "neighbors" to the fellowship.[63] They are not members of the fellowship but those outside, for whom the fellowship is to act in the priestly capacity of intercessors with God for the forgiveness of their sins.

Thompson argues that sin that does not lead to death is sin committed by members of the fellowship, as in 2:1–2, whereas sin that leads to death is the sin of the dissenters, thereby reinforcing her concept of duality in the text.[64] However, the character of God requires a corresponding morality in his children. He is the God who is love, who demonstrated that love by sending his own Son to make atonement for sin, so that sinners may be forgiven and restored to *koinōnia* with him (1:3, 6). The purpose of the proclamation of Jesus Christ incarnate in 1:1–3 is to bring sinners back into relationship with the eternal, holy, and pure God. There are no stark polarities with God because that would indicate that his mission to restore all things to him in Christ has somehow ended with the Johannine fellowship. On the contrary, the mission-heart of God continues to reach out to sinners in Christ and through his followers who reflect his love by interceding for their neighbors.

The distinction in the instruction in 5:16–17 is between interceding for those whose sin can be forgiven (it does not lead to death) and those whose sin cannot be forgiven (it leads to death). In the context of the Johannine fellowship, this category of sinner refers to those who have resolutely rejected God's forgiveness. It seems that the dissenters have fallen into this category. Forgiveness is impossible for them because they do not acknowledge that they are sinners (1:8). Consequently, they reject God's means of forgiveness through the propitiation provided by his Son (2:2) and display the characteristics of those who are given over to the evil one (3:8–9).

Therein, the Cain and Abel motif comes into play. Cain had an opportunity to repent and turn from his sin so that the Lord would have regard for him. But Cain refused to heed God's warning and rejected the word of life. He resolutely chose the way of the devil who has been sinning from the beginning (3:8). In the same way, the dissenters have followed the way of Cain and have rejected the word of life (forgiveness in Christ) held

---

[62] Georg Strecker, *The Johannine Epistles, Hermeneia: A Critical and Historical Commentary on the Bible* (Minneapolis: Augsburg Fortress, English translation, 1995), 202.

[63] Stott, *Epistles,* 190. This is not a widely held position. Smalley, for example, argues that the word *adelphos* used throughout the epistle describes the "orthodox Johannine community in its distinction from the heretics": in Stephen Smalley, *1, 2, 3 John*, Word Biblical Commentary 51 (Waco: Word Books, 1984), 189.

[64] Thompson, *1–3 John,* 142–143.

out to them. There is nothing more that can be offered to them. However, those who walk in the way of Abel, heeding the word of life, repenting of their sins, and living in love and holiness are those who reflect the character of their Father by loving those outside their fellowship for whom Christ died, including loving those who walk in the way of Cain and oppose them. Since Christ died for the sins of the world (2:2), the fellowship is to extend the love of Christ to all their neighbors by means of proclamation and intercessory prayer.

Conclusion

Therefore, the theological basis in 1 John for our being passionate about what we believe and passionate about loving those who disagree with us in an environment of religious conflict and violence is located in the character of God. The seemingly moral dilemma between love of the "brothers" and hatred of the "antichrists" suggested by a cursory reading of the epistle can be resolved by considering the epistle as prophetic Midrash Pesher on the Cain and Abel narrative of Genesis 4. God would have accepted the worship of Cain and would have restored him into relationship with himself, if he had approached God with a heart that was free from sinful motives. Cain was not prepared to do this and so bound himself to Satan's rebellious ways, leading to the first instance of religious violence.

The author of 1 John uses the Hebrew "protohistory" from Genesis 4 to explain the eschatological events in the Johannine fellowship. Those who are righteous like Abel are being persecuted by those who have chosen the way of rebellion like Cain. Yet, the righteous are not to respond to conflict and violence in equal proportion. Instead, they are to reflect the holy character of their Creator with whom they walk in *koinōnia*. They are to be passionate about the truth because God is truth, and Jesus Christ is the revelation of God's truth. At the same time, the self-sacrificing nature of the love of God calls them to love all people and to eagerly desire that they come to the knowledge of the truth. They are to proclaim the truth (1:3) and to pray earnestly for forgiveness for those who have not committed the ultimate sin of denying God's offer of restoration (5:16). The reason they do this is because they reflect God's love that is the mission-heart of God. Christians who experience religious conflict and violence for the sake of righteousness should, therefore, hold passionately to the truth about Jesus Christ, continue to love those who oppose them, and pray that the opposition will accept God's gracious offer of eternal life. In other words, the theological basis for loving in the face of religious conflict and violence is the mission-heart of God.

5.
"They Shall Not Inherit the Kingdom of God"— Is the Bible's Language of Judgment and Sin too Condemnatory to Patiently Deal with Human Sins?
An Evangelical Protestant Perspective

Rev. Daniel Funke
Pastor of Grace Baptist Church Govan
Glasgow, Scotland
Dr. Tomas Bokedal
Lecturer in N.T. Studies, King's College
University of Aberdeen, Scotland[65]

Introduction	74
A. Biblical Theological Reflections	75
1. Vital Distinctions	75
2. The Unbeliever's Need: Justification	76
3. The Believer's Project: Sanctification	76
4. 1 Corinthians 6	78
5. The Good News and the Bad	79
Conclusion on Biblical-Theological Reflections	80
B. Lutheran Approaches to the Bible's Language of Sin and Judgment	81
1. God Does Not Want Any to Perish	81
2. Defining Sin, Justifying Condemnation: Philip Melanchthon	82
3. Condemnatory Effects of Actual Sins: Johann Gerhard	84
4. Necessary Distinction between Law and Gospel: Carl Fredrik Wisløff	84
5. Consciousness of Sin—The Essential Condition for Understanding Christianity: Søren Kierkegaard	86
6. On Enjoying Less Than the Fullness of Human Life: Robert Kolb	88
Concluding Remarks	88

---

[65] Bokedal earned his ThD from Lund University, Sweden, one of the world's oldest universities; his MDiv, MA, and BA from the University of Gothenburg, Sweden; his DipHE from Sahlgrenska Academy; his DipHE from Chalmers University of Technology; and his PGCert from Gothenburg Psychotherapy Institute. He was a lecturer at the Lutheran School of Theology in Gothenburg, Sweden. He has published several articles and book chapters including, "Revelation: What Forms of Authority, and to Whom?" in *T & T Clark Companion to the Theology of Kierkegaard*, T & T Clark Handbooks, ed. Aaron P. Edwards and David J. Gouwens (London: T & T Clark/Bloomsbury, 2019), 279-298; and "Canon/Scripture," in *The Dictionary of the Bible and Ancient Media*, ed. Tom Thatcher, Chris Keith, Raymond F. Person, Jr., and Elsie R. Stern (London: T & T Clark/Bloomsbury, 2017). See t.bokedal@abdn.ac.uk.

Funke earned his MA in Divinity from the University of Aberdeen and is pastor of Grace Baptist Church Govan, Glasgow, Scotland. See dannofunke@hotmail.de.

Introduction[66]

As evangelical Protestant Christians, we believe that the Bible is authoritative and sufficient for all aspects of the Christian life and Christian ministry.[67] That view includes an understanding that, when dealing with human sins, the Bible is sufficient for addressing and dealing with them.[68]

Sin is a universal reality, and as a result of its gravity and consequences, all people ought to deal with their sins. This is certainly true on a personal level. Additionally, there is great need for ministers of the gospel to deal with the sins of their people. In preaching and counseling alike, there is opportunity to address sin, not because that is pleasant, but because it is necessary. And quite apart from the ministry, many Christian men and women will seek to address the sins of their friends and neighbors, parents, and children. What they need, before and above all else, is "judicial and moral cleansing."[69] They can find it in God's word. There we can find the way to deal with our sins, whether we are already in fellowship with God or not. And yet many would lament that the language of Scripture is somehow too strong, too critical, and too condemnatory to patiently deal with human sins.

There is no denying that the Bible's language of judgment and sin is strongly dichotomizing. Paul, for instance, tells us that "the unrighteous will not inherit the kingdom of God" (1 Cor 6:9).[70] And while those who "wash their robes ... have a right to the tree of life and ... may enter the city by the gates" (Rev 22:14), those who are "dogs and sorcerers and the sexually immoral and murderers and idolaters, and everyone who loves and practices falsehood" are outside the gates (v15).[71] Their "portion will be in the lake that burns with fire and sulfur, which is the second death" (Rev 21:8). Jesus himself used strong words throughout his ministry, as exemplified in his explanation of the parable of the weeds: "The Son of Man will send his angels, and they will gather out of his kingdom all causes of sin and all law-breakers, and throw them into the fiery furnace. In that place there will be weeping and gnashing of teeth" (Matt 13:41–42).

---

[66] The Introduction and Part A were written by Daniel Funke, with some of the references in the footnotes supplied by Tomas Bokedal.

[67] Cf. Robert Kolb, "The Bible in the Reformation and Protestant Orthodoxy," in *The Enduring Authority of the Christian Scriptures*, ed. D. A. Carson (Grand Rapids: Eerdmans, 2016), 100–01.

[68] On the clarity and sufficiency of Scripture, see, e.g., Robert D. Preus, *The Theology of Post-Reformation Lutheranism*, Vol 1: A Study of Theological Prolegomena (Concordia Publishing House, 1970), 309–15.

[69] Horatius Bonar, *The Everlasting Righteousness* (1st 1874; Edinburgh: Banner of Truth, 1993), v.

[70] See also Gal 5:19–21, Eph 5:5. Quotations are taken from the English Standard Version.

[71] See also Rev 21:27.

This language might make us wonder if there is still room to patiently deal with human sins. In this article, we set out to answer the question that heads this page—whether the Bible's language of sin and judgment is too condemnatory to patiently deal with human sin. In order to address this question, we propose that it is necessary to apply distinctions to our reading of the Bible. The key distinction is that of the sinner, whose biggest need is justification, and the saint, who, while still a sinner, seeks to grow in holiness. This might be an obvious distinction, but it will serve as the first big step in addressing the question at hand. We will then take a closer look at one relevant passage, 1 Corinthians 6. This will be followed by looking at the relationship of the Bible's language of sin and judgment with the Bible's presentation of the gospel, and how we must understand the good news in context. That will conclude the first part of the article. The second part will deal with the Evangelical Lutheran approaches to the issues at hand.

A. Biblical Theological Reflections
1. Vital Distinctions

It is paramount that we make vital distinctions when approaching the Bible's language of sin and judgment. We need to distinguish between who is in and who is outside of fellowship with God, or, to use Paul's language, who is "in Christ," and who is not.[72] In light of this dualism, we have to distinguish clearly between justification and sanctification. If these distinctions are not upheld (and kept in mind), any discussion of sin and judgment in the Bible will be simplistic and reductionistic.

These distinctions are, of course, found consistently throughout the Bible and are especially clear in the N.T. In the Gospels and Acts, we find those who are disciples and believers, and they are characterized by their abiding in Christ. Others do not believe and are not abiding in Christ. The language of abiding is very similar to that of Paul who prefers the idea of being "in Christ." And John, likewise, is writing to those who are in the light, and walk in the light, as opposed to those who are and walk in the darkness. The greatest need for sinners who are not "in Christ" is justification, while the great project for those who are "in Christ" is sanctification, which includes mortification of sin. These distinctions are necessary, both in the realm of biblical studies, as well as in the practice of pastoral ministry. How we approach a particular sin, both in our own lives and in the lives of others, depends on whether or not we are in Christ.

---

[72] Cf. C. F. W. Walther, *The Proper Distinction Between Law and Gospel*, trans. W. H. T. Dau (St. Louis: CPH, 1929).

2. The Unbeliever's Need: Justification[73]

The Bible constantly reminds the reader of the reality of personal judgment. The writer to the Hebrews reminds us that "it is appointed for man to die once, and after that comes judgment" (Heb 9:27). This judgment is universal and personal: "We will all stand before the judgment seat of God; for it is written, 'As I live, says the Lord, every knee shall bow to me, and every tongue shall confess to God.' So then each of us will give an account of himself to God" (Rom 14:10–12, cf. 2 Cor 5:10).[74] This fact of judgment, in light of the universality of sin and guilt, forces the reader to seek salvation, and this salvation is offered, throughout the Christian Bible, in the person and work of Jesus Christ.

The traditional Protestant idea of salvation is that of justification by faith. The sinner is freely justified by grace through faith, on the ground of the work of Christ alone. His righteousness is imputed to the sinner, while the sinner's punishment is imputed to Christ on the cross. This double imputation is at the heart of salvation in the Bible: "For our sake he made him to be sin who knew no sin, so that in him we might become the righteousness of God" (2 Cor 5:21).[75]

This is the great hope that the Bible offers to the sinner. It is an offer made to all people, in line with God's desire for all people to be saved (1 Tim 2:4, Ezek. 18:23, 32). And, so, men and women from all places can enter fellowship with God. This does not, of course, mean that the sinner ceases to sin. 1 John quite strongly argues against any suggestion that a Christian does not sin. The person making such a claim is a liar, and the truth is not in them (1 John 1:8, 10). The truth is that a Christian is, to borrow Luther's language, *simul justus et peccator*, or "at once justified and sinner."

3. The Believer's Project: Sanctification

A justified sinner is never merely justified. He is changed. He receives the Holy Spirit and is given a new heart, and therefore we can affirm, with James, that faith without works is dead (Jas 2:26). While Protestants have always affirmed that justification is by grace through faith, this faith is

---

[73] On justification by faith see, e.g., Article IV of the *Augsburg Confession* and chapter 11 of the *Second London Baptist Confession of 1689*.

[74] N. T. Wright, *Jesus and the Victory of God, Christian Origins and the Question of God,* Vol. 2. (London: SPCK, 1996), 1089, "There ought … to be no question about Paul holding firmly to a Jewish-style notion of a coming day of judgment."

[75] For treatment of a classic Protestant understanding of justification, see, e.g., Stephen Westerholm, *Perspectives Old and New on Paul: The "Lutheran" Paul and His Critics* (Grand Rapids and Cambridge: Eerdmans, 2004); idem, *Justification Reconsidered: Rethinking a Pauline Theme* (Grand Rapids and Cambridge, 2013); D. A. Carson, Peter T. O'Brien, and Mark A. Seifrid, eds., *Justification and Variegated Nomism*, 2 vols. (Tübingen: Mohr Siebeck, 2001 and 2004).

accompanied by a changed life. Robert Traill powerfully encapsulates this when he writes that "There is no difference between a justified and a sanctified man, for he is always the same person that partakes of these privileges." [76] A justified woman, in other words, is a woman being sanctified. And if she is sanctified, she has been justified. The two are a package deal and cannot be obtained separately (cf. Rom 8:30; 1 Cor 1:30, 6:11).[77]

This becomes an important foundation for our understanding of approaching the sins of the believer. A significant aspect of growing in holiness is taken up with limiting and killing personal sins. John is telling his readers that he is writing to them, in part, that they may not sin (1 John 2:1). Paul, likewise, exhorts us to put to death the deeds of the body: "For if you live according to the flesh you will die, but if by the Spirit you put to death the deeds of the body, you will live" (Rom 8:13). This mortification was central to the holiness movements of Lutheran Pietism and of Puritanism and has been a significant aspect of sanctification throughout church history.[78] Success, however, will not be absolute in this body, and there is, therefore, need for confession and repentance.[79]

That the life of the Christian should be marked by continual repentance was so important to Martin Luther, that he made that explicit in the first of his 95 theses: "When our Lord and Master Jesus Christ said, 'Repent,' he willed the entire life of believers to be one of repentance."[80] Confession is an important element of ongoing repentance, and should therefore be part of every Christian's dealing with past sins. One of the great promises made to Christians is that we are assured forgiveness if we confess our sins: "If we confess our sins, he is faithful and just to forgive us our sins and to cleanse us from all unrighteousness" (1 John 1:9). Mortification and confession, then, are the major ways in which a believer can prevent future sins and account for past sins.[81]

---

[76] Robert Traill (1642–1716), *Justification Vindicated* (1st 1692; Carlisle: Banner of Truth Trust, 2002), 8.

[77] For a Lutheran reading, see, e.g., *The Book of Concord: The Confessions of the Evangelical Lutheran Church*, ed. Robert Kolb, Tomothy J. Wengert, and Charles P. Arand (Minneapolis: Fortress, 2000), 565 and 660.

[78] See, e.g., John Owen (1616–1683), *Of the Mortification of Sin in Believers*, in *Works of John Owen*, Volume 6 (ed. William Goold; 1827; repr. Edinburgh: Banner of Truth, 1967).

[79] Contra movements that advocate for perfectionism.

[80] Translation of Thesis 1 found in Graham Tomlin, *Luther and His World* (Lion Hudson, 2012), 59.

[81] As for the balance between justification and sanctification in the believer in Lutheran thinking, see Harold L. Sankbeil, *Sanctification: Christ in Action: Evangelical Challenge and Lutheran Response* (Milwaukee: Northwestern Publishing House, 1989), 113.

The distinctions made in this section will be helpful in understanding how we can patiently deal with sin, even with an eye to the strong language of sin and judgment throughout the Bible. An example will highlight that point.

4. 1 Corinthians 6

The title that heads this chapter is a title taken from a few instances throughout the N.T. that portray salvation in exclusive terms. Some will inherit the kingdom of God, while others will not. One such instance is found in 1 Corinthians:

> Or do you not know that the unrighteous will not inherit the kingdom of God? Do not be deceived: neither the sexually immoral, nor idolaters, nor adulterers, nor men who practice, nor thieves, nor the greedy, nor drunkards, nor revilers, nor swindlers will inherit the kingdom of God. (1 Cor 6:9–10)

Paul is exhorting Christians to live at peace with one another, and a grievous practice among the Corinthian Christians is that they do not mind settling quarrels with one another in court. Following that discussion, Paul is writing the words already quoted. Paul is clear in his language. Those who are marked by a continual pattern of unforgiven sin will not inherit the kingdom of God.

It is important to remember the distinctions we have already made when approaching a text like that. Many men and women are marked by these patterns of sin. We can think of the businessman, who, because of his greed, is a workaholic, while neglecting his family. We can think of the woman, who is a con-artist, relieving all sorts of people of their money. And we can think of the man who outwardly is a great husband and father, and yet cheats on his wife every week with his co-worker. Paul assures us that men and women like that will not inherit the kingdom. Their patterns of being unrepentant sinners excludes them from this blessing. But they are not beyond the offer of salvation, and that becomes clear in the verse that follows those we have quoted above.

Paul reminds the Corinthian Christians that some of his readers fit the categories of sin he has mentioned: "And such were some of you." And the reason that they have now become heirs is that they "were washed ... sanctified ... justified in the name of the Lord Jesus Christ and by the Spirit of our God (v11). The Corinthian Christians have been justified and sanctified—and we may add that they are also in the process of being sanctified—and, as a result, their lives are changed.[82] While some of them have been marked by the patterns of sin, which Paul mentions in 6:9–10,

---

[82] The verbs in v11 are aorist verbs, and we should prefer to translate ἡγιάσθητε as being set apart.

they no longer are. The Spirit has been at work in their lives, and they have been fundamentally changed.

This leaves us with an important question: What happens when I sin, after I have been justified? We should expect that those who have been marked by a particular sin continue to struggle and wrestle with that sin after becoming Christians. But herein lies an important distinction. Those who are marked by sin are significantly different from those who struggle with it. We can draw a distinction, for instance, between the alcoholic who enjoys drinking, and who continues to drink even though knowing the possible consequences of such a behavior. The former alcoholic turned Christian, however, who relapses after struggling and fighting against his addiction is in a different category.[83] Sin is not evidence that someone is not right with God; however, an unrepentant lifestyle of sin is.[84]

1 Corinthians 6:9–10 is not a unique passage in Scripture. Galatians 5:21 and Ephesians 5:5 make similar points, and so do the last two chapters of the Apocalypse. Justification is not based on our works, but those who are justified live a life bearing fruit for God. It is in bringing together these concepts and the distinctions mentioned above that we can see how good works and justification by faith are perfectly harmonious.

5. The Good News and the Bad

One final argument is significant. The language of judgment and sin in the Bible is descriptive. We affirm that there *is* a final judgment, and that sin is exceedingly evil, because we read about their condemnation in the Bible. The language used might be harsh, but we affirm its necessity, because unless we know about sin and judgment, the gospel makes little sense.

The gospel, the good news, can only be fully understood in light of the bad news. In order to patiently deal with the sin of the unbeliever, therefore, we need to establish the condition in which the unbeliever finds himself. It should not surprise us that the major confessional documents of the Lutheran and Reformed traditions generally place a discussion of sin and judgment before a discussion of the remedy presented in Jesus Christ. This is beautifully done in the *Sum of Saving Knowledge*, a document often published alongside the Westminster Standards.[85] Heading *I* of that document is entitled, "Our woeful condition by nature, through breaking the Covenant of Works." Heading *II* is entitled, "The remedy provided in Jesus Christ for the elect by the Covenant of Grace." The second heading only

---

[83] Cf. also 2 Pet 2:20–22; and Walther, *Proper Distinction*, Thesis XVIII.

[84] Cf. Thesis X; and Rom 8:13.

[85] David Dickson (1583–1663), and James Durham (1622–1658), *Sum of Saving Knowledge: or, A Brief Sum of Christian Doctrine* (Edinburgh: Jonstone, Hunter, and Co., 1872; 1st 1650).

makes sense in the light of the first. The good news as presented throughout the Bible, likewise, only makes sense in the light of an understanding of judgment and sin. Paul's masterful articulation of the doctrine of justification of faith in Romans (Rom 3:21–26) is preceded by a discussion of sin and judgment. The contrast could not be any clearer, and the height of Paul's argument only makes sense in the light of what has preceded it in Romans 1:18–3:20; what is true for Paul's argument is certainly true for the Bible as a whole.

That Christ has secured an eternal redemption by entering the holy places by his own blood (Heb 9:12) only makes sense if we see a need of redemption. Atonement as a concept only makes sense in the light of our condition. Salvation as a central theme of the Bible can only be communicated if we know from what we are saved and rescued. It is the good news that allows us to patiently deal with sin, both for those outside, and for those within covenant boundaries. And if that is true, it is only through the Bible's language of judgment and sin that we find a way to patiently deal with human sins.

Conclusion on Biblical-Theological Reflections

Answering the question that heads this article is a twofold task. First, in order to deal with human sins, we make a vital distinction between the believer and the unbeliever. The greatest need of those who are not in fellowship with God is being right with God, and therefore having peace with God. Men and women in that situation need to be called to believe and repent. Those who are in fellowship with God are commanded to grow in holiness, and to confess and repent of their sins. If we do not keep this distinction in mind, we fail to see that the Bible's language of sin and judgment must be understood in context.

Second, we must remember that the good news throughout Scripture only makes sense in the light of judgment and sin. The Bible's language of judgment and sin, therefore, gives context to the proclamation of the good news of Christ crucified and risen. Rather than obstructing a patient approach to dealing with human sins, this language allows us to fully understand, and therefore fully apply, the remedy for sin. The answer is, therefore, a clear "No." The Bible's language of judgment and sin is not too condemnatory to patiently deal with human sin.

So far, we have considered two arguments from the Bible. In the second part we will add voices from church history and specifically from Lutheran church history to show how our answer lines up with the answers given by Lutheran theologians and pastors.

B. Lutheran Approaches to the Bible's Language of Sin & Judgment [86]
1. God Does Not Want Any to Perish

In the N.T., the stance on the themes of judgment and salvation is rather positive. We learn from the Gospel that "God did not send his Son into the world to condemn the world, but in order that the world might be saved through him" (John 3:17). The apostle Paul concurs. Having previously pointed the Galatian believers towards the curse Christ became in our place (Gal 3:13; 2 Cor 5:21), he ensures the readers of Romans that *there is no condemnation*—due to our shortcomings vis-à-vis God's law—*for those who are in Christ Jesus* (Rom 8:1). Paul asks: Who shall condemn, or bring any charge against, those who belong to Christ? He who loves us, who gave his own Son up for us, will he not patiently give us everything with him? Indeed, will anything in all creation be able to separate us from the love of God in Christ Jesus our Lord (Rom 8:31–39)?

On a basic level, God, who is a loving God (Rom 8:39, 2 Cor 13:11, 1 John 4:16), does not want condemnation at all, as expressed in the Lutheran *Formula of Concord*: God "'does not want any to perish but wants all to come to repentance' (2 Peter 3:9). As it is written in Ezekiel (33:11 and 18:23), 'As I live, I have no pleasure in the death of the wicked, but that the wicked turn from their ways and live.'"[87] Again, however, we recognize the dual sinner-saint pattern, or unbeliever-believer distinction, discussed in Part A: Either a life characterized by sin, judgment, and wrath (Rom 2:8f, 8:6–8), or a life lived in light of forgiveness, salvation, the good, and the noble (Rom 2:7 and 10, 3:20–26, 4:7, 5:1, 8:3f).[88] Regarding the former, for Lutherans it is important to underscore that God does not instigate sin and that

> All preparation for condemnation stems from the devil and human beings, through sin, and in absolutely no way from God. Since God does not want a single human being to be condemned, how then could he himself prepare a person for condemnation? For as God is not the cause of sins, so he is also not the cause of punishment or condemnation. The only cause of condemnation is sin, for 'the wages of sin is death' [Rom 6:23].[89]

---

[86] Part B and most of Concluding Remarks are authored by Tomas Bokedal.

[87] *The Book of Concord: The Confessions of the Evangelical Lutheran Church*, ed. Robert Kolb, Timothy J. Wengert, and Charles P. Arand (Minneapolis: Fortress Press, 2000), 653.

[88] On the relation between Rom 2:13 and 3:20, see Westerholm, *Justification Reconsidered*, 83f.

[89] *The Book of Concord*, 653.

Consequently, outside of Christ all sins are mortal, separating human beings from the living God.[90] A personal relationship with God, on the other hand, is only possible by means of forgiveness of our sins through faith in Christ.

Thus, an initial Lutheran response to our question—whether the biblical language about judgment and sin is too condemnatory to patiently deal with human sins—is a note of clarification:

1. God does not want anyone to be condemned,
2. There is no condemnation for those who are in Christ Jesus, rather God wants to give them everything with him,
3. Human sins (by deviating from the norms set by a holy and righteous God) are themselves the very reason for the biblical language about judgment and sin, and
4. In order to patiently deal with the human dilemma of sin, God, in an act of divine love towards humanity, sent his Son, who himself is without sin (1 John 4:10, 2 Pet 3:7–9, Heb 4:15), to atone for human sin (2 Cor 5:18f., Rom 5:10f., 1 Joh. 2:2) and be executed and condemned on a cross.

In the following I shall briefly discuss some aspects of this essay's topic as they appear in the works of five Lutheran theologians, namely Philip Melanchthon (defining sin, justifying condemnation), Johann Gerhard (condemnatory effects of actual sins), Carl Fredrik Wisløff (the necessary distinction between law and gospel), Søren Kierkegaard (consciousness of sin, the essential condition for understanding Christianity), and Robert Kolb (on enjoying less than the fulness of human life).

2. Defining Sin, Justifying Condemnation: Philip Melanchthon

In his theological treatise *Loci Communes*, Philip Melanchthon (1497–1560) defines the scriptural sense of the term *sin* as follows: "*sin* properly means something culpable and condemned by God unless there is forgiveness. This general description fits original sin and actual sin."[91] Melanchthon takes this as a compressed definition focusing exclusively on the relational dimension, namely the human guilt before God. In order to broaden the description to include as well the reason behind guilt, he widens the definition as follows:

> Sin is a defect or an inclination or an action in conflict with the law of God, offending God, condemned by God, and making us worthy of eternal wrath and eternal punishments, unless there be forgiveness. In this definition there are

---

[90] Philip Melanchthon, *Loci Communes rerum theologicarum*, trans. J. A. O. Preus (St. Louis, MO: Concordia Publishing House, 1992 (1543), 53. On the distinction between non-forgiven mortal sins in the unregenerate and forgiven venial sins in the regenerate (of which the latter do not drive out the Holy Spirit and faith); compare 126ff.

[91] Melanchthon, *Loci Communes*, 47.

elements, namely defect and inclination, which refer to original sin. The action includes all actual sins, inner and external.[92]

In this definition, which was previously approved by Luther,[93] the common element is understood to be "the conflict with the law of God," including not only actions (as the early Lutheran adversaries argued), but it also "condemns the darkness, defects and depraved inclinations in the nature of man" (cf. Rom 7).[94] According to Melanchthon, human reason understands that "wicked actions are against the law of God," but it ignores the ensuing wrath of God. Thus particular emphasis needs to be placed on the descriptive terms: "condemned by God," "offending God," and "making us worthy of wrath and punishment, etc." Melanchthon draws this definition from Gal 3:10: "Cursed is he that does not continue in all things which are written in the Law." We conclude from this that the biblical language about sin and judgment is properly condemnatory since God is offended and since he, in line with his divine will and nature, must condemn sin.

Melanchthon stresses that "sin is a far greater evil than human reason thinks."[95] Accordingly, the church reproaches not only external actions conflicting with the law of God, or with reason ("as philosophy does"); "but it reproves the root and the fruit, the inner darkness of the mind, the doubts concerning the will of God, the turning away of the human will from God and stubbornness of the heart against the law of God. It also reproves ignoring and despising the Son of God. These are grievous and atrocious evils, the enormity of which cannot be told. Therefore, Christ says, 'The Holy Spirit will reprove the world of sin.'"[96]

On a related epistemological note, Paul underscores the severity of sin triggered by God's law: "Through the law sin becomes exceedingly sinful" (Rom 7:13). This means that the law,

> shows the wrath of God, and when this is recognized, then we understand that our uncleanness is not a small evil but is something culpable, condemned, and cursed by God because terrible punishments follow. Since all this is the case, therefore as often as sin is mentioned, let this designation be discerned in the church; it speaks of judgment and of the wrath of God.[97]

---

[92] Melanchthon, 48.

[93] Johann Gerhard, *On Sin and Free Choice: Theological Commonplaces* (St. Louis: Concordia Publishing House, 2014).

[94] Gerhard, *On Sin and Free Choice*.

[95] Melanchthon, *Loci Communes*, 47.

[96] Melanchthon, 47.

[97] Melanchthon, 48.

With these definitions and considerations in mind, the God of the Bible—and the N.T. in particular (John 3:16–19)—is a God of patience and love towards human beings and their many shortcomings.

3. Condemnatory Effects of Actual Sins: Johann Gerhard

Johann Gerhard (1582–1637), one of the foremost Lutheran dogmaticians, spends several chapters on matters relating to sin and judgment. I shall here briefly bring to the fore only one point, namely his list of the condemnatory effects of actual sins.

Gerhard catalogues the negative effects of actual sins that help us understand why sins cannot be easily tolerated, and why, as a consequence, Scripture's language of sin is condemnatory:

I. The grief of conscience;
II. The wrath of God ("the wrath which You threaten over sinners is intolerable," Manasseh, v. 5);
III. A curvature, obliquity, and filthiness of the soul;
IV. Guilt ("No more remember my iniquities; erase my sins," Ps 25:7, 51:1);
V. Vicious habits inclining toward other sins ("whoever sins becomes a slave to sin," John 8:34), and
VI. Temporal and eternal punishments of all kinds.[98]

According to our primary distinction in Part A, God's wrath and punishments of all kinds are revealed against all sin and ungodliness (Rom 1:18ff.), whereas the righteousness of God is given patiently, sacrificially and freely to all who believe in the Son (John 3:16–19, Rom 4:25, 2 Pet 3:8–9, 1 John 2:2)—in the phrasing of *The Book of Concord*—to those who know "that he is the atoning sacrifice for our sin. Isaiah says [Isa 53:6], 'The Lord has laid on him the iniquity of us all.'"[99] Again, the heart of the gospel is portrayed against the backdrop of accumulating human sins, God's wrath and judgment, all necessary for understanding and appropriating the good news.

4. Necessary Distinction between Law and Gospel: Carl Fredrik Wisløff

Carl Fredrik Wisløff (1908–2004), an influential Norwegian Lutheran pastor and theologian, airs matters pertaining to our discussion in his 1946 book on Christian faith *Jeg vet på hvem jeg tror* ("I Know in Whom I Believe"). Salvation, Wisløff begins, is to receive forgiveness for one's sins (Ps 32, Luke 1:77, Rom 8:1).[100] The one who has not received forgiveness

---

[98] Gerhard, *Theological Commonplaces*, 112.

[99] *The Book of Concord*, 236.

[100] Carl Fredrik Wisløff, *Jag vet på vem jag tror: Orientering i kristen tro* (Göteborg: Kyrkliga förbundets bokförlag, 1992, frist 1946), 85f.

for their sin is lost since they are still under God's wrath. He then proceeds to the important Lutheran distinction between law and gospel.

From the time of Melanchthon and the *Book of Concord* in the 16th century, Lutherans discussed three uses of the law (God's requirement on human beings through his commandments), even though Luther at times tended to embrace only the first two of these: (1) *the civil use of the law*, promoting good order in society, and punishing evil; (2) *the pedagogical use of the law*, referring to the law's function in repentance (cf. Gal 3:24, in order for human beings to receive the gospel it is necessary that they first attain knowledge of their sin and need for forgiveness; and Rom 3:20, the law makes us aware of the accusation of our own consciousness, which then may lead to repentance and faith in the gospel); and (3) *the didactic use of the law*, teaching and reminding believers how they should live as Christians, promoting sanctification.[101] As Wisløff focuses mainly on the second of these, *the pedagogical use of the law*, its important accusatory function in repentance is presented through which God patiently deals with human sinfulness.

The way in which a human being is saved receives two answers from Scripture. On the one hand, by means of the law, if you want to be saved, keep the commandments—then you will live (Lev. 18:5, Luke 10:28, Gal 3:12)! On the other hand, by means of the gospel, we are saved without any good works whatsoever: "By grace you have been saved through faith. And this is not your own doing; it is the gift of God, not a result of works, so that no one may boast" (Eph 2:8f.).[102] Wisløff stresses that the law corresponds to our own human way of thinking, whereas the gospel comes to us as something new and foreign to human reasoning. The law refers to our own works; the gospel, on the other hand, "does not refer to myself but to Jesus. It says: He, Jesus, is your salvation. Jesus is your peace. He died for you, he loves you."[103]

By accusing us, the law makes us aware of the accusation in our own consciousness and our own sinfulness; its effect is thus first and foremost knowledge of sin (Rom 3:20, 4:15; Gal 2:19f, 3:24). Over against this accusatory effect of the law, the effect of the gospel is righteousness and faith apart from the law, of which the law and the prophets have testified (Rom 3:21). The gospel portrays Christ "as crucified" (Gal 3:1) to the one

---

[101] An interesting exercise in reflecting further around these three uses of the law may be to seek to apply them to some of the examples offered in Part A above.

[102] Wisløff, *Jag vet på vem jag tror*, 88f.

[103] Wisløff, 90f.

who is terrified over their sins; by hearing and receiving the gospel, salvific faith is graciously and patiently kindled in their heart.

A typical Lutheran response to our main question is thus: the biblical language about sin and judgment indeed is too condemnatory when our attention is one-sidedly directed to the law and its requirements, since the law accuses us and does not bring salvation, although it prepares the way for salvation (*the pedagogical use of the law*). Now, the alternative way of salvation through the gospel does not result in condemnation; instead, God here mercifully and patiently deals with human sins by the righteousness of Christ (Rom 3:21–31, 10:4; 2 Cor 5:21), the gifts of faith (Acts 10:43, Eph 2:8, Rom 6:23), and the Spirit (John 20:22; Acts 2; Rom 7:6, 8:9–11; 2 Cor 5:17; Gal 3:2), and by the means of grace, the believer's continuous use of word and sacrament.[104]

The proper distinction between law and gospel is key to Lutheran soteriology.[105] However, both law and gospel need to be proclaimed. In the law God confronts me, as one who is my opposite, with difficult, convicting questions: "Adam! Eve! Where are you (Gen 3:9)? Where is your brother (Gen 4:9)? Such questions convict me; what I am not conscious of comes into the light." God speaks in two different ways to human beings, through the law in which he speaks words of conviction against me, in the gospel in which he speaks for me. "The gospel is thus a 'different Word,' a second Word of God, which cannot be merged with the word of the law."[106]

According to Lutheran teaching, God's law, in its pedagogical function, thus deals with our sins by accusing us, whereas the gospel, grounded in Christ's righteousness, patiently and forgivingly embraces all believers, despite their many defects and struggles with sin.

In sum, scriptural language of sin and judgment used in relation to God's law has a natural place in Lutheran theological discourse, whether with regard to the law's civil–punishing, pedagogic–accusatory (emphasized above), or didactic function. It expresses divine truth and the truth of sinful human beings, and it begins telling us who God is—righteous, patient and loving. The gospel as a second Word of God depends on it.

5. Consciousness of Sin—The Essential Condition for Understanding Christianity: Søren Kierkegaard

The Danish Evangelical-Lutheran thinker Søren Kierkegaard (1813–55) occupies himself much with the notion of sin, not the least as an

---

[104] Wisløff, 92f.

[105] Cf. Walther, *Proper Distinction*.

[106] Oswald Bayer, *Martin Luther's Theology: A Contemporary Interpretation*, trans. Thomas H. Trapp (Grand Rapids: Eerdmans, 2008), 61.

epistemological category, echoing Luther on the noetic effects of the fall. For Kierkegaard, a true description of the divine–human relationship thus always needs accounting for regarding this present human predicament—that we are sinners. According to Kierkegaard's pseudonym Climacus, a human being is "in the state of, or is, untruth,"[107] and so radically in that state that she is incapable of acquiring the truth, unless the possibility is given her by Christ, "the God-in-time."[108] Again, as in Part A above, a necessary distinction between ignorant, unforgiven sinners and forgiven believers emerges at the heart of this discussion.

Human beings who are not yet in a personal relationship with God through faith in Christ—the God-in-time—are still in untruth and hence do not have the capacity to judge in matters relating to God, truth, and salvation (John 3:19, Rom 3:11). Since it is not clear to human beings what sin or divine judgment is, as they are in untruth, this needs to be revealed (cf. John 16:8). Whatever God chooses to reveal that pertains to judgment and sin is thus made known the way God, in his supreme freedom, chooses to reveal it, mainly through the God-man, Jesus Christ, as the center of scriptural revelation.

Furthermore, as Kierkegaard highlights the terrifying individual experience of encountering God's judgment over human sinfulness there is only one way out of the dilemma, from the human point of view, namely, total honesty on the part of the individual who encounters God: "to confess honestly before God where he is, so that he still might worthily accept the grace that is offered to every imperfect person—that is, to everyone."[109]

Kierkegaard (through his pseudonym Anti-Climacus) now makes a very interesting observation that directly relates to this essay's topic:

> The consciousness of sin is the essential condition for understanding Christianity. This is the very proof of Christianity's being the highest religion. No other religion has given such a profound and lofty expression of our significance—that we are sinners.[110]

So, to come back to our question, the Christian biblical language about sin and judgment is essential to Christian faith and rightly condemnatory, since ignorant, unforgiven human beings are not only in untruth, but are there by their own fault, having imprisoned themselves, and brought upon

---

[107] N. H. Søe, "Anthropology," in *Kierkegaard and Human Values*, Bibliotheca Kierkegaardiana, vol. 7, ed. George E. Arbaugh, Niels Thulstrup, Marie Mikulová Thulstrup (Copenhagen: C. A. Reitzels Boghandel, 1980), 27.

[108] Søe, "Anthropology," in *Kierkegaard*.

[109] Kierkegaard, *Practice in Christianity*, ed. Howard V. Hong and Edna H. Hong (Princeton: Princeton University, 1991), 67.

[110] Kierkegaard, *Practice in Christianity*, 68.

themselves unfreedom and guilt before God, thus having deserved God's wrath.[111] For believers, too, as we have seen, the law has an accusatory function, mainly in a pedagogical sense, in accordance with the Lutheran reading of Galatians 3:24, "the law was our guardian until Christ came, in order that we might be justified by faith," thus pointing us and leading us to Christ, "For Christ is the end of the law for righteousness to everyone who believes" (Rom 10:4).

6. On Enjoying Less Than the Fullness of Human Life: Robert Kolb

A quotation from the American Lutheran theologian Robert Kolb will round off our discussion:

> God is, according to the portion of the text of the Decalogue that Luther excerpts for his "close of the commandments" a "jealous" God. That is, God's love for his human creatures is so intense that he will not tolerate anything that harms or damages the human creature's enjoyment of the humanity God created for us. For God wants his people to turn their hearts and thus the orientation of their entire life, to him alone. Such is his love for us because only in him can we find the ultimate peace and joy that typifies Eden, the Shalom that is the perfect ordering of our lives for the fullness of the peace and joy that gives us every blessing and benefit.[112]

Thus, Kolb concludes, anything that trashes any part of our being human arouses God's wrath. God makes that clear throughout the Scriptures in order to recall people to him, to the

> loving and trusting relationship that is the good human life. This is evidence of God's deepest love for those whom he created for conversation and community with himself. A picture of God that suggests that he is indifferent to us when we are enjoying less than the fullness of human life is an ugly picture of him.[113]

Concluding Remarks

We began this article by making a vital distinction in Part A: There is a difference between the believer and the unbeliever, and this difference is vital in dealing with human sin and sins. The Bible has much to say to both and is therefore relevant to both groups of people. Rather than being too condemnatory to patiently deal with human sins, it is the only medium through which the remedy for human sins is communicated. According to Lutheran teaching, that medium is the scriptural word of God either alone or as effective in the sacraments. The Bible's language of sin and judgment is,

---

[111] Kierkegaard, *Philosophical Fragments*, ed. Howard V. Hong and Edna H. Hong (Princeton: Princeton University, 1985), 15 and 17.

[112] Robert Kolb, private email conversation, May 26th, 2017.

[113] Kolb, private email conversation, May 26th, 2017.

therefore, not too condemnatory to patiently deal with human sins, as it is set in the context of the revelation of the gospel.

In Part B, the following Lutheran emphases were unpacked as we further explored our question:

1. God does not want any condemnation, or anyone to perish, but wants all to come to repentance (2 Pet 3:9);
2. *Sin* properly means something culpable and condemned by God unless there is forgiveness;
3. The heart of the gospel is portrayed against the backdrop of accumulating human sins, God's wrath and judgment—all necessary for understanding and appropriating the good news;
4. God's law in its pedagogical function deals with our sins by accusing us, whereas the gospel, grounded in God's righteousness, patiently and forgivingly embraces all believers, despite their many defects and struggles with sin;
5. The consciousness of sin is the essential condition for understanding Christianity.

The way out of the dilemma of encountering God's judgment over human sinfulness is total honesty and confession before God on the part of the individual, in order that they might worthily accept the grace that is offered to every imperfect person—that is to everyone.

6.
"They Shall Not Inherit the Kingdom of God"— Is the Bible's Language of Judgment and Sin too Condemnatory to Patiently Deal with Human Sins?
An Anglican Perspective

Rev. Dr. Matthias Grebe
Post-Doctoral Researcher and Lecturer
Evangelisch-Theologische Fakultät
Rheinische Friedrich-Wilhelms-Universität
Bonn, Germany[114]

Introduction	91
A. Matthew and Paul on the Kingdom	93
1. "Theirs Is the Kingdom of Heaven"	93
2. "They shall not inherit the Kingdom of God"	97
B. Judgment, the Holy Spirit, God's μακροθυμία, and the Church	100
1. Judgment	100
2. Life in the Holy Spirit and God's μακροθυμία	103
3. The Messianic Mission of the Church	106
Conclusion	108

Introduction

> The servant fell on his knees before him. "Be patient with me," he begged, "and I will pay back everything." The servant's master took pity on him, cancelled the debt and let him go. Matthew 18:26

Since the time of the early Church, ethical teaching has ordinarily been positioned in terms of "practical precepts for everyday living." [115] Particularly in the first five hundred years of Christianity, during the time of

---

[114] Grebe earned his PhD at Cambridge under Professor David Ford and did post-doctoral research at the University of Bonn on his second monograph on theodicy. He has studied theology at Tübingen, Cambridge, and Princeton. He wrote *Election, Atonement, and the Holy Spirit:Through and Beyond Barth's Interpretation of Scripture*, foreword by David F. Ford (Oregon: Wipf and Stock, Princeton Theological Monograph Series; Pickwick Publication, 2014; 312 pp.), *After Brexit? The Church of England, the European Churches and the Future of European Unity* (Leipzig: Evangelische Verlagsanstalt, 2019; 160 pp.), and *Polyphonie der Theologie: Verantwortung und Widerstand in Kirche und Politik* (Stuttgart: Kohlhammer, 2019; 522 pp.). He has contributed several book chapters, including, "Revelation as Salvation: a Comparison of Revelation in Barth and Tillich" and "Jürgen Moltmann" in *Paul Tillich et Karl Barth: Antagonismes et accords théologiques*, ed. Mireille Hébert and Anne Marie Reijnen (Zürich: LIT Verlag, 2016; 231 pp.); "The Problem of Evil," in *The T & T Clark Companion to the Atonement*, ed. Adam J. Johnson (London: T & T Clark, 2017); "The Church of England and European Ecumenism: Making our Unity Visible," with Will Adam and Jeremy Worthen in his *After Brexit? ... European Unity*. He has published several articles including, "Jesus Christ: Victim or Victor? Revisiting Galatians 3:13 in conversation with Karl Barth and Scripture," *Communio Viatorum: A Theological Journal* 57 no. 3 (2015). See mgrebe471@gmail.com and grebe@uni-bonn.de.

[115] C. H. Dodd, *Gospel and Law: The Relation of Faith and Ethics in Early Christianity* (Cambridge: Cambridge University Press, 1951), 25.

creedal formulations, the question of *who* will inherit the Kingdom of God was at the forefront of the minds of preachers and theologians alike. This was to "safeguard" the Gospel and to exercise ecclesial discipline by highlighting those deemed to be "inside" or "outside" the realms of Christian orthodoxy.

The background of the early Church's ethical teaching lies in Judaism, which "adopted the interpretation of history put forward by the prophets of ancient Israel."[116] This interpretation of history was that history itself was propelled towards the eschatological messianic age and the event of the revelation of God's mercy and justice. This event would therefore simultaneously bring about "judgment and salvation, judgment absolute and salvation absolute, and would reveal the Kingdom of God, that is to say, the sovereignty of God over His world."[117] The early Church believed that this inauguration of the Kingdom of God, God's rule over the world, with its dual focus on both judgment and salvation, had occurred not by military force but by the obedient suffering of Jesus Christ, God's anointed one, in his life, death and resurrection. The early Jewish followers of Christ had found in him a

> continuation of Israel's vocation to imitate God and thus in a decisive way to depict God's kingdom for the world. Jesus' life was seen as the recapitulation of the life of Israel and thus presented the very life of God in the world. By learning to imitate Jesus, to follow in his way, the early Christians believed they were learning to imitate God, who would have them be heirs of the kingdom.[118]

The Church's understanding and teaching of the Kingdom of God resulted in an acute tension between the sense of "already" and "not yet" with regard to its fulfillment, which is apparent throughout the N.T.

The question addressed in this essay is whether the language we encounter in these N.T. writings in relation to judgment is too condemnatory, in such a way that there can be no space to deal patiently with human sin. This question will be attended to through two further questions:

1. Who will and will not inherit the Kingdom of God?
2. What does the Bible mean by sin and judgment?

And these questions will consider God's patience and suffering and Christ's call to follow him in the power of the Spirit.

---

[116] Dodd, *Gospel and Law*, 26.

[117] Dodd, 27.

[118] Stanley Hauerwas, "5. Jesus: The Presence of the Peaceable Kingdom," in *The Peaceable Kingdom—A Primer in Christian Ethics*, 2nd ed. (London: SCM Press, 1984), 78.

Within this undertaking, the first part of the essay will examine the Beatitudes in the Sermon on the Mount in Matthew's Gospel, and Paul's vice list of 1 Corinthians 6, which serve to identify those inside and outside the covenant (in the Beatitudes, Jesus highlights those who will inherit the Kingdom of God and to the Corinthians, Paul highlights those who will not). Furthermore, we will also see that Paul tells us that those people who will inherit the Kingdom of God will do so because of the work of Christ and the power of the Spirit within them, giving evidence of what life lived by the Spirit looks like. The final part of the essay, then, will investigate what Christian ethical living—empowered by the Spirit—looks like according to the Bible.

A. Matthew and Paul on the Kingdom

Before we investigate who *will not* inherit the Kingdom of God, let us first turn to the Sermon on the Mount in the Gospel of Matthew, one of the most cited and widespread N.T. texts, and particularly the Beatitudes. Here we can consider who—according to Jesus' preaching—*will* inherit the Kingdom of God.

1. "Theirs is the Kingdom of Heaven"

The *leitmotif* of Matthew's Gospel is found right at the beginning of Jesus' preaching, in chapter 4:17: "Repent, for the kingdom of heaven is near." Jesus' preaching of the Gospel, the "Good News," is closely linked to the messianic or eschatological event of the "Kingdom of God,"[119] and Jesus' mission, characterized in terms of God's kingdom, is "working within a Jewish context [...] united in its vision of God's comprehensive, peaceable rule."[120] Thus the 'Good News' (εὐαγγέλιον), which is coupled with τῆς βασιλείας, includes a call to repentance, thereby making a demand of people.

In the Sermon on the Mount in Matthew's Gospel, Jesus teaches his disciples, just as "Israel was taught by Moses, to be holy."[121] Jesus' revelatory words and commands not only announce God's Kingdom—God's saving activity in the world, which is good news—but his words and deeds, or rather his person and his deeds, complete the realization that the

---

[119] See also the parallels in the Good News for the oppressed between the Matthean Beatitudes and Isa 61, in W. D. Davies and Dale C. Allison, *The Gospel According to Saint Matthew: A Critical and Exegetical* Commentary, Volume I, The International Critical Commentary (Edinburgh: T & T Clark, 1988), 436–439.

[120] J. B. Green, "Kingdom of God/Heaven," in *Dictionary of Jesus and the Gospels,* ed. Joel B. Green, Scot McKnight, and I. Howard Marshall (Downers Grove: InterVarsity Press, 1992), 472.

[121] Stanley Hauerwas, "5: The Sermon," in *Matthew, SCM Theological Commentary on the Bible* (London: SCM Press, 2006), 58.

Kingdom is near (Matt 4:23). Thus, the sayings of the Sermon on the Mount are the interpretation of Jesus' life, and we might argue, with Stanley Hauerwas, that "that same life is the necessary condition for the interpretation of the sermon."[122]

In chapter 5, the Beatitudes are framed with the reward of the Kingdom of Heaven, which is given to those who are "poor in spirit" (5:3) and those who are "persecuted because of righteousness" (v. 10). Entering the Kingdom of Heaven or Kingdom of God is "equivalent to the divine gift of eternal life,"[123] and is positioned as incorporating all the other rewards;[124] in other words "4b, 5b, 6b, 7b, 8b, and 9b explicate the meaning of 'theirs is the kingdom of heaven.'"[125] The word μακάριοι, translated in the LXX with the word יְאַשְׁרֵי, describes the "nearly incomprehensible happiness of those who participate in the kingdom announced by Jesus" of those who have long awaited the fulfillment of salvation brought by God's Messiah.[126]

In the Beatitudes, the eschatological blessings of the Kingdom of God, or rather the "decisive pronouncements of the blessedness of those who receive the kingdom,"[127] are presented in a "proleptic present."[128] What this means is that the "kingdom of heaven will come to those who live thoroughly in *renunciation and want* for Jesus' sake" in the here and now.[129] In this way, the Beatitudes do not simply proclaim ethical principles—though they do contain "implied ethical exhortations," which become more explicit in the fifth and seventh Beatitudes—but in fact are a "description of the behavior of Jesus himself."[130] The focal point of the Beatitudes is the announcement of God's Kingdom;[131] they are in and of themselves the very constitution of a new salvific community *en Christo*, as the proclamation of these words bring the Kingdom of God into the present existence.

---

[122] Hauerwas, "5: The Sermon," in *Matthew*, 61.

[123] C. Hartsock, "Life, Eternal Life," in *Dictionary of Jesus and the Gospels*, 519.

[124] Among the Synoptic Gospels, Matthew is unique in his use of the phrase "kingdom of heaven". For an explanation of this novelty see J. B. Green, "Kingdom of God/Heaven," in *Dictionary of Jesus and the Gospels*, 473f.

[125] W. D. Davies and Dale C. Allison, *The Gospel According to Saint Matthew: A Critical and Exegetical Commentary*, 3 Vols. (Edinburgh: T & T Clark, 1988), 446.

[126] Donald A. Hagner, *Matthew 1–13, Volume 33A, Word Biblical Commentary* (WBC) (Dallas: Texas, Word Book, 1993), 91.

[127] Hagner, *Matthew 1–13*, 88.

[128] Davies and Allison, *The Gospel According to Saint Matthew*, 446.

[129] Dietrich Bonhoeffer, *Discipleship*, in *Dietrich Bonhoeffer Works*, vol. 4, ed. Geffrey B. Kelly and John D. Godsey (Minneapolis: Fortress Press, 2003), 103. Italics in original.

[130] Hagner, *Matthew 1–13*, 96.

[131] Hagner, 96.

Does Matthew's Sermon on the Mount, particularly the Beatitudes, advocate a legalism that denies an understanding of justification by faith we see in Paul? In Matthew's Gospel, we also encounter what in Pauline theology is summarized with "justification by faith"—"that childlike acceptance of God's gracious gift, undeserved and incapable of being merited"[132] (Matt 18:2–4). Those who inherit the Kingdom of God are not the ones who rely upon their own strength but those who trust in God and accept his promises and commands in an innocent, childlike way; those who have a faith that comes from knowing that it can accomplish nothing; those who humbly receive the complete unmerited gift of salvation offered by God in Christ's person and work.

How then are the Beatitudes meant to be understood? Do they exemplify unachievable Christian living, an idealized set of ethical principles? As Hauerwas highlights, "ecclesial practices that have legitimated questions about whether Jesus's teachings in the sermon are meant to be followed are but reflections of Christologies that separate the person and work of Christ."[133] When the Church assumes it is at home in the world, and exists for her own sake, then the Church loses the "eschatological character of Jesus's proclamation of the kingdom."[134] One result of this is that salvation is coined in individualistic terms and with satisfaction theories of the atonement, which focus on the work of Christ and make it "possible for the 'saved' to avoid the radical character of the discipleship depicted in Jesus's sermon."[135] According to this interpretation, salvation might appear to be all about accepting Jesus as "my personal savior," after which point the individual can then follow the teaching of the Sermon on the Mount.

This is problematic, however, because when salvation is construed in this way, the Sermon becomes "an ethic that is no longer constitutive of salvation," [136] and this represents little more than another form of Bonhoeffer's "cheap grace;"[137] discipleship following a set of doctrine or principles, thereby turning grace into a "general truth."[138] For Bonhoeffer, grace is understood as God's gift of forgiveness to humanity, and this gift has a name—the person of Jesus Christ.[139] According to Bonhoeffer, Jesus is

---

[132] W. F. Albright and C. S. Mann, *Matthew: Introduction, Translation, and Notes, The Anchor Bible* (New York: Doubleday, 1971), p. CII.

[133] Hauerwas, 5: "The Sermon," in *Matthew*, 60.

[134] Hauerwas, 60.

[135] Hauerwas, 60.

[136] Hauerwas, 60.

[137] See Bonhoeffer, *Discipleship*, 43–56.

[138] Bonhoeffer, 43.

[139] Bonhoeffer, 43.

the one preaching the Sermon, and thus the proclamation should not be separated from the preacher:

> The Sermon on the Mount is the word of the very one who is the lord and law of reality. The Sermon on the Mount is to be understood and interpreted as the word of God who became human.... Action in accord with Christ does not originate in some ethical principle, but in the very person of Jesus Christ.[140]

This means that from the "perspective of the entire Gospel the proclamation of the kingdom and the teaching about the behavior that God desires cannot be separated from one another, nor can the two of them be separated from Jesus."[141] Jesus' Sermon on the Mount is the Gospel of the Kingdom and the εὐαγγέλιον is the preaching of the earthly Jesus,[142] otherwise the Sermon "cannot help but become a law, an ethic, if what is taught is abstracted from the teacher."[143] Ultimately, therefore, preaching and teaching in Matthew are not related as "promise of salvation and imperative," but instead, the "imperative is also the goal of the 'proclamation,' and the 'teaching' also points to the kingdom."[144] Jesus' proclamation is a direct address, with ramifications in the eschaton: it is Christ's call to the people, which demands a concrete decision that leads either to a response of repentance or to rejection, i.e. finally resulting in preservation or condemnation.[145]

Furthermore, since the life of Christ comprises suffering, reconciliation, and cross-bearing, the disciples are called to ensure that their life does likewise. According to Bonhoeffer, Jesus is speaking the Beatitudes to "those who are already under the power of his [Jesus'] call,"[146] and it is this call to discipleship, which has made them poor, hungry, and tempted. Finally, whereas in other places, Jesus' words about the Kingdom of Heaven are linked with judgment and woe (Matt 7:12, 8:12, 13:41, 23:13), here they are phrased in positive terms (excluding the "woes" in the Gospel of Luke 6:24–26). In contrast, in Paul's first letter to the Corinthian Church, to which we will now turn, we encounter a decidedly more negative perspective,

---

[140] Dietrich Bonhoeffer, *Ethics*, in *Dietrich Bonhoeffer Works*, Volume 6, ed. Clifford Green (Minneapolis: Fortress Press, 2009), 231.

[141] Ulrich Luz, *Matthew 1–7: A Commentary, Hermeneia—A Critical and Historical Commentary on the Bible* (Minneapolis: Fortress Press, 2007), 169.

[142] See Luz, *Matthew 1–7*, p. 168f. Hauerwas laments that "Christian ethics has tended to make 'Christology' rather than Jesus its starting point," in *The Peaceable Kingdom*, 72.

[143] Hauerwas, "5: The Sermon," in *Matthew*, 59.

[144] Luz, *Matthew 1–7*, 169.

[145] Luz, 169, fn. 13.

[146] Bonhoeffer, *Discipleship*, 101.

namely the list of "unrighteous" people who shall *not* inherit the Kingdom of God.

2. "They shall not inherit the Kingdom of God"

The vice list in 1 Corinthians 6 of Paul's anathemas, which represents the negative conditions of those who will *not* "inherit the Kingdom of God," contrasts sharply to the virtue list of the Beatitudes in Matthew 5, and those who will be partakers and inheritors of God's Kingdom.[147] Because Paul assumes that God's Kingdom is a kingdom of righteousness, therefore "the unrighteous can have no part in it," since God's rule brings with it the "moral conditions that require a radical transformation of values and behavior for believers."[148]

Consequently, those who exhibit the sins listed in vv. 9–11 "cut themselves off" from God's rule and his Kingdom (the phrase "they will not inherit the Kingdom of God" bracketing either side of the catalogue of sins, or rather the different types of sinner),[149] and are therefore offered no "hope of divine inheritance."[150]

The vice list Paul offers here and elsewhere (see also Gal 5:19–21 and Eph 5:3–5) does not simply represent a subsidiary concern with regard to the Gospel he preaches on justification by faith, but is in fact very much at the center. This is apparent in the fact that the attributes contrast to both Christ's person and preaching of the Kingdom, and also to his work, which includes his death on the cross for humanity, bringing about the sinner's justification and sanctification through the forgiveness and washing away of sin—i.e. transferring her from one realm to another, from the slavery of darkness into the Kingdom of light (see Col 1:13 and 1 Pet 2:9). Thus, for Paul, living a life according to the vice list represents a life in direct opposition to and rejection of Christ.

Since some in the Corinthian Church were likely to have been married to pagan individuals and others were household slaves, many were understood to be mixing with those of "loose morals."[151] Paul therefore warns the Corinthian Church that if they persist in the same evils as "the wrongdoers,"

---

[147] See the Jewish "Two Ways" tradition, in Richard N. Longenecker, *Galatians*, Volume 41, *Word Biblical Commentary* (WBC) (Dallas: Word Book, 1990), 251.

[148] David E. Garland, *1 Corinthians*, Baker Exegetical Commentary of the N.T. (Grand Rapids: Baker Academics, 2003), 211.

[149] See Stephen J. Chester, *Conversion at Corinth: Perspectives on Conversion in Paul's Theology and the Corinthian Church* (London: T & T Clark, 2003), 134.

[150] Garland, *1 Corinthians*, 211.

[151] James Moffatt, *The First Epistles of Paul to the Corinthians*, The Moffatt N.T. Commentary (London: Hodder and Stoughton, 1938), 60.

they are in the same danger of not inheriting the kingdom.[152] Is this a hypothetical warning, since children of the Kingdom cannot be disinherited? Fee highlights that the "warning is real" and that those who are persisting with the same behavior as those already destined for judgment—those outside the community of faith—are "placing themselves in the very real danger of that same judgment."[153] Here, we also observe both Paul's pastoral concern that the Corinthian Church is allowing herself to be persuaded that "God cannot mean his moral demands seriously,"[154] as well as his patient invitation to them to change their behavior, and repeated reminding of them of God's promise of inheritance[155] and gift of salvation (*pro nobis*). This gift is that they are holy and thus already belong to God (v. 20—bought with a price) through the work of Christ (*extra nos*) and the Spirit (*in nobis*) and should therefore no longer live as the "wrongdoers." We see Paul's particular understanding of the relationship of ethics and grace when he urges the Corinthians to "Be who they already are by grace" and to "Stop behaving like the wrongdoers," calling the believers to turn away from behavior that may have matched who some of them *were*, but no longer *are*. Here he predicates the implied imperative on the prior work of Christ of justification and sanctification (see also Gal 5:1).[156]

The echoes of inheriting the Kingdom of God that form the background to verses 9–11—a piece of both paraenesis and encouragement—derive from the O.T. context of the Exodus and the giving of the Law (see Ex. 18 and 19, and Deut 1).[157] These passages explain that obeying the Law of the Covenant, enshrined in the Ten Commandments, will lead to God's people inheriting the land.[158] It is not, however, only the O.T. background of

---

[152] Gordon D. Fee, *The First Epistle to the Corinthians*, Revised Edition, *The New International Commentary on the N.T.* (NICNT) (Grand Rapids: Eerdmans, 2014), 267.

[153] Fee, *The First Epistle to the Corinthians*, 267.

[154] C. K. Barrett, *A Commentary on the First Epistle to the Corinthians* (London: Adam and Charles Black, 1968), 140.

[155] For the Exodus tradition see J. K. Howard, "Christ Our Passover: A Study of the Passover-Exodus Theme in 1 Corinthians," *The Evangelical Quarterly* (1969; see https://biblicalstudies.org.uk/pdf/eq/1969-2_097.pdf.), 97–108. In 2 Corinthians 6 vv.9–11 Paul connects the Kingdom of God and inheritance with a list of ten vices: see Roy E. Ciampa and Brian S. Rosner, *The First Letter to the Corinthians, The Pillar N.T. Commentary* (Grand Rapids: Eerdmans, 2010), 238. In the background to this passage are themes such as obedience to the covenant, a priestly kingdom and a holy nation.

[156] See Fee, *The First Epistle to the Corinthians*, 273, and Longenecker, *Galatians*, 225.

[157] See Ciampa and Rosner, *The First Letter to the Corinthians*, 238.

[158] See Ciampa and Rosner, *The First Letter to the Corinthians*, 238. We might wonder if there are similarities between the Decalogue and Paul's vice list. Paul might have reflected upon the Moses material typologically, as Ciampa and Rosner, *The First Letter to the Corinthians*, point out: "In vv. 9–11 Paul connects inheritance with a list of ten vices. Whereas the Decalogue and Paul's vice list overlap in content, the similarity is not so marked as to suggest dependence. It is not that Paul is giving a second

[*Footnote continued on next page*]

obedience to the Law which helps unlock the Pauline passage, but also the context of suffering. In the Exodus narrative, the people of Israel have just come out from slavery in Egypt and endured the wanderings through the wilderness, trusting in the promises of God. In this way, the two notions of *obedience* and *suffering* are central to understanding what Paul has in mind when he talks about inheriting the Kingdom. Entering into the Canaan and inheriting this Promised Land in the O.T. form the paradigm for understanding inheriting the Kingdom of God in the N.T. and are "held out as encouragement to fidelity and obedience in difficult circumstances in the knowledge that the wicked will one day face judgment when God's people are vindicated."[159] The "wrongdoers" however, will not inherit the Kingdom but instead face final judgment.

Judgment, as we will later further expound, must be seen here through the covenantal lens. In the Exodus story it was those who mourned and rebelled against Moses who were not allowed to enter the Promised Land and cut off from the community, either through direct divine judgment (see Num 16:31–32) or when instructed by Moses and Aaron (Exod 32:27–29). The O.T. covenantal passages about divine judgment can therefore be read typologically, as prophetic signs of judgment, which "serve as patterns for what is yet to come, especially the deliverance of the righteous and the destruction of the wicked."[160] The purpose of God's "pruning" the people is to separate and make them holy, so that they can enter into the Promised Land (see also John 15, where Jesus talks about the Father pruning his people). This "pruning," Paul says, has already taken place in the circumcision of Jesus Christ, and through being washed by him in his baptism (Rom 6:3 and Col 2:11). Here it is important to point out that Paul is not stipulating that no individual committing one of the sins could ever inherit the Kingdom, but rather that the ones at risk are those whose lives are characterized by sin—those who are unrepentant and thus in "persistent rebellion against God, not the temporary backsliding."[161] So with pastoral sensitivity, Paul reminds and affirms the Corinthians of who they are *in Christ*, and patiently encourages those who have lapsed to "change their ways so as to distance themselves as far as possible from such behaviors,"

Decalogue. Nonetheless, that Paul and Moses both gave God's people ten words to ensure they would receive their inheritance and becomes part of a kingdom is intriguing" (238).

[159] Ciampa and Rosner, 239.

[160] M. A. Seifrid, "Judgment," in *Dictionary of the Later N.T. and Its Developments*, ed. Ralph P. Martin and Peter H. Davids (Downers Grove: InterVarsity Press, 1997), 624.

[161] Ciampa and Rosner, *The First Letter to the Corinthians*, 243.

as those who will bear not fruit will eventually be cut off completely and "thrown away" and "face rejection in the final judgment."[162]

To re-emphasize: if the Covenant, and thus the Kingdom of God, is all about union with God—perfect fellowship with God in and through Christ's achievements—and if being part of this Covenant and Kingdom of God is contingent upon holiness and purity, then in this passage Paul is painting sin as essentially "self-living in the body," counter to the bodily resurrection life of Christ.[163] Honoring God with one's body entailing not exhibiting the vices listed, but instead joyfully enduring the suffering of the Beatitudes.

The next section will first involve an examination of God's judgment, before we turn to the Holy Spirit's application and how the sanctified community—the Church—whose chief cornerstone is Christ, joins in with the messianic mission of the Kingdom of God on earth through word and deed.

B. Judgment, the Holy Spirit, God's μακροθυμία, and the Church
1. Judgment

From Genesis to Revelation, God is seen as the "Judge of All" (Heb 12:23). But what does this understanding of judgment mean in Christological terms? According to the creedal profession of faith, it is Jesus who is the Judge, who after dying on the cross for humanity's sins and ascending to the right hand of the Father, will return for judgment. Jesus is not, as Barth famously put it,[164] the Judge judged in our place (in a passive sense), but, as I have argued elsewhere, Jesus is actually the eschatological Judge actively judging humanity (see John. 5:22).[165] Overall, his messianic task is to give life back to a world enslaved to sin and death—to be the light of the world. The N.T. can therefore be said to conceptualize judgment as restorative of God's original order of things. The negative side of Christ's judgment, as we will examine later, should consequently be understood as a "self-imposed fate for those who refuse to believe in his Son (3:16ff)."[166]

According to Jewish tradition, the eschatological Messiah who brings judgment is a comforter. In line with this tradition, Jesus makes reference to Isaiah 61:2, to a time when God will "comfort all who mourn" in Zion. This

---

[162] Ciampa and Rosner, 240.

[163] Moffatt, *The First Epistles of Paul to the Corinthians*, 69.

[164] See Karl Barth, *Church Dogmatics*, vol. IV, part 1 (Edinburgh: T & T Clark, 1956).

[165] See Matthias Grebe, 4, "Jesus Christ the Judge: Through and Beyond Barth," in *Election, Atonement, and the Holy Spirit: Through and Beyond Barth's Theological Interpretation of Scripture*, Princeton Theological Monographs Series 214 (Eugene: Wipf and Stock Publishers, 2014).

[166] Rudolf Schnackenburg, *The Gospel According to St John: Commentary on Chapters 5–12*, Volume Two (New York: Seabury Press, 1980), 105.

emphasizes that God's ultimate *mercy* will be revealed on the Day of Judgment, when the righteous will be declared children of God (Rom 8:17).[167] Yet, even though God's saving will always "prevails over his judgment," Jesus' coming also highlights two aspects of the divine: God's κρίμα (see John 3:17, 5:22–27, 8:15, 12:42) and God's saving purpose.[168] Furthermore, as Schnackenburg contends, "[i]f anyone rejects the one sent by God, their unbelief becomes judgment on them through their own guilt (John 3:18b, 12:48). This judgment leads to a division among people."[169] This division in the final judgment is clearly depicted in Matthew 25 in the separation of the sheep and the goats, a paradigm already present in the O.T. cultic Day of Atonement of Leviticus 16, where two goats face two very different kinds of fate—one, union with God, and one, eternal separation.[170]

Paul believes that the community of believers, the Church—in contrast to the pagan temples and shrines—is the temple of God, indwelled by the Spirit of God. He therefore highlights that the body of the believer is for God and not for self-gratification.[171] The believer is commanded to follow in the footsteps of Christ, to imitate him and commit to his teaching and reject all immorality, greed and idolatrous behavior, which for Paul are marks of pagan life. Furthermore, in light of the fact that the person (both body and soul—there is no dualism here!)[172] *in Christ*, bought at a price,[173] does not belong to oneself, but to God (v. 19f.), "to whom they must give account for everything," Paul particularly warns against sexual immorality.[174]

Through the lens of the Covenant, the body is understood to be the temple of God's presence (vv. 18ff.), the place to "bring glory to God and to sanctify his name."[175] Since sexual immorality is viewed as a sin against one's own body, Paul conceptualizes this as a direct sin against God. It is

---

[167] See Craig S. Keener, *A Commentary on the Gospel of Matthew* (Grand Rapids: Eerdmans, 1999), 166.

[168] Schnackenburg, *Gospel According to St. John* (II), 105.

[169] Schnackenburg, 105.

[170] See Grebe, *Election, Atonement, and the Holy Spirit*, 68–99.

[171] See Anthony C. Thiselton, *The First Epistle to the Corinthians: A Commentary on the Greek Text, The New International Greek Testament Commentary* (Grands Rapids: Eerdmans, 2000), 458.

[172] Here the term "soma" needs to be understood in a holistic sense, i.e. as indicative of the entire human being. For further detail see John A. T. Robinson, *The Body: A Study in Pauline Theology* (London: SCM, 1966).

[173] Schrage points out the theology of redemption from the O.T. and draws attention to the Hebrew term פדה (*padah*) and גאל (*ga'al*) behind ἀγοράζειν, in Wolfgang Schrage, *Der erste Brief an die Korinther: 1Kor 6,12–11,16*, Evangelisch-Katholischer Kommentar zum Neuen Testament (EKK), VII/2, (Düsseldorf: Benzinger/Neukirchner, 1995), 2:35–36.

[174] Thiselton, *The First Epistle to the Corinthians*, 475.

[175] Ciampa and Rosner, *The First Letter to the Corinthians*, 264.

not simply that God is offended because his holy temple is defiled, but from a covenantal point of view, the root of the problem goes deeper to the nature of God's love. If the core of the Covenant is about union with God, which Christ has won on the cross, then sinning in this way involves returning from the freedom won in Christ (Gal 5:1) to the bondage from which God has ransomed the believer in the first place. This is contrary to God's will for humanity, and Paul patiently pleads with the Corinthian Church to remember the Covenant promises of the Kingdom.

The judgment Jesus expounds is always an "assessment of what one's life declares about allegiance to Jesus and the God of Israel."[176] For Paul, the focus is on relationship with Christ, which in no way is seen to be in "conflict with his affirmation of judgment according to works. For he understands people's deeds as evidence of their character, showing whether their relation to God is fundamentally one of faith or unbelief."[177] Thus, doing the will of the Father—and in so doing, imitating the Son—becomes imperative for those who want to inherit the Kingdom of God and be granted eternal life. Judgment is, as highlighted in John 15's picture of Christ the vine and the Father the gardener, both a pruning and a cutting off process: all who bear good fruit (faith *with* works!) remain part of a strengthened vine and all those who do not, are cut away.[178]

Here we see that judgment is attributed with a positive sense—cleansing through separation—God judging by separating the pure from the impure, the wheat from the chaff (Matt 13: 24–30). According to Jesus (John. 9:39), judgment is positive for those who are Christ's disciples, as to "receive Jesus is to receive the light of the world; to reject him is to reject the light, to close one's eyes, and to become blind."[179] Jesus Christ, the High Priest, is the judge on the judgment seat (2 Cor 5:10) who judges (John 5:22). Thus, when Jesus said, "No one comes to the Father except through me" (John 14:6), what he means by "through me" is his judgment. In the unity of his person and work as judge, Jesus Christ becomes the "means of access to God who is the source of all truth and life;"[180] Jesus is the only "way" to eternal life and the entry "door" (John 10:9) to this life is his judgment.

---

[176] W. G. Olmstead, "Judgment," in *Dictionary of Jesus and the Gospels*, 460. See also Stephen H. Travis, *Christ and the Judgement of God: Limits of Divine Retribution in N.T. Thought* (Milton Keynes: Paternoster, 2008), 224–226.

[177] Stephen H. Travis, "Judgment," in *Dictionary of Paul and His Letters*, ed. Gerald F. Hawthorne, Ralph P. Martin, and Daniel G. Reid (Downers Grove: IVP, 1993), 517.

[178] See also Travis' argument on the "branches" in, *Christ and the Judgement of God*, 272.

[179] C. K. Barrett, *The Gospel According to St. John: An Introduction with Commentary and Notes on the Greek Text* (London: SPCK, 1960), 303.

[180] Barrett, *The Gospel According to St. John*, 382.

Since a person has to go *through* Jesus to get to the Father—i.e. through this "judgment of separation" of the High Priest (Matt 13 and 25)—this separation or "pruning" of the believer (see John 15) should be seen as salvific. Through Christ's command to follow him into discipleship, the Church is being cleansed (John 15:3).

Key to understanding how Christ's judgment should be seen as salvific is the fact that judgment is not simply the stating of an opinion, but the judgment brings about an action. Because judgment should be understood not simply as a statement of what is right or wrong, but rather as an act of performative speech, Jesus' spoken words bring about what he says, executing his commands to the disciples, just as God's words did in creation when he spoke the separation of light and darkness into existence. Thus, in his judgment, Jesus brings about the new creation, and the on-going sanctifying work of the Holy Spirit continues this work of "judgment of separation" in a Christian's life (John 16:8). This new life, Paul argues, is the new life of Christ through the Holy Spirit, and it is to this, which we will now turn.

2. Life in the Holy Spirit and God's μακροθυμία

The interpretation of the Law as it appears in the Gospels has often been seen as contrasting starkly to the interpretation of the Law as set out by Paul in his letters, and particular chasms have been identified between passages such as Matthew 5:17 (Jesus being the fulfillment of the Law) and Romans 10:4 (Jesus being the τέλος of the Law).[181] Whether or not we regard Jesus as the second Moses, who ascends a second mountain and teaches Israel to be holy,[182] he nevertheless still explains the Law and a New Covenant to his followers, thereby fulfilling the prophesy of Jeremiah 31:31–35. That the Law is written neither in stone nor with ink, but with the Πνεύματι Θεοῦ on the hearts of the believers (2 Cor 3:3), is also what "struck the imagination of Paul."[183] In Paul's letter, as well as in John's Gospel, we see an "ethical dualism that uses the terms σάρξ and πνεῦμα to express the antithesis of that dualism,"[184] originating not in Greek thought but having its background in the O.T..

According to Paul, the flesh opposes the life of the Spirit and the Spirit opposes the evil works of the flesh. Paul's understanding of this personal internal struggle (see Rom 7) can thus be encapsulated with the following: if a person chooses evil, the Spirit opposes him; if they choose good, the flesh

---

[181] See Longenecker, *Galatians*, 246.
[182] See Hauerwas, "5: The Sermon," in *Matthew*, 58.
[183] Dodd, *Gospel and Law*, 68.
[184] Longenecker, *Galatians*, p. 245.

hinders them.[185] Thus, in 1 Corinthians 11:1 Paul commands his readers, "Be imitators of me as I am of Christ" and elsewhere he calls them to "fulfill the law of Christ" (Gal 6:2), saying that he himself is "within Christ's law" (1 Cor 9:21), that is, the "new law" Jesus preached in the Sermon on the Mount.

Most significantly, however, this fulfilling of the Law or imitating Christ should not be understood legalistically, as for Paul, life by the Spirit is a life of freedom, which constitutes "a third way of life distinct both on the one hand from legalism and on the other from that which is characterized by a yielding to the impulses of the flesh."[186]

We see that Paul does not contrast the works of the flesh with a list of virtues, but instead with the life in the Spirit, for he is "contrasting two realms of existence—life in the Spirit which leads to the kingdom of God, and life in the flesh which leads to exclusion from God's kingdom."[187] For Paul, "the way of the Spirit is the way of freedom; the way of the Spirit is the way of love."[188] To be under grace is to be led by the Spirit, and to be led by the Spirit is what brings "simultaneous deliverance from the desire of the flesh, the bondage of the law, and the power of sin."[189] Ultimately, therefore, to be led by the Spirit is to walk by the Spirit—that is, to have the power to "rebut the desire of the flesh" and be increasingly "conformed to the likeness of Christ."[190]

For Paul, the Spirit not only transfers the believer from one realm of existence to another, but "also (1) sensitizes the believer to what is contrary to God's will, (2) gives to the believer an intrinsic standard of values, and (3) enables the believer to do what is good, with expressions of that goodness being for the benefit of others."[191] And wherever this new life in Christ through the power of the Spirit is present, the individual's "relationship with God and life lived as a Christian are begun, sustained, directed, and complete entirely by the Spirit."[192]

This new life in the Spirit is what some in the Corinthian Church had forgotten; Paul therefore had to remind them patiently that through baptism

---

[185] See Ernest De Witt Burton, *A Critical and Exegetical Commentary on the Epistle to the Galatians*, The International Critical Commentary (Edinburgh: T & T Clark, 1956), 302.

[186] Burton, *Commentary ... Galatians*, 302.

[187] Travis, *Christ and the Judgement of God*, 90.

[188] F. F. Bruce, *The Epistle to the Galatians: A Commentary on the Greek Text*, The New International Greek Testament Commentary (Grands Rapids: Eerdmans, 1982), 243.

[189] Bruce, *Galatians*, 245.

[190] Bruce, 245.

[191] Longenecker, *Galatians*, 247.

[192] Longenecker, 248.

and the proclamation of the word, they were already washed and clean. The gift of the Spirit in the here and now is thus the first fruit (ἀπαρχὴν, Rom 8:23) of the Kingdom of God and the guarantee (ἀρραβών, 2 Cor 1:22) of the future inheritance.[193]

Patience, μακροθυμία, is one of the fruits of the Spirit and thus a quality of God (Exod 34:6; Ps 103:8). In multiple instances, the Bible highlights God showing his patience towards humanity, particularly the impenitent (Rom 2:4, 9:22; 1 Tim 1:16; 1 Pet 3:20; 2 Pet 3:15).[194] Indeed, we already read in the Jewish Scriptures about God's patience, or longsuffering, when dealing with his people. The LXX translates מיפא דרא, God's being slow to anger (Exod 34:6), with μακρόθυμος. Here, μακροθυμία is seen as a gift of God, which "consists in His forgiveness (ἐξιλασμός),"[195] and spans between God's wrath and his grace. From this Jewish perspective, the term μακρόθυμος does not "imply renunciation of the grounds of wrath;" rather what it means is that "alongside wrath there is a divine restraint which postpones its operation"[196] until the measure of sins have been filled up for judgment. In Paul's writing, God's longsuffering is also related to his wrath (see Rom 2:4 and 9:22), and yet it is important to acknowledge that divine μακροθυμία stands alongside God's ὀργή, allowing ὀργή to be "freed from anthropomorphic misunderstanding."[197]

A quick look at the Gospel of Matthew gives us an example of God's patience with humanity. In the parable of the wicked servant in chapter 18, Jesus "both adopts and transcends the Jewish understanding of μακροθυμία."[198] We read that when an appeal is made by the debtor to the patience of the Κύριος, he cancels the debt of the servant, which transcends the Pharisees' casuistic theory of compensation.[199] Here God's mercy appears to be unlimited and God's μακροθυμία seems to consist in forgiving grace.

Yet as we continue in the passage, we learn that according to Jesus' teaching, God remains sovereign in his decision and judgment is not ruled out by any prior signs of his μακροθυμία. The picture Jesus gives us is that God's μακροθυμία is linked to a human obligation, namely that of human

---

[193] Bruce, *Galatians*, 251.

[194] Bruce, 253, and Longenecker, *Galatians*, 262.

[195] Johannes Horst, "μακροθυμία B. The Theological Significance of the Terms in the O.T. (LXX) and Later Judaism," in *Theological Dictionary of the N.T.*, vol. 4, ed. Gerhard Kittel, G. W. Bromiley, and Gerhard Friedrich (Grand Rapids: Eerdmans, 1964), 376.

[196] Horst, "μακροθυμία B," in TDNT, 377.

[197] Horst, 382.

[198] Horst, 379.

[199] Horst, 380.

μακροθυμία towards the neighbor. The idea of neighborly love would not have been new to his listeners, as it was rooted in Judaism. However, when he highlights in the parable that a "failure of readiness for μακροθυμία on man's part will necessarily call in question again the divine forbearance,"[200] Jesus augments and goes beyond his listeners' understanding of neighborly love.

Ultimately then, the parable in Matthew 18 provides the model for the Church to imitate Christ, patiently deal with the forgiven sinner and for "reintegration of the wrongdoer into the community's life."[201] It highlights the biblical truth of the two sides of the coin of μακροθυμία in the N.T.: (1) that God in Christ himself is the subject of divine longsuffering (1 Tim 1:16), dealing patiently with human sinners, and (2) that "love your neighbor" is an obligation in the missionary service of Christ's Church (2 Tim 3:10).

3. The Messianic Mission of the Church

The early Church assumed that by "imitating the 'Way' of Jesus, they were imitating the 'Way' of God himself. For the content of the kingdom and the means of citizenship turns out to be nothing more or less than learning to imitate Jesus' life through taking on the task of being his disciple."[202] An individual becomes a disciple not simply by following an ethical principle—this would just amount to "cheap grace"—but by following the way of Jesus, the way of "renunciation" as summarized in Mark 8:34 and 10:42–45, and the way exemplified in the Beatitudes. For Dietrich Bonhoeffer, Jesus is the human for others, serving his Church, and the Church is the community for others, serving those in need around her. Thus, the community of disciples inheriting the Kingdom of God follow the way of service for others, as opposed to the self-centered self-service exemplified in the list of vices.

And yet, as Bonhoeffer stresses, following Christ always entails a decision,[203] since "God's authority commands obedience. God's word comes to us with this command."[204] Since God's command to follow Christ always propels the disciple to be patient with one's neighbor (imitating God's patience with humanity's sin), the obedient disciple must also show a

---

[200] Horst, 380.

[201] Richard B. Hays, *The Moral Vision of the N.T.: Community, Cross, New Creation, A Contemporary Introduction to N.T. Ethics* (New York: Harper One, 1996), 102.

[202] Hauerwas, *Peaceable Kingdom*, 80.

[203] See Dietrich Bonhoeffer, *The Young Bonhoeffer 1918–1927*, in *Dietrich Bonhoeffer Works* (DBW), vol. 9, ed. Clifford J. Green and Marshall D. Johnson (Minneapolis: Fortress Press, 2002), 451.

[204] Bonhoeffer, *Young Bonhoeffer*, 496.

new readiness to offer "mercy to others," in response to Jesus' preaching that the "reception of forgiveness from God and granting of forgiveness to one's brother are inseparably connected. Without the latter, God's judgment reassumes it full validity."[205] Jesus exhorts his followers not to restrict their benevolence to those who love them, instead urging a "generosity beyond the closed circle of relationships."[206]

Jesus' ministry to sinners was therefore one of "restoration, rather than the condemnation and exclusion, of sinners through repentance ... he regarded table fellowship with sinners, especially the bitterly despised tax collectors, as an enacted parable demonstrating the open invitation to enter the kingdom to anyone who would receive his message."[207] The disciples are called to show the same love and generosity shown by the "creator god, who gives sunshine an rain to both Israel and the Gentiles,"[208] to those regarded as outside the covenant community, as Jesus regarded his followers as the "eschatological people promised in scriptures, through whom, in a manner yet to be explicated, the glory of YHWH would be revealed to the world."[209]

In fact, we see Jesus' patient concern for sinners in that he was "more critical of those who dismissed the sinners than of the sinner themselves because he saw in the efforts to marginalize persons a way of life that competed with his own message of the kingdom of God."[210] The apostolic message with the commission to make disciples of all nations points towards the fact that all of humanity are called to be Christ's disciples and to participate through the Spirit in his life, death, and resurrection, thereby inheriting the Kingdom of God. In Matthew's narrative, entering into the Kingdom is "predicated on one's conformity to the covenant with God, particularly on doing the Father's will."[211]

Here we are reminded of the importance of the twofold pastoral sacramental view of what the Church has practiced over thousands of years: (1) The Christian initiation into the community of the Church is through the "small gate" of baptism (Matt 7:13), when the old self dies with Christ, is

---

[205] Friedrich Büchsel, "κρίνω E. The Concept of Judgment in the N.T.," in *Theological Dictionary of the N.T.*, vol. 3, ed. Gerhard Kittel, G. W. Bromiley, and Gerhard Friedrich (Grand Rapids: Eerdmans, 1965), 937.

[206] M. F. Bird, "Sin, Sinner," in *Dictionary of Jesus and the Gospels*, 866.

[207] Bird, "Sin, Sinner," in *Dictionary of Jesus and the Gospels*, 867.

[208] N. T. Wright, *Jesus and the Victory of God, Christian Origins and the Question of God*: Volume 2 (London: SPCK, 1996), 444.

[209] N. T. Wright, *Jesus and the Victory of God*, 444.

[210] Bird, "Sin, Sinner," in *Dictionary of Jesus and the Gospels*, 865.

[211] Green, "Kingdom of God/Heaven," in *Dictionary of Jesus and the Gospels*, 475.

buried in his death, and then resurrected to new life, becoming a καινὴ κτίσις, and (2) The disciple's entrance through the "gate" and onto the "narrow road," with the task to μείνατε in Christ daily, on this on-going Eucharistic road of fellowship to salvation by faith with thanksgiving. Being in this "unique union with Christ in faith"[212] means that the disciple is called to imitate the master in her behaviour and follow in his footsteps daily, even if this means suffering. Being in union with Christ involves bearing one's own cross.

Equally, imitating the judge Jesus—who condemned sin in the flesh through his crucifixion and resurrection (Rom 8:3)—also means living a new life by the power of the Spirit, putting sinful flesh to death and conquering the sinful desires. Finally, for co-workers with Christ in God's vineyard, it also means preaching the Gospel of Christ's victory on the cross over sin and death, proclaiming his salvation as Good News to the suffering world, and thereby bearing fruit for the Kingdom. The person gains access to the Father through Christ, both by what he has achieved on the cross—judgment of sin—as well as through his final spoken judgment on the Last Day (Matt 25). The Church lives in this proleptic age between cross and final judgment, witnessing to the fact that Christ is King and Judge of the world.

Conclusion

The biblical texts examined above have shown the tension—already encountered by the early Church—of the "already" and "not yet" of God's Kingdom in the life of the believer; between (1) the theological indicative and ethical imperative of the Gospel as well as (2) the flesh opposing the Spirit. We saw that the indicative and imperative of the Gospel are both predicated on the prior work of Christ and the ethical application of that work to the lives of the believer by the Spirit.[213] Thus one's experience of God's grace and one's ethical behavior that evidences that grace are closely linked.[214]

We saw that the overall thrust of 1 Corinthians is Paul's opposition to "Roman influence in the church belonging to God in Corinth, particularly the archetypal Gentile sins of sexual immorality and idolatry." [215] Nevertheless, Paul's vice list enumerates not only the typical sins of the

---

[212] Rudolf Schnackenburg, *The Gospel According to St John: Commentary on Chapters 13–21*, Vol. 3 (New York: Crossroad/Herder, 1983), 99.

[213] Fee, *Corinthians*, 273.

[214] Fee, 273.

[215] Ciampa and Rosner, *The First Letter to the Corinthians*, 246.

contemporary pagans,[216] but also parallel Hellenistic-Jewish lists of vices.[217] These vices represent a number of attributes that do not enhance life or advance ethical living and love for the others, since they foster self-love and a selfish devotion—pure self-gratification that stamps out the sanctity and "vital spirit of love within the community."[218] The list thus reflects the behavior of those "outside the church" who are "guilty of open rebellion against God and destined for judgment."[219]

Furthermore, in light of the doctrine of union with Christ and the question of what a person can do with their body,[220] we saw that Paul "corrects the Corinthians' misapplication of Christian freedom and asserts that believers' bodies come under the lordship of the risen Christ."[221] This notion of union with Christ also highlighted the "inseparability of Christian identity and Christian lifestyle, or of theology and ethics."[222] For Paul, being *in Christ* means neither nomism nor libertinism, but instead must be seen a "highway above them both,"[223] as a "new quality of life based in and directed by the Spirit."[224]

---

[216] See F. W. Grosheide, *Commentary on the First Epistle to the Corinthians: The English Text with Introduction, Exposition and Notes*, The New International Commentary on the N.T. (Grand Rapids: Eerdmans, 1953), 140.

[217] See Barrett, *A Commentary on the First Epistle to the Corinthians*, p 140. See also E. A. Martens, "Sin, Guilt," in *Dictionary of the O.T.: Pentateuch*, ed. T. Desmond Alexander and David W. Baker (Downers Grove: InterVarsity Press, 2003), who contends that in the Pentateuch, particularly in the book of Deuteronomy, Israel is warned against certain actions, which were prevalent in Canaanite and surrounding cultures. These actions can be grouped in five categories: (1) idolatries (Deut 27:15); (2) human sacrifice (Deut 12:31); (3) sexual perversions such as homosexuality (Lev 20:13); (4) illicit business practices involving deception (Deut 25:13–16); and (5) dietary and clothing taboos (Deut 14:3; 22:5), p. 769. In Antioch (Acts 15:19–20) Paul pleads with the leaders of the church not to enforce Levitical law onto the Gentile believers. In Antioch, the church leaders agree that the Gentile Christian are freed from any Torah adherence with regard to cultic sacrificial rituals (such as circumcision), since the cultic demands of the Torah have been fulfilled once and for all in the life, death, and resurrection of Christ (1 Cor 5:7; 2 Cor 5:21). However, according to these leaders, Levitical laws that attend to ethical living, and specifically here sexual immorality, are not abolished but remain to be followed. See also Thomas Aquinas, who suggests we need to distinguish between moral, juridical, and ceremonial law in the O.T., and maintains that only the moral law is to be observed in Christians, as through his life and death, Christ fulfilled the juridical and ceremonial law. (*Summa Theologica*, part I–II Q.94).

[218] Moffatt, *The First Epistles of Paul to the Corinthians*, p. 61. See also Joseph A. Fitzmyer, S.J., *First Corinthians: A New Translation with Introduction and Commentary, The Anchor Yale Bible* (New Haven: Yale University Press, 2008), 250.

[219] Garland, *1 Corinthians*, 211.

[220] See here Calvin, who argues from lesser to greater: "The union of Christ with us is closer than that of husband and wife…For if a man who is joined to a wife in marriage ought not to have union with a prostitute, it is far more serious in the case of believers, who are not…one flesh with Christ, but one Spirit," in Ciampa and Rosner, *The First Letter to the Corinthians*, 260.

[221] Ciampa and Rosner, *The First Letter to the Corinthians*, 251.

[222] Thiselton, *The First Epistle to the Corinthians*, 458.

[223] Burton, *A Critical and Exegetical Commentary on the Epistle to the Galatians*, 302.

[224] Longenecker, *Galatians*, 246.

An examination of the Beatitudes highlighted that it is not only those who do no wrong, but also those who are willing to suffer righteously for the Gospel in the present, who are called children of God, and become inheritors of the future promise of the Kingdom (see Rom 8:17 or 2 Cor 4:17). The proclamation of the coming Kingdom of God is a "claim about *how* God rules and the establishment of that rule through the life, death and resurrection of Jesus."[225] It is a way of life that God has made possible *in Christ* for the here and now.[226] We saw that through Jesus' preaching, the Kingdom of God on earth is spoken into existence by the one who personifies the Kingdom of God in the flesh, Jesus Christ.

We also saw that patience in the Bible is not simply a virtue among others virtues, but part of the very nature of God. God as revealed in the Bible deals patiently with humanity just as a father deals patiently with his child. Since the fruit of the Spirit (Gal 5:22–23) is patience, one might even go so far as to say that the Spirit is God's patience for the Church. For this reason, Bulgakov has argued that it is through "the patience of the Spirit"[227] that the Church is sustained and marked.

However, a life lived in the Spirit is not only one empowered by the Spirit but one lived in direct command to bear fruit, manifested in patience towards one's neighbor. Therefore, the parable of the wicked servant in Matthew 18 highlights (1) that God deals patiently with human sin, (2) that Jesus places real significance on responding to God's patience in a loving way towards our neighbor, and (3) that in God's patience, the possibility of judgment is not ruled out.

We can therefore conclude with Fee that the Spirit's "genuinely transforming and empowering work is often left until the Eschaton, rather than experienced in the process of arriving there."[228] Paul warns his readers that although Christ offers security, to rely on grace in a way that appears to justify continued sinning is false, if not fatal. The Spirit's coming into the world is a turning point, transforming the present into the shape of the future realities and forcibly drawing all of world history towards the eschatological promise of God's peaceful reign. Paul also has the calling of holy covenant people in mind and is "*comparing habituated actions, which by definition can find no place in God's reign for the welfare of all, with those qualities in accordance with which Christian believers need to be transformed if they*

---

[225] Hauerwas, *The Peaceable Kingdom*, 83.

[226] Hauerwas, 83.

[227] Sergius Bulgakov, *The Comforter*, trans. by Boris Jakim (Grand Rapids: Eerdmans, 2004), 341.

[228] Fee, *The First Epistle to the Corinthians*, 274.

belong authentically to God's new creation in Christ."[229] We saw that he distinguishes between two groups of people—those who do evil and those who do good—with two possible destinies. When writing about people "not inheriting the kingdom of God" he implies that if "professing Christian persistently did evil rather than good they would show themselves not to be Christians and to be in danger of condemnation at the final judgment," as Christians are not exempt from this judgment, "precisely because its function is to show, by the evidence of people's deeds, whether they are in relationship to Christ or not (2 Cor 5:10)."[230] For Matthew, however, the issue of salvation is not "whether one is a sinner, but whether one has repented."[231] Ultimately therefore, Christ's final judgment of human sin is something that the disciple who turned to Christ in penitence and faith now eagerly awaits—the salvation of God's Kingdom, eternally fulfilled.

---

[229] Thiselton, *The First Epistle to the Corinthians*, 439.

[230] Travis, "Judgment," in *Dictionary of Paul and His Letters*, 517.

[231] Bird, "Sin, Sinner," in *Dictionary of Jesus and the Gospels*, 866.

7.
"They Shall Not Inherit the Kingdom of God"— Is the Bible's Language of Judgment and Sin too Condemnatory to Patiently Deal with Human Sins? *A Modernist Perspective*

Rev. Dr. John Michael Kiboi
Senior Lecturer in Theology
St. Paul's University, Limuru, Kenya[232]

Introduction	113
A. Problem: Polarities of God's Judgment and Mercy	114
1. Condemnatory Texts	114
2. Texts of God's Clemency	115
B. Three Perspectives on Condemnatory Texts	117
1. Particularism	117
2. Universalism	118
3. Annihilationism	122
C. Contradictions of the Three Perspectives	123
1. Nature of Hell as Non-being	123
2. Hell as a State of Shame	126
3. Conclusion on Three Perspectives on Condemnatory Texts	127
D. Alternative Perspectives	128
1. The Dialectical Nature of Biblical Doctrines	128
2. Divine Revelation as Instantaneous and Progressive	129
Conclusion	131

Introduction

The Bible presents two strands of revelation regarding the nature of God's dealings with humankind at the eschaton: 1) God's wrath over the sinner as unrelenting and 2) God forgiving and therefore likely to forgive sinners. Many see contradiction. Since God is the revealer of Himself, and

---

[232] Kiboi earned his PhD in dogmatic theology from the Catholic University of East Africa, Nairobi, Kenya; his MA from the University of Toronto; and his BD from St. Paul's University, Limuru, Kenya. He holds a certificate in counseling from the Stephen Ministries (CSM), Saint Louis, Missouri. He is a leader of St. Paul's University's PhD programme in Theology, in charge of faculty and post-graduate research and training clinics, head of systematic theology. He has published two books, *The Tripartite Office of Christ in the Light of Worgoondet: Towards a Sabaot Christology of Inculturation* (Nairobi: CUEA Press, 2017; 249 pp.) and *Assurance of Salvation: Towards a Cumulative Case Argument* (Latvia, European Union: Scholars' Press, 2018; 210 pp.). He has led many seminars and published several articles, including, "The Imperative of the Great Commission and the Quest for Christian-Muslim Relationship: Dialogue, Diapraxis, or Inculturation?" *African Christian Studies* (September 2015); "From a Post-Colonial Hermeneutic of Suspicion to a Dialectical Theology of Instantaneous and Progressive Divine Revelation," *African Christian Studies* (December 2015); "Inter-Religious Conflicts in 21st Century: Dialectical-Scepticism as a Panacea," *African Ecclesial Review* (March/June 2017); and "Towards a Theodicy of Divine Impotence as a Solution to the Problem of Evil," *African Christian Studies* 33, no. 2 (June 2017). See www.SPU.ac.ke and jkiboi@spu.ac.ke.

in Him there is no contradiction, the double revelation needs to be explained. We forward that since God is absolute truth and could not reveal Himself in contradiction, any appearance of contradiction belongs to the nature of the progressive pattern of revelation on the part of the faithful.

Is the Bible's language of judgment too condemnatory to patiently deal with human sins? This question is not new and has been dealt with in a variety of ways in the history of Christianity. We give a fresh systematic and analytical approach.

Clearly, the Biblical language on the fate of a sinner definitively sounds condemnatory, yet there are also texts in Scripture that could be interpreted differently (as tolerant). Donald G. Bloesch in discussing the doctrine of predestination observes that, "There are both universalistic and particularistic motifs in holy Scripture."[233] In this article, the particularistic motif is based on condemnatory texts whereas the universalistic motif is based on clemency texts and also drawn from logical and theological coherence. When these contradictory texts are encountered in the same Scripture, a dilemma is created for the believer.

The Bible presents two strands of texts—condemnatory and clemency—which in turn have given rise to various strands of interpretations, such as Universalism, Particularism, and Annihilationism. We will juxtapose the texts that are condemnatory against those that teach God's clemency on sinners. After exploring the existing interpretations of the two strands of Biblical revelations on the fate of the sinner in the eschaton, we will provide an alternative perspective that views the two strands as God's way of revelation that is both instantaneous and progressive. We propose this new perspective with an aim of finding pastoral solace in progressive divine revelation.

A. Problem: Polarities of God's Judgment and Mercy
1. Condemnatory Texts

Although the Scriptures have a lot of texts that are condemnatory and that emphasize God's justice, there are also a lot of texts that teach God's clemency. Beginning with condemnatory texts, we encounter caution against taking God's promises lightly.[234] Galatians 6:7 confirms the justice

---

[233] Donald G. Bloesch, *The Last Things: Resurrection, Judgment, Glory* (Downers Grove: IVP, 2004), 182.

[234] Regarding the fate of sinners, Rev 14:10–11, speaking of the antichrist it states, "They will also drink the wine of God's wrath, poured unmixed into the cup of his anger, and they will be tormented with fire and sulfur in the presence of the holy angels and in the presence of the Lamb. And the smoke of their torment goes up forever and ever." Isa 66:24 declares, "And they will go out and look upon the dead bodies of those who rebelled against me; their worm will not die, nor will their fire be quenched, and they will be loathed to all mankind." Deut 32:22 portrays hell as a place where God pours out His wrath

[*Footnote continued on next page*]

of God in rewarding people according to their deeds, and therefore people are cautioned against being deceived otherwise: "Do not be deceived; God is not mocked, for whatever one sows, that will he also reap." Various texts in the Old and N.T.s attest to the wrath of God and intensity of punishment in hell. Regarding the fate of sinners in the eschaton, Daniel 12:1b states:

> There shall be a time of anguish, such as has never occurred since nations first came into existence... many of those who sleep in the dust of the earth shall awake, some to everlasting life, and some to shame and everlasting contempt.

And 2 Thessalonians 1:9 states, "These will suffer the punishment of eternal destruction, separated from the presence of the Lord and from the glory of his might."

The Bible clearly teaches God's justice and depicts God as one who does not tolerate human sins. However, it should be noted that OT references to God's wrath are texts about the consequences of Israel breaking the covenant, which is indeed different from the wrath of God experienced at the eschaton. It should be further put into mind that the NT references are all dealing with the latter perspective on wrath and are more properly the focus of this study. Jesus teaches that God's word shall come to pass and not a single iota shall be removed. He also teaches that mountains shall pass away, but God's word shall be fulfilled as promised. This assertion makes it difficult for anyone to doubt these condemnatory texts, yet there are texts that stand opposed to them in the same Scriptures which, which we take as the same strength that God's word shall come to pass and cannot be ignored.

2. Texts of God's Clemency

What was said above about God's wrath can also be said about his mercy. In the OT, the context is always the Sinai Covenant and the object is Israel. Although God in the foregoing texts is depicted as wrathful and just, there are also texts in the same Scripture that portray God as being lenient to the sinner. He forgives even those who reject His grace. Here below follows a brief survey of such texts.

Many OT prophets began their proclamations declaring judgment, but later they proclaimed restoration. For instance, within Joel, there are both condemnatory and forgiving texts. Joel 1:1–2:11 prophesizes God's judgment and punishment on Israel, but in 2:12b hope is proclaimed: "Return to the LORD, your God, for he is gracious and merciful, slow to anger, and abounding in steadfast love, and relents from punishing." 1Chronicles 16:34 declares that God's steadfast love endures forever. This is

---

on the sinners. It says, "For a fire is kindled in my anger, and shall burn to the lowest *sheol* (hell); It shall consume the earth with her increase and set on fire the foundations of the mountains." Also compare Ps 34:21–22, Rom 8:1, John 3:18, Matt 25:46, Mark 9:43, Rom 6:23, 2 Thess 1:9–10, and Rev 21:8.

echoed by the Psalmist who sings of God's mercies as enduring forever (Ps 136:1–26).

In the prophecy of Jonah, God is set to punish Nineveh, but He sends Jonah to preach to them that he may warn them of impending judgment (3:4b); yet, when the king of that nation and its people repented of their sins, God had compassion on them and "God changed his mind about the calamity that he had said he would bring upon them; and he did not do it" (3:10). In chapter 4, Jonah protests God's change of heart in verse 4:2b, lamenting,

> That is why I fled to Tarshish at the beginning; for I knew that you are a gracious God and merciful, slow to anger, and abounding in steadfast love, and ready to relent from punishing.

Thus, in Joel and Jonah, we find the two attributes of God, justice and mercy, juxtaposed to each other.

Isaiah in the same manner declares God's wrath on His rebellious nation, but that is later followed by God's forgiving character. In Isaiah 5, the prophet passes judgment on the rebellious nation. He uses the imagery of a fruitless vineyard which, despite being well tendered, produced wild grapes (5:1–4). In verses 5–6 judgment is pronounced. The farmer is going to remove the hedge he had put around the vineyard. Now the vineyard is going to be ignored and will not be cared for, and it will be vandalized. In verse 7, the writer likens the house of Israel and Judah to the vineyard. But in chapter 27, he presents God as having changed His heart and now cares and protects the same vineyard. God's anger is then redirected against those who harm Israel and Judah—His vineyard. Although in verses 4–5, the assurance of protection is conditional, in verse 6 the prophet makes a quick reassurance. He declares, "In days to come Jacob shall take root, Israel shall blossom and put forth shoots, and fill the whole world with fruit." In Isaiah 43:25–26, the prophet reassures the people that when God forgives, He does not count the past sins on those He has forgiven: "I am he who blots out your transgressions for my own sake, and I will not remember your sins."

Observed from the texts above, one can infer a particular rhythm, warning, punishment, and redemption. It is evident that God's warning precedes His action (punishment). God first warns the transgressing nation of possible punishment. In many OT prophecies, although the nation is punished it is restored and not annihilated; this remnant theme abounds in the entire OT. Unlike the current era, OT period sins were punished within the time of the errant generation.

In many ways, the entire Bible story is that of warning, punishment, and restoration. For example, in the days of Noah, the nations are warned and then punished, but there is a remnant. In the days of Isaiah a similar theme and flow of rhythm is seen in warning, punishment, and restoration. The current era of Christ's prophecy has a warning which will be followed by punishment and a restoration in the eschaton.

How then does one reconcile the two opposing strands of revelation in the Holy Scripture? If we hold that all scripture is inspired by the Holy Spirit, then both strands must be inspired, and an attempt to reconcile opposing texts in the Scripture is dangerous as it may lead to emphasis of one over the other. Attempts have been made in the past to resolve the problem of texts that are condemnatory, that depict God's attributes contradictorily, by advancing theories regarding the fate of the sinner. Some of the traditional theories include particularism (the traditional view), universalism, and annihilationism.

Besides the traditional interpretations, new theological hermeneutics have proposed the nature of hell as a state of non-being and a state of shame. Jerry L. Walls avers that,

> These disputes hinge largely, of course, on different interpretations of scripture. Proponents of each of these positions can cite passages of scripture that, on the face of it at least, appear to support their view.[235]

He goes on to state that "Universalists and annihilationists as well as traditionists make the case that scripture, rightly interpreted, teaches their view."[236] He further notes that,

> This requires that each position offer a plausible interpretation of those texts that appear to support positions contrary to their own. For instance, advocates of the traditional view that hell consists of conscious eternal misery must provide an explanation of those texts that appear to support annihilation and show why they do not do so.[237]

B. Three Perspectives on Condemnatory Texts: Particularism, Universalism, and Annihilationism

1. Particularism

They are the traditional view that holds to a literal punishment for sinners and a reward for the saved in the eschaton.

The condemnatory texts point toward imminent punishment for obstinate sinners in the eschaton who are sent to hell. Particularism is the traditional defense of hell as a matter of divine justice.[238] They view hell as a state of eternal damnation for the sinners who rejected the offer of salvation. As we

---

[235] Jerry L. Walls, ed., *The Oxford Handbook of Eschatology* (New York/Oxford: Oxford University Press, 2010), 15.
[236] Walls, *Eschatology*, 15.
[237] Walls, 15.
[238] Walls, 15.

have already observed, there are several texts both in the OT and NT that explicitly teach the existence of hell and the eternal punishment of the sinners.

When salvation by grace is juxtaposed to condemnatory texts, especially Galatians 5:19–21,[239] the question arises, "Must inheritors of the Kingdom be perfect?" In responding to this question, Mark J. Edwards quoted 6th century Fabius Planciades Fulgentius as saying:

> Since God is righteous, such people do not obtain the kingdom of heaven so long as they do such things. But since God is merciful, the wicked, if they cease doing revolting things by which they try God's patience and turn to God in humble amendment; they do without doubt obtain the kingdom of God.[240]

According to Dieter Lührmann, Paul means by the Kingdom of God that "eschatological world in which God's righteousness will clearly be the order of the world" and such vices will not be entertained.[241]

The particularist First, based on the condemnatory texts found in the Bible, the argument raised by particularists is that God's word cannot go unfulfilled.[242] Matthew 24:35, Mark 13:31, Luke 21:33 all declare that "heaven and earth shall pass away, but my words shall not pass away." In regard to this promise, 2 Peter 3:7 states the means by which the earth shall be destroyed: "But by the same word the present heaven and earth have been reserved for fire, being kept until the Day of Judgment and destruction of the godless." Matthew 25 clearly teaches that the goats will have to be separated from the sheep (i.e., sinners from the righteous).

They argue that for God to be just, the two states of heaven and hell must exist. For God's attribute of holiness to be upheld, God has to punish sin. In other words, God's holiness cannot tolerate sin and sinners. For this reason, God has to separate Himself completely from sin and sinners. In sum, hell the reward for those who rejected the gospel invitation to life, and heaven is the reward for those who accepted the gospel of Jesus Christ and believed in the only Son of God (John 3:16–18).

2. Universalism

Although the Christian Holy Scripture teaches the ultimate triumph of kingdom of God, Origen was condemned and declared a heretic by the Church for postulating universal salvation, including the salvation of Satan.

---

[239] Paul lists particular sins and warns that whoever commits them will not inherit the kingdom of God. Such are sins of the flesh, viz., fornication, impurity, licentiousness, idolatry, sorcery, enmities, strife, jealousy, anger, quarrels, dissensions, factions, envy, drunkenness, and carousing.

[240] Mark J. Edwards, ed., *Ancient Christian Commentary on Scripture: N.T. VIII—Galatians, Ephesians, Philippians* (Downers Grove: IVP, 1999), 89.

[241] Dieter Lührmann, *Galatians: Continental Commentary* (Minneapolis: Fortress Press, 1989), 111.

[242] Cf., condemnatory texts already provided.

This practice of sanction has for many years made Christian theologians to keep away from declaring the non-existence of hell, despite many texts and theological interpretations that point towards universal reconciliation.

The theology of Universal Reconciliation is grounded in the theology of the Cross. If God's purpose and aim in the incarnation of Jesus Christ was to reconcile everything back to Himself, then Christ's death on the Cross was for all humankind a means of reconciling them back to their Creator. Thus, if by his death he conquered death and hell, then all must be reconciled to the Creator.

Bauckham quotes a Swabian revivalist Christoph Blumhardt,

> There can be no question of God's giving up anything or anyone in the whole world, either today or in all eternity. The end has to be: Behold, everything is God's! Jesus comes as the one who has borne the sins of the world. Jesus can judge but not condemn.[243]

Jürgen Moltmann, in line with this perspective, concludes regarding universal reconciliation by stating that:

> Judgment is not God's last word. Judgment establishes in the world the divine righteousness on which the new creation is to be built. But God's last word is 'Behold, I make all things new' (Rev 21:5). From this no one is excepted. Love is God's compassion with the lost. Transforming grace is God's punishment for sinners. It is not the right to choose that defines the reality of human freedom. It is the doing of the good.[244]

According to Paul Tillich, the doctrine of two-fold eternal destiny (i.e., salvation and condemnation) contradicts the idea of God's permanent creation of the finite as something "very good." His argument is based on the following syllogism:

> If 'Being' is good, nothing that 'is' can become completely evil. Human beings 'are' (i.e., they have being and is included in the creative divine love). Therefore, human beings cannot be completely evil because they are included in the creative divine love.[245]

People who subscribe to the universalist perspective argue that "He [God] does not retain his anger forever, because he delights in showing clemency" (Micah 7:18b). Similar theology resonates with Lamentations 3:22, "The steadfast love of the LORD never ceases, his mercies never come to an end." This theme is echoed in the NT in James 2:13 which states, "For judgment will be without mercy to anyone who has shown no mercy; mercy

---

[243] Richard Bauckham, ed., *God Will Be All in All: Eschatology of Jurgen Moltmann* (Edinburgh: T & T Clark Ltd, 1999), 47.

[244] Bauckham, *God Will Be All in All*, 47.

[245] Paul Tillich, *Systematic Theology* (Chicago: University of Chicago Press, 1951), 479.

triumphs over judgment." In Psalms 136, the Psalmist emphasizes the fact that "God's mercy endures forever."[246] They further argue that the NT declares that in the end every human being shall bow and confess to the Lordship of Jesus Christ to the glory of God the Father (Phil 2:9–11).

They also argue that since all God's attributes are eternal, his enduring love and mercy are also eternal and, therefore, from eternity He never willed damnation of humankind.

Actually, it is not in the eschaton that God's mercies will overcome His wrath. Since all things in God happen instantaneously, judgment and forgiveness already happened in His timeless realm (eternity), the extinction of hell already happened in His time; that is, the extinction of hell happened before the incarnation of Jesus Christ and eventual conquering of death and hell, an event that happened in time. In His eternal foreknowledge and eternal design for creation, God's redemption already happened in Jesus Christ.

This can be inferred from Bloesch's words, "Moreover, his triumph in his death and resurrection mirrors his original triumph at the beginning of all things, his victory at the creation where he brought the primordial chaos under control."[247] According to Bloesch, this triumphant grace shall persist into the eschaton in which God's grace shall eventually triumph over evil. Just as it happened at creation, where God's grace triumphed over chaos, at the eschaton, "God's victory over the chaos will be given additional confirmation in his second coming, which will bring worldly history to an end and supplant the kingdoms of this world by the kingdom of God."[248]

According to Bloesch, "Sacred tradition attests that God created all people for eternal life (Wisdom 2:23)." He goes further to observe that this point was discerned by Count Zinzendorf who averred, "All human souls ... are designed for salvation ... many more persons are saved than lost. The lost are the exceptions."[249]

Discussing the doctrine of (double) predestination, Bloesch holds that divine election is both universal as well as particular. He explains that "election is universal in its outreach and particular in its efficacy for faith."[250] According to him,

---

[246] If we understand "endure forever" to mean eternally, this will mean that in eternity, before creation of the universe, God's mercy endured; and that is why in eternity he begot His Son for the purpose of salvation of humanity – God was about to create. I.e., God's mercies endure from eternity to eternity, before creation to after judgment. This then means that after judgment, God's mercy triumphs over His wrath.

[247] Bloesch, *Last Things*, 216.

[248] Bloesch, 216.

[249] Bloesch, 215.

[250] Bloesch, 183.

All are elected to be in the service of Christ, but only some are destined for fellowship with Christ. The invitation goes out to all, but adoption is only for some. Unbelief is the reason for being barred from fellowship with Christ—God is the cause of our salvation; unbelief is the cause of our damnation.[251]

Although Bloesch holds this universal perspective of salvation, he takes into account texts that teach the dialectical nature of God and the texts in the Scripture that teach both God's mercy and God's jugement (cf. Isa 49:2; John 12:47–48; 2 Cor 2:15–16; Heb 4:12; Eph 6:17; Rev 1:16, 2:12, 16–17, 19:15).[252]

Bloesch notes that it was Aquinas "who sought to hold together the polarities of judgment and mercy in God's dealings with humanity."[253] Aquinas said, "Although in Justice God could deprive of existence and annihilate a creature that sins against him, yet it is more becoming justice that he keep (*sic*) it in existence to punish it."[254] Aquinas argued that, "In the case of annihilation, Justice would have no admixture of mercy, since nothing would remain to which he might show mercy; and yet it is written (Ps 25:10) that all the ways of the Lord are mercy and truth."[255] Some in the Catholic Church have inclined towards the doctrine of universal salvation as it can be inferred from the Catholic mystic Francois Fenlon who is quoted as having taught: "Thou grantest grace even to those who will forever experience the rigour of thy justice."[256]

Bloesch's stated clearly his position in regard to universalism:

> From my perspective hell as the outer darkness, eternal perdition, has been destroyed by the cross and resurrection victory of Christ, since he died for all and his gracious election goes out to all. The possibility of ontological separation from God has been cancelled by Jesus Christ through his universal atoning sacrifice. This kind of hell has been excluded from God's purposes. Yet an inner darkness remains as a sign and shadow of what has been overcome. To the rejected it appears to include the horror of eternal separation from God. The truth of the matter is that the pain in hell is due to the presence of God rather than to his absence, to his unfathomable love rather than to any abysmal hatred, or that is worse, gross indifference.[257]

---

[251] Bloesch, 183.

[252] Bloesch, 183.

[253] Bloesch, 217.

[254] Aquinas quoted in Bloesch, 217.

[255] Bloesch, *Last Things*, 217.

[256] Francois Fenelon, *Christian Perfection*, trans. Mildred Whitney Stillman (New York: Harper and Bros., 1947), 128. Quoted in Bloesch, 217.

[257] Bloesch, *Last Things*, 217.

Another argument for universal salvation by Bloesch is based on his understanding of Psalm 139:7–12: "Even if we make our bed in hell, Christ is there ready to restore us if we will only accept the fact that he has borne the judgment on sin in our place and in the place of all humanity."[258] Clearly, Bloesch's doctrine of universal salvation includes that Christ will save people even in hell. As if in conclusion, Bloesch declares, "In depiction of the last things that is fully consonant with the mysteries of Christian faith, we must affirm no ultimate dualism but instead a duality within an ultimate unity. There is no coeternal evil, but an evil that has been overturned by good."[259]

3. Annihilationism

Annihilation is the view that hell is a permanent once-and-for-all termination of the sinful soul, that it will be blotted out and be as though it never existed. According to this view, the unbeliever will cease to exist anymore with both the body and soul following the physical death. The view takes a literal view of biblical references such as, "The soul that sins shall die" (Ezek. 18: 4) and "the wages of sin is death" (Rom 6: 23).

This teaching is based on the argument that if God's ultimate purpose is to redeem the whole of his creation, then the existence of hell negates or defeats God's purposes. This is a thesis that builds on the doctrine of eternal punishment (unending suffering) as seemingly incompatible with the nature of God who is loving and merciful. They propose that hell is the final annihilation of the impenitent to preserve the view that God is loving and merciful and that annihilation will help answer the question of how God will ultimately achieve his goal of universal salvation.

The doctrine of annihilation finds support from some leading evangelicals, like John Stott who advances three scriptural arguments to support the idea of annihilation. The first thesis is that the doctrine of hell (or the idea of unending punishment) contradicts God's promises regarding final victory over *all* evil. The doctrine is also hard to reconcile with the teaching of the NT texts which suggest universal salvation.[260]

The second thesis is that the scriptural language indicates that the final fate of the wicked is destruction and not torture. This means that they will not continue existing in a form of perpetual suffering, but actually will be

---

[258] Bloesch, 218.

[259] Bloesch, 218.

[260] David L. Edwards and John Stott, *Evangelical Essentials: A Liberal—Evangelical Dialogue* (Downers Groove, DOWNERS GROVE: IVP, 1988), 312–320. Cf., John 12:32, "Christ will draw all humanity to himself"; Eph 1:10, "God will finally unite all things under Christ's headship"; Col 1:20, "God will finally reconcile all things to himself through Christ"; Phil 2:10–11, "every knee shall bow, every tongue confess"; and 1 Cor 15:28, "God will in the end be all in all."

destroyed. The imagery of fire, for example, signifies not suffering but *destruction.* Stott writes, "The main function of fire is not to cause pain, but to secure destruction, as all the world incinerators bear witness."[261]

The third thesis holds that the idea of an everlasting punishment is not compatible with what we know of divine justice as revealed in the scripture. Stott argues that it is unlike God's nature to subject one to a suffering experienced for all eternity (literally unending torture) for sins committed in time.[262]

Besides Stott's three theses, the other argument for annihilation is that sin deserves punishment. It is not, however, in God's intention or even of his nature to punish the sinner forever. The unrighteous will be judged and handed punishment commensurate with their sin. Then they will be annihilated after having suffered punishment commensurate to their sins.

C. Contradictions of the Three Perspectives
1. Nature of Hell as Non-being

There have been disagreements regarding the state of affairs in the hereafter, whether in heaven or hell. Theologians have argued that it is not reasonable to anticipate the temperatures in hell or the pleasant state of affairs in heaven since the descriptions in the NT seem to contradict.[263] There have also been disputes on whether fire exists in hell at all. Even those who hold onto the tradition of the existence of fire in hell have questioned its nature. They have also questioned the length of punishment in hell. What will be the nature of bodies burning in hell?

Recently the Church of England in its "Doctrine Commission of the Church of England" did away with hell fire, replacing it by "total non-being." They declared "Hell is not eternal torment, but it is the final and irrevocable choosing of that which is opposed to God so completely and so absolutely that the only end is total non-being."[264] This perspective can easily be mistaken for annihilationism. Yet all that the Anglican Church is stating is that since God is the source of human being, once the sinner alienates the self from their source of being, i.e., from the Being of God, they lose their source of being and the result is them becoming "non-being."

According to Jürgen Moltmann,

---

[261] Edwards and Stott, *Evangelical Essentials*, 312–32.

[262] Edwards and Stott, 312–320.

[263] "Reinhold Niebuhr warned against speculating on the 'furniture of heaven' and the 'temperature of hell,'" quoted in Bloesch, 229.

[264] *The Mystery of Salvation: The Story of God's Gift* (London: Church House Publishing, 1995), 199, in *God will be All in All: Eschatology of Jurgen Moltmann*, ed. Richard Bauckham (Edinburgh: T & T Clark Ltd, 1999), 43.

'Fire' and 'annihilation' are merely metaphors for an inescapable remoteness from God, or for a God-forsakenness from which there is no way out. Hell is not supposed to be an eternal concentration camp from which there is no release, even by death. On the contrary, it is supposed to be 'the ultimate affirmation of the reality of human freedom.'[265]

This is in agreement with the Doctrine Commission whose stand is that "the reality of hell (and indeed of heaven) is the ultimate affirmation of the reality of human freedom."[266] Moltmann holds that, "The logic of hell is nothing other than the logic of human free will, in so far as this is identical with freedom of choice."[267] God in love preserves our human freedom to choose between Him and rejecting Him. This is the essence of heaven and hell—choosing God or rejecting God in total freedom.

God, whose nature is love, preserves human freedom, for freedom is the condition of love. For this reason, the human is free either to choose God or reject God. When humans in this freedom choose God, they choose heaven; when they reject God, they reject heaven and choose hell. God in His utmost love grants the human choice. Thus, heaven and hell are human choices, and God's demonstration of His uttermost love is in letting that which He loves have their choice.

In other words, God, who is love, sets the object of His love—human beings—free to choose. Human beings in their freedom make choices which land them either in heaven (epitome of eternal being) or in hell (epitome of eternal non-being). Thus, hell is the state of permanent humans' rejection of God and God's permanent acceptance of their rejection, while heaven is the state of humans' permanent choice of God and God's permanent acceptance of that human choice of choosing Him in their love and freedom.

In sum then, God does not designate some people to heaven or hell, for hell does not exist as a *place* of torment but as a *state* of humans rejecting their source of being and acceptance of state of rejection by God.

However, the question that arises from this perspective would be: If hell or heaven are the result of humans exercising their freedom to choose God or reject His gospel offer of salvation, how many people have such freedom of choice today? And as Moltmann would ask, "What happens to the people who never had the choice, or never had the power to decide?"[268]

Given that there are many people in the world that do not have both the capacity and the opportunity to exercise freedom of choice, due to their

---

[265] Richard Bauckham, ed., *God will be All in All: The Eschatology of Jurgen Moltmann* (Edinburgh: T & T Clark, 1999), 45.
[266] Bauckham, *God will be All in All*, 45.
[267] Bauckham, 44.
[268] Bauckham, 44–45.

state, that dilemma renders the argument for the existence of hell as a product of human freedom of choice invalid. Therefore, it behooves us to redefine the nature of hell.

If the ultimate state of existence will be either heaven or hell, where will the earth and all other beings who have not "chosen" be? In heaven or in hell? This question is complicated by the fact that a God of love cannot annihilate the earth or send it to hell when it did not have the capacity and freedom to choose like other humans had or did. Yet, 2 Peter is explicit on the fate of the entire universe, stating emphatically,

> But the day of the Lord will come like a thief, and then the heavens will pass away with a loud noise, and the elements will be dissolved with fire, and the earth and everything that is done on it will be disclosed.

The question also arises from the argument that if God declared at the end of creation that all that He had created was good, how is He in His love going to annihilate that which was declared good?

If we go by Moltmann's concept of hell as that which is already defeated, then the nature of hell needs to be either redefined or rethought. Moltmann says, "Christ suffered the 'inescapable remoteness from God' and the 'God-forsakenness' that knows no way out, so that he could bring God to the God-forsaken."[269] He goes ahead to state that Christ "suffered the torments of hell so that for us they are not hopeless and without escape."[270] He argues that by Christ descending into hell, he took hope to the place where all who enter must abandon hope.[271] Thus, if Christ has dealt death and hell a lasting blow ("Through his sufferings Christ has destroyed hell. Hell is open: "Hell where is thy victory?" 1 Cor 15:55),[272] it has no more powers, then we really need to apply new hermeneutics to the doctrine of hell and the qualifications for entry into heaven. When Christ entered hell and through His victorious resurrection, hell was opened up and no longer has capacity to confine anyone in it.

Based on the above, hell only exists as that which has no capacity to confine anyone, and sinners are not found in it since they have become "non-being" after losing the source of their being—God. Arguably, hell can only exist if there are some occupants in it. Since the occupants' nature is that of "non-being," then hell's nature too is that of "non-being." The syllogism resolves itself: hell cannot continue existing if its occupants are non-being, nor can hell exist as non-being, for non-being does not exist.

---

[269] Bauckham, 46.
[270] Bauckham, 46.
[271] Bauckham, 46.
[272] Bauckham, 46.

2. Hell as a State of Shame

Unlike those who hold that heaven as the total presence of God and hell as His absence,[273] those who hold that since God is omnipresent, then God is present in hell in His love too. According to Luther, "Even hell, no less than heaven, is full of God and the highest Good."[274] Knowing that God is love and that God continues loving despite adamant rejection, even into hell, this knowledge is the cause for the sinner's torment.

The torment will not be due to any form of fires or exclusions but of shame that they did not heed the invitation, very much as expressed in Prov 25:21–22, which states, "If your enemies are hungry, give them bread to eat; and if they are thirsty, give them water to drink; for you will heap coals of fire on their heads" (see also Rom 12:20). God who exhorts us to continue showing love even to our enemies is our example Himself. Luther held that God's love remains even in deathly and hellish pain.[275] By God continuing to show His steadfast love even in hell, the adamant sinner will be tormented by the fact that they rejected God.

But for how long will this shame last?

In line with our earlier argument of hell as a state of non-being, we should also postulate that since God in eternity begot His Son for the purpose of conquering that same hell, hell is only spoken of as enduring as that which is already conquered. Essentially, it is only God's love and mercies that endure forever. Therefore, hell can only be spoken of as enduring as that which expresses God's eternal love.

Since God is light, and wherever God is there light abounds, we can say hell will not be an epitome of suffering due to fire but a suffering due to shame that the sinner will be exposed to. The sinner's past evil done in secrecy shall be exposed by God's light to the public, and thus the nature of suffering will be that of shame.[276] The sinners in the eschaton will seek to hide their evil acts, and the only place they think is suitable is in hell. They think this is the place where the light of God is absent. They forget that God's omnipresence will light them, exposing their evil and subjecting them to shame. In line with this position, Bloesch states, "But this is precisely

---

[273] Bloesch, *Last Things*, 221.

[274] Ewald Plass, ed., *What Luther Says* (St. Louis: Concordia, 1959), 2.6.28, quoted in Bloesch, 222.

[275] *Luther's Works*, ed. Jaroslav Pelikan (St. Louis: Concordia, 1958), 14:143, quoted in Bloesch, 223.

[276] Sinners do not like performing their evil acts in the light but in darkness (cf. John 3:16–f). After evil acts, they wish these acts were never brought to the light. For this reason, they hide from God's light. After sinning in the Garden of Eden, Adam and Eve were filled with shame and sought to hide themselves from the condescending righteousness of God.

what hell is; being exposed to the light that redeems even when darkness is much preferred."[277]

Furthermore, on the question of how long shall this shame last, it appears to be a question of categories of time: the heavenly versus the earthly categories of time. Since time in heavenly realm is eternal, in other words timeless, we can say the duration in hell will be eternal. Yet, this should not be understood as forever. When heavenly categories are literally interpreted using earthly categories it creates a categorical problem.

Secondly, it should be understood that "God afflicts sinners not to annihilate or ruin them but to show them the error of their ways, to chastise them and also to drive them to repentance."[278] For this reason, we can argue that hell does not endure forever because God desires that by feeling the sting of His anger, sinners will be restrained and corrected. It should also be noted that, since God's punishment is not sheer vengeance but holy love, and since hell is related to both God's justice and his mercy, the punishment of the guilty is tempered by God's mercy. Therefore, hell cannot endure forever.[279]

Isaiah 60:11 and Revelation 21:25 speak of the gates of heaven being continually open. If the gates of heaven are continually open, then to whom are they open? There are theologians who hold onto universal salvation in which "even when one is in hell one can be forgiven."[280] Thus, given the character of God as loving and forgiving, He possibly will not allow human beings to suffer under His watch forever.

3. Conclusion on Three Perspectives on Condemnatory Texts

Particularism goes against God's intrinsic nature of justice. How can sins committed in temporary time find its punishment in the eternal realm? It depicts God as unjust and a sadist who enjoys seeing His creation suffer. Thus, it contradicts both God's nature as forgiving and the teaching that God's mercy endures forever overcoming His wrath. In other words, particularism ignores the existence of texts of God's clemency and only emphasizes God's wrath.

Universalism overlooks the biblical condemnatory texts and emphasizes texts of clemency. If we hold that the entire Bible is Spirit breathed, then no particular texts should be emphasized over and above the others, or ignored for that matter, yet that is what universalism does. Moreover, interpretations

---

[277] Bloesch, *Last Things*, 224.

[278] Bloesch, 225.

[279] Bloesch, 225.

[280] Bloesch drawing an inference from Eduard Thurneysen, *Dostoevsky*, trans. Keith R. Crim (Richmond: John Knox Press, 1964), 66, in Bloesch, *Last Things*, 227.

where the devil is forgiven have been condemned by most of the orthodox and evangelical Churches' best theologians.

Although annihilationism attempts to reconcile particularist and universalist perspectives, it fails at the same time to uphold the biblical teachings that—in the end—all creation shall bow before Christ and confess that Christ is Lord. Holding the two perspectives in tension leads to defeatism; God ends up saving only a handful of His creation and annihilates the rest, which is in any case a larger proportion.

Since the Bible has Scriptures in tension between condemnatory and clemency, a twenty-first century theologian needs to be honest. Through historical criticism and source criticism, we have learned that such tensions exist as a result of the Biblical compilers not wanting to leave out any tradition, included contradictory traditions in the same Bible. With the teaching that all scripture is inspired, the compilers of the texts that became canonized may have feared excluding some of the texts (or shown that some may have been earlier traditions that were later amended or traditions held in different regions or times).

Therefore, any of these perspectives of God's dealings with His creatures (humankind) could be right as long as it has biblical backing and theological coherence. Therefore, it is advisable to put into consideration the entire biblical teaching and Church tradition when interpreting any particular text. We should be aware of texts opposed to those that appeal to us.

D. Alternative Perspectives
1. The Dialectical Nature of Biblical Doctrines

The Bible appears to contain some verses that oppose each other and which led to the appearance of paradox of interpretations like universalism and particularism regarding God's love and justice. The classic tension seems to rise from the doctrine of God's grace, which teaches that human beings shall be saved by God's grace, and that is taught in the same Scripture which teaches human responsibility (all human beings shall account for their deeds).

Holding these two doctrines together creates a dilemma and anxiety. The question is, do I work for my salvation or do I wait upon God's grace to save me? Christian Scripture teaches both divine sovereignty and human responsibility: i.e., although God is in control (doctrine of providence), human beings are still the captains of their own actions and therefore responsible and accountable for them. It is thus evident that whereas the Bible abounds in texts that teach conditional salvation, there are those that teach unconditional salvation.

Another example of doctrines standing opposed to each other is that of Election versus Reprobation. Some theologians like St. Augustine and

Calvin taught the doctrine of divine election. According to these theologians, their interpretation of Romans 9 was that God elected in eternity and created those to be saved and predestined others for damnation. According to some critics of this doctrine, the doctrine of double predestination portrays God as unjust, a character that is inconsistent with God's true nature.

Yet even Augustine realized the complicated tension, teaching that regarding the atoning work of Christ, saying, "Without God we cannot; without us, he [God] will not." [281] He meant that God who created humankind without their cooperation or participation in the process that cannot save humankind without the human being's participation in the process of salvation. He went ahead to state, "He who created you without your help, will not save you without your cooperation."[282] This runs against his view of Romans 9 and against Calvin's doctrine of undeserved grace and the irresistibility by the elect, as summed in the Calvanist acronym TULIP.[283]

The Scriptures are inspired by the Spirit of God, and each should be revered in equal measure. What do we do with texts that depict God as wrathful versus those that depict Him as forgiving or lenient with the sinners (condemnation vs clemency)? Since God is Pure Act and He is the absolute truth (John 14:6f), He cannot contradict Himself—never has and never will. Therefore, these traditions seem to stand opposed to each other, and we need to better coherence.

2. Divine Revelation as Instantaneous and Progressive

We propose that revelation is both instantaneous and progressive in nature, leading a solution between the above outlined tensions. In an article on equality in Kenya, Hazel Ayanga said, "Any cursory reading of the Bible shows that it contains both positive and negative teaching on gender equality." [284] Thus, according to Ayanga, the Scriptures hold seemingly contradictory doctrines at tension without making an effort to resolve them. I did some work on this in an article on post-colonial hermeneutics, arguing that although the Bible appears to teach contradictory themes, it is because

---

[281] Augustine, *Nature and Grace* (415). Cited in Bloesch, 185.

[282] Augustine, *Sermons*, 169.13. Cited in Bloesch, 185.

[283] *T*otal Deprivation; *U*ndeserved Grace; *L*imited Grace; *I*rresistible Grace; *P*ersevering Grace.

[284] Hazel Ayanga; "Inspired and gendered: The Hermeneutical challenge of teaching gender in Kenya"; cf., H. Jurgens Hendriks, Elna Mouton, L. D. Hansen, Elisabet Le Roux, *Men in the Pulpit, Women in the Pew? Addressing Gender Inequality in Africa.* EFSA (Institute for Theological and Interdisciplinary Research) (Sun Press, Stellenbosch, 2012), 86.

God's revelation, although instantaneous, the human beings' understanding of these apparently contradicting doctrines is progressive.[285]

Various Biblical accounts depict divine revelation as dialectical in nature. The two kinds of texts—condemnatory and clemency—co-exist in the same Scriptures and demand an explanation. Although it is biblical to claim that God is wrathful, it is not rational, nor is it biblical to claim that His wrath endures forever. Such a claim would also contradict God's character of love. The Bible is clear on the question of God's wrath; God's wrath does not endure forever as His grace/mercy does. This evidence thus disqualifies the particularist argument for eternal damnation of the sinner.

Our contention is that although God's wrath consumes like fire, it does not last forever. Based on this understanding, we could conclude that His wrath is overcome by His grace—this is the nature of instantaneous and progressive revelation. God who reveals Himself as wrathful also reveals Himself as gracious and forgiving, instantaneously. The question of how long would God's wrath lasts creates a problem of categories. In the hereafter, time does not exist; therefore, since "forever" belongs to the category of time (as we experience it here on earth), it does not apply in the hereafter.

The condemnatory texts that reveal God's character as wrathful should be taken as belonging to an earlier human understanding of who God is, which with time has received new clarity.[286] Therefore, the earlier condemnatory texts should be understood pedagogically as one that served its purpose in the remote situations till the clarifications were made in Jesus Christ himself. The O.T. revelation of God as condemning served before Jesus came to clarify that God is love through his incarnation, life, suffering, death, and resurrection; God who loves, self-empties Himself of His glory to condescend and live among His creation, influence their morals through his teachings and life example, and dies on the Cross on their behalf—the supreme example of love. How can such a God abandon them at the end?

To bolster our argument that divine revelation is both instantaneous and progressive, we could draw lessons from biblical exegetes. In an article

---

[285] John M. Kiboi, "From a Post-Colonial Hermeneutic of Suspicion to a Dialectical Theology of Instantaneous and Progressive Divine Revelation," *African Christian Studies* 31, no. 4 (December 2015): 24–53.

[286] In the Bible we have many doctrines which seem with time to have received new understanding: e.g., in the OT, the Spirit of God is initially understood to be impersonal, *ruach* (wind); but later as the revelation gets clearer, it is discovered that the Spirit of God is God and therefore personal (cf. Gen 1:1ff, and Ps 139). The Genesis 2 creation account depicts God as creating from pre-existing material, while chapter one presents creation as being created from nothing. Similarly, initially God is perceived to be revengeful, but later He is understood to be forgiving and loving (cf. Jesus' beatitudes re-interprets the Old Jewish laws, e.g., an eye for an eye to forgiving one's enemy).

published in the *African Christian Studies*, it is observed that the Genesis 1 account of creation is a post-exilic version of the older Genesis 2 account. The exegetes claim that it was during exile when Jews found that the Gentile creation accounts competed with their creation account that they (Jews) developed their version (Gen 1) which depicts their God as superior to the Gentile gods who could not create *ex nihilo* like theirs. From such biblical exegetes' perspectives, we can argue for progressive revelation that the chronological revelation is the process by which that which was initially revealed and was obscure becomes clearer.[287]

Therefore, God's revelation is instantaneous but also progressively unfolds itself to us in time. Through this gradual revelation we get to know Him and His will better. We can conclude that the condemnatory texts were human, crude, and primitive interpretations of who God is; and as the revelation became clearer later, human beings came to know God as merciful and forgiving. This later clarification in the human mind does not however cancel the earlier revelation but elucidates it and naturally replaces it.

Conclusion

All along we have been battling with the question whether the Bible's language of judgment and sin is too condemnatory to patiently deal with human sins. We juxtaposed the contradictory condemnatory versus clemency texts within a survey of the existing perspectives of particularism, universalism, and annihilationism. Therein we saw how the interpretation of non-being and state of shame emanated into some contradictions. We argued that condemnatory texts belong to an earlier primitive human understanding of God's revelation (God's nature), much of which was instantaneously revealed in that ancient time. Then we showed how those texts demonstrating God's clemency most powerfully belong to the later clarified revelation of God's nature. We proposed one way to resolve the tensions from the interpretations of the two strands of texts though the demonstration that God's revelation is both instantaneous and progressive in nature—God is love!

---

[287] John M. Kiboi, "From a Post-Colonial Hermeneutic of Suspicion to a Dialectical Theology of Instantaneous and Progressive Divine Revelation" *African Christian Studies* 31, no. 4, (December 2015): 36.

8.
Does the Roman Catholic Church's Language of Sin Make Pastoral Care of Victims too Difficult?

Fr. Dr. Daniel Ude Asue
Catholic Priest and Chaplain
U.S. Army, 10th Mountain Division[288]

Introduction	134
A. Popular Beliefs vs. Catholic Teaching	135
1. Abortion	136
2. Contraceptives	136
3. Homosexuality	137
4. Celibacy vs. Sexual Abuse	139
B. Catholic Theological Currents	139
1. The Struggle between the Cross and the Incarnation	139
2. Theology of the Incarnation	139
3. Theology of the Cross	140
C. Pastoral Language and Approaches	141
1. Pope Francis' Pastoral Language	141
2. Language of God's Love and Mercy	142
3. Paradoxical Language of God's Love and Justice	143
4. Language of Sin and Liberation	143
D. Doctrinal Language and Pastoral Applications	145
Conclusion	147

---

[288] Asue earned his PhD in Practical Theology from St. Thomas University, FL. He has been a chaplain for the U.S. Air Force; vicar priest for St. Anne Catholic Church, Sunset, CA; as well as a vicar for a few other churches and a hospital chaplain. He was the editor of *The Catholic Star*. He has written *Bottom Elephants: Catholic Sexual Ethics and Pastoral Practice in Africa: The Challenge of Women Living within Patriarchy & Threatened by HIV-Positive Husbands* (Washington, DC: Pacem in Terris Press, 2014; 346 pp.) and chapter two, "The Evolution of Christian Feminist Ethics as a Demand for Social Justice," in *The Kpim of Feminism: Issues and Women in a Changing World*, ed. George Uzoma Ukagba, Obioma Des-Obi, and Iks J. Nwankwor (Victoria, Canada: Trafford Publishing, 2010; 599 pp.). He has published several articles, including "Evolving an African Christian Feminist Ethics: A Study of Nigerian Women," *International Journal of African Catholicism* 1, no. 2 (Summer 2010); "Muslim Youths in Search of Identity in Nigeria: The Case of Boko Haram Violence," *International Journal of African Catholicism* 3, no. 1 (Winter 2012); "Remodeling Catechesis in Post Vatican II African Church: A Generation Approach," *Asian Horizons, Dharmaram Journal of Theology* 6, no. 3 (Sept., 2012); "How Does an African Polygamist Experience Grace in the Catholic Church?—A Hermeneutical Retrieval of Tertullian," *Hekima Review* 48 (May 2013); "Divine Revelation in Africa: Challenges of Intercultural Hermeneutics and Inculturation Theology," *Hekima Review* 49 (January 2014); "Sexual Violence, Contraceptive Use, and the Principle of Self-Defense in Marriage," *Hekima Review* 50 (May 2014); "Faith-Based Organizations and the Women's Empowerment Process in Nigeria: An Assessment of the Catholic Women Organization in Tivland," *International Journal of African Catholicism* 6, no. 2 (Winter 2015.); and "Ecumenical Tensions among Nigerian Christians: Lessons from Vatican II," *International Review of Mission* 105, no. 2 (Nov. 2016). See frdanielasue@bedeva.org and asue1ng@yahoo.com.

Introduction

The Roman Catholic Church in her over two-thousand-year-old history has been effective in relating to people on the fundamental questions of life and providing meaning to their lives. However, acknowledging that the church is both divine and human, it is pertinent that the church constantly balances the theology of the incarnation and the theology of the cross that undergird Catholic theological discourse in attending to the concerns of the people of the time. This balance will result in appreciating their challenging experiences and speaking the language of the people.

In order to speak the language that is most understandable to the people, the Second Vatican Council moved from the Latin-dominated liturgy to the vernacular. For instance, in 1965, the Second Vatican Council (Vatican II) expressed the need to put "the Gospel at the service of common concerns,"[289] and to be much more meaningful to people:

> To carry out such a task, the Church has always had the duty of scrutinizing the signs of the times and of interpreting them in the light of the Gospel. Thus, in language intelligible to each generation, she can respond to the perennial questions which men ask about this present life and the life to come, and about the relationship of the one to the other. We must therefore recognize and understand the world in which we live, its explanations, its longings, and its often dramatic characteristics.[290]

The above quotation from a pastoral document of Vatican II highlights a number of things that are pertinent to pastoral language in the Catholic Church: (a) the aim is on interpreting "signs of the times" by making the Gospel much more meaningful, (b) the process is by rendering the message to a language that is intelligible to people, and (c) respond to the perennial questions concerning this life and the life to come.[291] This is critical in the sense that the gospel is not just about the here and now but it has a spiritual side to it that goes beyond the here and now. Christian proclamation of the gospel must be conscious of this and focus on establishing God's kingdom on earth "as it is in heaven" (Matt 6:10).

In proclaiming the gospel and making it much more meaningful to the people, there arises the struggle between maintaining doctrinal purity and evolving good pastoral language for people in different situations.[292] There

---

[289] Joe Tremblay, "Speaking the People's Language," *Catholic New Agency* (May 04, 2012), www.catholicnewsagency.com/column/speaking-the-peoples-language-2133/.

[290] Vatican II Council, *Gaudium et Spes,* no. 4.

[291] Tremblay, "Speaking the People's Language."

[292] See Joseph Bai, "One Reality Two Languages: The Relationship between Pastoral Language and Doctrinal Language," in www.academia.edu/4147144/One_Reality_Two_Languages_The_Relationship_between_Pastoral_Language_and_Doctrinal_Language.

is a possibility on the one hand, that we as a church may be disconnected from the yearnings of a people, be misinterpreted or respond to our own questions, and therefore not attend to the questions of the people. On the other hand, there is also the possibility of dilution of doctrines or a reducing of doctrinal integrity in submission to a culture in the name of speaking the language of the people. Having been involved in several ministries and apostolates, I can tell that all the rank-and-file of Catholics have a hard time making heads or tails out of the average ecclesiastical documents or even papal encyclicals. As a result, they resort to what is oftentimes contrary to what the Catholic Church teaches; namely, popular beliefs which tersely put are sound bites and twisted presentations of the church's message.

How is the Catholic Church going to ensure that the message is properly heard especially by those who are victims of certain situations? Suffice it here to also mention that this paper is conscious of the fact that some people make conscious choices and then turn around to play the victim card. Merely because people have jumped onto the victimhood ship, it does not follow *ipso facto* that they are victims. With that in mind, in order to explore the question, "Does the Roman Catholic Church's language of sin make pastoral care of victims too difficult?"—this paper argues that the first place to begin is to look at what people believe about Catholic beliefs, what exactly the church teaches, and then what is perceived by some as controversy.

A. Popular Beliefs vs. Catholic Teaching

There are certain teachings of the Catholic Church that have provoked opposition from the general culture in the western world. While these teachings are in line with the values from the global south (Asia and Africa) and Central America, they appear controversial in North America and Western Europe. This was evident at the synod on family that was concluded in Rome in October 2015. Some of these teachings border on issues of abortion, contraception, homosexuality, women's ordination, euthanasia, death penalty, and clergy sex abuse. This section highlights the four most common ones that are always in the media. Popular beliefs appear to be different from what the official teaching holds about them. The aim is to assess to what extent the Catholic teaching has been understood in the first instance before interrogating the logic of pastoral language and doctrinal language. The four issues examined are abortion, contraceptives, homosexuality, and clergy sexual abuse, and thereon we will place popular belief and Catholic teaching side by side.

1. Abortion

Popular Belief: The Catholic Church is against reproductive rights and discriminates against women by valuing the life of the child over the mother.

Catholic Teaching: Every human life is sacred and must be respected from the womb to the tomb. Human life begins at the very moment of conception and develops into maturity expectedly after a nine-month period. "Direct abortion, that is to say, abortion willed either as an end or a means, is gravely contrary to the moral law."[293] Understood in this way, even rape and incest are not grounds for abortion. What then are women who find themselves in these circumstances supposed to do?

There is provision for possible pastoral scenarios. For example, therapeutic abortions (for healing purposes) that do not directly target the life of the child are permissive in Catholic moral tradition.[294] This often applies in cases of ectopic pregnancy or when expectant mothers are to undergo major surgeries. This means the doctors are not directly causing the death of a fetus. By not directly causing the death of a fetus, the church makes a distinction between causing death and allowing the process of certain death to continue to the end, knowing fully that doctors cannot do the impossible.

For example, a pregnant woman suffers a heart attack, and a possible emergency surgery requires an anesthesia that would likely result into spontaneous abortion of the unborn fetus as a consequence of such medical procedure. It is still morally permissive to go ahead with the medical procedure. Here, it is the woman's body that is doing the act of ejecting the fetus as an effect of the medical procedures of the doctors who are trying to save both the lives of the mother and the fetus. There is no direct aim at killing the baby. So, when the baby dies naturally, no sin is committed. On the other hand, if the doctors or nurses directly target and take the life of the baby, especially for social or economic reasons, that is considered murder and the taking of an innocent life: "Formal cooperation in an abortion constitutes a grave offense."[295]

2. Contraceptives

Popular Belief: The Catholic Church is misogynist and controlling, thereby dictating to families and women on what to do with their bodies. Women's freedom is at stake!

---

[293] *Catechism of the Catholic Church*, no. 2271.

[294] *Catechism of the Catholic Church*, nos. 2274 and 2275.

[295] *Catechism of the Catholic Church*, no. 2272.

Catholic Teaching: Catholic teaching situates sex within marriage and holds that sexual acts are to be opened to fertility (procreation).[296] It further upholds the depth of human sexuality which includes procreation, education of children, and mutual complementarity of spouses.[297] The Catholic Church accepts family planning and encourages her members to do so. Vatican II teaches that couples should "thoughtfully take into account both their own welfare and that of their children, those already born and those which may be foreseen."[298] The problem lies with the sort of family planning method that one wishes to undertake. The church favors natural family planning as against artificial family planning methods.[299] "A common purpose does not make morally equal all the possible means of achieving that same purpose."[300]

One of the major grounds for non-acceptance of contraceptives like the pill is that they are *abortifacient*; i.e., they cause the uterus to eject potentially fertilized eggs or prevent their being fertilized. The Catholic Church believes that human life begins right from the first moment of conception, and every person has the right to life. One cannot therefore value the life of one person over another. However, there are certain times that couples are in a dilemma and a tension might ensue. For example, what happens in HIV situations? A condom may be a possibility. According to Anthony Fisher, the archbishop of Melbourne in Australia, not all condom use results in contraception. A HIV-positive couple may use condoms to reduce the risk of HIV transmission during infertile periods without the intention of preventing conception.[301] Pope Benedict made a similar pronouncement in regards to the usage of condoms by prostitutes in certain circumstances to prevent the transmission of HIV.

3. Homosexuality

Popular Belief: The Catholic Church is anti-gay, homophobic, and is being discriminatory against homosexuals.

Catholic Teaching: The Catholic Church is not anti-gay but pro-traditional marriage. Catholic theology upholds the traditional understanding of marriage, which is between one man and one woman. Genital sex is only permissive within such a marital union and aimed at procreation, education

---

[296] *Catechism of the Catholic Church*, no. 2271.

[297] *Catechism of the Catholic Church*, no. 2332.

[298] Vatican II Council, *Gaudium et Spes,* no. 50.

[299] Pope Paul VI, *Humanae Vitae,* nos. 10 and 14.

[300] Daniel Ude Asue, *Catholic Sexual Ethics and Tiv Women: A Case-study of Pastoral Practice in Regards to HIV/AIDS* (PhD. Dissertation, Miami, FL: St. Thomas University, 2012), 204.

[301] Anthony Fisher, "HIV and Condoms within Marriage," *Communio* 36, no. 2 (2009): 345.

of children, and mutual complementarity of spouses.[302] Pope John Paul II specifically taught that sexuality is the means by "which man and woman give themselves to one another through the acts which are proper and exclusive to spouses."[303]

The *Catechism of the Catholic Church,* however, does not support discrimination of homosexual persons. It rather teaches respect for homosexual persons and acknowledges that is an experienced deep-seated tendency and inclination,[304] which its psychological genesis is largely unexplained and may not be freely chosen.[305] Since people are often not responsible for their inclinations (orientations), but only grow into an awareness of it, which "constitutes for most of them a trial. They must be accepted with respect, compassion, and sensitivity."[306]

Gay rights movements decry the *Catechism of the Catholic Church*'s (No. 2357) teaching on homosexuality as disordered and say it contributes to gay discrimination. But this is not the intent of the church. In common usage the word *disordered* suggests a breakdown, ailment, or other related negativities. In a technical philosophical-theological context within the church's teaching, *disordered* refers to the failure of a thing to "achieve fully or at all the goal to which it ought to have been directed."[307] The church's use of *disordered* identifies among other forms of causalities the final cause (i.e., a purposeful cause) which is concerned with the goal of human sexuality. "In this specific framework, Church teaching identifies the ultimate purpose of human sexuality as procreative, a rather remarkable conclusion that coincides with the conclusion of biological science."[308]

The church sees depravity and disorder not only in homosexuality, but also in masturbation, because they do not attain the ultimate goal of human sexuality.[309] This position connects a long Christian moral tradition that comes from a historical narrative of divine revelation: "All human sexuality shares a common history identified in faith with implications for life today. Revelation and faith tell us that human sexuality is created good, marked by sin, and, finally, redeemed in Christ."[310]

---

[302] *Catechism of the Catholic Church,* 2nd edition, no. 2332.

[303] John Paul II, *Familiaris Consortio,* no. 11.

[304] *Catechism of the Catholic Church,* 2nd edition, no. 2358.

[305] *Catechism of the Catholic Church,* 2nd edition, no. 2357.

[306] *Catechism of the Catholic Church,* 2nd edition, no. 2358.

[307] Louis J. Cameli, *Catholic Teaching on Homosexuality* (Notre Dame: Ave Maria Press, 2012), 29.

[308] Cameli, *Catholic Teaching on Homosexuality,* 29.

[309] *Catechism of the Catholic Church,* 2nd edition, no. 2352.

[310] Cameli, *Catholic Teaching on Homosexuality,* 31.

4. Celibacy vs. Sexual Abuse

Popular Belief: Mandatory celibacy is responsible for the sexual abuse among the Catholic clergy, and sexual abuse is enormous among the rank and files of the Catholic clergy. Some argue, the Church is unduly denying abled young men and women the right to live, express and enjoy their sexual capacity.

Catholic Teaching: Celibacy is freely undertaken by members of the clergy in the Latin rite,[311] and in the Eastern Churches "while bishops are chosen solely from among celibates, married men can be ordained as deacons and priests."[312] Among the twenty three rites in the Catholic Church, only the Latin rite has mandatory celibacy which is never imposed but freely chosen. People still have an option of becoming Catholic priests under the Eastern rites. That being said, there is no specific studies at the moment that directly link pedophilia with celibacy. And it is critical to note that the majority of Catholic celibate priests have never abused children or adults; hence, it is imperative to avoid sweeping conclusions and acknowledge the moral integrity of most priests. That said, the victims of priestly abuse are to be treated with tenderness and not subjected to emotional torture.

B. Catholic Theological Currents

1. The Struggle between the Cross and the Incarnation

There is a struggle between the theology of the cross (contrast between world wisdom and divine wisdom) and a theology of the incarnation (sympathy to human values).[313] "As Christian anthropology resonates between finding self by sincere gift of self (GS #24), so also the two theologies resonate between Incarnation (finding self) and Cross (sincere gift of self)."[314]

2. Theology of the Incarnation

The theology of the incarnation focuses on God breaking into the world: "and the word became man and dwelt among us" (John 1:14). In giving an account of the Christian revelation there is emphasis on the humanity of Jesus. Christian revelation believes that Jesus, the Christ was truly human and God. How best to understand this has been a source of tension in

---

[311] *Catechism of the Catholic Church*, no. 1579.

[312] *Catechism of the Catholic Church*, no. 1580.

[313] James C. Livingston et al., *Modern Christian Thought, Volume II: The Twentieth Century*, 2nd Edition (Minneapolis: Fortress, 2006), 262.

[314] Robert A. Connor, "The Truth will Make You Free," Personal Blog, April 7, 2009, http://robertaconnor.blogspot.com/2009/04/theology-of-incarnation-theology-of.html.

Christian history. The Council of Nicaea (325) upheld the doctrine of the Trinity and taught that Jesus as the Son is one in being (*ousia* – subsists) with the Father (*homo-ousios* – consubstantial).[315] The Council of Ephesus (431) clarified that Christ has two natures (divine and human), and is truly and fully divine and human; and therefore Mary is the Mother of God (*theotokos*). The Council of Chalcedon (451) affirmed the two natures in Christ but the existence of only one Person who is divine.

> The Council of Constantinople III (680–681) preferred to speak of the human nature dynamically in terms of the human will, but that the protagonist of that dynamism is not the will but the divine Person. Hence, both the human and the divine will form one 'Yes' that is the 'Yes' of the Person.[316]

The essence of this brief doctrinal survey is to bring forth the importance of the human will in our response to the gospel. In looking for a language for pastoral formulation, Catholic theology must take into cognizance good strategies for the conversion of the human will. Often, those who emphasize the human nature moving towards divinity (God) tend to be sympathetic to the failings of people as part of being human. While it is acceptable, excess emphasis on failing humanity without taking into cognizance the human will and freedom excuses all failings and leaves a person with no responsibility. Take away freedom and responsibility and you kill humanity!

3. Theology of the Cross

The theology of the cross is about the divine activity in human salvation and human response to God's saving event. In the words of Benedict XVI:

> the theology of the Cross is not a theory; it is the reality of Christian life.... Christianity is not the easy road; it is, rather, a difficult climb, but one illumined by the light of Christ and by the great hope that is born of him.[317]

We are led to an awareness of who God is and how God saves us. Indeed, God gives us divine graces by treating us not as we deserve but as God would have us be. As humans with freedom and freewill, we need to corporate with the graces of God. The theology of the cross opens us to the reality of "a dynamic, topical, anti-world conception of Christianity, a conception which understands Christianity not only as discontinuously but constantly appearing breach in the self-confidence and self-assurance of

---

[315] Joseph T. Lienhard, SJ, "*Ousia* and *Hypostasis*: The Cappadocian Settlement and the Theology of 'One *Hypostasis*,'" in *The Trinity: An Interdisciplinary Symposium on the Trinity*, ed. Stephen T. Davis, Daniel Kendall, and Gerald O'Collins (New York: Oxford University Press, 2002), 99–122.

[316] Robert A. Connor, "The Truth will Make You Free."

[317] Benedict XVI as cited by the Prelate of Opus Dei, Javier, "Letter from the Prelate" (April 2009), Opus Dei's official website, http://opusdei.org.au/en-au/document/letter-from-the-prelate-april-2009/.

man and of his institutions, including the Church."³¹⁸ At no point are we to be self-serving and conceited, but we must accept our brokenness and beseech God's throne of mercy. We are to accept ourselves as sinners before we could implore God's mercy. "Whoever says he has no sin is a liar" (1 John 1:10), and it is while we were sinners that Christ died to save us (Rom 5:8).

For good pastoral language, the two theologies must complement one another.

> The two fundamental structural forms of 'incarnation' and 'cross' theology reveal polarities which cannot be surmounted and combined in a neat-looking synthesis without the loss of the crucial points in each; they must remain present as polarities which mutually correct each other and only by complementing each other that they point towards the whole.³¹⁹

Ratzinger (Pope Benedict XVI) decrying the overt tilt toward theology of the incarnation, for instance, urges the theology of the cross and challenges the direction of contemporary Roman Catholic theology as it seeks the path of *aggiornamento* after Vatican II Council. He sees elements of relativism in the ongoing discourse and argues against relativism "as a false interpretation of the ideological presuppositions"³²⁰ of events in the modern world. For him, relativism robs faith of its claim to truth without providing a vision of human dignity while accepting pluralism as the interplay of church, society, and politics. He rejects relativism and skepticism as opposed to truth and humanity's bond to the truth. In-between is the problem of privatization of religion. Underlying such privatization is moral relativism which is not viable for Christians who seek to be faithful to their faith and professional lives. The Christian mandate is clear that Jesus wants his followers to make a difference in the world in their public lives. As Pope Benedict XVI further explains truth is now personal, no one is wrong, sin is relegated to the background, and positive reinforcement is fast becoming the new god. How do we then fashion a language that takes into cognizance the two theologies and be countercultural while at the same time using good pastoral language?

C. Pastoral Language and Approaches
1. Pope Francis' Pastoral Language

How then do we correct the deficiencies of relativism enunciated by Pope Benedict XVI in the preceding section? The papacy of Pope Francis

---

[318] Benedict XVI [Joseph Cardinal Ratzinger], *Introduction to Christianity*, 2nd Edition (San Francisco: Ignatius Press, 2004), 170.

[319] Benedict XVI, *Introduction to Christianity*, 170.

[320] James C. Livingston, Francis Schussler Fiorenza, Sarah Coakley, James H. Evans Jr. *Modern Christian Thought: The Twentieth Century*, vol. 2 (Minneapolis: Fortress, 2006), 263.

has attempted a solution in this regard. Pope Francis has not changed doctrines but uses simple language that people can relate to. Remember that church documents are classics. So, the language simultaneously serves multi-purpose needs, namely, it has to stand the culture of the time, it has to rise above it, and it has to address people universally without being tied to a particular culture. These documents need not to be too long or ambiguous, thereby saying one thing and another at the same time. To minimize the secular media's misrepresentation of the church, this paper suggests ways that could keep them classic, simple and not challenging in terms of precision. Learning from Pope Francis, this paper proposes a critical incorporation of the following elements in the church's pastoral language.

2. Language of God's Love and Mercy

The language of God is love, and love is obviously encouraged in pastoral application. As stated by Pope Francis, the church is obliged to "proclaim mercy as God's merciful love, revealed in the same mystery of Christ," and we are likewise obliged "to have recourse to that mercy and to beg for it."[321]

However, the difficulty comes when people are no longer challenged to change their lives. The gospel should challenge people to leave their comfort zones. Unfortunately, many people are increasingly "seeking the psychological comforts of religion without making sacrifices."[322] Aside the tidbits one gets from the media that mischaracterize the Roman Catholic Church as being "hard," "rigid," and "out of touch," one commentator says of the homilies that they are purely therapeutic.[323] This is turning the gospel into a jolly affair amounting to sentimentality and self-satisfaction which cannot be the hallmark of Christian life. As Paul encouraged young Timothy as bishop of Ephesus: "proclaim the word; be persistent whether it is convenient or inconvenient; convince, reprimand, encourage through all patience and teaching" (2 Tim 4:2). Mercy without repentance is cheap grace. Thus, John Paul II puts it this way:

> Mercy is manifested in its true and proper aspect when it restores to value, promotes and draws good from all the forms of evil existing in the world and in man. Understood in this way, mercy constitutes the fundamental content of the messianic message of Christ and the constitutive power of His mission.[324]

---

[321] Pope Francis, *Misericordiae Vultus*, no. 11.

[322] Rod Dreher, "I'm Still Not Going Back to the Catholic Church," *Time* (September 23, 2013), http://ideas.time.com/2013/09/29/im-still-not-going-back-to-the-catholic-church/.

[323] Dreher, "I'm Still Not Going Back."

[324] John Paul II, *Dives in Misericordia*, no. 6.

3. Paradoxical Language of God's Love and Justice

God is loving and merciful, and at the same time God is just and calls us to repentance. As echoed in the Magnificat, God's "mercy is from age to age on those who fear him" (Luke 1:50). This is not instilling an intimidating fear in people; rather, it is an attempt to spark a sense of awe that gives rise to reverential fear and the worship of God through true repentance. There is a difference between contrition and attrition in Catholic theology. Contrition means someone is truly sorry for a sin, remorseful, and is ready to change. Attrition is the acknowledgement of sin with a sorrow over sin without being ready to change. It also means a conditional repentance informed by fear or favor. Since Christianity is geared towards a change of heart to become a better disciple, Catholic theology cherishes a good act of contrition over attrition. As Pope John Paul II taught, the tragedy of the modern world is the loss of the sense of sin which blocks us from seeking repentance.[325]

4. Language of Sin and Liberation

One of the underlying metaphors in the Roman Catholic *use of language* in relation to freedom is "captives need to be liberated from sin." At the onset of his papacy, Pope Francis called for a church of mercy by urging us to get people on the margins into the mainstream. He calls the church a field hospital where the wounded can be treated. At the same time the pope's teaching on divine mercy needs to be properly understood. Employing the pope's *hospital* and *cure* metaphors, one would say the nature of the *cure* in the church's *hospital* needs to be discerned. For instance, "Anesthesia is a kind of medicine that masks pain, but it is not the kind of medicine that heals the underlying sickness."[326] Conversion to God as the goal of the Christian life "is always the fruit of the 'rediscovery' of ... [God], who is rich in mercy."[327] Thus John Paul II submits: "Authentic knowledge of the God of mercy, the God of tender love, is a constant and inexhaustible source of conversion, not only as a momentary interior act but also as a permanent attitude, as a state of mind."[328]

Henri de Lubac observes that modern ideologies have often created a neutral optimism that is usually backed up by humanistic sciences, and is used to draw us away from the reality of sin to the point of making excuses from every wrong act we commit as human beings. The resultant attitude is an attempt to couch reality—especially of sin—in a language that

---

[325] John Paul II, *Reconciliatio et Paenetentia*, no. 18.

[326] Dreher, "I'm Still Not Going Back to the Catholic Church."

[327] John Paul II, *Dives in Misericordia*, no. 13.

[328] John Paul II, *Dives in Misericordia*, no. 13.

emasculates such reality but does not advance personal spirituality. Thus, while authentic Christianity draws us into a relationship with God and with fellow human beings and inspires contrition for our shortcomings, modern ideologies on the other hand make us want to dance away from this relationship and rather focus on adapting to secular interlocutors to comfort our consciences and escape responsibility. In this process we want to make sin to appear palatable and tolerable. We need not be obsessed with the question, "How shall we present the idea of sin so that it may be credible?"[329] One does not need to be a Christian to know that sin is inherent in the human condition. The good news is that the weaknesses of the human condition and the evil ingrained have been conquered in Christ.[330] Jesus Christ did not shy away from preaching the austere nature of the gospel. However, he brought sin and grace side by side. St. Paul put it this way, "despite the increase of sin, grace has far surpassed it" (Rom 5:20).

Christians are to be watchful for an emerging form of pharisaism that does not want to hear the words of pardon and reconciliation. While repetition of mercy is acceptable and praised, it should not emasculate the growing revolt against the mention of the word sin. The words of Jesus "neither do I condemn you" are echoed and appreciated, the remaining part of "go and sin no more" should equally be appraised and no longer deliberately omitted. People condemn sin everywhere and every day, but no one wants to own up. Once people are reminded of personal sins, they revolt, and the focus turns to social sins which are embedded in structures. Who are those behind these structures in society? While commending those who look forward to collective salvation, there is again the danger of a Christian misrepresentation of the general salvation of the world: the salvation attained in Christ has a personal touch. It is not just the sins that happen in society, but how we personally partake in them both by omission or commission that matters.[331] Pope John Paul II puts it thus:

> We cannot however forget that conversion is a particularly profound inward act in which the individual cannot be replaced by others and cannot make the community be a substitute for him. Although the participation by the fraternal community of the faithful in the penitential celebration is a great help for the act of personal conversion, nevertheless, in the final analysis, it is necessary that in this act there should be a pronouncement by the individual himself with the whole depth of his conscience and with the whole of his sense of guilt and of

---

[329] Henri de Lubac, *A Brief Catechesis on Nature and Grace*, trans. Brother Richard Arnandez, F.S.C. (San Francisco: Ignatius Press, 1984), 130.

[330] Lubac, *Catechesis on Nature and Grace*, 131–133.

[331] Lubac, 134–138.

trust in God, placing himself like the Psalmist before God to confess: "Against you ... have I sinned [Psalm 51:4]."[332]

This then means that in drawing out the pastoral language of sin the social effects of sin cannot triumph the personal guilt and effects that personal sin imputes. At the same time, there is need to balance the doctrinal language with the pastoral language so that the sinner will not shy away from what is supposedly the gospel but he/she is challenged to embrace alongside with repentance and the cross that goes with it. How do we go about that?

D. Doctrinal Language and Pastoral Applications

The difficulty of applying pastoral language consists in putting forth doctrinal statements that give people a clear and understandable meaning of what is being taught. Sometimes, this allows misrepresentation of the harder elements of deep doctrine.

Some people tend to misrepresent the church based on misconceptions and without truly searching the church's experts, and then even blame the church for being silent. This often applies to discussions on abortion. For instance, the official teaching of the Catholic Church does not accept abortion in whatever form including therapeutic abortion, nevertheless, it is permissive when the life of the mother is in danger and the abortion is not directly willed. The same can be said of rape.

During the 2012 elections in USA, rape was a big issue that raised a problem for the Catholic Church in spite of the fact that the *Catechism of the Catholic Church* describes rape as an "intrinsic evil" and an offence against the sixth commandment with grave consequences.[333] Thus the U.S. Catholic Bishops' *Ethical and Religious Directives for Catholic Health Care Services* states that, "A woman who has been raped may defend herself against a conception resulting from sexual assault."[334] Catholic theology does not oblige a raped woman to allow the natural potential for conception to take its course as is the case in consensual sex. "The forced introduction of sperm is an act of aggression she may resist even through means that prevent the creation of new life."[335] Granted that many rape treatments recommend anti-fertility medications within 72 hours, Catholic theology encourages victims to seek help within 24 hours to prevent pregnancy.

---

[332] John Paul II, *Redemptor Hominis*, no. 20.

[333] *Catechism of the Catholic Church*, 2nd ed., no. 2356.

[334] United States Conference of Catholic Bishops, *Ethical and Religious Directives for Catholic Health Care Services*, 36.

[335] Massachusetts Catholic Conference, "Emergency Contraception," accessed on February 27, 2014, www.macatholic.org/emergencycontraception.

The emphasis is on stopping ovulation. Therefore, care should be taken to avoid abortion in the process of preventing pregnancy during rape. Even though drugs like Ovral may inhibit ovulation there are many contraceptives that affect the endometrium of the uterus resulting into an expulsion of an already conceived ovum.[336]

At this stage, the expulsion of an already conceived ovum becomes an abortion which is unacceptable practice in Catholic moral teaching.[337] "Here, there should be reasonable certainty that ovulation has not taken place and is not about to occur."[338] As briefly discussed, the main problem in understanding Catholic doctrines comes from what is not said rather than what is said. Church officials should try to explain more clearly the distinctions, and journalists need to report what is said, and be more careful to avoid misinterpretations.

Despite the highly sounding philosophical and theological language, which is very precisely worded, pastoral/practical theologians should strive to be clear and relevant in contextualizing and applying the pastoral message. We are not talking about toning down the doctrinal message itself, but we are trying and must truly try to meet people where they are pastorally and as much as possible in their everyday language. Today's culture is saturated by media sound bites, and an average person does not have the time to reflect on abstract theological truths that may appear dry and not directly related to their daily circumstances and dire needs in a tension-filled society. The continuous use of abstract language does no justice to the gospel or truly help recipients who are yearning to hear words of consolation and hope in the midst of stressful living.

One of the criticisms against papal encyclicals and ecclesiastical documents is that they are thick voluminous readings. They are actually carefully worded documents by the academics in the church, and rather short in academic schools. While academics in church is integrated with a deep faith and devotion to the gospel academics in schools often do not highlight faith in their studies. The church then, strives to meet the academic need of rational precision with brevity, while trying to make each discourse relatable to the masses. Yet, some critics will demean the precision as pretentious, as if those critics have never seen Supreme Court decisions. And, truly, some of the church's best pieces might actually appear too high

---

[336] Daniel Ude Asue, "Sexual Violence, Contraceptives Use, and the Principle of Self-Defense in Marriage," *Hekima Review* 50 (2014), 119.

[337] Vatican II, *Gaudium et Spes*, sec. 51.

[338] Asue, "Sexual Violence, Contraceptives Use, and the Principle of Self-Defense in Marriage," 119.

for some laymen and lose some critical relevance. That is the place of the local priest to astutely make relevant for their parishes those precise pieces.

In this regard, the efforts of Pope Francis are commendable since his encyclicals are stripped of exotic language but with simple theological finesse. At the same time, there is some work to be done. For instance, the most recent papal encyclical, *Laudate Si* by Pope Francis has 40,859 words long (including footnotes). "However, St. Paul's Letter to the Romans is a little over 9,000 words. Even as the inspired Word of God, this New Testament document is rarely read from the first to the last chapter by Catholics."[339] The implication is that these high church documents

> may appeal to the clergy, professors and theology enthusiasts ... but ... do not accommodate the average person trying to get through a busy day. Perhaps, this is one of the reasons why we are losing people to the world; they just don't understand what we are saying nor do they have time to read what we have to say.[340]

We have the challenge, then, of translating the language and meaning of the church's most definitive statements on doctrine and practice into the everyday language of the masses, and thus make the doctrinal statements much more applicable in a pastoral fashion to all of the infinitely complex crises of the Christian in the world.

Conclusion

The doctrinal positions of the Catholic Church are worked out in carefully, precisely worded terms; and the pastoral language from Rome can and should and is often translated into the everyday language of the people. Yet, when that translation does not take place locally, the result is a misrepresentation of authentic Catholic teaching. Some even misconstrue media sound bites to be the official teaching of the church, and some of the media is decisively anti-Catholic and even anti-Christian. To address this, theologians need to balance the theology of the incarnation and the theology of the cross that undergird Catholic theological discourse. In the balance, their pastoral language can evolve in such a way that is always mindful of the community's language as the local priests teach and relate the church doctrines. This does not mean in anyway a dilution of the doctrines or a reducing of doctrinal integrity in submission to a culture. Rather, this is a studied pastoral language which should include these benchmarks:

---

[339] Tremblay, "Speaking the People's Language."
[340] Tremblay.

1. Language of God's love and mercy,
2. Paradoxical language of God's love and justice, and
3. Language of sin and liberation.

While not merely trying to make people feel good or trick people into pricking their consciences, a more authentic pastoral care that is true to Catholic doctrine should challenge them to repentance without dampening their spirits. As such, we raise their hopes for salvation in Jesus whose message carries both condemnation of sin and divine grace. This requires a gentle translating of our precise theological language from a classical finesse into an everyday pastorally sensitive theology and ministry that relates well to and helps the average person in the pew to understand, appreciate and be transformed by it.

9.
Is the Roman Catholic Theology of Sin too Judgmental?

Professor Robert Fastiggi
Roman Catholic Professor of Systematic Theology
Sacred Heart Major Seminary, Detroit, Michigan[341]

Introduction	149
A. How Does the Catholic Church Determine What Is Sinful?	151
B. The Nature of Sin and Different Kinds of Sin	153
C. Sin, Repentance, Confession, and Mercy	155
D. The Sacrament of Penance and Reconciliation Is a Sacrament of Mercy	157
Conclusion	159

Introduction

The topic of this essay might suggest a need for a defense or a rebuttal. Whenever a group is charged with being excessive in some way—with being too much this or too much that—members of that group might grow resentful and accuse those who raise the question of dealing in stereotypes. As a Roman Catholic, or more specifically a Catholic of the Roman or Latin Rite,[342] I do not take any offense at the question. I believe it is an important

---

[341] Fastiggi earned his PhD and MA from Fordham University, Bronx, New York. He has been executive editor of the 2009–2013 supplements to the *New Catholic Encyclopedia* and the co-editor of the English translation of the 43rd edition of the Heinrich Denzinger's *Enchiridion Symbolorum: A Compendium of Creeds, Definitions and Declarations of the Catholic Church*, edited by Peter Hünermann (St. Ignatius Press, 2012; 1,450 pp.). He has done research in Paris and Montréal, and took part in a study-tour of Saudi Arabia and Bahrain sponsored by the National Council for U.S.-Arab relations. He is the author of *The Natural Theology of Yves de Paris* (Scholars Press, 1991); *The Mystical Theology of the Catholic Reformation—An Overview of Baroque Spirituality*, co-author with José Pereira (University Press of America, 2006; 309 pp.); *What the Church Teaches about Sex—God's Plan for Human Happiness* (Huntington: Our Sunday Visitor Press, 2009; 174 pp.); *Called to Holiness and Communion: Vatican II on the Church*, co-editor with Fr. Steven Boguslawski (Scranton: University of Scranton Press, 2009; 300 pp.); co-editor with Judith Marie Gentle, *De Maria Numquam Satis—The Significance of the Catholic Doctrines on the Blessed Virgin Mary for All People* (University Press of America, 2009; 204 pp.); *St. Paul, the Natural Law, and Contemporary Legal Theory*, co-editor with Jane Adolphe and Michael A. Vacca (Lexington Books, 2012; 254 pp.); *The Sacrament of Reconciliation: An Anthropological and Scriptural Understanding* (Chicago/Mundelein: Hillenbrand Books, 2017; 176 pp.); *Catholic Sexual Morality* (Wipf and Stock, 2018); *Ludwig Ott: Fundamentals of Catholic Dogma*, trans. and reviser (Baronius Press, 2018; 569 pp.); *Equality and Non-discrimination: Catholic Roots and Current Challenges*, co-editor with Jane F. Adolphe and Michael A. Vacca (Pickwick Publications, 2019; 246 pp.); and *Virgin, Mother, Queen: Encountering Mary in Time and Tradition*, co-author with Michael O'Neil (Ave Maria Press, 2019; 192 pp.). See www.SHMS.edu and fastiggi.robert@shms.edu.

[342] The word Roman Catholic is widely used to refer to those who are in communion with the See of Rome under the Pope or Roman Pontiff. There are also Eastern Rite Catholics (e.g. Chaldean, Maronite,

[Footnote continued on next page]

issue to explore. After all, some former Catholics I know have left the practice of their religion because they believe the Catholic Church judges matters to be sinful that are not sinful, or they themselves feel unfairly judged because they are divorced and remarried, homosexually active, or in support of legal abortion. There is also the popular idea promoted by writers like James Joyce (1882–1941) that the Roman Catholic Church is especially obsessed with sexual sins and, therefore, is responsible for a repressed and unrealistic attitude toward human sexuality.

Because of these fixed ideas about an overly judgmental Roman Catholic view of sin, many people in the media as well as celebrities rejoiced in Pope Francis' words of "who am I to judge" in reference to those struggling with homosexual inclinations. It seems, though, that many people did not read the entire answer Pope Francis gave to the reporter, Ilze Scamparini, in response to a question regarding the alleged private life of Monsignor Battista Ricca and the existence of a "gay lobby" in the Vatican. [343] Pope Francis responded during the July 28, 2013 press conference on the flight returning to Rome from World Youth Day in Rio de Janeiro, and he first noted that the investigation into the alleged private life of Msgr. Ricca found nothing that had been alleged.[344] He went on to note, "If a person, whether it be a lay person, a priest or a religious sister, commits a sin and then converts, the Lord forgives, and when the Lord forgives, the Lord forgets, and this is very important for our lives." After this, Pope Francis commented on the alleged "gay lobby" in the Vatican in this way:

> So much is written about the gay lobby. I still haven't found anyone with an identity card in the Vatican with "gay" on it. They say there are some there. I believe that when you are dealing with such a person, you must distinguish between the fact of a person being gay and the fact of someone forming a lobby, because not all lobbies are good. This one is not good. If someone is gay and is searching for the Lord and has good will, then who am I to judge him? The Catechism of the Catholic Church explains this in a beautiful way ... The problem is not having this tendency, no, we must be brothers and sisters to one another, and there is this one and there is that one. The problem is in making a lobby of this tendency: a lobby of misers, a lobby of politicians, a lobby of masons, so many lobbies. For me, this is the greater problem.

---

and Byzantine) who are in full communion with the Pope but are not of the Roman or Latin Rite. The matter is further complicated by the fact that Eastern Orthodox Christians and many Anglicans consider themselves "Catholic" but not "Roman Catholics."

[343] The allegations against Msgr. Ricca stemmed from his time working in the Vatican Nunciature in Montevideo, Uruguay. See Sandro Magister, "The Prelate of the Gay Lobby" in *Chiesa* (July 18, 2013): http://chiesa.espresso.repubblica.it/articolo/1350561?eng=y, accessed December 20, 2013.

[344] The text of the July 28, 2013 press conference can be found on the Vatican website at: http://w2.vatican.va/content/francesco/en/travels/2013/outside/documents/papa-francesco-gmg-rio-de-janeiro-2013.html, accessed December 20, 2016.

The way Pope Francis addresses the reporter's questions—both with regard to Msgr. Ricca and with respect to the alleged "gay lobby"—helps us understand the Catholic theology of sin and judgement. Francis first notes that when people commit sins and convert, the Lord forgives them. He does not deny that homosexual actions are sinful.[345] The existence of this sin or any sin, however, must be balanced with the recognition of God's forgiveness and mercy toward those who repent. If a person is struggling with some sin and "is searching for the Lord and has good will" we should not judge. In other words, we must realize that only God can judge the inner heart and culpability of any individual. Moreover, only God can judge a person's soul after death. We can, though, make judgments with regard to what actions are objectively wrong or sinful.

A. How Does the Catholic Church Determine What Is Sinful?

How, though, does the Catholic Church determine which actions are sinful and which are not? Here we must realize that the Catholic Church understands herself as "the Body of Christ,"[346] and she must be faithful to the teachings of Christ and Sacred Scripture. In this regard, the Catholic Church does not believe her teaching authority or Magisterium is above the word of God. [347] Instead, the Magisterium serves the Word of God, "teaching only what has been handed on, listening to it devoutly, guarding it scrupulously and explaining it faithfully in accord with a divine commission and the help of the Holy Spirit."[348] The Catholic Church's theology of sin, therefore, is believed to be based on Sacred Scripture and Sacred Tradition as authoritatively interpreted by the Magisterium of the Church. [349] Moreover, the Catholic Church also believes that the moral norms of Scripture are confirmed by the natural law of "right reason," which reflects the works of the divine law engraved into the human heart.[350]

---

[345] In other contexts, Pope Francis makes it abundantly clear that he fully endorses what the *Catechism of the Catholic Church*, n. 2357–2359 teaches about showing "respect, compassion, and sensitivity" to persons with homosexual tendencies while recognizing that homosexual acts can never be justified. See Pope Francis, *The Name of God is Mercy: A Conversation with Andrea Tornielli* trans. Oonagh Stransky (New York: Random House, 2016), 61–62 and Pope Francis, post-synodal apostolic exhortation, *The Joy of Love* (New York and Mahwah, N.J.: Paulist Press, 2016), 178, n. 251.

[346] See the *Catechism of the Catholic Church* [henceforth, CCC] (Washington, DC: US Conference of Catholic Bishops, 1997) n. 787–795. See also Rom 12:4–5 and 1 Cor 12:12–31.

[347] The Magisterium or teaching authority of the Church is believed to reside in the Roman Pontiff and the bishops in communion with him.

[348] Vatican II, *Dei Verbum*, the *Dogmatic Constitution on Divine Revelation* (Nov. 18, 1965), n. 10.

[349] See above and the CCC, n. 84–95.

[350] See CCC, 1956 and Rom 2:14–15.

Many Christians today, including some Catholics, believe that the moral standards of the Bible reflect a certain cultural framework.[351] These might accept the general moral principles taught by Jesus (e.g., charity), but they believe that many particular biblical moral teachings need to be evaluated in light of contemporary empirical science.[352] They also ask why some moral teachings of the O.T. are ignored—e.g., prohibitions against sowing a vineyard with two different kinds of seeds, or plowing with an ox or an ass harnessed together (Deut 22:9–10)—while others, such as the prohibition against homosexual relations (Lev 18:22), are upheld strictly.[353]

The Catholic response to these points relies on the distinctions made by St. Thomas Aquinas (c. 1225–1274) between the various types of law in the O.T. While the moral law expressed in the Ten Commandments remains for all time, the ceremonial laws and the judicial laws no longer apply. As Aquinas writes: "We must, therefore, distinguish three kinds of precept in the Old law; viz., moral precepts, which are dictated by the natural law; ceremonial precepts, which are determinations of the Divine worship; and judicial precepts, which are determinations of the justice to be maintained among men."[354] Unlike the moral law, which continues in force forever, the ceremonial laws represent temporary laws connected with O.T. worship. These laws ceased their binding force after Christ's passion and resurrection established a new form of worship.[355] The judicial laws of the O.T. were laws that regulated the affairs of people living in a particular place and time. As such, they were contingent and time-bound, and their binding force does not last forever.[356]

If there is a question whether a particular law from the O.T. is still in force, the Catholic Church relies first on the N.T. to see whether the law was explicitly abrogated and secondly on discernment as to whether the law was ceremonial or judicial rather than moral. The Catholic Church also believes she is bound by the teachings of Christ and the N.T. Thus, when Christ forbids divorce and remarriage in Mark 10:2–12, Luke 16:18, and Matthew

---

[351] See Anthony Kosnik et al. *Human Sexuality: New Directions in American Catholic Thought* (New York: Paulist Press, 1977), especially pages 7–32. It should be noted that the Holy See's Congregation for the Doctrine of the Faith sent a letter with some critical observations about this book to the President of the U.S. Conference of Catholic Bishops on July 13, 1979: http://www.vatican.va/roman_curia/congregations/cfaith/documents/rc_con_cfaith_doc_19790713_mons-quinn_en.html (accessed December 20, 2016).

[352] Kosnik, *Human Sexuality*, 53–77, 211–213.

[353] Kosnik, *Human Sexuality*, 10.

[354] St. Thomas Aquinas, *Summa Theologica*, I–II, q. 99 a. 4 in *St. Thomas Aquinas: Summa Theologica* trans. Fathers of the English Dominican Province (Allen: Christian Classics, 1981), 1034.

[355] *Summa Theologica*, I–II, q. 103, a. 3.

[356] *Summa Theologica*, I–II, q. 104, a. 3.

5:32 and 19:9, the Catholic Church believes she is bound to his teachings.[357] The same is true with the other moral teachings of Christ summed up in the Sermon on the Mount (Matt 5–7), as well as the moral teachings of St. Paul and the other writings of the N.T. The moral teachings of the Ten Commandments or Decalogue continue to have normative application, and they form the basis for Catholic catechetical instruction on moral norms.[358]

B. The Nature of Sin and Different Kinds of Sin

What exactly does the Catholic Church mean by sin? In the *Catechism of the Catholic Church*, we find these basic definitions:

1. "Sin is an offense against reason, truth and right conscience";
2. Sin "is failure in genuine love for God and neighbor caused by a perverse attachment to certain goods";
3. Sin is "an utterance, a deed, or a desire contrary to the eternal law."[359]

Sin is also variously described as "an offense against God" and "disobedience."[360]

In the O.T., the most common Hebrew terms for sin are *hāttā'*, which means, "missing the mark; *pesha'*, which means rebellion, and *'awōn*, which means iniquity or guilt.[361] In the N.T., the main term for sin is *harmatia*. John the Baptist refers to Jesus as the "Lamb of God, who takes away the sin (*harmatia[n]*) of the world."[362] Jesus tells the paralytic, "Child, your sins (*hamartia[i]*) are forgiven" (Mk 2:5). In the N.T., we find other words for sin such as lawlessness (*anomia*; e.g. Rom 4:7); darkness (*skotos*; e.g. John 8:12) and injustice (*adikia*; cf. Rev 22:11).[363]

The Bible reveals that certain sins lead to spiritual death and exclusion from God's kingdom (cf. Deut 30:17; Matt 25:41–46; 1 Cor 6:9–10; Gal 5:19–21; Rev 21:8 and 22:15). Such sins are called mortal sins because they

---

[357] The so-called exceptive clauses in Matt 5:32 and 19:9 for *porneia* are understood in reference either to certain forms of lewdness (e.g. incest), which render the marriage unlawful from the start, or to unions that are not truly marriages but examples of fornication (*porneia*). See Robert L. Fastiggi, *What the Church Teaches about Sex: God's Plan for Human Happiness* (Huntington: Our Sunday Visitor, 2009), 51–53.

[358] See the CCC, 2083–2557.

[359] CCC, 1849; for the third definition, cf. St. Augustine, *Contra Faustum* 22: PL 42, 418; St. Thomas Aquinas, *Summa Theologica* I–II, 71, 6.

[360] CCC, 1850.

[361] Cf. William E. May, *An Introduction to Moral Theology*, Second Edition (Huntington: Our Sunday Visitor, 2003), 186.

[362] John 1:29. Here the reference is to the "sin" of the world, but in the *Agnus Dei* of the Mass, Jesus is invoked as the "Lamb of God who takes away the sins (*peccata*) of the world." The "sin of the world" can be understood as original sin that Jesus takes away at baptism. But it's equally true that He takes away personal sins as well.

[363] May, *An Introduction to Moral Theology*, 186.

are deadly to the life of grace and justification. The classical text for the distinction between venial (non-deadly) sins and mortal (deadly) sins is 1 John 5:16–17: "There is such a thing as deadly sin.... All wrongdoing is sin, but there is sin that is not deadly."

The Catholic Church also distinguishes between original sin and personal sin. The fall of Adam and Eve left human nature in a state "deprived of original holiness and justice."[364] This deprivation of holiness and grace is passed on through human propagation and is sometimes described as a "stain" on the soul or an inborn "guilt." The Catholic Church, however, does not believe that original sin has "the quality of a personal fault in any of Adam's descendants."[365] Instead, it is a sin "contracted" but not "committed"; it is "a state and not an act." Original sin, therefore, can only be understood as sin "in an analogical sense."[366]

Original sin has left human nature in a wounded state subject to ignorance, suffering, bodily death, and the "inclination to evil that is called 'concupiscence.'"[367] Concupiscence is the tendency to sin, but it is not sin itself. It manifests itself, however, in the tendencies of self-assertion (pride), lust, and greed.[368] It is sometimes described as "the tinder or fuel for sin" (*fomes peccati*). In spite of its influence, concupiscence can be overcome by the grace of Christ.[369]

Unlike original sin, personal sin involves a freely chosen "thought, word, deed or omission"[370] contrary to the law of God. Sin engages the intellect and the will,[371] and it only takes on the quality of a sin when the person freely chooses to transgress the moral law. Sins can be due to ignorance (lack of knowledge); weakness (giving in to strong passions); or malice (emerging from an evil will or desire to harm).[372] Most sexual sins proceed from weakness rather than malice, and in sins of passion, full and deliberate consent of the will may more easily be lacking.[373] Moreover, when the

---

[364] CCC, 404.

[365] CCC, 405.

[366] CCC, 404.

[367] CCC, 405.

[368] 1 John 2:16: "For all that is in the world, sensual lust, enticement for the eyes, and a pretentious life, is not from the Father but is from the world": sometimes called the "threefold concupiscence."

[369] CCC, 1264; cf. Council of Trent (1546): D–H, 1515.

[370] CCC, 1853.

[371] Cf. Dominic Prümmer, O.P., *Handbook of Moral Theology*, trans. J. G. Nolan (New York: P. J. Kenedy and Sons, 1957), no. 158, p.67.

[372] Prümmer, O.P., *Handbook of Moral Theology*, 68, no. 159.

[373] Cf. Congregation for the Doctrine of the Faith [CDF], *Declaration on Certain Problems of Sexual Ethics, Persona Humanae*, December 29, 1975, no. 10, in *Vatican Council II: More Post Conciliar Documents*, ed. Austin Flannery, O.P. (Collegeville: The Liturgical Press, 1982), 494.

moral law is transgressed because of ignorance there might not be any sin involved if the person is not culpable for his or her ignorance.

Sins that are repeated over and over again lead to "perverse inclinations, which cloud conscience and corrupt the concrete judgment of good and evil."[374] Such perverse inclinations are called vices or bad habits that "have arisen through the repetition of acts."[375] Based on St. John Cassian (c. 360–433) and St. Gregory the Great (c. 540–604), the Catholic Church traditionally has identified seven capital sins or vices. These vices are called "capital" because "they engender other sins, other vices."[376] The seven capital sins are pride, avarice, envy, wrath, lust, gluttony, and sloth (or *acedia*).[377]

C. Sin, Repentance, Confession, and Mercy

The Catholic Church is faithful to the biblical message of repentance for the forgiveness of sins, for the call to repentance is a major theme of the Bible. John the Baptist is shown in the Gospel of Mark as proclaiming a "baptism of repentance for the forgiveness of sins" (Mark 1:4). Jesus begins his public ministry by proclaiming: "This is the time of fulfillment. The kingdom of God is at hand. Repent, and believe in the gospel" (Mark 1:15). In Mark 6, Jesus sends out the Twelve two by two to cure the sick, drive out demons, and preach "repentance" (Mark 6:12). At the end of the Gospel of Luke, Jesus sends out his disciples to preach "repentance for the forgiveness of sins" to all the nations, beginning from Jerusalem (Luke 24:46–47).

The principal Greek word in the N.T. for repentance is *metanoia*, which is used 24 times as a noun, and an additional 34 times in its verbal form of *metanoeō*.[378] Although *metanoia* is usually translated as "repentance" (as in Mark 1:4 and Luke 24:47), it literally means "a change in thinking"[379] or a "change of mind."[380] The N.T. also uses the Greek verb *metamelomai* six times. This verb means "to regret" or "feel sorrow." Regret or sorrow can be a true expression of repentance, but it also requires a desire for forgiveness from the Lord.

The N.T. links repentance to faith in Jesus and to baptism. St. Paul, in his farewell speech at Miletus, says: "I earnestly bore witness for both Jews and Greeks to repentance and to faith in our Lord Jesus Christ" (Acts

---

[374] CCC, 1865
[375] Prümmer, 75, no. 171.
[376] CCC, 1866.
[377] CCC, 1866.
[378] A. Boyd Luter, Jr. "Repentance: N.T." in *The Anchor Bible Dictionary*, vol. 5, ed. David Noel Freedman (New York: Doubleday, 1992), 672.
[379] Luter, "Repentance," 674.
[380] Luter, 672.

20:21). Jesus responds to the great faith of the people and cures the paralytic, saying: "Child, your sins are forgiven" (Mark 2:5). Faith, though, also leads to repentance and baptism. In his speech at Pentecost, Peter tells those gathered: "Repent and be baptized, every one of you, in the name of Jesus Christ, for the forgiveness of your sins; and you will receive the gift of the Holy Spirit" (Acts 3:38).

After baptism there is still the possibility of sinning. This is why the Catholic Church, along with the Eastern Orthodox Churches, has the Sacrament of Penance or Reconciliation.

Baptism is "the instrumental cause" of justification,[381] but the Sacrament of Penance is "the second plank [of salvation] after the shipwreck of lost grace."[382] According to St. Paul, there are certain sins that can deprive believers of the kingdom of God (1 Cor 6:9–10; Gal 5:19–21). Baptism brings salvation (1 Pet 3:20–21), but deadly sins committed after baptism can deprive those baptized of "the kingdom of Christ and of God."[383] In light of this possibility, the Council of Trent anathematized those who claim "that a man once justified cannot sin again and cannot lose grace."[384]

The Catholic Church believes that Christ knew the baptized could lose the grace of justification so he "instituted the sacrament of penance for those who fall into sin after baptism."[385] After Christ's resurrection, he breathed the Holy Spirit on his disciples and said: "Receive the Holy Spirit. Whose sins you forgive are forgiven them, and whose sins you retain are retained" (John 20:22–23). Because only God can forgive sins (Mark 2:7), Jesus needed to breathe the Holy Spirit on his disciples so they could be ministers of divine forgiveness. This power to forgive sinners is also expressed by the power of binding and loosing (Matt 18:18) and the power of the keys given by Christ to Peter (Matt 16:19).[386] When Jesus speaks of "binding and loosing," he is using "rabbinic technical terms that can refer to the binding of the devil in exorcism" and "to the juridical acts of excommunication and

---

[381] Council of Trent, *Decree on Justification*, chapter 7 as cited in *Compendium of Creeds, Definitions, and Declarations on Matters of Faith and Morals*, 43rd. ed., ed. Heinrich Denzinger and Peter Hünermann (San Francisco: Ignatius Press, 2012), [henceforth D–H], n. 1529.

[382] Tertullian, *De paenitentia*, 4, 2: cited in D–H, 1542.

[383] Eph 5:5; see also 1 Cor 6:9–10, Gal 5:19–21, and 2 Pet 2:20–22.

[384] Council of Trent, *Decree on Justification*, canon 23: D–H, 1573.

[385] Council of Trent, *Decree on Justification*, canon 23: chapter 14: D–H, 1542.

[386] These are the Scriptures cited by the Council of Trent in its *Doctrine on the Sacrament of Penance*, chapter 5 in support of the belief that "our Lord Jesus Christ left priests to represent him as presiding judges to whom all mortal sins into which the faithful of Christ would have fallen should be brought that they, through the power of the keys, might pronounce the sentence of remission or retention of sins" D–H, 1679.

definitive decision making."[387] The Catholic Church understands the power of the binding and loosing as the power given by Christ to priests who "represent him as presiding judges" so they "might pronounce the sentence of remission or retention of sins."[388]

Many people wonder why Catholics believe that mortal sins must be confessed to a priest rather than directly to God. The Catholic Church, however, believes she is being faithful to Christ who gave the apostles the authority of binding and loosing, and this authority has been passed on by apostolic succession to bishops and to priests. James 5:16 says "confess your sins to one another" so there are occasions in which it is appropriate to confess wrongdoings to those who are not priests. The power of binding and loosing sins in the Sacrament of Penance, however, is possessed only by bishops and priests by means of apostolic succession. This is clearly seen in John 20:22–23 when Jesus breathes the Holy Spirit upon the disciples and says: "Receive the Holy Spirit. Whose sins you forgive are forgiven them, and whose sins you retain are retained." Priests could only know what sins to forgive and what sins to retain if they hear the confession of penitents. Priests, of course, do not have authority by themselves to forgive sins. In granting absolution to sinners and assigning penances, they are acting in the person of Christ the head, *in persona Christi Capitis.*[389]

D. The Sacrament of Penance and Reconciliation Is a Sacrament of Mercy

The Catholic theology of sin is not intended to make people feel guilty any more than the Gospel witness of the forgiveness is intended to make people feel guilty. Guilt is a human emotion that is felt when we believe we have done something wrong or hurt someone else. Jesus came to into the world to reconcile sinners to God. The forgiveness of sins is at the heart of the Gospel. Baptism brings about the forgiveness of sins, which is why the Nicene-Constantinopolitan Creed has the believer say: "I acknowledge one baptism for the forgiveness of sins."[390] Christians, though, sin after baptism, and the Sacrament of Penance, which is also called the Sacrament of Reconciliation, is the means by which the sinner can receive forgiveness from Christ through the ministry of priests.

In the early Church and throughout the much of the Middle Ages penances for mortal sins were often very severe. Many times, sinners were

---

[387] Benedict T. Viviano, "The Gospel According to Matthew" in *The New Jerome Biblical Commentary*, ed. Raymond B. Brown, S.S. et al. (Englewood Cliffs: Prentice Hall, 1990), 659.
[388] Council of Trent, *Doctrine on the Sacrament of Penance*, chapter 5: D–H, 1679.
[389] CCC, 1548.
[390] D–H, 150.

required to do public penances and would only be welcomed back to the Eucharist after doing these long penances. It was often believed that the performance of the penance itself, i.e. the satisfaction for the sins committed, was the real efficient cause of reconciliation with God.[391] St. Thomas Aquinas, however, said that it was the absolution imparted by the priest that brought about the forgiveness; the penance was intended to serve as a means of spiritual healing for the sinner and a way of making reparation for the temporal effects (or punishments) caused by the sins committed.[392] The Council of Trent in 1551 affirmed the teaching of Aquinas in this regard. As Bernhard Poschmann writes:

> The primary importance of the Council for the development of dogma consists in the fact that it sanctioned definitively the teaching that had been inaugurated by St. Thomas and had soon become general, that the sacrament is the efficient cause of the forgiveness of sins. Moreover, it swept away forever the theory of the merely declarative character of absolution.[393]

The teaching of Trent meant that the sinner could be assured of forgiveness of sins by the absolution of the priest as long as there was an honest confession of sins, adequate sorrow,[394] and a firm purpose not to commit the sins in the future. The performance of the penance was primarily medicinal, but it also served to repair the temporal effects brought about by the sins.

In recent years, the emphasis on the Sacrament of Reconciliation has been on an encounter with God's mercy. Pope Francis has made mercy one of the main themes of his pontificate, and he described the Sacrament of Reconciliation as a way people can "touch the grandeur of God's mercy with their own hands."[395] Pope Francis affirms the traditional Catholic theology of sin, but he articulates it in the context of God's mercy. As he writes:

> The Church condemns sin because it has to relay the truth: "This is a sin." But at the same time, it embraces the sinner who recognizes himself as such, it welcomes him, it speaks to him of the infinite mercy of God. Jesus forgave even those who crucified and scorned him. We must go back to the Gospel. We find it speaks not only of welcoming and forgiveness but also of the "feast" of the

---

[391] Bernhard Poschmann, *Penance and the Anointing of the Sick* trans. Francis Courtney, S.J. (New York: Herder and Herder, 1964), 141.

[392] Poschmann, *Penance*, 168–178.

[393] Poschmann, 202.

[394] Trent taught that even imperfect sorrow or attrition, which was motivated by the fear of divine punishment, was sufficient to receive forgiveness of sins. Cf. D–H, 1678.

[395] Pope Francis, *Misericordiae Vultus*, Bull of Indication of the Extraordinary Jubilee of Mercy(April 11, 2015), n. 17. This Bull is published as an appendix to Francis, *The Name of God is Mercy: A Conversation* with Andrea Tornielli, trans. Oonagh Stransky (New York: Random House, 2016).

returning son. The expression of mercy is the joy of the feast, and that is well expressed in the Gospel of Luke: I tell you, in just the same way there will be more joy in heaven over one sinner who repents than over ninety-nine people who have no need of repentance (Luke 15:7).[396]

The judgment of God is ultimately one of mercy and forgiveness. The Church, though, must teach the truth and identify sins as sins. Of course, there are many factors that might mitigate the culpability for certain actions that are objectively wrong.[397] As the *Catechism of the Catholic Church* teaches: "The promptings of feelings and passions can also diminish the voluntary and free character of the offense, as can external pressures or pathological disorders."[398] The judgment that certain actions or omissions are sinful is another way of saying that certain actions and omissions are spiritually harmful. God wants what is best for his sons and daughters. Sin, by its nature, wounds and destroys charity, which is the highest theological virtue (1 Cor 13:13).

Conclusion

This essay has attempted to address the question: "Is the Roman Catholic theology of sin too judgmental?" The answer I believe is "no." The Roman Catholic theology of sin would only be overly judgmental in the eyes of those who find the teachings of the Gospel to be too judgmental. As explained above, the Catholic Church tries to be faithful to the moral law of Christ as revealed in Sacred Scripture. Unfortunately, many people identify certain prohibitions by the Church as merely ecclesiastical prohibitions when, in fact, these prohibitions are grounded in Sacred Scripture. The Church does not invent the moral law, but receives this law from God, who teaches this law through divine revelation and the natural law.

The Catholic theology of sin, to be properly understood, must be seen not so much as a theology of judgment but as a theology of mercy. As Pope Francis teaches: "Let us not forget that mercy is doctrine. Even so, I love saying: mercy is true."[399]

Judgments, of course, must be made. Penitents must examine their consciences and judge (or determine) whether or not they have sinned or been fully responsible for the wrongdoings committed. Priests also must form judgments about the culpability of the penitents who come to them and what penances would be spiritually beneficial to them. The Magisterium of the Church must judge or determine what teachings of the revealed moral

---

[396] Pope Francis, *The Name of God is Mercy*, 50.
[397] CCC, 1860.
[398] CCC, 1860.
[399] Pope Francis, *The Name of God is Mercy*, 62.

law endure for all time and what laws in the Bible are merely ceremonial or judicial for the times in which they were articulated. God's mercy is more powerful than any sin committed because Jesus came to reconcile sinners to God. Sinners, though, must be willing to confess their sins with humility and trust in God's mercy.

We must remember that God is the ultimate judge. When we die, we are all placed before the light of God who judges with perfect justice and perfect mercy. God is merciful to sinners as long as they entrust themselves to his mercy.

10.
Was Jesus' Language of Judgment and Sin too Condemnatory for him to Deal Graciously with Human Sin?— A Reflection from the Matthew's Gospel

Professor Wayne Baxter
N.T. & Greek Heritage College and Seminary
Cambridge, Ontario, Canada[400]

Introduction 161
A. The Matthean Final Judgment: Who? 163
B. The Matthean Final Judgment: How? 165
Conclusion 169

Introduction

Scholars have long recognized judgment as a central motif in the Gospel of Matthew.[401] Indeed, some of the most rigorous dominical sayings concerning divine judgment originate from the First Gospel:

> For I tell you, unless your righteousness exceeds that of the scribes and Pharisees, you will never enter the kingdom of heaven (5:20).... For if you forgive others their trespasses, your heavenly Father will also forgive you; but if you do not forgive others, neither will your Father forgive your trespasses (6:14–15).

Does this stringent attitude the Matthean Jesus exhibits towards personal righteousness and sin extinguish any hope for people in the Day of Judgment? U. Luz, for one, has argued that the inclusio of Matthew 1:23 and 28:20—the twin promises of God's presence—suggests that grace

---

[400] Baxter earned his PhD from McMaster University, Hamilton, Ontario, Canada, and his MDiv from Trinity Evangelical Divinity School, Deerfield, IL. He has pastored Christian and Missionary Alliance churches in Windsor and Ottawa, and a Canadian Baptists of Ontario and Quebec church in Mississauga. He has taught part-time at Wilfrid Laurier University, King's University College (UWO), and McMaster University. He wrote *Growing Up to Get Along: Conflict and Unity in Philippians* (Rapid City: Crosslink, 2016; 142 pp.); *We've Lost. What Now? Practical Counsel from the Book of Daniel* (Eugene: Wipf & Stock, 2015; 158 pp.); and *Israel's Only Shepherd: Matthew's Shepherd Motif and His Social Setting* (T & T Clark, 2012; 228 pp.).
See www.HeritageCambridge.com and wbaxter@heritageseminary.net.

[401] For example, the standard Greek word group used in the N.T. to convey judgment is kri/nw/kr i/na /kr i6 ij . These appear in the Synoptic Gospels a total of 33 times: once in Mark, 13 times in Luke, and 19 in Matthew. For recent examinations of the theme of judgment in Matthew's Gospel, see Anders Runesson, *Divine Wrath and Salvation in Matthew* (Minneapolis: Fortress Press, 2015) and D. Marguerat, *Le Jugement dans l'Evangile de Matthieu* (2nd ed., Geneva: Labor et Fides, 1996).

predominates over judgment.[402] Other commentators appeal to N.T. texts like John 3:16-17 or Romans 8:1 to counterbalance these harsh Matthean logia, but it remains highly unlikely that Matthew's original audience had access to these or other such offsetting texts. The present study seeks, therefore, to examine whether Jesus' language of judgment prohibits him from dealing graciously with sin from a solely Matthean perspective.

While many passages in Matthew address the topic of judgment,[403] and each deserves an analysis, this study focuses on the Final Judgment pericope in Matthew 25:31-46 for several reasons.[404] From a source-critical perspective, the Final Judgment passage is exclusively Matthean and without parallel in the Olivet Discourses of Mark and Luke, thus presenting a uniquely Matthean window into the question of judgment. Narrative-critically speaking, if the Olivet Discourse, with its strong eschatological orientation, represents the climax of Jesus' teaching in the First Gospel,[405] then the logical flow within this discourse suggests that the Final Judgment pericope forms the apex to this climax.[406] Finally, from an ideological point of view, the cataclysmic day of God's judgment remains a central motif in the works of many O.T., Second Temple, and N.T. authors.[407]

Although Matthew's messianic depiction of Jesus in the Final Judgment pericope is an important feature to this text,[408] the exegesis of Matthew 25:31-46 in this study will focus specifically on the recipients of Jesus' judgment and the criterion for his judgment, which will help to shed significant light on the question of Jesus' ability to deal graciously with sin. The study will then conclude by offering some pastoral reflections on judgment and grace in light of Jesus' teaching in Matthew 25:31-46.

---

[402] U. Luz, *Matthew 21—28: A Commentary*, Hermeneia: A Critical and Historical Commentary on the Bible, trans. J. Crouch, ed. H. Koester, (Minneapolis: Fortress Press, 2005), 290-93. Luz, however, overplays his hand regarding the role of this inclusio for Matthew. For a brief critique of Luz's position, see Andrew Angel, "Inquiring into an Inclusio—On Judgment and Love in Matthew," *Journal of Theological Studies* 60, no. 2 (October 2009): 527-30.

[403] E.g., Matt 5:21-26, 7:1-6, 21-23, 13:24-30.

[404] For a detailed history of interpretation of Matt 25:31-46, see S. Gray, *The Least The Least of My Brothers: Matthew 25:31-46: A History of Interpretation*, SBLDS 114 (Atlanta: Scholars Press, 1989).

[405] Whereas the other major discourses deal primarily with ethics, Torah interpretation, mission, and God's kingdom, the Olivet Discourse deals with Jesus' Second Coming and the Final Judgment.

[406] The first part of the Olivet Discourse treats the Second Coming (Matt 24:1-41); the next section deals with how to wait for Jesus' return (Matt 24:42-25:30); the final section discusses what happens when he does return (Matt 25:31-46).

[407] In the O.T., see, for example, Isa 66; Joel 2:1-11; Zeph 1:14-2:3; and Mal 4; among Second Temple works, see, for example, *1 Enoch* 100-108; *Testament of Abraham* A 10-14; and 1QWar Scroll. N.T. texts that speak of Final Judgment include 2 Cor 5:10-11, 2 Pet 3:3-9, Jude 6, and Rev 20:11-15.

[408] For an examination of this particular issue, see W. Baxter, *Israel's Only Shepherd: Matthew's Shepherd Motif and His Social Setting*, LNTS 457 (London: T & T Clark, 2012), 150-51.

A. The Matthean Final Judgment: Who?

The identity of the recipients of judgment in Matthew 25:31–46, i.e., "all the nations" (pa/nta ta \eqnh), has been hotly debated. W. D. Davies and D. Allison list the most serious positions as all non-Christ-believers (Jews and Gentiles), all non-Christ-believing Gentiles, and all of humanity.[409] There is some commonality between these major views. All agree, on the one hand, that the eschatological judgment in view is not limited to one locale: it involves people from many geographical locations;[410] and, on the other hand, each position acknowledges that individuals are judged.[411] But key to the present study is the identity of "all the nations."

Besides 25:32, Matthew uses "all the nations" (pa/nta ta\eqnh) in 24:9, 14, and 28:19. In the similarly eschatologically oriented chapter 24, "all nations" explicitly refers to "the whole world" (o#h|t h|=oikoumenh|).[412] "All" in 24:9 and 14 probably refers to Gentiles, but in an inclusive way: "every nation without exception" (including Israel),[413] rather than exclusively, i.e., "every other nation" (every nation except Israel). The subsequent discourse points in this direction: according to 24:16–20, the disciples continue to live and evangelize in the land of Israel—since it is from there that they must flee—when all of the signs of the End transpire.

In the other occurrence of "all the nations" in the final chapter of the Gospel, the disciples are commanded after the resurrection to make disciples of "all the nations" (pa/nta ta\eqnh). Some scholars try to exclude Israel from 28:19; but 10:23 and 23:39 do not allow for this exclusion: according to the former text the mission to Israel will continue until the Parousia, while the latter logion clearly presupposes that Jerusalem will eventually see Jesus again—because of the continuing mission to Israel by some Christ-

---

[409] W. D. Davies and Dale C. Allison, *The Gospel According to Saint Matthew*, ICC, 3 vols. (Edinburgh: T & T Clark, 1988–97), 3:422.

[410] Cf. the survey of U. Luz, "The Final Judgment (Matt 25:31–46): An Exercise in 'History of Influence' Exegesis" in *Treasures New and Old: Recent Contributions to Matthean Studies*, ed. D. Bauer and M. A. Powell (Atlanta: Scholars Press, 1996), 271–310.

[411] S. Brown suggests that pa/nta ta eqnh represents Matthean redaction of a parable taken up by Matthew that originally dealt with the judgment of individuals (Brown, "Faith, the Poor and the Gentiles: A Tradition-Historical Reflection on Matthew 25:31–46," *Toronto Journal of Theology* 6, no. 2 (1990), 174–75). Both Brown and J. Michaels assert that the grammatical peculiarity of a masculine pronoun (au)ouj) used to refer to a neuter noun (eqnh) supports the contention of the nations being judged as individuals (Michaels, "Apostolic Hardships and Righteous Gentiles: A Study of Matthew 25:31–46," *Journal of Biblical Literature* 84, no. 1 (1965), 28, n. 6.

[412] In 24:14b, "all the nations" (pa=in toi= eqnesin) is grammatically parallel with "the whole world" (o#h t h|=oikoumenh).

[413] While Matthew can use eqnh as a point of contrast with Israel (e.g., Matt 10:5–6), he can equally use it in close association with Israel (e.g., Matt 4:12–15).

believers.[414] It seems most probable, then, that "all the nations" in 25:32 would possess this same inclusivity that appears in the Evangelist's other deployments of the phrase: every nation including Israel will be judged.[415]

J. Donahue argues that the linguistic context supports the notion that Jesus' disciples be identified with those judged (i.e., the sheep and the goats), like in the parable of the virgins (25:1–13) and the parable of the talents (25:14–30).[416] In other words, in Donahue's view Christ-believers are being judged. If the Final Judgment pericope was purely a parable—like 25:1–13 and 25:14–30—this assertion would hold. But as numerous scholars rightly maintain, 25:31–46 is technically not a true parable,[417] and is more likely an apocalyptic discourse.[418] As apocalyptic discourse 25:31–46 would function less as parenesis and more as consolation for persecuted people.[419] L. Cope's comment on the passage bears repeating:

---

[414] The basis for their exclusion, according to many of these scholars, would be Matt 21:43: "Therefore I tell you that the kingdom of God will be taken from you [the nation of Israel] and given to a nation (eỉqnoj[i.e., the Gentiles]) producing the fruit of it"; see, for example, G. Stanton, *A Gospel for a New People: Studies in Matthew* (Edinburgh: T & T Clark, 1992), 151–52, and U. Luz, *The Theology of the Gospel of Matthew* (Cambridge: Cambridge University Press, 1995), 119–20. Matthew 10:23b reads: "For truly I tell you, you will surely not complete the cities of Israel until the Son of Man comes." Matthew 23:39 reads: "For I tell you [= Jerusalem] will not see me from now on until you say, 'Blessed is the one who comes in the name of the Lord.'"

[415] G. Buchanan in his *Matthew, Mellen Biblical Commentary*, 2 vols. (Lewiston: Edwin Mellen Press, 1996–97) suggests that Gentiles are not in view here, as they are in the Missionary Discourse, but rather, Diaspora Jews. There are, however, a number of weaknesses with his position. Because Buchanan perceives a close parallel with *1 Enoch* 62–63, where the ruling class (i.e., kings, governors and the like) are punished before the Son of Man, he believes that Matthew probably has rulers in mind with "nations." This, however, is unlikely because in *1 Enoch* unlike in Matthew sheep-goat imagery is never invoked. Furthermore, it is doubtful that "nations" represent the ruling class because this is not the usual reading for t a\eṭnh. When Matthew refers to the Gentile ruling class, he always differentiates between them and t a\eṭnh (10:18; 24:9). If Matthew had the ruling class in mind he probably would have used hġemwñ as he does elsewhere (2:6; 10:18; 27:2, 11, 14, 15, 21, 27; 28:14). While Buchanan correctly links pañt a t a\eṭnh of 25:32 with pañt a t a\eṭnh of 28:19, he incorrectly limits the recipients of the apostolic commission in 28:18–20 to "Judaized Gentiles" (i.e., Palestinian Gentiles) to the exclusion of non-Judaized (non-Palestinian) Gentiles. Yet, would post-70 CE Jewish messianic communities recognize this sort of distinction among non-Christ-believing Gentiles? Buchanan also seems to ignore the apocalyptic elements of 25:31–46, which would support a more grandiose scene of judgment involving "all the nations" of the world.

[416] John R. Donahue, "The 'Parable' of the Sheep and the Goats: A Challenge to Christian Ethics," *Theological Studies* 47 (1986), 9–13.

[417] Davies and Allison, for example, call Matt 25:31–46 an "eschatological testament" because of the many features it shares with Jewish and Christian apocalypses (*Matthew*, 3:326); cf. J. Court ("Right and Left: The Implications for Matthew 25:31–46," *N.T. Studies* 31 [1985]: 223–33) who also acknowledges the importance of recognizing the "apocalyptic revelation-discourse" character of the pericope for interpretative purposes.

[418] Cf. G. Stanton, *A Gospel for a New People*, 221–30, who discusses the common thrust between Matt 25:31–46 and texts with similar social settings like *4 Ezra*, *1 Enoch* and *2 Baruch*.

[419] See G. Stanton, *A Gospel for a New People*, 228.

Perhaps it is impossible to say conclusively who 'all nations' are, but it is possible to say who they are *not*. From the pronouncements of vss. 40 and 45 it is clear that those who have been given or refused hospitality are not a part of the judgment proceeding and that they are 'the least of these my brethren.' . . . 'All the nations' are those *other than the brothers of the Son of Man*.[420]

All of these observations, then, suggest that "all the nations" excludes Christ-believers but includes non-Christ-believing Gentiles and non-Christ-believing Jews. Thus, according to this Matthean pericope, in the day of Final Judgment Jesus the eschatological king will judge all unbelievers—Jews and Gentiles.[421] But what is his criterion for judgment?

B. The Matthean Final Judgment: How?

"All the nations" will be judged according to their deeds of mercy or lack thereof: "I was hungry and you gave me something to eat, I was thirsty and you gave me drink, I was a stranger and you gathered together with me; naked and you clothed me, I was sick and you visited me, I was in prison and you came to me" (vv. 35–36). These acts of charity commonly appear in early Jewish writings.[422] The Evangelist may be drawing upon Isaiah 58:7, where the prophet chastises his people for practicing their religion without any regard for social compassion: "[You should] share your bread with the hungry, and bring the homeless poor into your house; when you see the naked, to cover them, and not to hide yourself from your own kin." But these deeds apply equally to Gentiles, as evidenced by the penitent confessor in the pre-Second-Temple era text, the Egyptian Book of Dead: "I have appeased God by [doing] his will. I have given bread to the hungry, water to the thirsty, clothes to the naked, and a boat to the shipwrecked" (chapter 125, Plate 32).[423] The criterion for judgment described in 25:31–46, then, applies to both Jews and Gentiles.[424]

---

[420] Lane Cope, "Matthew XXV:31-46: 'The Sheep and the Goats' Reinterpreted," *Novum Testamentum* 11 (1969), 37 (his emphasis).

[421] While Christ-believers are not judged in this scene, this does not imply that there is no final judgment for them. Since belief in multiple judgments is common in Second Temple Judaism and first-century Christ-belief (e.g., *L.A.B.*; *4 Ezra*; *Testament of Abraham*; *Revelation*), Matthew probably would have also affirmed multiple judgments (judgment of Christ-believers appears elsewhere in his Gospel, albeit with less elaboration); but only one is envisioned in 25:31–46: unbelievers. Thus, while 25:31–46 is popularly called the "Final" Judgment, it should not be considered the only judgment.

[422] Cf. the survey in Davies and Allison, *Matthew*, 3:425–28, of early Jewish texts that include similar lists of deeds of mercy.

[423] See E. A. W. Budge, *The Egyptian Book of the Dead: The Papyrus of Ani Egyptian Text Transliteration and Translation* (New York: Dover Publications, 1967), 205.

[424] Further, the language of patriarchal blessing ("you who are blessed of my Father") and of inheriting a foreordained kingdom (v. 34) refers to the Abrahamic covenant (cf. Matt 1:1c), and can apply equally to Jews and Gentiles: see, for example, Paul's appeal for Gentile inclusion in the Abrahamic Covenant in Romans 4 and Galatians 3.

According to Matthew, Jesus' Final Judgment is based upon performing deeds of mercy, specifically, to "one of these brothers and sisters of mine, the least of them" (ἑνὶ τούτων τῶν ἀδελφῶν μου τῶν ἐλαχίστων). The "elative superlative,"[425] τῶν ἐλαχίστων, functions adjectivally, describing the extent or scope of ἑνὶ τούτων τῶν ἀδελφῶν μου, thus yielding the meaning, "one of these brothers and sisters of mine, *even* the least of them." Similarly, Brown understands the second genitive as functioning in apposition to the first giving the sense, "these brothers and sisters of mine, the least," or "these brothers and sisters of mine, that is to say, the least." Thus, "the two expressions, 'my brothers' and 'the least,' refer to the same group, rather than the latter being a subset of the former."[426]

The composition of this particular group has received various interpretations. Davies and Allison summarize the possibilities as: everyone in need—whether Christ-believer or not; all Christ-believers; Jewish Christ-believers; Christ-believing missionaries; or Christ-believers who are not missionaries.[427] To identify this assembly, two things must be considered. First, of its 31 occurrences in the Gospel, Matthew typically deploys ἀδελφοί ("brother") to denote either a biological relationship [428] or discipleship. [429] Given this tight correlation, it would be a mistake to understand "brother" here as simply anyone "down on their luck," since Matthew plainly deploys the term only for people who relate to Jesus in a direct and specific way. Second, Matthew employs ἐλάχιστοι ("least") only two other times: once referring to Bethlehem (2:6) and once referring to the commandments of the Law (5:19). In both of these instances the term is used to convey the smallness of a particular subject in order to show the overall significance of either the subject or the object to which it is related. [430] Here in 25:40, ἐλάχιστοι, then, would convey the overall significance of Christ-believers: even the slightest one has immense worth in God's eyes.[431] Thus, it would seem best to identify this group with Christ-

---

[425] N. Turner, *Syntax*, vol. 3, in J. Moulton, *A Grammar of N.T. Greek* (repr., Edinburgh: T & T Clark, 1993), 31.

[426] Cf. Brown, "Faith," 173.

[427] Davies and Allison, *Matthew*, 3:428–29.

[428] See Matt 1:2, 11; 4:18, 21; 10:2, 21; 12:46–48; 13:55; 14:3; 17:1; 19:29; 20:24; 22:24–25.

[429] See Matt 12:49–50; 18:15, 21, 35; 23:8; 28:10; and probably 5:22–24, 47; 7:3–5.

[430] Hence, in the case of the former, Bethlehem cannot be considered the "least" among the rulers of Judah anymore because of the renown it will receive as the birthplace of the messiah. In the latter, those who teach others to break even the "least" of the Law's commandments cannot expect to receive favour because of the overwhelming significance of the Law—"not the smallest letter or stroke shall pass away from the Law until all is accomplished."

[431] Cf. the lost sheep logion in Matt 18:12–14. The saying is similar to Matt 11:11, where the "least" (μικρότερος) in the kingdom of heaven is greater than the greatest of the prophets, viz., John the Baptist.

believers generally,[432] and not, as some argue, to those serving specifically as missionaries or prophets.[433] In other words, for Matthew, the ultimate criterion for Final Judgment will be based on how people ("the nations") have treated any of Jesus' followers, whether great or small.

Two questions follow from this interpretation. First, why would Matthew cast Final Judgment in such a disciple-centric way? His phrasing of the criterion for judgment would provide a greater sense of vindication for the Mattheans. Because 25:31–46 is an apocalyptic discourse, it functions as encouragement to persevere in the face of opposition.[434] In discussing the relevance of the genre of apocalyptic discourse for the interpretation of 25:31–46, Stanton writes,

> Apocalyptic regularly functions as consolation for groups which perceive themselves to be under duress. Apocalyptic language is also often used to reinforce attitudes of group solidarity amongst minority groups at odds with society at large; clear lines are drawn between 'insiders' and 'outsiders' ... [it] provides hope of ultimate vindication for the powerless and oppressed people of God.[435]

Matthew's disciple-centric description of the criterion for Final Judgment would offer hope in their persecution.

The second question is similar: Can "how Christ-believers are treated" serve adequately as the decisive factor at the Parousia? The criterion's sufficiency rests in the central belief that Christ's presence resides with his followers. Christ's abiding presence with his disciples is evidenced by the phrase, "inasmuch as you did it to these brothers and sisters of mine, the least of them, you did it to me" (v. 40, cf. v. 45). This idea is stated more explicitly in 18:20: "For where there are two or three who assemble in my name, there I am in their midst." This notion of Christ's presence manifesting with his followers finds its parallel in the Book of Acts. When Jesus confronts Saul for persecuting the church (Acts 9:1–2), he asks him, "Saul, Saul, why are you persecuting me?" (9:4b), followed by his declaration, "I am Jesus whom you are persecuting" (9:5b). That followers of Jesus—and not just Jesus—can form the criterion of judgment in the

---

[432] Whereas e)la/xistoj conveys the significance of the disciples, the related term, mikroj, seems to be no more than a synonym for "followers of Jesus" (cf. Matt 10:42; 18:6, 10, 14).

[433] So, for example, Luz, "Final Judgment," 301–305, Donahue, "Sheep and Goats," 25, and Brown, "Faith," 172–73.

[434] Scholars have long recognized the persecution Matthew's community experienced: e.g., R. Gundry, *Matthew: A Commentary on His Handbook for a Mixed Church Under Persecution* (2nd ed., Grand Rapids: Eerdmans, 1994) and Douglas R. A. Hare, *The Theme of Jewish Persecution of Christians in the Gospel According to St. Matthew*, Vol. 6 of Monograph Series of the Society for N.T. Studies. (Cambridge: Cambridge University Press, 1967).

[435] G. Stanton, *A Gospel for a New People*, 228.

Eschaton should not be unexpected. Within Matthew's own narrative this principle has already been anticipated by the Missionary Discourse, where the rationale for this criterion for judgment appears explicitly: "The one who receives you receives me, and the one who receives me receives the one who sent me" (10:40). Cope calls this the "halakhic principle of agency," whereby the commissioned agent is considered the equivalent of the person being represented. [436] Acceptance of the messenger—evidenced by hospitality—presupposes prior acceptance of the sender, viz., Jesus. Conversely, rejection of the messenger, demonstrated by a lack of hospitality, presupposes prior rejection of the sender. Clearly for Matthew, hospitality towards Christ-believers bears Christological significance.

Because the presence of Christ resides with his disciples, whoever accepts and shows hospitality towards them is rewarded, but whoever rejects and fails to show hospitality to them receives divine punishment. Does that then mean that the more common measure of faith in Christ does not factor into the Final Judgment? Brown argues that within the context of Matthew and in a post-Easter setting, faith in Christ would surely be presupposed.[437] The reaction of the sheep and goats (vv. 37–38, 44) seems to move the audience in this direction of presupposed faith. When the king acknowledges their deeds (or their lack thereof), each group is astonished, completely unaware of the true significance of their works. Their incognizance precludes salvation by works: people who seek to earn divine reward would only be too aware of their deeds; they would quite self-consciously feed the hungry, refresh the thirsty, clothe the naked, and the like. The king's pronouncement would not have caught them off guard—they would have expected the king to know of their charity. Furthermore, their lack of awareness suggests that they performed these deeds without any specific intentionality—they did what came natural for them. Final judgment merely represents the outworking of Jesus' words regarding the heart:

> The good person brings good things out of a good treasure, and the evil person brings evil things out of an evil treasure. I tell you, on the Day of Judgment you will have to give an account for every careless word you utter; for by your words you will be justified, and by your words you will be condemned (Matt 12:35–37).

But just as words accurately signify the heart, so also does a person's deeds. Thus, the king judges the deeds of the nations in regard to the Matthean

---

[436] Lane Cope, "Matthew XXV," 40. Buchanan refers to the messengers as "ambassadors" (*Matthew*, 2:52–53). This principle of agency appears most frequently in the fourth gospel (e.g., John 10:30; 12:44–45; 14:9, 24).

[437] S. Brown, "Faith"; cf. J. Ramsey Michaels, "Apostolic Hardships," 28.

community, because their deeds offer a clear reflection of the heart in regard to Jesus: deeds of mercy towards Christ-believers demonstrate a prior acceptance of Jesus, while the absence of deeds reveals an antecedent rejection of Jesus.

Conclusion

The apocalyptic discourse of Matthew 25:31–46 teaches that Jesus will judge all non-Christ-believing Jews and Gentiles based on the extent to which they, prior to his Parousia, demonstrated hospitality to his followers—deeds which signify their de facto acceptance or rejection of Jesus. But does this narrow interpretation of 25:31–46 preclude any present-day application? While Donahue argues that the "least of my brothers" refers strictly speaking to Matthean missionaries, he nonetheless insists that "this does not make the pericope into a sectarian ethic with little relevance for contemporary ethics or homiletics. Rather, engagement with Matthew's understanding of discipleship gives the pericope a richer dimension than its contemporary generalized use allows."[438] Given the task of the present volume to make pastoral theology relevant in the modern world, there are a number of important implications of the Final Judgment pericope as it relates to the question of the relationship between divine grace and human sin.

First, while the Final Judgment speaks explicitly of unbelievers being sent away to "eternal punishment," not all are condemned: the righteous enter "eternal life." In other words, while the scope of Christ's judgment is universal, not all are universally condemned. That some will be saved in the Day of Judgment does offer some hope. Second, while the risen Christ resides in heaven, presently separated from earthly, human experience and thereby vulnerable to the charge of being an unsuitable judge for humanity—i.e., of being unfair—because of this detachment, this pericope teaches that people encounter Christ directly through his followers. Thus, God has given people the opportunity to face their accuser (so to speak) directly through his people. How they treat Jesus' followers closely correlates to their beliefs about Jesus: a life reflecting deeds of mercy towards Jesus' followers demonstrates acceptance of Jesus, while the absence of charity reveals rejection of him.

Third, many moderns protest, "What about people who have never heard the gospel?" The Final Judgement pericope responds twofold to this complaint. On the one hand, people will not be judged according to what they do not know but according to what they do know—which is a direct

---

[438] John R. Donahue, "Sheep and Goats," 25.

manifestation of their beliefs about Jesus, or more broadly, God. On the other hand, clearly, not everyone who has never heard the gospel will face eternal condemnation: only the "goats," but not the "sheep." All are not outright universally condemned.

Fourth, Jesus deals graciously with human sin through the agency of his disciples. Despite the narrow interpretation offered here, as John Donahue comments, Matthew's audience is not absolved from care for the poor and needy of the world:

> According to the rabbinic mode of argument from the 'lesser to the greater,' Matthew speaks of pagan virtues in such a way that Christians should surpass them (5:43–48). If the pagans are to be concerned for the hungry, etc., how much more Christian disciples?[439]

The devout reader in any era, then, would surely seek to apply this text on a personal and practical level; and as they performed these deeds of mercy to society's less fortunate, Christ, through his abiding presence among his people, extends his grace to people, treating them graciously and not as their sins deserve.

Therefore, is Jesus' language of judgment and sin too condemnatory to deal graciously with human sin? While a comprehensive answer to this question would need to take into account the rest of the Gospel witnesses, and while a cursory glance at the scene of Final Judgment in Matthew 25:31–46 might suggest a negative response, upon closer examination, despite his stern view of judgment, Jesus does indeed deal graciously with sin.

---

[439] John R. Donahue, "Sheep and Goats," 28; cf. M.-A. Chevallier, "Note à propos de l'éxegèse de Matt 25:31–46," *Revue des Sciences Religieuses* 48 (1974): 398–400.

Part Two:
Pastoral Theology in Human Need

11. Addressing Spiritual Lethargy: A Biblical, Theological, and Homiletical Approach
    Dr. Rock M. LaGioia 172
12. Midwifing Model of Pastoral Care with Addicted Persons
    Rev. Dr. Myrna Thurmond-Malone 181
13. Practical Theology/Spirituality and Fostering Healthy Human Relationships in the Workplace
    Rev. Dr. Hundzukani Portia Khosa-Nkatine 195
14. "Women Don't Like Nice Guys"—Dating, Attraction, and Christian Values: Teaching Our Young People How to Fall in Love
    Dr. Walter S. Chung and Dr. Stephanie Chung 203
15. Judgmental Attitudes and Their Impact on Our Pastoral Effectiveness
    Kevaughn Mattis 215
16. Ethics of Judging between Truth and Love when the Absolutely Right Choice Is Elusive
    Rev. Dr. Michael G. Maness 231
17. The Church as Alternative Community: A South African Perspective
    Professor Godfrey Harold 253
18. Church and State in Ethiopia: Contribution of the Lutheran Understanding of the Community of Grace
    Dr. Samuel Yonas Deressa 265

11.
Addressing Spiritual Lethargy:
A Biblical, Theological, and Homiletical Approach

Dr. Rock M. LaGioia
Professor of Pastoral Studies and
Director of Doctoral Programs
Grace Theological Seminary
Winona Lake, Indiana[440]

Introduction 172
A. Biblical Approach to Spiritual Lethargy 173
   1. The Church in Ephesus 173
   2. The Church in Laodicea 174
B. Theological Approach to Spiritual Lethargy 176
C. Homiletical Approach to Spiritual Lethargy and Sermon Series 178
Conclusion 201

Introduction

Called to care for and cure souls, pastors invest a significant amount of time and energy addressing a malady which can be diagnosed as spiritual lethargy. The Apostle Paul urged the Thessalonians to avoid succumbing to spiritual lethargy: "so then let us not sleep as others do, but let us be alert and sober" (1 Thess 5:6).[441] Paul also attempted to rouse those saints in Rome who were in a moral stupor: "The hour has come for you to wake up from your slumber" (Rom 13:11, NIV). Peter the Apostle warned believers about the prowling adversary (1 Pet 5:8). In the face of ever-present spiritual danger, all believers must be "in a wakeful activity" taking great pains to be watchful.[442]

Spiritual lethargy may be defined as a state of indifference and/or inertia regarding one's own spiritual growth and vitality. A. W. Tozer describes

---

[440] LaGioia earned his DMin, MDiv, and ThM from Trinity Evangelical Divinity School, Deerfield, IL. He wrote the articles on "Blackwood, Andrew Watterson," "Chapman, John Wilbur," "Chappell, Clovis Gilham," Jefferson, Charles Edward," "Jowett, John Henry," "Lee, Robert Greene," "McClain, Alva J.," "McGee, John Vernon," "Marshall, Peter," "Robinson, Haddon W.," and "Talbot, Louis Thomson" in *Encyclopedia of Christianity in the United States*, ed. George Thomas Kurian and Mark A. Lamport (Lanham: Rowman & Littlefield Publishers, 2016; 2,664 pp.); "Anticipating Christ's Return." in *Bulletin for Intercultural Studies of Grace Theological Seminary* 12 (December 2013); and "Victory Over Trials and Temptations." in *Selah: Pause and Think* (Grace Publishing House, 2013). See www.Grace.edu/academics/seminary/faculty/lagioia and lagioir@grace.edu.

[441] All Scripture quotes are from the *Updated New American Standard Bible* unless noted.

[442] Arnold G. Fruchtenbaum, *The Messianic Jewish Epistles: Hebrews; James; 1 and 2 Peter; Jude* (San Antonio: Ariel Ministries, 2005), 379.

this condition well: "there is little communion and little joy in the Lord. To have a cold heart with little pity, little fire, little love and little worship is spiritual lethargy."[443]

Some of the most common symptoms of spiritual lethargy include any combination of the following:

- Chronic indulgence in sinful thoughts and actions;
- Little or no desire to pray;
- Engagement in exclusively Christ-less entertainment;
- Avoidance of personal accountability;
- Decreased appetite for Bible study;
- Selfish and materialistic orientation;
- Reluctant and sporadic church attendance.

Some of the above symptoms may be difficult to detect even by observant and discerning pastors. For example, a person who is languishing in spiritual lethargy may still engage in some form of religious activity, albeit in a perfunctory manner. Further, those symptoms do not heal easily. However, pastors should be encouraged by the fact that none of them are incurable. This article will approach spiritual lethargy from three perspectives: biblical, theological, and homiletical.

A. Biblical Approach to Spiritual Lethargy

The Bible instructs pastors on how to address spiritual lethargy when that lethargy affects those under the pastors' spiritual care. All churches have at least a few members who are dying spiritually. One of the pastor's responsibilities is to wake up and exhort the sleeping and to help restore the dying. By the grace of God, a living remnant can restore a dying church.

1. The Church in Ephesus

The Ephesian Christians were active workers who persevered and remained morally upright. They were theologically orthodox and discerning in doctrinal matters. Despite these commendable qualities, the Ephesian church neglected something essential: "But I have this against you, that you have left your first love" (Rev 2:3).

To work hard and to persevere do not necessarily guarantee a robust love for Jesus. Neither does being morally upright and theologically astute. The Ephesians did not hate Christ, but their love for Him had lost its depth and fervency. Their once vibrant faith degenerated into a cold orthodoxy. The

---

[443] A. W. Tozer, *The Dangers of a Shallow Faith: Awakening from Spiritual Lethargy* (Bloomington: Bethany House, 2012), 20, 55.

Good Shepherd urged His sheep and contemporary pastors should urge their flocks to return to their first love.

How does a Christian with an indifferent heart return to Jesus? The Son of God told the Ephesian church: "Remember therefore from where you have fallen" (Rev 2:5a). Protestant Reformer Peter Martyr Vermigli referred to the memory as "a priceless treasury and faithful guardian of past events."[444] Every believer has the capacity to search and retrieve from their "priceless treasury" memories that recall what their relationship with Christ was like.

Pastors should attempt to stir the memory of the lethargic believer to stir the heart. The following questions may help:

- Do you remember what it was like when you first fell in love with Christ?
- Do you recall the spiritual exhilaration you experienced when you told others about your Savior?
- Do you remember the wonderful sense of anticipation as you scheduled times to converse with Christ?
- Do you recall the tears of gratitude and spontaneous praise to your Creator as you gazed at a sunset or other magnificent vistas of God's creation?

After challenging the Ephesian church to remember their former condition, Jesus commanded them to "repent" of their present condition (Rev 2:5b). Speaking the truth in love, the pastor can challenge the lethargic person as follows: Change your mind immediately about your sinful indifference toward Christ! Determine now to break away from your lifeless religiosity! Reverse the cooling trend by taking steps to rekindle your love for Christ!

In addition to remembering their former condition and repenting of their present condition, Jesus urged the Ephesian believers to resume their former conduct: "do the deeds you did at first" (Rev 2:5c). The deeds they did at first were prompted by love not obligation. With a heart freshly revived, the deeds would now be done with renewed enthusiasm and a deeper sense of satisfaction.

2. The Church in Laodicea

Tragically, there is no commendation for this lukewarm church. Indeed, out of all seven churches in Asia Minor, the church in Laodicea received the severest rebuke. The Great Physician diagnosed their spiritual infirmity: "I

---

[444] John Patrick Donnelly, ed., *Peter Martyr Vermigli: Life, Letters, and Sermons*, The Peter Martyr Library, vol. 5 (Kirksville: Thomas Jefferson University Press, 1999), 234.

know your deeds, that you are neither cold nor hot; I would that you were cold or hot" (Rev 3:15).

The spiritually "cold" person is likely "an unbeliever who has rejected the gospel openly and aggressively."[445] The spiritually "hot" person is a fervent and enthusiastic follower of Jesus Christ. The spiritually "lukewarm" person is a self-professed Christian who is indifferent. Spiritual lethargy has terrible implications: "to profess Christianity while remaining untouched by its fire is a disaster. There is more hope for the openly antagonistic than for the coolly indifferent."[446]

Many under-shepherds tolerate the indifference of the spiritually "lukewarm" person. By contrast, the spiritually "lukewarm" person makes the Great Shepherd vomit: "So because you are lukewarm, and neither hot nor cold, I will spit you out of my mouth" (Rev 3:16). Pastors who understand its dangers will not tolerate spiritual lethargy.

Jesus identified the Laodicean church's boastfulness and blind self-sufficiency as further evidence of their lukewarm complacency. "Because you say, 'I am rich, and have become wealthy, and have need of nothing,' and you do not know that you are wretched and miserable and poor and blind and naked" (Rev 3:17). The church in Laodicea grossly overestimated its spiritual condition. Pastors must offer a frank and sobering diagnosis of the lethargic person's true state of health.

In His grace Jesus offered the Laodicean church a remedy for spiritual lethargy. The first ingredient in Jesus' remedy is "gold refined by fire, that you may become rich" (Rev 3:18a). Situated in a wealthy financial center, the Laodicean church needed to buy gold from Christ. The gold symbolized "high quality faith, a faith capable of withstanding trials and one that results in works."[447]

The second ingredient in Jesus' remedy for spiritual lethargy is "white garments so that you may clothe yourself, and that the shame of your nakedness will not be revealed" (Rev 3:18b). The Laodiceans needed to clothe themselves in white garments to cover their spiritual nakedness and avoid shame at Christ's return. The white garments represent a new heart inclined toward righteous acts done in faith.

The third ingredient in Jesus' remedy for spiritual lethargy is "eye salve to anoint your eyes so that you may see" (Rev 3:18c). The Laodiceans needed spiritual discernment from the Great Physician. Only He could open their eyes to their true spiritual condition.

---

[445] Robert L. Thomas, *Revelation 1–7: An Exegetical Commentary* (Chicago: Moody, 1992), 306.

[446] Leon Morris, *Revelation* (Rev ed.; TNTC; Grand Rapids: Eerdmans, 1987), 82.

[447] Thomas, *Revelation 1–7*, 314.

When counseling those who lack these three ingredients, pastors may encourage them to examine themselves to determine whether or not they have truly received Christ as Savior.

After communicating His displeasure over the spiritual lethargy of the Laodiceans, Jesus expressed His love for them: "Those whom I love, I reprove and discipline" (Rev 3:19a). The least deserving of the seven churches, the Laodiceans were corrected and instructed by Jesus because of His great love for them. Pastors would be wise to temper their correction and instruction with genuine expressions of love.

This section on a biblical approach to spiritual lethargy represents a very small sampling of the abundant and relevant biblical data. Pastors are encouraged to engage in a comprehensive study. The next section on a theological approach to spiritual lethargy is also limited.

B. Theological Approach to Spiritual Lethargy

The Apostle Paul commanded Titus, "But as for you, speak the things which are fitting for sound doctrine" (Titus 2:1). "Sound" (ὑγιαινούσῃ healthful) doctrine promotes spiritual health. Thinking rightly about God is an antidote to spiritual lethargy in that it fosters healthy thinking and living. Among the numerous reasons a person might become spiritually lethargic, the most fundamental cause is a deficient view of God's character as expressed through His attributes.

> The best way to learn about God's character is to study His attributes revealed in Scripture and in His Son. An attribute is an essential characteristic or quality of a person, thing, or group.[448]

Holiness is an example of one of God's attributes. A correct understanding of God's holiness can improve the spiritual health of a believer who is under the dark cloud of spiritual lethargy. Grudem defines God's holiness as "The doctrine that God is separated from sin and devoted to seeking his own honor."[449]

Isaiah the prophet was not spiritually lethargic. Yet, when he had a life-changing encounter with the Holy One, Isaiah became painfully aware of his need for further sanctification. In fact, his personal encounter with the Holy One caused Isaiah to become burdened over his sin and the sin of his people.

In the year of King Uzziah's death, Isaiah entered the temple and received a life transforming vision. Attempting to describe his vision, Isaiah recorded, "I saw the Lord sitting on a throne" (Isa 6:1b). Who specifically

---

[448] Charles R. Swindoll and Roy B. Zuck, eds., *Understanding Christian Theology* (Nashville: Thomas Nelson, 2003), 955.

[449] Wayne Grudem, *Systematic Theology: An Introduction to Biblical Doctrine* (Grand Rapids: Zondervan, 1994), 1243.

did Isaiah see sitting on the throne? In John 12:40–41, after quoting Isaiah 6:10, the Apostle writes, "These things Isaiah said because he saw His glory, and he spoke of Him." Whose glory did Isaiah see? "The Adonai whom Isaiah beheld at that moment was the divine being who is incarnated in Jesus."[450]

Isaiah reported that "Seraphim stood above Him" (Isa 6:2a). These fiery ones were moral beings hovering in close proximity to the brilliant countenance of the sovereign Holy One. Each of these moral beings had "six wings: with two he covered his face" (Isa 6:2b). The seraphim could not even glance at the Holy One!

"And one called out to another and said, 'Holy, Holy, Holy, is the LORD of hosts, the whole earth is full of His glory'" (Isa 6:3). The Holy One is unique in His ethical purity. He is sovereign, set apart and unlike any other man including Isaiah. This encounter with the Holy One had a profound impact upon Isaiah. In fact, the phrase "the Holy One of Israel" appears only six times in the rest of the Bible. However, in the book of Isaiah, it appears twenty-six times!

Isaiah recalls, "And the foundations of the thresholds trembled at the voice of him who called out, while the temple was filling with smoke" (Isa 6:4). The praise of God's holiness by the Seraphim was powerful enough to rock the foundation stones which supported the doorposts. Likely, Isaiah was prostrate with his face on the floor by the doorway of the Temple. Isaiah was overwhelmed!

"Then I said, 'Woe is me, for I am ruined!'" (Isa 6:5a). Painfully aware of his desperately sinful state before the Holy One, Isaiah felt doomed to die! Why specifically? "Because I am a man of unclean lips" (Isa 6:5b). When we become burdened over our sin, it is wise and spiritually healthy to confess our sins in a specific and concrete manner. A correct understanding of God's holiness can be life-changing as we become burdened over sin.

Further, while encountering the Holy One we become burdened for service.

> Then one of the seraphim flew to me with a burning coal in his hand, which he had taken from the altar with tongs. He touched my mouth with it and said, "Behold, this has touched your lips; and your iniquity is taken away and your sin is forgiven" (Isa 6:6–7).

Isaiah had just confessed, "I am a man of unclean lips" (Isa 6:5b). The Holy One met Isaiah right at the point of his need. Today, He does the same for the spiritually lethargic. Convinced that he was about to be struck dead

---

[450] Frederic Louis Godet, *Commentary on John's Gospel* (Grand Rapids: Kregel, 1978), 795.

because of his sin, Isaiah instead received divine grace. God's grace is a powerful motivator for service.

"Then I heard the voice of the Lord, saying, 'Whom shall I send, and who will go for Us?'" (Isa 6:8a). Isaiah was not coerced nor even addressed. Yet, because he was overwhelmed by divine grace, Isaiah volunteered to serve The Holy One. "Then I said, 'Here am I. Send me!'" (Isa 6:8b). Isaiah was so burdened for service that he volunteered before he read the job description. While encountering the Holy One, we become burdened for service.

When addressing the needs of the spiritually lethargic, pastors need to teach them the practical implications of sound doctrine. The attributes of God such as His holiness, love, grace, mercy, goodness, omniscience, omnipresence, and immanence all have practical implications. For example, God is omniscient. He knows when our hearts are lethargic and is aware when we are merely going through the motions.

Furthermore, exploring and teaching the practical implications of other doctrines (sin, sanctification, prayer, etc.) will also bear fruit. For example, studying the doctrine of sin will help the spiritually lethargic understand that our fallen nature does not want to worship God or pray because our sinful hearts cater to our fleshly desires. Therefore, our flesh must be subdued daily as we concurrently avoid the influence of the world and the devil.

C. Homiletical Approach to Spiritual Lethargy and Sermon Series

God has spoken in the Scriptures. Therefore, they exist to be made known. The Apostle Paul asks,

> How then will they call on Him in whom they have not believed? How will they believe in Him whom they have not heard? And how will they hear without a preacher? (Rom 10:14).

The purpose of all preaching is to bring a personal encounter between the God of the Word and the hearer of the Word. "So, faith comes from hearing, and hearing by the word of Christ" (Rom 10:17).

After telling Timothy that all Scripture is God-breathed and "profitable for teaching, for reproof, for correction, for training in righteousness" (2 Tim 3:16b), Paul issued a solemn charge: "preach the word; be ready in season and out of season; reprove, rebuke, exhort, with great patience and instruction" (2 Tim 4:2). God's Word is the basis for the solemn charge to preach God's Word. Preaching is God's primary and unique means by which His Word is brought effectively to all people including the spiritually lethargic.

Sermon Series: "Addressing Spiritual Lethargy"

Our gracious God has breathed out a multitude of Scripture passages which either directly address or indirectly relate to the problem of spiritual lethargy. The suggested sermon series below is merely one example of what such a series might look like:

Series Title: "Addressing Spiritual Lethargy"

I. Sermon, Rev 3:1–6: "An Unexpected Wake-Up Call"
   Theme: A Living Remnant Can Restore a Dying Church
   A. Remember How Eagerly You Embraced the Gospel (vv.1–3a)
   B. Keep Strengthening Faltering Church Members (v.3b)
   C. Turn At Once from Spiritual Lethargy (vv.3c–6)

II. Sermon, Rev 2:1–7: "You Have Left Your First Love"
   Theme: Return to Your First Love!
   A. Remember Your Former Condition (vv.1–4, 6, 5a)
   B. Repent of Your Present Condition (v.5b)
   C. Resume Your Former Conduct (vv.5c–d, 7)

III. Sermon, Rev 3:14–22: "Neither Cold nor Hot"
   Theme: Christ Has the Remedy for a Lukewarm Heart
   A. Acquire from Christ a Purified Faith (vv.14–18a)
   B. Acquire from Christ a Heart Inclined toward Righteous Acts (v.18b)
   C. Acquire from Christ Spiritual Discernment (vv.18c–22)

IV. Sermon, Isa 6:1–8: "Transformed by God's Holiness"
   Theme: Encountering the Holy One is Life-Changing!
   A. Encountering the Holy One, We Become Burdened over Sin (vv.1–5)
   B. Encountering the Holy One, We Become Burdened for Service (vv.6–8)

V. Sermon, Hosea 11:1–11: "The Love of God Our Father"
   Theme: God the Father Loves His Children!
   A. God the Father Nurtures His Children (vv.1–4)
   B. God the Father Disciplines His Children (vv.5–7)
   C. God the Father has Mercy on His Children (vv.8–9)
   D. God the Father Restores His Children (vv.10–11)

VI. Sermon, 2 Cor 12:1–10: "My Grace is Sufficient for You"
   Theme: God's Grace in Christ is Sufficient for Our Every Need
   A. God's Grace Provides Christ-Like Humility (vv.1–7)
   B. God's Grace Provides Spiritual Strength (vv.8–10)

VII. Sermon, John 15:1–7: "Spiritual Vitality through Abiding in Christ"
   Theme: Believers Must Abide in Christ
   A. Abiding in Christ Results in Spiritual Cleansing (vv.1–3)
   B. Abiding in Christ Results in Abundant Fruitfulness (vv.4–6)
   C. Abiding in Christ Results in Effective Prayer (v.7)

Conclusion

As we defined spiritual lethargy and identified its most common symptoms, we addressed it from three perspectives: biblical, theological, and homiletical. In the section on a biblical approach to spiritual lethargy, our study was limited to two biblical passages which are instructive for pastors who want to know how to address spiritual lethargy in the lives of those under their care.

Revelation 2:1–7 notes some commendable qualities that were still evident in the Ephesian church. Yet, the Ephesian Christians had left their first love, Jesus Christ. To reverse the cooling trend, pastors must urge the spiritually lethargic to take the following steps to rekindle their love for Christ: 1) remember your former condition, 2) repent of your present condition, and 3) resume your former conduct with a renewed enthusiasm.

The contents of Revelation 3:14–22 were sent to the lukewarm church in Laodicea. Pastors who understand the dangers of such a lukewarm condition should resolve to never tolerate spiritual lethargy in the lives of those whom they serve. Rather, they should offer a frank diagnosis and stir a sense of need within them. Each lethargic person should be urged to seek Christ for the following: a robust faith, a new heart inclined toward righteous acts, and spiritual discernment. Finally, pastors should balance their corrective activities with genuine expressions of love.

The section on a theological approach rests upon the conviction that sound doctrine is a healthy antidote to spiritual lethargy. One root cause is a deficient view of God's character. God's holiness serves as an instructive model for searching out the practical implications of relevant doctrines in addressing the needs of the spiritually lethargic. A correct understanding of God's holiness can move the complacent to become burdened over sin and burdened for service. In addition to God's attributes, doctrines such as sin, sanctification, and prayer can also help the spiritually lethargic.

The section on a homiletical approach is undergirded by two complementary convictions: first, God has spoken in the Scriptures, and second, preaching is God's primary means by which His Word is brought effectively to all people, including the spiritually lethargic. The sermon series, "Addressing Spiritual Lethargy," is offered as merely one example of how to approach the subject from the pulpit. Pastors are encouraged to search the Scriptures and construct a sermon series which directly addresses the issue of spiritual lethargy within their congregations. Spiritual vitality in the pulpit will help cure spiritual lethargy in the pew.

12.
Midwifing Model of Pastoral Care with Addicted Persons

Rev. Dr. Myrna Thurmond-Malone
Founder and Director, MHT Family Life Center
Riverdale, Georgia[451]

Introduction 181
A. Exploring Addiction 182
B. Transference and Countertransference and Uncovering
    the Root of Addiction 185
C. Midwifing: A Womanist Approach to Pastoral Counseling 188
D. Four Verbatims in the Midwifing Model of Pastoral Care 192
Conclusion on the Midwifing Model of Pastoral Care 193

Introduction

This article begins with an examination of addiction—behavioral addiction—and a brief history of when the American church began to get involved in helping persons with addictions. In my writing, I consider the painful memories shared by several counselees that endured traumatic experiences and whose addictions were instituted as their means of survival. I highlight cultural transference and cultural countertransference, as well as my approach of midwifing developed through research, group sessions, integrating self-psychology, narrative, and womanist theology. The integration of each provides the framework of my midwifing methodology. The information and resources utilized in the article are an accumulation of my ten years of experience and education working and providing care to a diverse population grappling with addiction.

As an ordained clergy, licensed Christian counselor and therapist, certified pastoral counselor, chaplain, and anger management specialist, I have provided care for a broad spectrum of persons—from the incarcerated

---

[451] Thurmond-Malone earned her ThD in Pastoral Care and Counseling, Columbia Theological Seminary, Decatur, Georgia, and her MDiv from the Interdenominational Theological Center. She is a licensed Christian counselor and a board-certified pastoral counselor. She is listed in Best Marriage Therapists in Riverdale at Marriage.com. She has been a chaplain and grief counselor for Metro State Women's Prison and adjunct professor at the Interdenominational Theological Center where she taught Clinical Introduction to Psychology of Pastoral Care. She has written *Midwifing—A Womanist Approach to Pastoral Counseling* (Oregon: Pickwick, 2019; 182 pp.), based upon her 2015 Columbia Theological Seminary ThD diss. She is the co-author with Alisha Tatem, Brandy McMurry, and Quanika Bynum of *Daughters of the Desert—The Journey Towards Letting Go, Surrendering, and Trusting God* (Scotts Valley: CreateSpace, 2015) and *Selah—Reflections on Sabbath and Self-Care* (CreateSpace, 2015). See www.MHTFamilyLifeCenter.org and RevMyrnaMalone@mhtfamilylifecenter.org.

and homeless, the poor and middle class, to the professional. The material presented in this article represents a technique of pastoral care that is focused on

1. Creating a safe and sacred space,
2. Power of telling and sharing one's narrative, and
3. Re-authoring one's narrative.

The technique affirms that each of the three parts helps to facilitate the opportunity for hope, wholeness, transformation, liberation, empowerment, re-authoring, and the development of a secured sense of self. Lastly, I illustrate the benefits of a midwifing approach when providing care to persons battling addiction due to the deeper issues of trauma.

For the counselees presented in this article, substance or behavior was developed in order to cope with harmful memories. The whole is intended for pastoral care professionals within a clinical and/or educational setting. The view represented is meant to shift attention from the addict to a focus on understanding the need for the substance or behavioral addiction. Further, the purpose is to explore the narrative of the person and the importance of journeying alongside the counselee as they unpack the reasoning of their addiction, explore self-love through self-care, and become whole and transformed by integrating negative and positive experiences. This will lead to liberation and empowerment, allowing the counselee self-acceptance through affirmation, re-authoring their narrative, and learning healthier ways of coping.

A. Exploring Addiction

The American Association of Addictive Medicine states,

> Addiction is a primary, chronic disease of brain reward, motivation, memory, and related circuitry. Dysfunction in these circuits leads to characteristic biological, psychological, social, and spiritual manifestations. This is reflected in an individual pathologically pursuing reward and/or relief by substance use and other behaviors.[452]

In *Mental Health and Mental Disorders: An Encyclopedia of Conditions, Treatments, and Well-Beings*, edited by Len Sperry, addiction is also defined as,

> the compulsive use of a habit-forming substance or the irresistible urge to engage in a behavior despite harmful consequences and as a chronic disease of

---

[452] Len Sperry, *Mental Health and Mental Disorders: An Encyclopedia of Conditions, Treatments, and Well-Beings* (Santa Barbara: Greenwood, 2016), 17.

the brain which involves compulsive and uncontrolled pursuit of reward or relief with substance use or other compulsive behaviors.[453]

Behavioral addiction refers to repeatedly engaging in behavior(s) that are destructive and result in harmful consequences.[454] When persons succumb to the control of substances or behaviors and become addicted, their judgment becomes impaired and their interpersonal relationships are affected, as are their emotional and spiritual internal self.

The practice of seeking to understand and help addicted persons began with the addiction to alcohol. In 1913 an assembly of religious leaders known as the Oxford Group gathered to create a space of healing for persons suffering from alcohol addiction. In 1935, their practices became more popular through Alcoholics Anonymous (AA), which adopted their model. The Oxford Group described itself as "a movement of vital personal religion working within the churches to make the principles of the N.T. practical a working force today."[455]

However, before 1913, the idea that human character can be changed can be traced back as early as the 1730s to Jonathan Edwards and John Wesley. Author and researcher Glenn F. Chesnut writes,

> What Edwards and Wesley discovered was that human character could be changed. One could take the story of a person's life, and with the aid of God's grace, change the way the story ended.[456]

This concept of changing the way the story ends has been highlighted through narrative theology and narrative therapy.

Pastoral theologian Edward Wimberly ascribes to the power and the liberative means of a narrative approach to providing pastoral care, which he highlights in his teaching and writings. In *Recalling Our Own Stories*, Wimberly emphasizes that the use of narrative in scripture aides the counselee in drawing from problematic texts and journeying toward empowerment and deconstruction. His method explores the counselee's life and helps them to get at their presenting problem. This technique helps the counselee to define and/or get to the root of the problem and affirm space for a new narrative, deconstructing negative internal and external scripts. Wimberly's approach helps the counselee to see God at work in their life.

---

[453] Sperry, *Mental Health*.

[454] Sperry, *Mental Health*, 18.

[455] Dick B., *The Oxford Group and Alcohols Anonymous: A Design for Living That Works* (Kihei, Maui: Paradise Research Publications, Inc., 1998), 146–147.

[456] Glenn F. Chesnut, *Changed By Grace: V. V. Kitchen, the Oxford Group, and A.A.* (Lincoln: Universe, 2006), xii.

Michael White and Michael Epstein contend that "mapping the influence of persons" and "reorganizing their experience" encourages them to externalize the problem.[457] The narrative process helps the counselee to externalize themselves as the problem and see the problem as the problem. It allows for the listener as well as the storyteller to witness the story and create a new story through externalizing and re-authoring. I assert that the fundamental healing component in one's narrative is the *telling* and the *hearing*. This demonstrates the value and humanity of the person telling the story and asserts their value through the hearing of the story.

Reflecting on the change that began in the 1730s, and the later re-storying, provides insight today for pastoral care professionals who create an atmosphere of hope that will resonate with those who suffer with addiction, stirring within the counselees hopefulness. This hopefulness is critical. Receiving care and assistance in an environment hopeful of new possibilities of change allows counselees to gain confidence that they can overcome their addiction and begin again without the stronghold of addiction taking charge of their life. Sperry affirms that providing hope is a crucial dimension for addiction counselors as they offer themselves as "living proof" of hope. Most addiction counselors are individuals who overcame the control of their addiction and use their experiences to assist and care for persons who struggle with addiction.

Although most everyone who provides care to the addicted has been an addict themselves, the counselor must be able to demonstrate what Heinz Kohut terms "vicarious introspection."[458] For Kohut, vicarious introspection is the emphasis on empathy and introspection and should be used as tools in psychoanalysis to study the human experience and the core self of the counselee. This allows the pastoral counselor or pastoral care provider the opportunity to understand what the counselee has experienced through the lens of the counselee. To provide pastoral care and counseling, one must not focus on the addict, but on the addiction. The counselor must try to identify the underlying reasons or circumstances that led the counselee to seek to a resolution to a particular behavior (or substance abuse) in order for the counselee to cope or deal with problematic internal and external factors.

Empathy is valuable in counseling, even invaluable to providing care to persons who wrestle with addiction, because an empathic approach emphasizes contextual human understanding rather than technical competence. Thus, the pastoral counselor or pastoral care provider can

---

[457] Michael White and Michael Epstein, *Narrative Means to Therapeutic End*, (New York: W. W. Norton, 1990), 17–18.

[458] Heinz Kohut, *How Does Analysis Cure?* (Chicago: University of Chicago Press, 1984), p. 175.

"walk in the addict's shoes" and provide interpretation that coincides with their experience, rather than simply pathologizing their perspectives. Therefore, the goal of helping persons with addiction is not about beating them over the head with their addiction but listening and practicing an empathetic understanding in order to gain insight into their pain, hurt, and into their internal/external unresolved self or shame; this will create a "cohesive self" and spiritual growth.

When persons suffer from addiction, they usually feel humiliated, shameful, and defeated. Therefore, one goal for pastoral care professionals should be to help the counselee give voice to their shame and provide a space for healing. Gershen Kaufman asserts that persons who suffer from addiction tend to hate themselves, have a lack of resolve and inner strength, and those result in failed relationships and unmet interpersonal needs.[459]

B. Transference and Countertransference and Uncovering the Root of Addiction

For a different lens in re-evaluating pastoral counseling to persons living with addiction, we explore the importance of self-awareness for the pastoral care provider. The role of discernment is important. We explore cultural transference and cultural countertransference in the therapeutic encounter to help the counselee as they find the courage to uncover what is beneath or at the root of their addiction.

Educator, pastoral theologian, and counselor Archie Smith, Jr. uses the term "bleed through" as he explores and discovers something that is covered up.[460] Smith asserts that "pentimento" occurs when the past is not dealt with, but is forgotten or covered over.[461] Smith's framework provides an awareness of how one covers up (or over) that which one cannot deal or cope. Covering over one's traumatic and painful memories will eventually lead to "the bleeding" into their present, and that "bleeding" leads to addiction when they can no longer cope with the hurt from the past. For the pastoral care professional who wishes to help, assist, and journey alongside persons who request care, Smith's process emphasizes the creation of an atmosphere that allows the counselee to lament and to uncover what may have led to their addiction.

---

[459] Gershen Kaufman, *The Psychology of Shame: Theory and Treatment of Shame-Based Syndromes*, 2nd ed. (New York: Springer, 1996), 122–23.

[460] Archie Smith, Jr., *The Relational Self: Ethics and Therapy from a Black Church Perspective* (Nashville: Abingdon, 1982), X.

[461] Pentimento is the technique of removing the top layer of paint to reveal a painting underneath. Smith uses the term as a means of "covering up a canvas previously painted," causing the experiences of their life to "bleed through."

Pastoral counselors who create safe and sacred spaces for persons to cry out:
1. Assist the counselee to value their experience,
2. Acknowledge their pain,
3. Make space for healing to occur which promotes hope, and
4. Furthermore, they help them develop a healthy core self.

A safe and sacred space allows the counselee to reflect on the strength of their faith and rebuild their trust in and relationship with God, inviting them to pursue healthier ways of coping and moving them from surviving to thriving. This framework allows the pastoral professional to disengage from a moral model in order to become aware of cultural transference and cultural countertransference.

Cultural awareness helps the pastoral care provider to avoid stumbling upon cultural boundary violations. That happens when the counselor or therapist imposes his/her values and notions regarding a wide range of social and cultural matters upon the analysis and counselee. According to Salman Akhtar, that occurs when the counselor ignores the counselee's cultural background, the counselor ignores his/her own cultural background, or the counselor ignores the effect of his/her own cultural background on the counselee. [462] Foremost, Akhtar asserts the counselor must take into consideration the cultural identity of the counselee. He writes, "Cultural identity is the core self-representation that is aligned and affiliated with the norms and attitudes, values, and communication idioms of a group of people." [463] Akhtar, expressing John Spiegel's definition, sees cultural transference and countertransference

> as [one's] respectively feelings, fantasies, and attitudes a patient [counselee] might have towards the analyst's [counselor] ethno-racial group or an analyst [counselor] may have towards the patient [counselee] ethno-racial group.[464]

Akhtar asserts one's perception of another's culture is transgenerationally conveyed as a result of one's historical relationship towards an ethno-racial group, consequently hindering interpretation during the therapeutic encounter. [465] Charles Gelso and Jeffrey Hayes write:

> Cultural countertransference (and transference) [are] culture-related distortions of the patient [counselee] or rigid interpersonal behaviors rooted in his or her

---

[462] Salman Akhtar, *Comprehensive Dictionary of Psychoanalysis* (London: Karnac Books, 2009), 64.

[463] Akhtar, *Dictionary of Psychoanalysis*.

[464] Akhtar.

[465] Akhtar.

[the therapist] direct or vicarious experience with members of the patient's [counselee] group [occurring when the counselee holds onto perceptions that don't apply to the counselee]. [466]

Addictions: A Comprehensive Guidebook outlines the need for awareness of transference if operating under the moral model. Alleging that when working with persons who desire to overcome their addiction, the use of naming and blaming may stem from the counselor's cultural identity (religion, race, gender, etc.) and their attempt to avoid uncomfortable feelings.[467]

Clinicians Leslie C. Jackson and Beverly Greene expand the scope of cultural transference to encompass the

> emotional reactions of a client to the therapist based on the client's sense of who the therapist is, culturally, with respect to race, ethnicity, religion, gender, age, social class, and other factors ... cultural transference looks beyond race to acknowledge other obvious differences between the client and the therapist, and it allows for "cultural" reactions by a client to a therapist who is similar with respect to race and gender. [And] cultural countertransference as the therapist's emotional reactions to the client based on the client's race, ethnicity, religion, gender, age, social class, or the like ... [anything] that gets in the way of seeing the client more clearly.[468]

Jackson and Green go further, discussing the "real relationship" that occurs in the therapeutic space between the counselee and the pastoral counselor. The real relationship is the realistic relationship established between the counselee and the counselor, and not the one of fantasy.

Womanist pastoral care author Markeva Hill writes,

> As counselors, we are trained to follow the transference thread that leads us through the labyrinth of the unconscious back to the scene of the crime(s). Once there, we assist in reconstructing the past in order to make sense of the present and create new meaning and options for the future [of the counselee].[469]

These are not easy to see and require a lot of clinical training.

Each explanation of cultural transference and cultural countertransference illustrates the need for cultural awareness when providing pastoral care and counseling to anyone. This awareness will not only allow for a therapeutic alliance to be developed, it also allows the

---

[466] Charles Gelso and Jeffrey Hayes, eds., *Countertransference and the Therapist Inner Experience: Perils and Possibilities* (Mahwah: Lawrence Erlbaum, 2007), 134.

[467] Barbara S. McCrady and Elizabeth E. Epstein, eds., *Addictions: A Comprehensive Guidebook*, (New York: Oxford University Press, 1999), 445.

[468] Leslie C. Jackson and Beverly Greene, eds., *Psychotherapy with African American Women: Innovations in Psychodynamic Perspective and Practice* (New York: The Gilford Press, 2000), 20, 24.

[469] MarKeva Gwendolyn Hill, *Womanism Against Socially-Constructed Matriarchal Images: A Theoretical Model Toward a Therapeutic Goal* (New York: Palgrave MacMillan, 2012), 70.

counselee to open up and reflect on what purpose the addiction serves, leading them to develop a healthy core self. This, suggests Kohut, is the ultimate goal of therapy—the development of a healthy and balanced self or "cohesive self." Kohut speaks of the cohesive self as a psychic structure that becomes harmonious, vigorous, and energetic. In other words, it is an integrated self that is able to develop a structured/organized self. [470]

C. Midwifing: A Womanist Approach to Pastoral Counseling[471]

The term womanism was coined in 1982 by African American author and activist Alice Walker. [472] However, we draw on Delores Williams' definition of womanism, who declares that womanist theology is a

> prophetic voice concerned about the well-being of the entire African American community, male and female, adults and children ... attempts to ... affirm ... challenge all oppressive forces. [473]

A womanist framework values the importance and uniqueness of the counselee, serving as a conduit to empower and journey with the counselee. It enables the counselee to cultivate their own true identity separate from what has been imposed on them via socialization, miseducation, and other external forces that may have led to their addiction. Hill asserts, "Womanism is able to empower pastoral counselors with the tools of healing and assist them in joining the counselee in a manner that would prove to be non-threatening for both counselor and counselee."[474]

Additionally, we assert that womanism seeks to create a safe space that allows the counselee to explore their defense mechanisms and current coping skills, eventually helping to un-armor defensive and protective mechanisms by becoming aware of the root to their addiction. It seeks to dialogue with culture, socialization, and spiritual, religious, as well as with theological beliefs, as the counselee examines their story and the birth of their addiction.

Finally, a womanist framework provides a holistic, healing approach as it creates space for the counselee to share, hear, and acknowledge their story; and, in turn, it helps them to affirm a stronger self-identity as they embrace their humanity and begin to integrate their experiences, moving from

---

[470] Heinz Kohut, *How Does Analysis Cure?* (Chicago: University of Chicago, 1971), 99–100.

[471] Myrna Thurmond-Malone, "Midwifing: A Womanist Approach to Pastoral Counseling, Investigating the Fractured Self: Slavery, Violence, and the Black Woman" (ThD diss., Columbia Theological Seminary, 2015).

[472] Alice Walker, *In Search of Our Mothers' Gardens* (New York: Harcourt, 1983).

[473] Delores Williams, *Sisters in the Wilderness: The Challenge of Womanist God-Talk* (Maryknoll: Orbis Books, 1993), 67.

[474] Markeva Gwendolyn Hill, *Womanist against Socially-Constructed Matriarchal Images: A Theoretical Model toward a Therapeutic Goal* (New York: Palgrave Macmillan, 2012), 69.

fractured selves to wholeness and taking control of their addiction. A womanist framework includes the pastoral functions of nurturing, empowering, liberating, and reconciling.[475]

The role of pastoral counselor as midwife is inclusive of these pastoral functions and provides support, meeting counselees where they are. This allows for the counselee to transition from a state of survivor mode to a thriving mode, thereby facilitating the creation of a safe and sacred space that allows the counselee to get through their challenging life experiences.

This framework also speaks of the power of language to transform and create healing. In some folklore writing, the midwife is referred to as "conjurer" or "sistah conjurer." Valerie Lee noted how sistah conjurer is a term that, rather than

> dismissing the women as superstitious or incompetent, gives them historical and personal agency [and] conjurer is a magical means of transforming reality.... It is a healing event ... taking healing as a metaphor for spiritual power ... emphasize[ing] the restorative potential ... locating in language a new curative domain. [476]

A recent study on the role of midwives illustrates how midwives empower women by meeting them where they are, which in turn allows them to "get through" the birthing process.[477] This perspective provides a construct to engage the pastoral counselor on the benefits of meeting the counselee "where she/he is" in order to facilitate empowerment, thus allowing the entire person to be present in the therapeutic encounter of good, bad, and uncomfortable issues that may need to be explored when getting to the root of addiction. The midwifing perspective suggests that the pastoral counselor must be in a position to hold, care for, and handle the issues that are part of the counselee's narrative.

We interpret the midwife as being able to create as a sacred and safe holding environment. This allows persons who are addicted to bring their entire being and life experiences into the therapeutic encounter, giving them the confidence by assuring them that their voices and stories will be honored and supported through the telling and sharing of difficult and traumatizing life experiences.

The narrative and midwifery experience of Margaret Charles Smith highlights the struggles of black women for whom she cared, and her ability

---

[475] Carroll Watkins Ali, *Survival and Liberation: Pastoral Theology in African American Context* (St. Louis: Chalice Press, 1999), 8–9.

[476] Valerie Lee, *Granny Midwives and Black Women Writers: Double-Dutched Readings* (New York: Routledge, 1996), 14–17.

[477] Tracey Cooper and Dame Tina Lavender, "Women's Perceptions of a Midwife's Role: An Initial Investigation," *British Journal of Midwifery* 21, no. 4 (August 2013): 268.

to hold all that their "lived reality" represented as she cared for them and created a space to prepare for the birthing. Linda Holmes writes,

> Mrs. Smith's skills as a midwife stood up to many of the challenges she faced, allowing her, as black folks often say, to 'make a way out of no way.' ... Mrs. Smith met few problems that she couldn't solve.[478]

Womanist and women's healthcare provider Arisika Razak explains her experience of a midwife as someone who stands "as witness, companion, and helper.... My work [as a midwife] demonstrated the immense contradictions under which women live."[479] Razak goes on to share how her experience as a midwife created a holiness experience, whereby the face of God was able to be experienced in the birthing process.[480]

The counseling birth process in midwifing would be to journey alongside persons that struggle with addiction, allowing them to develop a functional process for externalizing—giving birth, if you will—to their life experiences that may have led them to become addicted. Therein, such allows them to encounter the face of God through the telling, thereby creating space for new life. A midwifing therapeutic approach is aware of the importance of creating a safe and sacred space that allows the pastoral counselor to build trust with the counselee in order to hear each story.

Valerie Lee highlights the trust aspect of midwifing throughout her book, *Granny, Midwives, and Black Women Writers: Double-Dutched Readings*, as she explores the perception of midwives from those for whom she provided care. About the midwife Miss Mary, Lee writes, "When patients saw the midwife coming, they thought they saw heaven! They thought the midwife could ease their burdens for them."[481] This suggests not only the perception of the midwife's healing aspect, but also her connection to God and a feeling of safety and trust engendered for women in her care. Engaging the voice of Holmes, who writes, "the ability to summon the Holy Ghost for support, guidance, and 'miracle working' ... midwives frequently assumed the meditative state of prayer in preparation of attending a birth."[482] Lee explores the "high and holy calling" of granny midwives who felt they received a "call from the Lord" to do midwifery, thereby relying upon the spiritual dimensions of God to use their gift of "catching the baby."[483]

---

[478] Margaret Charles Smith and Linda Janet Holmes, *Listen To Me Good: The Life Story of an Alabama Midwife* (Columbus: Ohio State University Press, 1996), 88.

[479] Arisika Razak, "Embodying Womanism," in *Ain't I a Womanist Too: Third-Wave Womanist Religious Thought*, ed. Monica A. Coleman (Minneapolis: Fortress Press, 2013), 218.

[480] Razak, "Embodying Womanism."

[481] Lee, *Granny Midwives and Black Women Writers*, 86.

[482] Smith and Holmes, *Listen To Me Good: The Life Story of an Alabama Midwife*, 88.

[483] Lee, *Granny Midwives and Black Women Writers*, 82–83.

For this pastoral counselor, "catching the baby" can be used as a metaphor for the pastoral counselor's ability to not only offer a container, but also to be able to hold the narratives of the counselee as the counselee themselves fill the container.[484] We believe that when we establish trust and safety, the counselee is more likely to permit their entire being into the counseling session and share their narrative. The pastoral counselor as midwife creates a therapeutic environment facilitating the counselee's undoing of the walls that may have been developed in the course of coping with a life that led to addiction. The pastoral counselor must have the fortitude to hold and engage the stories shared for the development of a counselee's healthy core self, allowing re-storying and healthier coping skills.

For that safe and sacred space to occur, the pastoral counselor must develop a position of empathy. Empathy allows for the counselee to keep their walls down and be open to engage their story with the pastoral counselor, allowing the counselor and counselee to examine further the counselee's defense mechanisms. Lee's use of the metaphor "double-dutched readings" illustrates empathy as she places herself, as well as other folklore and literary writers, in the shoes of those who provide care. The desire was to tell the stories not from the writers' lens, but rather to tell the stories through the lens of those of the actually gave care in the folklore story—quite ingenious. Lee and other writers, such as Morrison, do not change the narrative to fit the experiences of today, but hold the story in the light in which the giver shared their experiences.

Thus, midwifing is an attempt at listening and understanding the stories and experiences through the lenses of those giving birth, that is, those who need to deliver and even get deliverance. When providing care to persons suffering from addiction the focus is not on the addiction, but on the story surrounding, behind, or beneath the addiction, as well as the thoughts, feelings, and perceptions that the counselee may have internalized as a result of their experience and/or addiction. This posture creates a sacred and safe space, allowing the counselee's narrative to be heard and defenses to let down, and this offers assurance that it is safe to tell their story, even *deliver* their story into the kind and gentle and empathic hands of an experienced pastoral care midwife—one the counselee trusts with their most intimate and painful experiences.

In other words, there is healing in the telling and the "delivery" of the story. It allows the pastoral counselor and counselee to reflect on the story. The *delivery* helps to free the addicted from the pain of the story and

---

[484] Lee, 84.

develop a healthier defense mechanism. The counselee can then inspect their defense mechanisms, which allows them to explore and get to the root of their armoring and the root of their addiction. This positions the counselee to gain insight into their inner self and how their armoring has played a role in their addiction, identity, and relationships. Exploring the "why" helps to externalize negative feelings and thoughts that may have prevented them from building a healthier self-image and relationships with others, creating hope and the willingness to replace the negative addiction with healthier ways of coping.

Midwifing allows counselees to explore their need to escape negative memories such as sedative scripts of shame. A sedative script looks at a scene while paying attention to the negative and while disregarding other parts of the scene.[485] The telling of their story authorizes counselees to honor their voice, story, and identity, thus allowing them to become empowered and deconstruct negative sedative scripts. Through listening and affirming, pastoral counselors have the ability to journey with the counselee to un-armor—again, to "deliver"—and to thereby re-story a new beginning. This allows the counselee to not only uncover painful memories, but to move past the old negative behaviors that create feelings of inadequacy.

This Midwifing Pastoral Care helps to empower the counselee to recognize their humanity. When this occurs, they are able to become empowered and thereby liberated from negative experiences and from the stronghold of their addiction.

D. Four Verbatims in the Midwifing Model of Pastoral Care

The following four statements come from real-life sessions with hurting people and reflect the benefits of the midwifing approach, the names changed to preserve anonymity. Coming from a variety of backgrounds and ethnicities, educated and non-educated, poor and middle class, they all confess to be spiritual or Christian. Each shared their reluctance of counseling, being afraid that they might be judged; they wanted to forget bad memories and did not want to be typed as crazy. Lastly, each shared that there was not adequate space in which they could openly share their experiences and feelings.

> **Jessica:** I struggle with identity. It's hard to look in the mirror because of what happened to me during my childhood. I use sex so I could have control because I didn't have it growing up. I questioned God and how could He allow this to happen to me. Where was he? I didn't think of me having a lot of sex as an

---

[485] E. Virginia Demos, ed., *Exploring Affect: The Selected Writings of Silvan S. Tomkin* (New York: Cambridge University Press, 1995), 389.

addition I just wanted to be numb. But counseling is helping. I feel safe and I'm learning how to define me even though I was molested.

Jeff: I was pretty excited about counseling after our first session. You seemed sincere, and that made me feel safe. It feels good to talk about my dreams and not live in the past. I have been able to recognize triggers that lead me to drink or be mean to others. I'm learning to love myself.

Samantha: You know I took what you said to me last session and I wrote a letter to my father and shared how he hurt me. Even though he is dead, it helped me to get it out of me. I realize that I used food to replace what I didn't get from my dad and this week instead of turning to food I wrote the letter. It made me feel like I'm finally getting control.

Keisha: Growing up in Mississippi during segregation was hard. I hated being black. When I left for college I didn't know it could be worse, but it was. When I was at a frat party I was raped. I have been holding that in for so long. I felt dirty and ugly and was ashamed. I couldn't go to church or tell my parents, so I started getting high and drinking.

The relevance of the midwifing approach in a modern world focuses on how healing and wholeness can occur as persons who struggle with addiction receive adequate care through a culturally empathic therapeutic encounter. The pastoral counselor willingly hears the stories through the counselee's own lenses, affirming their narratives, and facilitating deconstruction of their negative and harmful life experiences. In so doing, a safe and sacred space for addicted persons helps "deliver" them from negative coping and "embraces" a re-authoring of their narrative.

Conclusion on the Midwifing Model of Pastoral Care

In conclusion, midwifing is a concept that provides guidance, affirmation, compassionate care and support for those who seek care. It fosters empowerment and liberation, allowing persons to connect with self, community, and God. Midwifing is aware of the impact that one's culture and socialization have on the development of the structure of one's self. Midwifing is an effective method as it

1. Establishes a safe therapeutic space that allows the counselee to construct a therapeutic alliance,
2. Postulates a position of empathy allowing the counselee to feel free to open up and explore their defense mechanisms,
3. Allows the counselee to experience the therapist as affirming, understanding, and non-threatening,
4. Recognizes their humanity,

5. Enables the counselee to become empowered and liberated in order to deconstruct negative identification, strongholds, and/or behaviors, and
6. Develops a healthy core self and relationship with the community, allowing the counselee to see themselves in the image of God as they develop a mature self through repairing self-deficits.

Lastly, wholeness becomes possible as the pastoral counselor creates the space for experiences of the counselee to be heard.[486] With hope all along the way, the addicted move from a fractured self to a whole self that embraces their humanity and their self-worth, allowing them ultimately to see themselves in the image created by God—even truly loved and fearfully and wonderfully made.

---

[486] Pamela Cooper-White, *Braided Selves: Collected Essays on Multiplicity, God, and Persons* (Eugene: Wipf and Stock, 2011).

13.
Practical Theology/Spirituality and Fostering Healthy Human Relationships in the Workplace

Rev. Dr. Hundzukani Portia Khosa-Nkatine
Lecturer in Practical Theology
University of Pretoria, South Africa
Chaplain, South African Military Health Services[487]

Introduction 195
A. Practical Theology Enhances Human Relations 196
B. Human Relations.. 197
   1. Effectiveness of Practical Theology 197
   2. Challenge to Practical Theology... 199
      a. What is going on?... 200
      b. Why is this going on?... 200
      c. What ought to be going on? 201
      d. How might we respond?... 201
Conclusion 201

Introduction

We spend most of our time at work, and how we relate with the people that we spend most of our time with has a huge influence on how we view life. When one speaks of practical theology, we often limit its effectiveness to our churches, our congregations, and even our families. Practical theology should also have an effect in our workplaces and how we build human relations. Even though we are not of the world, we live in the world, and good human relations are important. This paper will focus on fostering healthy human relationships in a workplace.

In most parts of South Africa when the term "spirituality" is mentioned, it is believed to be a term only fit for Christians. This can bring division among people of different religious groups. With the growing number of churches being established in South Africa, Christianity has become debatable, especially among non-believers. So, if one were to bring Christianity into the workplace, which tradition or school of thought would the organization bring, and what would be the basis of that choice? Would

---

[487] Khosa-Nkatine earned her PhD from the University of Pretoria, South Africa. She is the author of *Developing a More Inclusive Liturgy Praxis for the Evangelical Presbyterian Church in South Africa* (Rita, Latvia: Lambert Academic Publishing, 2017; 160 pp.) which is based upon her Master of Theology thesis seen here, https://repository.up.ac.za/bitstream/handle/2263/46075/Khosa_Development_2014.pdf. She is a chaplain at South African Military Health Services (SAMHS), and researcher and lecturer at the University of South Africa (Unisa). See www.UP.ac.za and hundzukhosa@gmail.com.

the Reformed tradition be good enough for everyone? Would the Pentecostal be good enough? Charismatic? There are several types of Christian churches, and outside the Christian tradition, we have Judaism, Buddhism, Islam, and more. Browning (1985, p. 15) argues that practical theology must be more than methodological: it must actually do theology to illuminate Christian practices in the midst of life's concrete problems and issues.

A. Practical Theology Enhances Human Relations

According to Marilyn Naidoo (2014, p. 3) in the Christian tradition, spirituality is not just seen as human wellbeing or meaning. It is a deeply lived experience of the person and of nature of God in every aspect of life; it is a primary orientation. Okon (2007, p. 2) argues that while it is not correct to use the words "culture" and "society" interchangeably, it is appropriate to emphasize that there is a symbiotic relationship between the two concepts. Okon furthermore argues that while culture is a system of norms and values, a society is an independent, self-perpetuating human group with a territory and a shared culture. He says that human society is a system of interrelationships that links people together, and no culture can exist either without society, or independent of society, and society is not a reality unless it exists within a context of culture. Good human relations are enhanced in practical theology as Steyn and Masango (2011, p. 2) argue that theology should meet the praxis of pastoral care for the people it seeks to serve, for pastoral care interprets human need. This interpretation points to a theological and hermeneutical analysis of pastoral problems. Practical theology's effectiveness in fostering healthy human relationships is not limited to just one religion or to a certain culture. We do not live in a country of just one religion. South Africa is a very diverse country, sometimes called a rainbow nation.

According to Wepener (2014, p. 8), worship as body language was and still is the most significant feature of the change or "reform" in worship in Sub-Saharan Africa. This includes the dancing, singing, the playing of a variety of musical instruments along with other bodily gestures. He quoted a certain Pastor Daramola of the RCCG: "When we Africans gather for worship, we make a noise, it is embedded in us. We just have to make a noise and shake our bodies."

Klein in Baloyi (2013, p. 14) invites every local church to become a centre of healing and transformation through holistic counselling services. When a local church becomes a centre of healing and transformation, it should not be limited to its own members but should extend to outsiders as true reflection of Christianity. Serving all is practical theology fostering healthy human relationships.

B. Human Relations

Naidoo (2014, p. 1) argues that we live in the transition period between the old definition of work as mere survival and the new definition of work as a livelihood. We agree with Naidoo (2014) when she further argues that workplace spirituality has the potential for leadership development: it allows employees and leaders to act from personal truth, integrity, values, and ethical practices. When practical theology is applied in the life context of people who spend more time at work than they do at church, they will foster those same values, morals, principles in their workplace. This helps develop leadership in the workplace.

Without even preaching, the leader teaches his or her team through example the importance of healthy human relations. Moxley in Naidoo (2014) argued that with the accelerating force of global, societal, and organizational changes come the call for a more holistic leadership that integrates the four fundamental arenas that define the essence of human existence:

1. Body (physical),
2. Mind (logical or rational thought),
3. Heart (emotional, feelings), and
4. Spirit.

1. Effectiveness of Practical Theology

According to a book written by Faranani Facilitation Services, organizational culture is a set of shared beliefs, values, and norms that influence the way members think, feel, and behave. Culture is created by means of terminal and instrumental values, heroes, rites and rituals, and a communication network. The primary method of maintaining organizational culture is through the socialization processes by which individuals learn the values, expected behaviors, and social knowledge necessary to assume their roles in the organization. How many companies start the day off with a morning prayer, or even a moment of silence? The aim of practical theology is not to turn companies into churches but to help individuals carry their full humanity into their workplace. Their spiritual life should not be left at church on Sundays, and employers do well to recognize that.

According to Beyers (2010, p. 1), the dominant religion of the west has been Christianity. The result is that a Christian (Western) understanding of religion dominated that scholarly field. A Christian theology of religions led western scholars to arrange religions in a hierarchical structural implying that some religions were inferior to others. In his research, Cas Wepener (2014, p. 9) observed in many worship services in AICs and Pentecostal churches what Stephen Ellis and Gerrie Ter Haar call "spectacular forms of hyperkinetic trance," speaking in tongues and the sharing of visions and dreams (sometimes about the visiting researcher). Practical theology should aim at teaching people of different religions how to live with one other without being judgmental of the next person's faith.

Social media shows how people differ even in the same religion. In Christianity for an example, some still love their traditional type of churches, while others want the loud music and drum type of churches. And Christians prefer different types of pastors. Practical theology plays an active role in empowering people to embrace the diversity in Christianity. There is a lot of hate speech on social media, and maybe it is because people focus more on belonging to a certain congregation then belonging to the body of Christ which is all of us in our diversity.

Dreyer and Pieterse (2010, p. 1) describe several alternatives:

> The role of religion in the public sphere also causes problems for theologians. It is possible, for example, to summarise broad patterns in Protestant theology in reaction to the Enlightenment and the loss of a religious worldview. Generally speaking, orthodoxy clings to its traditional theological positions; Pietism flees from rational criticism of religion to the safe harbour of the subjective religious experiences of the individual; liberal theology tries to reconcile the Christian message with the views of the Enlightenment by digging out the core message of Christianity from the Bible and building hermeneutical bridges for the understanding of the message by modern minds; and political theology accepts the principles of the Enlightenment and tries to show that the Christian faith is in line with this thinking if we understand it as realizing the ideals of modern people: liberation from oppressive structures and political oppression, eradication of poverty and restoration of human dignity (cf. Jonker 2008, pp. 135–137). There are mixed models of these extreme positions in Protestant theology, but a brief overview of the theological reactions shows the intensity of the theological debate in its efforts to digest the radical cultural changes that have taken place in the church in the past three hundred years.

One cannot ignore the challenges that come with religious exercises in the workplace. This might create discomfort to other members whose religion might be against the practices of others. The aim of practical theology in this context is not to promote a certain religion, but it is rather to use the pastoral care common to all religions to promote healthy human relations in society at large.

Pastoral care seeks to improve human relations while respecting a person's faith, even regardless of the faith (or lack of faith), with an underlying look to God and without the caregiver denying his or her own faith.

Felicity Kelcourse (2002, p. 146) says that pastoral counselling can be understood as a form of prayer, through faith hearing another attend to that of God in them. However, due to diversity in the workplace, the practice of pastoral counselling with biblical texts is not always applicable to all employees. Pastoral counselling therefore should not be limited to just one religion. It is wrong to limit pastoral counselling exclusively to Christians or to a certain group of people. Comfort and care can and must cross religions without proselytizing or judging.

The study of theology does not only cover Christian beliefs, but it also involves a brief introduction into different religious groups found within the scholars' country. Pastors should therefore be open to becoming care givers with sensitivity to matters of faith and a sensitivity to a diversity of religions in the workplace and in community. Denton in Naidoo (2014, p. 2) argues that research suggests that when considering how to bring spirituality into the workplace, organisational cultures need to be transformed collectively, and this should be done by transforming leadership where spiritual practices and values are incorporated into culture of the organisation.

2. Challenge to Practical Theology

There are at least six challenges to practical theology:

1. To explore sensitivity to different religious practices and rites within the workplace;
2. To study other religious beliefs and practices rather than focus on just one religion;
3. To explore ways to bridge the gap between Christians and other religions in the workplace;
4. To explore ways to bring men, work, and family together;
5. To explore ways theology can be more relevant to everyday struggles in the workplace professionally;
6. To explain the different disciplines within the study of theology (practical theology, pastoral care, liturgical studies, family counseling, trauma counseling, dogmatic, church history, missiology, systematic theology, liberation theology, black theology, OT & NT studies, etc.)

According to Dreyer and Pieterse (2010, p. 1), there are many questions regarding the role of religion in the public sphere. How must we deal with the issues of religious education in public schools? How do we deal with different religious calendars in our business life? How should we view prayers at public gatherings? How do we deal with religious groups' petitions regarding the death penalty, abortion, same-sex marriage? How do we deal with atheists' claims to freedom of speech? These demonstrate the presence of religions in the public sphere.

Practical Christian theology attempts to not merely preach the gospel, but to "care" for the person as a human being first without prejudice to that person's religion. One cannot expect a Christian to teach Islam, but a

Christian can give human care to a Muslim without being threatened by that Muslim's faith.

In order to explore this research, Osmer's approach to practical theology will be used (2008, p. 4):

- What is going on?
- Why is this going on?
- What ought to be going on?
- How might we respond?

Osmer (2008, p. 4) regards these as of utmost importance when dealing with practical theology research. We give a few proposed answers to these questions in the context of this paper.

a. What is going on?

One of the basic human rights in South Africa is for one to have the freedom of choice of religion, yet some feel that this right is discriminated against at work. People feel as though they are being forced to shy away from their spiritual practices in their workplace. When then does this basic human right start and when does it end? The spirituality in the workplace is limited mostly to Christians, and Christianity is often seen as the rightful choice of religion in South Africa. Some workplaces also limit workers' practice of their religious beliefs due to the rules that come with working in a certain company. When other religions enter a mostly Christian work place, there is no small dilemma.

b. Why is this going on?

The dilemma is complicated when the Christian faith has the highest percentage of adherents in South Africa. Religion is often seen as divisive and unhelpful in the work environment. Consequently, there has often been a failure in one or more of the six challenges just mentioned.

Even though all employees do not often belong to the same religious faith, they often have to deal with the faith issues the majority of the employees belong to. When your boss is a Christian, he might at the end of the day in his speech end by saying "May God bless you" or "we thank God for a project well done." Statements such as these might bring discomfort to an employee who does not believe in God (for whatever reasons they might have). When looking at the country of South Africa as a whole, Christian holidays are celebrated and acknowledged more than any other religion in the country. This might limit knowledge and even the practice of holidays celebrated by other religions.

c. What ought to be going on?

Organizations need to be well informed and aware of other religious groups, their rights, and their rituals. They also need to be sensitive when speaking about faith, values, and morals. It is wrong for any organization to assume values, morals, faith, and ethics are the same for all employees. The point of argument is not to change any organization into a church or spirituality society. But employees should have the right to pray or not to pray, to believe or not to believe, and the *right* to talk of a different god or believe differently without offending others. And those of faiths different from the majority ought to have the *right* to believe and practice without persecution for their faith.

d. How might we respond?

One also needs to find a theory on how to sensitize a freedom of spirituality in the workplace. The mostly Christian South African universities need to create awareness that includes other religious groups in its studies. When we talk of pastoral care givers, it is not only limited to Christians. We can respond theologically by doing more research on other religious faiths. Organizations can also include five minutes of "silence" every day at work to allow individuals to talk to their gods in a way that is not harmful to others and to the organization. Organizations can also organize annual events where employees are taught or introduced to different faiths outside of the organizations.

Conclusion

Dreyer and Pieterse (2010, p. 6) state that if we, as religious people representing the churches, want to join the public debate on the burning issues in South Africa society, we have to accept our secular state, our constitution with its liberal values of a modern state, and renounce any claim to a monopoly on power.

According to Scott Manetsch (2013, p. 94), Calvin and his colleagues believed pastoral ministry to be of especially "crucial importance" for the life of the community. Kelcourse (2002, p. 146) says that pastoral counselling can be understood as a form of prayer. He adds (2002) that in therapy an interpersonal dialogue is formed between the pastoral counsellor and counselee where God is present. Today, some of the weakness of pastors and care givers is that they tend to preach about what they are told or heard, and that makes it hard for people to come forward to their pastors without fearing their story might be part of the sermon on a Sunday morning. A wise pastor cares and is careful to guard all confidential information.

We agree with Baloyi (2013) that the church should become a centre of healing and not a show. Klein in Baloyi (2013, p. 14) invites every local church to become a centre of healing and transformation through holistic counselling services. The psychological help that modern society affords can help those who are overtaken by the dangerous fanatics who turn Christian faith upside-down with people eating grass, snakes, drinking fuel, or having "DOOM" sprayed in their face all in the name of healing. Pastoral care for these can gently lead them into the fold of a more wholesome and true Christian faith.

Even with all the challenges that Christianity faces in this context, a practical theology can have a positive effect in fostering healthy human relations.

14.
"Women Don't Like Nice Guys"—
Dating, Attraction, and Christian Values:
Teaching Our Young People How to Fall in Love

Dr. Walter S. Chung
Director and Professor of Online Programming,
Eastern University, St. Davids, PA
and Coordinator of Applied Behavior Analysis,
The Chicago School of Professional Psychology

Stephanie Chung
Chair and Professor of Special Education and
Co-founding Director of Online Applied Behavior Analysis
Cairn University, Langhorne, PA[488]

Introduction 203
A. Theology of Love 204
   1. Love Is the Central 204
   2. Nature of Love 204
   3. Forms of Love 206
B. Major Research Findings of Love in Psychological literature 206
C. Teaching Young People to Love 208
   1. Find Secure Love in God 208
   2. Cultivate Agape Love 210
   3. Practice Erotic Love within the Boundary of Marriage 211
   4. Develop Skills to Maintain Love 212
   5. Seek God's Guidance 212
Conclusion 213

Introduction

Is it true that women don't like nice guys? This question is so popular that a Google search can easily yield over 640 million results.[489] If women truly dislike nice guys and instead turn their attention to "bad boys," who

---

[488] Walter Chung, PhD, BCBA-D, CRC, LPC, LBS, is the founding director and professor of the Online Counseling Program and coordinator of Applied Behavior Analysis Concentration, Eastern University, and adjunct professor, Online Applied Behavior Analysis Program, The Chicago School of Professional Psychology (TCSPP). He was professor and director of professional practice in applied behavior analysis for The Chicago School of Professional Psychology between 2016 and 2018. At the same time at Cairn University, he and his wife, Dr. Stephanie Chung, co-founded the first fully online Christian Master's Degree program in applied behavior analysis in the world (focusing on Autism) and that included a board-certified behavior analyst program. See www.eastern.edu/walter-chung and wchung@eastern.edu.
Stephanie Chung, EdD, BCBA, LBS, is Chair and Professor of Special Education Department, Co-founding director of Online Applied Behavior Analysis Programs, Cairn University. See schung @cairn.edu and https://cairn.edu/team/stephanie-chung/. They have co-authored several technical articles, and both serve as reviewers of several technical journals.
[489] Google asked on April 21, 2020.

are in fact narcissistic and dominant, then it will be a challenge to convince the young generation to value and live with the biblical perspective of love. In their book *Mating Intelligence Unleashed: The Role of the Mind in Sex, Dating, and Love*, psychologists Glenn Geher and Scott Barry Kaufman (2013) reviewed many existing scientific studies of mating and presented a more optimistic conclusion. Bad boys with aggressive and manipulative characteristics are actually not considered attractive by women. When women state that they dislike nice guys, they are referring to those "overly nice and submissive guys" who tend to lack self-confidence (p. 192). In fact, women prefer men who display not only the characteristic of assertiveness (i.e., confidence) but also the virtue of agreeableness or kindness (p. 183). At least two implications can be drawn from these research findings: (a) It is acceptable to be godly, because nice guys do not necessarily finish last; and (b) the church has the role of educating young people about falling in love and building a healthy long-term relationship in the midst of inundations of false ideas of love from a variety of different sources, especially social media.

Therefore, the purpose of this paper is to develop an understanding of love based on the Bible and examine how existing research aligns with the biblical perspective of love. We will then propose how the theology of love can be practically applied to teach our young people how to fall in love.

A. Theology of Love

1. Love Is the Central

To understand love correctly, we should begin with the Bible. As revivalist David J. Lewis (1900) once stated, "Love is the center of all God's dealings, and all of His laws; as love is the center of the Bible, the center of Christianity" (p. 265). Specifically, the Bible provides us with detailed information about the nature of love and forms of love in our relationships.

2. Nature of Love

From the Bible, we first learn that love is good because it originates from God. In 1 John 4:7, the Apostle John wrote that "love is from God ... for God is love." Oswald Chambers (1985) further elucidated the meaning of this scripture by emphasizing "the eternal fact that God is love, not, God is loving. God and love are synonymous. Love is not an attribute of God, it is God; whatever God is, love is" (p. 12). In the Book of Genesis, the climax of creation occurred on the sixth day when God created man and woman to experience His love through intimate fellowship with Him and enjoy their love for one another through marriage (Gen 1: 26–31, 2:18–24). Love was created by the Lord and was a beautiful reflection of His image because "God, as Trinity, exists in a fellowship of love" (Ferguson, 1987, p. 31). Love was also perfect and good, indicated first through the intimate fellowship between humans and God (Gen 2:15–20) and then later through the transcendent interaction between husband and wife (Gen 2:23–24). The implication of being created in God's love is that man and woman were created with the desire and ability to love, as well as to develop healthy relationships with others. The constant, intimate fellowship with God provided man and woman with a sense of security, acceptance, and significance. In perfect love, they did not feel any shame (Gen 2:25) and "the result was a totally secure self-image, which is possible only when one's identity is totally in God" (Kirwan, 1984, p. 76).

The second truth we derive from the Bible is that love can become agonizing and grotesque when distorted by sin. The fall of Adam and Eve (Gen 3) ushered sin into the world and produced negative repercussions on human beings and their relationship with God. Sin has swept darkness and corruption into the perfect, loving relationship among human beings who, in their depravity, have become competitive, incapable of empathizing, rebellious against authority, and unable to love (Erickson, 1992). This warped relationship among human beings is clearly illustrated by Genesis 3:11–16. Van Leeuwen (1990) argued that one implication of this broken human relationship in marriage is that male's original dominion over his wife and family has now become male domination. Sherlock (1996) echoed Van Leeuwan's view, emphasizing that even though the relationship between men and women continues, the original loving partnership "has turned into rivalry" and "dominion has become corrupted into exploitation" (pp. 42–43).

Theologian Millard Erickson (1992) believed that sin has further distorted the identity of human beings. After the fall, human beings have assumed the identity of sinners before God (Rom 3:23), possessing characteristics such as enslavement, flight from reality, denial of sin, self-deceit, insensitivity, self-centeredness, and restlessness. Kirwan (1984) postulated that the three essential characteristics of human identity after the fall are rejection, shame, and weakness or helplessness. He elaborated on the meaning of Genesis 3:7–10 as below:

> When Adam told God that he hid because he was afraid, he was saying in essence, "I have lost God, so I no longer belong. I am afraid and insecure". He was also saying, "I have lost perfection, so I no longer feel a sense of self-esteem. Instead I feel guilty and ashamed."... Adam was God's foreman, commissioned to subdue the earth and able to live in happiness without fear . . . Now he no longer had that strength. He undoubtedly felt inferior and insignificant. (pp. 81–82)

In other words, human beings have been stripped of their sense of security and harmony as fully illustrated in Genesis 3:7–10. Such feelings of shame, weakness, fear, and insecurity cripple their ability to enjoy fellowship with God and loving relationships with one another.

The third truth we gain from the Bible is that the goodness and beauty of love distorted by sin have been redeemed and restored by Jesus Christ. In describing Christ's redemption, Dillistone (1983) wrote, "By identifying Himself with humans in their temptations, trials, hopelessness, suffering and death [Jesus] paid an immeasurably costly price and brought into being a new humanity, bearing His own image and committed to following His example" (p. 488). Christ's redemptive work brings a new reality to humankind which includes not only the restoration of the relationship between God and human beings but also reconciliation among humans (Sherlock, 1996). Through the redemptive work of Jesus Christ, human beings regain the ability to love and enjoy its goodness and beauty. As theologian, Sinclair B. Ferguson (1989) stated, "The key to such restoration lies in the recovery of man to his original honor, dignity, privilege and responsibility. Reconciling all things to God, therefore, means fundamentally restoring to man the image that he reflected perfectly at creation but later marred by his sin" (p. 10).

3. Forms of Love

Other than the nature of love, the Bible also informs us that love is multifaceted. In his classic book *The Four Loves*, C. S. Lewis (1960) thoughtfully analyzed the four types of human love including affection (*storge*), friendship (*phileo*), erotic love (*eros*), and love of God (*agape*). Many bible scholars such as Charles Stanley (2015) and John Piper (1975) agreed with Lewis's belief that different types of love can be found in the Bible. For instance, sacrificial love (*agape*) is beautifully expressed in John 3:16, brotherly and friendship love (*phileo*) can be found in Hebrews 13:1, and romantic or erotic love (*eros*) is fully illustrated in Song of Solomon 1:1–4. These forms of love have been well discussed in many pieces of Christian literature for centuries.

B. Major Research Findings of Love in Psychological literature

Since the 1970s, psychologists have begun to pay attention to the scientific study of love and intimate relationships. Researchers approached the topic from various perspectives, and some research findings provided interesting evidence to illustrate and support the biblical perspective of love. For example, based on the attachment theory of love, psychologists conducted a number of studies and found that adults who have insecure attachment patterns (e.g., feeling anxious about relationships or avoiding relationships) tend to have a less positive experience of love and greater relationship dissatisfaction, echoing the biblical truth that the feelings of shame, fear, and insecurity due to sin can weaken the human ability to enjoy loving relationships (Shaver, Hazan, and Bradshaw, 1989). Attachment psychologists believe that insecure adults, who struggled in their relationship with their parents during childhood, hold pessimistic beliefs and expectations for their love relationship. Therefore, they have greater chances of experiencing relationship conflicts and domestic violence due to their failure in controlling their anger, jealousy, and pain. On the contrary, individuals with secure attachment are optimistic about their love relationship and are more willing to tolerate differences as well as work through problems. Consequently, they are able to have "more stable romantic and marital relationships, greater intimacy, higher relationship satisfaction, and stronger commitment to their partners and families" (Shaver, Mikulincer, and Feeney, 2009, p. 495).

The *Love-Styles Theory and Triangular Theory of Love* assert a similar theme that love is multifaceted, consistent with what Scripture has already revealed through the ages. The Love-Styles Theory was proposed by Alan Lee in 1970s. Through extensive literature review and interviewing of subjects about their past love experiences, Lee (1977) identified six common love styles which include *agape* (selfless love), *eros* (passionate love), *mania* (obsessive and jealous love), *ludus* (game-playing love), *pragma* (practical love seeking compatibility in social and personal qualities), and *storge* (friendship or companionship love). Research indicated that the most affirming love style is agape, the least preferred love type is *ludus*, and people tend to date those who share a similar love style (Hahn and Blass, 1997). However, some love styles, such as mania and ludus, or storge and mania, have difficulties finding an appropriate match since the expectations are so different that conflict is inevitable (Lee, 1988).

The Triangular Theory of Love was proposed by Robert Steinberg in the mid-1980s. According to Steinberg (1986), love consists of three components which are intimacy (i.e., close and bonded feelings), passion (i.e., romantic, physical and sexual drives), and commitment (i.e., decision to love and maintain the loving relationship). Eight types of love can be generated by the different combinations of these three components which include nonlove (casual relationships, absence of all three components), liking (intimacy alone), infatuation (passion alone, "love at first sight"), empty love (commitment alone), romantic love (intimacy and passion), companionate love (intimacy and commitment), and consummate/complete love (intimacy, passion and commitment). Steinberg believed that some types of love, such as fatuous love, infatuated love, and empty love are unhealthy and highly vulnerable to distress. Consummate love is the healthiest type of loving relationship even though it is difficult to be attained and maintained.

To further validate the aforementioned research findings about love in psychology literature, we conducted a large scale survey among emerging adults (i.e., age 18–25 as defined by Jeffrey Arnett, 2000) to examine their love styles attitude, their sense of attachment, and how the two variables may relate to their marital/dating relationship satisfaction. A total of 445 emerging adults participated in the study and completed various standardized instruments, such as the Relationship Questionnaire (Bartholomew and Horowitz, 1991), the Love Attitudes Scale—Short Form (Hendrick, Hendrick, and Dicke, 1998), and the Relationship Assessment Scale (Hendrick, Dicke, and Hendrick, 1998). The results of one-way ANOVA analysis indicated a preference for three types of love: *eros* (passionate love), *agape* (altruistic love), and *storge* (friendship love) are significantly more popular or preferable than the *pragma* (practical love), *mania* (possessive, dependent love), and *ludus* (game-playing love). A stepwise regression analysis showed that an emerging adult who has a secure attachment pattern, stronger *eros* and *agape* love, and has less *ludus* and *mania* love will have a higher chance of experiencing a satisfactory relationship with his/her partner/spouse. In sum, our study not only confirmed the existence of love types but also validated the importance of having secure attachment and certain love styles (i.e., *agape* and *eros*) in marital/dating relationship satisfaction.

C. Teaching Young People to Love

Both the biblical perspective of love and research findings concerning love from the psychological literature provide at least the following five implications for the church to teach young people how to fall in love: (1) find secure love in God, (2) cultivate agape love, (3) practice erotic love within the boundary of marriage, (4) develop skills to maintain love, and (5) seek God's guidance.

1. Find Secure Love in God

Since the sense of secure attachment plays a key role in successful loving relationship, it would be beneficial for the church to help young people understand and internalize their identity in Christ. Doing so increases their sense of security in relationships and diminishes the chances of exhibiting anxiety or avoidance. This may also enable them to take more appropriate approaches to their loving relationships. It is important to have young people come to the realization that they are created to be God's beloved. This love is graphically portrayed in the parable of the lost son in Luke 15:11–31, as well as in Ephesians 1:4 which declares that God has intentionally created each individual to be His Beloved: "Long before [God] laid down earth's foundations, He had us in mind, had settled on us as the focus of His love, to be made whole and holy by His love" (New American Standard Bible).

So, what is the best way to guide young people into experiencing the love of God? To experience the love of God, young people should learn to embrace God's messages of love in the Bible, believing them as truth. The Bible paints a radical image of God's view of His children which should translate into their view of themselves and others. Through flowing words and beautiful descriptions of the Lord's divine love, Zephaniah 3:17 captures this picture: "The LORD your God ... will exult over you with joy, He will be quiet in His love, He will rejoice over you with shouts of joy." This verse clearly depicts the abundant devotion and tenderness that God possesses for His people. Rather than turning His face away in shame of His children's failures or sins, the Lord boasts of His love for them through His shouts of joy. This unchanging, rejoicing love of God for the young person provides the value to his/her existence. Because he/she is already loved by the Creator, there is no need for the person to strive to be accepted by the world and meet its ever-changing expectations. Through Christ's work on the cross, God has accepted him/her completely (Heb 10:14). For young people, this truth can shatter their chains of insecurity and usher them into a golden future where they can feel free to be who they are without fear of rejection. This freedom can help spark new motivation for positive behaviors in the young person's interaction with his/her partner.

Another practice that may enrich young people's experience of God's love is taking time to revitalize their spirit by basking in God's all-embracing love throughout the day. In exhorting Christians to keep themselves in the love of God, Oswald Chambers (1985) elucidated, "Keep means work. It is not a lazy floating, it is work" (p. 19). It may benefit young people if they pause to hear God whisper "My Beloved" to them, as well as meditate on how God watches over them with complete joy. Henri Nouwen (2002) stated:

> [Experiencing our Belovedness] means letting the truth of our Belovedness become enfleshed in everything we think, say, or do.... Every time you feel hurt, offended or rejected, you have to dare to say to yourself: These feelings, strong as they may be, are not telling me the truth about myself. The truth, even though I cannot feel it right now, is that I am the chosen child of God, precious in God's eyes, [and] called the Beloved from all eternity. (pp. 45, 49)

Furthermore, Nouwen advised Christians to always give thanks to God for choosing them as His Beloved. In other words, young people need to constantly lift up praises to the glorious God for His wondrous love. As C. S. Lewis (1994) explained, praising God begets more joy and celebration in each Christian: "I think we delight to praise what we enjoy because the praise not merely expresses but completes the enjoyment; it is its appointed consummation ... [The] delight is incomplete till it is expressed" (p. 179). Therefore, exuding streams of praise and thanksgiving to God will more completely express and release within the young people the full fountain of joy and celebration.

2. Cultivate Agape Love

Agape love refers to the love that is sacrificial and completely dedicated to the well-being of another person (Stanley, 2015). In other words, agape love is a selfless or altruistic love. We are called to "walk in the way of love, just as Christ loved [*agape*] us and gave himself up for usas a fragrant offering and sacrifice to God" (Eph 5:2). *Agape* lovers choose to love in abundance and do not expect anything in return. Other characteristics of agape lovers include being patient and non-emotional, forgiving, non-demanding, willing to support others, and believing in honesty in relationships (Hahn and Blass, 1997). J. A. Lee (1998) believed that *agape* love is difficult to be practiced in adult dating or marital relationships due to the "enlightened self-interest that pervades the ideology of our commercial, political, and even educational institutions. A gentle, patient, caring love without motives of self-interest is difficult to find even in those helping professions supposedly organized to supply it in the form of healing and therapy" (p. 48). To help young people cultivate agape love by overcoming their self-interest, we can recommend them to practice the self-management model based on Galatians 6:7–8: "Do not be deceived; God cannot be mocked. A man reaps what he sows. Whoever sows to please their flesh, from the flesh will reap destruction; whoever sows to please the Spirit, from the Spirit will reap eternal life."

Assume Brad and Julie have planned to enjoy a date at the theaters and watch the movie "Rogue One—A Star War Story." They agree to meet at 7:00 pm. Brad waits for Julie at the gate, but she does not arrive until 7:45 pm. At that moment, Brad has two choices laid out before him. He can decide to please the flesh, serve himself, and manipulate Julie by screaming at her and storming away. However, he could also choose to please the Spirit, serve God, and minister to Julie by listening to her and ensuring that she is safe.

However, good intentions can be challenging to maintain. Brad may be able to lovingly minister to Julie on days that he feels that he can be kind and sacrificial toward her. However, on other days, he may find himself struggling and wanting to give in to his flesh and belittling her instead. Similarly, Julie may also work diligently at being patient and understanding but may also find herself battling the urge to quarrel with Brad when he gets demeaning. Both feel that the standard is too high to reach. Like Paul, they say that "I do not understand what I do. For what I want to do I do not do, but what I hate I do" (Rom 7:15). However, thank God that He did not save us for us to live the perfect Christian life or show Christian love through our own striving. Along with our salvation, He has given us the power to live godly lives. In John 15:5, Jesus said, "I am the vine; you are the branches. If you remain in me and I in you, you will bear much fruit; apart from me you can do nothing." Demonstrating agape love is fruit that we will bear if we abide in Christ through constantly connecting with Him through prayer and letting His life flow into our lives. When we feel a struggle coming on, we lift up our hearts to Jesus and focus on Him, trusting that He will carry us through that very moment and the next and the next until we experience victory.

3. Practice Erotic Love within the Boundary of Marriage

Erotic love refers to passionate love, and the experience is normally emotional, intense, and affectionate (Hahn and Blass, 1997). Due to the high psychophysiological involvement and experiential salience, Steinberg (1986) perceived that passionate love is not only necessary for short-term relationships but is also moderately important for maintaining long-term relationships. However, passionate love tends to have low stability, especially when erotic lovers believe in "love at first sight" while expecting "intimacy, including sexual intimacy, right from the beginning of a relationship" (Hahn and Blass, 1997, p. 597). Engaging in sexual intimacy outside of marriage not only contradicts the counsel of Scripture (e.g., Gal 5:19,

1 Cor 6:18) but also leads to the pitfall of increasing one's chances of divorce. For example, analyzing the data from the three waves of the National Survey of Family Growth collected between 2002 and 2013, Wolfinger (2016) found that women with zero to one sexual partner before marriage were the least likely to divorce, as compared to women with two or more sexual partners before marriage. Even for the women who married in the 1990s and had one sexual partner before marriage, their odds of divorce were 75% higher than the women who married as virgins. For women married in the 2000s, the odds of divorce for those who had one sexual partner before marriage increased to 154% compared to their peers who married as virgins. Therefore, practicing erotic love within the boundary of marriage is not only biblical but also allows young couples to reap the rewards of a lasting marriage. As such, the church can provide guidance toward cultivating a relationship that honors biblical boundaries by using principles such as those advocated by Cloud and Townsend (2000) in their book *Boundaries in Dating*. Cloud and Townsend suggested that dating individuals should learn to recognize the signs of speeding too quickly into physical intimacy, the possible contributing factors of being too hasty, the advantages of delaying sex until marriage, and the strategies they can adopt to slow down the physical over-involvement during dating.

4. Develop Skills to Maintain Love

To have a successful dating relationship, both J. A. Lee (1988) and Steinberg (1988) believed that a person should identify his/her preferred style of love and then find a partner with the love style that will match his/her choice. In addition, supports need to be provided for couples to resolve any love style differences. However, Lee (1988) warned that couples who share similar love styles may not necessarily experience a lasting relationship (e.g., both partners have the ludus love style). A person's love style preference may also change as a result of time, specific situations, and experience. Therefore, it is valuable for dating young individuals to learn the skills that will maintain their loving relationships.

Byrne and Murnen (1998) suggested that three factors play a key role in promoting and sustaining a loving relationship: similarity (in values, attitudes, beliefs, interests, and personality), positive evaluation (in words and behaviors), and continuous excitement and stimulation (in various aspects of life together). Jeffery H. Larson (2000) further advised dating individuals to assess ten similarities in their relationships which are significant predictors of marital satisfaction. These ten similarities include the importance of marriage, the perception of gender roles, career development, finance (i.e., material wealth), autonomy (i.e., the extent of individuality and privacy in marriage), sex expectations, family planning, couple boundaries (i.e., the extent of disclosing marriage issues to others), religious beliefs and practice, and general background characteristics (e.g., ethnicity and race, socio-economic status, age, educational level). Other specific skills young individuals may need to learn are skills for communication, conflict resolution, flexibility (e.g., sharing leadership equally, switching roles or responsibilities), and creating intimacy. All these are the strengths of happy couples identified by Olson and Olson (2000) after they surveyed 5,153 happily married couples and 5,127 unhappily married couples.

5. Seek God's Guidance

Young people today are not only eager to have a dating partner but are also willing to seek one through online dating. According to the Pew Center Research, online dating among young adults age 18 to 24 has surged up from 10% in 2013 to 27% in 2015, a triple increase (Smith and Anderson, 2016). The results of the Pew Research Center survey also indicated that 23% of adults agree that people who use online dating sites are desperate. Whether this is true or not, one important exhortation from God's Word is to "trust in theLORD with all your heartand lean not on your own understanding; in all your ways submit to him, and he will make your paths straight" (Prov 3:5–6). Although young people would do well to follow the above principles for establishing a godly and positive love relationship, the most important principle of all is to trust and seek God's guidance. The God who created us in our mother's womb, ordained our days before one of them came to be, and also sent His Son to be a Sacrifice to redeem us from our sins is intimately involved in every aspect of our lives, even our love and marriage life (Psalm 139:13–16; John 3:16).

Conclusion

Even though nine out of ten people marry by age 50 in the U.S., the projected divorce rate is estimated to be 40 to 50 percent, and the rate of divorce risk is even higher for those who are remarried (American Psychological Association, n.d.). For young people who live in a culture of divorce in the midst of a rising generation of narcissism among millennials (Pedersen, n.d.), it is a challenge to learn how to love and develop healthy long-term loving relationships. It is imperative for the church to hold on to the biblical truth of love, recognize the scientific research findings that are consistent with the biblical perspective of love, and support the young people to love successfully by finding their secure love in God, cultivating agape love, practicing erotic love within the boundary of marriage, developing essential skills to maintain love, and above all, seeking God's guidance.

A great treasure unfolds for a couple who respects God's truths and that dedicate themselves to highest forms of true love.

15.
Judgmental Attitudes and Their Impact on Our Pastoral Effectiveness

Kevaughn Mattis
Founder and Director, *Testamentum Imperium*[490]

"I like your Christ, I do not like your Christians.
Your Christians are so unlike your Christ."
Mahatma Gandhi[491]

Introduction 215
A. Personal Journey in Grace 216
   1. My History in Seventh-day Adventism 216
   2. Realizing the Struggle between Grace and Duty 216
   3. Approaching a Balance Based upon God's Revelation 217
   4. The Problem of Law and Idolatry 218
B. Three Ways to a Higher Quality of Pastoral Care 219
   1. Return to Transcendence 219
   2. Emphasize Covenantal Relationship with God and His Faithfulness ... 221
   3. Acknowledge the Continuing Struggle with Sin Despite the
      Spirit's Work in Covenant Relationship with God 224
Conclusion on Our Pastoral Effectiveness 229

Introduction

One of the most frequently expressed criticisms of Christianity in modern times is that it cultivates moral contempt and divisiveness. These sentiments are essentially held in two schools of thought:

1. **First,** there are those who are deeply troubled by the judgmental attitudes of Christians and who believe that certain traditional doctrines and schools of thought are responsible for that. However, this conviction does not lead them to reject the Christian faith in toto.
2. **Secondly,** there are those who view Christianity as a judgmental religion in its essence. It naturally produces hateful and hypercritical people. They

---

[490] Mattis earned his LLB with honors from the University of London, UK, and his LPC from BPP Law School, Manchester, UK, and he practices law in Trinidad, Tobago. He founded *Testamentum Imperium* (Great Testament) around 2005 with requests for articles on the security of the Christian believer from scholars all over the world, www.PreciousHeart.net/ti. Of the first volume's 80 articles, 13 articles were published in *Perspectives on Eternal Security: Biblical, Historical, and Philosophical*, Foreword by H. Wayne House, edited by Kirk R. MacGregor and Kevaughn Mattis (Wipf and Stock, 2009; 238 pp.). Volume 2 received 122 articles, volume 3 received 161 articles, and articles are nearly complete for volumes 4 and 5. This appears to be one of the largest collection of articles on the Great Testament of Christian eternal security anywhere in the world.
   See destinyfromthebeginning@hotmail.com.
[491] See www.searchquotes.com/search/Judgmental_Christians/2/.

believe that Christianity or religious belief as a whole should be discarded as an outdated worldview of a past era in human evolution. In this chapter, we will address the first school of thought.

A. Personal Journey in Grace
1. My History in Seventh-day Adventism

Growing up in the Seventh-day Adventist Church in the Caribbean, our denomination has affirmed the Reformation doctrines of *sola fide* and *sola gratia*, and yet the assurance of salvation has proven to be an elusive congregational experience in the church's history.[492] In no small way, this elusiveness results from the difficulty of trying to hold together the doctrines of *sola fide* with the more traditional versions of the Seventh-day Adventist doctrine of the heavenly sanctuary/investigative judgment and its remnant eschatology.[493] By definition, the remnant constitutes the saved amongst humanity. The defining mark of this group is that they manifest an intense degree of faithfulness and loyalty to God in the midst of a sin-enslaved world that persecutes them. In the final chapter of human history, the believers who remain faithful to the commandments of God, including the seventh-day Sabbath (Seventh-day Adventists), will be persecuted by the world governed by the anti-christ until Christ delivers his saints into eternal glory and judges the world at the second coming. As an adherent of traditional Seventh-day Adventism I viewed my faith as an indictment on Protestantism which had failed to complete the Reformation of the church by developing a robust doctrine of sanctification and rejection of the idolatrous practice of viewing Sunday as the Lord's Sabbath day.

This theology caused me deep anguish. Was I to think that every believer who attended church on Sunday was lost? Was I correct to believe that God's remnant would only consist of professing believers whose faithfulness was obvious and exceptional?

2. Realizing the Struggle between Grace and Duty

One lesson keenly learnt from my own ecclesial experience is the sobering reality that affirming the doctrine of "Righteousness by Faith," as we Adventists call it, does not secure an enduring and meaningful assurance of salvation. To make the point more generally, affirming the doctrines of *sola gratia*, *sola fide* and *solo Christos* do not guarantee the eradication of legalism—given the fact that one's theology of grace has to give account for the warning passages in scripture and the reality of judgment according to

---

[492] That is, *sola fide*, "by faith alone"; and *sola gratia*, "by grace alone."

[493] A definition of the traditional doctrine of the heavenly sanctuary/investigative judgment may be found at the ministry for former Adventist established by Dale Ratzlaff, Life Assurance Ministries, See http://lifeassuranceministries.com/investjudg.html.

works. Furthermore, attempting to affirm the unconditionality of grace in the midst of the frustration and angst of dealing with nominal and unremorseful professing believers is a task easier said than done.

3. Approaching a Balance Based upon God's Revelation

Without claiming any superior insight on the subject, my more reflective moments have led me to a train of thought regarding why so many of us desire to be grace filled and Christ centered but often end up being sectarian and judgmental. It seems to me that our failure to be a more gracious community is in part consequent upon the fact that divine transcendence has not properly shaped our theologies of grace.[494] We believe that through scripture, God has accommodated to our creaturely incapacity to know Him. His word enlightens our ignorance and permits us to make clear and certain (and perhaps at times even infallible) judgments about what the parameters and limits of God's redemptive graces truly are, and what humans beings must and must not do in order to become the beneficiaries of God's saving mercy. So, on the one hand, we affirm that God is unlike anything we know, that his ways are "above our ways," incomprehensible, and that we cannot truly understand or fully grasp God's essence.[495] Yet, on the other hand, we believe that through God's gracious self-revelation of his law and character, we can know God's judgments and predict his actions. Consequently, our doctrine of divine transcendence has not deeply shaped our theology of the grace of God. In other words, saving grace is no longer an inscrutable mystery[496]

---

[494] See support of this in William Carl Placher's *The Domestication of Transcendence: How Modern Thinking about God Went Wrong* (Westminster John Knox, 1996), esp. chapter 6, "The Domestication of Grace," 88–110. There indeed appears to be a relationship between the domestication of transcendence and the domestication of God's grace.

[495] See the article, "The Ineffable, Inconceivable, and Incomprehensible God: Fundamentality and Apophatic Theology," Jonathan D. Jacobs; www.MarcSandersFoundation.org/wp-content/uploads/Jacobs-Phil-Fundamentality-and-Apophatic-Theology.pdf. See also Karl Barth's notion of God as, "wholly other" in, *The Westminster Handbook to Karl Barth*, edited by Richard E. Burnett (Louisville: Westminster John Knox Press, 2013), 220–222. The term was first coined by Rudolf Otto in his *The Idea of the Holy*, 2nd ed., trans. John W. Harvey (Oxford, England: Oxford University Press, 1958), but was later attributed to Barth for his role in developing the idea.

[496] In Pádraic Conway and Fáinche Ryan's, eds., *Karl Rahner: Theologian for the Twenty-first Century* (Peter Lang AG, Internationaler Verlag der Wissenschaften; 2010), 45, the authors said: "Rahner believers that it is the anthropomorphic nature of the religion of this era, its abundance of man-made rules and regulations that make it difficult for people of the twentieth century to listen to, to believe in religion, and thus to have faith in God. Mystery is recognized as the missing link in Rahner's world, but a mystery which is welcoming, some-what fathomable. Balance, as always is the key. Rahner is warning against a too facile attempt to explain all that is, for this is not what will lead us to God. This is an appeal to Christians to remember God in the midst of rules and regulations, to remember that faith is not built on law but on mystery."

4. The Problem of Law and Idolatry

The Pauline Epistles and the Gospel narratives of Jesus have gifted to us a deep psychoanalytical insight into the way that we as human beings often engage in the idolatry of worshipping the law in the place of the lawgiver.[497]

Any system of righteousness that is ultimately rooted in law will stir the very heart of man to rebel. This is the counterintuitive logic of the gospel. And one of the clearest ways in which the law has caused us as believers to rebel is through divisiveness and overly judgmental attitudes of exclusion (Gal 5:15). Testimony to this is found in Tony Richie's article, "A Pentecostal Take on Islamophobia":

> Expulsion or banishment is at the core of the fallen human condition. Adam and Eve's exile is decisive and definitive for us all. "Banished" (*ṣālaḥ*) is the same language used of Abraham's action that "sends away" Ishmael and other possible rivals to Isaac (Gen 21:14; 25:6). It describes the scapegoat that is expelled from the camp of Israel (Lev 16:10). Still stronger is "drove" (*gāraš*) in Genesis 3:24, which also describes God's exile of Cain (4:14) and Sarah's charge to Abraham to "get rid" of the slave girl Hagar with her son (21:10). It is the language of divorce and dispossession (e.g., Exod 33:2; Deut 33:27). Is it some small coincidence that these incidents involve irrational fear and implacable strife against the other? Perhaps deep in each human being resides an abominable instinct, arising out of fallen, sinful nature, which casts out and drives others away in twisted reenactment of their own haunting sense of exclusion, otherness, and alienation. Matthew's Gospel teaches us that the danger of ultimate exclusion is not imaginary (Matt 8:12; 22:13; 25:30). But Jesus himself endured for us the darkness outside (Matt 22:53; 23:44; compare Heb 13:11, 13) and now all may stand before an open gate (Rev 21:25). If incessant anxiety over our innate sense of separation from God and each other is our damnation, then there is salvation too. Thus I agree with Miroslav Volf in Exclusion and Embrace, on the essentiality of reconciliation for the reality of Christian salvation. Exclusivist tendencies often stem from unconscious psychological and sociological concerns over one's own ultimate exclusion or inclusion. One who has the prerogative and power to exclude others does not see him/herself present among the excluded.[498]

Ritchie is typical of those striving to explain the ramifications of our fallen nature. Some tendencies to "exclude" certainly stem from our fallen nature and complicate our perceptions of God's grace.

---

[497] See for example, John 5:39 and Rom 10:1–10.

[498] Tony Richie, "A Pentecostal Take on Islamophobia," *Evangelical Interfaith Dialogue* (Evangelicals and Islamophobia: Critical Voices and Constructive Proposals; Fall 2016), 40. See https://fullerstudio.fuller.edu/wp-content/uploads/2016/10/Evangelicals-and-Islamophobia-Fall-2016.pdf.

Chris Vlachos articulated well the problem of humanity and the law in his book, *The Law and the Knowledge of Good and Evil*.[499] Vlachos focused on the law-critical statement of 1 Corinthians 15:56, "The sting of death is sin, and the power of sin is the law." According to Vlachos, the law plays a "catalytic role" with regard to sin: i.e., while the law is not the cause of sin, it serves as a catalyst which exacerbates existing sin. For Paul, the catalytic function of the law was not only active at Sinai (Rom 5:20), but existed since Eden, where the prohibition not to eat of the tree of knowledge triggered lurking evil into action. By premising the catalytic role of the law in Eden, Paul was establishing the Edenic commandment-sin scenario as archetypal: human failure occurs whenever the law encounters Adamic flesh. Such a theology of sin/law casts fresh light on Romans 6–7, where deliverance from the law occupies a central role in Paul's discussion of sanctification. According to Vlachos, "If it were law that drew the serpent out of the bush, then it would be freedom from law that necessarily and inevitably de-fangs sin and leads to good works."[500] Paradoxically, sin spawns in a "legal" climate (Rom 7:5), whereas righteousness flourishes in a "lawless" environment (Rom 7:6).[501]

B. Three Ways to a Higher Quality of Pastoral Care
1. Return to Transcendence

If we are to overcome our judgmental attitudes, we will have to find biblically grounded reasons for tempering our tendencies to hastily exclude professing believers from the family of God whenever their lives do not meet our approval. Given the course taken by this chapter, such biblical reasons can be found in nourishing our soteriology with a remedial dose of transcendence. The relationship between unfathomable grace and divine transcendence may be found in the dialogues between Moses and God in the Book of Exodus. In Exodus 3:14, at the scene of the burning bush, Moses asks God for His name. In response, God replies that, "I am that I am." In further dialogue with Moses in Exodus 33, God accedes to Moses' request to reveal His glory in a way that relates the Glory of God to God's Name and Goodness. More particularly, God's Name and Glory is revealed through His freedom to be merciful to whom He wills: "I will cause all my

---

[499] Chris Alex Vlachos, *The Law and the Knowledge of Good and Evil: The Edenic Background of the Catalytic Operation of the Law in Paul* (Wipf and Stock, 2009). Vlachos also articulated this view in "Law, Sin, and Death: An Edenic Triad? An Examination with Reference to 1 Corinthians 15:56," *JETS* 47, no. 2 (June 2004), 277–98.
See www.ETSJETS.org/files/JETS-PDFs/47/47-2/47-2-pp277-298_JETS.pdf.

[500] Vlachos, *Law and the Knowledge*.

[501] Vlachos, *Law and the Knowledge*. See also the references to "law" in Gal 5:18–23.

goodness to pass in front of you, and I will proclaim my name, the LORD, in your presence. I will have mercy on whom I will have mercy, and I will have compassion on whom I will have compassion" (Exod 33:19). On Exodus 33, O.T. scholar Peter J. Gentry states as follows:

> In a chiastic structure 'A B A' we have the word glory in verses 18 and 22 on either side of the explanation in verse 19: "I will cause my goodness to pass before you and proclaim my name." This explanation reveals that the glory of Yahweh can be described or discussed under two categories: the name of Yahweh and the goodness of Yahweh. If we consider the initial request in v. 13, where Moses says "show me your way," it would seem that the goodness of Yahweh in v. 19 is synonymous with the way of Yahweh in v. 13.
>
> Exodus 33:13 show me your way
> Exodus 33:18 show me your glory
> Exodus 33:19 I will cause my goodness to pass
>   before you and proclaim my name
> Exodus 33:22 when my glory passes by
>
> We may conclude then that the glory of Yahweh can be described under two categories: the name of Yahweh and the way of Yahweh…. Yahweh says in v. 20, "you cannot see my face" and reiterates in v. 23, "you will see my back, but not my face." The term "face" (פָּנִים) here entails a different figure of speech from that used in v. 14. By means of anthropomorphism, an analogy is drawn between the knowledge one may have of a human by a frontal view in which one can behold the face and a view of the backside which does not reveal the person in the same way. Thus Yahweh is using this figure of speech to instruct Moses that as a human, he cannot have full knowledge of God, but he can nonetheless have a true knowledge, albeit a partial knowledge.
>
> Exodus 33:20 "you cannot see my face"
> Exodus 33:23 "you will see my back but not my face"[502]

In her lecture, "Naming God and the Techné of Language: Can we Name God Wrongly?" Cambridge theologian Janet M. Soskice also reflected on Moses' encounter in dialogue with God in Exodus.[503] She underlined the fact that God's name—"I am who I am," *ego eimi ho on*—had been turned into a metaphysical abstraction in some Christian schools of thought: mercy

---

[502] Peter J. Gentry, "'The Glory of God': The Character of God's Being and Way in the World: Some Reflections on a Key Biblical Theology Theme" *Southern Baptist Theological Journal* 20, no. 1 (2016), 149–161; http://equip.sbts.edu/wp-content/uploads/2016/08/SBJT-20.1-Gentry-Gods-Being-Way.pdf. Gentry raises an important question in this piece, "The revelation of the glory of Yahweh in Exodus 33–34 leaves the reader engulfed in mystery and creates a major tension in the storyline of Scripture. How can *ḥesed* and *'ĕmet* describe the name or very being of God, since this Hebrew word-pair normally describes covenant relationships? A short answer is that the way God relates with His creation, e.g. in covenant, reflects and displays the nature of His being. In more abstract theological terms, God in His economy (i.e. what we see of His dealings in the world) is none other than God in His essence (i.e. how He is in Himself)."

[503] See www.youtube.com/watch?v=RS2ESOb8Kal.

had been excluded from among the essential attributes of God (Exod 3:14). However, Soskice argues that *ego eimi ho on* should be more precisely read as, "I am with you and will be with you" (Exod 33:12–21). What God is in His eternal being we cannot know, but we can know God in whom He is for us. And who is God for us but the God of Mercy? Soskice references Walter Kasper's theological affirmation that through the Exodus dialogues between God and Moses, it is revealed that Mercy is the very Name of God not invented by man but given to us by God.[504] Relating this insight to our discussion, if God has made His name and glory known to us through His freedom to have "mercy on whom He will," how can we use God's law to definitively shut each other out of the family of God? Would not this presume that we can see the Face of God contrary to the Exodus 33 narrative?

2. Emphasize Covenantal Relationship with God and His Faithfulness

Following from the above conversation on Exodus, we need to reconsider our covenant relationship with God as believers. For if, in some sense, we come to a partial knowledge of God's glory and God's name through His being in covenant with us, it begs this question: How do we understand our covenant relationship with God? In a gem of an article titled, "Covenant and Narrative, God and Time," Jeffrey J. Niehaus articulated that God has made covenants with humans which have been central to the progress of salvation history (Adamic, Noahic, Abrahamic, Mosaic, Davidic, and New covenants).[505] The O.T. presents the divine covenants in a narrative structure in which all of God's covenants with humanity are conducive toward the new covenant. The new covenant is the one covenant that endures into eternity fulfilling whatever was required, hoped for, or promised in the earlier covenants which were in fact paving the way for the new and everlasting covenant in human time.

This raises a few interesting questions about the implications of biblical covenants. The O.T. covenants are patterned after that of the Suzerain vassal treaties common in the Ancient Near East. The Sinai Covenant (Exod 19–24; 32–34) is an example of such a suzerain-vassal treaty/covenant where much emphasis falls on the obligations of the vassal (Israel) to perform the will of the Suzerain (Yahweh); i.e, the vassal agrees to perform upon an oath to the suzerain. Failure to pursue the obligations of the

---

[504] Cardinal Walter Kasper brought this point to life in his German publication on Mercy translated into English, *Mercy: the Essence of the Gospel and the Key to Christian Life* (Mahwah: Paulist Press, 2014).

[505] Jeffrey J. Niehaus, "Covenant and Narrative, God and Time," *Journal of the Evangelical Theological Society* 53, Vol. 3 (September 2010), 535–59. See www.etsjets.org/files/JETS-PDFs/53/53-3/Niehaus_JETS_53-3_pp_535-559.pdf.

covenant would result in the nation (not just certain individuals) being laid open to the curses affixed to the covenant. On the other hand, compliance would guarantee the blessing mentioned in connection with rewards of obedience contained within that covenant.

The Noahic and Abrahamic covenants, and others like them, are not limited solely to the vassal's obligations (human obligation), but also entail unilateral obligations that the Suzerain (Yahweh) has freely entered into and has committed Himself to perform. What is peculiar (perhaps unique) about this type of covenant is that although it follows the Suzerain-vassal pattern, the emphasis is placed on the obligations of the Suzerain. As O.T. scholar David Noel Freedman writes concerning the Abrahamic covenant:

> The covenant is formally of the suzerainty type, since the stipulations are imposed upon only one of the parties, who in turn is bound by oath. Strikingly, it is the suzerain who is obligated, not the vassal. The covenant is initiated by the suzerain and is unconditional in the sense that no demands are imposed upon Abraham.[506]

The co-existence of these variations in the covenants creates a tension in scripture. For one thing, Israel was unable to keep its obligations to God under the Mosaic covenant and has been judged by God as deserving of the covenant's curses. Yet, God promised to fulfill His commitments to the Abrahamic covenant (and by extension, unfaithful Israel). So, on the one hand, we have Israel's breach of the Mosaic covenant which leaves the nation under the covenantal curses of Deuteronomy. Yet, however, through the Abrahamic covenant, God has promised to protect and preserve Israel without conditions. How can these two covenants stand together? Freedman answers that the tension is resolved by the new covenant itself:

> In the new age of the covenant—the new spirit and the new life—the conflict between the two covenant types is resolved in reciprocal fulfillment. Yahweh's irreversible commitment to Israel flows into the blessings which he bestows on an obedient people who, through the power of his Spirit, fulfill all the requirements of the covenant.[507]

Freedman's reasoning is that God's faithfulness and enabling power are the cause and source of the believers' covenant faithfulness; as such, God's faithfulness and power are indispensable for affirming the doctrine of eternal security and the perseverance of the saints for many Baptist,

---

[506] David Noel Freedman, "Divine Commitment and Human Obligation," *Interpretation* 18 (1964), 425.

[507] David Noel Freedman, *Divine Commitment and Human Obligation, Vol. 1: Ancient Israelite History and Religion* (Grand Rapids: Eerdmans, 1997), 178.

Reformed and Evangelical theologians.[508] It also provides a sound premise upon which a theology of *sola gratia* may be fashioned.[509]

Yet, such grace-centered biblical and systematic theology does not and has not guaranteed grace-centered pastoral care. On many occasions throughout church history, the heirs of the Reformation, though affirming the assurance of salvation in *sola fide* and *sola gratia* have fallen into legalism. Take the Puritans as a case in point. Trevin Wax, Managing Editor of The Gospel Project for LifeWay Christian Resources, detailed in his article, "Beware the Puritan Paralysis," the following about some forms of Puritan pietistic practice:

> Though the Reformers sought to emphasize the assurance we can have because of God's grace in election and salvation, their descendants sometimes undercut the beauty of assurance by stressing the fruit of sanctification more than the fact of justification. Self-examination was a "descending into our own hearts" to root out every possible sinful tendency and desire. Beware the paralysis that comes from this type of introspection. If our goal is to discover, analyze, and root out every aspect of sinfulness in our hearts, then we will never come to the end of the task. Satan loves to take the tender conscience and stir up doubt of salvation, doubt of sanctification, and doubt of progression in holiness. Then, he turns the gaze of the introspective person inward, where the dark recesses of our hearts continue to lead to darker recesses still. Instead of living in the shining light of

---

[508] For example in Gordon D. Fee's *Paul, the Spirit, and the People of God* (Grand Rapids: Baker Academic, 1996.), chapter 9, "Conversion: Staying In (Part 1) The Spirit and Pauline Ethics," he said, "I grew up in a church where the buzz phrases 'eternal security' and 'once saved, always saved' were bad news. People who believed so, I was told, even if they did not intend it, encouraged 'easy-believism' and 'cheap grace'; that is, people believed in Christ for salvation but failed to exhibit it in their lives. They were eternally secure, so why get uptight about how they lived? Only later did I learn that this language was a popular distortion of Calvin's perseverance of the saints. Calvin believed (rightly so) that God enables his holy ones, his saints, to persevere to the end, and in that sense, they were secure-eternally. Unfortunately, what was sometimes advocated as Calvinism often did offer false security to unbelievers, people who wanted a passport to heaven without becoming citizens. Nothing could be further from Paul's perspective. Salvation has to do with both getting in and staying in. To get saved means to be joined to the people of God by the Spirit; and to be saved means to live the life of heaven on earth, also by the Spirit-walking in the Spirit, being led by the Spirit, sowing to the Spirit. The Spirit who implants the faith by which we believe (2 Cor 4:13) is the same Spirit whose fruit in our lives includes faith (Gal 5:22), meaning now 'faithful walking in God's ways.' Merely optional righteousness is unthinkable. What does it mean, then, to live in the Christian community and in the world as the people of God? That is what ethics is all about, which is what this chapter is all about. To be sure, life in the Spirit means far more than just ethical behaviour. The whole of life under the new covenant is now lived in and by the Spirit, including worship, one's relationship to God, and everyday life itself."

[509] For an excellent work which defends the thesis that divine enablement is the basis of salvation in the N.T. corpus see Charles H. Talbert and Jason A. Whitlark's *Getting "Saved": The Whole Story of Salvation in the New Testament* (Grand Rapids: Eerdmans, 2011). This work seeks to answer the question, "Is the covenant relationship sustained by a sense of personal gratitude for God's past gift of conversion—or is post-conversion faithfulness itself an ongoing gift from God?" The editors Talbert and Whitlark together with Scott J. Hafemann adhere to the doctrine of the perseverance of the saints. Clifford A. Barbarick and Michael W. Martin may be classified as Arminians who like I. Howard Marshall take the assurance of salvation seriously.

gospel truth, the gospel that dispels all this darkness and grants us a new heart, we travel deeper and deeper into the cavernous rooms of our remaining sin. Meanwhile, our missiological effectiveness is thwarted. We talk about grace, sing about grace, read about grace, and hear sermons about grace, but at the end of the day, we are paralyzed, not free. [510]

As Wax illustrates, a radical focus upon one's failure to be absolutely holy in thought and practice can deeply undercut one's assurance of salvation, and thereby undermine one's belief in sola fide and sola gratia.

3. Acknowledge the Continuing Struggle with Sin Despite the Spirit's Work in Covenant Relationship with God

At times, the practical result of affirming that the Spirit empowers genuine believers to fulfill the requirements of God's law has been to restrict God's saving grace to professing believers whose lives meet our own approval. However, if we are to truly return to God's transcendence, it is incumbent upon us to interpret our salvation experience through the Christ event and not through introspective human reason. While we must strive to observe the work of the Spirit in our lives, our pneumatology must complement our Christology. In his monumental work, *The Doctrine of Justification*, James Buchanan made the salient point that one of the most subtle errors that diminishes the fruit of assurance which the Protestant doctrine of justification should bring is that of substituting the inner work of the Spirit for the righteousness of Christ imputed to us:

> There is, perhaps, no more subtle or plausible error, on the subject of Justification, than that which makes it to rest on the indwelling presence, and the gracious work, of the Holy Spirit in the heart. It is a singularly refined form of opposition to the doctrine of Justification by the imputed righteousness of Christ, for it merely substitutes the work of one divine Person for that of another; and it is plausible, because it seems to do homage to the doctrine of Grace, by ascribing to the presence and operation of the Holy Spirit the production of faith, and all the effects which are ascribed to it, whether these belong to our Justification or to our Sanctification. It is the more difficult to expose and refute error, when it presents itself in this apparently spiritual form, than when it comes before us in its grosser and more common shape, as a doctrine of justification by works, because it involves some great truths which are held as firmly by those who advocate, as by those who abjure, the Protestant doctrine of Justification. Yet, subtle and plausible as it is, and difficult as it may be to disentangle the error from the partial truth which is involved in it, nothing can be more unscriptural in itself, or more pernicious to the souls of men, than the substitution of the gracious work of the Spirit in us, for the vicarious work of Christ for us, as the ground of our pardon and acceptance with God; for if we are

---

[510] Trevin Wax, "Beware the Puritan Paralysis," The Gospel Coalition (November 20, 2012). See https://blogs.thegospelcoalition.org/trevinwax/2012/11/20/beware-the-puritan-paralysis/.

justified solely on account of what Christ did and suffered for us, while He was yet on the earth, we may rest, with entire confidence, on a work which has been already 'finished'—on a righteousness which has been already wrought out, and already accepted of God on behalf of all who believe in His name,—and we may immediately receive, on the sure warrant of His word, the privilege of Justification as a free gift of God's grace through Christ, and as the present privilege of every believer, so as at once to have 'joy and peace in believing.' Whereas, if we are justified on the ground of the work of the Holy Spirit in us, we are called to rest on a work, which, so far from being finished and accepted, is not even begun in the case of any unrenewed sinner; and which, when it is begun in the case of a believer, is incipient only,—often interrupted in its progress by declension and backsliding—marred and defiled by remaining sin—obscured and enveloped in doubt by clouds and thick darkness,—and never perfected in this life, even according to the low standard of a relaxed law, if that law is supposed to require any definite amount of personal holiness in heart and life. For these reasons, it is of the utmost practical importance, to conceive aright, both of the Mediatorial work of Christ, and of the internal work of His Spirit, in the relation which they bear to each other, under the scheme of Grace and Redemption.[511]

In our efforts to guard the grace of God from licentious abuse, we sometimes interpret the new covenant as though it were a conditional contract: unless new covenant benefactors attain a certain observable degree of sanctification, their profession of faith is false or their salvation is lost. However, the new covenant is not a conditional contract. In the new covenant, we have the Son, who is as Isaiah prophesied, "A *covenant* of the people" (Isa 42:6, 49:8). John makes the same point when he says, "For the law was given through Moses; *grace and truth* came through Jesus Christ." (John 1:17). In John 1:17, "grace and truth" (in Hebrew *ḥesed* and *'ĕmet*) are shorthand for the whole nature of covenant (as a part-for-the-whole expression in the O.T.) and are now to be found in the Son, who in effect embodies the covenant, and thus also, God's covenantal relationship with his people. The very God who is free to have mercy and compassion "on whom He will" in Himself embodies the new covenant! We must therefore exercise caution in reading the scriptures contractually and not in a covenantal fashion, for priority must be given to God's grace (Rom 5:20).[512]

---

[511] James Buchanan, *The Doctrine of Justification: An Outline of its History in the Church and of its Exposition from Scripture, Lecture XV Justification; It's Relation to the Work of the Holy Spirit* (Edinburgh: T & T Clark, 1867; Solid Ground Christian Books, 2006; 540 pp.), 387–88. See https://books.google.com/books?id=Px0DAAAAQAAJandprintsec=frontcoverandsource.

[512] The difference between a contractual and a covenantal relationship with God was a key tenet of the theology of James B. Torrance and in recent times, by N.T. scholar Douglas Campbell in his *The Deliverance of God: An Apocalyptic Rereading of Justification in Paul* (Grand Rapids: Eerdmans, 2013).

This caution is necessary because the child of God still possesses his Adamic sin nature and needs the righteousness and mercy of Christ as much now as he did in his pre-conversion state. This truth has been ably educed by Greek scholar Daniel B. Wallace in his articles on Romans 3:21–26. In Romans 3:23, when Paul says that "all" have sinned and fall short of the glory of God, we often take that verse as referring to man in his pre-conversion state. However, Wallace ably argues that the "all" of Romans 3:23 refers to believers only.[513] Therefore, Paul switches between the aorist (past) tense to the present tense: "for all *have sinned* and *fall short* of the glory of God." This tense change is significant. It indicates that all believers *have* sinned and *still continue* to fail to reach God through our own righteousness. *We are still totally depraved sinners!* "All have sinned and still continue to fall short." How is such a motley crew to be saved? In part 2 of his article, Wallace continues, "How are we—whose past lives are summarized by sin and whose present lives are still mired in it—to be saved? Paul answers this in v. 3.24—'being freely justified by his grace through the redemption that is in Christ Jesus.'" Paul's theological affirmation is that a man is saved on the same basis, both before and after conversion, "freely by grace through the redemption that is in Christ Jesus," because both sinner and saint suffer with the same sin condition and need the same kind of mercy now as we did before conversion.[514]

It is for this reason that we must fashion our theology of grace in a manner that takes into account the mystery of God's mercy and the continuing reality of sin in the lives of the redeemed. On the one hand, in Matthew 7:21, Jesus says that *not everyone who says* to me, "*Lord, Lord,*"

---

[513] Daniel B. Wallace, "What Does it Mean to be Justified? A Brief Exposition of Romans 3:21–26," Part 1, https://bible.org/article/what-does-it-mean-be-justified-brief-exposition-romans-321-26-part-1 (2007); "What Does it Mean to be Justified? A Brief Exposition of Romans 3:21–26," Part 2, https://bible.org/article/what-does-it-mean-be-justified-brief-exposition-romans-321-26-part-2 (2007). In part 1 of his article, Wallace argues, "Paul has just defined the 'all' in v 22: 'all who believe.' The same 'all' are most likely in view here too. Perhaps the reason that most interpreters see the groups as different is that Paul does not qualify the 'all' in v. 23, while he qualifies it in v. 22 ("all who believe"). Thus, two different 'alls' seem to be in view. However, it is typical of Paul and of Greek in general not to define the 'all' in the second mention. Greek is a more economical language than English and as such it does not need to repeat words and phrases as much as English does. As for Paul, his style is often to establish the meaning of the group in the first sentence, then simply keep the discussion with the 'all' for the rest. Verse 24 starts off with a participle in Greek; it is not a new sentence but is rather a subordinate clause to the preceding. (The NET Bible makes it start a new sentence but only because of the length and complexity of the Greek.) The implication? Those who are justified freely (v. 24) are the 'all' of v. 23. *If* the 'all' are *all* sinners, then everyone is justified. Salvation is universal, regardless of what one believes. But this view stands in direct contradiction with the testimony of the NT: 'there is no other name under heaven by which people can be saved'; more specifically, Rom 3:22, 'the righteousness of God comes… to all who believe.' When Paul prays for his fellow Jews in Rom 9, he wishes that he could be sent to hell if that would save but one of them! Why would this even be contemplated if everyone is saved?"

[514] Wallace, "What Does it Mean," Part 2.

will enter the kingdom of heaven, but only the one who does the will of the Father in heaven. However, in Matthew 13:8, Jesus also tells us that the seed which fell on good soil and yielded a crop, some a hundredfold, some sixty, and some thirty. Now, there is evidence that even a thirty-fold harvest would have been a miraculous thing in ancient Palestine[515] One might therefore argue that all believers must manifest a miraculously exorbitant degree of good works in order for their salvation to be genuine. But can we honestly trust ourselves to distinguish between a false believer and a genuine believer who is producing a thirty-fold harvest?

The Parable of the Wheat and the Tares in Matthew 13:24–30; 36–43 gives us just that sort of caution. In the Pauline Epistles we see the vice lists (1 Cor 6:9–10; Gal 5:19–21; Eph 5:3–5), and hear that those who practice such sins will not inherit the kingdom of God. The warnings are sober and must be heeded by all. Yet, in 1 Corinthians 6:15–20 Paul acknowledges that some believers have fallen into the kind of sexual sin that is mentioned in the vice list (6:9–10), and yet the Apostle appeals to their new identity and union with Christ as the reason to flee such sins. In Galatians, Paul's acknowledges that believers who desire to do good wrestle with their sin nature (Gal 5:13–18) and may be weak and in need of a fellow brother to aid them (Gal 6:1–2). In Ephesians 4:30, Paul acknowledges that believers may grieve the Spirit by which they are sealed till the day of redemption. In the Book of James, an epistle written to show that genuine faith is a faith that produces works, the author uses Rahab as an exemplar of saving faith while she is still identified with the lifestyle of a harlot! In Hebrews 12:14, we are called to pursue peace with all men and holiness without which no one shall see the Lord. Yet, the Hebrew Epistle reminds us that we all need the chastening love of God to produce that fruit (Heb 12:6–11).

On 1 Thessalonians 5:9–10, N.T. scholar Richard H. Bell argued for the assurance of salvation despite our moral lapses:

> Paul is therefore not saying in 5:10 that whether we are alive or dead at the second coming we will be with Christ (even though he believed this was the case as 1 Thess 4:13–17 makes clear). His point in 5:9–10 is quite different. The meaning of the Greek verbs suggest the following. God has destined us not for wrath (i.e. not for condemnation) but for salvation. This is achieved through Jesus Christ who died for us. The consequence is that whether we are morally awake or morally asleep we may live with him. This is assurance indeed. Our salvation does not depend on ourselves. It depends entirely on God. All of us, if we are honest, know those times when we are "morally asleep." God wants us to

---

[515] James R. Edwards, *The Gospel According to Mark* (Grand Rapids: Eerdmans, 2001), 129, fn. 42. See R. K. McIver, "One Hundred-fold Yield-Miraculous or Mundane? Matthew 13:8, 23; Mark 4:8, 20; Luke 8:8," *New Testament Studies* 40, no. 4 (October 1994): 606–8.

do good works. That is clear in Paul and clear in the teaching of the Reformers. But our salvation does not depend on good works. Even in those times when we are morally asleep we can be assured of our salvation.[516]

Dispensationalist theologian, Charles Caldwell Ryrie gave a very balanced view on the subject of assurance of salvation and works as the evidence of the new birth in his now near classic *So Great Salvation*:

> Every Christian will bear spiritual fruit. Somewhere, sometime, somehow. Otherwise that person is not a believer.... Having said that, some caveats, or cautions, are in order. First, this does not mean that a believer will always be fruitful. Certainly we can admit that if there can be hours and days when a believer can be unfruitful, then why may there not also be months and even years when he can be in that same condition? Paul exhorted believers to engage in good works so they would not be unfruitful (Titus 3:14). Peter also exhorted believers to add the qualities of Christian character to their faith lest they be unfruitful (2 Pet 1:8). Obviously, both of those passages indicate that a true believer might *be* unfruitful. And the simple fact that both Paul and Peter exhort believers to be fruitful shows that believers are not always fruitful. Second, this does not mean that a certain person's fruit will necessarily be outwardly evident. Even if I know the person and have some regular contact with him, I still may not see his fruit. Indeed, I might even have legitimate grounds for wondering if he is a believer because I have not seen fruit. His fruit may be very private or erratic, but the fact that I do not see it does not mean it is not there. Third, my understanding of what fruit is and therefore what I expect others to bear may be faulty and/or incomplete. It is all too easy to have a mental list of spiritual fruit and to conclude that if someone does not produce what is on my list that he or she is not a believer. But the reality is that most lists that we human beings devise are too short, too selective, too prejudiced, and often extrabiblical. God likely has a much more accurate and longer list that most of us do. Nevertheless, every Christian will bear fruit; otherwise he or she is not a true believer. In speaking about the judgment seat of Christ, Paul says unequivocally that every believer will have praise come to him from God (1 Cor 4:5).[517]

Heeding Ryrie's wise insight, our graciousness should outweigh our judgment.

---

[516] Richard H. Bell, "Salvation from the Wrath to Come: An Exposition of Romans 5:9 and 1 Thessalonians 5:9," *Testamentum Imperium* 1, (2005–2007), 5. The view espoused by Bell on which my argument relies appears to be the minority view of the interpretation of the text. See www.PreciousHeart.net/ti/2007/003_07_Bell_Romans_5_1Thess_5.pdf.

Another able defense of the minority view is given by Thomas R. Edgar in, "Lethargic or Dead in 1 Thessalonians 5:10?" *Chafer Theological Seminary Journal* 6, no. 4 (October–December 2000). See http://chafer.nextmeta.com/files/v6n4_3.pdf.

[517] Charles Caldwell Ryrie, *So Great Salvation: What It Means to Believe in Jesus Christ* (Moody, 1977; Victor, 1989), 41–42 of chapter 5.

Conclusion on Our Pastoral Effectiveness

A return to a reliance on God's transcendence and the mystery of grace would enhance the field of pastoral theology! For one thing, it would compel us to deeply come to terms with the outrageous fact that we worship a God who desires a certain kind of obedience to His Majesty - which is, above all, a loyalty rooted in love (Jer 31:33–34; 32:40; Gal 5:6; 1 John 4:18). This kind of obedience cannot be nurtured if we readily retreat to the warning passages of scripture each time that a believer's life disappoints us. We therefore have to be more patient, gracious, and prayerfully reflective in the way in which we seek to foster sanctification, knowing all too well that genuine believers can and do struggle with sin.[518] This could only come from affirming a gospel message that gives priority to the mercy of God and therein lies the best way to enrich our pastoral effectiveness - a rejuvenated gospel of mercy.

In conclusion, if we as believers become more gracious in the way in which we address sin within the community of grace, bearing in mind our own depravity, there is a greater likelihood that that gracious encounter in community will spill over to the unbeliever (Luke 7:36–50, esp. 47). Finally, we would be equipped with a more coherent message and lifestyle in an age where pastoral theology, Christian living, and apologetics must go hand in hand.

Soli Deo Gloria!

---

[518] See Steven L. Porter's article, "The Gradual Nature of Sanctification: Σάρξ as Habituated, Relational Resistance to the Spirit," http://themelios.thegospelcoalition.org/article/the-gradual-nature-of-sanctification-as-habituated-relational-resistance-to.

16.
Ethics of Judging between Truth and Love when the Absolutely Right Choice Is Elusive

Rev. Dr. Michael G. Maness
Retired Senior Clinical Chaplain
Texas Department of Criminal Justice
Managing Editor, *Testamentum Imperium*[519]

Love cherished in the soul on earth will be to us the *foretaste* of and the *preparation* for that world which is a world of love and where the Spirit of love reigns and blesses forever.[520]

Jonathan Edwards, 1852

Introduction: Commander Bucher Lied to Save Lives in 1968 232
A. Love in Christ's Competence and Its Greatest Work 233
B. Four Ethical Systems Compared 235
    Chart 1. Ethical Systems Compared 235
    1. On NCA—Rakestraw's Non-Conflicting Absolutism 236
    2. On GA—Geisler's Graded Absolutism 236
    3. On P—Smith's Principleism 237
    4. DA—Maness' Dynamic Absolutism, an Ethic of Love 237
C. Deontology and Teleology—"Time" Critical to "Rightness" 238
    Chart 2. Essence of Deontology and Teleology 239
D. Absolutes United in Love and Eternity 240
    1. Absolutes Positively Stated Expressions of Love 240

---

[519] Maness earned his DMin from New Orleans Baptist Theological Seminary (1997), MDiv from Southwestern Baptist Theological Seminary, Fort Worth (1990), and BA from Criswell Institute for Biblical Studies, Dallas (1985). He retired as a senior clinical chaplain from the Texas Department of Criminal Justice (20 years). In 1999 he led Texas MHMR, TYC, and TDCJ staff chaplains in a legislative push that got them their first pay-group raise in 40-plus years, then in 2007 led TDCJ chaplains in an effort that gained back 25 staff chaplain positions, and in 2011 led the effort that saved the Texas prison chaplaincy from zero budgeting, chronicled in *How We Saved Texas Prison Chaplaincy 2011* (2015; 414 pp.). His latest book *When Texas Prison Scams Religion* (2022; 894 pp.) exposes 25 years of nefarious dealings with religion in TDCJ, especially as TDCJ followed Louisiana's Angola in the abuse of buying faith with favor from prisoners, *totally* ignoring psychopathy, and more defending the profession of prison chaplaincy. Over 100 articles and eight books on a host of topics include *Would You Lie To Save a Life?—A Theology on the Ethics of Love* (2007; 432 pp.), of which this paper is a summary; *Heart of the Living God* (2004; 728 pp.); *Character Counts—Freemasonry USA's National Treasure and Source of Our Founding Fathers' Original Intent* (2007; 448 pp.); *Ocean Devotions—From the Hold of Charles H. Spurgeon* (2008; 440 pp.); *Heaven—Treasures of Our Everlasting Rest* (2004; 132 pp.); *Queen of Prison Ministry—Story of Gertha Rogers, First Woman to Minister on Texas Death Row*, with foreword by ret. TDCJ Exec. Dir. Wayne Scott (2008; 100 pp.); and *Precious Heart, Broken Heart—Love and the Search for Finality in Divorce* (2003; 192 pp.). His web domain, www.PreciousHeart.net, links over 100k resources and hosts perhaps the largest collection of data on prison chaplaincy in the world. He has been managing editor of *Testamentum Imperium* for over 15 years, www.PreciousHeart.net/ti, publishing the work of 300-plus scholars from around the world.

[520] Jonathan Edwards, *Charity and Its Fruits: Christian Love as Manifested in the Heart and Life* (Scotland: Banner of Truth Trust, 2000; 1st 1852), 322, italics mine.

    2. Love Struggles in the Small Window of Time 241
    3. Love's Infinity of Variables on the Concourse of Time 243
        Chart 3. Unique Arenas of Individuals 243
E. Love's Simplicity Amid Eternal Complications 244
    1. Manifold Struggles between Legality and License 244
        Chart 4. Love's Struggle between Legality and License 244
    2. Teleological and Deontological Analysis of Love's Choice 245
        Chart 5. Teleological-Deontological Analysis of Choice 246
    3. Five Implication of Chart 5—the Fuller Elegance of Perfected Love 248
Conclusion: Love and Truth Converge on the Concourse of Life 250
    Chart 6. *Imago Dei* Trinity of Human Abilities in Love 251

Introduction: Commander Bucher Lied to Save Lives in 1968

All of us have deep human needs for Love and Truth in our lives; these bring to us the greatest treasures in our lives, and these also bring great moral dilemmas. This chapter is a condensation of my book, *Would You Lie to Save a Life?*[521] A few paragraphs herein reflect an entire chapter in that book. During its 20 years of refining, two other books arose concurrently from within its research like two long rivers of additional source material.[522] The writing took place over most of my 20-year career as a state-employed chaplain over a large Texas prison and can barely be touched here. More could and *should* be done to incorporate into our penal systems the professionalism resident in the vast healthcare and military chaplaincies.[523] As documented, many states do not value freedom of religion or pastoral care enough to vigorously support the prison chaplaincy profession.[524]

In sum, this is all about the *ethics* of the absolutes of Love and Truth. As in my book *Would You Lie to Save a Life?*, I capitalize Love, Truth, Responsibility, and Right Choice throughout to highlight their status. Love wins, but not easily, and the most judgmental struggle to stay afloat.

The North Koreans hijacked the USS *Pueblo* in January of 1968. They brutally beat the crew. After credibly threatening to kill *Pueblo* crew and

---

[521] Michael G. Maness, *Would You Lie to Save a Life—a Theology on the Ethics of Love*, with illustrations by Gustave Doré (AuthorHouse, 2007; 432 pp.).

[522] Maness, *Heart of the Living God: Love, Free Will, Foreknowledge, Heaven: a Theology on the Treasure of Love* (AuthorHouse, 2004; 728 pp.) and *Character Counts—Freemasonry USA's National Treasure and Source of Our Founding Fathers' Original Intent* (AuthorHouse, 2007; 448 pp.).

[523] Please see the bibliography "Army, U.S." for their massive volumes on the chaplaincy corps from 1791 to the present—no other like them, but there should be. Though most of Texas prison chaplaincy history has been deleted, save those data at www.PreciousHeart.net/chaplaincy/, if its modus operandi continues, all its history will die too, a terrible waste of massive documented human concern.

[524] See my books, *How We Saved Texas Prison Chaplaincy 2011—Immeasurable Value of Volunteers and Their Chaplains* (2015; 414 pp.) and *When Texas Prison Scams Religion* (2022; 894 pp.). See Larry VandeCreek and Laurel Burton, "Professional Chaplaincy: Its Role and Importance in Healthcare," *The Journal of Pastoral Care* 55, no. 1 (Spring 2001): 81–97, a landmark joint statement of the five largest chaplaincy bodies representing 10,000-plus members, www.PreciousHeart.net/chaplaincy /Chaplaincy_Healthcare.pdf, and all of it and more applies equally to prison chaplaincy.

fireman Howard Bland, the youngest of the crew, Commander Lloyd M. "Pete" Bucher signed a "confession" that *lied* about spying in North Korean water—he saved their lives.⁵²⁵ I dare say most of us would have done the same. The Koreans held the *Pueblo* crew hostage for 11 more months forcing them refine their "confession," which turned into a hilarious comic of absurdities listed in Bucher's stunning and entertaining autobiography.⁵²⁶

Bucher fought for decades, and he finally won for his crew their POW Medals in May of 1990. In 1973, a movie on their ordeal won two 26th Primetime Emmy Awards, with Hal Holbrook playing Bucher and winning both the Best Actor and the Best Actor of the Year awards. Sadly, the *Pueblo* remains a commissioned ship in the U.S. Navy while parked as a tourist attraction in Pyongyang, North Korea's capitol, moored on the Potong River near their Monument to the Victorious Fatherland.⁵²⁷ Mercy! We should tow it home, and the remaining *Pueblo* crew asked President Trump to do just that in 2018.⁵²⁸

I interviewed Commander "Pete" Bucher in the summer of 1997 at the Black Angus Steakhouse in San Diego. With us were his fellow crew member, Chief Communications Technician James F. Kell, and my friend, Lt. Col. Will Duke. Great interview. Even those decades later, Kell believed Bucher saved their lives.⁵²⁹ Bucher died on January 28, 2004, and a print of one of his many paintings of a sailing ship hangs in my home office.

What is the *absolutely* Right Choice in Bucher's dilemma over denying Truth and lying to save life in Love for his fellows? In short, we are not as competent as Jesus and could not find the *absolutely* Right Choice, though one is always available, just as one was for Jesus. Every decision is short of Jesus' competence. We show how "time" itself has a place in the "rightness" of the choice, and we show how every choice must include the teleological, even the eschatological to be an *absolutely* Right Choice this side of heaven; that is, *no choice* can be *right* without considering the future, and for the Christian no choice can be right without Love *and* a view to heaven.

A. Love in Christ's Competence and Its Greatest Work

In the decades since I wrote the first paper on this in seminary in about 1989, I have offered the dilemma around tables of preachers and teachers

---

[525] Lloyd M. Bucher, *Bucher: My Story*, with Mark Rascovich (Doubleday, 1970; 447 pp.).
[526] Bucher, *Bucher: My Story*.
[527] Craig S. Coleman, "North Korea Unveils USS *Pueblo*: American Ship Captured in 1968 Now On Display as Tourist Attraction," *Korea Times* (May 3, 1995).
[528] FOX News reported on September 22, 2018, "USS *Pueblo* spy ship crew tell Trump to bring the vessel home from North Korea," at www.FOXNews.com/us/uss-*Pueblo*-spy-ship-crew-tell-trump-to-bring-vessel-home-from-north-korea, accessed December 17, 2019.
[529] See www.USS*Pueblo*.org for more.

dozens of times. Quickly, the room divides. A minority of diehard Truth-sayers contrast with the liars, and predictable discussions ensue. Some defend the Truth in all scenarios, and those are often the most judgmental, sometimes even arrogant, stabbing, "Speak the Truth in Love" (Eph 4:15). To *think* and *feel* is often too much trouble for those land-lovers unacquainted with the roiling depths of the ocean's worst moral weather. Dietrich Bonhoeffer acidly said:

> It is only the cynic who claims "to speak the truth" at all times and in all places to all men in the same way, but who, in fact, displays nothing but a lifeless image of the truth. He dons the halo of the fanatical devotee of truth who can make no allowance for human weaknesses; but, in fact, he is destroying the living truth between men. He wounds shame, desecrates mystery, breaks confidence, betrays the community in which he lives, and laughs arrogantly at the devastation he has wrought and at the human weakness which "cannot bear the truth." He says truth is destructive and demands its victims, and he feels like a god above these feeble creatures and does not know that he is serving Satan.[530]

This reflected the shame of Nazi fundamentalism in 1940s Germany.

Beyond 1 Corinthians 13 and our hearts, the intersecting pathos between the theologians, philosophers, poets, and song writers contributes to Love's vitality and wealth and its connection to eternity.[531] James Moffatt's magisterial classic *Love in the New Testament* shows the coming of age of Love from the ancients through its new birth in Bethlehem.[532] Moffatt noted how some portions of Christianity can only be understood from the "inside."[533] A sad Truth permeates Jesus' words "no greater Love has anyone than this, to give their life for a friend" (John 15:13). Really? Must one *die* for the best of Love to be seen? Sometimes that is the only infallible proof of Love. For the one giving their life, the future of the loved one becomes supreme! *Sacrifice* is Love's greatest work and the heart of the gospel. Our "citizenship" is at the same *time* in heaven (Phil 3:20), and so over the long haul on earth, then, Love's eternal nature extends into heaven where the need for the word *Truth* will cease.[534] That is, the *need* for the

---

[530] Dietrich Bonhoeffer (1906–1945), *Ethics*, ed. Eberhard Bethge (New York: Macmillan, 1955): 328–329. He opposed Nazi crimes and was hanged on April 9, 1945, 21 days before Hitler's suicide.

[531] Cf. Paul Tillich's *Eternal Now* (New York: Scribner, 1963) and Amos Yong's *Spirit of Love: A Trinitarian Theology of Grace* (Waco: Baylor University Press, 2012),

[532] James Moffatt, *Love in the New Testament* (London: Hodder and Stoughton, 1929): 32–33, "When Christianity begins, we find ... the Church conscious of a new relationship to God ... the most central and simple term heard 'Love.'... It was in their group that for the first time the word was heard, *God is Love*." We have not seen an equal to this masterpiece on Love for the N.T. Christian.

[533] Moffatt, *Love in the New Testament*, 321–322.

[534] Maness, *Heaven—Treasures of Our Everlasting Rest* (AuthorHouse, 2004). Cf. Richard Baxter's masterpiece *The Saints' Everlasting Rest—The Blessed State of the Saints in Their Enjoyment of God in Glory* (London: Rob. White, 1649, 856 pp.; see http://digitalpuritan.net/richard-baxter/ for all of Baxter's

[Footnote continued on next page]

word Truth will cease in heaven, for there will be no falsehood in the eternal world of purely perfected Love. We will touch that again later.

B. Four Ethical Systems Compared

NCA	**Robert Rakestraw's Non-Conflicting Absolutism:** [535]	
	Absolutes Never Conflict, chooses the impending right, being right	
GA	**Norman Geisler's Graded Absolutism:** [536]	
	Absolutes are Graded, chooses the greater good, exempting wrong	
P	**Ebbie Smith's Principleism:** [537]	
	Absolutes Conflict, chooses the greater good, accrediting wrong	
DA	**Michael Maness' Dynamic Absolutism:**	
	Absolutes Never Conflict, chooses greater good, and guilt remains	

Chart 1. Ethical Systems Compared

Consciously or not, most evangelicals will fall into one of these four systems, perhaps most of the world. Our dilemma here is about our Responsibility to Love and to tell the Truth at the same *time!* My experience debating this leads me to stress our Responsibility to:

Love and tell the **Truth** at the **Same TIME**

We are not free to choose one absolute if two have a bearing upon a dilemma, and we contend Love always has a bearing, even eternally.

---

work), Millard J. Erickson's *Basic Guide to Eschatology* (Baker, 1998; 200 pp.), Jürgen Moltmann's *Theology of Hope—On the Ground and the Implications of a Christian Eschatology* (SCM, 1967; 346 pp.), Moltmann's *The Coming of God—Christian Eschatology* (Fortress, 1996; 420 pp), Joseph Ratzinger/Pope Benedict XVI's *Eschatology: Death and Eternal Life*, 2nd Ed. (Catholic Univ. of America Press, 2007; 1st 1988; 307 pp.), and Nicholas Wright's *History and Eschatology: Jesus and the Promise of Natural Theology* (Baylor Univ. Press, 2019; 365 pp.). Cf. fn. 557.

[535] Robert V. Rakestraw, "Ethical Choices: A Case for Non-Conflicting Absolutism," *Criswell Theological Review* 2, no. 2 (Spring 1988): 239–267, www.PreciousHeart.net/love/Rakestraw-1988.pdf.

[536] Norman L. Geisler, *Christian Ethics—Options and Issues* (Grand Rapids: Baker, 1989; a revision of his *Ethics—Alternatives and Issues* (Zondervan, 1982, through 13 prints from 1971–82): 113–132. See more on Geisler at his Southern Evangelical Seminary (SES) at www.SES.edu at https://ses.edu/about-ses/our-history/, which was founded in 1992 by Geisler and Ross Rhoads, former evangelist and then Pastor of Calvary Church in Charlotte. Geisler continues to isolate himself from his peers and criticism, as seen in his recent resignation from the Evangelical Theological Society (outlined in an interview in *Criswell Theological Review* 1:2 (Spring 2004): 139–145; and is criticized further in my book, *Heart of the Living God: Love, Free Will, Foreknowledge, and Heaven: a Theology on the Treasure of Love* (AuthorHouse, 2004). In his presidential intro to his own seminary (as of 6-5-2004), he said students come to his seminary because "they can get something here [SES] that they cannot get anywhere else, namely, training under some of the top apologists and Bible teachers in the country to evangelize the world and to defend the historic Christian Faith." So he really knew how to *grade*.

[537] Ebbie C. Smith, "The Ten Commandments in Today's Permissive Society: A Principleist Approach," *Southwestern Journal of Theology* 20, no. 1 (Fall 1977): 42–58. He taught ethics for many years at Southwestern Baptist Theological Seminary. This article in its earliest draft was a paper presented in his class at SWBTS, and for the book I secured his and John P. Newport's endorsement.

1. On NCA—Rakestraw's Non-Conflicting Absolutism

Robert Rakestraw's Non-Conflicting Absolutist—NCA—would tell the Truth in Commander Bucher's dilemma, for there are "no exceptions" to telling the Truth (except silence).[538] Very deontologically, Rakestraw states,

> If, as we believe, an absolute is a universally-binding moral norm or directive which admits of no exceptions or exemptions outside of the absolute itself, then we must maintain that when a conflict situation arises in which specific absolutes are brought to bear upon the decision, whatever else we may do, we cannot disobey, lay aside, or transcend any of these divine absolutes.[539]

While agreeing to that, we challenge Rakestraw's prior claim that "the ends *never* justify the means."[540] That becomes inextricably linked to a claim of competence in making Right Choices, even to a claim of competence equal to Jesus. Another problem is his application: NCA denies the integration of teleology (ends) in the determination of the Right Choice. NCA would tell the Truth, for Bucher's conflict is simply between a lie and the Truth. Therein for NCA, Love has little-to-zero relevance and no decisive impact in Bucher's dilemma regarding the Right Choice! That is *not* how the world turns. That is not how we *live*.

2. On GA—Geisler's Graded Absolutism

Norman Geisler's Graded Absolutism (GA) would lie, and the saving of lives is considered a higher absolute than Truth in his scheme of grading.

> There are higher and lower moral duties—for example, Love for God is a greater duty than Love for people. These ... sometimes come into unavoidable moral conflict; in such conflicts we are obligated to follow the higher moral law; when we follow the higher moral law *we are not held responsible* for not keeping the lower one [italics mine].[541]

Geisler's GA easily negates Bucher's problem. Saving life is *higher* than maintaining a small Truth. GA is convincing if one reads nothing else. GA's core rests upon nine pages of loosely fitting paragraphs in his revised *Christian Ethics*. The problem with GA is two-faced: he claims to value the absoluteness of absolutes with a straight face, then he crooks his face to say he must "grade" the absolutes. His gradation contains an elitism, especially when he briefly expounds upon the "traceability" of laws to God's nature. Where is Love? He never articulates the place of Love. Geisler has the

---

[538] Rakestraw, "Ethical Choices," 239–240.

[539] Rakestraw, 255.

[540] Rakestraw, 252, italics mine.

[541] Norman Geisler, *Christian Ethics—Options and Issues* (Grand Rapids: Baker Book House, 1989; a revision of his *Ethics—Alternatives and Issues* [Grand Rapids: Zondervan, 1982, through 13 prints from 1971–82]): 132, last paragraph of his section on section (113–132, 9 pages) on graded absolutism. See also Geisler, "Biblical Absolutes and Moral Conflicts," *Bibliotheca Sacra* (July 1974): 219–228.

amazing ability to determine the gradation. Unintentional or naïve, still his gradation unequivocally assails the *absoluteness* of absolutes in a quagmire of specious reasoning. Geisler does not work very hard on clarifying either his ability or his gradation, though he tries to answer a few objections because he knows something is awry. His "absolute in its *sphere*" and "when there is a conflict" indicate that his GA is an ethic where "conflicting absolutes" is itself *the* absolute.[542] Undressed, that is cold and windy.

Sphere here, sphere there—"Trust me, sweet darling" makes as much sense. Make the sphere clear. Even a high strato-*sphere* would be better than the nebulous, invisible, and intractable GA spheres. What does *sphere* mean? How is the "very gradation ... absolute"? What is "absolute" about a gradation, even in a strato-sphere?

Where does breathable atmosphere end and outer space begin?

3. On P—Smith's Principleism

Ebbie C. Smith is a Principleist (P) who would lie to save lives, and P accredits the lie. P admits that the lie is short of God's ideal and allows for both complexity and the wrongness of the lie. P would later accredit the wrong, making the whole package okay for the good that the choice accomplished, following the precedents in the cases of Rahab and the Hebrew midwives. Unlike NCA and G, P does not find the absolutely Right Choice. P will seek "the reasons a command was given and the ideals behind the law."[543] Therein, P makes room for Love's struggle with a solid deference to God.[544] It was for Smith I wrote the first paper on this, working on my master's degree circa 1989.

4. DA—Maness' Dynamic Absolutism, an Ethic of Love

Maness' Dynamic Absolutism (DA) claims there are times when the absolutely Right Choice in perfect Love is too hard to find. There are no conflicting absolutes, yet still dilemmas befall us where there *appears* to be a conflict. The astronomical difference between the *actuality* and the *appearance* of a conflict is unfurled here between the two absolutes of Love and Truth. In the *appearance* of a conflict, when we are unable to see clearly and the clouds are thick, there always remains a third absolutely Right Choice in perfect Love where no conflict exists—as it was for Jesus.

---

[542] Geisler, *Christian Ethics*, 124, "God does not change.... Furthermore, each particular command is *absolute in its sphere*.... Absolute in order of priority"; cf. "Biblical Absolutes," 219. Italics mine.

[543] Smith, "Ten Commandments," 4; He also says a method of finding ideals behind the Law is similar to the linguistic principle of "dynamic equivalence" in translating, *Syllabus*, 57–59.

[544] Smith, "Ten Commandments." Cf. T. B. Maston, *The Christian, the Church, and Contemporary Problems* (Waco: Word Books, 1968): 187: "It should be remembered ... the lesser of two evils involves some evil, which means that the evil in the decision is to be kept under the constant judgment of the perfect ideal."

In Bucher's dilemma, the demands of Love *appear* to be greater than the demands of Truth. Subjective and impossible to fully articulate, yet the signing of a scrap of paper to save life—*criminy*—demands much from Love and depresses a lot from Truth. Still, it is just an *appearance* of conflict. For Jesus would be more competent. Differing competences are seen in all vocations. A banker may see ten ways to invest, a policeman five ways to respond, and a surgeon three ways to cure where the normal person may see none. Jesus always knew, and we are not as competent.

C. Deontology and Teleology—"Time" Critical to "Rightness"

Every Right Choice involves both *teleology* and *deontology,* and so time itself becomes an integral element in the rightness of every choice. Like many philosophical words, these pull together rich concepts having few clear perimeters. In my book, we detailed their history to condense their essential meanings.[545] Fundamentalists often snub "ends" with a grimace, and in doing so mulch the teleological nature of the Golden Rule.[546]

In addition to arguing for the existence of God, the teleological arguments have served to argue for immortality and creationism.[547] With the cosmological argument, William Lane Craig has argued for creation and the existence of God, and his arguments are supported with a sophistication that at times requires some understanding of physics, and no one has written

---

[545] See H. Richard Niebuhr, "The Meaning of Responsibility" in Wayne G. Boulton, Thomas D. Kennedy, Allen Verhey's *From Christ to the World—Introductory Readings in Christian Ethics* (Grand Rapids: Eerdmans, 1994): 195–204 (referencing Niebuhr's *The Responsible Self* [New York: Harper and Row, 1963]): 200–201, 203. See *Encyclopædia Britannica* (Premium Service, 2004): s.v., deontological ethics, which included Immanuel Kant and W. D. Ross; and s.v., teleological ethics, which included Thomas Hobbes, Jeremy Bentham, John Stuart Mill, Henry Sidgwick, Herbert Spencer, Niccolò Machiavelli and the 19th-century German Friedrich Nietzsche. See Stephen Darwall, *Deontology* (Hoboken: Blackwell, 2003): 1–2, his intro.

[546] See Maness, *Would You Lie to Save a Life?* chap. 5.B.2. "Is the Golden Rule Absolute?"

[547] See Neil A. Manson's masterful *God and Design—The Teleological Argument and Modern Science* (London: Routledge, 2003; 376 pp.), J. D. Barrow and F. J. Tipler's *The Anthropic Cosmological Principle* (Oxford: Oxford Univ. Press, 1986), and William A. Dembski's two fine books, *No Free Lunch—Why Specified Complexity Cannot be Purchased without Intelligence* (Lanham: Rowman and Littlefield, 2002) and *The Design Inference—Eliminating Chance through Small Probabilities* (Cambridge: Cambridge Univ. Press, 1998). See this very readable inquiry, with up-close interviews, by Dembski and Michael Ruse, eds., *Debating Design: from Darwin to DNA* (Cambridge: Cambridge University Press, 2004). See also William Lane Craig's *Philosophy of Religion—a Reader and Guide* (New Brunswick: Rutgers University Press, 2002; 634 pp.); Michael J. Behe's *Darwin's Black Box—the Biochemical Challenge to Evolution* (New York: Simon and Schuster, 1998 [1st 1996]; 307 pp.); and Jane Maienschein and Michael Ruse's *Biology and the Foundation of Ethics* (Cambridge: Cambridge University Press, 1999; 336 pp.). "Intelligent Design" has some top-flight advocates that evolutionists too often refuse to countenance.

more on foreknowledge than Craig.[548] The teleological arguments for God and for the "ends" of a grand design have elegant ethical implications.[549]

Classical Theists argue that God has exhaustively settled *all* of the future. Such makes mush out of most of the N.T. view that God is *still* working in the world today. Some of the future is settled, like the return of Christ and our future heavenly rest, yet some of the future is not settled. Importantly, the future is *not* settled above God's ability to save today and *not* settled above God's ability to prevent a victim's tragedy tomorrow. No one's destiny is so settled that God cannot work today. We have not been given a fake sense of hope in the Bible, and nowhere are we asked to *fake* hope.

Father Time is not greater than Father God.

Genuine Love *demands* that every lost soul and future victim can have an authentic hope *today* that God can save, that the future is not totally set; worse, those who argue for "settled" almost *totally* exclude Love.[550]

Because deontology and teleology are critical, even burdensome words, here are two condensed definitions:

DEONTOLOGY: "Dutiful" because of inherent "Rightness"
    and so ... "Means" are chosen regardless of "Ends"

TELEOLOGY: "Rightness" chosen in view of "Consequences"
    and so ... "Ends" are usually chosen over "Means"

Chart 2. Essence of Deontology and Teleology

---

[548] No one has done more research on foreknowledge, I believe, than William Lane Craig; here are just a few of his books (not including his many articles): *The Only Wise God—The Compatibility of Divine Foreknowledge and Human Freedom* (Eugene: Wipf and Stock, 2000; 157 pp.), *Time and Eternity—Exploring God's Relationship to Time* (Wheaton: Crossway, 2001; 272 pp.), *Divine Foreknowledge and Human Freedom—The Coherence of Theism, Omniscience* (Leiden: Brill, 1990; 360 pp.), *The Problem of Divine Foreknowledge and Future Contingents from Aristotle to Suarez* (Leiden: Brill, 1997; 298 pp.), *The Cosmological Argument from Plato to Leibniz* (New York: Macmillan, 1980; 305 pp.), and *The* Kalam *Cosmological Argument* (New York: Macmillan, 1979). See also Craig and Quentin Smith's *Theism, Atheism, and Big Bang Cosmology* (Oxford: Clarendon Press, 1995).

[549] Some of these arguments intermingle with natural theology. Cf. Marvin Halverson and Arthur A. Cohen, ed., *A Handbook of Christian Theology* (Nashville: Abingdon: 1972 & 1980, 1st 1958), 246–256, esp. articles on "Natural Law" by Samuel Enoch Stumpf and "Natural Theology" by David Cairns.

[550] We compared both sides in *Heart of the Living God: Love, Free Will, Foreknowledge, Heaven: a Theology on the Treasure of Love* (AuthorHouse, 2005; 728 pp.). Clark H. Pinnock's novel and conservative-shaking *Most Moved Mover: A Theology of God's Openness* (Baker, 2001; 218 pp.) is a seminal contribution, though some evangelicals have twisted openness beyond reason. Cf. Bruce A. Ware's pointed *God's Lesser Glory: The Diminished God of Open Theism* (Crossway, 2000; 240 pp.), John S. Feinberg's massive *No One Like Him: The Doctrine of God* (Crossway, 2005; 879 pp.) and John M. Frame's likewise massive *The Doctrine of God: A Theology of Lordship* (P & R, 2002; 896 pp.) powerfully challenge openness but Ware, Feinberg, and Frame almost *totally* exclude Love. Compare John P. Newport, *Life's Ultimate Questions* (New York: W Pub./Harper Collins, 1989; 644 pp.): 443–452; and Colin Brown, *Philosophy and the Christian Faith* (Westmont: IVP, 1969): 24–30.

In their connotations, deontology has carried with it a huge aspect of inherent "rightness," and teleology has carried with it a huge aspect of using ends in "method." Without the loss of any deontological values, the N.T. brought us to and tied us to a teleological/eschatological worldview.

Love's highest work in the teleological. The watcher in the night tower is Responsible for the city within the walls of his or her watch. The watcher's Responsibility looks ever forward into the future of the night with a vigilance to the threatening horizon. We Love and disciple others *on* the concourse of time with a constant vigilance *down* the concourse of time into the future. Clearly then, *without* encountering consequences—and the end in heaven—as crucial to the determination of the "rightness" of a choice, there is no real Love at all. We argue that Love has never been wholly/solely deontological, for Love's highest nature is seen in the teleological, and even toward glory in the eschatological hope of heaven.

D. Absolutes United in Love and Eternity
1. Absolutes Positively Stated Expressions of Love

Absolutes need positively articulated statements.[551] All of the universal absolutes are pre-Fall principles and will continue to exist without change as a part of God's nature.[552] Love and the absolutes are not mere divine expectations. Love is an absolute and also the *vehicle* of the other absolutes, and so Truth is not truly identical with or truly separate from Love. The absolutes express a facet of Love connected to eternity, and principles like the Golden Rule help their expression.

The sum of all absolutes is the good and unhindered *will* of God. Newman Smyth said, "The good ... the right" is the "will of God."[553] Carl F. H. Henry said, "The idea of the good must be identified with the will of God"; furthermore, "The man who does the will of God does what is intrinsically good. At the same time, he does that which will yield to him his greatest personal happiness as well as best promote the general welfare."[554] Emil Brunner said, "The Good is simply and solely the will of God. But the will of God is the will of God for the Kingdom.... Nothing is good save union with the sovereignty of God through this will."[555] Karl Barth said,

---

[551] Cf. Ebbie Smith, *Syllabus*, 14; he explains the meaning through positively stating them.

[552] Carl F. H. Henry, *Christian Personal Ethics* (Grand Rapids: Baker, 1977; 1st 1957; 615 pp.): 264, "Even unfallen man needed supernatural revelation in order to have some content of an approved morality.... From the very outset of human life, the ethical situation was defined by duties and convictions that were not accessible from natural reason alone."

[553] Cf., Newman Smyth, *Christian Ethics* (New York: Charles Scribner, 1908): 68–70 and 170–174.

[554] Henry, *Christian Personal Ethics*, 189 and 209–218: Rom 12:2, the perfect will of God; cf. 278–349: chapters 12 and 13 on the biblical particularization of the will of God.

[555] Emil Brunner, *The Divine Imperative* (Louisville: Westminster, 1947; 728 pp.), 56; cf. 132–151.

"Good means sanctified by God."[556] All these and more are being pleasing to God, *being* like Christ: many parts are linked together to form a contiguous whole, the single absolute of *loving* obedience to God.

Therefore, "Do not murder, lie, steal, or commit adultery" reflect the absolutes—as Laws given *in* time—but are not in and of themselves absolute. The absolutes are "loving, being truthful, sharing, respecting, and being pure"—*being* like Christ. Love and the absolutes had relevance in eternity past and have relevance throughout the eternal future for God and Christ; biblical absolutes are universal and timeless, for they had their origin in the eternal nature and absolute righteousness of God. The Decalogue did not exist from eternity; yet it will remain for eternity as a part of divine Truth, as Jesus said (Matt 5:18). Once in full reception of our inheritance of perfect Love and imperishable righteousness—after heaven has begun—the Law's purpose will cease in eternity to have *ethical* relevance as a separate entity for ethical light and guidance into Love and God's will. The need for Ten Commandments will cease in heaven, for God Himself will be our light.

Is Truth itself just one of the absolute manifestations of Love? We think so. Truth has a seemingly absolute practicality for us here on earth. Yet, the glory of heaven will be a more natural life in Love and Truth than Adam and Eve had before their Fall. Heaven is not a return to Eden, but a new and far superior life. With glorified bodies and God as our light, the word *Truth* will no longer be consciously needed in a life with zero lies, as Truth itself becomes an inherent part of our life, as much as light is now and more so when God becomes our light. We will perfectly *Love* for the rest of our everlasting loving lives.[557] Therein, the need for the word *Truth* will cease in the land totally absent of falsehood, the land where only the Truth lives, the heavenly land of perfected eternal Love.

2. Love Struggles in the Small Window of Time

The most painful aspects of the Bucher's dilemma are seen in the small window of time where the crisis peaks. We have four Christian views in

---

[556] Karl Barth, *Ethics*, trans. Goeffrey W. Bromiley (New York: Seabury, 1981): 16.

[557] See Michael G. Maness, *Heaven—Treasures of Our Everlasting Rest* (Bloomington: AuthorHouse, 2004) and its bibliography here: www.PreciousHeart.net/bibs/Heaven_Bib.htm. Compare Richard Baxter (1615-1691), *The Saints' Everlasting Rest—The Blessed State of the Saints in Their Enjoyment of God in Glory* (London: Rob. White, 1649, 856 pp.; London: Rob. White, 1649, 856 pp.; see http://digitalpuritan.net/richard-baxter/ for *all* of Baxter's work); Alister E. McGrath, *A Brief History of Heaven* (Hoboken: Wiley-Blackwell, 2003); J. Oswald Sanders, *Heaven: Better by Far—Answers to Questions About the Believer's Final Hope* (Grand Rapids: Discovery House, 1993); Millard J. Erickson, *Contemporary Options in Eschatology* (Grand Rapids: Baker, 1977); Jerry L. Walls, *The Oxford Handbook on Eschatology* (Oxford: Oxford University Press, 2010); and, C. S. Lewis' masterful, *The Great Divorce: A Fantastic Bus Ride from Hell to Heaven—a Round Trip for Some, but Not for Others* (New York: Macmillan, 1946). Cf. fn. 534.

DA, P, GA, and NCA, and we have the great *appearance* of a conflict between the absolutes of Truth and Love in the saving of life.

> **Small Window of Time OPENS** at the point where the Koreans calloused and believed they *must* murder, and importantly it opens at the point where Bucher and his men *perceive* that the Koreans *will* murder.

> **Small Window of Time CLOSES** after Bucher decided to sign the lying confession ... or was killed.

When the Time Zone of hope for rescue passes—when this Small Window opens—Bucher and his men believe and have become *convinced* that they have come to an end. The young *Pueblo* fireman Howard Bland is first. All the Koreans want is a lying signed confession to being in Korean *water*. Lie about being in the wrong *water*! The window closes when Bucher makes a choice ... or when Bucher himself is killed.

Bucher is given a pen to sign the confession. A murder hangs in the air dependent upon the scratch of his pen. If he waits any longer—in his understanding—death will result; the Small Window opens. That determination is critical. If he signs the confession, at least in this Time Zone—as *Bucher* believes—he and his men will not be killed. After a visit to the North Korean torture chamber, here are Bucher's own words:

> The name was read from the list ... Fireman Howard Bland ... youngest crew member. Would these animals dare kill him before my eyes? The vision of that tortured South Korean hanging from a strap with his compound fracture, blinded eye and multiple contusions reappeared on the wall of the room in full, horribly vivid reality. Yes, this breed of politics did not give a damn about the life or death of their own kinsmen—let alone any round-eyed Americans! I could not even contemplate leaving Bland's life at their mercy for the sake of my signature on a scrap of paper containing nothing but blatantly obvious lies and propaganda.... I had resisted as long as I could, but now I could do none other than finally give in to a totally foreign brutality. I made up my mind: '**All right ... I will sign.**' [The colonel hissed and thrust the pen into Bucher's hand, instructing the others to help Bucher.][558]

What a struggle of Love! Even waiting was a choice; at this time *waiting* appeared to be a fatal choice, where young fireman Bland would be *killed*. At the precise moment that Commander Bucher made the choice to sign and took the pen, all of them entered into a new Time Zone—saved to live—and the Small Window closed. In that Small Window, we see more clearly how Love and Truth *appeared* to collide (my book extrapolated many details). Bucher could not find the absolutely Right Choice, but he did choose *life*, in

---

[558] Lloyd M. Bucher, *Bucher: My Story* (Doubleday, 1970), chapter XII, 227–253. Brackets mine, reflecting "hissed" used by Bucher while condensing his larger context. Bold mine.

Love for his crew over Truth: and that appears to be the closest we can get, as least on this side of heaven. We are not as competent as Christ.

3. Love's Infinity of Variables on the Concourse of Time

Regarding our obligations to Love, we cannot give up our search for a cure to cancer, and we should not give up on Bucher's dilemma until we have found the absolutely Right Choice in perfect Love. Ethics is the science of "what we ought to do," even when the cancers of hate flood the world. Nations in world wars have staked their futures upon what they considered "right." This played out horrifically in the Ukraine in 2022.

Love is even more important than any science, for there is no scientist who would trade his or her discovery of the greatest formula (or cure) for the *Love* of his or her family. Reverse that, and we see that the reason the scientist searches is *because* of Love for his family and all our families.

On the battlefield struggling to find Love, you and I work within our unique selves and unique situations that are different from every other person in millions of ways with respect to psychology, experience, spirituality, and general knowledge. Each unique person is placed into several unique arenas at the same *time*, as seen below.

---

1. A UNIQUE Historical/Social Time Frame
2. A UNIQUE Set of Circumstances within that Time Frame
3. A UNIQUE Set of Relationships—with God and with Others
4. A UNIQUE Personality & Psychology & Moral Fortitude
5. A UNIQUE Set of Drives & Fears & Physical Fortitude
6. A UNIQUE Fund of Knowledge
7. A UNIQUE Set of Abilities.
   —And each of these are changing every hour of every day.

Chart 3. Unique Arenas of Individuals

There are more ways to categorize these. *All* these unique arenas are in intensive view at the same *time* by the person *in* a death-defying crisis.[559]

The unique arenas are an integral part of the whole enterprise of Love and ethics—in searching for the "right" choice—where a unique person is impelled in unique dilemmas to apply teleological principles like the Golden Rule. All the effort is *dynamic* within the confines of Truth and with a heart

---

[559] Cf. Helmut Thielicke, *Theological Ethics, Volume 1: Foundations*, ed. William H. Lazareth (Philadelphia: Fortress Press, 1966): 578, "Ethics ... is similar to that in medicine. The problems do not arise with the ordinary cases, but in the borderline cases, those involving transitions or complications. It is the abnormal rather than the normal case which brings us up against the real problems. Hence the real test, even in respect of foundational principles, is whether an ethics has been proved in the crucible of the borderline situation and emerged with even deeper insights."

of Love that teleologically seeks first the kingdom of God. *Dynamic* means the ever-looking vigilance within the ever-changing—living—uniqueness that unfolds down the concourse of time for each person. Hence, that is why we call our ethic *Dynamic* Absolutism.

"Time" is critical. In looking back or ahead to the future for the rightness of a given choice, God judges not only one's understanding but also judges the constricting elements of time. God judges the entire house, not just the Small Window of time.

Dynamic Absolutism (DA) forwards that the element of "time" is critical to the determination of "rightness" in every situation, making the teleological a *necessary* ingredient in every Right Choice. If we do not, we deny the ethical practicality of faith, hope, and Love, as they all *point beyond themselves* in their own definitions and beyond ourselves in our use of them on the concourse of time. Not a mere Responsibility, God has given us the *gift* of contemplating the future. Made in the image of God, our hope in heaven is as sure as the promises of God. With teleological principles like the Golden Rule, and with Love's eternal connections, we have one foot on earth and one in heaven, ethically, and so a Right Choice in perfect Love is somehow *in time* connected to our thinking of tomorrow's heaven.

E. Love's Simplicity Amid Eternal Complications
1. Manifold Struggles between Legality and License

Four ethical systems justify a choice: NCA tells the Truth; GA, P, and DA lie in Love to save life. See below how they line up rather neatly with respect to Love's struggle between legality and license.

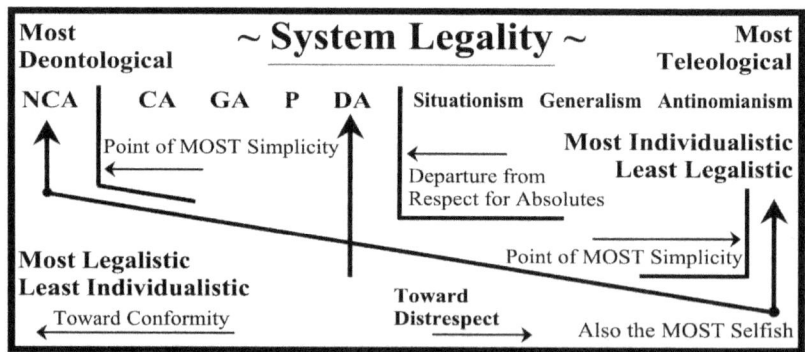

Chart 4. Love's Struggle between Legality and License

The "most legalistic/least individualistic" on the far-left contrasts with the "least legalistic/most individual" on the far right.[560] Somewhere between

---

[560] Obviously, "right" or "left" has no ethical bearing, as the chart can be easily reversed.

them is the line of departure from a respect of absolutes (center), and moving right of that line is an *increasing* departure from a respect for absolutes. Those farthest to the right do walk the wasteland of the lawless antinomian caveman and criminal. In Chart 4, the four systems line up neatly into comfort zones within legality and individualism.[561] As the most deontological, NCA is the most comfortable in legality and least comfortable in individuality. NCA and the others betray how much each consider deontology *with* or *without* teleological concerns. If NCA's maxim "the end *never* justifies the means" is true, then the Golden Rule not only appears useless but *is* useless.[562] (CA is in the book.) Next, GA takes confidence in its ability to *grade* and *exempt* absolutes, followed by P who accredited a saving lie as "right." DA follows as the most teleological.

2. Teleological and Deontological Analysis of Love's Choice

The complexity in Chart 5 below tackles three questions:
1. How do the choices by DA, P, GA, and NCA relate to the deontological and the teleological aspects inherent in their choices?
2. How do the deontological and the teleological aspects relate to each other?
3. Are there any implications from these relationships?

Dealing with these questions cause complication to metastasize into at least 8 quadrants of Responsibility for DA, P, and GA, and 8 quadrants for NCA; and those 16 contrast with the 8 quadrants in the supermarket scenario in which all four make the same choice. Positively said, the grid shows the artfully interwoven nature of a single precious choice—we are fearfully and wonderfully made (Ps 139:14). Chart 5 shows the elegant complications in the delicate ethical relationships within Bucher's choice to Love with a lie; therefore, his choice is at the same *time*:

—Deontologically *wrong* because of the inherent value of Truth,
—Deontologically *right* because of the inherent value of Love,
—Teleologically *wrong* because of the long-term effects normally associated with Lying against Truth, and
—Teleologically *right* because looking forward in Love saves lives.

Chart 5 below was a big grizzly bear and hard to take down. Every choice can be broken down into fundamental parts between the deontological and the teleological. The best part of Chart 5 is also its most subtle, for it also reveals the many ethically elegant facets of Love *in* action.

---

[561] Cf. Geisler, *Christian Ethics*: situationism, 43–62; generalism, 63–78; antinomianism, 29–42. Situationism usually holds to one absolute like Love that is relative. Generalism/utilitarianism does not believe in absolutes but does in ethical laws with good results. Antinomianism does not believe in any objective criteria at all, from God or utility, and therein nearly everything is individually relative.

[562] Rakestraw, "Ethical Choices," 251–52, italics mine.

Teleological / Deontological Analysis of Choices											
Commander Bucher's Dilemma								**Theft at Supermarket**			
Lie may save the lives; Truth may bring murder								Ch *clear* for all systems			
Each System Chooses #1 Over #2	DA, P, GA Choices 1. Lie & Save L./Love [Ch 1] 2. Truth & Murder				NCA Choice 1. Truth &/or Murder [Ch 2] 2. Lie & Save Life/Love				DA, P, GA & NCA Ch T/Honesty & M/Hunger [Ch 3] L/Theft & S/Satiation			
	More Teleological Ch				More Deontological Ch				More Deontological Ch			
Top Row Over Left Side Column	G		G		G		G		G		G	
	Tel Ch	Deon Ch	Tel Ch	Deon Ch	Tel Ch	Deon Ch	Tel Ch	Deon Ch	Tel Ch	Deon Ch	Tel Ch	Deon Ch
<top row over>	S	S	L	L	T	T	M	M	T	T	M	M
G Tel Ch	T	T	T	T	S	S	S	S	S	S	S	S
<top row over>	S	S	L	L	T	T	M	M	T	T	M	M
G Deon Ch	T	T	T	T	S	S	S	S	S	S	S	S
<top row over>	S	S	L	L	T	T	M	M	T	T	M	M
B Tel Ch	M	M	M	M	L	L	L	L	L	L	L	L
<top row over>	S	S	L	L	T	T	M	M	T	T	M	M
B Deon Ch	M	M	M	M	L	L	L	L	L	L	L	L
Column Totals for G & B Choices Respectively	L = 0 T = 4 M = 4 S = 8		L = 8 T = 4 M = 4 S = 0		L = 4 T = 8 M = 0 S = 4		L = 4 T = 0 M = 8 S = 4		L = 4 T = 8 M = 0 S = 4		L = 4 T = 0 M = 8 S = 4	
Grand Totals for G & B Choices Together	L = 8 T = 8 M = 8 S = 8				L = 8 T = 8 M = 8 S = 8				L = 8 T = 8 M = 8 S = 8			
~ Abbreviations ~	Tel G Ch = One a system determines is "Right" from Consequences Deon G Ch = One a system determines is "Right" in itself										
Tel = Teleological Deon = Deontological	Tel B Ch = One a system determines is "Wrong" from Consequences Deon B Ch = One a system determines is "Wrong" in itself										
DA = Dynamic Absolutism P = Principleism GA = Graded Absolutism NCA = Non-Conflicting Absolutism				G = Good B = Bad Ch = Choice				L = Lying T = Truth M = Murder S = Saving Life / Love			

Chart 5. Teleological-Deontological Analysis of Choice

See color version at www.PreciousHeart.net/love/Chart-24-a.jpg > [563]

---

[563] Note that Chart 5 here is Chart 24 in my book, *Would You Lie to Save a Life?*, and the color version that helps distinguish the divisions at www.PreciousHeart.net/love/Chart-24-a.jpg.
   Notice "Ch 3" is a third scenario of Supermarket Theft contrasted in the book.

The color version allows more detail in the divisions. See that DA, P, and GA chose a more Teleological Choice in 8 quadrants, and that NCA chose a more Deontological Choice in 8 quadrants.

In "Ch 1" in the first upper-left quadrant, see that S is over T, indicating that Saving Life with Love was chosen over Truth, and that is basically interpreted at a G-Tel-Ch = Good Teleological Choice over a B-Tel-Ch = Bad Teleological Choice. In the first upper-left quadrant, because Love and Truth both have uniquely good teleological aspects, the choice to Love is a *good* teleological choice that was chosen over the *good* teleological elements that are usually associated with Truth. And so forth goes the variations in each of the 8 quadrants of each system, DA, P, GA; and likewise in "Ch 2" within NCA's 8 quadrants in Bucher's dilemma. This is a first in many ways. The full relevance of the totals remains to be developed, along with the possibility of other quadrants. After the choice is made, see how each choice is either *more* teleological or *more* deontological, and each contains both a greater good and a lesser evil.

While skinning the grizzly bear, and trying to *chart* the relations, it took some time to discern the "teleological bad choice" of Truth, which we ethically connected to the likelihood of murder in Bucher's dilemma.

When we scraped the bear hide for curing, we saw subtle variations *within* each choice. Each choice has 16 relations of continuums (this-over-that) in the 8 quadrants. Each choice of the four systems, then, yields 32 fundamental elements of unique ethical finesse within each choice of NCA, GA, P, DA; that is, each of the 32 elements in each of the four systems vary slightly one from another. Therefore, the 32 elements illuminate a unique ethical strand within each of the four ethical systems; furthermore, within the four systems, we *then* see at least 128 uniquely finessed and truly elegant fundamental points of view within Bucher's single dilemma.

Looking at the left set of the three choices illustrated in Chart 5, where DA, GA, and P chose to lie to save a life, we see several perspectives in each of the 16 continuums in the 8 quadrants. A long-term good softens a long-term bad when we choose to Love (a specific right) to save life with a lie (a specific wrong). Here, a more teleological Truth (of Love) was chosen over a more deontological Truth (telling Truth and not lying), based primarily on the greater demands of Love over the demands of Truth in our Responsibility to look ahead and *down* the concourse of Time. Exclusively for DA, the lie was still wrong (deontologically) but less wrong than murder (teleologically); or, and importantly, the Truth was more wrong (teleologically viewing Bucher's partial responsibility in a prospective murder) than the lie (deontologically viewing Love in saving of lives).

We scraped the bear hide much more in the book. Once a system makes a choice, the choices can be charted. Prima facie, this almost appears like splitting a frog's hair, but is not. The grizzly bear hide in Chart 5 renders neatly, even elegantly 32 elements in 16 continuums in 8 quadrants of complex relations between the teleological and deontological jewels of each system's choice: and that is at least 128 unique and elegant elements among all four systems in the single dilemma of Commander Bucher.

In summary, the DA choice to Love with a lie that saves life was *as close* to the absolutely Right Choice in perfect Love as we were capable of finding—this side of heaven. Furthermore, Chart 5 is the perspective of DA, for NCA does *not* view Truth as a participation in murder, as hard to understand as that appears here to DA. Murder is the DA judgment upon the NCA option, because NCA would choose Truth even if murder was the reasonably expected result inside the **Small Window of Time**. With teleology and with DA's *"time* critical to *rightness,"* we conclude that if Bucher had chosen NCA's Truth, then that would have forced to Bucher some culpability in murder. We believe Bucher felt the same.

That chart was a big grizzly bear to skin. But once stretched out, its wondrous symmetry made the heart warm as it laid bare the elegant complexity of each unique choice, and it makes Love exponentially richer—all of this elevating higher Christ's holiness. There may be a better way to skin that bear. But there it is, taken out of the wild and on display, in a way, the first mapping of four choices' genome with their 128 fundamental elements in the grandeur of their teleological and deontological elegance.

The bear hunt is not over. For Bucher's honor, we need to continue to search for more of this bear's kin still hibernating in the Alaskan mountain ranges of ethical complexity. Let's continue to hunt for the elusive absolutely Right Choice in perfect Love in Bucher's dilemma.

3. Five Implication of Chart 5—the Fuller Elegance of Perfected Love

While Chart 5 proves little in itself—just a bear hide after all—the chart does show in one look a multitude of relationships in two significant areas of complexity hitherto unexplored:

1. *Many* interrelations of the teleological and the deontological natures of one choice chosen over another choice;
2. *Many* of the relations of a specific choice made by each system.

Herein, we saw clearer our **Responsibility to Love** at the fundamental level. The chart reduces a lot of rhetoric in the attempt to picture the fine relations between the teleological and the deontological, and surely there are more relations. Though fine, even subatomic, the distinctions between the quadrants illustrate the complex elegance of 32 elements of each system's *best* choice. And even though three of the systems make the same choice—GA, P, DA—each of those three justifies their choices in a *different* manner. Furthermore, the 32 elements resident in all four systems of NCA, GA, P,

DA showcase the extraordinary *minimum* of 128 fundamental elements. Moreover, if we ever find the elusive Right Choice, oddly enough, it will not have 16 continuums with 32 elements, for the *absolutely* Right Choice has no "bad" elements; the Right Choice will have only 2 quadrants with 4 continuums, with 8 good fundamental elements (and no bad ones).

Importantly, if we do find the Right Choice, we assume it will be clear, something that all Christians can see and agree upon. Just like when Jesus asked, "Let him who has no sin, cast the first stone" (John 8:7), "rightness" *immediately* became crystal clear to all; immediately, all agreed that all were sinners. So then, similarly, once the Right Choice is clearly seen, the other systems' choices fall off the chart, including mine. Stripped of 24 elements, what remains is the absolutely Right Choice that has at least 8 good fundamental elements. Therefore, regarding Love in ethics, there are at least five implications that Chart 5 illuminates concerning Love's depth.

- **1st**—On the nature of the totals found—Is there a bridge between a choice and that choice's rightness supplied by *math*?
- **2nd**—On how it undergirds our conviction that each system's choice has elements that are *both* teleological and deontological.
- **3rd**—On the nature of *choosing* itself and how every choice has an emphasis that is either more teleological or more deontological.
- **4th**—On the ease of finding decision once the Right Choice has been found to be *elusive* and beyond grasp at the critical *time*, inside the Small Window.
- **5th**—On what Chart 5 *does not* say—that when many right options are available, decision-making should *still* be as complicated for each individual.

Chart 5's complex relations bring speculation. When Distinguished Professor Stephen Hawking said, "We have, as yet, had little success in predicting human behavior from mathematical equations," he was talking about extrapolating the final spin of atoms and bridging the gaps between the physical, the biological, and the volitional.[564] We adduce from these totals a small implication about a bridge between a choice and that choice's "rightness," a bridge supplied by math, even if perturbing and elemental.

If there is substance to a math bridge, one is forced to wonder what other developments could be made from math. Einstein and colleagues figured on paper first the nature of the atomic bomb. The angles of a triangle are only *perfect* in the equation $a^2+b^2=c^2$—thank you, Pythagoras.[565]

Love still found a way through the complex and elegant symmetry between all the teleological and the deontological elements of Bucher's

---

[564] Stephen Hawking, *A Brief History of Time* (New York: Bantam, 1988): 168.

[565] The Pythagorean Theorem: "The sum of the squares of the legs of a right triangle equals the square of its hypotenuse."

choice. What other mysteries are there to Love's divine symmetry? What Chart 5 helped me see more clearly is a difference between two views of life in general: a focus on *hunting* good is better than a focus on *avoiding* bad. We want to live our life "to Love" more than "to avoid hate." At first, that was hard to articulate, and the scraping of the bear skin was demanding and really stunk. Spiritually speaking, we are far better off *loving* God and others as a mode of life than we would be in the near impossible focus of trying to discern and then *avoid* Satan's wiles. We give more in the book.

Though the Right Choice eluded us in Bucher's dilemma, we still had guidance, for in Love and through DA we proceeded with clear teleological principles like the Great Commands and the Golden Rule as we sought first God's kingdom. Chart 5 does not say straightforwardly, but it does certainly reveal more of the height of Christ's holiness. Have not *all* sinned and come short of Christ's competence? Who can make *any* choice as competently? Therefore, every choice *short* of Jesus' has a unique complication with a still beautifully elegant symmetry of at least 32 fundamental elements.

Furthermore, that does not mean that anyone must articulate any of the 32 elements in order to live well. One does not need the ability to explain the law of gravity to know that carelessness on a roof top can result in a broken bone should one fall off. An Olympic ice skater needs not to know an iota of physics to do a triple axel. There is a large difference between explaining Love and *Loving*. Best of all and any day of the week, God and our family and friends prefer the *Love* over any ability to explain Love. The real measure of Love is how careful the person is with respect to what they do understand and with respect to what they actually *do* in Love and Truth.

Conclusion: Love and Truth Converge on the Concourse of Life

In my book *Would You Lie to Save a Life?*, we also detailed seven fine lines between God's sovereign abilities and our free will, and we discerned at least 23 variables in every decision this side of heaven.[566]

The natural-born ability to Love is converted and even connected to heaven when we are spiritually born again; thereafter, Love never dies and always looks ahead and down the concourse of time, even and necessarily heavenward. On earth, our ethical struggle is a sacred trust in Love with a somewhat open future in our divine gift to make unique choices in a grand stewardship of time. In our *Imago Dei*, all humans are spiritual beings with two natural-born innate God-like abilities:

---

[566] See Maness, *Would You Lie to Save a Life?*, chap. 15.B.1 and chap. 1.B.2 with Chart 33. Seven fine lines are between: 1. God's sovereignty and free-will participation, 2. God's light and our rebellion, 3. deontological and teleological in *every* absolute, 4. when a person is or is not responsible for others, 5. a high or low degree of responsibility decides the teleological or deontological choice, 6. fruitful and redundant study, and 7. between valuable ethical deliberation and wasting *time*.

(1) to Love and (2) to make unique choices in time every time. Believer or not—every person is born with these two abilities.

Once spiritually born again, our natural-born *Imago Dei* abilities *to Love* and *to make unique choices* are miraculously freed and spiritually rewired— i.e., reconciled to God. Our faith, hope, and Love are no longer merely and solely earth-bound endeavors. Our highly treasured abilities *to Love* and *to make unique choices in time* are enriched even turbocharged through our living real-time spiritual relationship with God. We have been raised from the dead with a higher ability to Love; we are freed and set loose to more fully exhibit our *Imago Dei* on earth in view of our heavenly inheritance. Once born again, our natural-born *Imago Dei* abilities increase, and a third ability appears in our life with the perception of a Scarlet Thread that links us to the *potential* of choosing absolutely Right Choices in perfect Love—a Scarlet Thread unique to every person—as it was for Christ who followed His Scarlet Thread fully and without error. Therefore, our born-again *Imago Dei* includes a trinity of divinely gifted human abilities in Love:

1. **Our ability to Love,**
2. **Our ability to make unique choices in time, a stewardship of time,**
3. **Our ability to see and touch the availability of a Scarlet Thread of absolutely Right Choices in perfect Love.**

Chart 6. *Imago Dei* Trinity of Human Abilities in Love

When a person becomes a Christian, their *Imago Dei* abilities are freed, as if we learned to fly, and more so, for we are transformed from an earthly disconnected person—in the dark—into a heaven-bound child of God. We receive a portion of our eternal inheritance on earth, and so once *born* of and *related* to God—being *in* Christ—our Love is given a resurrection ability, an eternal caliber of endurance, and a philosophical depth that connects Love to eternity itself. We possess eternal life *this* side of heaven. Therein, we are divinely freed from darkness and divinely empowered to perceive a Scarlet Thread of absolutely Right Choices in perfect Love that unfurls before us down the concourse of time on earth toward heaven.

Because of the clouds, we often do not find the thread. God Himself bears witness with our spirit that we are his children, entitled to a peace that passes understanding, something a non-Christian cannot know. Our ability to Love reaches beyond earth toward heaven. Though we only know in part, we look for the promised treasure that—then—we shall enjoy in heaven when we shall become like Christ, obtaining a competence that was solely Christ's on earth; in heaven, we shall be able to *always* grasp the Scarlet Thread forevermore, *always* choosing unique absolutely Right Choices in perfect Love every second of *time* throughout our everlasting loving lives.

Our Love and our ethic are eschatological, or they are nothing. But you do not have to tell that to two people in Love. You only have to tell those who wish to analyze Love.

Christians are mountain climbers, struggling with Love all the way to the top. In mountain climbing, we must be careful. We need to watch our steps so that those below will not be hit by a disturbed stone. We certainly need concern for system making, lest we trip others up unknowingly. We have seen what devastation that carelessness causes, as with those who *grade* absolutes and make the very gradation absolute. We have also seen those who lift their own maxim of "the end never justifies the means" over the absolute of Love. Those are devastating to Love, turn our relationships into investigations, and they rather categorically short circuit Love.

Furthermore, my position on the mountain is never measured in competition with other climbers. If I succumb to the temptation to believe I am higher up than another, then that just might mean that the air got too thin, and I am not getting enough oxygen to my brain. I might be getting light-headed. I should take a break, look at the map again, and get my head back together. Lest I go out of my mind, or worse, pass out and fall off the mountain of Love altogether. Mountain climbing is dangerous, especially if you lose your way or lose your mind. Do not lose the map.

Do not get lost in the snow, and there is a lot of snow.

We can always Love. The greatest gift of God to humanity is Love—see His Son—the heart of two Great Commands. The simplest point also becomes infinitely profound and freeing. Look at Bucher's horrendous *ethical* dilemma and Viktor Frankl's tortures as a Jewish prisoner of the Nazis, and see that **we *can* still Love in hell on earth.**

In all of its beauty and vast golden treasure, Love places our hearts in two *times* at once. We Love God and others on earth, and at the same *time* our hearts look down the concourse of time for how to Love tomorrow in faith, hope, and Love, all in view of our heavenly home—in Christ connected to eternity. Our progress in faith, hope, and Love is a sacred trust and stewardship of *time* bequeathed to us at creation and recharged after our spiritual resurrection. Our being made in the Image of God and then being raised to a new freedom as a new creation are manifested most exquisitely in our ability to make unique choices in an eternally-connected Love and to be Loved uniquely—every time, all of the time, even throughout the rest of our everlasting loving lives. As for now, we struggle together to do our best to exhibit faith, hope, and Love, but the greatest of these is eternal Love.

17.
The Church as Alternative Community: A South African Perspective

Professor Godfrey Harold
Principal and Senior Lecturer in Systematic Theology
Cape Town Baptist Seminary, South Africa
Distinguished Fellow, B. H. Carroll Theological Institute
Irving, Texas[567]

Introduction 253
A. Early Judaic Alternative Communities and the Church 255
B. The Present South African Context... 256
C. The Expression of the Church as Alternative Community in South Africa.. 257
   1. Church that Breaks Down Barriers.. 257
   2. Reconciliatory Church and Restitution.. 258
   3. Compassion of the Church 260
   4. Love from the Church 262
Conclusion 263

Introduction

In 1994, when the African National Congress was elected into power by the true majority, South Africa emerged from a state of legislated racial speratedness known as apartheid into a democratic state. During the apartheid era, the church adopted this system either explicitly or implicitly by adpoting a "policy of no comment." However, there were some sporadic voices from within the church: Allan Boesack, Bishop Desmond Tutu, Beyers Naudé, and David J. Bosch who opposed this heretical system and called for an alternative community. The alternative community had to confront this oppressive system that dehumanised the majority. The

---

[567] Harold earned his PhD from the University of Western Cape, Cape Town, South Africa; his Th and MRE from Trinity Graduate School of Apologetics and Theology; and his MTh, BA, and BT (Honors) from University of Zululand, Kwazulu Natal, South Africa. Harold is the managing editor for the *South African Baptist Journal of Theology*, associate researcher at the University of Pretoria, and serves on the editorial board of *Pharos Theological Journal*. He has been an adjunct professor in the Faith amd Heritage cluster and supervised a PhD student for the B. H. Carroll Theological Institute, Irving, Texas. He has published over 28 peer-reviewed articles in national and international theological Journals, including "The Christian and Suffering: A Philosophical Question and a Pastoral Response," *Midwestern Theological Journal* 4, no. 2 (2006): 93-100; "An Evangelical Response to Postmodernism," *The South African Baptist Theological Journal* 16 (2008): 61-65; "Affirmative Action as an Approach to Economic Restitution in Post-Apartheid South Africa: a Reading of Luke 19:1-10," *The South African Baptist Journal of Theology* 25 (2015): 25-43. He is the author of *The Apostolic and Prophetic Reformation: A Critical Study* (Rita, Latvia: Lambert Academic Publishing, 2017; 117 pp.). He recently wrote the chapter "The Story of the Indian Church in South Africa" in *Diaspora Christianities: Global Scattering and Gathering of South Asian Christians*, ed. Sam George (Minneapolis: Fortress Press, 2019; 200 pp.). See www.ctbs.org.za and godfrey@ctbs.org.za.

alternative community, more so for Bosch, had to be confrontational and liberative; she would not recuse herself to personal piety but to gospel performance. This type of movement had to be revolutionary in its engagement, but not violent. Pillay (2015) said,

> in South Africa under apartheid the human community was separated and destroyed by racial and economic oppression. The task of the church is to rebuild this human community. Some 20 years after the establishment of a democratic South Africa it is questionable whether we are succeeding in the endeavour of building such a community.

This chapter suggests that the church in this present dispensation should see herself as an alternative community in order to address through prophetic utterance and creative action the challenging issues that impinge upon the Imago Dei and the dignity of being human.

The *Cambridge Dictionary* defines *alternative* "as something that is different from something else, especially from what is usual," and it defines *community* as "people living in one particular area or people who are considered as a unit because of their common interest, background or nationality." For the church in South Africa to become alternative in this new dispensation, she must call herself to address the human needs in response to and in light of "the active presence of God for the life of the world" (Craig Dykstra and Dorothy Bass, 2002, p. 18). The church as an alternative community forms practices that are communal, yet unique, by demonstrating through her enactments that she is God's redemptive movement within society. The church becomes the embodiment of the living presence of God that is revealed through her actions because of grace and a continuing relationship with God through the Holy Spirit. Miroslav Volf (2002, p. 255) indicates this most clearly: "human beings are made participants in divine activity and therefore are inspired, empowered and obliged to imitate it (Grace)."

John Swinton (2006, p. 83) describes Christian engagement as the "resonance of grace" that occurs in response to the human experience of divine grace. Such practices are designed to sustain faith and hope in a context that often appears hopeless and less than grace-filled. The practices of the *alternative community* thus forms the constituent and critical element in the country or city in that the living of life itself becomes incarnational when the church lives in the light of and in response to God's gift of abundant life. The key to success is practice. It is not enough just to know what to do, but to do it. By consistently doing, practice becomes a habit; moreover, Christian practice is not mere actions, but something reflective of who we are—we are a people of reconciliation, compassion, and love. We must become a people who are dependent on God because we know God.

Before we engage the practice of an alternative community, attention is drawn to the existence of early Judaic alternative communities.

A. Early Judaic Alternative Communities and the Church

During the times of the earthly ministry of Jesus, the Jewish nation was under the control of the Roman Empire (30 B.C. to AD 70). Before the Roman control of Israel, the Jews were under the governance of the Greeks (330–30 B.C.). During this time alternative communities developed within common Judaism like the Sadducees who helped with the Hellenization and the Pharisees who maintained a legalistic religiosity that prevented Hellenistic spirituality from contaminating their religion. The Essenes isolated themselves from all public life by becoming ascetic, and the Jewish Zealots rebelled against the Greco-Roman empires and took up arms.

Within common Judaism, another community developed around AD 30 called the church—*ekklesia*, "those called out" as from their homes to a specific place, occurring 111 times in the N.T. The word for church has at least two backgrounds, the classical Greek and the Old Testament. Millard Erickson (1999, p. 1041) states in classical Greek the word finds its expression in *ekklesia* and is found as early as Herodotus, Thucydides, Exenophon, and Euripides. It refers to a *polis* (city). In the secular sense, the word refers to a political gathering, an assembly of persons, or those called together by a herald: or simply, it is a meeting of people. The Greco-Roman usage of the term *ekklesia* refers to a political gathering. Thus, the Christian usage of the term *ekklesia* is radically different from how the Roman-Greco world used and understood it.

From the O.T., the etymology resonates more with the Hebrew word *kahal* that is employed in the Septuagint to infer those gathered by God. Hans Kung (1986, p. 82) states, "By taking over the term *ekklesia*, the early Christian community made its claim to be the true congregation of God, the true community of God, and the true eschatological people of God. Related to *ekklesia*, two times in the N.T. the word *kurisakos* used for those 'belonging to the Lord.'"

The Christian church is that community of people called into being by the life and resurrection of Jesus (Hans Kung, 1981, p. 75). James Cone (1986, p. 115) argues "the identity of the church found in Jesus. To ask 'What is the church' is also to ask 'Who is Jesus' for without Jesus the church has no identity." Thus, without the raising of Jesus from the dead, the church has no meaning. With the affirmation of faith that Jesus is what he claimed to be, the Messiah, a new alternative community was born—the church.

At the center of the church's teaching, stands Jesus, the Messiah, Man, resurrected Lord and Saviour. True God and true man, the Lord of the cosmos. Thus, the New Testament teaching was that Christians should now live the way of Jesus (Matt 16:24). Christians are called to model Jesus everywhere, privately and in the public square. Therefore, understanding the gospel that Jesus proclaimed underlines the practice of the church. The gospel makes clear that it is the "gospel of the kingdom." This gospel calls all people, and those who "enter do so by sheer grace" (Sider, 2007, p. 171).

This new alternative community that Jesus formed requires of his followers to live by a new radical ethic that asks Christians to minister to the oppressed and to the marginalized, to challenge the privileged or wealthy, to reject the way of violence, and to love our enemies. Those who become part of this community do so by responding in faith to Jesus Christ and his message, which brings them into salvation. Thus, this new way of life in Jesus Christ includes a relationship with God through Jesus Christ and a new economic relationship with others (Luke 19:9) as demonstrated when Zacchaeus responded to the message of Jesus. This new community also has a new social order, where racial and social hostility is overcome by the power of the resurrected Christ (Gal 3:28). R. J. Sider (2007, p. 173) states that the church is visible, public, and in some very real sense a political reality. Both the economic sharing and the rejection of ethnic division were so visible that it drew non-Christians to embrace Christ.

B. The Present South African Context

The present South African context is one of a burgeoning democracy that is fast becoming one of the most unequal countries in which to live. In South Africa, 26 million out of the 55 million citizens are now living below the poverty index of two dollars a day. T. Shabala, CEO of Standard Bank, brought this out most clearly,

> Most black South Africans—and most Africans in particular—remain severely disadvantaged compared to white South Africans. 4% of adult Africans have a tertiary qualification; 25% of white South Africans do. Throughout the South African economy, 70% of top managers and 59% of senior managers are white. The unemployment rate among Africans is 28.8%; among white people, it is 5.9%. 61% of white South Africans live in households that spend more than R10 000 a month; only 8% of Africans can spend that much. 16% of Africans live in extreme poverty and regularly suffer hunger; 99.9% of white South Africans are better off than that.

Over the last few months, South Africans have witnessed a rise in protestation. The year 2016 began with a flurry of racist comments on social media, and the majority of South African youth are becoming disillusioned with the present ANC-led government. While most South Africans want to live in harmony with each other, this desire is being frustrated by the legacy of apartheid leading to hatred.

To this tension the church must respond, not in living an "ascetic" life by disconnecting herself and becoming otherworldly, but by immersing and identifying herself with the struggles of the majority in post-apartheid South Africa. To become the voice of the voiceless and the marginalised, the church must become the prophetic conscience of the government. The church must share the message and defend the oppressed. The church as an alternative community in post-Apartheid South Africa is to be the catalyst for the flourishing of others, thus requiring her to affirm the bonds of common humanity. This calls for the active caring for justice and for the common good, flowing from identification with the needs and rights of others. Thus, "solidarity is not a state of affair or goal, but a virtue that impels the church into action" (Cochran, 2007, p. 5).

The church of Jesus Christ is a liberated and separated people, whose faith in Christ is a life lived in the presence of the Creator. This critical awareness of God's presence manifested through the Church calls for an ethical responsibility to ask what should be done to restore the dignity of the once oppressed majority. The words of Emil Brunner (1937, p. 164) are apropos:

> The true being of man, therefore, can mean nothing else than standing in the love of God, being drawn into his love for man. This means living life as a community which derives its source in God through Christ which is directed towards other human beings and the interest of others.

In other words, this understanding sees "being" as a gift of the Creator God, who has revealed himself through Jesus Christ, which also is a recognition that the end of humanity is an active discipleship of love for God and neighbour. Thus, the church becomes a model which a wounded country can follow. While the church lives in a secular culture, it does not in any sense transcend the culture around them; quite to the contrary, the church challenge injustices, thereby becoming a hopeful and hope-filled alternative.

C. The Expression of the Church as Alternative Community in South Africa

1. Church that Breaks Down Barriers

Here we deal with the features that must be demonstrated in the life of the church if she wants to live as an alternative community in post-apartheid South Africa. The expression of the church must be undergirded by our understanding of Scripture that clearly calls us to love one another. Immanuel Kant (1947, p. 7) put it very clearly:

> For love as an inclination, cannot be commanded. However, kindness done from duty, also when no inclination impels it, and even when it is opposed by a natural and unconquerable aversion, is practical love, not pathological love. It

resides in the will and not in feeling, in the principle action and not in tender sympathy; and it alone can be commanded.

This love has its first expression in the action of Jesus on the cross, which gives birth to the *Missio Dei* that finds expression through the actions or praxis of the church in faithful communion with God, the One who acts. Andrew Root (2014, p. 81) states that in *participatio Christi* the church participates in God through Jesus Christ. It affirms our cooperation with the divine life that our life is hidden with Christ in God. Thus, God's being is given in God's acts, and God's act is the revealing of the Godself for the sake of ministry (K. Barth, 1961, p. 85). Thus, when the church engages in ministry as the body of Christ, it reflects the being of God as a moved being. God moves towards humanity in the shape of ministry, as an invitation to take action and share in another's being. This act of God is seen in reconciliation. Therefore, Root (2014, p. 94) argues that ministry as the act of God is the event of God's being coming to humanity. This takes shape in the Christ action in what Root terms the *Christopraxis* of the church. When the church expresses compassion, it expresses the Being of God.

The expression of this alternative community—the church—is thus one of engagement in the internal (spiritual) and external (socio-political) through the prophetic engagements that speak to institutional structures that keep people separated. The community as the church acts out through creative and compassionate acts that demonstrate love at its fullest.[568] John Frame said, "For the Christian life is not only a matter of following rules of morality, but a dynamic experience: living in a fallen world, in fellowship with the living God" (2008, p. xxv). One of the tests of the authenticity of the church's claim to transcendence or to be counter-cultural is its capacity to represent in its congregation a "socially heterogeneous" people (James Cone, 1986, p. 119). This is a community that reflects Jesus Christ as the One who breaks down barriers that separate people.

2. Reconciliatory Church and Restitution

The fundamental message of the church is reconciliation. Brenda Salter McNeil (2015, p. 22) states that "reconciliation is an ongoing spiritual process involving forgiveness, repentance and justice that restores broken relationships and systems to reflect God's original intention for all creation to flourish." The church becomes prophetic when it creates and sustains a reconciled and reconciling community. The task of the prophetic ministry of the church is to nurture and nourish an alternative consciousness to the

---

[568] By prophetic, we agree with John W. de Gruchy, *Liberating Reformed Theology* (Grand Rapids: Eerdmans, 1990), 19: "A theology that is socially critical and world transformative, that is, one that explicity relates the Word of God to the social and political context within which it is proclaimed."

dominant culture around us (Bruggeman cited in McNeil, 2015). Reconciliation with God must be demonstrated by genuine reconciliation within the church and by continuing a ministry of reconciliation to the world. M. Volf (1999) calls this the Pauline concept of social reconciliation. Such a community of reconciliation is then the alternative hoped for in South Africa to help reconcile the tension with the surrounding context and culture of separateness.

As South Africa becomes more socially and racially separated, the church should structure herself to become an alternative conscience and as needed even counter-cultural. In the place of justice and righteousness, normal society brandished violence and oppression and call it justice. Dietrich Bonhoeffer (2005, p. 63) encapsulated this function of the church well:

> The church is the place where witness is given to the foundation of all reality in Jesus Christ. The church is the place where it is proclaimed and taken seriously that God has reconciled the world to himself in Christ. The space of the church is not there in order to fight for territory, but precisely to testify to the world that it is still the world, namely the world that is loved and reconciled by God.

While the church pursues justice and reconciliation, it defines its mandate in biblical terms and thus rejects all forms of violence, manipulation, and injustice. Liberation then is not a mere political movement and power struggle. The message of reconciliation of the church is to preach the good news about the peace Christ brings, reconciling man to God, man to man, and bringing harmony with God's creation. This is what Ernest Conradie (2013, p. 27) calls cosmic reconciliation. Reconciliation is thus with God, with the Church, and with those who have been sinned against.

How then is reconciliation to be enacted? The church as alternative community must be agents of spiritual and racial reconciliation that is more than mere words, but a reconciliation that demands action. Vuyani Vellem (2013, p. 111) underscores that if justice becomes subservient to reconciliation, then reconciliation is just cognitive, something that aborts the true reconciliation. Vellem said what is needed is the discovery of reconciliation through experience.

It is through restitution that I believe this is possible. In a previous article that I co-authored with Clayton Alexander (2015), I state that when the church fully understands the impact that three decades of separateness had on the masses and the degradation it caused, making people non-persons, the church is required to make practical engagements. Vellem terms it the "logic of experiential clarity regarding reconciliation," therefore, if reconciliation is to be fully realized, then restitution has to be made. This is where the church can challenge the government to speed up its programme of Land Reform that seeks to turn around what happened when certain racial groupings of the church in South Africa benefited unethically from the 1913 Land Act. However, the church as an agency of peace must condemn any form of violence and bloodshed in the re-appropriation of land.

Reconciliation requires that restitution be made to those who suffered under an evil system by the church herself. Restitution is perhaps the most human part of the reconciliation process, and restitution requires that we give up something, which brings us to a better understanding of the suffering that apartheid caused to the majority. When the church as the community of God leads this process, it does so from a place of compassion.

3. Compassion of the Church

In Exodus 33, Moses requests Yahweh to show his glory; that request was denied because no man can see God and live. Yet, God did reveal to Moses who He is as a loving and compassionate God. The church is thus called to reveal the character of God demonstrated through her acts of compassion and love. This, therefore, requires that a definition of compassion be explored and applied to the South African context. The church in South Africa can become what all other communities aspire to be: a loving, caring, and compassionate community.

Davies (2001, p. 17) states that compassion calls for the radical decentring of self, and putting at risk, in the free re-enactment of the dispossessed condition of those who suffer. Compassion, I believe, begins with the recognition of the other as created in the image of God, and because of this understanding the self assumes the burden of the other. It is here Davies (2001, p. 17) argues that in recognizing the veiled presence of God's image in the other that we come to understand our identity.

Nouwen, McNeil, and Morrison state that the word compassion means to "suffer with." Compassion requires one to enter into spaces where one identifies with the weak, vulnerable, and powerless. Compassion means a full immersion in the condition of being human. Therefore, compassion is not simple pity, but finds its purest expression unfolding in the incarnation of God.

God's compassion becomes our compassion. This principle of self-denying or "kenotic love" (Davies 2001, p. 21) touches all levels of human experience and tries to make social harmony a possibility. This radical manifestation calls then for reflection of personhood. Thus, the church as the alternative community seeks to see the image of God in all persons in society. This calls for a radical shift from theology to ministry. B. Stone (1996, p. 43) elaborates that "ministry has a three-fold character: it is a response to grace, it is participation in grace, and it is an offer of grace." Through the ministry of the church, the work of restoration of the image of God in us is extended to the rest of the world. This calls for a very intentional *entering into* the suffering of the other, on behalf of the oppressed, and working on behalf of their liberation.

The church as an alternative community reflects their knowing of God in two ways, namely, theologically and practically. I believe the latter is a stronger demonstration of our love for God. R. M. Brown (1984, p. 69) states this very clearly,

> This notion is so strange to us that 'knowing God' is a matter of deed rather than word, that one could affirm God without saying God's name or deny God while God's name is on our lips is not so strange to the Bible.

This is seen most clearly in Matthew 25:31–46 that distinguishes between knowing God and knowing about God. James qualifies this even further by mocking those who claim to have faith but who fail to take care of the marginalized in society: "You believe that God is one. You do well; the demons also believe and shudder" (Jas 2:19). Mere knowledge about God cannot replace living faith which is also living a compassionate life.

Compassion is brought into focus by asking the question: "What is it to be created in the image of God (*Imago Dei*)?" This "image" is given by God and is central to human dignity because the central theological issue in human dignity is the merciful, compassionate God. This understanding compels the church as an alternative community to be confrontive and transformative by speaking against institutional and economic barriers that keep people separated. The church in South Africa must assume the responsibility to see people as children of God, created in His image rather than being dictated to, and to see people through the socio-economic and political policies of the land. The church in South Africa must become a place where people who were once stripped of their humanity and dignity may find hope and restoration of that lost human dignity. The church becomes the prophetic voice that speaks out against poverty that forces people to live in situations of inferiority and bondage in relation to those to whom they remain dependent and enslaved.

Poverty is just the starting point of the attack on the image of God. The reality in South Africa is that poverty is overwhelmingly Black. Four hundred years of colonization and oppression have ravaged Blacks. Being robbed of that element of freedom of movement and of relationships has had crippling economic effects.

The church is called to a ministry that balances itself between support and development. Development ministries equip and enable those who are poor to provide for themselves. B. Meyers (1999, p. 14) noted that the church who understands its true identity as children of God and who have recovered their true calling is a "faithful and productive" steward of the "gifts from God for the well-being of all." Tim Chester (2013, p. 156) used Ezekiel 34 to affirm the need for development ministries in that God condemns the shepherds of Israel, and not for provide, but for failing to strengthen the weak.

The church bears a certain responsibility to the poor and oppressed. God's community is called to defend the cause of the poor, the needy, and those who have no social and economic power. The church works for the physical and social needs of people, not as though this was the primary need or exclusive task, but as its testimony of a redeemed, holy, and alternative society. In the end, when the church shows compassion, it demonstrates the heart of God and is concerned with sharing God's love in words and deeds.

Another assault on the "image of God" and human dignity is racism in the South Africa. J. Grant (1992, p. 49) writes:

> Politically, racism disenfranchises; socially it ostracizes; culturally it degrades and robs the people of those characteristics that make them a people; religiously it brainwashes and indoctrinates so that the oppressed people believe not only that it is impossible for God to like them or for them to image God, but that God ordains racist oppression.

The church as an alternative society must speak out against these issues that blur the image of God in persons by creating a community of faith where these differences do not impede fellowship and love one for another. When the church is governed by this vision, the church will have adequate theological resources to resist the temptation to become accomplices in racial and socio-economic segregation (Volf, 1999, p. 19). Thus, through the acts of compassion, the church becomes agents of reconciliation, where human flourishing takes place. St. Augustine *On the Trinity* writes, "God is the only source to be found any good thing, but especially by those which make a man good and those which will make him happy; only from him do they come into a man and attaches themselves to a man." Human beings truly flourish in this alternative community, when love is demonstrated as God becomes the centre of our lives. A human being ought to be loved, and the only way to properly love is to love people in God (Volf, 2011, p. 58).

4. Love from the Church

Scripture calls us to love God and our neighbour (Mark 12:29–31), and God is love and loves unconditionally. The triune God provides a model for human love. The life and practice of the church in response to God's love are summarized in Mark 12:29–31. Hence the term "living in love" is not something a community can achieve by their own efforts or in their own strength, but something that happens to them in faith and from God and when one loves God. God loving us is a decisive element in the life of love. By being loved by God the church understands what it means to reflect the reality of God and to demonstrate the reality of love in all we do.

Conclusion

When the church reverses her desire to conform to the world, and she more authentically lives out her *Imago Dei*, the action of the church is the movement that is not her own, but God's own being in love—and and through Him, we can truly love one another in actions.

The reason the church can make a difference in the world is because of Christ, who made the difference by becoming man and fulfilling the just requirements of God in reconciling humankind to God. This act of love, compassion, and reconciliation demonstrated in the life of Christ, the head of the Church, leaves us an example to follow through empowerment by the Holy Spirit, who leads us into all truth and therefore in to a life of love for others.

18.
Church and State in Ethiopia: Contribution of the Lutheran Understanding of the Community of Grace

Dr. Samuel Yonas Deressa
Assistant Professor of Theology and the Global South
Concordia University, St. Paul, Minnesota[569]

Introduction	265
A. The State in Ethiopia: the Dynamics of "Center" and "Periphery"	266
B. Public Engagement of Ethiopian Churches	271
C. Church as Community of Grace	273
D. Church's Role in Engaging the Public	278
Summary	281

Introduction

Ethiopia is currently suffering political unrest from broad social, economic, and political grievances shared by many citizens, particularly the two largest ethnic groups, the Oromo and Amhara. Citizens are being imprisoned, tortured, and killed for demanding their God-given human rights. According to a recent Human Rights Watch report in 2016, the country has registered a high death toll and mass arrests.[570] The present government, which promised democracy and prosperity when coming to power twenty-five years ago, has turned out to be one of the most brutal and dictatorial regimes Africa has ever seen.

Changing the Ethiopian situation requires all kinds of institutions, religious and non-religious, to be involved in public matters. A large number

---

[569] Deressa earned his PhD from Luther Seminary, St. Paul; his MDiv from Ethiopian Graduate School of Theology, Addis Ababa, Ethiopia; and his BTh from Mekane Yesus Seminary, Addis Ababa. He serves as a pre-seminary coordinator for the Department of Theology and Ministry, Condordia University, and has been on the faculty of Mekane Yesus Seminary, Addis Ababa, Ethiopia. He has written, *The Life, Works, and Witness of Tsehay Tolessa and Gudina Tumsa, the Ethiopian Bonhoeffer* (Minneapolis: Fortress Press, 2017; 299 pp.); *Cultural Ethics and Inter-Religious Coexistence and the Ethiopian Context: The Case of Karrayyu Oromo* (Addis Ababa, Ethiopia: Makane Yesus Seminary, 2011; 92 pp.); edited, *Revisiting the History, Theology, and Leadership Practice of the Ethiopian Evangelical Church Mekane Yesus, Journal of Gudina Tumsa Theological Forum* (Minneapolis: Lutheran University Press, 2016; 174 pp.); and wrote and edited, *Emerging Theological Praxis* (Minneapolis: Lutheran University Press, 2012; 140 pp.). See www.CSP.edu/person/dr-samuel-deressa/ and Deressa@csp.edu.

[570] Human Rights Watch, "Such a Brutal Crackdown: Killing and Arrest in Response to Ethiopia's Oromo Protests." See www.hrw.org/report/2016/06/16/such-brutal-crackdown/killings-and-arrests-response-ethiopias-oromo-protests, accessed 11/02/2016.

of non-religious institutions are already participating to determine Ethiopia's future both within and outside the country, including opposition parties, civic organizations, journalists, academicians, and political activists. Religious institutions, however, are being criticized for ignoring their public responsibility by remaining silent.

The approach of religious institutions (the church in particular) to Ethiopian public life can be described in two ways:

1. They are either more closely identified with the government than the people they serve, or
2. They are totally withdrawn from the public life of the community.

The Ethiopian Orthodox Church (EOC) worked hand and glove with the government following the "Christendom" model. As Paul Balisky has rightly noted, leaders of this church "viewed all of Ethiopia, whether pagan or Muslim, as their domain."[571] At present, even though the EOC does not follow the "Christendom" model; it continues to work closely with the government. After 1991, some evangelical churches also joined the EOC by declaring allegiance with the government. On the other hand, some Pentecostal and evangelical institutions consider their mission to be only evangelic work focused on "soul saving." With a narrow definition of the Great Commission, they emphasize spiritual services over the social, economic, and political roles of a church.

This paper explores the Ethiopian churches' approach to public life and proposes a prophetic challenge to social, economic, and political fragmentation resulting in the violation of human rights in Ethiopia. In sum, we will describe briefly the church and state relationship in Ethiopia from the time of the state's formation and Luther's understanding of *sola gratia* and the church as a community of grace. Lastly, informed by Luther's understanding of a church as a community of grace, we propose how the church can bring healing to the fractured Ethiopian community.

A. The State in Ethiopia: the Dynamics of "Center" and "Periphery"

Ethiopia came into existence when the Emperor Menelik II of Showa conquered the areas in the southern part of today's Ethiopia between 1886 and 1894. Some scholars describe Menelik's act as the expansion of his kingdom or "reunification of modern Ethiopia" rather than a colonial act that left the southern people under subjugation.[572] This incident, however,

---

[571] Paul Balisky, "Ethiopian Church and Mision in the Context of Violence," in *Mission in the Context of Violence*, ed. Keith E. Eitel (Pasadena: William Cary Library, 2008), 226.

[572] Oyvind M. Eide, *Revolution and Religion in Ethiopia: The Growth and Persecution of the Mekane Yesus Church, 1974–85* (Oxford: J. Currey, 2000), 15.

resulted in a radical change in the life of the conquered people. The people living in these areas were subjected to brutal, systemic, socio-economic exploitation, and political subjugation by those in authority. [573] Patrick Gilkes emphasizes that Menelik's "expansionist" policy "brought extensive slave trading, loss of land, the status of serfs for themselves, onerous burdens of taxation and corrupt and inefficient government."[574]

The land in the conquered territories was distributed among the soldiers, local administrators, and the EOC. The landowners built a system in which they were able to exact tribute and tax from the peasants who lived on those lands. It was named the *gebbar* system: the Amharic word *gebbar* is translated as "tribute giver." The conquered people were forced to pay tax or tribute to the landlords. In other words, Menelik introduced a tributary mode of production, whereby there existed "a structural relationship where peasant communities are in the possession of the land they till, but the production is collected by outside rulers who appropriate portions of peasant surplus by exacting a tribute."[575]

Oyvind Eide, in *Revolution and Religion in Ethiopia*, defines the Ethiopian community from two perspectives: the "center" and the "periphery."[576] These metaphors are used by many researchers to describe the socio-cultural and socio-political context created by emperor Menelik. In short, the dichotomy is utterly predatory in nature. Those in Ethiopia described as the "center" are communities that have been beneficiaries of the political and economic system of the country for the last few centuries. At the "center" are ruling parties, which were predominantly from one tribe in the northern part of the country and from the Ethiopian Orthodox Church (EOC). Those on the "periphery," however, are those people who are oppressed and marginalized by a system that only favors those that are at the "center." In other words, Ethiopia today as formed by Emperor Menelik has a clear dichotomy between the subjugator and the subjugated, the subjugator as a "center" that subjugates the "periphery."

Upon coming to power in 1931, Haile Selassie I (1931–1974) named himself the Elect of God and the Conquering Lion of the Tribe of Judah, and he sought to lead the country into a new age of modernization. He

---

[573] Arne Tolo, *Sidama and Ethiopian: The Emergence [of] the Mekane Yesus Church in Sidama* (Uppsala: Uppsala universitet 1998), 61; Ulrich Braukämper, *Geschichte Der Hadiya Süd-Äthiopiens: Von D. Anfängen Bis Zur Revolution 1974* (Wiesbaden: Steiner, 1980), 443.

[574] Patrick Gilkes, *The Dying Lion: Feudalism and Modernization in Ethiopia* (New York: St. Martin's Press, 1975), 205.

[575] Michael Ståhl, *Ethiopia, Political Contradictions in Agricultural Development* (Uppsala: Political Science Association in Uppsala, 1974), 10.

[576] Eide, *Revolution and Religion in Ethiopia*, 12.

introduced the first constitution in Ethiopia as a first step towards achieving his goal. In this constitution, he included a section dealing with the need to reform the land tenure system as part of his plan to "modernize" Ethiopia.[577]

Selassie introduced a new taxation system under a centralized government structure. Feudalism replaced a tributary mode of production. According to the feudal mode of production, the rulers were given the right to appropriate the land, and peasants were reduced to tenants in such a way that they were attendants to the rulers or the landowners. According to studies conducted on this tenant system, the tenants were required "by law to hand over up to three-fourths of their produce to landlords, who often were absentee."[578] This huge burden on the peasants continued to favor the landlords (rulers) rather than the tenants, and the livelihood of the peasants came under the mercy of their rulers. In this system, the landlords became the "center" of the system, and those at the "periphery," the southern people, were forced again into paying heavy taxes. Injustice and poverty continued to prevail over the people.

The feudal government also introduced the concept of modernization to Ethiopia. In the dynamic imperial politics, becoming "modern" (*zemenawinet*) or "civilized" required one to adopt an Orthodox Christian identity.[579] As Asmarom Legesse rightly indicates, "*Ethiopia glorified her Sabean, Jewish, and Christian heritage at the expense of her African identity. As the result, the remaining people of Ethiopia, the Cushitic and Nilotes, were viewed as alien and inferior.*"[580] Therefore, as Christopher Clapham accurately explains, "participation in national political life [demanded] assimilation to the cultural values of the Amhara core: the Amharic language, Orthodox Christianity and a capacity to operate within the structures and assumptions of a core administration."[581] Scholars refer to this action by the government as *Amharanization* of the empire.

Selassie's imperial regime ended in September 1974 and was replaced by what eventually became a Marxist-Socialist regime known as the Derg (1974–1991). The first two years of the socialist government gave hope to the oppressed people. In 1974, the Derg published a manifesto with a ten-

---

[577] Ta'a Tesema, *The Political Economy of Western Central Ethiopia: From the Mid-16th to the Early-20th Centuries*, PhD diss. (Michigan State University, 1986), 209.

[578] "Ethiopian Measures for Rural Transformation," a report from the Ministry of Agriculture and Settlement (Addis Ababa, Ethiopia: Ministry of Agriculture and Settlement, February 1978), 5.

[579] Donald L. Donham, *Marxist Modern: An Ethnographic History of the Ethiopian Revolution* (Berkeley: University of California Press, 1999), 128.

[580] Asmarom Legesse, *Oromo Democracy: An Indigenous African Political System* (Lawrenceville: Red Sea Press, 2000). Italics in the original.

[581] Christopher S. Clapham, *Transformation and Continuity in Revolutionary Ethiopia* (Cambridge: Cambridge University Press, 1988), 21.

point program emphasizing the "themes of equality, self-reliance, the indivisibility of the nation, state control of the economy, and the elimination of landlordism."[582] Separation of church and state was officially declared. Equal status of all religions before the law was emphasized. The feudal system was eradicated, and the Derg formed peasant associations (*Geberemaheber*) at the grass-roots level. Marxist-Leninist ideology became a general framework in which Ethiopian history, economy, cultures, religions; and societies were analyzed in academic institutions.

The Derg, however, was no better than the previous governments. According to Markakis, the Derg can be characterized as "garrison socialism" in reference to its ideological orientation and military background.[583] Despite its Marxist-Leninist orientation, nation building continued the previous imperial approach that continued the distinction between the "center" and the "periphery." This division was enforced by following the ideology of previous Ethiopian emperors with an uncompromised position on religious unity as a means for securing the national unity of the country.[584] The Socialist government like its predecessors adopted the same tradition and legitimized the superiority of the "center" (Amhara culture and EOC traditions). Just as in the previous hegemonic governments, the Derg regime also declared a manifesto emphasizing that the ruling party is determined to "aim at the united country without ethnic, religious, linguistic, and cultural differences."[585] All forms of ideologies that seemed either to question or to challenge the homogenized and inherited Empire of Ethiopia were subverted. With the inherited legacy of imposition and absolutism, Ethiopia became a militarist state under the dictatorial leadership of Mengistu Hailemariam.

At the formation of the present government in 1991, a historic opportunity seemed to present itself to the Ethiopian people. A multi-party democracy was introduced for the first time in Ethiopian history, and religious freedom was granted as a constitutional right. The administrative structure of the country was divided into nine member states of the Federal Democratic Republic of Ethiopia (FDRE) demarcated on the basis of settlement patterns, language, and the consent of the people concerned. According to the Ethiopian Constitution, Article 39, the unconditional right of self-determination, including secession, is given to nations, nationalities,

---

[582] Donham, *Marxist Modern*, 26, 129.

[583] See introductory section in John Markakis, *National and Class Conflict in the Horn of Africa* (Cambridge: Cambridge University Press, 1987).

[584] J. Spencer Trimingham, *The Christian Church and Missions in Ethiopia (Including Eritrea and the Somalilandsz* (London: World Dominion Press, 1951).

[585] Eide, *Revolution and Religion in Ethiopia*, 17.

and the people.[586] This constitution defines nations, nationalities, and peoples as "group(s) of people who have or share a large measure of a common culture, or similar customs, mutual intelligibility of language, belief in a common or related identities, and who predominantly inhabit an identifiable contiguous territory."[587] While Amharic is constituted as a working language of the federal government, regions are allowed to use their local languages in primary education and local administration.

During the transitional period of the current government, the constitution as a whole and the way the country is structured (the federal system) gave a positive impression to many Ethiopians. It was widely perceived that Ethiopia had finally eliminated the system that divided the nation as a "center" and "periphery." Several believed the country was transitioning from a dictatorial regime to one of freedom and democracy.

What happened, however, was a change of the "center" and the "periphery." The Tigrians, who were at the "periphery" of the previous regimes, became the "center," while the Amharas and all other tribes were left at the "periphery" of the system. The minority Tigrians, a mere 6% of the total population, controlled the economic and political dynamics of the country. They used ethnic federalism to keep all other states apart as a means of control. They knew that their existence would be endangered if other nations united, and therefore they used this system to evoke divisions, hatred, and enmities between these groups. Ethiopia's violent clashes between people of different ethnic groups testifies to this reality.

Today Ethiopia is still crippled from a lack of democracy. The government has not been able to abide by the constitution it ratified. Many agree that not enough was done to make the constitution practical. The transition from a dictatorship to a democratically elected government did not materialize. As Samuel Huntington tried to suggest, this probably happened because "Ethiopia has no democratic traditions" in the first place.[588] Elections held in the last three decades (1995, 2000, 2005, 2010, and 2015) indicate that the government's intention has not been to dedicate itself to real democracy that it had promised to the people. Those elections were characterized by compulsion, threats, imprisonments, and unfavorable treatment of non-EPRDF candidates.

In 2016, massive demonstrations in several parts of Ethiopia have been going on against the ruling government, including Oromoia and Amhara

---

[586] Quoted after the English translation from the Amharic original of the FDRE constitution, 1994.

[587] Federal Democratic Republic of Ethiopia (1994) Constitution, ratified by the National Constituent Assembly, 8 December 1994, Art. 46 and 47.

[588] Huntington Samuel, "Political Development in Ethiopia: A Peasant-Based Dominant-Party Democracy," in *Report to USAID/Ethiopia on Consultations with the Constitutional Commission* (1993).

regional states. Thousands of protestors have been killed and tens of thousands jailed and tortured. Oromiya is the largest regional state in Ethiopia, and the Oromo is the largest ethnic group (34% of the total population). The Oromo have been demanding their basic human rights for years and claim that they have been deprived of social, cultural, economic, and political rights, and have been reduced to second-class status within the Ethiopian empire for so long.

B. Public Engagement of Ethiopian Churches

Ethiopia is a country of diverse religions. Among these religions, Christianity was the first to be welcomed in the fourth century C.E. to the royal court. From there it gradually penetrated the common people. This created a phenomenon whereby the Ethiopian Orthodox Christianity became a state religion from its beginning until the coming of the socialist government in 1974.

Evangelical churches, however, started at the same time King Menelik conquered and annexed territories beyond the Abyssinian border. It began with the arrival of Swedish Evangelical Mission missionaries in 1868, and their subsequent effort to evangelize the Oromo through indigenous missionaries in the early twentieth century. These indigenous missionaries were liberated Oromo slaves and Eritrean priests. These first converts to the evangelical faith later became pioneer missionaries who translated the scriptures into Oromo, planted schools, and preached the good news of Jesus Christ to the people at the "periphery," the marginalized and oppressed communities.

The EOC started in the palace, at the center of the empire, while evangelical Christianity started among those at the "periphery." In other words, the EOC theology and service related to the privileged communities while the evangelicals preached to a people that had been deprived of cultural, economic, and political rights. The latter had been reduced to second-class status within the Ethiopian empire.

For evangelicals, their places of preaching became the foundation upon which Lutheran congregations were established, which could be considered the strong foundation for the start of evangelical churches in Ethiopia.[589] Most evangelical churches in Ethiopia, including the Ethiopian Evangelical Church Mekane Yesus (EECMY), the largest Lutheran church in the world

---

[589] Gustav Arén, *Evangelical Pioneers in Ethiopia: Origins of the Evangelical Church Mekane Yesus* (Stockholm: EFS Förlaget/Addis Ababa, Evangelical Church Mekane Yesus, 1978), and Fakadu Gurmessa, *Evangelical Faith Movement in Ethiopia: Origins and Establishment of the Ethiopian Evangelical Church Mekane Yesus*, trans. Ezekiel Gebissa (Minneapolis: Lutheran University Press, 2009).

with a membership of 8.7 million, were born out of those communities at the "periphery."

The EOC functioned as a state church until 1991 and still considers itself an ally of the government. One of its roles as a state church was to legitimize the power and actions of the kings. When Ethiopia was constituted in its present form, Menelik's actions were legitimized by the state church. In fact, the EOC used the opportunity to expand its spheres of influence. The church gave divine sanction to Menelik's act in conquering the territories of other people.[590] During feudalism, the EOC played a similar role by legitimizing Haile Selassie's policy of integration (assimilation), which demanded religious and language homogeneity for nation formation.

Some research indicates the EOC's mission to the conquered south was mainly politically motivated, with little or no interest in evangelism.[591] For them, Christianization was understood as tantamount to a civilizing mission, and therefore the EOC's mission was directed towards "civilizing" the conquered people. According to Negaso Gidada and Donald Crummey, this missionary approach of the EOC placed "very strong pressure" on the southern people, since "only adherence to Christianity could give access to 'civilized' status and an equal footing with other Christians who were, in fact, the overlords."[592]

During the military government, the EOC worked hand in hand with the government. As Donham notes, "The result was cultural reaction in which Marxist-Leninism was overlaid on Old Orthodox Christian notions of the nation."[593] In order to implement its policy with regard to religious unity, the Derg officially began to back the EOC financially; 1,729 patriarchate workers of the EOC received an annual subsidy of two million pounds as salary, while its higher officials received a monthly allowance of eleven thousand pounds from the Ministry of Finance.[594]

Yet the evangelicals were persecuted by the central government for decades. As churches emerged from the communities at the "periphery" of

---

[590] Haile M. Larebo, "The Ethiopian Orthodox Church and Politics in the Twentieth Century: Part I" *Northeast African Studies: Incorporating Ethiopianist Notes Northeast African Studies* 10, no. 3 (1987): 379; Donald Levine, *Greater Ethiopia: The Evolution of a Multiethnic Society* (Chicago: University of Chicago Press, 1974), 151.

[591] Tibebe Eshete, *The Evangelical Movement in Ethiopia: Resistance and Resilience* (Waco: Baylor University Press, 2009), 694.

[592] Negaso Gidada and Donald Crummey, *The Introduction and Expansion of Orthodox Christianity in Qélém Awraja, Western Wälläga, from About 1886 to 1941* (Addis Ababa: Addis Ababa University, 1972), 111.

[593] Donham, *Marxist Modern*, 137.

[594] Haile Larebo, "The Orthodox Church and the State in the Ethiopian Revolution," *Religion in Communist Lands* 14, no. 2 (1986): 153.

the empire, they suffered with the people. They were labeled as *mete haymanot*, which means "foreign" religions and anti-revolutionaries. Under the banner of the national unity, which government officials thought could only be attained through religious and cultural uniformity and with the EOC behind them, the government harassed the evangelical Christians. [595] Sidelined by the government from having any kind of role within the system, evangelicals were considered threats to Ethiopian ideology. Christian church leaders who tried to engage the government were imprisoned, tortured, and killed. Many considered politics as a matter of life and death and preferred not to be involved.

The evangelical Christian response to such reactions from the government has been different. Some churches, particularly the EECMY, have actively engaged the public in the past, regardless of the fact that its active participation sometimes resulted in mistreatment of its members. In the last thirty years, however, these churches have been silent at best or blessed the system at worst. When it comes to non-political affairs, the EECMY as well as other evangelical churches have been actively engaged in social and development activities. By opening schools, hospitals, and other social service institutions, they serve communities that demand a response to the multifaceted forms of injustice that condemn many persons to hunger, disease, unemployment, ignorance, displacement, and violent deaths resulting from civil conflicts, developmental stagnation, and so on. Some evangelical and Pentecostal churches, however, have adopted a non-political position founded on a theology that emphasizes evangelism as merely bringing a person to faith.

C. Church as Community of Grace

Ethiopian society is still in crisis, and many faithful men and women still too often fail to find appropriate responses to their life problems. What has the church to offer this society? The Lutheran understanding of grace speaks emphatically about the Christian's responsibilities to each other and to the public. It speaks to divisions between people of different ethnic or racial groups and structural injustices that have fractured the community. Luther's theology of *sola gratia*, grace alone, sets a premise for how a church as a community of grace can live out its prophetic role in public.

What is grace? The phrase *sola gratia* has been used by theologians since the time of the Reformation to indicate that justification and salvation can only be attained by faith, not by any works on humanity's part. In Romans 5:15, where Luther found a warrant, Paul writes: "how much more did

---

[595] Eide, *Revolution and Religion in Ethiopia*, 149.

God's grace and the gift that came by the grace of the one man, Jesus Christ, overflow to the many." Grace is a transforming mercy and gift of God. It is God's favor, mercy, and gratuitous good will "toward humankind redeemed by Christ and it enters lives through the word of the Gospel, which offers and effects genuine union with Christ."[596]

As Robert Jenson has noted that the right approach to understanding the meaning and significance of grace is through a theology of the triune God's self-giving. Based on the Apostle Paul's description of grace as the favor and gifts that God bestows on God's creation, he argues that grace is nothing but the self-giving God.[597] God the Father, "the ungifted giver," gives himself in Christ and the Holy Spirit; this is the grace given to or bestowed on human beings and the whole creation. Jenson's description of grace correlates with Luther's emphasis that the triune self-giving of God is foundational for understanding grace and its implication for the ongoing creative work of God.[598] Luther explains,

> These are the three persons and one God, who has given himself to us wholly and completely, with all that he is and has. The Father gives himself to us, with heaven and earth and all the creatures, in order that they may serve us and benefit us. But this gift has become obscured and useless through Adam's fall. Therefore the Son subsequently gave himself and bestowed all his works, suffering, wisdom, and righteousness, and has reconciled us to the father, in order that restored to life and righteousness, we might also know and have the father and his gifts. But this grace would benefit no one if it remains so profoundly hidden and could not come to us.[599]

According to Jenson, "Christ as word is both *extra nos* (outside us) and *qua fide in nobis* (as faith in us), and just only in this simultaneity he is the act of grace."[600] Christ is the Word of God that is addressed to human beings as *extra nos* (outside of us), and a Word that unites humanity with the triune God through faith. When the human soul is addressed by this Word, it is united with the triune God in faith. As Luther states,

> To cloth oneself with Christ is to cloth oneself with justice, truth, [and] grace. If you clothe yourself with Christ and Christ is the Son of God, you too are the

---

[596] Stephen Duffy, *The Dynamics of Grace: Perspectives in Theological Anthropology* (Michael Glazier, 1993; Eugene: Wipf and Stock. 2007), 190.

[597] Robert Jenson, "Triune Grace," in *The Gift of Grace: The Future of Lutheran Theology*, ed. Niels Henrik Gregersen et al. (Minneapolis: Fortress Press, 2005).

[598] Schwobel Scristoph, "The Quest for an Adequate Theology of Grace and the Future of Lutheran Theology: A Response of Robert W. Jenson," in *The Gift of Grace: The Future of Lutheran Theology*, ed. Niels Henrik Gregersen et al. (Minneapolis: Fortress Press, 2005), 35.

[599] Martin Luther, "Word and Sacrament," in *Luther's Work*, ed. Robert Fischer and Helmut Lehmann, vol. 37 (Philadelphia: Muhlenberg Press, 1961), 366.

[600] Jenson, "Triune Grace," 27.

children of God. Christ cannot be separated from us, nor we from him, since we are one with him, in him as the members are one in and with their head.[601]

This Word also evokes a transformation and leads to the experience of faith from within—which Jenson refers to as Christ being in us. In other words, as Luther states, "the soul of the one who clings to the word in true faith is so entirely united with it that all the virtues of the word becomes virtues of the soul also."[602] As God created the world by His Word, God also gives himself to His own creation in grace through the same Word.

The Spirit, on the other hand, is God's freedom that liberates humanity from within individuals in enabling them to love each other and their neighbors. As Luther states, "The Holy Spirit comes and gives himself to us also, wholly and completely. He teaches us to understand" Jesus' work in our lives and "helps us receive and preserve it, uses it to our advantage and impart it to others, increases and extends it" in, by, and through grace.[603]

What is a community of grace? A community of grace is a coming together of those who are loved by God unconditionally and therefore join in solidarity and share with one another the transforming grace of God. They let themselves be strengthened and transformed by the grace of the triune God and become an embodiment of God's grace to each other and to their neighbors. Grace enables each individual to be freed from egoistic self-love and to connect with his or her neighbor. Such community is created in a context where God's grace is communicated through the proclaimed gospel and administrated sacraments.

This community is called a missional community of grace—a church. For Luther the missional community of grace—the church—is the assembly of all believers among whom the Gospel is proclaimed and sacraments are properly administered.[604] The Augsburg Confession describes *word* and *sacrament* as the "means of grace." The word "means" refers to how and where grace happens. It happens when the word is preached and sacraments are administered within and among the believing community, the missional community of grace.

The church as a community of grace experiences God's grace through, by, in, and with the Word and the Spirit. God's grace is experienced in the relationship of humans with the triune God as well as with each other. Such a relationship is experienced when the sacraments are administered within a

---

[601] Cited in Duffy, *Dynamics of Grace*, 188.

[602] Martin Luther, "The Freedom of a Christian, 1520," in *Luther's Work*, ed. Harold J. Grimm and Helmut Lehmann, Vol. 31 (Philadelphia: Muhlenberg Press, 1957), 24.

[603] Luther, "Word and Sacrament," 366.

[604] Augsburg Confession, Article VII.

believing community. Humans are restored in forgiveness and blessing which results in a healing of the relationship and transformation among human beings.

The community of grace is described in the Apostles' Creed as the *communio sanctorum*, the "communion of saints." Luther's account of the Eucharist provides us with a comprehensive view of this communion and its practical expression. The gospel, according to Luther, is what leads to the "communion of saints." The gospel mediates the Holy Spirit, who "calls, gathers, enlightens, and sanctifies the whole Christian church on earth and preserves it in union with Jesus Christ in the one true faith."[605] In other words, it is the gospel mediated by the Spirit that opens the way for us to share the life of the Triune God, by virtue of which we are also enabled to commune with each other and share God's grace. Luther's argument regarding the significance of the gospel is similar to Scot McKnight's definition of the gospel: "The Gospel is the work of God to restore humans to union with God and communion with others, in the context of a community for the good of others and the world."[606] It is within this definition of the church that we find a more comprehensive and practical explanation of what it means for the church to be a missional community of grace.

According to Luther, "the significance or effect of this sacrament is fellowship of all the saints."[607] To take part in Holy Communion is to have fellowship with Christ and all the saints.[608] In the Eucharist, the Triune God shares Godself with us through bread and wine, and "we become united with Christ, and are made one body with all the saints." As Luther contends, while partaking in the Blessed Sacrament of the Holy and True Body and Blood of Christ, "all the spiritual possessions of Christ and his saints are shared with and become the common property of him who receives this sacraments."[609] Furthermore, according to Luther in eucharistic fellowship, "We are [also] to be united with our neighbors, we in them and they in us."[610] Quoting Luther,

---

[605] Eric Gritsch and Robert Jenson, *Lutheranism: The Theological Movement and Its Confessional Writings* (Philadelphia: Fortress Press, 1976), 124. Small Catechism II, 6.

[606] Scot McKnight, *Embracing Grace: A Gospel for All of Us* (Brewster: Paraclete Press, 2005), 12.

[607] Martin Luther, *The Blessed Sacrament of the Holy and True Body and Blood of Christ, and the Brotherhoods*, ed. Theodore Bachmann and Helmut Lehmann, vol. 35 (Philadelphia: Muhlenberg Press, 1960), 50.

[608] Luther, *Blessed Sacrament*, 59.

[609] Luther, 51.

[610] Luther, 51.

> To receive these sacraments in bread and wine, then, is nothing else than to receive a sure sign of this fellowship and incorporation with Christ and all saints. It is as if a citizen were given a sign, a document, or some other token to assure him [her] that he [she] is a citizen of the city, a member of that particular community.[611]

For Lutherans, there exists a connection between the Eucharist and the life and ministry of the church. When we participate in Holy Communion as a community of grace, we take part in "his life and good works, which are indicated by his flesh."[612]

To participate in Holy Communion means to share the life of the Triune God (his abundant love and blessing) with the whole of creation, which is manifested through our involvement in the ongoing creative work of God. In taking the blood under the wine, we also take part in "his passion and martyrdom, which are indicated by his blood."[613] We take part in the suffering of Christ that was meant for our salvation, and in the suffering of the whole creation. The Eucharist is the way God offers God's self to the whole of creation, and this is what we call grace. The believing community responds with thanksgiving. The thanksgiving offered to God is then as such:

> What sacrifices then are we to offer? Ourselves, and all that we have, with constant prayer.... Whereby we are to yield ourselves to the will of God, that He may do with us what He will, according to His own pleasure.[614]

In Eucharistic fellowship, all profits and costs are shared. In other words, as joy, support, protection, and so on are shared (between God, humanity, and the whole of creation), suffering is also shared within such fellowship. As God partakes in the joys and suffering of creation, the believing community does the same.[615] In Luther's own words, "In this sacrament, man is given through the priest a sure sign from God himself that he is thus united with Christ and his saints and has all things in common [with them], that Christ's suffering and life are his own, together with the lives and sufferings of all the saints."[616]

Eucharistic fellowship is a fellowship that requires willingness to share others' burdens and suffering. It is through the practice of such sharing that the Christian community of grace is formed. As Luther explains, in the

---

[611] Luther, 51.

[612] Luther, 60.

[613] Luther, 60.

[614] Martin Luther, *A Treatise on the N.T., That Is, the Holy Mass, 1520*, ed. Theodore Bachmann and Helmut Lehmann, vol. 35 (Philadelphia: Muhlenberg Press, 1960), 98.

[615] Luther, *Blessed Sacrament*, 51–52.

[616] Luther, 51–52.

Eucharist, "Christ has given his holy body for this purpose, that the things signified by the sacrament—the fellowship, the change wrought by love—may be put into practice."⁶¹⁷ We encounter God in and through each other's life. By carrying each other's burden with the love of Christ, we form a communal culture through which each member is formed into the likeness of Christ. As Luther emphasizes, "By the means of this sacrament, [grace is communicated in that] all self-seeking love is rooted out and gives place to that which seeks the common good of all; and through the change wrought by love there is one bread, one drink, one body, one community."⁶¹⁸ For Luther, to experience such transformation, one must:

> Take to heart the infirmities and needs of others, as if they were [one's] own. Then offer to others strength, as if it were their own, just as Christ does for [him/her] in the sacraments. This is what it means to be changed into one another through love.... To lose one's own form and take on that which is common to all.⁶¹⁹

D. Church's Role in Engaging the Public

Therefore, the social implication of the Lutheran understanding of a church as a community of grace has several applications in real life. Grace as a self-giving of the triune God relates the faith in the Trinity with a practical expression of that faith at all levels of social life. Understanding the church as a community of grace also helps us constructively and critically engage with the role of church in public in the Ethiopian context.

The major problem in Ethiopia is that there exists a distorted relationship among people of different ethnic groups. As clarified above, the political dynamics of the country have created a fractured community, grouped primarily into the "center" and the "periphery." It is vital for the church to address the question how Christian communities in Ethiopia are able to naturalize and provide healing to communities affected by so much oppression.

In view of grace founded on the self-giving of the triune God, this grace restores broken relationships in human communities with the purpose of creating "a universal community in which the love revealed in Christ seeks the fulfilment of all things in such a relationship to one another that what flows from the life of each enriches the life of them all."⁶²⁰ In other words, grace is the activity of God to make the human community whole. This speaks directly to the Ethiopian fractured community.

---

⁶¹⁷ Luther, 60.
⁶¹⁸ Luther, 67.
⁶¹⁹ Luther, 61–62.
⁶²⁰ Harold Ditmanson, *Grace in Experiance and Theology* (Minneapolis: Augsburg, 1977), 60.

How does the church as a community of grace live out its responsibility in restoring the divided communities? The churches in Ethiopia have not been able to provide an answer for at least two reasons: because they are 1) either too closely identified with the government or 2) have withdrawn from public engagement. On the first, the EOC has been serving hand and glove with the government following the "Christendom" model, legitimizing the oppressive governments. Even though the EOC has lost such status under the current government, it still identifies itself with the government at the "center," giving itself an image of patriarchy. On the second, some evangelical and Pentecostal churches follow the teaching that the gospel has nothing to do with social and political engagement. In their ministry, they emphasize evangelism over social, economic, and political services. At worst, they perceive their Christian responsibility as a solely "soul saving" enterprise. Neither of these two positions is supported by what it means to be a community of grace. They are contrary to the foundational teaching of Christianity in loving and serving our neighbors.

Those transformed by God's grace are to reach out to their neighbors and the whole world and empower them in every sphere of their human life. This understanding of God's grace and its implication in our social life negates both the Ethiopian churches' patristic approach in the EOC and the evangelical churches' social work that limits its mission to evangelism. The churches' mission in every context should be the same, which is participating in God's ongoing creative work by sharing God's grace with every human being, and that leads to empowerment and the transformation of individuals and communities. As Leonardo Boff clearly articulates, "Finally, the grace of God is to be seen in our invisible certainty that we are nurturing a new kind of society more worthy of human beings and God."[621]

The main problem with churches that follow the "Christendom" model is that they present themselves more as masters and Lords rather than as servants. However, as mentioned, grace is founded on the triune God's self-giving, which means that God's intention to bestow his grace on humans is founded in the sacrifice he made by offering his Son as a sacrifice. Christ, God's gift to humanity, came as a servant and shared this grace by laying down his life for all. The church shares this grace the same way, by serving others as servants. As it is written, "Whoever wants to be great among you must be your servant" (Mark 10:44). We are not called to be masters over others, but to serve others. As Luther states, a Christian should "empty himself [and] take upon himself the form of a servant [so that he is able] to

---

[621] Leonardo Boff, *Liberating Grace* (Maryknoll: Orbis, 1979), 86.

serve, help, and in every way deal with his neighbor as he sees that God through Christ has dealt and still deals with him."[622] Quoting Luther,

> A Christian lives not in himself, but in Christ and in his neighbor. Otherwise, he is not a Christian. He lives in Christ through faith, in his neighbor through love. By faith he is caught up beyond himself into God. By love he descends beneath himself into his neighbor.[623]

When it comes to evangelical churches, on issues concerned with the public, they argue that submission is the only option, as described Romans 13.[624] But Christians have immensely more to offer in situations of oppression than merely service and solidarity. To bring justice to social, economic, and political relations in Ethiopia, the church should participate in the work of the triune God because, as Luther contends, God "does not work in us without us, because he has created and preserved us that he might work in us and we might cooperate with him, whether outside his Kingdom through his general omnipotence or inside his Kingdom by the special virtue of his Spirit."[625] In other words, changing or reversing the Ethiopian problematic situation is the work of the triune God in which the church is invited to take part by the power of the Spirit.

A few evangelical churches, particularly the EECMY, have a legacy of critically engaging governments in the past. However, the present leaders have now chosen to follow other evangelical churches by limiting their ministry within the four walls of the church. The EECMY is being criticized for its unhelpful quietness in the face of a brutal government. As Luther indicated in his 1523 essay, "Temporal Authority: To What Extent It Should Be Obeyed,"[626] there is a limit to submitting to authorities. Therefore, the church should refrain from sanctioning an unjust and dictatorial government. When citizens are faced with harsh empires, the church is expected to rebuke such a system. As Gary Simpson rightly argues, "While publicity's rebuke comes from God, God does not work immediately, but rather through earthly means. God rebukes 'immediately.' In this sense,

---

[622] Luther, "Freedom of a Christian, 1520," 366.

[623] Luther, 371.

[624] Olana Gemechu, *A Church under Challenge: The Socio-Economic and Political Involvement of the Ethiopian Evangelical Church Mekane Yesus* (Rita, Latvia: Lambert Academic Publishing, 2013).

[625] Martin Luther, "The Bondage of the Will," in *Luther's Work*, ed. Philip S. Watson and Helmut Lehmann, vol. 33 (Philadelphia: Fortress Press, 1972), 243.

[626] Martin Luther, "Temporal Authority: To What Extent It Should Be Obeyed, 1523," in *Luther's Work*, ed. Walther I. Brandt and Helmut Lehmann, vol. 45 (Philadelphia: Muhlenburg Press, 1962).

publicity is the vehicle that installs the fear of the Lord, which is the beginning of wisdom and wise politics."[627]

As a community of grace, Ethiopian churches are called to renounce their complacency and silence and evaluate their lack of family spirit, their unwillingness to share, and their lack of active solidarity with persons struggling to break free from misery and oppression. This is not simply about doing charitable works among the needy, but it has to do with being courageous enough to confront the systems—be it political, social, economic, etc.—and confront rather prophetically in loving grace.

Summary

Christianity has enormous human and material resources (people, buildings, etc.), communication and social networks, and very rich and dynamic spiritual and cultural traditions and modes of thought and practice which have centrally informed democratizing movements such as the anti-apartheid struggle in South Africa or the freedom movement in the American south. Thus, theology has the potential to enrich our understandings of both the complexity and the vast agentic potential of the human person.

The Lutheran theology of grace can help address the divisive social, economic, and political structure in Ethiopia. Grace, founded on the self-giving of the triune God, is experienced through the Word and participating in the sacraments, which then brings transformation in our individual lives as well as our communal life. The church as a community of grace participates in the ongoing creative work of God and, by doing so, presents itself as a means through which God bestows his transforming grace for the betterment of the community.

Sharing this grace with our society as a community of grace requires the church to engage the public. The Ethiopian churches that have either identified themselves with the oppressive government or have withdrawn from politics have thwarted God's purpose to share His life with all creation through the church. As Christians, we focus on Christ and His sacrificial love for all humanity. In Christ, we are given the crisp and clear picture of what it means to give ourselves and of ourselves to others as a community of grace. Grace is God's gift of himself to other people in need, and so too should the church present itself, especially in Ethiopia.

---

[627] Gary Simpson, "Retriving Martin Luther's Critical Public Theology of Political Authority for Global Civil Society," in *Theological Practices That Matter*, ed. Karen L. Bloomquist (Minneapolis: Lutheran University Press, 2009), 163.

Part Three:
Pastoral Theology in Human Suffering

19. When Sickness Heals: Pastoral Reflection on Finding Meaning in Suffering
    Dr. Dana Costin-Stelian and Dr. Siroj Sorajjakool 284
20. Finding (or Missing) God and Meaning in Suffering
    Dr. Erhard S. Gerstenberger 299
21. Ecclesiology and Theodicy: Bonhoeffer's Sanctorum Communio as Response to Human Suffering
    Dr. Maury Jackson 317
22. The God of All Comfort: Karl Barth and Hope in Suffering
    Rev. Dr. Nathan D. Hieb 339
23. Disability and Suffering?—Pastoral and Practical Theological Considerations
    Dr. Amos Yong 361
24. What Kind of Response Can Pastoral Theology Give in the Midst of Suffering?
    Dr. HyeRan Kim-Cragg 379

19.
When Sickness Heals:
Pastoral Reflection on Finding Meaning in Suffering

Dr. Dana Costin-Stelian
Chaplain and Counselor, Charter Hospice
Palm Desert, California
Dr. Siroj Sorajjakool
President, Asia Pacific International University
Muak Lek, Thailand[628]

Introduction 285
A. What Is Spirituality? 286
B. Illness, Miracles, and Meaning 288
C. The Developmental Task in Illness 290
D. Integration in Behavioral and Social Sciences 293
Conclusion 297

---

[628] Costin-Stelian earned her PhD, MA, and BA from the University of Bucharest, Romania; and her MS from Loma Linda University, California. She has served as assistant professor of sociology for the University of Bucharest and a researcher with the Romanian Academy of Science. She has written *Roma Children Between Survival and Success* (Bucharest, Romania: Expert Publishing House, 2009) and several articles, including two chapters, "The Health Status of Roma Population" and "Family Planning in Roma Families," in *Roma People in Romania*, Catalin Zamfir and Marian Preda (Bucharest, Romania: Expert Publishing, 2001); and "Formative experiences," in *The Youth of the First Decade: The Challenges of the 90's*, Ioan Marginean (Bucharest, Romania: Expert Publishing House, 1996). See www.LinkedIn.com/in/danacostinstelian and dana.stellian@gmail.com.

Sorajjakool is serving as the President of Asia-Pacific International University in Thailand and also remains an adjunct professor at Loma Linda University where he was professor of religion, psychology, and counseling, and held several other positions over the last 20 years. He has written many books, including *Human Trafficking in Thailand: Current Issues, Trends, and the Role of the Thai Government* (Silkworm Books, 2013); *When Sickness Heals: The Place of Religious Belief in the Practice of Healthcare* (Templeton Foundation Press, 2006); *Child Prostitution in Thailand: Listening to Rahab* (Haworth Press, 2002), *Wu Wei, Negativity, and Depression: The Principle of Non-trying in the Practice of Pastoral Care*, foreword by Professor Ann Ulanov, Christiane Brooks Johnson Memorial Professor of Psychiatry and Religion, Union Theological Seminary (Haworth Press, 2001); with Mark F. Carr, Julius J. Nam, and Ernest Bursey, eds., *World Religions for Healthcare Professionals*, 2nd ed. (Routledge, 2017; 1st 2009), a textbook for Loma Linda University, CA, since 2009, and by Adventist University of Health Science, Florida; and with Henry Lamberton, eds. *Spirituality, Health, and Wholeness: An Introductory Guide for Healthcare Professionals* (Haworth Press, 2004), also a textbook at Loma Linda since 2004. He has written many chapters and articles, including those in *Sacred Spaces, Journal of the American Association of Pastoral Counselors, Journal of Pastoral Theology, Pastoral Psychology, Journal of HIV/AIDS and Social Services, The Journal of Pastoral Care, Catalyst: Journal of the Institute for Interdisciplinary Studies, Religions, Journal of Religion and Health, Journal of Pastoral Care and Counseling*, and *Golden Teak: Humanity and Social Sciences Journal*. See ssorajjakool@llu.edu and Siroj@apiu.edu.

Introduction

Tragedy disrupts! It disrupts the flow of normality and the logic of cause and effect; it disrupts the flow of time because it can make the future disappear and the past irrelevant; it disrupts faith and spirituality because in the face of tragedy values are challenged and meaning is lost. Most of us have lived through tragedies like this: the death of a loved one that meant the world to us, a debilitating illness or accident, a war that took away our freedom, or a natural disaster that destroyed our home. In the midst of heart-wrenching tragedy, when you gasp for air as you stare into the abyss that swallowed your world, you cannot believe that tomorrow is possible. And yet tomorrow always comes. With the sunrise, a new day, and a new world is born. A world in which the new normal holds together pain and comfort, war and peace, light and darkness, loss and love, death and dreams, fear and safety, anguish and joy, heartbreak and happiness. As the soul tries to find its way in this new world, it starts a new journey to find meaning, because we need meaning as much as we need air. And as we continue our journey, and leave behind the question "Why?" a new question emerges: Can we find meaning in pain?

This essay—based on the concept from the book *When Sickness Heals*—is a succinct and updated presentation of a theory asserting that severe illness comes with a "developmental task" regarding the role of religion and spirituality in the patient's experience, because "sickness can bring about changes in existential meaning and thus offer healing to the soul."[629] As we looked at the continuously growing body of research on spirituality and health, we realized that the main focus is on the health benefits of a vigorous spiritual life (including prayer, meditation, scripture reading, and fellowship with the community of believers, etc.). The reality of our encounters with cancer patients, however, revealed a much richer and more complex relationship between spirituality and faith. In our experience, patients with strong faith in a God who have everything under control, took longer to recover emotionally than patients who looked at cancer as a random event. This provoked us to reconsider the philosophical and theological literature focusing on the role of the non-being (understood as the negative elements of life: illness, pain, loss, death) in the journey of faith.

This theory is based on two propositions: First, we understand spirituality as a quest for meaning. This quest is ontological in nature: is there *a priori* knowledge in a Kantian sense? Also, at the ontological level, there is a sense of transcendence which coexists with the quest for meaning.

---

[629] Siroj Sorajjakool, *When Sickness Heals: The Place of Religious Belief in Healthcare* (Philadelphia: Templeton Foundation Press, 2006), xii.

These two intertwine in coexistence, and the two forces of transcendence and the quest for meaning define the meaning of our spirituality (beliefs and symbols) and the practice of our religion (rituals). Second, illness challenges our sense of meaning—and with it—our sense of transcendence. Because meaning is the homeostasis of the soul, whatever challenges that has to be reconfigured and reintegrated. And this is by definition a developmental task. This is why we break away from the traditional research focusing on the positive impact that spirituality and religion have on one's health and psychosocial wellbeing and argue that the healing power of spirituality goes beyond wellbeing. We believe meaning has the power to heal even when there is no possibility of recovery from a terminal illness. We believe healing is possible, even when there is no cure.

A. What Is Spirituality?

From the primal religions that speak about something beyond the material world to the richness of spirituality expressed in different cultures, forms, rituals, and beliefs; from Christianity to Islam, from the Mosaic tradition to African religions, from Buddhism to Hinduism, the golden thread of a powerful spiritual quest binds together the phenomenal world with something beyond matter and facts.

Working with cancer patients (at different times and in different units) we both observed that most new patients can fit in one of two categories: those who ask "Why?" and those who believe the illness is part of a bigger plan, God's plan. When children ask "Why?" they do it in order to make sense of an unknown world. As adults, we ask the same question for the same reason: to make sense of a world that lost its meaning after an incurable diagnosis, a devastating loss or trauma. When trauma is too disturbing to be processed consciously, it might be processed unconsciously through recurring dreams. "Bad dreams are attempts to make sense of bad experiences"[630] writes Bulkeley. This longing for making sense and meaning takes us back to Ludwig Wittgenstein's argument that there has to be a limit to thought; there are things that can only be shown (not said) because they are outside of the limits of language. These things belong to the realm of transcendence.[631] The same quest for something beyond the palpable reality emerges in Friedrich Nietzsche famous quote: "The riddle which man must solve." Is it possible that this intrinsic, powerful need to make sense of our

---

[630] Kelly Bulkeley, *Transforming Dreams: Learning Spiritual Lessons from the Dreams You Never Forget* (New York: John Wiley, 2000), 58.

[631] Ludwig Wittgenstein (1889–1951), *Tractatus Logico-Philosophicus*, intro. Bertrand Russell (1872–1970) (New York: Harcourt, Brace; London: K. Paul, Trench, Trubner, 1922); trans. C. K. Ogden (London/New York: Routledge, 1992); trans. D. F. Pears and B. F. McGuinness (London/New York: Routledge, 1994, 2001, 2014).

experiences within the phenomenal world is in fact the basis of what we call "spirituality"?

Researching and reflecting on writings that explore the depths of the soul, we were surprised to discover the rich diversity of authors confirming our intuition that spirituality is an existential quest for meaning. As Killen and de Beer write, "We are drawn to meaning. We need meaning as much as we need food and drink." We need to make "the truest and richest meaning possible of our lives."[632] We need to make sense of our reality, and in the process we create poetry and science, art and technology, philosophy and architecture, cultures and societies. Then we also need to make sense of ourselves. Maybe this is what the great mystic Rumi was trying to do when he wrote: "You dance inside my chest,/ where no one sees you./ But sometimes I do, and that/ sight becomes this art."[633] Maybe this "dance inside my chest" is what leads us to search for "the meaning to which we belong."[634] And this search points us to something bigger than ourselves as we ask with Pascal, "Who has put me here? By whose order and direction have this place and time been allotted to me?"[635]

As we already mentioned, our understanding of spirituality weaves together the ontological sense of meaning and the sense of transcendence. This ontological drive toward meaning leads us in a quest for self-knowledge. As we struggle to understand ourselves, we also discover within the structure of our being, a sense of transcendence.

This drive for meaning is most essential in challenging times. Because it is here that we realize how limited our certainty and our control over the circumstances are. Certainty is limited not only because knowledge is limited but also because we do not move from the margins toward the center of understanding God and reality. But rather we are a moving part in a mechanism. We are an intrinsic part of reality, changing it and being changed in return. In this paradigm, the religious commitment is to embrace reality and "make a better society, a safer community, a more compassionate humanity, and better citizens."[636]

Control, on the other hand, is limited because experience tells us that religion cannot always fix the problem. When the amulet, the ritual, or the prayer fails us, and their purpose to protect us from evil slips from us, we

---

[632] Patricia O'Connell Killen and John de Beer, *The Art of Theological Reflection* (New York: Crossroad, 1994), x.

[633] Rumi, *The Love Poems of Rumi*, ed. Deepak Chopra (New York: Harmony Books, 1998), 62.

[634] Siroj Sorajjakool, *When Sickness Heals: The Place of Religious Belief in Healthcare* (Philadelphia: Templeton Foundation Press, 2006), 5.

[635] Blaise Pascal, *Pascal's Pensées* (New York: E. P. Dutton), 1958.

[636] Sorajjakool, *When Sickness Heals*, 18.

finally discover a bigger God, a God that cannot be controlled by our rituals. God's way might remain an incomprehensible mystery, but as we give up control, we gain comfort. In embracing this mystery of God, we move away from the linear line of thought that builds a wall in the world, a wall that cuts through the core of our being and separates right from wrong, good from evil, smart from foolish, us from the others. And as we understand that we are in the same time and the "wall" is not that solid—that right and wrong, good and evil, smart and foolish, the brother and "the other" are not truly severed—we gain hope for healing and wholeness. We might lose rituals, or claims of absolute truth, and even religion, but maybe this would be our chance to re-gain a sense of transcendence and a deep meaningful spirituality.

B. Illness, Miracles, and Meaning

In the lonely hours of the night, between tears and pain, between the bitterness of the potion and the unquenchable thirst, on a modern hospital or on a bed of straw under the sky, someone lays awake searching and struggling. This is where theological reflection happens: not in churches or seminaries, but in hospitals and hospices, in nursing homes and mental health institutions. Why? Because illness and suffering play an important role in the quest for meaning.

Pan was diagnosed with germ cell cancer and did not respond well to treatment. The whole family engaged in merit-making rituals with the hope for a cure, and Pan himself became a novice monk. His mom was a strong believer in religious rituals, faithfully practicing them all her life, so it seemed reasonable to expect that gods would be there for her when she needed their help. But despite the prayer and rituals, Pan's situation did not improve. He begged his parents to let him go, and he finally passed away. He was seventeen-years-old. Pan's mom became discouraged, and she doesn't go to the temple as often as she used to. Something went wrong. There was dissonance between her beliefs and her reality. How can one make sense of this?

Pain is a powerful element in spirituality. It creates poetry, music, and art, theology and philosophy, devoted believers and atheists. In the Christian paradigm, pain can be a punishment for sin, or a test of faith. In the Buddhist wisdom, the problem of suffering is at the core of the Four Noble Truths: Life *is* suffering. To be *is* to suffer. We suffer because we have desire. In this paradigm, the way out of suffering is to give up desire, wants, and expectations. Buddhists understand life as a movement from being to nonbeing, it is our desire to cling to life that throws us back into the cycle of birth and re-birth. The only way out of the cycle of suffering is to achieve nonbeing, and that is not an easy task!

As chaplains in the oncology unit, we shared many sacred moments with our patients, and we often listened to them say, "I don't know why I have to go through this. But I believe there is a purpose in it. Everything happens for a reason, I just haven't figured what the reason is, yet!"

Prior to traumatic events, we define meaning in relation to all positive and normative elements. Illness, crisis, and trauma challenge this understanding. In our own experiences of trauma and depression, in the midst of intense mental agony, a thought came again and again:

> There had better be something good come out of this! Because without something good coming out of it, this pain doesn't make any sense! And without a sense, what reason do we have to go forward?

When there is no meaning and no sense to suffering, life loses its purpose and becomes unbearable. But the opposite is also true: sense and meaning make suffering bearable. This is exactly what Roger Schmidt suggests when he writes:

> Sociologist Max Weber (1864–1920) saw religion as a way of investing life with meaning in response to those features of human existence, suffering, evil, and death that are not resolvable in scientific terms. As anthropologist Clifford Geertz observed, religious symbol systems provide a context for making suffering "bearable, supportable, something, as we say sufferable."[637]

After interviewing fifteen individuals with terminal illnesses, Patricia B. Fryback and Bonita R. Reinert wrote: "Finding meaning is particularly important when a person is facing a serious illness, because the illness itself causes permanent changes in life that force a re-evaluation of any previously assumed meaning."[638] When trauma takes over our life, it chases the meaning away. But the need for meaning is ontological, so the lack of it is more unbearable than the pain or the death itself. This is why in the early stages of coping with trauma people often yearn for miracles because miracles normalize life and restore meaning.

A retired minister was diagnosed with cancer, and he became very sad and depressed. He called the whole family together. After reading the story of Jacob wrestling with God (Gen 32: 22–32), he told us:

> I'm not asking you to pray that God's will be done. I ask you to struggle with God. Just like Jacob did. Never let go. Struggle until God answers our prayer. Never let go.[639]

---

[637] Roger Schmidt et al., *Patterns of Religion* (Belmont: Wadsworth, 1999), 9, esp. chap. 3, "Tribal Religions in Historical Times."

[638] Chana Ullman, "Cognitive and Emotional Antecedents of Religious Conversion," *Journal of Personality and Social Psychology* 43, no. 1 (1982): 182–92.

[639] Sorajjakool, *When Sickness Heals*, 29.

The longing for a miracle immediately after an incurable diagnosis is an attempt to regain meaning by eliminating the illness and returning to the previous life. At this point, meaning and illness are not compatible concepts, as the pre-illness existential recipe for meaning does not include negative elements. As most people find comfort in believing in an all-knowing and benevolent Higher Power that has everything under control, they expect this Higher Power to act in their favor and to fix the problem.

Another element at play in longing for a miracle in the face of death is the coping mechanism of denial. Elisabeth Kubler-Ross's advice for us is to journey with the sick and dying even into denial, to go where they want to go and to be where they want to be. There can be a deep sense of reality in fantasy. There is much truth to be learned when a dying patient plans her wedding or when a paraplegic discusses a time in the future when he'll go surfing. Fantasy is sacred, and it should be treated as such. It connects us to the basic instinctive root of our being, and, in a sense, forms an integral part of our souls.[640]

When we are broken, fantasy makes us whole. However, believing in miracles is not the same with being in denial. For a person of strong faith, God is God and miracles are possible. But the hardest part to do is to *let* God be God and accept that miracles are as random as cancer is. And when the miracle does not happen, a new journey to find meaning begins, a journey that includes several dueling elements: health and sickness, joy and suffering, and life and death.

C. The Developmental Task in Illness

When my (DCS)—larger-than-life—father became paraplegic at age 60, we first prayed for a miracle. Shortly after that he said, "This is not life!" So he started praying for death. Yet, neither healing nor death came. He lived thirteen more years at home, cared for by my mother. He went through a short denial, a long anger, and a dark depression until he emerged on the other side. He found familiar joys and meaning in nature, ideas, and friends; but he also found unexpected meaning in being the only grandfather my daughter knew, or in being the subject of a documentary which raised awareness about Lyme disease and saved many lives in the process. Shortly before he passed away, my mother asked, "Are you upset with God?" Unable to speak, he shook his head and smiled.

This is the developmental task of illness: the movement from the incompatibility of meaning and illness to their integration; the transition from the existential desire to remove pain and suffering to the experience of

---

[640] Sorajjakool, *When Sickness Heals*, 29.

finding meaning while suffering. How do we get here? Why do we make this journey? Richard Rice is right on point when he writes, "Because suffering threatens the very meaning of life, an effective response to suffering must help us recover that meaning."[641] Rachel Naomi Remen adds weight and value to this perspective:

> The language of the soul is meaning. We may first discover the soul when life events awaken in us the need for meaning. In serious or chronic illnesses, even people who have never considered this dimension of experience before instinctively reach for a personal meaning in events that have disrupted their lives. Meaning helps us to see in the dark. It strengthens the will to live in us.[642]

Yet, maybe, meaning is even more than language; maybe it is the intrinsic matter of the soul. When illness, trauma, and pain threaten life as we know it, we begin to realize that the only unbearable thing here is the lack of meaning. When the miracle doesn't come and the cancer doesn't go away, something's got to give; and the only "disposable" is the old recipe for meaning—the one that takes no bitterness. Integrating "non-being" (non-normative, negative elements) in the new formula for meaning making is an upstream journey.

In our society this might look like driving the wrong way on a freeway. We live in a world of "Miss Universe" and "The Sexiest Man Alive," a world of excessive positive thinking and extreme makeovers, a world where the rich and famous set standards and values, and the poor are always neglected, ignored, and forgotten. Even death has become an opportunity for entertainment: a "show off" and a "show down". We don't know how to talk about excruciating pain, about smelly wounds that don't heal, and bleeding that doesn't stop. Nor can we talk about losing ourselves as we lose our hair, our jobs, and our hope.

And yet, the man gasping for air in room 11 is the handsome Italian she fell in love with 35 years ago. The barely alive woman in room 6 is someone's mother and someone's teacher. The heart attack patient in room 20 bed 2 is a young doctor. And the severely disabled child in room 13 is the apple of someone's eyes. This is who we are as human beings: forceful and frail, smart and stupid, fearless and fearful, beautiful and broken, all in the same time. When we finally understand and embrace this truth, we may finally discover what Henri Nouwen calls ecstasy:

---

[641] Richard Rice, *Suffering and the Search for Meaning. Contemporary Responses to the Problem of Pain* (Downers Grove: IVP Academic, 2014), 23.

[642] Rachel Naomi Remen, *My Grandfather's Blessings: Stories of Strength, Refuge, and Belonging* (New York: Riverhead Books, 2000), 28–29.

It is a joy that does not separate happy days from sad days, successful moments from moments of failure, experiences of honor from experiences of dishonor, passion from resurrection. This joy is a divine gift that does not leave us during times of illness, poverty, oppression, or persecution. It is present even when the world laughs or tortures, robs or maims fights or kills. It is truly ecstatic, always moving us from the house of fear into the house of love, and always proclaiming that death no longer has the final say.[643]

It is obvious by now that the developmental task of illness is both psychological and theological in nature. "Because suffering is unavoidable, theodicy is inescapable,"[644] writes Rice. In this journey we might be well served by his advice "to identify suffering as a mystery, rather than a problem."[645] Albert Y. Hsu understands that as he writes, "Despite all our questioning, perhaps there simply aren't any answers to the why questions. Maybe we don't know why, and we can't know why. Maybe that's all we know."[646]

As we leave behind the unanswerable "Why?" a new question comes along: Who? Who are we? Who is God? Most of us start our journey with an all-loving, all-powerful, and all-knowing God. But when suffering comes along, something's got to give, and we get to choose our non-negotiable quality of God. Nevertheless, when the amulet, the ritual, or the prayer fail to bring us the miracle we hoped for, it is hard to hold on to the idea of an all-powerful and all-knowing God. Yet, his love is still there, walking with us "through the valley of the shadow of death,"[647] giving us strength and peace, never letting us feel alone, or forgotten.

Rabbi Harold S. Kushner, the author of the best-seller *When Bad Things Happen to Good People*, walked this road.[648] As a Jew he was a carrier of the Abrahamic blessing; as a rabbi, he was a strong believer in an all-powerful God in control of the world. But this theodicy collapsed when his fourteen-year-old son died of an incurable disease. Reflecting on his new-found understanding of the Twenty-third Psalm, he wrote, "It doesn't say 'I will fear no evil' because evil only happens to bad people. It says there is a

---

[643] Henri J. M. Nouwen, *Lifesigns: Intimacy, Fecundity, and Ecstasy in Christian Perspective* (New York: Image Books, 1966), 99.

[644] Rice, *Suffering and the Search for Meaning*, 39.

[645] Rice, 24.

[646] Albert Y. Hsu, *Grieving a Suicide: A Loved One's Search for Comfort, Answers and Hope* (Urbana, Illinois: InterVarsity Press, 2002), 89.

[647] Psalm 23:4.

[648] Rabbi Harold S. Kushner, *When Bad Things Happen to Good People* (New York: Schocken Books, 1981; 20th Anniversary Ed., 2001).

lot of evil out there, but I can handle it because God is on my side."[649] Later on, the 9/11 events deepened his conviction that "God's promise is that whenever we have to confront the unfairness of life, he will be with us."[650]

"The discovery that the worst experiences can ultimately enhance our lives, often comes as a surprise"[651] for the patient, for the family, and sometimes, even for the chaplain. As I was looking at the fairly young woman receiving chemotherapy, I couldn't believe the serenity on her face. "What gives you strength?" I asked.

"I am Buddhist," she answered. "For Buddhists there is a time to be born, a time to grow, a time to get older, get sick and die. If the treatment works, then I get to live longer, if not, then it's my time to die," she said with a smile. "But I'm already a lucky one because I came back as human and I got to live until now."

She went on to explain that coming back as human meant that she did well in a previous life and accumulated enough merits. Living another life as a human gave her the chance to do better, which meant more merits and better chances for the next life. As I was listening to her, I understood that in the end it does not matter *when* we die, what really matters is *how* we live. A priceless gift from a dying Buddhist patient was given to an almost-living Christian chaplain. As I pondered her answer, Rice's words came to mind: "Perhaps God is uniquely near to us when we suffer horrendously, and the value of that closeness outweighs the cost of suffering."[652]

D. Integration in Behavioral and Social Sciences

It is hard to say what led us to the idea of integration in the first place. Part of it grew out of our professional experience as chaplains as we journeyed together with our patients "through the valley of the shadow of death."[653] Another part was personal experience, theological reflection, and intuition, steeped in our rich cultural and religious backgrounds. As the idea of integration started to take shape, we finally came to recognize its pattern in familiar religious symbols and theological writings, as well as in different theories and research from the field of behavioral and social sciences.

If we look at Freud's psychoanalytical theory of personality, there is strain, separation, and antagonism everywhere: from the tension between *life instincts* and *death instincts*, to the conflict between inner drives and social

---

[649] Cited by Kristin E. Holmes, "23rd Psalm Holds Answers to Many of Life's Questions," *The Riverside Press-Enterprise* (Oct. 25, 2005): B12.

[650] Holmes, "23rd Psalm."

[651] Rice, *Suffering and the Search for Meaning*, 62.

[652] Rice, 73.

[653] Psalm 23: 4, KJV.

demands; from the competition for psychic energy between Id, Ego, and Super-Ego, to the mysterious dance between consciousness and the unconscious.[654] Erik Erikson's psychosocial perspective on development builds on Freud's developmental stages. Each one of Erikson's stages start with an existential question, and it is characterized by a psychosocial crisis in connection with a significant relationship. The psychosocial crisis is a battle between two elements, one positive and one negative.

1. Infancy – Trust versus Mistrust,
2. Early Childhood – Autonomy versus Shame and Doubt,
3. Preschool age – Initiative versus Guilt,
4. School Age – Industry versus Inferiority,
5. Adolescence – Identity versus Role Confusion,
6. Young Adulthood – Intimacy versus Isolation,
7. Middle Age – Generativity versus Stagnation, and
8. Later Life – Integrity versus Despair.[655]

The person who masters each developmental task will emerge from the stage with a virtue that will be carried on all their lives. If the person fails, the struggle is not resolved.[656] The biggest challenge according to Erikson's model is the impossibility to move from the negative side of development to the positive one in the upper stages. The only way to do it is to go back and re-live every failed stage until one masters them all.

The next generation of psychoanalysts that followed Freud, starting with Melanie Klein, formulated the object relations theory. "Splitting"—an essential concept in this theory—describes the organization of mental life in early infancy by a strict separation between "good" and "bad." As a result, the "objects" that populate the child's "inner landscape" are rigorously divided into two categories: good or bad (father, mother, siblings, self, deity).[657]

Freud, Erikson, and Klein weave together positive and negative elements in the tapestry of our being. However, the pattern is black and white; there are no greys, and no integration. Pamela Cooper White on the other hand, is the master of integration. First, she understands human beings as both good

---

[654] Gerald Corey, *Theory and Practice of Counseling and Psychotherapy* (Brooks/Cole, Cengage Learning, 2013, 2009), 64–66.

[655] See Erik Erikson, *Childhood and Society* (New York: W. W. Norton, 1950, 1985), *Insight and Responsibility: Lectures on the Ethical Implications of Psychoanalytic Insight* (Norton, 1964), and with Joan M. Erikson, *The Life Cycle Completed: Extended Version* (Norton, 1998).

[656] Corey, *Theory ... Psychotherapy*, 69–71, 94.

[657] Pamela Cooper-White, *Many Voices: Pastoral Psychotherapy in Relational and Theological Perspective* (Minneapolis: Augsburg Press, 2011), 52–54, 104.

and "vulnerable," made in the image of God, and "inescapably alienated from God."[658] She embraces a "relational understanding of persons as multiple, mutable, fluid and always in process."[659] She transforms the transference and counter-transference into "shared wisdom."[660] She speaks about "the ambiguities of evil," and concludes that:

> Evil cannot finally be split off from human affairs, not our own, not anyone's. The depressive position acknowledges the tragic and poignant reality that all seeming opposites, including good and evil (mother, breast, father, me) are finally held together. When splitting begins to be healed and projections are withdrawn and reincorporated into the conscious life, to whatever extent that is fleetingly possible, evil can be understood as a tear in the very fabric of the good itself, and not apart from it.[661]

In this context,

> Our work as clinicians is to facilitate the healing of splitting, whether the narcissistic splitting of emptiness; compulsive behavior and disavowal; or the post-traumatic splitting of projection, terror, and fragmentation—or our own counter transferential splitting in the form of trying to remove the speck from our patient's eye while ignoring the log on our own (Matt7:3).[662]

In other words, our job as clinicians, chaplains, and pastoral theologians is—ultimately—to facilitate integration. As we turned to research we have found social science studies that support this perspective. One of them is David Karp's qualitative study documenting the four stages that chronically depressed people go through. Karp studied fifty individuals and concluded that in the first stage that most depressed people think that the cause of their depression is outside themselves (relational context, economic or political circumstances, natural or social environment, crisis, etc.). In the second stage, people realize that their depression even though influenced by the context is not determined by it. They cannot blame it on the context, and it doesn't go away with the context. In the third stage, the longest one, people look for a cure, researching and trying different psychotropic medications and therapeutic approaches. Finally, most chronically depressed people realize that depression might get better, but it will never go away. With this

---

[658] Cooper-White, *Many Voices*, 40.

[659] Cooper-White, *Many Voices*, ix.

[660] Pamela Cooper-White, *Shared Wisdom: Use of Self in Pastoral Care and Counseling* (Minneapolis: Fortress Press, 2004).

[661] Cooper-White, *Many Voices*, 131.

[662] Cooper-White, 131.

realization comes a certain sense of acceptance, a deeper spirituality, and a feeling of empowerment that makes depression itself more manageable.[663]

Johnny Ramirez Johnson, Carlos Fayard, Carlos Garberoglio, and Clara Jorge Ramirez studied the relationship between faith and emotions. They asked fifty-eight breast cancer patients to use six basic emotions (three positive in love, joy, surprise; and three negative in anger, sadness and fear) to describe their faith. Most patients (82.9 percent) used positive emotions in relation to their faith; but the most interesting finding is that the negative emotions were also part of the conversation, and this indicates "the need to understand religious faith as a construct that encompasses negative as well as positive emotions."[664]

Another qualitative study by Kelvin Thompson, Leigh Aveling, Art Earl, and Sorajjakool focused on the relationship between meaning and chronic pain. For most of the fifteen participants in the study, the initial definition of meaning did not include negative elements but rather was seen as a cumulus of "productive activities and positive relationships." As the chronic pain settled in, these people experienced multiple losses in meaning making activities and relationships. Medication restored some sense of normality and meaning but also had the unintended consequence of dependency and addiction. As the patients explored the connections between pain, addiction, and unresolved emotions like anger, guilt, or grief, they also started to understand that there is no prescription for meaning. Instead of trying to make their new life fit into the old recipe for meaning, they learned to "doctor" the recipe and create meaning in their present situation. As one patient said, "It's learning to live life on life's terms."[665]

She was a wife and a mother of two young children, and she was dying of cancer. I spoke, and prayed, and cried with friends and family members. But with her, I felt at a loss for words. When she brought God into the conversation, I dared to ask: "Where is God in this story?" She smiled like she was sharing a secret: "I thank God every day that it's me, not my children." She was right. She was holding a secret, the mystery, and the wisdom of integration: to be grateful for life in the face of death; to find healing in the midst of incurable illness.

---

[663] David Karp, *Speaking of Sadness: Depression, Disconnection, and the Meaning of Illness* (Oxford: Oxford University Press, 1996).

[664] Johnny Ramirez Johnson et al., "Is Faith an Emotion? Faith as a Meaning-Making Affective Process: An Example from Breast Cancer Patients," *American Behavioral Scientist* 45, no. 12 (August 2002): 1839–53.

[665] Siroj Sorajjakool, Kelvin Thompson, Leigh Aveling, and Art Earl, "Chronic Pain, Meaning, and Spirituality: A Qualitative Study of the Healing Process in Relation to the Role of Meaning and Spirituality," *The Journal of Pastoral Care and Counseling* 60, no. 4 (Winter 2006): 369–78.

Conclusion

Marilyn McCord Adams writes, "In the crucifixion, God identified with all human beings" on both sides of the horrendous evil. As a victim of horrendous evil, he identified with all the victims, giving them a chance to find meaning in their suffering by sharing in the suffering of God. And as a victim of a "cursed" death, Christ became symbolically synonymous with the perpetrators of evil. This perspective will give the perpetrators a chance to seek and embrace forgiveness, and also to forgive themselves.[666]

In *Letters and Papers from Prison* Dietrich Bonhoeffer asks "who Christ really is, for us today?"[667] Bonhoeffer's answer brings a dramatic change of paradigm. Instead of a God of the unknown, the "God of the gap," he offers us a God in what we know and experience, a God "at the centre of life, not when we are at the end of our resources."[668] A God fully revealed in Jesus Christ; a powerless and suffering God, "who wins power and space in the world by his weakness."[669] In this context, Bonhoeffer's "religionless Christianity" is a chance to free Christ from the prison of religion and church and to offer him to the world, not as "an object of religion, but.... really the Lord of the world."[670] Just like Christ, people are also "freed from false religious obligations and inhibitions," because to be a religionless Christian does not mean to make oneself a "sinner, a penitent, or a saint" but rather "to share in God's suffering at the hands of a godless world."[671] In this context, Christian life is a continuous clash (or balance) between two questions:

1. In what way are we "religionless-secular" Christians?
2. In what way are we the "ecclesia"?[672]

The answer is a call to discipleship and fellowship. It is not a call to special favor, but a call to suffering. It is not a call to power, but to powerlessness. It is not a call to a partial *religious act* or ritual, but a call to the fullness of faith. It is not a call to holiness through separation from the world, but a call

---

[666] Marilyn McCord Adams, *Horrendous Evils and the Goodness of God*, Cornell Studies in the Philosophy of Religion (Ithaca: Cornell University Press, 2000), 166.

[667] Eberhard Bethge, *Dietrich Bonhoeffer: A Biography*, Rev. Ed. (Minneapolis: Fortress Press, 2000), 863–864.

[668] Dietrich Bonhoeffer, *Letters and Papers from Prison* (New York: Simon and Schuster /Touchstone, 1997), 312.

[669] Bonhoeffer, *Letters ... from Prison*, 361.

[670] Bonhoeffer, 281.

[671] Bonhoeffer, 361.

[672] Bonhoeffer, 280.

to wholeness through "this-worldliness."[673] Bonhoeffer's conclusion is that "Jesus calls men, not to a new religion, but to life."[674]

At nineteen-years-old she was the single mother of a toddler, and a cancer patient. "How did cancer change you?" I asked. "It made me see more. Before, I never thought about people who suffer. I knew they existed, but I didn't want to see them. Now, I see them." The developmental task of serious illness and suffering is a very personal journey. But maybe in the end, we all grow. And as we learn to hold together good and evil, life and death, cancer and kids, chemo and Christmas, our reality grows with us becoming more encompassing. And as our reality expands, and we learn to make meaning from being and nonbeing alike, our lives become richer as our soul and our relationships deepen. And as the soul grows and ripens into wholeness, our inner eyes open toward transcendence, and we discover a different, more personal God—a God who can heal the soul of the incurable patient, a God who stands with us in the face of horrendous evil, a God who loves us with an "everlasting love" that goes beyond sickness, suffering, and death.

> The LORD hath appeared of old unto me, saying,
> Yea, I have loved thee with an everlasting love:
> therefore with lovingkindness have I drawn thee.
> Jeremiah 31:3

---

[673] Bonhoeffer, 369–370, Bonhoeffer admits to have borrowed and embraced the concept of "this-worldly life" from Luther.

[674] Bonhoeffer, 362.

20.
Finding (or Missing) God and Meaning in Suffering

Dr. Erhard S. Gerstenberger
Professor Emeritus of O.T. Literature and Theology
University of Marburg, Germany[675]

Introduction	299
A. Biblical Witnesses: Manifold, Not Homogeneous	301
1. Suffering Is Normal, Integral to Life, Undebatable	301
2. Suffering Is Reward for Misbehavior, Error, Rebellion, Sin, & Violations of Rules	302
3. Suffering Is Unjustified, Senseless, Arbitrary	303
a. What Would Ancient People Do when Confronted with Life-hazards?	303
b. Basic Issue of Ethical Perturbations in Difficult Passages	303
B. Finding or Missing God	311
1. How Dare We to Describe Finding/Missing of God in Tribulations without End?	311
2. There Is a Great Need to Reflect on the Seekers of God	312
3. Finding or Missing God in the Contemporary World	312
a. Lost in Persecution, Torture	313
b. Lost in Sickness, Frailty, Disease	313
c. Lost in Despair, Depression	314
d. Lost in Calamities and Catastrophes	314
e. Lost in Doubts, Unbelief, Remorse	315
f. Lost in Hate—Saved through Love	315
Conclusion	316

Introduction

Some preliminary remarks are in order. For one, our thinking, talking, writing about God always is a precarious, even a dangerous undertaking. Not because we have to fear divine wrath, but much more so because we are likely to overestimate our capacity to meaningfully perform such kind of

---

[675] Gerstenberger retired from Marburg University in 1997. He continues teaching the Hebrew Bible on a more leisurely scale both inside Germany and abroad, within church communities and academic settings. He is the author of many books and over 300 articles, including *Suffering* (1980; 272 pp.); *Yahweh—The Patriarch: Ancient Images of God and Feminist Theology*, trans. Frederick J. Gaiser (Minneapolis: Fortress Press, 1996; 168 pp.), *Psalms 1—with an Introduction to Cultic Poetry* (1988; 262 pp.), *Psalms 2 and Lamentations* (2001; 566 pp.), *Theologies in the O.T.* (2002; 372 pp.), and *Woman and Man* (1981; 252 pp.). For his 80th birthday in 2012 two of his colleagues published a collection of 42 articles spanning 50 years of teaching and writing (half in English, half in German, one in Portuguese): Ute E. Eisen and Christl M. Maier, eds., *Erhard S. Gerstenberger: Die Hebraeische Bibel als Buch der Befreiunjg*, which translates into English after his name into "*The Hebrew Bible—a Book which Liberates*" (Ausgewaehlte Aufsaetze, 2012; 718p; openaccess@bibsys.uni-giessen.de): published by Justus-Liebig-Universitat, Giessen, Germany, online every article, http://geb.uni-giessen.de/geb/volltexte/2012/8601/. See his bibliography http://geb.uni-giessen.de/geb/volltexte/2012/8838/pdf/Gerstenberger_Bibliographie.pdf or www.PreciousHeart.net/ti/Gerstenberger-Bibliography.pdf, over 300 articles in 18 pages from 1961–2012, put together by Michaela Geiger. See gersterh@staff.uni-marburg.de.

God-taLuke The Scriptures are full of warnings over against arrogant postures of theological knowledge: "We know only in part, and we prophesy only in part" (1 Cor 13:9).[676] God's encompassing presence is so much beyond our grasp that the psalmist moans: "Such knowledge is too wonderful for me; it is so high that I cannot attain it" (Ps 139:6). And prophets describe their impressions of encounters with God with great reluctance, as in Ezekiel 1:26, "something like a throne," "like sapphire," "like a human form," etc. The incomprehensiveness to humans regarding the depth and width and height of God should be kept in mind. Theological thinking and speaking should always be founded on this basic insight: we cannot possibly know and understand *fully* the ways of the Lord nor HIS/HER qualities (names and gendered pronouns in relation to God betray already the incompatibility of human language and divine reality, cf. Deut 4:16).

Two, not every bad situation can be blissfully resolved. We have to consider despair and failure, even utmost senselessness and bitter injustice in human life and society. They are to be encountered in faith (cf. Kohelet/Ecclesiastes), perhaps even in rebellion against God (cf. Job). Believers are saved—others are lost in the Bible. Destiny from the beginning is a human effort to explain the enigmas transcending our limited understanding. It was John Calvin, among others, who seriously wrestled with the question, whether all the course of history and its myriads of biographies were determined from the beginning of time.[677] But the Swiss reformer also acknowledged the shortcomings of human knowledge and reason.[678] Thus we may consider many doctrinary debates as fundamentally precarious. They do claim absolute validity while they are only partial, contextual, limited efforts to articulate some important truths. The basic theological insight is: humans are ignorant of the Divine (Ps 139:1–6).

Three, the gross balance of premature deaths and crippled lives on this globe may well overcome the positive counterparts of happy, healthy, peaceful existence, considering exemplar centuries like the 20th and the beginning of the 21st. The Second World War alone, ignited by Hitlerist fanatics in Germany, cost about 60 millions of mostly innocent victims. Post-war times, partially taking shape under slogans like "Make love, not war" and "Not ever again!" did not develop as peacefully as war-torn citizens in many states hoped. Facts and figures of gruesome battles, deadly concentration camps, but also of terrible catastrophes like the great tsunami

---

[676] NRSV, as will be all future quotations unless stated otherwise.

[677] Cf. *Institutio Christianae Religionis*, book III, ch. 21–23.

[678] *Finitum non capax infiniti*: "The finite is unable to harbor the infinite"; cf. Nicolaus Cusanus, *De docta ignorancia* (Kues, Germany: n.p., 1440).

of 2006 remind us of so much undeserved and totally insensate suffering. Not to forget countless millions of people, especially children in their early years, who perish continuously because of lack of nourishment, medicaments, clean water, education, knowledge, etc. Add the growing number of disturbed, rootless, derailed, addicted, radicalized, hopeless young persons especially in the industrialized societies and the global masses of mostly southern inhabitants of this globe who are in want of the most essential goods of daily survival. The balance of welfare on this globe is quite gruesome. If eight billionaires own as much as 3.6 billions of lower income people on this globe, there must be something basically wrong.

A. Biblical Witnesses: Manifold, Not Homogeneous

Jewish-Christian Holy Scriptures are the fundament of our respective communities of faith and to some extant also of Islam and other religions (cf. Bahai, Zulu groups, Mormons, etc.). The Jewish and Christian Bible contains a large harvest of Ancient Near Eastern and Egyptian traditions reaped in the 10th century B.C. through the 2nd century A.D by successive faith communities, commencing with Ancient Israel of the pre-monarchic, dynastic, exilic-postexilic periods and the shorter epoch of Early Christianism (cf. *Biblische Enzyklopaedie*, 1996ss). The body of those recognized and authorized writings has been every now and then arranged and re-arranged by successive communities of faith under the guidance of the Spirit as the normative set of documents comprising the experiences of our ethnic and spiritual ancestors with their God. Such collections of faith-documents (Holy Scriptures) are by necessity pluriform, spiritually and theologically varied, polyphone and layered; they have to be interpreted in their primary and subsequent settings and in interpretations as well as in regard to their contemporary meanings. What different attitudes and experiences with severe suffering can we encounter in the different layers of Biblical tradition?

1. Suffering Is Normal, Integral to Life, Undebatable

Depending on life-situations and perspectives on suffering we find in the Biblical writings some basic indifference or even fatalistic acceptance of evil conditions. "The rich and the poor have this in common: the Lord is the maker of all" (Prov 22:2, cf. v. 7). However, other passages vehemently denounce poverty as disgrace in the eyes of the Lord. As the following investigations will turn out, other great evils are sickness, famines, war and violence, being mobbed in one's own community, fear of demons, and forsakenness by one's personal God. They all can fall into the category of inevitable shortcomings of human life. Most all of Ecclesiastes thinks about the unexplainable evils and deficits while seeing no solution to these enigmas (cf. Eccl 1:12–18; 2:18–23; 3:1–8, 16–22; 4:1–4, etc.). Narrative, legal, psalmic, and prophetic literatures only partially tolerate the corrupt state of affairs (cf. Isa 40:6–8, 21–24). They overwhelmingly try to explain bad living conditions, especially live-threats, and speak up against their causes.

2. Suffering Is Reward for Misbehavior, Error, Rebellion, Sin, and Violations of Rules

First of all, some important ancient Israelite and subsequent Christian witnesses (as well as countless Ancient Near Eastern contemporaries) wrestle with their personal destiny. At the brink of death they cry: "My God, my God, why have you forsaken me?" (Ps 22:1[679]). There were countless causes known to the ancients which might have initiated fatal developments in a person's biography. Adam's and Eve's urge for divine knowledge and super-human power (a trait of all humanity?) makes for their expulsion from paradise under miserable conditions (Gen 3; cf. the tower of Babel, Gen 11:1–9, confusion of language, strife). Personal guilt finds its revenge (Judg 15:1–8, 16:28–30). Kings suffer from their personal misdeeds as well as in their collective function (cf. 2 Sam 11–12, 24:10–17). Each incident of personal guilt and punishment in the Bible is a case all on its own.

Numerous are the tendencies to rationalize on the relationship between personal behavior and bad fates, as will be shown later. One dominant theory, especially in wisdom literatures of the Ancient Near East including the Bible, is the belief that humans by their misdeeds create a destructive sphere around themselves which eventually will engulf the evildoer and his fellow-men (cf. Koch 1955). Phrases like "his [the victim's] blood may come over him [the murderer]" (cf. Josh 2:19; Judg 9:24; 1 Sam 1:16; 1 Kgs 2:32–33, etc.) are indicative of the power of spilled blood; in other cases it is the ensuing curse of a stricken family (cf. Judg 17:2) which is to hunt the agent of 'awen, 'wel, ḥaṭṭā't, to'ebah, ra'ah, ḥāmās, raeša', dāmīm and more Hebrew designations of destructive deeds.[680]

Old Israelite concepts of "revenge," then, as well as the other examples given above, indicate that personal perpetrations never are seen as isolated acts. They always involve other people, be it as victims or partisans (kinship) of a perpetrator. Guilt, sin, damage, injustice, etc., are performed or staged by individuals, but in ancient times the collective dimensions always are extant. In consequence, there is a broad acknowledgment also about families, groups, cities, nations, which by common transgressions can commit wrongdoings, habitually or incidentally. In these cases collective

---

[679] Hebrew MS v. 2; mind the difference of Greek and Hebrew verse-numbers in the Psalter.

[680] Cf. the relevant articles in G. Johannes Botterweck, Helmer Ringgren, Heinz-Josef Fabry, *Theological Dictionary of the O.T.* (Stuttgart/Grand Rapids: Eerdmans, 1973ss).

bodies are liable to divine punishment because there was hardly any human institution capable to judge communal wrongs. The prophets' wholesale indictments were ordered by God. Clear enough, however, is the biblical attitude over against collective wrongdoings: they cause much distress for lowly people and need to be stopped (cf. Am. 1:3–2:16, Lev 25:25–55, Jer 46–51, Lam 1–5). The exact ligations between sin and punishment, however, are always debatable. No mathematical formula is applicable. Jesus calls attention to this fact in Luke 13:1–5.

3. Suffering Is Unjustified, Senseless, Arbitrary

a. What Would Ancient People Do when Confronted with Life-hazards?

In Biblical exegesis, one should not only consider the sacred text but also the circumstances in which it was recited. This "life situation" (German *Sitz im Leben*) does decisively shape, according to Hermann Gunkel and many others, the meaning and message of the text itself. Ancient Israelites as well as many other contemporary peoples of the Near East (and many tribal societies around the globe to this day) would consult diagnostics and healers of different specialization whenever grave dangers or life-threats were imminent (Gerstenberger 2009). When a child went sick, when famine would rise to a breaking point, or when war-situations became unbearable people would seek a "man of God," a "seer," a "medium" (literally: "mistress of a spirit," 1 Sam 28:7), "medical expert," etc. (cf. 1 Kgs 14:1–3, 2 Kgs 4:18–24, Num 22–24, Isa 38:21) in order to cope with those serious situations. Inevitably, the experts would try to apply medical and ritual means, as can be seen in a few OT narratives (cf. Isa 38:21, 2 Kgs 4:30–35). Babylonian sources tell us in great detail how ritual healing was practiced (cf. Maul 1994; Heessel 2000). Prayers of the sufferer, intoning complaint, petition, confidence, imprecation, and vow were part and parcel of the healing ritual. Most probably, the "complaints of the individual" in the Psalter, 30 to 40 in number, originally belonged into the context of healing ceremonies (cf. Ps 102 headline; Pss. 22, 31, 35, 38, 51, 55, 59, 69, etc. with their allusions to physical and social ills).

b. Basic Issue of Ethical Perturbations in Difficult Passages

Treating the calamities of individual sufferers was the professional task of the healer. And in general, experienced professionals were quite effective. The real challenges of faith arise when they failed, and suffering became totally inexplicable. Efforts to explain failure would prove fruitless, and the continuing ills would counteract hope. Weak, dubious, and misleading as all rational explications of distress may seem, as long as they give only a faint idea of being right or possible they often do have an assuaging effect. Every pastor can tell stories about bereaved or despaired people who clung to a minimal reasoning to give plausibility to the dreary and painful happenings. When, however, all counselling is doomed or becomes senseless—is everything lost? Does God disappear completely from the scene? Compare Psalm 22:1–2. Dead-end streets of human biographies are perhaps test cases for trust in God.

What is so surprising and rewarding with Biblical witnesses is that they already know of the fundamental, existential impasses of life, and they do not hide them. Christian preaching may have a tendency to emphasize saved lives or a successful prayer for deliverance. Suicidal rates are perhaps corresponding to the degree of comfort a suffering person may achieve. In any case, the lesson from the O.T. complaint psalms cause us to think. They give the impression that the prayers for specific cases of illness, hostility of neighbors, demonic possession, being robbed and exploited normally will be accepted by the Lord (cf. Pss. 38, 41, 91, 9/10). They move from invocation, complaint, to affirmations of confidence to petitions and vows of giving due thanks for salvation (cf. Barth 1997). We do not know how often each prayer was used and the supplicant heard. Certainly, however, to some extant salvation from death was not achieved, but the outcome of the healing ritual was:

- "O my God, I cry by day, but you do not answer ..." (Ps 22:2)
- "I am weary with my moaning, every night I flood my bed with tears ..." (Ps 6:6)
- "[wicked] stoop, they crouch, and the helpless fall by their might. They think in their heart, 'God has forgotten, he has hidden his face ...'" (Ps 10:10–11)
- "I am ready to fall, and my pain is ever with me ..." (Ps 38:17)
- "Each evening they come back, howling like dogs and prowling about the city ..." (Ps 59:6, 14)
- "They gave me poison for food, and for my thirst they gave me vinegar to drink ..." (Ps 69:21)

Hundreds of affirmations within these complaints sound very desperate, but most all the prayers end up in hopeful or even triumphant tones. Some of the cries for help, however, seem to be wrapped in blank despair, notably Psalm 88. Was the text damaged in the course of tradition? Is something missing? Regardless, the end of Psalm 88 is devastating.

(1) Hard to say whether or not Psalm 88 is incomplete

Clear enough is the fact that it has been used for centuries in the same form we now find it in the Hebrew Bible. It starts out with a regular invocation: "... incline your ear to my cry" (v. 2). After this the whole prayer is an endless repetition, in growing resentment, of complaints and contestations challenging the good care and responsibility of God for the supplicant (vv. 3–9a, 9b–12, 13–18). "I am counted among those who go down to the Pit" (v.4); "I am like ... the slain that lie in the grave, like those whom you remember no more" (v. 5); and "You have put me in the depth of the Pit" (v. 6). Life has come to an end by God's arbitrariness, the cord to family and friends has been cut (vv. 8, 18), because down there in the abyss God is absent (vv. 10–12). A renewed outcry to the Lord (v. 13) does not amend the situation of being lost. The horrified question "why do you cast me off?" (v. 14) confirms isolation and hopelessness. "Wretched and close to death from my youth up, I suffer your terrors; I am desperate (v. 15 [Hebrew MT = 16] is textually difficult: "desperate" = *'apunah*, is a unique word in the Hebrew Bible). Being shunned by one's intimate fellows does seal the condemnation of the supplicant (v. 18). And there is not a simmer of optimism in this psalm (cf. Pss. 44, 89, 137 with urgent questions and desperate pleas at the end). Hopelessness is part of Biblical witness!

(2) Somewhat different stance in rebellious prayers of Jeremiah[681]

In all probability they have been formulated by late composers in order to portray the inner feelings of the prophet during his turbulent times of activity. Jeremiah in their view was commissioned by Yahweh to a very difficult task of announcing the decline of the Davidic kingship over against the Babylonian onslaught and beyond (cf. Jer 1:4–10). The prophet, however, is in the line of other reluctant messengers of God (cf. Jonah 1:3; Exod 3:11–12, 4:10–13; Isa 6:5; Judg 6:11–17). Do the prayers of Jeremiah revolt against his commissioning? Does the message he has to proclaim meet heavy resistance, for political or for religious reasons? Or both? People are threatening the prophet's life (in line with some narrative parts of the book of Jeremiah and with a good number of Psalms; cf. Jer 11:19, 21; 15:11; 18:19; 20:10). The prophet cries for urgent relief and destruction of the enemies; he wrestles with God, and even accuses Him with treachery (Jer 15:18, 20:7). The climax is the last of the so-called "confessions": a desperate cry to be caught with the Word of the Lord, which forces him to speak out against his own will.

> For the Word of the Lord has become for me a reproach and derision all day long. If I say, "I will not mention Him, or speak any more in his name," then within me there is something like a burning fire shut up in my bones; I am weary with holding it in, and I cannot. (Jer 20:8b–9).

Furthermore, after a short hymnic praise, which may well be the composer's insertion (20:13), the prophet all but collapses. He curses the day of his birth (20:14–18; cf. Job 3:3–12). That means: he wants to annihilate himself together with any relationship he has with God.

---

[681] Jer 11:18–12:6; 15:10–18, 19–21; 17:14–18; 18:19–23; 20:7–18.

(3) Lamentations is a collective liturgy (except Lam 3) dealing with the frustrations of suffering.

Invasion of foreign troops, destruction of city and temple, violence of the victors, famine, homelessness, and the lack of divine protection create an atmosphere of near total despair. Of course, the book of Lamentations, a composition of high literary quality (acrostic lines!), was composed for and used in lament ceremonies after the fall of Jerusalem and the burning down of the temple (cf. Zeph 7:2–7, 8:19). The predominance of mourning and lament, therefore, is justified. The massive preponderance of descriptions of death, violence, famine, sometimes articulated by the voice of "virgin Jerusalem" herself, is unusual, also in comparison to Sumerian City Laments (cf. O'Connor 2003). Lamentation 1, 2, and 4 are filled with laments, bitter questions, and accusations against God. Only in Lamentations 4:22 a little glimmer of hope appears ("he will keep you in exile no longer"), and ch. 5 is stylized as a communal petition with confession of former guilt: "Our ancestors sinned; they are no more, and we bear their iniquities" (5:7). Then, drastic descriptions of suffering continue, unhampered (5:8–18). A very brief hymnic interlude (5:19) is followed by more incisive, distrustful questions: "Why have you forgotten us completely? Why have you forsaken us these many days?" (5:20). The final plea for help is immediately counteracted by a mental reserve: "Restore us to yourself, O Lord.... unless you have utterly rejected us, and are angry with us beyond measure" (5:21–22). In this fashion the lament falls out of the framework of normal complaint and petition. It leaves open whether or not God will re-establish normal relations with his people. A possibility of final rupture remains open, just like in some prophetic speech: Hosea 1:6–8 (renounced in 2:1–3); Amos 2:4–8, 5:18–20, 8:1–3, 9:1–4 (partially revoked in 9:11–15); Isaiah 5:1–7; and Jeremiah 2, etc. What kind of liturgy is Lamentations if there is a built-in chance of failure?

(4) Job against his "friends"

The book of Job is composed of several different parts. The narrative frame (Job 1–2, 42:10–17) and the inserted speeches of the Lord (Job 28, 38:1–42:9) are remarkably distinct against the debates Job has his "visitors" or "friends" (Job 3–27, 32–37), and then inserted is Job's resentful monologue against God (Job 29–31). Obviously, the narration of Job's trials and restitution voice a strong conviction that God may severely test a human being with plagues hard to bear (1–2, 42:10–17). Yet, on the instigation of a satanic counsellor? This itself poses problems. If that person resists the temptation to turn away from his supreme protector, then he will be rewarded manifold. The poetic part of the book containing heated dialogues with four self-styled friends and counsellors purports to demonstrate an exemplar relationship of a frustrated individual who resents that painful, obscure divine guidance, which he experiences as arbitrary, unfair, burdensome, repressive (Job 3–27, 32–37). Also mind that the precise calamities of Job 1–2 are never mentioned in the dialogues.

Other ancient Middle Eastern literatures brought forth similar pieces of "Jobian" suffering and challenging the deities. The O.T. Job begins his revolt with that suicidal self-curse (3:2–26) which also closes the prayers of Jeremiah. He outright rejects the many consoling and admonishing words of his counsellors. They want to convince him of the superior justice and goodness of God, who supposedly always administers chastisements for good, even if for hidden reasons. Instead of complaining, Job should accept all hardships and repent unknown sins. And this is exactly what the spiritual revolutionary does not want to do. He insists on his own righteousness, which makes divine punishments unwarranted, and he directly accuses God of arbitrariness and tyranny:

> I will say to God: Do not condemn me; let me know why you contend against me…. you seek out my iniquity and search out for my sin, although you know that I am not guilty (Job 10:2, 6–7a).

God has put Job in the wrong (19:6), the consequences are terrible:

> He has stripped my glory from me … he breaks me down on every side, and I am gone … he has kindled his wrath against me … his troops … have thrown up siege-works against me … He has put my family far from me … my relatives and my close friends have failed me (Job 19:9–14).

Relationships to God and to fellow humans have been broken. "My breath is repulsive to my wife; I am loathsome to my own family. Even young children despise me" (Job 19:17–18a).

(5) Suffering is ordained for betterment, a toil to receive honor and well-being

Job's friends Eliphaz, Bildad, Zophar, and afterwards Elihu present traditional theologies in this exemplar debate on "who is righteous?" (Job 4–5, 8, 11, 15, 18, 20, 22, 25, three rounds of speeches by the first three opponents with Zophar missing in the third round; 32–37, one rambling theological discourse of Elihu). They drone away without acknowledging a single argument of the afflicted one. Their main argument is, essentially: God cannot inflict unjust punishments, because our cherished doctrines make Him an unflinching eternal and sovereign judge who detests fooling around with his clients (they obviously do not know Job 1–2). If God is genuinely just and only just throughout, Job's misery must have different origins. They can only be determined by the ancient's belief in the doctrine of "reward and punishment." Somebody who suffers must identify the true

reasons of his plight in his or her own biography. Sufferers are bearing their guilt in the form of divine retribution:
- "Can mortals be righteous before God?" (Job 4:17);
- "Do not despise the discipline of the Almighty" (Job 5:17);
- "Does God pervert justice? ... If your children sinned against him, he delivered them into the power of their transgression" (Job 8:3–4);
- "See, God will not reject a blameless person" (Job 8:20);
- "You say: 'My conduct is pure ... but O that God would speak ... and that he would tell you the secrets of wisdom!'" (Job 11:4–5);
- "You are doing away with the fear of God.... For your iniquity teaches your mouth" (Job 15:4–5);
- "Is not your wickedness great?" (Job 22:5).

Some social misdeeds are pointed out (v. 6–9), to be refuted by Job in 23:12 and extensively in 29–31. Ever more the friends repeat their creed: "How then can a mortal be righteous before God?" (25:4; cf. 33:12; 34:10–12, 21–26). The friends in all their talking rely on the superior wisdom and justice of God who does punish only the wicked; he helps the blameless and rehabilitates the repentant (cf. the proposed prayer ritual by a professional mediator in 33:12–28). So, the "friends" defend God's equity and righteousness ("theodicy"), but they totally fail to realize that humans are able only to imagine precarious human standards of justice. To measure God by earthly norms simply misses all divine dimensions. God declares Job to have spoken rightly about Him, accepting the charges of arbitrariness (cf. Job 42:7).

The way other layers of the Job tradition wrestled with this traditional theology is both remarkable and disturbing. In Job 38–41, God himself is cited to use much of the friends' theology of majesty: God is immensely superior to human reasoning, therefore untouched by earthly grumblings. This argument pushed aside when the Job's counsellors spoke, now convinces the "righteous sufferer" (42:1–6). He concedes that God is right (42:5–6). But, in a different line of argumentation, where Elihu is not mentioned any more, God seems to revert himself confronting the "friends" with a harsh verdict: "you have not spoken of me what is right, as my servant Job has" (42:7). The traditionalists, good theologians as they were, have to offer penitentiary sacrifice and depend on Job's intercession to be restored. These are bewildering interpretations of an unsolvable theological problem. God cannot act in such a contradictory manner, can He? The lesson to be learned from the compilation of different reasonings in the book of Job simply is this: We all may voice our own insights and convictions in regard to extreme suffering, but we should know, that they all are far from the comprehensive and uniform truth to which we aspire. Human knowledge of the divine is fragmentary, ambiguous, and very limited at best.

(6) Skeptic theology all around (Kohelet/Ecclesiastes)

Some other parts of the Bible of similar attitudes notwithstanding, the book of Ecclesiastes (Hebrew name: *Kohelet*) is an outsider among canonical literature. It does propagate theological insights not common in the Torah, prophets, and writings, nor in the N.T. The book certainly is not a uniform presentation of coherent teachings, much rather it is a collection of mainly skeptical views on the vanity of earthly values like property, honor, happiness, labor, justice, success, knowledge, etc. Some parts are clad in argumentative discourse, often in the first person singular and partly in the guise of Solomon, king in Jerusalem (cf. Eccl 1:12–18; 2:1–11, 12–26; 3:9–22; 6:1–6; 7:23–29; 9:1–2, 11–16), others present proverbial sentences, admonitions or prohibitions (cf. Eccl 5:1[Hebr. 4:17]–12[Hebr. 5:11]; 7:1–14, 16–21; 10:1–4, 8–20; 11:1–6). The whole of life seems so transitory, fragmentary, full of frustrations, that only short termed pleasures may be counted as worthwhile and a gift of God:

> Enjoy life with the wife whom you love, all the days of your vain life that are given you under the sun, because that is your portion in life and in your toil at which you toil under the sun (Eccl 9:9).

(7) Suffering as programmatic meaninglessness, emptiness, forlornness

We have met, so far, several different attitudes against suffering, in particular to the dead-end-roads of despair, forsakenness, and utter helplessness of the believer. Are there chances to meet God in such situations? How could this come true? And, after all: What does it mean to find or miss God? Who is able to judge whether or not a person has met or lost his/her Divine creator, redeemer, father, friend? The book of Ecclesiastes, in contrast to all its skepticism, seems to offer a first glimmer of hope in a dreary reality. Ancient Near Eastern thought and faith opened this avenue already centuries before the teachers of Israel. A Sumerian collection of sayings and exhortations bears the title: "Vanity, nothing but vanity" (Alster 2005, pp. 266–287). God, in all these wisdom writings, is not a personal being, talking with and meeting people. Rather, he dispenses mysterious destinies, unaccountable portions of well-being and/or hardships. Human senses and thoughts cannot fathom God's decisions. People must accept what they receive from him in the fleeting stream of their short lives. Sure enough, there are other passages in the Bible which stress the transiency of existence (cf. Pss. 39, 90) or the instabilities and corruption of life (cf. Pss. 14, 73, 94). *Kohelet*, on principle, casts serious doubts on the ideal of a harmonious life under the guidance and protection of a benign deity. The book of Job, on the other hand, in part chastises God's arbitrariness to the point to make him renounce theological doctrines of just retribution and redemption of sinners. Both writings, then, are really far away from what we commonly understand by a normal relationship of any human being to his or her God.

(8) Jesus and Paul as sufferers

Quite often it has been observed in Christian and other interpretations of Scripture that the N.T. uses wide and exhaustive concepts of the O.T. in order to articulate its new messages under the name of Jesus Christ. The passion story of the gospels thus has been thoroughly composed most of all in the light of O.T. psalms (Pss. 22, 31, 35, 69, 110, 118), prophetic texts (cf. Zeph 9:9, 11:13, 12:10, 13:7; Dan 7:13) and in particular of 2nd Isaiah's figure of the "Servant of the Lord" (cf. Isa 42:1–9, 49:1–7, 50:4–11, 52:13–53:12). Chances of frustrations and failures are high in all these accounts. Only the faith message of resurrection, conceived in the mental context of separate physical and spiritual worlds does relieve the anxiety-stricken followers of Jesus (cf. Matt 28:1–10; Mark 16:1–8; Luke 24:1–12; John 20:1–18). Death in their mind has been overcome by "New Life" in Christ. Henceforth, the sufferings, death and resurrection of Christ acquire an encompassing, mythical, and redemptive meaning for the Christian churches. The conceptions of suffering in the passion stories corresponds to the insights of Isaiah 53:1–12. Jesus' death was the utmost sacrifice God Himself made to compensate for the sins of mankind: "When you make his life an offering for sin, he shall see his offspring and prolong his days ... The righteous one, my servant, shall make many righteous" (Isa 53:10–11). The ultimate sacrifice will atone for the multitude (Heb 9:23–10:18).

It is especially the apostle Paul who developed and refined the concept of suffering. He takes pains to demonstrate on the basis of Hebrew Scriptures that from the beginning humankind has fallen into disobedience and rebellion (cf. Rom 1:18–3:20).

> All have sinned and fall short of the glory of God; they are now justified by his grace as a gift, through the redemption that is in Christ Jesus, whom God put forward as a sacrifice of atonement by his blood, effective through faith (Rom 3:23–25).

In accordance with his mystical understanding of the church as "body of Christ" (1 Cor 12:12–31), he prolongs the sufferings of Christ into his own life and commissioning: "the sufferings of Christ are abundant for us.... If we are being afflicted, it is for your consolation and salvation" (2 Cor 1:5–6). The ongoing hardships of apostles and other Christian believers do have a positive meaning for everybody concerned (cf. 1 Pet 3:17–19; 5:1, 9). Suffering, in the eyes of early Christians was a gateway to the coming glory and fullness of life. It did merge with the initial torments of O.T. prophets like Jeremiah, the "Servant of the Lord" in 2nd Isaiah, Jesus Christ, and the martyrs of all times (cf. Sobrino 2002). Tortures and traumas are destructive and painful, but they do not signify the end of all hope. In itself, Christ's suffering was brutally senseless. As a substitute sacrifice, it became absolutely meaningful for his followers. But the individual and collective Christian conscience nevertheless retained the problems of theodicy. Few have been able to "put their own ailments under the cross" and be content with their sometimes very troublesome destinies.

(9) Biblical witness in overview

The multi-faceted picture of suffering we get in the Bible is very heterogeneous, but it seems universal. Paul in sum speaks of the whole (!) creation groaning and longing for salvation (Rom 8:18–25). From ancient times onward humans have been aware of the ills of earthly conditions. Depending on cultural and historical circumstances, they all longed for betterment in all realms of life. Supplications of the death-threatened individual (cf. complaint Psalms) often are met by trust in temporary restoration of health and well-being; but there are notions of possible failure visible in quite a few texts. Some Psalms and the Book of Job doubt that God applies fair play on his believers. They are afraid of divine arbitrariness and do articulate freely their anxieties. Skeptic wisdom, especially the Ecclesiastes, makes the fragility of life its concern. The latter constructs a minimal theology on the basis of *carpe diem*, "use the daily opportunities" and be content with what you are given. N.T. witnesses, in the wake of O.T. prophecies and the preaching of Jesus rely on a creative significance of suffering which will end soon and turn into boundless joy within an apocalyptic renewal of heaven and earth (cf. Zeph 12–14; Isa 9, 11, 24–27, 60–62, 65:17–25, etc.). Christian writers, also under the influence of Zoroastic and late Greek apocalyptic imaginations, laid great emphasis on the crash of the old world and a renewal of the universe (cf. Mark 13; 1 Cor 15:35–58; Apoc. 6–22, etc.). Horrible torments had to be undergone until the breakthrough could be reached.

B. Finding or Missing God

1. How Dare We to Describe the Finding or Missing of God in Tribulations without End?

We first have to think about the meaning of "finding God." The presupposition of this concept surely is the "loss of God" testified by the Scriptures and in some of the ancient writings outside Israel. But what does this phrase mean? And how is God conceived of so that He may be separated from his creatures to "get lost" or "remains remote" as some Psalms complain? Should we not consider at least a second way to "find" God (besides a first and often considered normative "return of the prodigal son," Luke 15:11–32) in the search for the lost sheep performed by the

Great Shepherd (Matt 18:10–14)? The basis for all these conceptions is very human indeed, as if God were an emotive person reacting against bad behavior of his creatures or clients. The imagination of our biblical forebears painted God as king, warrior, judge, father, creator, elder, shepherd, midwife, wisdom, etc., and sometimes even in impersonal terms as storm, breath, spirit, fire, depth and the like. Psalm 139:7–12 protests against all identifications of God, maintaining that his inexorable "presence" transcends every localization, so that nobody ever can escape him. Deuteronomy 4:15–20 warns against all and every likeness of God with earthly entities. God, who cannot be likened to anything in the same vein cannot be forsaken or put into a distance. So, what is "finding God" like? Can He be found? Will we be found, every one of us, by Him? Or are we only talking about erroneous human sentiments to feel distanced, shut away, banned and forlorn in relation to God?

2. There Is a Great Need to Reflect on the Seekers of God

Since genuine God-Talk of any kind is always metaphorical—our language is unable to partake in the otherness of God's reality—faith and theology are thrown back to earthly dimensions. Indeed, we are completely on the human side especially when uncertainties arise. The heavenly voice "Keep away from God's presence" (cf. Exod 19:21–24; Deut 5:22–27) and the unapproachability of the Divine are configurations of theological minds. This is true also for the priestly idea of God's deadly presence in the Holy of Holies (cf. Lev 16:15–19). Criteria of "finding God" are to be established by human thinking, feeling, ascertaining. We need to rely on shaky signs of God's nearness and benignancy. Some of the most popular ones are the questions: "Does God (according to my knowledge and insight) treat me justly and friendly?"—this is the age-old issue of theodicy. Another one runs: "Am I behaving correctly in the eyes of God?"—amounting to the problems of righteousness and justification. Other signs of God's nearness include confessions and actions of faith. Sufferings of many kinds are sometimes apt to unsettle even firm convictions: "Stretch out your hand now and touch his bone and his flesh, and he will curse you to your face," says the Satan to the Lord about righteous Job (Job 2:5). Quite a true recognition of human mores!

3. Finding or Missing God in the Contemporary World

Biblical witnesses must be tested in our own world. There certainly are many situations in which women and men of faith have been feeling tested as to their steadfastness regarding their life-programs, confessions, and humanitarian engagements. What are such adverse, utterly threatening conditions able to do to the victims? Many may be discouraged and cross the lines, abandoning their beliefs. But it seems a whole lot of them remain upright, and we may include heroines and heroes of all creeds and convictions.

Do they meet their God in such final challenges? They often risk their lives in defense of justice and love; the list of those who actually *lose* is very long. In the hour of death, or of utter depravation, what are their thoughts? What are *our* thoughts?

a. Lost in Persecution, Torture

In recent times perhaps more so than in some preceding centuries, minority religious, ethnic, and gender groups here and there have been hunted down, abused, massacred, enslaved. Nadia Murad Basee and Lamija Aji Bashar, two Yesidi women, recently receiving the Sakharov Prize, spoke before the United Nations about their sufferings. They felt confirmed and strengthened in their battle for the persecuted. Countless martyrs in Latin America remained firm in their plights and struggles for the underprivileged. From Pakistan, Malala Yousafzai survived a shooting and continued her work for discriminated women. Old Mahatma Gandhi and Nelson Mandela became illustrious pioneers of perseverance in troubled times. Dietrich Bonhoeffer, outstanding Protestant fighter against Hitlerism, prisoner in a concentration camp, in the face of death composed the hymn: "Von guten Mächten treu und still umgeben" (Surrounded faithfully and silently by benign powers). Jehuda Bacon, survivor of the Nazi-holocaust, and many others like him, dedicated the rest of their lives to testify against racism and hate, in order to build a better world of solidarity and equality of all human beings. Singular examples of a wonderful trust in the Lord?

We should not forget, however, millions of people who did lose their faith in a just God. Could anybody judge that they missed their goal?

b. Lost in Sickness, Frailty, Disease

Amazing progress in modern medicine has not done away with human problems of high-grade physical sufferings. What to do if causes of illnesses stay undetectable, pains remain unbearable, decay of cells and nerves cannot be stopped, death is demanding its toll, even—*horribile dictum*—at an early age? Our ideal images of a wholesome and blessed life, given by God to His favorites, falls into pieces when we carefully observe human realities. Openly and under the surface there is so much absurd suffering going on in almost all societies and groups that world views of harmony, complacency, and peace are shattered. Henning Luther, a young theologian who died at the age of 46 years from a HIV infection, plausibly spoke about the "fragmentariness" of life, which we must take into account as a normal possibility, and even the reality for too many. Others have reflected upon physical and mental deficiencies which must be tolerated as a divine "gift" and which must *not lead* to discrimination by the self-declared "sound" ones (against e.g., Lev 21:16–24). Human conceptions of holiness and wholeness are no safe matrixes of exclusion or disdain.

c. Lost in Despair, Depression

Many sufferers end up in a dead-end road perceiving no exit, seemingly lost without hope. Suicides are high in our world, depending among other reasons on cultural patterns and the intensity of the crises. Remarkably, many calm and rational thinkers do put an end to their own lives knowing about their social responsibilities, even their obligations over against God. (Those who committed suicide under the impact of their guilt, like Joseph Goebbels, Adolf Hitler, Hermann Goering, etc., need to be discussed separately). A case in question is that of the famous Austrian writer Stefan Zweig, who died in 1942 together with his wife, by their own decision, after fleeing Nazi Germany. He talked and wrote about his imminent departure from life, arguing that there was no hope for him and the world to achieve betterment of the ongoing hellish conditions of war, brutality, injustice, and persecution.

Jochen Klepper was a successful, very soft-spoken writer, servile to government authority, yet ousted by the Nazis from his jobs. When they threatened to deport his Jewish wife and her daughter, the three of them committed suicide after painful deliberations about the legitimacy of such an action before God.

Consciously renouncing the gift of life: Can this be a way out of severe suffering and a means to find God? To pull the ripcord and disappear from the scene, instead of suffering martyrdom, could that mean to "miss God"?

d. Lost in Calamities and Catastrophes

For many humans, life does end abruptly, without much forewarning. All ages of victims are involved, from the youngest to the oldest. There is not much difference in man-made or natural (divine?) causes for sudden deaths. Millions and millions of people never had a chance to ask for God. Did they miss Him? Before one's last breath, is there any last moment in a human life where one takes an instantaneous balance of everything that happened during their lifetime? Even a last-second evaluation of all of one's life *including* a full recognition of God's overwhelming grace, acceptance, and love? In one last moment! But why are we concerned about such kinds of reckoning, if the Biblical witnesses quite often insist: "The Lord, the Lord, a God merciful and gracious, slow to anger and abounding in steadfast love and faithfulness" (Exod 34:6; cf. Pss. 103:8, 111:4, 145:8; Luke 6:36; Heb 2:17; James 5:11, etc.)? To engage God in prayer and service in order to achieve graciousness, peace of mind, and basic trust have been good biblical practices through the ages. Secularized persons and groups do not care for religious certainty but quite often manage to acquiesce in their fates and circumstances and accept the comforting voices of their friends to rest in peace.

e. Lost in Doubts, Unbelief, Remorse

Biblical testimony is manifold in portraying human rebellion, waywardness, treachery against neighbors and against strangers, and, last but not least, over against his or her own self. Human beings have been at odds ever more with their own cognitive and technical achievements. Horst Eberhard Richter (1979), renowned psychotherapist and social philosopher, described our times after the "dethronement" of God in vivid terms. Humans now feel abandoned, forlorn, and compelled to take over all positions of the Almighty. But they get thoroughly confused, unable to fill their self-imposed role. The apprentices are overburdened by those magisterial tasks, they fall mentally sick, and they ruin themselves. Uncertainties and anxieties abound in present-day civilizations. Seeking God and finding only one's lonely self? Is that the destiny of modern mankind? Is the universe empty of any empathic Divine? Even agnostics and atheists may find consolation and meaning in unheard of agonies (cf. Heym 1942).

f. Lost in Hate—Saved through Love

Incredibly, the Bible does tell very much, perhaps too much, about hate. God, at times and places, is an irascible ruler who revenges and destroys his enemies (cf. Deut 32:39–42; Pss. 11:5, 45:8, 94:1–3, etc.). Invariably, the followers of Yahweh adopt similar attitudes (cf. Pss. 89, 24, 119:104, 113, 139:21, etc.), so that hating adversaries and wishing them and their families bad luck, pestilence, and death become a pattern of thought. Even the prophets (cf. Jer 18:19–23) and kings (cf. Ps 18:16–50) have adopted hostile patterns. And they enter into prayers of petition. Since most ills of suffering individuals were attributed to demonic or evil-minded human action, the curing process included the elimination of the enemy influence. This fact explains a lot about the condemnation and cursing passages in individual complaints in the Bible (cf. the extreme example in Ps 109). On the other hand, collective Psalms of complaint dwell on military action by Yahweh and his people (cf. Judg 5; Pss. 44, 89).

In short, ancient Near Eastern belligerence (fight for fertile lands and resources of water) and population-growth (fertile crescent!) also cultivated a system of violent power and ruthless revenge that were handed down to Christian (after Constantine) and Islamic communities. Those are opposed to strong sentiments of social justice, solidarity, and "love" of neighbor and the resident foreigners.

In our times, states and empires on a Christian or Islamic basis inherited those political traditions. Populistic leaders preach nationalism, chauvinism, ethnic ideologies, technical and economic hegemonies. Hate has a large and self-destructive part in these developments. How can we escape the doom of rational and responsible politics? Meet God and stand up for global solidarity and love? Christ himself and many Christians did overcome hate by sympathy with those who chose to be enemies of a few, of many, or even of everyone.

Conclusion

The menaces of unexplainable suffering are manifold both in the Bible and in modern times. Also, the attitudes and strategies to cope with these attacks on spiritual equilibration vary with great and ongoing concerns, because the basic questions remain unsolved. What does it really mean to be in concordance with God? To seek and find Him when the right relationship seems to be lost? And how do we define a "stable relationship" with the Divine? Does it suffice to "trust in the Lord and Savior Jesus Christ" as the Heidelberg catechism spells it out? Can we rely on our own feeling of being accepted regardless of our merits and actions and confessions? Does our dubious record of obedience to the Word of God disqualify us? Should we define a "reconciliation" with God in terms of unconditional trust in Him, no longer being concerned about anything which might befall us, leaving behind all concerns and speculations about a "happy end"? Some believers and non-believers have been able to do just that. The best answer, however, to the vexing questions of unbelievable suffering is the insight that we are freed from any pressure to "find" or "meet" God, because He already has found us.

21.
Ecclesiology and Theodicy: Bonhoeffer's *Sanctorum Communio* as Response to Human Suffering

Dr. Maury Jackson
Associate Professor of Practical Theology
H.M.S. Richards Divinity School
La Sierra University, Riverside, California[682]

Introduction 317
A. Theodicy and the Limits of Bonhoeffer's Theological Method 319
    Table 1. Typology of Approaches to Theodicy, Pt. 1 322
B. Primal Rupture, Collective Persons and the Principle of
    Vicarious Representation 323
C. God's New Will and Purpose for Humanity: Sanctorum Communio 329
    Table 2. Typology of Approaches to Theodicy, Pt. 2...................................... 331
D. Sacramental Basis of Therapeutic Ministry: Who Holds the Office? 332
    Figure 1. Three Sociologically Concentric Circles & Centers of Activity 335
Conclusion: Note on the Paradox of *Sanctorum Communio* and Apocatastasis 336

Introduction

The final sentence in Dietrich Bonhoeffer's doctoral dissertation reads as follows: "In the community of love and in the unity of faith it [the church] endures and it knows 'that the *sufferings* of this present time are not worth comparing with the glory about to be revealed to it.'"[683] However, while one might imagine based off of this quotation that the topic of suffering was an important theme in the rest of his work, a reader would be hard pressed to

---

[682] Jackson earned his DMin from Claremont School of Theology, CA; his MA from California State University, Los Angeles; and his MDiv from Seventh-day Adventist Theological Seminary, Andrews University, Berrien Springs, MI. He has served as pastor on the Atlantic and Pacific coasts. His several published works include: "Shepherding Public Discourse Practices: Homiletic Form Aligned to the Logic Operative in Racial Rhetoric and Public Theological Discourse for Secular Liberal Democracies," *Cultural and Religious Studies* 4, no. 9 (September 2016); "Causality Principle as the Framework to Contextualize Time in Modern Physics," *International Journal of Humanities and Social Science Invention* 5, no. 6 (June 2016), 1–22; "Moral Education and the Adventist Print Media," *Adventist Today* 22, no. 4 (Fall 2014), 12–17; "When Anger Heals: A Christian Response to the Global Healthcare Debate," *Adventist Today* 21, no. 1 (Winter, 2013), 04–09; "The Heresy Tertullian Overlooked: On Prescription against the Apologist's Use of Rhetoric," *Spes Christiana* 22–23 (2011–2012), 15–30; "Sketching an Adventist Vision for Global Mission" *Adventist Today* 20, no. 2 (March–April, 2012), 16–19; and "Answering the Call for a Sacred Conversation on Race," *Spectrum Magazine* 36, no. 3 (Summer, 2008), 42–50. See https://lasierra.edu/divinity and mjackson@lasierra.edu.

[683] Dietrich Bonhoeffer, *Dietrich Bonhoeffer Works, Volume I, Sanctorum Communio: A Theological Study of the Sociology of the Church* (Minneapolis: Fortress Press, 2009), 289. Emphasis mine.

find any explicit discussion by him on "the sufferings of this present time." In fact, if one searches the subject index in the 2009 Fortress Press edition of *Sanctorum Communio*, they will be directed to only three reference entries for the word "suffering."[684] One of those refers not to Bonhoeffer's own words, but to the afterword written by Joachim von Soosten.[685] A second citation is to Bonhoeffer's discussion of "the punitive character of the suffering of Jesus," highlighting "Christ's action as vicarious representative" action, which secures the renewal of humanity.[686] The third and final entry comes in the middle of a section on the topic of the limitlessness of Christian love.[687] In this briefly extended section, Bonhoeffer discusses the theme of suffering in the context of the duty to share one another's burdens. To summarize, within a book of almost three hundred pages, Bonhoeffer manages to use only five pages to address explicitly the subject of suffering.

Despite the scarcity of the term "suffering" in the work, the concept itself is present, however implicitly, throughout his arguments. Not only does it provide the backdrop to Bonhoeffer's extensive essay, but it seems quite appropriate that it does. Suffering, after all, provides the backdrop to our daily existence. And wherever the matter of suffering is presented, all people—atheists, Christian apologists, religious philosophers, and misotheists—ask the question, "Why?" Sometimes this "why?" question is asked from the distance of a detached, often academic observer; however, philosophical arguments that achieve logical clarity typically miss the mark for those not afforded a reprieve from the very real angst of suffering. The way a person frames the question "why?" bespeaks that person's hopes for this life. For some who have surrendered to the contingency and chance of life, they simply ask, "Why me?" But for others, who believe that God is active, present, and participating (some might even say intervening) in our world, they ask, "Why God?" To suffer is both to be physically harmed and to experience an emotional wound. Those who suffer have the double effect of harm: they feel the injury, as well as the emotional hurt that accompanies it. To suffer, in short, is evil.[688] Can one justifiably believe in God's existence in the face of this evil?

---

[684] Bonhoeffer, *Bonhoeffer Works*, 370.

[685] Bonhoeffer, 304. Soosten writes: "Who the neighbor is, the suffering other for whom Christians must care and whom they must defend, is determined solely by the One whom the Christian obediently follows in faith."

[686] Bonhoeffer, 155.

[687] Bonhoeffer, 179–182.

[688] My colleague Reverend Dr. Matthew Burdette retorts that this strikes as too broad a statement. According to him, to suffer is to experience the actions of another without the freedom to say no: being a creature always involves suffering, since we are subject to powers greater than our ability to resist. He writes (in an email), "Is this evil? I am not sure. I think one can say, 'To suffer harm is to experience

[Footnote continued on next page]

In his work, I argue that Bonhoeffer shapes a Christian pastoral care response for those who are suffering, if not an answer for how to justify God's existence in the face of such evil. In what follows, I will 1) sketch how Bonhoeffer's theological method reframes the theodicy response by 2) exposing the primal rupture to human community and 3) discovering a principle latent in the community of sinners; that is, the principle of collective ethical action, which 4) God creatively employs in the redemptive work of Christ to institute God's will for the salvation of humanity. And in the end, all this is done in order to 5) provide a sacramental basis for the therapeutic ministry of the Church's pastoral office.

A. Theodicy and the Limits of Bonhoeffer's Theological Method

In this first section, in order to draw out the implicit theodic logic of Bonhoeffer's argument in *Sanctorum Communio*, I will attempt to show how he breaks with traditional Western philosophical approaches to theodicy. While traditional approaches to theodicy ask the question of how God can exist if evil exists, Bonhoeffer appears throughout his work to ask:

> "How does God act in the world to respond
> to those who suffer evil?"

What will be shown is that Bonhoeffer's answer to that question "socializes" the problem: it is viewed as a problem that can only be responded to "by," "from," and "in" a communal context. In this way Bonhoeffer's response anticipates those clinical pastoral paradigms that recognize suffering in relationship to their communities.[689]

The therapeutic ministry of the pastor has drawn heavily from the cognate discipline of psychology;[690] this has occurred to such a great extent that one could wonder whether theological curriculum should include more courses in psychology. While some might view this suggestion with suspicion, others, like John Cobb Jr., view this trend more charitably. In his postscript to a debate on theodicy by four of his faculty colleagues, Cobb writes:

---

evil.' a person always suffers *something*. The thing may be evil, but I am not sure the reality of suffering is itself an evil." It might be helpful to remind ourselves of the philosophical distinction of natural evil from moral evil. For me, the evil *in* suffering is the evil *of* suffering: that we have this kind of existence. Only an ultimate response is a true theodic response to "suffering," in this since of the word.

[689] My colleague Marlene Ferreras directed my attention to the work of Sharon Thornton: "People suffer in relationship to communities, not apart from them," in Sharon G. Thornton's *Broken Yet Beloved: A Pastoral Theology of the Cross* (Atlanta: Chalice Press, 2002), 127.

[690] This very trend in the therapeutic sources that modern pastors draw from has been challenged by Thomas C. Oden, *Kerygma and Counseling: Toward a Covenant Ontology for Secular Psychotherapy* (Philadelphia: The Westminster Press, 1966).

> One reason pastors have turned to psychology for help in answering (or not answering) the question, Why?, is that most theologians give them no help.... I am astounded—and somewhat put off—by the audacity of philosophers ... who undertake to tell us what God was thinking before there was a world! I would prefer that pastors not take their cue from that.[691]

Yet it is debatable to what extent one should draw from the cognate discipline of psychology in pastoral theology. Such a method appears problematic when the question arises as to how much should individuals' specific experiences inform theological reflection.[692] To the extent that pastoral studies assist in this conversation between theology and human experience, one must evaluate whether to place the emphasis on the tradition or contemporary experience. Bonhoeffer appears to anticipate this challenge, and yet he does so by trying to reframe the purpose of Christian theology in a way that makes it more practically relevant. He undertakes this reframing by placing ecclesiology at the center of the system. What does the presence of Christ, existing as the community of the Church, mean for the justification of God's existence in the face of evil? In other words, does being a person in the body of Christ reconstruct our experiencing? Is the Christ-community a healing salve or is it more of a social placebo when it comes to providing any curative to the world's suffering, let alone providing any answers to the problem of evil?

This might be the best way to form a working question for any treatment of the theme of theodicy in the broader work of Dietrich Bonhoeffer. That is, of course, if it is even possible to trace an explicit theme. Obviously his dissertation did not address some abstract treatment of "the problem of evil" (in general), nor did he address concerns about individual angst with suffering. In his own words, the problem he is directly concerned with is "the problem of a specifically Christian social philosophy and sociology."[693] Bonhoeffer breaks with a longstanding tradition in religious thinking when it comes to the question of theodicy. After all, he wrote explicitly,

> The question of why evil exists is not a theological question, for it assumes that it is possible to go behind the existence forced upon us as sinners.... The theological question does not arise about the origin of evil but about the real

---

[691] John B. Cobb, Jr., "The Problem of Evil and the Task of Ministry" in *Encountering Evil: Live Options in Theodicy*, ed. Stephen T. Davis (Atlanta: John Knox Press, 1981), 173.

[692] Gordon Lynch, "The Relationship between Pastoral Counseling and Pastoral Theology" in *The Blackwell Reader in Pastoral and Practical Theology*, ed. James Woodward and Stephen Pattison (Malden: Blackwell Publishing, Ltd, 2000), 228.

[693] Bonhoeffer, *Bonhoeffer Works*, 22.

overcoming of evil on the Cross; it asks for the forgiveness of guilt, for the reconciliation of the fallen world.[694]

This statement appears to contradict the ordinary Western philosophical position that, for example, the philosopher of religion Stephen T. Davis advocates, who argues that "the problem of evil is a problem for *theism*."[695] For Davis and others like him, theological methodology can and must conjecture beyond the point of our broken condition and inquire after the possibilities available to God in the divine eternity.

It appears that, unlike Davis and according to Bonhoeffer, our sinful existence functions like the point of singularity in big-bang cosmology; that is, theological method breaks down or dissolves into speculation prior to the fallen human condition. We don't have the tools for any methodology to go behind our fallenness? On the face of it, Bonhoeffer's statement about the existence of evil suggests that our job is not to ask the "why?" question, but to act for good in light of the reality of God's mission, revealed in the Christ-community. One may wonder whether this response to the problem of evil is an avoidance strategy, one that would disqualify Bonhoeffer from being counted among the various protest theodicies.[696] Rather than trying to make explicit theoretical sense of the problem, Bonhoeffer presents the church as the divine therapeutic curative for the problem of suffering in our fallen world. However, Bonhoeffer's response does suggest an implicit theological reasoning about suffering.

In an effort to draw out the logic of his implicit theodicy, it is helpful to lay out (in table form) how different approaches to theodicy correspond to an implicit sacramental image and so an implied therapeutic curative.[697] For example, if the response to the problem of evil is to claim that God has a perfect plan, then the sacramental image can be modeled as imagining that we live in a world shared with the Lord of nature and history, which implies a therapy for the one who experiences suffering of remembrance: bringing back to mind that God is in control. The passage from Isaiah 46:9–11 informs the curative like a pharmacopeia, as seen in the following table.[698]

---

[694] Dietrich Bonhoeffer, *Creation and Fall Temptation: Two Biblical Studies* (New York: Collier Books, 1959), 76.

[695] Stephen T. Davis, ed. *Encountering Evil: Live Options in Theodicy* (Atlanta: John Knox Press, 1981), 2.

[696] Cf. Claire Messud, *The Emperor's Children* (New York: Vintage Books, 2007), 457.

[697] As noted to me privately by my friend and colleague, Reverend Dr. Matthew Burdette, the word sacramental used here, more accurately, suggests an implicit construal of the God/world relationship.

[698] I am aware that the notion of "therapeutic curative" is problematic. I am using it in an ordinary and not in the technical sense of the term. I am also aware that pastoral care goes beyond Seward Hiltner's concepts of "healing, sustaining, and guiding." Again, healing is only one of the multiple ways

[*Footnote continued on next page*]

Table 1. Typology of Approaches to Theodicy, Pt. 1[699]

Title of Response	6 Types of Responses		
	Sacramental Image	Therapeutic Curative	Bible Text
Perfect Plan	Lord of Nature/History	God's in Control	Is 46:9–11
Freewill Defense	Good and Bad Apples	Cooperate with God	Josh 24:15
Soul Making	The Vine Pruner	God's not finished: Yet	1 John 3:2
Open Theism	His Eye is on the Sparrow	God's responsive Love	1 John 4:8
Finite Theism	God/world Interdepend	Involve not Intervene	Gen 1:26
Protest Theodicies	"My God, Why Have..."	Challenge God	Amos 7:3

All this has been said to make note of how difficult it is to trace the theme of theodicy in Bonhoeffer's collected works. It is even more difficult to trace this theme specifically in *Sanctorum Communio*. Nevertheless, given the fact that Gottfried Wilhelm Leibniz, who coined the term theodicy, wrestled with some of the same questions and issues that Bonhoeffer takes up in his dissertation, we may find some reason to continue an investigation into Bonhoeffer's theodic intuitions.[700] In many ways, Bonhoeffer does not fit neatly into the standard types of theodic answers, and yet he draws from each of them to some degree. For instance, he insists on identifying the will as necessary for the dignity of the human person,[701] and so one could be tempted to view his approach to theodicy as a species of the freewill defense. Yet he also insists on both the reality and the actualizing fulfillment of the sovereign purposes of God in the new humanity,[702] which might tempt us to view his approach to theodicy as a

---

of naming and providing pastoral caring responses. See, Seward Hiltner, *Preface to Pastoral Theology: The Ministry and Theory of Shepherding* (Nashville: Abingdon Press, 1958).

[699] The creation of this table was inspired, in part, by the book written by Richard Rice, *Suffering and the Search for Meaning: Contemporary Responses to the Problem of Pain* (Downers Grove: IVP, 2014).

[700] In Gottfried Wilhelm Leibniz's Part One of his *Theodicy: Essays on the Goodness of God and the Freedom of Man in the Origin of Evil* (CreateSpace Independent Publishing Platform, 2015, 1st 2005) writes: "Having so settled the rights of faith and of reason as rather to place reason at the service of faith than in opposition to it, we shall see how they exercise these rights to support and harmonize what the light of nature and the light of revelation teach us of God and of man in relation to evil. The difficulties are distinguishable into two classes. The one kind springs from man's freedom, which appears incompatible with the divine nature; and nevertheless freedom is deemed necessary, in order that man may be deemed guilty and open to punishment. The other kind concerns the conduct of God, and seems to make him participate too much in the existence of evil, even though man be free and participate also therein. And this conduct appears contrary to the goodness, the holiness and the justice of God, since God co-operates in evil as well physical as moral, and co-operates in each of them both morally and physically; and since it seems that these evils are manifested in the order of nature as well as in that of grace, and in the future and eternal life as well, nay, more than, in this transitory life."
See www.philvaz.com/apologetics/LeibnizBestPossibleWorldTheodicy.pdf.

[701] Bonhoeffer, *Bonhoeffer Works*, 67; 80ff.

[702] Bonhoeffer, 165.

species of the perfect plan vision. Whatever theodic vision we are able to draw from Bonhoeffer's *Sanctorum Communio*, it would be an error in judgment if we fail to recognize that Bonhoeffer's vision is not derived from the usual Western approach to theological method, which exhibits that particular "audacity of philosophers ... who undertake to tell us what God was thinking before there was a world!"[703]

Having explored Bonhoeffer's unique approach to theodicy and its demand for a communal therapeutic response to suffering, I will now turn to how he employs the theological symbols of sin and "the Fall" in order to provide an adequate anthropological and sociological account of the empirical phenomena that can inform a social philosophy.

B. Primal Rupture, Collective Persons and the Principle of Vicarious Representation

In this section, in order to draw out the implicit theodic logic of Bonhoeffer's argument in *Sanctorum Communio*, I will first offer an exposition of his understanding of sin, the only category that explains the radical social rupture resulting in individual disaster. Secondly, I will show how Bonhoeffer employs this theological symbol "sin" to interpret the phenomena we witness in our shared human condition. It soon becomes apparent that the biological concept of the species is inadequate and unable to define the moral and spiritual dimensions of human experience. Bonhoeffer includes these dimensions and the individual and social phenomena arising from them in his more adequate theological definition of the human species. This account of the entire species contends for a version of humanity that includes its personal and social expression. Adam, in short, is both collective and individual.

Pursuing the theme of theodicy in Bonhoeffer's theological study of the sociology of the Church displays how the dominant Western approach to theodicy may be misguided, and for this reason: framing the problem abstractly, generally, even simply as "the problem of *evil*," that can be addressed by any lone thinker outside of the community. Bonhoeffer's investigation precludes this approach from the start; it is not that simple. An individual cannot wrestle with the question of theodicy apart from a communal cry. Bonhoeffer's *Sanctorum Communio* reframes the problem. His concern is not the problem of evil *per se*, but "the problem of a Christian sociology."[704] According to Bonhoeffer, Christian faith requires

---

[703] John B. Cobb, Jr., "The Problem of Evil and the Task of Ministry" in *Encountering Evil: Live Options in Theodicy*, ed. Stephen T. Davis (Atlanta: John Knox Press, 1981), 173.

[704] Dietrich Bonhoeffer, *Dietrich Bonhoeffer Works, Volume I Sanctorum Communio: A Theological Study of the Sociology of the Church* (Minneapolis: Fortress, 2009), 32, carrying from fn. 3 on p. 30.

commitment to certain beliefs about the nature of community, which stand in opposition to established values and beliefs in sociological epistemology. Bonhoeffer's concerns address the problem of evil indirectly—which may be the only way to address it. The problem comes at an awkward angle through the reality that is forced upon us.

What is that reality? For Bonhoeffer, it is the reality of sin, which he describes as "utmost solitude," "radical separation," or the "isolated position" that each person comes to recognize.[705] Bonhoeffer describes "original sin" as a "rupture," "fall," and "separation"[706] where what was lost was community with God and others. This community with God defines our primal community where our individual identities are secure. We must not forget that, for Bonhoeffer, social community is the primal community; that is, the human person always already presumes a community. Moreover, in Bonhoeffer's system, the primal community is not the subject of protology, but of eschatology: it is not a subject of speculation about origins, but one of sustaining a future hope.[707] In light of this, Bonhoeffer draws a strong contrast between, on the one hand, the person-concept of the primal human state and, on the other hand, the person-concept of fallen humanity, i.e., the one "who does not live in unbroken community with God and humanity, but who knows good and evil."[708] The dependent clause, "but who knows good and evil," indicates how acute the challenge is of addressing the theodicy problem in *Sanctorum Communio,* or in any of Bonhoeffer's works.

Initially, it appears that Bonhoeffer has gone back on his claim that we cannot know humanity prior to the fall, that he is, as it were, inquiring after that for which he lacks the tools of inquiry. He appears to speak of a primal human state "behind the existence forced upon us as sinners," which would open the door to questions of how one can justify the existence of God in the face of evil. According to Bonhoeffer, our fallen state came as a result of our knowledge of evil: to live in the fallen state is to be broken from community with God and humanity as a result of knowing good and evil.[709]

---

[705] Bonhoeffer, *Bonhoeffer Works*, 145.

[706] Bonhoeffer, 61.

[707] Bonhoeffer, 64–65: "Thus we have sketched the archetype of the church. While the theological problem presents little difficulty, *the methodological issues become more complicated by relating social philosophy and sociology* to the doctrine of the primal state. Here, too, it cannot be a matter of developing speculative theories about the possibility of social being in the primal state not affected by evil will. Instead, methodologically, all statements are possible only on the basis of our understanding of the church, i.e., from the revelation we have heard. Thus social-philosophical and sociological problems can be dealt with in the context of theology not because they can be proved generally necessary on the basis of creation, but because they are presupposed and included in revelation."

[708] Bonhoeffer, 44.

[709] Bonhoeffer has more to say on this subject in *Creation and Fall* where he writes, "*Imago dei*—Godlike man in his existence for God and neighbor, in his primitive creatureliness and limitation; *sicut*

[*Footnote continued on next page*]

This suggests that theodic concerns emerge with a certain epistemological rupture that occurred at the fall. This is not "before" the fall nor "after" the fall; what "contemporaneously occurs" constitutes what he seems to mean by "fall."

What further rescues his argument is his claim that the doctrine of the primal state belongs to the study of eschatology and not to the study of protology. In speaking of the doctrine of the primal state, Bonhoeffer writes: "In the logic of theology as a whole it belongs with eschatology."[710] In this way he does not go "behind the existence forced upon us as sinners," rather he embraces it, writing that "The doctrine of the primal state is hope projected backward."[711] Living in hope is not to go "behind the existence forced upon us as sinners," but it is to work within it.

When Bonhoeffer seeks out the ways that the *peccatorum communio* (community of sinners)[712] can inform/be formed-into the *sanctorum communio* (community of saints), he uncovers the recalcitrance of this reality of sin that is forced upon us. He writes: "The reality of sin and the *communio peccatorum* remain even in God's church-community; Adam has really been replaced by Christ only eschatologically, επ ελπιδι (in spe) [in hope]. So long as sin remains, the whole of sinful humanity also remains in every human being."[713] This universality of sinful humanity is key to Bonhoeffer's interpretation of original sin.

In addressing original sin, Bonhoeffer ties individual culpability with the universality of sin, but he does not do so through a biological inheritance. In this way, he is able to preserve the dignity of humankind. He writes:

> When the human race is understood by means of the biological concept of the species, the ethical gravity of the concept of culpability is weakened. We must

---

deus—Godlike man in his out-of-himself knowledge of good and evil, in his limitlessness and his acting out-of-himself, in his underived existence, in his loneliness. *Imago dei*—that is, man bound to the Word of the Creator and living from him; *sicut deus*—that is, man bound to the depths of his own knowledge about God, in good and evil; *imago dei*—the creature living in obedience; *sicut deus*—the creator-man living out of the division of good and evil." Dietrich Bonhoeffer, *Creation and Fall: A Theological Interpretation of Genesis 1–3* (New York: Collier Books, 1959), 71.

[710] Bonhoeffer, *Bonhoeffer Works*, 58.

[711] Bonhoeffer, 60–61.

[712] It is reasonable at this point to ask, if sin is isolating, how is there a community of sinners? Clearly, from his quote on page 213, no easy answer can be given: "Among human beings there is no such thing as a pure, organic community life." 1) One might argue that here lies the paradox of being in Adam: each member warring against the others, and being bound together in mutual hatred, 2) one might argue that the grace of God allows for the remnants of genuine community to exist under sin (albeit in a fractured way), or 3) one might argue that when he speaks of a community of sinners, Bonhoeffer uses the word community loosely to stand for a society of sinners.

[713] Bonhoeffer, *Bonhoeffer Works*, 124.

thus discover a Christian-ethical concept of the species. The issue is how to understand the human species in terms of the concept of sin."[714]

Here Bonhoeffer suggests that sin defines the Christian faith's theological anthropology. This anthropology strangely relates the individual with the social, and yet it honors the dignity of the human person by holding the individual accountable. Original sin displays a theological anthropology in which there is no stand-alone human individual, and yet this universality does not mean the erasure of discrete individuals. Bonhoeffer notes, "The human being, by virtue of being an individual, is also the human race.... Thus all humanity falls with each sin, and not one of us is in principle different from Adam; that is, everyone is also the 'first' sinner."[715]

The individual's moral culpability presents to us the image of persons as "monads," in Leibniz's use of the word, who represent the race of people in a disturbing way.[716] Every person has sinned, and in that sin, each represents, in his or her person, that common human experience of fallenness. Because of the fall, our monadic existence is ruptured to the point that it even breeds a social and philosophical vision that is as distorted as our evil condition stands.[717] In other words, as broken monads our ideas are also fractured. What defines the species of humanity as a whole, finally, is the characteristic feature of belonging to that unique creation where individual moral agency involves the moral status of all others; individual moral culpability inescapably and morally implicates all others in the human community by uniquely deforming the ontic basic-relationship, imposing a radical separation between people. At this juncture, we see how our ontological rupture also rips at the epistemological level.

It is individual social atomism, the belief "that selves are encapsulated entities"[718] that is the primary antagonist in Bonhoeffer's understanding of the effects of original sin on epistemology.[719] The epistemological form of the primal rupture is manifested in philosophical atomism, which creates a conceptual chasm that cannot reconcile our ontological isolation with its very attempts to explain our isolation through a social philosophic construct. For a working definition of atomism, Brian Fay says it is the "thesis that the

---

[714] Bonhoeffer, 111–113.

[715] Bonhoeffer, 115.

[716] Bonhoeffer, 79. "Clearly, Leibniz's image of the monad may serve to clarify these social basic-relations. This is an image of individual beings who are completely self-contained—'monads have no windows'—and yet conceiving, mirroring, and individually shaping all of reality, and, in so doing, discovering their being."

[717] Bonhoeffer, 116.

[718] Brian Fay, *Contemporary Philosophy of Social Science: A Multicultural Approach* (Malden: Blackwell Publishers, 1997), 47.

[719] Fay, *Philosophy of Social Science*, 33.

basic units of social life are self-contained, essentially independent, separated entities."[720] Fay frames the logical force of philosophical atomism by raising the question, "Do We Need Others To Be Ourselves?"[721] Atomism is a social philosophy that employs a kind of methodological individualism: "It accounts for social phenomena ultimately in terms of individual acts and choices."[722] Yet, for Bonhoeffer, this philosophy distorts the distortion because it is only partially true. In fact, the universality of sin is an empirical phenomenon that precludes this sort of atomism; were this atomism true, sin would not be universal, but only afflict those individuals who willingly chose to sin.

Bonhoeffer prefers to speak about the human monad in such a way that the social and the personal are irreducibly implicated in each other. Nothing is prior to the social, including the knowledge of the individual subject. Bonhoeffer writes: "To attempt to derive the social from the epistemological category must be rejected as a μεταβασις εις αλλο γενος (change to a different category). It is impossible to reach the real existence of other subjects by way of the purely transcendental category of the universal."[723] According to Bonhoeffer, the reality of God is where one begins; the primal state is where we have unmediated community with God and humanity.[724] He writes, "Community with God by definition establishes social community as well."[725] According to Bonhoeffer, the problem with the various theories about social relations is that the concept of the divine relation to humanity embedded in them is problematic. The Aristotelian God is impersonal, the Stoic God is formal, the Epicurean God is utilitarian, and the Cartesian God is solipsistic.[726]

For Bonhoeffer, philosophical atomism is not simply a conceptual antagonist derived from an alternative sociological theory, it is theologically important to lay bare (or expose) the notions implied in the concept of philosophical atomism because: *"The concepts of person, community, and God are inseparably and essentially related."* [727] In short, Bonhoeffer's answer to the question of whether or not we need others to be ourselves is no and yes. We don't simply need "others" to be ourselves; we need a

---

[720] Fay, 30.
[721] Fay, 30.
[722] Fay, 31.
[723] Bonhoeffer, *Bonhoeffer Works*, 45.
[724] Bonhoeffer, 63.
[725] Bonhoeffer, 63.
[726] Bonhoeffer, 36–41.
[727] Bonhoeffer, 34.

particular "Other" to be ourselves, that is, to be ourselves we need God.[728] Because the concepts of person, community, and God are so interconnected, Christian theology must develop its own concept of the person that does not presume philosophical atomism. Personhood cannot be abstracted from community. And in order to understand the basic constituents of this community, Bonhoeffer sees it as necessary to discuss the subject of the human spirit, which he defines as *"the bond of self-consciousness and self-determination that documents its structural unity*; this spirit can be *formally defined as the principle of receptivity and activity."*[729] His definition requires another component, i.e., the function of human spirit, where he describes it as "effective in acts of thinking, self-conscious willing, and feeling."[730] So he writes: "The term 'Christian concept of person' will now be used for the concept of person that is constitutive for the concept of Christian community and is presupposed by it."[731] In Bonhoeffer's thinking, the concept of person already implies the concept of Christian community. Here, we begin to see his sacramental image emerge for an additional row to our table. Early in his dissertation, Bonhoeffer makes clear that he is not attempting to capture an empirical social realm in the human being, but is tracing the metaphysical or the philosophical precedents that are indispensable to any empirical account of social relations;[732] now we can see how the universality of sin implies an ethical solidarity with all sinful humanity, the collective fallen person, i.e., old Adam.

The notion of a collective person, in which all individual persons are in ethical solidarity, suggests a primitive concept of *the principle of vicarious representative action*. This principle implies that in addition to individual culpability, there can also be corporate culpability and that an individual or a group of individuals are able to act on behalf of a larger community. An understanding of this principle is needed to make sense, for example, of Bonhoeffer's saying,

> The human being, by virtue of being an individual, is also the human race.... Thus all humanity falls with each sin, and not one of us is in principle different from Adam; that is, everyone is also the 'first' sinner.[733]

---

[728] Bonhoeffer, 80. "God does not desire a history of individual human beings, but the history of the human *community*. However, God does not want a community that absorbs the individual into itself, but a community of *human* beings. In God's eyes, community and individual exist in the same moment and rest in one another. The collective unit and the individual unit have the same structure in God's eyes."

[729] Bonhoeffer, 67.

[730] Bonhoeffer, 67.

[731] Bonhoeffer, 44.

[732] Bonhoeffer, footnotes on page 40 [#20] that continues to page 41.

[733] Bonhoeffer, 115.

Bonhoeffer is able to speak of "the ethical personality of collective persons" and of the possibility of regarding "the collective person as an ethical person, that is, to place it in the concrete situation of being addressed by a you."[734] He supports this concept in a way that preserves the dignity of individuals and their moral choices. Paradoxically, despite ethical solidarity among all persons, he asserts that even at a time when the collective person comes under judgment, individuals can escape it. He writes:

> But this must not lead us to reject the very idea of judgment being passed on the collective person. We learned that the community as a collective person exists from God to God (see above) and that it must be conceived as being established through the will of God, and as such standing at the last judgment. This idea can also be found in the N.T. (Chorazin, Bethsaida, Capernaum, Matt 11:21ff.; the address to the churches in Revelation 2 and 3, esp. 3:10 and 3:16). That God can condemn a collective person and at the same time accept individuals who are part of it, and vice versa, is an idea that is as necessary as it is incomprehensible.[735]

Bonhoeffer takes the time to illustrate that *the principle of vicarious representative action* is firmly established in the Holy Scriptures. Not only does Bonhoeffer support this idea of *the principle of vicarious representative action* in a way that honors the dignity of individuals and collective persons, he also supports the notion of corporate culpability by drawing on additional biblical images and metaphors. He refashions the Pauline image of fallen humanity as a corporate unit, calling it "humanity-in-Adam." He reinvokes the call of Israel to be the "people of God." He receives anew Isaiah's confession, "I am a person of unclean lips and dwell in the midst of a people of unclean lips." He recalls the words, of the divine messenger, in the story of the destruction of Sodom, "For the sake of ten I will not destroy them." Bonhoeffer's purpose for drawing on the biblical texts and imagery is to invite all, in the corporate Adam of the fall; that is, the community of sinners to hear that they are being addressed by the call of God for a new corporate humanity in the story of Jesus Christ.[736]

C. God's New Will and Purpose for Humanity: Sanctorum Communio

Only an ultimate response is a true theodic response to suffering. According to Bonhoeffer, the Church, as the divine reality, refashions collective humanity and therefore shows us what God intends for

1. The real (as opposed to the phenomenal) basic-relatedness of human beings;

---

[734] Bonhoeffer, 118.
[735] Bonhoeffer, 284.
[736] Bonhoeffer, 121.

2. The sociality of the human spirit, which is present before any act of an individual or group of individuals exercise their will(s) to be in community; and
3. The real (as opposed to phenomenal) ethical basic-relations that forms empirically existing communal relations.[737]

Due to how these concepts are modified in the new creation of God in the Church, we might now be able to use interchangeably the term "community of saints" with the notions "community-of-the-cross" and "community-of-God's-Realm" in order to provide insight into an assumed therapeutic curative implied in Bonhoeffer's doctoral dissertation.

Bonhoeffer writes that "God pledges to be present within the church-community." [738] He details the difference between what he calls the "empirical church" and what he calls the "essential church." Clifford Green notes, "It is clear that Bonhoeffer does not regard *Gemeinde* [the German word for local community] as a theological term for a Christocentric community and *Kirche* [the German word for church] as merely a sociological term for describing an empirical, religious institution."[739] While it is important to keep the concepts of the empirical and essential church distinct, they are nevertheless inseparable. This is because the church is one; there is only one church. The church is the one body of Christ. And for Bonhoeffer, we should not think of the metaphor of *body* with the image of an organism in *mind*. The church as the body of Christ should be thought of functionally. [740] The church is where the presence of Christ exists as community. With the church, God undertakes his first therapeutic act for humanity, acting to heal the primal rupture in history and to do so beyond history.[741]

The topics of community and church are important not simply because we empirically observe a common experience of human sinfulness that relates our personal culpability with ethical solidarity. More importantly, as

---

[737] Bonhoeffer, 124–125.

[738] Bonhoeffer, 229.

[739] Clifford J. Green, "Editor's Introduction to the English Edition" of *Dietrich Bonhoeffer Works, Volume I Sanctorum Communio: A Theological Study of the Sociology of the Church* (Minneapolis: Fortress Press, 2009), 16.

[740] Bonhoeffer, *Bonhoeffer Works*, 225. Bonhoeffer writes: "Is the body of Christ as a whole thus primarily present in the universal church, so that all individual congregations would be members only of this body? The N.T. says nothing of this kind. The question is also theologically misguided since it understands *the concept of the body of Christ* simply in an organic and physical sense, whereas it in fact expresses the presence of Christ and the work of the Holy Spirit in his church-community. The concept of the body in this context is not a *concept referring to form* but to *function*, namely the work of Christ (concerning the 'body' of the collective person....)."

[741] Bonhoeffer, 155: "*Christ's action as vicarious representative* can thus be understood from the situation itself. It is simultaneously 'within concrete time' and the 'for all times.'"

Bonhoeffer writes, "This experience does not in any way constitute sociality; rather, sociality exists before the experience and independently of it."[742] God's act to cure at the social level—God's act itself—is that place of primary concern. Here, we come to appreciate what is central to Bonhoeffer's conceptual development, that is, "the ethical personality of collective persons."[743] Can the collective person behave as an ethical agent being addressed by another? For Bonhoeffer, the story of Israel as a collective people becomes paradigmatic to the answer of this question.[744] It happened in Israel and it now happens again in the *Sanctorum Communio*.

In the incarnate life and work of Jesus, God begins the work of restoring humanity, in history, by receiving the actions of one individual on behalf of a larger community. Bonhoeffer does not speak of substitutionary atonement. Christ's work in history begins a work that continues in the life of the church-community. God receives the actions of the one individual as the vicarious representative action which establishes God's new humanity, joining persons together into a new collective person, that is, into the collective that is Christ existing as community. E. H. Robertson captures this when he writes, "The saving act of Christ is then seen, not only as the reconciling of man to God, but also as the restoring of the torn fabric of humanity."[745]

The implied theodic vision of the communion of saints affords us the ability to add an additional row of a sacramental image onto our previous table.

Table 2. Typology of Approaches to Theodicy, Pt. 2

Title of Response	7 Types of Responses		
	Sacramental Image	Therapeutic Curative	Bible Text
Perfect Plan	Lord of Nature/History	God's in Control	Is 46:9–11
Freewill Defense	Good and Bad Apples	Cooperate with God	Josh 24:15
Soul Making	The Vine Pruner	God's not finished: Yet	1 John 3:2
Open Theism	His Eye is on the Sparrow	God's responsive Love	1 John 4:8
Finite Theism	God/world Interdepend	Involve not Intervene	Gen 1:26
Protest Theodicies	"My God, Why Have..."	Challenge God	Amos 7:3
Sanctorum Communio	Christ Existing as Community	Present Suffering ≠ Future Glory	Rom 8:18

---

[742] Bonhoeffer, 116–117.
[743] Bonhoeffer, 118.
[744] Bonhoeffer, 119, footnote 26.
[745] E. H. Robertson, *Dietrich Bonhoeffer* (Richmond, VA: John Knox Press, 1967), 14.

When viewing this table, it is important to remember how Bonhoeffer organizes his theological thinking. For him, "The doctrine of the primal state is hope projected backward."[746] Living in hope is not to go "behind the existence forced upon us as sinners," but is to work within it. It is for this reason that he can distinguish between the realization of the church and the actualization of the church. For Bonhoeffer, the reality of the church cannot be theologically questioned. If the church comes from God, "It must be revealed."

> Revelation of God's will is necessary because the primal community, where God speaks and the word becomes deed and history through human beings, is broken. Therefore God must personally speak and act, and at the same time accomplish a new creation of human beings, since God's word is always deed. *Thus, the church is already completed in Christ, just as in Christ its beginning is established.*[747]

What is realized, first in the life and ministry of the person of Jesus of Nazareth (as *the vicarious representative actor*), and ultimately in the eschaton, is being actualized in history, in the collective person of the community of saints. God immerses the divine purpose into human history, where the sufferings of the present time take place. This empirical history, with its empirically present church, is the arena of divine action. Yet the communal nature of the church shows that divinity also has in view another arena, for God is not confined to history. Bonhoeffer writes: "Because of the eschatological character of community, which it shares with history, the deepest significance of community is 'from God to God'."[748]

D. Sacramental Basis of Therapeutic Ministry: Who Holds the Office?

Therefore, the community of which Bonhoeffer speaks is the communion of saints already realized in the eschaton; that is, the Church already is, and it becomes actualized within history.[749] Again, I repeat, only an ultimate response is a true theodic response to suffering. Bonhoeffer defines social community as a community of will,[750] because the will of community shapes the objective spirit of the church, and it is necessary to identify the unique objective spirit that offers a unique category for sociologists to study.

---

[746] Robertson, *Bonhoeffer*, 60–61.

[747] Robertson, 142.

[748] Robertson, 101.

[749] John Milbank expresses a similar thought when he writes, "The church itself, as the realized heavenly city, is the telos of the salvific process." *Theology and Social Theory: Beyond Secular Reason* (Oxford: Blackwell Publishing, 1993), 403.

[750] Bonhoeffer, *Bonhoeffer Works*, 86: "Community is a community of wills, built upon the separateness and difference of persons, constituted by reciprocal acts of will, finding its unity in what is willed, and counting among its basic laws the inner conflict of individual wills."

Nevertheless, they cannot investigate this sociological group with their usual theoretical tools. According to Bonhoeffer, if one desires to study the church as a subject of sociology, it becomes important to take seriously the eternal word of God, in Christ, that takes form in history: "The word is the sociological principle by which the entire church is built up."[751] This community is the one in which the will of God in Christ is operative from beginning to end.[752] Bonhoeffer writes: "Objective spirit is thus to be regarded as the connection between historical and communal meaning, between the temporal and spatial intentions of a community. Objective spirit is will exerting itself effectively on the members of the community."[753] For Bonhoeffer, the will of God for humanity becomes the will of the members of the communion of saints.[754]

This communal will is always a will to love. This communal will is one where all have heard and responded to the apostle's admonition to "Let the same mind be in you that was in Christ Jesus" (Phil 2:5). And it was God's loving will, turned in the direction of his suffering creation, that caused God in Christ to join in their suffering. This was not simply for the purpose of participating in their reality, but, more importantly, to make the divine eschatological reality for them actualized within their historical context of suffering. God, in Christ, "unite[s] all individuals in himself, and act[s] before God as their vicarious representative."[755] This kind of vicarious representative action presents us with more than an ethical actor (although Bonhoeffer still believes that there is an ethical reason to accept this kind of vicarious representation).[756] This vicarious representative action presents us with a theological concept (this is where sociology and theology are necessarily linked in the sociological study of the church).[757] It is at this point that we realize the *sanctorum communio* is also identified as the "*community-of-the-cross*, which contains within itself the contradiction of simultaneously representing utmost solitude and closest community."[758]

---

[751] Bonhoeffer, 246.

[752] Bonhoeffer, 247.

[753] Bonhoeffer, 99.

[754] Bonhoeffer, 141–142. Bonhoeffer asserts: "The church is God's new will and purpose for humanity. God's will is always directed toward the concrete, historical human being. But this means that it begins to be implemented *in history*. God's will must become visible and comprehensible at some point in history. But at the same point it must already be completed. Therefore, it must be revealed."

[755] Bonhoeffer, 148.

[756] Bonhoeffer, 156. Bonhoeffer writes: "It is true, the doctrine of vicarious representative action includes more than our ethical posture, but we *ought* to let our sin be taken from us, for we are not able to carry it by ourselves; we *ought not* reject this gift of God...and only for the sake of this love ought we abandon our ethical position of responsibility for ourselves."

[757] Bonhoeffer, 156–157.

[758] Bonhoeffer, 151.

This loving will of God acts upon, and is acted upon by, each member of the community. It finds expression in the "plurality of spirit, community of spirit, and unity of spirit."[759]

For Bonhoeffer, the historical form of the church community can be modeled by sociologists as having the empirical form of three concentric circles. The smallest of the three, the inner most circle, is the church as a confessing community. The objective center of this community is the table of the Lord's Supper: this is where it identifies itself as the *community-of-the-cross*. This community is surrounded by and encompassed in a community of wills. The focal point of this community is the preaching of the cross: a preaching that must always be worldly in its call for willing followers. This is where it identifies itself as the *community-of-the-word*. This community of wills is surrounded by and encompassed into the widest circle; that is, the popular community, representing all of those who are baptized.[760] The *community-of-the-baptized* is the outermost expression of the empirical form of the historical actualization of the reality of Christ existing as community. In light of this historical form of the community, it becomes all the more clear how John Milbank can write that, "The life of the saints is inherently social, because it is the opposite of a life of sin, which is the life of self-love."[761] It is this social phenomena that models community in ways that go beyond the coercive political societies.[762] Yet and still, the social data that exert influence on the individual members, i.e., values, norms, structure…etc. are fully present in the community where Christ is present. The following figure models the three concentric circles where God's active love is at work in and for our suffering world.

---

[759] Bonhoeffer, 274.
[760] Bonhoeffer, 247.
[761] Milbank, *Theology and Social Theory*, 402.
[762] Milbank, 402.

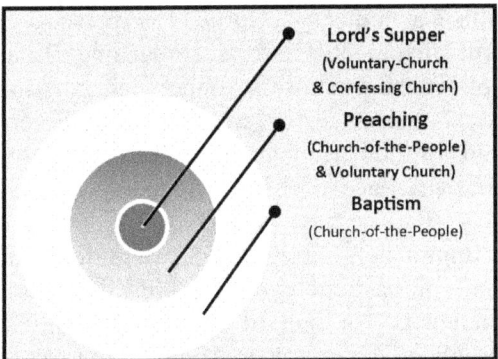

Figure 1. Three Sociologically Distinct Concentric Circles & Their Centers of Activity

Bonhoeffer lays out these details in order to provide a definite description of the corporate body of Christ, and he does so in a way that preserves the integrity of the collective mission of God, while at the same time preserving the integrity of each individual missioner.

- Christ is present in this communal body.
- Christ is present with each member of this body.
- Christ is present, caring, and healing the rupture that took place at the moment of the fall.

This means that God's primary response to the problem of suffering is to be present where those who suffer. The church is a sacrament of the body of Christ.[763] The church is the visible sign of an invisible grace.[764]

What we have discussed thus far leads us to recognize that the unique theodic response of Bonhoeffer is not *that* he presents the *Sanctorum Communio* as a response to human suffering, but it is *the way that* this offer uniquely shapes the divine response to human suffering. Thomas Oden frames clearly the unique challenge that Christian ministry must clarify when he frames the issue with the question whether Christian ministry is primarily sacramental or primarily therapeutic.[765] The Christian who offers pastoral care to the suffering one must be clear about what is more

---

[763] Milbank, 182.

[764] This is the way that the thoughts of Saint Augustine have commonly been summarized: "On the subject of the sacrament, indeed, which he receives, it is first to be well impressed upon his notice that the signs of divine things are, it is true, things visible, but that the invisible things themselves are also honored in them, and that that species, which is then sanctified by the blessing, is therefore not to be regarded merely in the way in which it is regarded in any common use." *Nicene and Post-Nicene Fathers*, vol. 3, p. 312.

[765] Thomas C. Oden, *Pastoral Theology: Essentials of Ministry* (New York: HarperCollins Publishers, 1983); cf. *Transforming Practice: Pastoral Theology in an Age of Uncertainty*, 2nd ed. (Eugene: Wipf and Stock, 2002).

fundamental to his/her ministry efforts. The presence of Christ is the foundation for all therapeutic efforts. Preaching, [766] administering the sacraments of baptism and the Lord's Supper, engaging in pastoral care and counseling, political resistance, or whatever else becomes necessary to bandage the wounds of the hurting are all based upon, rooted in, and framed by the sacramental presence of Christ in the world through the church community.

Furthermore, Emmanuel Lartey, who offers four ideal types in the historical paradigm of pastoral care, captures this work of God in the "priesthood of believers" in one of his paradigms. He has named an approach that Bonhoeffer's work prefigures, namely, the communal-contextual approach. According to Lartey, "This approach reacts against the clericalization, clinicalization, and individualization of pastoral care and pastoral theology. Practitioners employing this model seek to restore these disciplines to their roots within communities of faith." [767] Bonhoeffer prefigures this model because for him the unique divine response comes only in a context where there is the priesthood of all believers (non-clericalization), where there is no space fabricated at a distance from emergent suffering (non-clinicalization) for the whole race of humanity (non-individualization). It is in this context that the new Adam is called to wait upon others during the time we wait in hope.

Conclusion: Note on the Paradox of *Sanctorum Communio* and Apocatastasis

The realm of Christ is the realm of God. This is the hope of the Christian realized in the eschaton. Bonhoeffer's reference, in the final paragraphs of his dissertation, to 1 Corinthians 15:24 places the story of the Church in the larger drama of the story of God. He does not quote the verses before and after, yet they stand behind the essential argument throughout his entire essay.

> For as all die in Adam, so all will be made alive in Christ. But each in his own order: Christs the first fruits, then at his coming those who belong to Christ. Then comes the end, when he hands over the kingdom to God the Father, after he has destroyed every ruler and every authority and power. For he must reign until he has put all his enemies under his feet. (1 Cor 15:22–26).

---

[766] See Dietrich Bonhoeffer, *Worldly Preaching: Lectures on Homiletics* (New York: Crossroad Publishing Company, 1991); cf. Maury Jackson and Horace Crogman, "Shepherding Public Discourse Practices: Homiletic Form Aligned to the Logic Operative in Racial Rhetoric and Public Theological Discourse for Secular Liberal Democracies" in *Cultural and Religious Studies* 4, no. 9 (September 2016).

[767] Emmanuel Lartey, *Pastoral Theology in an Intercultural World* (Eugene: Wipf and Stock Publishers, 2006), 123.

What happens is that God's first response to human suffering in the person of Jesus is then followed by the *sanctorum communio*, and then finally God finishes the work in the eschaton. As Bonhoeffer says: "What has become reality here is not the *ecclesia triumphans* [church triumphant], but the Realm of God extending throughout the whole world."

It is the "all" in the Corinthians passage and the realm of God extending throughout the "whole world" in Bonhoeffer's next to the last paragraph of his book that introduces a more troubling question, which he does not fully address, but clearly hints at an answer: the problem of *apocatastasis* (the salvation of all). Like the term "suffering," in the index of his work, so too the term "*apocatastasis*" only has three references.[768] The first time that this word is mentioned is in a footnote where Bonhoeffer is critical of Friedrich Schleiermacher's motives for why we should love everybody, namely, because they share the divine spirit. Here Bonhoeffer challenges this reasoning: "This line of argument is methodologically impossible, since apocatastasis [the salvation of all] can at most be the very last word in eschatological reflection, but not as the self-evident point of departure for any theological argument."[769] The second time that this word appears is in a note on a deleted section from his earlier publication that is referenced as *Sanctorum Communio A*. Again, this reference is in connection with challenging Schleiermacher's method of placing the doctrine of apocatastasis as a point of departure in his theological argument.

But what do we make of Bonhoeffer's third use of the term, in light of his words that "apocatastasis can at most be the very last word in eschatological reflection"? One may be tempted to think that for Bonhoeffer this last word in eschatological reflection is a speculative word, but it is much more than that. The last word is a word of hope. For Bonhoeffer, the hope of the church is a hope for the universal salvation of all. Bonhoeffer speaks of "the inner necessity of the idea of apocatastasis" as an unresolvable paradox.[770] Here we see why this unresolvable paradox must be the Christian eschatological hope:

> The strongest reason for accepting the idea of apocatastasis would seem to me that all Christians must be aware of having brought sin into the world, and thus of having the sins of humanity on their conscience. Justification and sanctification are inconceivable for anyone if that individual believer cannot be assured that God will embrace not only them but all those for whose sins they are responsible.[771]

---

[768] Bonhoeffer, *Bonhoeffer Works*, 360.
[769] Bonhoeffer, 171.
[770] Bonhoeffer, 286.
[771] Bonhoeffer, 287.

Here, for Bonhoeffer, universal salvation cannot be a category of developmental psychology encroaching into theological method. God does not save everybody because we are all going to die short of our next stage of moral, psycho-social, or faith development (and it would be unjust to punish some, but not others).

For Bonhoeffer, universal salvation is a hope based upon the sacramental presence and healing activity of the new Adam: where a vicarious representative collective called the *sanctorum communio* leads individuals within it to intercede on behalf of another recognizing that no one stands alone, but the community "leads *a single life*."[772] This novel sociological structure is where you find that community of love perfected. It is that collective person known as the body of Christ or the new Adam, who like Moses and Paul[773] would

> ask God to accept or condemn him together with his people…. and he curses himself out of community with God and from his people to the place of damnation, where they are, precisely because he truly loves both community with God and his people, which means, because he is obedient to the command that we should unreservedly surrender ourselves to the neighbor.[774]

If Bonhoeffer is forced to join the theodicy debate as philosophers have put forth the question of why there is evil, he wants to know who is asking the question! This question asked, by the old Adam, implies that this human is complicit in sin and responsible for suffering and evil. If this question is asked by the new Adam, the presence of Christ existing as community, it's a hope for an eschatological fulfillment of the mission of God in the community of the cross. And it is this and only this hope that can justify God's existence, while evil exists. For Bonhoeffer, this vision of *the sanctorum communio* is the only one that can know "that the sufferings of this present time are not worth comparing with the glory about to be revealed to it."[775]

---

[772] Bonhoeffer, 185.
[773] Bonhoeffer, 184. Bonhoeffer references Exod 32:32 and Rom 9:1.
[774] Bonhoeffer, 184.185.
[775] Bonhoeffer, 289. Cf. Rom 8:18, the NRSV reads "revealed to us."

22.
The God of All Comfort:
Karl Barth and Hope in Suffering

Rev. Dr. Nathan D. Hieb
Pastor, Monmouth Chinese Christian Church,
Monmouth, New Jersey
Adjunct Professor of Theology,
Alliance Theological Seminary, Nyack, NY
Adjunct Assistant Professor of Mission Theology and Urban Studies
Fuller Theological Seminary, Pasadena, CA [776]

Introduction 339
A. God's Mercy and Compassion 340
B. God Consoles Those Who Suffer 344
C. God Confronts the Source of Affliction 345
D. God Removes the Suffering Caused by Sin 350
E. Our Pastoral Response 352
F. The Cross We Bear 355
G. The Consolation We Receive 357
Conclusion—The God of All Comfort 358

Introduction

³Blessed be the God and Father of our Lord Jesus Christ, the Father of mercies and the God of all consolation,⁴ who consoles us in all our affliction, so that we may be able to console those who are in any affliction with the consolation with which we ourselves are consoled by God.⁵ For just as the sufferings of Christ are abundant for us, so also our consolation is abundant through Christ.

II Corinthians 1:3–5, NRSV

Pastoral ministry entails entering into and sharing the suffering of those to whom we minister. Yet, pastors are not simply fellow-sufferers. Our ministry to those in affliction displays a specific ordering, direction, and shape determined by our call to point to the one who bore all suffering on

---

[776] Hieb earned his PhD in systematic theology from Princeton Theological Seminary, NJ; his MDiv and MA from Fuller Theological Seminary, Pasadena, CA; and his BA in Philosophy and Urban Studies from the University of Minnesota. He has ministered for twenty years among immigrant congregations, the urban poor, and youth countercultures in New Jersey, Los Angeles, and Minneapolis. He has served on ministry projects in Central Asia, East Asia, South Asia, South East Asia, Europe, and Latin America. He is the Pastor of the English Congregation of Monmouth Chinese Christian Church in Middletown, New Jersey, as well as Partnering Adjunct Professor of Theology at Alliance Theological Seminary, New York, and Adjunct Assistant Professor of Mission Theology and Urban Studies at Fuller Theological Seminary, Pasadena, California. He is the author of *Crucified in a Suffering World: The Unity of Atonement and Liberation* (Minneapolis: Fortress Press, 2013; 240 pp.). See www.MCCC.org/mccc/ and ndhieb@gmail.com.

the cross, sets us free from affliction-causing sin, and invites us to join him in his ministry of consolation. In pastoral ministry, we learn that the cross and the counseling room, the death of Christ and the liberation of the sin-scarred soul, reconciliation with God and a future of service for us all, are not separate motifs in the great story of our faith. Rather, they are deeply interrelated and inseparably united in a dynamic event completed once for all on the cross of Jesus Christ, yet encountered anew and afresh in the lives of those who follow Him.[777]

Karl Barth's theology demonstrates this unity by tracing the interconnection between two pastoral tasks often regarded as functionally separate: the proclamation of Christ's atoning work and the consolation of those who suffer. The first task addresses the spiritual plight of humankind, the relational rupture caused by sin, and the reconciliation with God achieved through Christ's victory over sin and death on the cross. The second task engages the existential crises endured by all people and offers God's peace and hope in the midst of affliction. Here I suggest that Karl Barth's theology of the cross aligns to the character, ordering, and structure of pastoral ministry described in 2 Corinthians 1:3–5. Put another way, 1:3–5 encapsulates, in broad brush strokes, the main contours of Barth's theology of reconciliation and its outworking in the life of the church. Reading this Scripture passage alongside Barth's theology of the cross highlights the practical, pastoral dimension of his thought, and his deep ministerial sensitivity toward those who suffer. Even though Barth's doctrine of reconciliation offers more than this in its sweeping account of Christ's incarnation, ministry, and death in relation to his prophetic, priestly, and kingly offices, Barth's theology of the cross is never less than a pastoral response to human affliction. Barth demonstrates how pastoral ministries of consolation find their basis within the doctrine of atonement, and the atonement finds its outworking in ministries of consolation.[778]

A. God's Mercy and Compassion

"Blessed be the God and Father of our Lord Jesus Christ, the Father of mercies and the God of all consolation ..." – 2 Corinthians 1:3

God's response to human suffering begins with the mercy and compassion eternally present within Godself and revealed to us in the

---

[777] George Hunsinger examines the "once for all" and "again and again" dimensions of sanctification in "A Tale of Two Simultaneities: Justification and Sanctification in Luther, Calvin, and Barth," in *Evangelical, Catholic, and Reformed* (Grand Rapids: Eerdmans, 2015), 189–215.

[778] In this article, I extend in new directions the arguments that I presented in *Christ Crucified in a Suffering World: The Unity of Atonement and Liberation* (Minneapolis: Fortress, 2013).

ministry of Jesus Christ. Barth examines these themes when he considers God's eternal perfections in "The Mercy and Righteousness of God" (*Church Dogmatics* II/1), and Christ's ministry of compassion to the afflicted masses in "The Royal Man," (*Church Dogmatics* IV/2). Indeed, the two cannot be separated, for Christ's ministry to the poor and needy reveals God's compassion to us, and the eternal mercy of God provides the ground and basis of Christ's earthly ministry. I will first sketch Barth's view of God's mercy, and then examine his treatment of Christ's ministry of compassion.

In *Church Dogmatics* II/1, Barth discusses "The Perfections of the Divine Loving" expressed in the pairings of grace and holiness, mercy and righteousness, and patience and wisdom.[779] Each of these divine perfections coinheres inseparably and indivisibly within the unity of God, "the One who loves in freedom."[780] Yet, God's unitary being "is lived out by Him, and therefore identical with a multitude of various and distinct types of perfection." [781] God's diverse perfections remain indivisibly joined in perichoretic unity within God's being. They intertwine with and elucidate each other. Yet, they each also attest to unique facets of the diversity of God's unitary being.[782]

In Barth's discussion of God's love, grace, and mercy in "The Mercy and Righteousness of God" (*Church Dogmatics* II/1), we find striking evidence of God's compassion upon those in need. God's love expresses itself in God's decision to enter into relationship with us. God's grace is an aspect of God's love characterized by "the free inclination of an unconditionally superior towards one who is unconditionally subordinate."[783] God's mercy is God's choice to enter into, experience, and remove "the distress of another."[784] Barth underscores the close association among these concepts when he claims that divine mercy relates to "the very centre of the concept of divine love and its specific determination as grace." Furthermore, "Divine love bears necessarily the character of mercy."[785]

---

[779] Karl Barth, *The Church Dogmatics* II/1, ed. G. W. Bromiley and T. F. Torrance, trans. W. B. Johnston, T. H. L. Parker, Harold Knight, J. L. M. Haire (New York: T & T Clark, 1957), 351–439. Immediately after this discussion, Barth outlines "The Perfections of the Divine Freedom," which include God's unity and omnipresence, constancy and omnipotence, and eternity and glory. See *CD* II/1, 440–677.

[780] Barth, *Church Dogmatics* II/1, 322–323.

[781] Barth, 322.

[782] Barth, 368. Barth describes both the unity and diversity of God's being: "the being of God in itself is really one in real plenitude."

[783] Barth, *Church Dogmatics* II/1, 369.

[784] Barth, 377.

[785] Barth, 369.

God expresses His mercy by entering into, sharing, and removing human suffering. Indeed, Barth claims that God bears humanity's suffering within God's own heart. Barth therefore rejects divine impassibility, the claim that God cannot suffer, for this would reduce the personal God revealed in Jesus Christ to an "impersonal absolute" whose interactions with the world are "mathematical or mechanical."[786] God's merciful love prompts God to bear our suffering in Godself.[787] God turns to us in mercy, makes our sin God's "own intimate concern," [788] and chooses to bear both our sin and the suffering it entails. In doing so, God experiences the full depth and magnitude of sin, which we are incapable of experiencing. Barth argues that, "Our suffering for sin has not touched us, and cannot touch us, as it touches Him."[789]

Christ's earthly ministry consistently reveals the mercy and compassion within God's heart.[790] Even before Christ bears and removes humanity's sin and sin-caused suffering on the cross, Christ turns to those who suffer, feels profound compassion for them, and alleviates their distress. In *Church Dogmatics* IV/2, Barth reminds us that when Jesus sees the shepherdless masses, he is filled with compassion for them (ἐσπλαγχνίσθη).[791] Barth writes, "[Jesus] was not only affected to the heart by the misery which surrounded Him—sympathy in our modern sense is far too feeble a word— but it went right into His heart, into Himself, so that it was now His misery."[792] Jesus bears human misery in its true depth and intensity, which are beyond our capacities to bear, causing all other instances of suffering to exist as reflections of his own.[793] In this way, Barth's interpretation of human suffering is thoroughly Christocentric. Christ takes up and bears human suffering so completely that humanity may no longer understand its

---

[786] Barth, 370.

[787] Barth has Schleiermacher in mind when he writes, "The source of the feeling of sheer dependence has no heart. But the personal God has a heart. He can feel and be affected. He is not impassible." Barth, *Church Dogmatics* II/1, 370. See also Colin E. Gunton, *Becoming and Being*, 201–202.

[788] Barth, *Kirchliche Dogmatik* II/1 (Zürich: Theologischer, 1980), 456.

[789] Barth, *Church Dogmatics* II/1, 374. Elsewhere Barth writes, "The sorrow which openly or secretly fills the heart of man is primarily in the heart of God." Barth, *Church Dogmatics* IV/2, 225.

[790] Barth describes the reliability of God's self-revelation in Jesus Christ: "[Jesus] was on earth as God is in heaven." Karl Barth, *The Church Dogmatics* IV/2, ed. G .W. Bromiley and T. F. Torrance, trans. G. W. Bromiley (New York: T & T Clark, 1958), 184.

[791] Barth, *Church Dogmatics* IV/2, 184–187. See also Albert Dahm, *Der Gerichtsgedanke in der Versöhnungslehre Karl Barth*, vol. XLVII, Konfessionskundliche und Kontroverstheologische Studien (Paderborn: Verlag Bonifatius-Druckerei, 1983), 134.

[792] Barth, *Church Dogmatics* IV/2, 184.

[793] Barth writes, "The cry of those who suffered was only an echo. ... Jesus had made it His own." Barth, *Church Dogmatics* IV/2, 184.

own suffering apart from God's merciful love revealed in Christ's incarnation, ministry, death, and resurrection. As he takes up and bears humanity's affliction in compassionate love, Christ also acts decisively to relieve it. In his miracles, Jesus addresses people "with whom things are going badly," people in desperate need of consolation in their suffering. These miracles unmask humanity's actual situation of profound need, which is "like a great hospital whose many departments in some way enfold us all."[794]

Although the effects of sin, and the suffering sin causes, permeate human life as we now know it, when Christ turns to relieve human affliction he does not simply address spiritual conditions but regards "the whole man in … his 'natural' existence in the narrower sense, his physical existence."[795] While affirming the connection between humanity's fall into sin and the suffering we now experience,[796] which we will consider further in section IV, Barth notes that when Jesus turns to heal those in affliction he usually does not mention their sins.[797] Rather, Christ regards them as sufferers first, people who indeed are also sinners but whose suffering requires immediate intervention. In this way, Christ's miracles reveal the opposition of God's merciful love to all that causes human suffering and distress.

In Jesus Christ, God stands in solidarity with suffering humanity and "enters the field against this power of destruction in all its forms."[798] Humanity, suffering under the effects and consequences of sin, remains the object of God's primary concern.[799] Barth writes, "[The Son of Man] goes right past sin, beyond it and through it, directly to man himself; for His purpose is always with man."[800] By turning with compassion toward suffering humanity in order to relieve humanity's distress, Jesus Christ demonstrates God's deep desire to comfort, console, and liberate the people

---

[794] Barth, *Church Dogmatics* IV/2, 221.

[795] Barth, 222, revised.

[796] Barth, 223. Elsewhere Barth writes, "Sin as such is not only an offence to God; it also disturbs, injures and destroys the creature and its nature. And although there can be no doubt that it is committed by man, it is obviously attended and followed by suffering, i.e., the suffering of evil and death." Karl Barth, *The Church Dogmatics* III/3, ed. G. W. Bromiley and Thomas F. Torrance, trans. G. W. Bromiley and R. J. Ehrlich (Edinburgh: T & T Clark, 1960), 310.

[797] Barth notes exceptions, such as Christ's healing of the paralytic in Mark 2:1–12. Of this passage, Barth writes, "The obvious aim of the story is to bring out the connexion of Jesus' miracles with His proclamation." Barth, *Church Dogmatics* IV/2, 223.

[798] Barth, *Church Dogmatics* IV/2, 225, revised.

[799] Barth, 227. On 225–226, he writes, "[The Son of Man] goes right past sin, beyond it and through it, directly to man himself; for His purpose is always with man."

[800] Barth, 225–226.

God loves.[801] In this way, Jesus Christ reveals and confirms the Father's "mercies" and "consolation" extended to us (II Corinthians 1:3).

B. God Consoles Those Who Suffer

"who consoles us …" – 2 Corinthians 1:4a

As Christ's miracles relieve the immediate causes of human affliction, and thereby reveal the mercy eternally present within God, so Christ's confrontation with the sin at the source of humanity's suffering demonstrates the depth and effectiveness of God's consolation. In Jesus Christ, sinful and suffering people encounter the compassion of God. Indeed, Christ's incarnation, ministry, death, and resurrection form the original pastoral act to which all other pastoral ministries exist as an echo and reflection.

God in Jesus Christ "consoles us in all our affliction …" (2 Cor 1:4a) by not only addressing the surface-level symptoms or the most visible features of our distress, but also by addressing the root of the problem. Sin separates humanity from God and destroys the fellowship with God for which we have been created. Barth describes sin as humanity's "headlong [rush] into nothingness, into eternal death,"[802] as "nothingness," as the "impossible possibility," and as the "ontological impossibility." [803] Sin constitutes humanity's greatest dilemma, for it is "the ground of humanity's hopeless destiny in death," and "the source … of the destruction which threatens humanity." Because sin ruptures humanity's relationship with God, Jesus Christ's reconciling work overcomes both this separation and the destruction sin entails. He does so "by treading the way of sinners to its bitter end in death" and thereby removing sin, and the eternal death to which sin leads, from humanity.[804] Apart from God's intervention in Jesus Christ, humanity remains helplessly unable to free itself from its self-chosen destruction.

In order to console those who suffer, we must draw near to the afflicted and open our lives to them as we humbly accept their invitation to enter their lives. In the archetypal, determinative pastoral act, reflected and echoed in all subsequent moments of pastoral ministry, God the Son draws near to suffering humanity in Jesus Christ by becoming fully human without

---

[801] Barth, 225: "The activity of the Son of Man, as an actualisation of His Word and commentary on it, necessarily has the crucial and decisive form of liberation, redemption, restoration, normalization." See also p. 232.

[802] Karl Barth, *The Church Dogmatics* IV/1, ed. G. W. Bromiley and Thomas F. Torrance, trans. G. W. Bromiley (Edinburgh: T & T Clark, 1956), 213.

[803] Karl Barth, *The Church Dogmatics* IV/3.1, G. W. Bromiley and Thomas F. Torrance, trans. G. W. Bromiley (New York: T & T Clark, 1961), 178–179.

[804] Barth, *Church Dogmatics* IV/1, 252–253, revised.

ceasing to be fully God. Christology, in this way, provides the foundation for reconciliation, and by extension, for the pastoral ministry that proclaims and demonstrates this reconciliation. In "The Way of the Son of God into the Far Country" (*Church Dogmatics* IV/1), Barth offers several presuppositions that form the core of his Christology, which anchors "everything that follows"[805] and "which, at all costs, we must accept and affirm."[806] First, God in Jesus Christ is the One who acts and who alone reconciles humanity with God. "When we have to do with Jesus Christ we have to do with God."[807] Christ's exclusively unique status as God and human entails that Christ's person and work reveal the being and act of God. Therefore, when Christ draws near to those in need and acts with compassion toward those in distress, we see God in flesh extending mercy to sinful, suffering humanity. Second, in Jesus Christ, God acts within the contexts and processes of human life and culture, within "the sphere of human and world history."[808] Here Barth emphasizes God's nearness to humanity, the proximity God attains by entering into human life in the person of Jesus Christ. Third, Barth argues that Jesus Christ reveals God to us in his humiliation and suffering: "Everything depends ... on our seeing and understanding ... the proper being of the one true God in Jesus Christ the Crucified." In light of this, we must "accept the humiliation and lowliness and supremely the obedience of Christ as the dominating moment in our conception of God." Jesus Christ reveals God's condescending, compassionate, and pursuing love by standing in "solidarity with the creature," by "bring[ing] help where there is no other help," and by setting humanity free from its sin and suffering.[809]

C. God Confronts the Source of Affliction

"in all our afflictions ..." – 2 Corinthians 1:4b

God in Jesus Christ draws near to us by taking on human flesh, acting within human history, and revealing Godself to us. Christ then confronts the source of humanity's affliction: its sin-caused separation from God. Karl

---

[805] Barth, 211.

[806] Barth, 197. As Gustaf Aulén aptly states, "The Incarnation is the necessary presupposition of the Atonement, and the Atonement the completion of the Incarnation." Gustaf Aulén, *Christus Victor: An Historical Study of the Three Main Types of the Idea of Atonement*, trans. A. G. Hebert (New York: Macmillan, 1961), 151. For more on the inseparability of Christ's person and work, see George Hunsinger, "Karl Barth's Christology: Its Basic Calcedonian Character (1999)," in *Disruptive Grace: Studies in the Theology of Karl Barth*, (Grand Rapids: Eerdmans, 2000), 131–132, fn 2.

[807] Barth, 198.

[808] Barth, 198.

[809] Barth, 199.

Barth speaks of this process in "The Judge Judged in Our Place" (*Church Dogmatics* IV/1), and "Jesus is Victor" (*Church Dogmatics* IV/3.1).

Scripture employs diverse metaphors to portray the reconciliation of humanity with God in Jesus Christ. In "The Judge Judged in Our Place," Barth describes atonement using four forensic statements that he then re-expresses in priestly terms. Through these statements, Barth attempts to explain how "Jesus Christ was and is 'for us'"[810] by acting "as our Representative and Substitute."[811] First, "Jesus Christ was and is for us" because he took our place as the judge. According to Barth, "All sin has its being and origin in the fact that humanity wants to be its own judge."[812] Often we are tempted to view ourselves as judges qualified to declare ourselves innocent and others guilty. "Not all people commit all sins, but all people commit this sin which is the essence and root of all other sins."[813] Jesus Christ enters "that place"[814] in which humanity has set itself up as the judge, and removes humanity from this place, for the right to judge belongs to God alone. As Christ takes his rightful place as the judge, the substitutionary logic of atonement, and Christ's solidarity with afflicted humanity, begin to come into view: by reclaiming the place of the judge, Jesus Christ saves us from ourselves,[815] and demonstrates that "He is radically and totally for us, in our place."[816] Corresponding to the forensic imagery of Christ as the judge, Barth depicts Christ as the High Priest who serves as humanity's "mediator and representative" before God.[817] By achieving reconciliation between humanity and God, the great atonement foreshadowed by the ministry of the Levitical priesthood in the O.T., Jesus offers humanity "peace with God, access to Him, and hope in Him (cf. Heb 10:19f with Rom 5:1f)."[818]

Second, "Jesus Christ was and is for us" by taking our place as sinners. Because our decision to judge ourselves and others constitutes "our basic sin," and "All our other sins, both small and great, derive ultimately from this source,"[819] the place of the judge has become the place of sinners. When

---

[810] Barth, 231.

[811] Barth, 230.

[812] Barth, 220; see also 231.

[813] Barth, 220, revised.

[814] Barth, 232, where Barth speaks of "that place where every person is in his inner being supremely by and for himself."

[815] Barth, 216–217.

[816] Barth, 232.

[817] Barth, 275.

[818] Barth, 276–277.

[819] Barth, 235.

Jesus takes back the place of the judge, which rightfully belongs to him as God, he also occupies the place of sinners as the sinless one standing in representative solidarity for all sinners. By doing so, Jesus "gives Himself ... to the fellowship of those who are guilty," makes "their evil case His own," and bears their "accusation and sentence."[820] Jesus removes humanity from the place of its sinful judging, and in doing so Jesus also removes sin from humanity, making it his own along with "the accusation, the judgment, and the curse which necessarily fall on us there."[821] As God, Jesus Christ judges sin. As human, Jesus Christ bears God's judgment to spare the people God loves from suffering the penalty for sin.

Third, "Jesus Christ was and is for us" because he suffered and died. Christ's death is unique and unrepeatable in several ways. First, Jesus did not merely suffer his death passively. He also "willed" this event. Therefore, Christ's death was both a passion and an action. Second, Jesus' death occurred at "a very definite point in world history which cannot be exchanged for any other." This contextual anchoring prevents his death from being viewed as a timeless myth. In fact, the historical particularity of Christ's death grounds its universal relevance. Third, in light of the hypostatic union, "this human action and suffering" is "the passion of God Himself," which cannot be said of any other instance of human suffering.[822] If Jesus were only human and not also divine, then his crucifixion would not be unique at all; it would fade into human history as simply another instance of brutal suffering and death. By making this claim, Barth in no sense intends to minimize either human suffering in general or the specific forms of physical suffering experienced by Jesus on the cross.[823] Rather, he is arguing that the singularity of Christ's death lies elsewhere than in the magnitude of his physical suffering. The exclusive uniqueness of Christ's suffering and death derives from "the person and mission of the One who suffered there."[824] In Jesus Christ, God enters into and experiences suffering and death as a human person. As a unique and unrepeatable act, Christ's

---

[820] Barth, 236.

[821] Barth, 236–237.

[822] Barth, 245.

[823] Indeed, Barth acknowledges the profundity of every experience of suffering: "Even if it is only the whimper of a sick child it has in it as such something which in its own way is infinitely outstanding and moving and ... something which we can even describe as shattering." Ibid., 246. Christ, in his suffering, experienced the shattering crisis common to all instances of human suffering. Because of this, the intensity of Christ's physical suffering points to his solidarity with afflicted humanity, and the uniqueness of his suffering lies elsewhere.

[824] Barth, *Church Dogmatics* IV/1, 246.

passion "objectively" and "decisively" changes humanity's relationship with God[825] by reconciling "the world with God."[826]

On the cross, God in Jesus Christ confronts "the destruction which threatens all creation and every individual," "eternal death," "the power of that which is not," and "sin itself and as such." Because Jesus uniquely "wrestle[s] with" sin, suffering, and death on the cross, "His passion has a real dimension of depth which it alone can have in the whole series of human passions." God in Jesus Christ overcomes the sin that separates humanity from God and the "corruption" that arises as the result of sin. "In the place of all people He has Himself wrestled with that which separates them from Him. He has Himself borne the consequence of this separation to bear it away."[827] Jesus Christ's suffering and death, grounded in the exclusive uniqueness of his person as God and human, achieves the reconciliation of the world with God.[828]

Barth's priestly portrayal of atonement integrates the second and third elements of his forensic account (Christ took our place as sinners, and Christ suffered and died): Christ is both the "one true Priest" who offers the sacrifice for sin, and he himself is the "one true sacrifice." As Priest, Christ removes humanity's sin by offering himself as the eternally effective sacrifice.[829] As he does in his forensic depiction, Barth places expiation (i.e. the removal of sin and sinners) at the center of his priestly account of atonement. Through Christ's sacrifice on the cross, God "shed our wicked blood in His own precious blood" and "kill[ed] our sin in His own death."[830] By removing our sin and ourselves as sinners, Jesus removes the obstacle to our reconciliation with God and unites us in fellowship with our Creator.

Fourth, "Jesus Christ was and is for us" because he acted rightly before God. Jesus displays his righteousness in the place of human disobedience by acting "justly in our place."[831] On the cross, Christ acts in "the fulness of a positive divine righteousness" which reveals "the free love of God effectively interposing between our enmity and Himself."[832] Jesus provides in himself "the obedience of the creature" to God, which is the righteousness

---

[825] Barth, 245.

[826] Barth, 246–247.

[827] Barth, 247, revised.

[828] Barth, 251–252. For Barth, the "decisive" means of reconciliation is expiation, i.e. the removal of sin and of ourselves as sinners (pp. 253–254).

[829] Barth, 277.

[830] Barth, 280.

[831] Barth, 273.

[832] Barth, 257.

humanity lacks.[833] He does this in our place by acknowledging God as the Judge, accepting the rightness of God's judgment against sinners, bearing this judgment as humanity's representative before God, and thereby reconciling humanity with God.

In priestly terms, Christ is the "perfect sacrifice" that takes the place of "all the sacrifices offered by people."[834] The perfection of Christ's sacrifice consists of his obedience to God's will by which he converts disobedient humanity to God in his own person and puts to death humanity's sin in his own death.[835] Furthermore, the removal of sin and the establishment of human righteousness in Jesus Christ inaugurates the social transformation of human community: "The doing of evil ceases..... The violent are now restrained, the orphans are helped to their right and the cause of the widow is taken up (Isa 1:16f)."[836]

Christ further consoles us in our affliction through the victory he attains on the cross, which Barth describes in "Jesus is Victor," (*Church Dogmatics* IV/3.1). Here Barth describes the atonement in royal imagery within a section of the *Church Dogmatics* devoted to Christ's prophetic office. This placement indicates that Christ's victory (royal office) provides the content of Christ's prophetic self-witness.[837] As Jesus prophetically declares humanity's reconciliation with God, a clash ensues between the "light" he reveals and the utter darkness of humanity's sinful condition.[838] In this conflict, the light of Jesus Christ exposes darkness for what it is and attacks "sin, death and the devil" with "the incomparable, living, effective and penetrating sword of Heb 4:12."[839] People themselves do not constitute the darkness opposed by Jesus Christ, though darkness deeply influences humanity. Instead, Jesus Christ "attack[s] and force[s] on the defensive" an element within humanity that opposes reconciliation.[840] Jesus extends his grace to people while confronting "the resisting element in [them]" that opposes God's grace.[841] At every point, this conflict exhibits a clear

---

[833] Barth, 257.

[834] Barth, 281, revised.

[835] Barth, 281–282.

[836] Barth, 281.

[837] See Colin E. Gunton, *The Actuality of Atonement: A Study of Metaphor, Rationality and the Christian Tradition*, (Grand Rapids: William B. Eerdmans, 1989), 78. John Webster, *Barth's Moral Theology: Human Action in Barth's Thought* (Edinburgh: T & T Clark, 1998), 139.

[838] For this reason, Christ's prophetic ministry may be described as "a history of conflict." Barth, *Church Dogmatics* IV/3.1, 237.

[839] Barth, *Church Dogmatics* IV/3, 238, see also 239.

[840] Barth, 251, see also

[841] Barth, 272.

direction, in which light confronts darkness, and an assured conclusion, in which Jesus Christ victoriously inaugurates the peace, joy, and freedom of reconciliation with God.[842] Even though this conflict rages, and we experience Christ's victory as a "'still' and 'not yet'"[843] reality under the current conditions of our lives, Jesus Christ ensures the final outcome due to his "unconditional superiority" as the Word of God.[844]

D. God Removes the Suffering Caused by Sin

"in all our afflictions ..." – 2 Corinthians 1:4b

For Barth, God in Jesus Christ "consoles us in all our afflictions" (2 Corinthians 1:4b) by healing both the relational rupture between God and humanity, and the suffering caused by sin. To understand the full consolation achieved through Christ's cross in Barth's thought, we must first examine the connection between sin and suffering.

In "The Mercy and Righteousness of God" (*Church Dogmatics* II/1), Barth highlights three links between sin and suffering. First, sin intrinsically entails suffering, and misery inseparably adjoins sin.[845] One cannot sin without the sinful act damaging the sinner in such a way that the sin in and of itself becomes a form of suffering. Second, sin leads to suffering as the "punishment" and "judgment" of sin.[846] Third, suffering is the consequence and inevitable result of sin.[847] Sinful choices lead to painful outcomes. As a consequence of sin, affliction may arise not only due to one's own sin but also as the result of the sin of others. Though all remain sinners before God, those who suffer the undeserved consequences of other people's sin suffer innocently. This recognition opens the door for theological discussions of

---

[842] Barth, 237–238, 246–248, 251–252.

[843] Barth, 262–263.

[844] Barth, 266–267.

[845] Barth, *Church Dogmatics* II/1, he said, "Arrogance is seen as pitiable folly, the usurpation of freedom as rigorous bondage, evil lust as bitter torment." See also Barth, *Church Dogmatics* II/1, 144, 220, and 436.

[846] Barth, *Church Dogmatics* II/1, 371. Elsewhere, *Church Dogmatics* II/1, 253, Barth said, "We can say indeed that [Jesus Christ] fulfils this judgment by suffering the punishment which we have all brought on ourselves." See also *CD* III/3, 275; *CD* IV/1, 12, 553; *CD* IV/2, 223. Wolf Krötke, *Sin and Nothingness in the Theology of Karl Barth*, ed. David Willis, trans. Philip G. Ziegler and Christina-Maria Bammel, vol. 10, *Studies in Reformed Theology and History* (Princeton: Princeton Theological Seminary, 2005), 79; see also 77–78, 81. David Lauber, *Barth on the Descent into Hell: God, Atonement and the Christian Life* (Aldershot: Ashgate, 2004), 36. Bruce L. McCormack, *For Us and Our Salvation: Incarnation and Atonement in the Reformed Tradition*, ed. David Willis-Watkins, *Studies in Reformed Theology and History* (Princeton: Princeton Theological Seminary, 1993), 30–32.

[847] Barth, *CD* II/1, 371. See also Karl Barth, *CD* III/3, 310–311; *CD* IV/1, 436. Karl Barth, "Poverty," in *Against the Stream: Shorter Post-War Writings, 1946–52*, ed. Ronald Gregor Smith (New York: Philosophical Library, 1954), 245. Dahm, 134–135. Krötke, 68.

"victims" (i.e. those who suffer innocently) and of "injustice" (i.e. the sinful actions that cause the suffering of victims).[848]

When considering forms of suffering arising from random, accidental events or "natural evils," we usually cannot identify an unjust human cause. When Jesus' disciples see a blind man in John 9:2–3, they ask, "Rabbi, who sinned, this man or his parents, that he was born blind?" Jesus' response is instructive: "Neither this man nor his parents sinned; he was born blind so that God's works might be revealed in him" (NRSV). Likewise, we cannot assign blame. Christ's words suggest that certain types of suffering are not directly caused by prior sin, neither the sin of the sufferer nor the sin of others. Furthermore, Barth reminds us that, in light of Christ's atoning work, the question of human guilt in relation to certain forms of human suffering, like genetic defects or natural disasters for which no one is directly responsible, becomes groundless. All are guilty of sin, and Christ offers his righteousness to all.[849] At the same time, in "The Pride of Humanity" (*Church Dogmatics* IV/1),[850] Barth argues that humanity's sin causes "the irruption of chaos" within "the sphere of creation."[851] Although no specific person may be blamed for random maladies, natural disasters, or devastating accidents, sinful humanity as a whole twists God's good creation, and this distortion then leads to various afflictions in the natural order. In this way, sinful humanity collectively bears some responsibility for the suffering caused by natural evils.

According to Barth, when Christ confronts sin on the cross, he also confronts human affliction in the diversity and complexity of its forms, including the suffering caused by random accidents and natural disasters. Christ's crucifixion "reveal[s]" the significance of seemingly every form of human suffering, even "the great catastrophes of nature and history."[852] Natural evils, whose relation to prior sin is not self-evident, receive similar status under the current, fallen conditions of our lives as the affliction directly caused by unjust human action. When Jesus Christ removes sin, and the suffering arising from sin, he opens the way for the healing of human affliction in all its forms.[853]

---

[848] George Hunsinger, "The Sinner and the Victim," in *T & T Clark Companion to the Doctrine of Sin*, edited by Keith L. Johnson and David Lauber, (New York: T & T Clark, 2016), 433–450.

[849] See Karl Barth, "Johannes 9, 13 (1938)," in *Karl Barth Gesamtausgabe: Predigten 1935–1952*, ed. Hartmut Spieker and Hinrich Stoevesandt (Zürich: Theologischer Verlag Zürich, 1996), 115–118.

[850] Barth, *Church Dogmatics* IV/1, revised.

[851] Barth, 436.

[852] Barth, *Church Dogmatics* II/1, 395.

[853] While maintaining the connection between sin and suffering, Barth complexifies the picture further by speculating that natural death and some accidents would still occur in a sinless state as part of

[*Footnote continued on next page*]

E. Our Pastoral Response

"so that we may be able to console those who are in any affliction with the consolation with which we ourselves are consoled by God."

– 2 Corinthians 1:4c

Barth argues in "The Mercy and Righteousness of God" (*Church Dogmatics* II/1) that God calls humanity, upon whom God has mercy, to respond by extending God's mercy to others. As John Webster writes, "Grace is imperatival." [854] Christians must recognize the ethical responsibility given to all people that corresponds to God's reconciling work in Jesus Christ. Simply put, God's righteousness determines the character of the human righteousness God requires. Throughout the O.T., we see that God consistently acts to aid "the poor, the widows and orphans, the weak and defenseless."[855] Likewise, through the incarnation of Jesus Christ, God turns to sinners whose inability to achieve God's righteousness reduces them to desperate need.[856] Christians recognize that in God's sight they themselves are "the poor and wretched," and therefore they recognize the deep solidarity that binds them to all who are poor and afflicted around them, as well as their duty to respond in mercy by consoling sufferers and alleviating their affliction.[857] The human righteousness that responds in obedience to God's call conforms, therefore, to God's righteousness by possessing "necessarily the character of a vindication of right in favour of the threatened innocent, the oppressed poor, widows, orphans and aliens."[858] This human righteousness entails "a very definite political problem and task,"[859] "a political attitude," and "a political responsibility,"[860] determined

---

God's good order of creation. He calls this the "'shadow side' of creation.'" Barth, *CD* III/3, 350. See also Karl Barth, *Church Dogmatics* III/1, ed. G. W. Bromiley and T. F. Torrance, trans. O. Bussey J. W. Edwards, Harold Knight (Edinburgh: T. and T. Clark, 1958), 372, 380–382; Karl Barth, *The Church Dogmatics* III/2, ed. Geoffrey W. Bromiley and Thomas F. Torrance, trans. Geoffrey W. Bromiley Harold Knight, J. K. S. Reid, R. H. Fuller (Edinburgh: T & T Clark, 1960), 598, 631–632; Barth, *CD* III/3, 297. Because we do not live in a sinless state, we cannot imagine sinless physical death or accidents. Within the fallen conditions of our lives, Barth argues that all suffering maintains a connection to sin. Sin amplifies and distorts the natural evils that may have existed in an unfallen state, rendering their original, unfallen character inaccessible to our fallen imaginations.

[854] John Webster, *Barth's Ethics of Reconciliation* (Cambridge: Cambridge University Press, 1995), 51.

[855] Barth, *CD* II/1, 386; see also 387; William Werpehowski, "Karl Barth and politics," in *The Cambridge Companion to Karl Barth*, ed. John Webster, (New York: Cambridge University Press, 2000), 236–237.

[856] Barth, *Church Dogmatics* II/1, 387.

[857] Barth, 387.

[858] Barth, 386.

[859] Barth, 386.

[860] Barth, 387.

by the human need the Christian encounters. Those who recognize God's mercy and righteousness in Jesus Christ cannot view human need without understanding that they are "made responsible to all those who are poor and wretched in [their] eyes, that [they are] summoned ... to espouse the cause of those who suffer wrong." Christians seek to console those in affliction through alleviating their distress for the simple reason that Christians see their own spiritual poverty before God in the world's material poverty.[861] Profound solidarity, therefore, infuses the Christian's interaction with the vulnerable, the poor, the distressed, the grieving, and the oppressed. As they recognize their solidarity with the afflicted, Christians receive the obligation to do all they can to relieve misery as an extension of the mercy they themselves have received. Any other response by Christians to those who suffer, Barth argues, constitutes a rejection of their own justification.[862]

We may draw further insights regarding the Christian duty to console those who suffer from "The Way of the Son of God into the Far Country," (*Church Dogmatics* IV/1). Philippians 2:7–8 describes Christ emptying himself in humility by "taking the form of a slave, being born in human likeness" and by being "obedient to the point of death – even death on a cross," (NRSV). Christ's downward movement in humility, though, cannot be separated from his upward movement: "Therefore God also highly exalted him and gave him the name that is above every name ..." (Phil 2:9). Philippians 2:3 instructs Christians to display "the same mind ... that was in Christ Jesus ..." Therefore, the movement of *kenosis*, which entails humility and exaltation, extends from Christ to encompass those who follow "in His steps" by "looking to Christ and His way as an example."[863] Profound implications result for Christian ministry and ethics as Christ leads us "from the heights to the depths, from riches to poverty, from victory to defeat, from triumph to suffering, from life to death ..." We live and serve under the sign of the cross "in fellowship with the Crucified."[864] By grounding the Christian's service in Jesus Christ's *kenosis*, Barth avoids valorizing self-sacrifice as an end in itself.[865] Christians have only one goal: following Jesus

---

[861] Barth, 387.

[862] Barth, 387.

[863] Barth, 189. Barth speaks of the "law" of humility as "the one binding law for both the Head and the members, for Jesus and His people, and because for Jesus therefore also for His people." Barth, *CD* IV/1, 189.

[864] Barth, *Church Dogmatics* II/1, 190. George Hunsinger relates Christ's *kenosis* in Barth's thought to the "enemy-love" at "the heart of the gospel." Hunsinger, "The Politics of the Nonviolent God: Reflections on René Girard and Karl Barth (1998)," in *Disruptive Grace: Studies in the Theology of Karl Barth*, (Grand Rapids: Eerdmans, 2000), 35, 37–38.

[865] Barth, *Church Dogmatics* II/1, 191–192.

Christ wherever he leads. Their path will move downward in obedience and service, yet along this path they will also arise in newness of life.[866]

Christian service occurs within the broader context of participation in Christ's prophetic work, which Barth addresses in "The Vocation of Humanity," (*Church Dogmatics* IV/3.2).[867] Jesus Christ's "self-declaration" establishes the Christian vocation of witness to the "Word of reconciliation," the joyful news of humanity's union with God in Jesus Christ.[868] Christians then find themselves incorporated within a "community of action"[869] in which they are called, which "means being given a task," and led into vocation, the "execution of this task."[870] Christian vocation consists of speech and action that witness to Jesus Christ's reconciling work.[871] This "twofold ... unity" follows the pattern of ministry established by Christ's incarnation, ministry, death, and resurrection by which he models "speech which is also action ... and action which is also speech."[872] Although Christ's proclamation often precedes and elucidates his actions, both contain his "self-declaration."[873] In a similar way, Christians attest to Christ's self-revelation and the reality of reconciliation with God through speech and action. In fact, both activities communicate the same content, for when Christians act they declare "the same thing in another way, with the speech of their acts, with their hands as well as their lips."[874]

One way that Christians proclaim with their actions the reality of humanity's reconciliation with God is through diaconal service, which demonstrates with unique clarity the liberation from affliction made possible

---

[866] Christians experience *kenosis* and exaltation in analogy to, and in participation with, Christ's *kenosis* and exaltation. Their *kenosis* is their humble service to others, and their exaltation is their reconciliation with God, which entails their vivification and liberation. Barth follows Calvin in regarding *participatio Christi* as the basis of Christian sanctification. Barth, *CD* IV/2, 581.

[867] Barth, *Church Dogmatics* IV/3.2, 481–680, title revised.

[868] Barth, 481–482. See also Webster, *Barth's Moral Theology*, 142. George Hunsinger, *How to Read Karl Barth: The Shape of His Theology* (New York: Oxford University Press, 1991), 275.

[869] Barth, *Church Dogmatics* IV/3.2, 597.

[870] Barth, 573–574.

[871] Barth, 860–862.

[872] Barth, *Church Dogmatics* IV/3.2, 862. In an early essay, Barth writes, "Jesus by word and deed opposed the material misery which *ought not to be*. Indeed, he did so by instilling persons with the Spirit which transforms matter. ... He worked from the internal to the external. He created new men in order to create a new world." Karl Barth, "Jesus Christ and the Movement for Social Justice (1911)," in *Karl Barth and Radical Politics*, edited by George Hunsinger, (Philadelphia: Westminster, 1976), 28, italics in original.

[873] Barth, *Church Dogmatics* IV/3.2, 862.

[874] Barth, *Church Dogmatics* IV/3.2.

by Jesus Christ.[875] While recognizing that poverty takes many forms,[876] and that every aspect of Christian life must exhibit the character of service, Barth follows the tradition in calling the church's ministries to aid those in physical and economic distress "the diaconate" (from διακονία). [877] Christians console those who suffer by "explicitly accept[ing] solidarity with the least of little ones ... with those who are pushed to the margin ... with fellow-creatures who temporarily at least, and perhaps permanently, are useless and insignificant and perhaps even burdensome and destructive."[878] According to Matthew 25, the church through its diaconal service declares these people to be the "brothers [and sisters] of Jesus Christ" and attests to God's solidarity with suffering humanity through the incarnation. If the church neglects this task, then "even though its proclamation of Christ is otherwise ever so powerful, it stands hopelessly on the left hand among the goats" and its witness becomes "futile."[879]

Diaconal ministry remains intrinsically modest, because the tremendous amount of unmet need in our world will continually overshadow its accomplishments. In addition, because diaconal ministry serves those furthest removed from the world's attention and concern, it occurs without fanfare or acclaim in the unsung, unnoticed acts that console those forgotten and abandoned by others. This service constitutes one form of "the good deed which corresponds to the good Word," which permits "the good Word to be understood in the fulness of its truth."[880]

F. The Cross We Bear

"For just as the sufferings of Christ are abundant for us ..." – 2 Corinthians 1:5a

Christians quickly discover that their proclamation of Christ's reconciliation, through word and deed, increases their own need for

---

[875] Barth's comments on Christian diaconal service occur within the context of a broader examination of various ministries given to Christians as part of their prophetic vocation of witness. These ministries, like prophetic witness itself, always entail both speech and action. For Barth, speech always precedes and elucidates the meaning of the action. Although diaconal service seems to emphasize Christian action, we must regard this service as action inseparably united to speech. Therefore, the proclamation of the gospel (evangelism) and ministries that promote social justice (diaconal service) must operate hand in hand. Cf. Barth, *Church Dogmatics* IV/3.2, 865–901.

[876] Barth, *Church Dogmatics* IV/3.2, 243, where Barth acknowledges that poverty may appear in sociological, physical, relational, intellectual, and spiritual forms.

[877] Barth, 889: "Diaconate means quite simply and generally the rendering of service."

[878] Barth, 891.

[879] Barth, "The Christian Community and the Civil Community," in *Against the Stream: Shorter Post-War Writings, 1946–1952*, ed. Ronald Gregor Smith, (New York: Philosophical Library, 1954), 34, 46, 47. See also Jane A. Barter, "A Theology of Liberation in Barth's *Church Dogmatics* IV/3," *Scottish Journal of Theology*, 53 (2000): 174.

[880] Barth, *Church Dogmatics* IV/3.2, 892.

consolation as they follow in the costly steps of the Crucified. As an inseparable aspect of their prophetic witness, Christians receive a cross in analogy, correspondence, and witness to Christ's cross.[881] Due to the exclusive uniqueness of Christ's person and work, Christians do not in any way contribute to the reconciliation of the world with God that Christ accomplishes no matter how similar their suffering may appear on the surface to Christ's own. Nevertheless, Christians do experience an echo, a reflection, and an aftershock of Christ's affliction as they step forward in faithful witness to the reconciliation Christ accomplishes.[882] As mentioned previously, this acknowledgment in no way entails the valorization of suffering, as though it were an experience to be sought out. Christians possess a firm grasp of life's true character, purpose, and value, and therefore see suffering's destructiveness in its true light. In response, they rightly avoid suffering whenever possible. Yet, the "life-movement"[883] of sanctification leads along a path that will be intersected, literally "crossed through,"[884] by the affliction inseparable from discipleship. "To save his life [the Christian] must surrender and lose it. He will not seek or induce this loss. It will come to him."[885]

Three sources cause this suffering. First, the world responds harshly to the consoling proclamation of humanity's reconciliation with God, which it perceives as "monstrous presumption and insolent demand."[886] In the "Yes" of reconciliation with God, proclaimed by Christians, the world hears God's "No" toward its attempts to construct a godless life.[887] The world then responds by declaring its own "much more energetic No," and reacts with "oppressive counter pressure" to the "pressure" it perceives in Christian witness.[888] Christians in this way often suffer the world's negative response to their joyful, consoling proclamation. Second, affliction comes upon

---

[881] Barth, *Church Dogmatics* IV/2, 609–613. Christians bear a cross in the form of persecution, the suffering and death intrinsic to human life, and temptations in the form of severe doubts.

[882] Barth, *Church Dogmatics* IV/2, 598–605. In this section, Barth carefully enumerates the differences between Christ's cross and the Christian's cross. Christ alone reconciles humanity with God, Christ alone experiences God's rejection, Christ is uniquely exalted, and Christ alone bears his cross in spotless obedience.

[883] Barth, *Church Dogmatics* IV/2, 601–602. See Stanley Hauerwas, *Character and the Christian Life: A Study in Theological Ethics* (San Antonio: Trinity University Press, 1985), 208–209.

[884] Barth, *Church Dogmatics* IV/2, 602. Barth speaks of the cross (das Kreuz) "crossing through" (*durchkreuzen*) the believer's life. Karl Barth *Kirchliche Dogmatik* IV/2, (Zürich: Theologischer, 1980), 680.

[885] Barth, *Church Dogmatics* IV/2, 603.

[886] Barth, *Church Dogmatics* IV/3.2, 620.

[887] Barth, 622.

[888] Barth, 623.

Christians because of their refusal to avoid the reality of their calling as Christ's witnesses, or to change the content of their witness.[889] Instead of offering "easy and cheap" words, they proclaim God's "Yes" to humanity, which "is necessarily enclosed in the No which [humanity] never like[s] to hear."[890] Finally, Christians suffer because they enter deep fellowship with Jesus Christ along their path of prophetic witness, and this fellowship entails affliction "grounded ... in the affliction of Jesus Christ."[891] Christians witness to a world "shaken and threatened to its foundations" by Christ's self-witness.[892] As they point to Christ, therefore, Christians bring upon themselves the same opposition the world directs against him, and their suffering distinctly reflects his own.[893]

G. The Consolation We Receive

"so also our consolation is abundant through Christ." – 2 Corinthians 1:5b

Christ mercifully consoles Christians in their suffering. While their own well-being must never motivate Christians in their vocation of witness, for their life circumstances remain subordinate to their calling,[894] Barth argues that they will nonetheless experience the confirmation of "the content of [their] witness"[895] in the form of "the benefits which Christ has won for the whole world and for all people."[896] By selflessly proclaiming the world's reconciliation with God, and bearing the affliction that attends their prophetic vocation, Christians advance their "own best interests."[897] For Barth, the consolation of liberation encompasses both the spiritual and material dimensions of life as a holistic experience of the benefits of salvation granted to Christians through union with Christ.[898]

---

[889] Barth, 626.

[890] Barth, 627.

[891] Barth, *Church Dogmatics* IV/3.2, 634 and 639. Cf. George Hunsinger, "The Politics of the Nonviolent God," 39.

[892] Barth, *Church Dogmatics* IV/3.2, 634.

[893] In *Church Dogmatics* IV/2, 607–609, Barth examines the four-fold sanctifying function of the Christian's cross. Through their suffering, they gain humility, a reminder of the punishment they have been spared, increased faith, obedience, and love, and certain "verifications" of God's activity in their lives due to their increased dependence upon the Holy Spirit. These confirmations of God's activity may take the form of works that are "more tested and purified and substantial, and may indeed be better and greater, than ever before."

[894] Barth, *Church Dogmatics* IV/3.2, 652.

[895] Barth, 648–649.

[896] Barth, 651–652, revised.

[897] Barth, 653.

[898] George Hunsinger notes that Barth follows Luther and Calvin by interpreting I Corinthians 1:30 to mean that "Only through union with the person of Christ c[an] his saving benefits be received, for

[*Footnote continued on next page*]

Counterintuitively, this consolation flows to Christians as they subvert their own self-actualization by stepping forward in selfless service to God and their neighbors. A mutually reinforcing dialectic then unfolds in which the Christian serves "God who points him to his neighbour" and "his neighbour who points him to God."[899] By serving God and suffering humanity through the proclamation in speech and action of humanity's reconciliation with God, Christians experience the reality of the message they proclaim, the consolation of their own liberation, which entails "peace and joy, and even great peace and great joy."[900] In this way, although Christians will not seek their own liberation as they proclaim reconciliation, they will nevertheless receive liberating consolation as an intrinsic aspect of their prophetic vocation of witness.

Conclusion—The God of All Comfort

Karl Barth's theology of the cross traces God's pastoral consolation in Jesus Christ, which establishes the content and pattern of our pastoral ministries today. The God of all comfort turns to us in mercy and consoles us in our affliction by confronting and removing the source of our distress, the sin that leads to our suffering. Our compassionate God then calls us to extend the consolation we have received by proclaiming, through speech and action, humanity's reconciliation with God to those around us. As we do so, we bear the affliction and liberation that accompany our vocation of witness. Our ministries to those who suffer occur under the sign of the cross, and God's consolation flows in and through those who tread in the footsteps of the Crucified. Karl Barth's theology of reconciliation in this way aligns to the character, ordering, and structure of 2 Corinthians 1:3–5, and reveals the pastoral commitment that undergirds Barth's thought. Furthermore, Barth demonstrates the deficiency of isolating ministries of consolation from their basis in the doctrine of atonement on one hand, and, on the other hand, of speaking of Christ's cross without reference to its pastoral implications. Understood in this way, the atonement enfolds pastoral concerns, such as our entrance into others' suffering for their consolation, and pastoral ministries point to the cross of Jesus Christ, where God entered into human suffering for the salvation and consolation of the world.

Christ and his benefits [a]re one." George Hunsinger, "Barth on Jesus, Lord of Time (Hebrews 13:8)," in *Evangelical, Catholic, and Reformed*, George Hunsinger (Grand Rapids: Eerdmans, 2015), 260.

[899] Barth, *Church Dogmatics* IV/3.2, 652.

[900] Barth, 654.

23.
Disability and Suffering?—
Pastoral and Practical Theological Considerations

Dr. Amos Yong
Dean, School of Mission and Theology
Professor of Theology and Mission
School of Intercultural Studies
Fuller Theological Seminary, Pasadena, California[901]

Abstract	361
Introduction	362
A. Why "Suffering" Is a Bad Word in Disability Rights and Disability Studies Circles	364
B. Why Suffering Is a Problem for People with Disabilities	367
List 1. Four Social Constructs of Disability	369
C. "Four Fences" in Providence and in Pastoral Theology of Suffering Disability	371
List 2. Four Fences of Disability in Divine Providence	371
List 3. Four Fences on a Theology of Suffering Disability	371
D. "Suffering Disability": Redemptive Pastoral Praxis	374
Conclusion	377

Abstract

"Suffering" is a difficult topic at the crossroads of disability studies and pastoral care. On the one hand, people with disabilities want to clearly

---

[901] Yong earned his PhD from Boston University; his MA from Portland State University, Portland, Oregon; and another MA from Western Evangelical Seminary, Portland, Oregon. This article was first published "Disability and Suffering? Pastoral and Practical Theological Considerations," *Journal of the Christian Research Institute on Disability* 4, No. 1 (2015): 27-42, and permission was granted to republish in this book. He has published several books and over 200 articles, including *Theology and Down Syndrome: Reimagining Disability in Late Modernity* (Baylor University Press, 2007; 465 pp.); *The Future of Evangelical Theology—Soundings from the Asian American Diaspora* (IVP Academic, 2014; 255 pp.); *Renewing Christian Theology—Systematics for Global Christianity*, with Jonathan A. Anderson (Baylor University Press, 2014; 477 pp.); *Spirit of Love: A Trinitarian Theology of Grace* (Baylor University Press, 2012; 246 pp.); *The Bible, Disability, and the Church: A New Vision of the People of God* (Eerdmans, 2011; 161 pp.); *Cambridge Companion to Pentecostalism* (Cambridge University Press, 2014; 358 pp.); *Interdisciplinary and Religio-Cultural Discourses on a Spirit-Filled World—Loosing the Spirits*, co-edited with Veli-Matti Kärkkäinen and Kirsteen Kim (Palgrave Macmillan, 2013; 262 pp.); *Pneumatology and the Christian-Buddhist Dialogue—Does the Spirit Blow through the Middle Way?* Studies in Systematic Theology 11 (Brill, 2012; 359 pp.); *The Cosmic Breath—Spirit and Nature in the Christianity-Buddhism-Science Trialogue*, Philosophical Studies in Science and Religion 4 (Brill, 2012; 299 pp.); *The Spirit of Creation—Modern Science and Divine Action in the Pentecostal-Charismatic Imagination*, Pentecostal Manifestos 4 (Eerdmans, 2011; 252 pp.); *Who is the Holy Spirit? A Walk with the Apostles* (Paraclete Press, 2011; 231 pp.); *The Spirit Poured Out on All Flesh—Pentecostalism and the Possibility of Global Theology* (Baker Academic, 2005; 320 pp.); *In the Days of Caesar: Pentecostalism and Political Theology—The Cadbury Lectures 2009* (Eerdmans, 2010; 397 pp.), and *Beyond the Impasse—Toward a Pneumatological Theology of Religions* (Baker Academic, 2003; 207 pp.). See amosyong@fuller.edu.

distinguish impairments from the sense of suffering, urging that the latter does not necessarily follow the former. This is in part a reaction to historically paternalistic attitudes manifest in and through pastoral care directed to people with disabilities. This paper focuses on how to empower appropriately discerning pastoral praxis so that ecclesial ministry occurs *with* people with disabilities and their families/caregivers rather than only *to* them. Such an approach unfolds in solidarity with the genuine suffering of people with disabilities rather than perpetuates the kind of social stigmatization that causes existential and psychological pain even for those who do not otherwise suffer physically.

Introduction

It is often assumed that disability and suffering are interconnected.[902] This paper seeks to problematize the connections, albeit not just theoretically or theologically but in order to empower more appropriate religious and especially Christian praxis. Four parts follow:

A. Clarify why an uncritical equation of the two is problematic especially in light of contemporary disability rights and disability studies perspectives;
B. Explore how suffering follows disability, although not always as presupposed by those who are temporarily able-bodied (i.e., those who do not have disabilities[903]);
C. Sketch a pastoral theology of disability in dialogue with disability perspectives that minimizes the explicitly theological warrants for connecting suffering and disability; and
D. Propose a dual model of disability ministry and praxis in the face of real and perceived suffering.

The goal is to complicate the normate[904] assumptions linking disability and suffering in order to attend more appropriately—both in theory and practice—to such matters in ecclesial or faith communal contexts.

---

[902] This is reflected, for instance, in the title of Larry J. Waters and Roy B. Zuck, eds., *Why, O God? Suffering and Disability in the Bible and the Church* (Wheaton: Crossway, 2011). The contents of the book itself are more nuanced, and the decision on the title may reflect more the publisher's assumptions about how to market the book. But even in this case, that is precisely the point being made.

[903] Those in the disability rights movement have developed a new nomenclature regarding those different than they as the "temporarily able-bodied," i.e., those who are born dependent and, if they were lucky or blessed enough to live into old-age, will come again into dependency on others; see Kimberly Willis's guest editorial introducing the term to a theological audience, "Persons with Disabilities and the Temporarily Able-Bodied: Becoming the Body of Christ," *Liturgy* 23, no. 2 (2008): 1–2.

[904] "Normate" refers to that "socially constructed ideal image" through which definitive humanity is envisaged and the approximation toward which confers authority and power; it is therefore the unquestioned "glasses" through which temporarily able-bodied people see, evaluate, and engage the world, resulting in negative perceptions of and actions impacting people with disabilities. See Kerry H. Wynn, "The Normate Hermeneutic and Interpretations of Disability within the Yahwistic Narratives," in *This Abled Body: Rethinking Disabilities in Biblical Studies*, ed. Hector Avalos, Sarah J. Melcher, and Jeremy Schipper (Atlanta: Society of Biblical Literature, 2007), 91–101, esp. 92.

Before moving on, it is important to briefly define key terms and situate these reflections autobiographically. Disability as understood in the existing scholarly literature is not an obvious notion. It is standard within the field to distinguish *impairment* from *disability*, with the former pertaining to limitation or lack of certain physical, intellectual, or sensory capacities, and the latter involving the social, economic, and other disadvantages experienced as a result. A person could be profoundly deaf or severely hearing impaired, for instance; but if she could afford a cochlear implant or worked at her home computer as a manuscript editor, then she would not be considered as having a hearing disability. Yet the line between impairment and disability is not hard and fast; those who are chronically ill, as another example, may because of their condition perform sub-optimally as an employee but not be able to document their condition to qualify for disability status. The point is that there is both a personal and biological aspect to impairment even as there is a social dimension of understanding of how such impinges on human interactions in the broader context of public life.[905]

The final caveat is the important admission that I approach this topic not from firsthand experience of "suffering disability."[906] To be sure, the scare quotes around the phrase itself should signal that there is more to disability and impairment than what suffering is assumed to be, precisely what this paper is designed to elaborate. Nevertheless, I myself do not have an impairment, my 20-400 vision notwithstanding (alleviated by my corrective lenses for sure), so in that sense I do not have the same right as a person with a disability to speak to the topic at hand.[907] The extent of my experience of disability is having grown up with and cared for a younger brother with Down Syndrome. This has led me to reflect extensively on disability, especially from a religious and theological perspective.[908] The

---

[905] On the social aspects of disability, see Colin Barnes and Geof Mercer, *Exploring Disability: A Sociological Introduction*, 2nd Ed. (Cambridge: Polity Press, 2010), ch. 2; cf. Carol Thomas, *Female Forms: Experiencing and Understanding Disability* (Buckingham: Open University Press, 1999), ch. 3.

[906] Note that when "suffering disability" is used in relationship to people with disabilities, this does not presume (as under normate conditions) that all people with disabilities suffer from or merely because of their condition; instead it is used as shorthand in the rest of this paper to refer to those who actually suffer—or perceive themselves as suffering—whether physically, existentially, or in any other way, from their impairing conditions.

[907] In previous generations, people with disabilities were spoken for by others, but with the advent of the civil rights movement, followed quickly by disability rights awareness, people with disabilities are advocating for themselves and generally are suspicious that those without disability are adequately able to speak on their behalf; see, for instance, the manifesto by James I. Charlton, *Nothing about Us without Us: Disability Oppression and Empowerment* (Berkeley: University of California Press, 1998).

[908] My scholarly training is in religious studies and theology and my published work has been in systematic and constructive theology; my two books on disability are *Theology and Down Syndrome: Reimagining Disability in Late Modernity* (Waco: Baylor University Press, 2007) and *The Bible*,

[*Footnote continued on next page*]

following does not pretend to be the final word at the intersection where disability meets suffering; it is intended merely to be a catalyst for discussion and perhaps a prompt for attitudinal, behavioral, and practical adjustment, especially as that pertains to those ministering not only *to* but also *with* people with disabilities for the cause of the Christian gospel.

A. Why "Suffering" Is a Bad Word in Disability Rights and Disability Studies Circles

For the temporarily able-bodied, that disability and suffering are intertwined seems obvious. These associations are no doubt even stronger within religious, especially Christian, contexts. After all, there is a long history of Christian care for people with disabilities, stretching back through the medieval hospitals to the rise of monastic movements over 1500 years ago, which identified the vulnerable on the margins of society and sought to provide for their needs.[909] Many of those who were found in such hospice and hospital environments could not care for themselves and were stigmatized if not discriminated against by society.[910] In more recent times, people with disabilities have been publicly portrayed, through the freak-show and other media, in negative terms: as abnormal, even inhuman, objects of the temporarily able-bodied gaze.[911] Even with regard to the so-called "invisible disabilities"—i.e., impairments of the brain or the mind, including those related to learning disabilities, which are not obviously perceived—what is experienced of or known about them leaves the temporarily able-bodied anxious, even fearful.[912] Set in historical perspective, then, it may be at least understandable why people generally believe disability is causally related to suffering. The temporarily able-

---

Disability, and the Church: A New Vision of the People of God (Grand Rapids: William B. Eerdmans, 2011), among other published articles and papers.

[909] See Andrew T. Crislip, *From Monastery to Hospital: Christian Monasticism and the Transformation of Health Care in Late Antiquity* (Ann Arbor: University of Michigan Press, 2005), esp. 115–16; cf. Mark P. O'Tool, "The *povres avugles* of the Hôpital des Quinze-Vingts: Disability and Community in Medieval Paris," in *Difference and Identity in Francia and Medieval France*, ed. Meredith Cohen and Justine Firnhaber-Baker (Farnham: Ashgate, 2010), 157–73.

[910] Note the play on words in Edward Wheatley's *Stumbling Blocks before the Blind: Medieval Constructions of a Disability* (Ann Arbor: University of Michigan Press, 2010), which is suggestive of the unkind attitudes directed toward and oppressive social realities erected vis-à-vis the—in this case, visually—impaired.

[911] I discuss the freak show in my *Theology and Down Syndrome*, 82–86; cf. Paul Martin Lester and Susan Dente Ross, *Images that Injure: Pictorial Stereotypes in the Media* (Westport: Praeger, 2003), and Robert Bogdan, Martin Elks, and James A. Knoll, *Picturing Disability: Beggar, Freak, Citizen, and Other Photographic Rhetoric* (Syracuse: Syracuse University Press, 2012).

[912] This is especially the case with mental illness, for instance, since those so-afflicted often exhibit bizarre behaviors for no identifiable reason; see also Michael L. Perlin, *The Hidden Prejudice: Mental Disability on Trial* (Washington, DC: American Psychological Association, 2000), and Amy Simpson, *Troubled Minds: Mental Illness and the Church's Mission* (Downers Grove: IVP, 2013).

bodied obviously do not want to become dependent on the care of others, be made a spectacle before others, or be subject to awkward behaviors that are socially inexplicable or unacceptable.

The problem, of course, is that temporarily able-bodied presuppositions are shaped by their normate anxieties and biases, and these have been at least relativized, if not challenged, by disability vantage points. The disability rights movement of the last generation has opened up public space for the registration of disability voices and experiences that have questioned temporarily able-bodied assumptions, [913] and the epistemological, methodological, and theoretical lenses generated by such perspectives have propelled the recent emergence of disability studies as a scholarly field of inquiry. From this horizon, disability theorists have sought to uncouple the fact of human impairment and the sense of suffering. At least three major problems have been identified with how the temporarily able-bodied link the two.

First, whatever the existential sense of suffering experienced by people with disabilities, temporarily able-bodied perceptions of those with impairments often results in stereotypical and prejudicial attitudes toward them.[914] While perhaps little can be done about personal prejudice, the normate position of temporarily able-bodied persons in society means that they have political and especially economic power over those with disabilities and often exercise the latter in discriminatory ways in employment contexts.[915] So if normate conventions regarding impairment might be innocuous enough at the attitudinal level, they are downright harmful because personal stigmatization is reinforced by what they can and cannot do, and these often lead to exclusion of people with disabilities from employment opportunities. While the temporarily able-bodied may be sentimental about the presumed suffering of people with disabilities, there are real socioeconomic and other structural inequalities that constrain the latter quality of life and intensify whatever other experience of suffering may already be felt.

The second problem with temporarily able-bodied suppositions is that their attitudes toward those perceived as suffering are not actually harmless. Instead, the goodwill intended by temporarily able-bodied people in response motivates a kind of paternalism that can also be dangerous. The

---

[913] Fred Pelka, *What We Have Done: An Oral History of the Disability Rights Movement* (Amherst and Boston: University of Massachusetts Press, 2012).

[914] Douglas Biklen and Lee Bailey, eds., *Rudely Stamp'd: Imaginal Disability and Prejudice* (Washington, DC: University Press of America, 1981).

[915] Peter Susser and Peter J. Petesch, *Disability Discrimination and the Workplace*, 2nd ed. (Arlington: BNA Books, 2011).

movement to sterilize women with intellectual disabilities in the first half of the twentieth century is an extreme but important example.[916] No doubt some were genuinely concerned about the welfare of their friends or loved ones who were susceptible to getting pregnant but without the capacity to adequately raise their children. However, the state, with public backing, acted on this front in ways that violated the dignity and humanity of these most helpless. To be sure, temporarily able-bodied paternalism oftentimes manifests itself not in such violent ways, but is urged as a means to achieve other moral goods.[917] But this raises another problem with how the temporarily able-bodied construe suffering in relationship to disability: that people with disabilities are treated as passive recipients dependent on temporarily able-bodied charity and sympathy rather than as having their own agency and personhood.[918]

A third concern is understandably related to the very definition of disability, which connotes some kind of inability or incapacity. Here, the proper human response, temporarily able-bodied or otherwise, is to help, to assist with whatever cannot be done. This is all well and good except when the person is reduced to what he or she lacks. Normate discourse thus often does not think twice about talking about "the blind, lame, and deaf" as if that were the only important or essential feature about such individuals.[919] If the "people first" language of "people with disabilities" is designed to respond to such reductionist categorizations by foregrounding the full humanity of those not temporarily able-bodied,[920] that still is insufficient to overthrow the normate postulation that such individuals lack capacity or agency and are helplessly reliant on the charitable benevolence of others.[921]

---

[916] See Sharon Morris, "'Human Dregs at the Bottom of Our National Vats': The Interwar Debate on Sterilization of the Mentally Deficient," in *Social Histories of Disability and Deformity*, ed. David M. Turner and Kevin Stagg (New York: Routledge, 2006), 142–60.

[917] See the arguments back and forth in *Mental Retardation and Sterilization: A Problem of Competency and Paternalism*, ed. Ruth Macklin and Gaylin Willard (New York: Plenum Press, 1981).

[918] Henri-Jacques Stiker, *A History of Disability*, trans. William Sayers (Ann Arbor: University of Michigan Press, 1999), ch. 4; Doris Zames Fleischer and Freida Zames, *The Disability Rights Movement: From Charity to Confrontation* (Philadelphia: Temple University Press, 2001); and Nora Ellen Groce, *From Charity to Disability Rights: Global Initiatives of Rehabilitation International, 1922–2002* (New York: Rehabilitation International, 2002).

[919] This stems also from scriptural discourse—e.g., S. John Roth, *The Blind, the Lame, and the Poor: Character Types in Luke-Acts* (Sheffield: Sheffield Academic Press, 1997), that is in turn perpetuated unthinkingly by temporarily able-bodied people.

[920] See Tanya Titchkosky, "Disability: A Rose by Any Other Name? 'People-First' Language in Canadian Society," *Canadian Review of Sociology and Anthropology* 39, no. 2 (2001): 125–40.

[921] Even those writing as informed by disability perspectives have difficulty breaking beyond this stereotype. For instance, Lynne M. Bejoian, Molly Quinn, and Maysaa S. Bazna, "Disability, Agency and Engagement: Three Wisdom Traditions' Call to Be Radically Available," in *Disability and Religious Diversity: Cross-cultural and Interreligious Perspectives*, ed. Darla Schumm and Michael Stoltzfus

[*Footnote continued on next page*]

The point is not to undermine the motivation for acts of kindness and generosity, but to sever the temporarily able-bodied inference that those presumed suffering with disabilities survive merely or only as passive recipients of the aid of others.[922]

B. Why Suffering Is a Problem for People with Disabilities

Almost three decades ago, a younger Stanley Hauerwas put the question about suffering in relationship to disability, especially to intellectual disability, squarely on the table.[923] To begin, while suffering might include the experience of pain, it ought not be assumed that all suffering involves pain. In fact, some forms of suffering experienced by people with disabilities are devoid of physical pain and have to do instead with the sense of loneliness of alienation from others. Further, while the root meaning of suffering involves being forced to submit to a set of circumstances, human sufferers are not merely passive endurers but can also embrace their lot in a more active sense.[924]

With regard specifically to those with intellectual disabilities, however (in those days, the acceptable nomenclature was the "mentally handicapped," which is in the title of Hauerwas's book), the point was pressed: should all suffering be avoided? Remember that this was the time in which biomedical technology was increasingly able to identify fetuses with Down Syndrome and other congenital impairments, and the option was emerging about whether women or couples wanted to carry their children through to term or prevent their birth as well as their anticipated life of suffering. Hauerwas' counter, however, was that the suffering of the "mentally handicapped" was less the issue than that of their mothers or parents, especially the stigma of bearing such babies and then the inconveniences of raising these less-than normally developing children in an individualistic society that emphasizes independence and self-sufficiency.[925]

(New York: Palgrave Macmillan, 2011), 177–99, recognize that people with disabilities are agents in their own right (esp. 193–94) but the predominant thrust of this article is directed toward mobilizing the agency of non-disabled people to act inclusively toward the former.

[922] Thus societal discourse needs also to shift from that of organizational "agencies" acting on behalf of those passive because of intellectual disabilities—e.g., Paul Wehman, John Bricout, and John Kregel, "Supported Employment in 2000: Changing the Locus of Control from Agency to Consumer," in *Mental Retardation in the 21st Century*, ed. Michael L. Wehmeyer and James R. Patton (Austin: Pro-ED, 2000), 115–50—to recognition that included in this group of people are many capable of self-understanding and self-advocacy to some degree so more of a mutuality than currently exists between such service organizations and those with disabilities and their families can emerge.

[923] Stanley Hauerwas, *Suffering Presence: Theological Reflections on Medicine, the Mentally Handicapped, and the Church* (Notre Dame: University of Notre Dame Press, 1986).

[924] Hauerwas, *Suffering Presence*, 28.

[925] Hauerwas, ch. 9.

Within the broader framework of Christian faith, the problem is not the suffering of people (infants/children) with intellectual disabilities or their families but the lack of a sufficiently rich understanding of the church as a truly open-hearted community that is capable of being hospitable to and welcoming of such families so that these children are valued and embraced just as they are.

Still, there is no doubt that with regard to the severely or profoundly disabled, there is some suffering, even pain, involved, just as there is no denying that parents of such infants and children—even those who are only more moderately disabled—are faced with often inconceivable challenges related to their care and provision.[926] Further, it is also clear that those with severely debilitating diseases or injuries, including people stricken with chronic pain and chronic illness, not to mention severe mental impairment and profound intellectual disability, suffer at different levels of intensity.[927] Last but not least, the experience of later onset disability is particularly challenging since it requires developing or older adults not only to adjust to new bodily or sensory incapacities but also to reorient themselves psychologically and existentially toward a new self-identity.[928] In all of these ways and more, it is downright unjust to minimize or overlook the suffering experienced and involved.

While not dismissing the suffering that attends to some, if not many, experiences of disability, I want to challenge the biomedical paradigm within which such suffering is often defined. Following Hauerwas's lead, but extending it variously, what I will argue is that suffering is often individualized according to a biomedical diagnosis: an infant is presumed to suffer because of being born with Down Syndrome; a toddler is thought to suffer because of his polio; the hearing impaired are believed to suffer because of their being hard of hearing; the visually impaired are assumed to suffer because they have to get around using canes or guide dogs; the paraplegic must obviously suffer because she has to use a wheelchair, etc. In each case, the suffering follows from the biomedical impairment, and

---

[926] One of my doctoral students, a mother of a son with disability, writes eloquently from that perspective: Mary Fast, "A Theodicy of the Cross: Where is God in the Suffering of Disability?" PhD diss. (Virginia Beach: Regent University School of Divinity, 2015).

[927] See Martin Osterweis, Arthur Kleinman, and David Mechanic, eds., *Pain and Disability: Clinical, Behavioral, and Public Policy Perspectives* (Washington, DC: National Academy Press, 1987), esp. part III; Paul W. Power and Arthur E. Dell Orto, *Families Living with Chronic Illness and Disability: Interventions, Challenges, and Opportunities* (New York: Springer, 2004); and Erin Martz and Hanoch Livneh, eds., *Coping with Chronic Illness and Disability: Theoretical, Empirical, and Clinical Aspects* (New York: Springer, 2007).

[928] E.g., Shane Clifton, *Husbands Should Not Break: A Memoir* (prepublication copy available from the author at Shane.clifton@ac.edu.au).

society—those temporarily able-bodied—is mobilized to develop technological and other interventions in order to alleviate the related incapacities and the attendant suffering conditions.

But what if the social model of disability were applied to understanding suffering instead?[929] Without ignoring the biomedical aspects of impairment, the social model emphasizes that disability is as much if not more on some occasions a social construction and process of socialization:

1. Disability defines and responds to impairing conditions according to cultural conventions;
2. Disability imprisons those with impairments within economic constraints;
3. Disability limits opportunities according to certain sociopolitical structures; and
4. Disability confines some people within architectural or geographic environments.

List 1. Four Social Constructs of Disability

Applied to the notion of suffering, the social model insists that human suffering unfolds socially, often according to interpersonal, relational, and wider cultural dynamics.[930] In this framework, people with disabilities suffer less because of their physical, intellectual, or sensory limitations than because they are unable to live up to normate expectations regarding living independently, achieving life quality, attaining vocational goals, and manifesting economic success.[931] On the flip side, the temporarily able-bodied make assumptions about those who are different, impose labels on them, and implement social, medical, and other policies undergirded by normate values that constrain rather than enable the flourishing of people with disabilities.[932]

Note then that the sense of suffering has as much to do with the self-perception of failing to live up to the values and expectations of others. More to the point, then, the suffering of people with disabilities in these

---

[929] A brief but substantive overview of the social model is provided by Tom Shakespeare, "The Social Model of Disability," in *The Disability Studies Reader*, 2nd Ed., ed. Lennard J. Davis (New York: Routledge, 2006), 197–204; see also note 4.

[930] Ranjan Roy, *Social Relations and Chronic Pain* (New York: Kluwer Academic/Plenum, 2001); cf. Irmo Marini and Mark A. Stebnicki, eds., *The Psychological and Social Impact of Illness and Disability*, 6th ed. (New York: Springer, 2012).

[931] As depicted by James M. Rotholz, *Chronic Fatigue Syndrome, Christianity, and Culture: Between God and an Illness* (Binghamton: Haworth Press, 2002).

[932] Dietmut Niedecken's work not only shows who people with disabilities (the learning impaired in this volume) are reduced to their condition, but also how religious, social, medical, and other presuppositions combine to support eugenic practices (in the Nazi German context) allegedly for the common good; see Niedecken, *Nameless: Understanding Learning Disability*, trans. Andrew Weller (New York: Brunner-Routledge, 2003).

instances has to do with an internalized sense of failure. Some people with disabilities thus define themselves according to such expectations and self-identify in negative terms as those *not able to do*—or *disabled from doing*—this or that. The social model helps us to understand how society's treatment of individuals leads them to view themselves as others see them: they are "disabled"—or incapable of this or incapacitated with regard to that—and come to see themselves as helpless, unable, and dependent (perhaps more in their own minds than in reality) on others. Some people with disabilities come to pity themselves, given the sympathy bestowed upon by them by a normate world,[933] while others lose their dignity as human beings through being treated paternalistically as "less than" by the temporarily able-bodied. How do people with disabilities retain their sense of self-esteem when the normate world devalues their existence?[934]

Religiously and theologically, people with disabilities also suffer because of how their condition is understood and what the community of faith expects of them. Not only do they have to contend with questions (oftentimes not actually asked, but surely thought) like: Why did this happen to you?—as if some sin or demonic etiology could "explain" the presence of impairment—but they also begin to believe that their lack of faith, for instance, is one, if not the primary, contributing factor to their persisting condition. Even if not embracing such a self-understanding, they have to exemplify the Christ-like character expected of those on the path of sanctification, so that means not complaining about their situation, or needing to project an "overcomer's mentality" to those in the community of faith. And if at all successful in this regard, people with disabilities become icons, even sacraments, of divine virtue, patience, and fortitude in the eyes of the temporarily able-bodied faithful, and this results in another set of standards or expectations foisted upon the impaired. After all, if St. Paul said that, "God is faithful, and he will not let you be tested beyond your strength, but with the testing he will also provide the way out so that you may be able to endure it" (1 Cor 10:13, NRSV), and if "you" are impaired, then obviously "you" must have been given a special grace to endure such disability.

---

[933] See the discussion of "Pity as Oppression in the Jerry Lewis Telethon," in Beth A. Haller, *Representing Disability in an Ableist World: Papers on Mass Media* (Louisville: The Advocado Press, 2010), ch. 7; for a first-person perspective, see Angela Victoria Lundy, "Off the Pillow of Self-pity," in *Amazing Gifts: Stories of Faith, Disability, and Inclusion*, ed. Mark I. Pinsky (Herndon: Alban Institute, 2012), 188–90.

[934] Jenny Morris, *Pride Against Prejudice: A Personal Politics of Disability* (London: Women's Press, 1991).

C. "Four Fences" in Providence and in Pastoral Theology of Suffering Disability

This section begins to develop a pastoral approach to the experience of suffering disability by focusing on theological reorientation. In previous work, I had initiated reflection related to such a task by retrieving and re-appropriating the Chalcedonian theological method.[935] I compared how the early church fathers protected the mystery of the incarnation utilizing apophatic or negative language about how *not* to talk about the nature of Christ: e.g., Christ's divine and human natures were merely asserted to be *without confusion, without change, without division, without separation*, known also as the "four fences" of the Chalcedonian confession. So in like manner, rather than deploying cataphatic or positive descriptions of the Christological reality and rather than make presumptive affirmations about what is theologically ambiguous, Christians are better advised to recognize what is *not* known about disabilities in the context of pastoral care. Hence, I suggested that these "four fences" of the mystery of Christ could translate into "four fences" regarding disability in relationship to divine providence:

1. God's will is *not* arbitrary;
2. Divine providence and creaturely responsibility are *not* mutually exclusive;
3. Divine willing is *not* opposed to the laws of nature; and
4. Proper Christian pastoral care should *never* presume to provide any definitive theological explanations for disability.

List 2. Four Fences of Disability in Divine Providence

The point is that a more humble approach is needed, one that acknowledges there is much that is *not* understood theologically, even as trust and faith in God ought to be nurtured.

Building on this platform, let me suggest "four fences" toward a theology of disability in the context of pastoral care for people and their families suffering disability.

1. God's sovereignty does *not* mean God is the direct cause;
2. Though a fallen world, sins are *not* directly linked to disability;
3. All sickness is *not* derived from Satan or demons;
4. Pastoral agents should *not* resort to sovereignty, sin, or Satan as the first or foremost cause of any disability.

List 3. Four Fences on a Theology of Suffering Disability

First, God's sovereignty does *not* mean that God is the direct cause of disability in any specific case. Yes, scripture periodically suggests that God is the cause of impairments, including as when Yahweh rhetorically pressed

---

[935] See my *Theology and Down Syndrome*, 167–69.

Moses: "Who gives speech to mortals? Who makes them mute or deaf, seeing or blind? Is it not I, the Lord?" (Exod 4:11). However, there are many instances of those with sickness or impairment across the scriptures which etiology is not linked with God's sovereign will. Mephibosheth, was "crippled in his feet" because of an accident (2 Sam 4:4), Trophimus is simply said to have been "left ill in Miletus" (2 Tim 4:20), and there are more. My point is simply that we can never know any specific disability as having been directly willed by God—unless God says so explicitly—and therefore we should not tell people with disabilities that their suffering, if such is experienced, is divinely sanctioned. Divine sovereignty does not need to translate into a view that every specific event in the cosmos is part of God's particular intention.[936]

Second, that we live in a sinful and fallen world does *not* mean that human sins are directly linked to disability in any case. Yes, there might be obvious occasions when creaturely choices bring about impairing consequences, as with fetal alcohol syndrome. Yet even here, the appropriate pastoral response does not make this point and leave things at that. Sensitivity to the scriptural connections between sin and disability in general[937] should alert pastoral caregivers to the reality that many believers continue asking, as did the disciples upon encountering the visually impaired man: "who sinned, this man or his parents, that he was born blind?" (John 9:2). Jesus' response is crucial for present purposes: "Neither this man nor his parents sinned; he was born blind so that God's works might be revealed in him" (9:3). We will return in a moment to the latter clause of Jesus' reply. For now, what needs to be emphasized in the context of pastoral care, especially when interacting with those who are suffering, is that sin and disability are related only in the general sense that we live in a fallen world, and not necessarily in any individual case. If people come to realize, through introspection, that their experience of suffering disability can be gleaned from to make life adjustments and better choices, then pastoral agents can help them process these thoughts; but proper pastoral care should not begin by tying the experience of suffering disability too

---

[936] Here I am partial, as a Wesleyan, to the idea that God does not have a blueprint for every single cosmic development, but rather oversees things sovereignly and yet also preveniently and generally; see also Gregory A. Boyd, *Is God to Blame? Moving beyond Pat Answers to the Problem of Evil* (Downers Grove: IVP, 2003), esp. ch. 2.

[937] I discuss the scriptural texts that perpetuate these associations in my *The Bible, Disability, and the Church*, 18–24.

tightly with sin.[938] It is not only presumptive but also judgmental from a normate vantage point.

Third, that there are some scriptural passages that suggest sickness and impairments derive from the work of Satan and his demons does *not* mean that disability is so derivative in any particular case. Even if "the Accuser" tormented Job and even if Jesus responded to the deaf-mute by exorcising an evil spirit, that neither justifies the "devil-behind-every-impairment" notion nor warrants the assumption that epilepsy is of demonic provenance. This is not to say that the human experience of impairment is devoid of a spiritual dimension. Of that, there is no doubt, for the biblical principalities and powers are intertwined with the structural evils that plague the political, social, and economic domains of human life and relationship,[939] and in that sense are entangled also with the disabilities caused by war, famine, and poverty. Yet this general cosmological perspective does not validate pastoral approaches that see Satanic attack as the root cause of suffering disability. Amidst grappling with the challenges of life, people with disabilities and their families ought not to have to bear the additional burden that they are under spiritual assault from dark and destructive cosmic forces. Although such an approach is limited by and large to Pentecostal and charismatic communities, yet the explosive growth of this kind of Christianity worldwide indicates that unless specifically countered, this can become the dominant popular understanding of impairment and disability.[940]

Fourth, last but not least, pastoral agents should *not* resort to sovereignty, sin, or Satan first and foremost when caring for those suffering disability, and similarly, disability should *not* be presumed to be meant or designed for the sanctification of the afflicted. The point is not to deny that people with disabilities as well as their caregivers are in need of sanctification; all

---

[938] See A. Wati Longchar, "Sin, Suffering, and Disability in God's World," in *Disability, Society, and Theology: Voices from Africa*, ed. Samuel Kabue, Esther Mombo, Joseph Galgalo, and C. B. Peter (Limuru, Kenya: Zapf Chancery, 2011), 47–58, esp. 50–56.

[939] See my *In the Days of Caesar: Pentecostalism and Political Theology—The Cadbury Lectures 2009*, Sacra Doctrina: Christian Theology for a Postmodern Age series (Grand Rapids: William B. Eerdmans, 2010), ch. 4, for explication of these interconnections.

[940] For further discussion of disability in pentecostal-charismatic Christianity as such interfaces with indigenous cultural worldviews, see Yong, *Theology and Down Syndrome*, 130–40, and *The Bible, Disability, and the Church*, ch. 3. For informed Pentecostal approaches to these matters, see John Christopher Thomas, *The Devil, Disease and Deliverance: Origins of Illness in N.T. Thought*, Journal of Pentecostal Theology Supplemental series 13 (Sheffield: Sheffield Academic Press, 1998), esp. ch. 9. Other Pentecostal theologies of disability and pastoral care are emerging that do not rely on demonic etiologies—e.g., Steven M. Fettke, *God's Empowered People: A Pentecostal Theology of the Laity* (Eugene: Wipf and Stock, 2011), ch. 4; and Jeff Hittenberger, "Receiving God's Gift of a Person with Special Needs: Amos Yong's Theology of Disability," in *The Theology of Amos Yong and the New Face of Pentecostal Scholarship: Passion for the Spirit*, Global Pentecostal and Charismatic Studies 14, ed. Wolfgang Vondey and Martin W. Mittelstadt (Leiden: Brill, 2013; 306 pp.), 141–59.

people, especially Christian believers, can use an added dose of divine holiness in their lives. However, popular piety sometimes thinks there must be a rationale for the existence of impairment or disability, and if the blame cannot be put on God, sin, or the devil, then it must serve providential purposes related to the individual's spiritual journey. Perhaps the sanctification of this person's life will also be exemplary for others, or enables solidarity among those so suffering. All that is well and good. But the point to be emphasized is that even if those suffering disability come these conclusions on their own, these conclusions should *not* be first or presumed by the temporarily able-bodied pastors and counselors.

This same caveat of allowing people with disabilities to come to their own informed perspective applies for the other three "fences." Those suffering disability can, through earnest wrestling with the scriptures among other resources,

- Come to embrace their experience as somehow providentially ordained;
- Come to the conviction that they are under some kind of spiritual onslaught;
- Take these as prompts to reexamine their personal, moral, and spiritual lives. [941]

My argument is not that pastoral agents cannot be in conversation about such matters with those suffering disability; rather, I insist that such "explanations" not be where the discussions begins, imposed on people with disabilities by the temporarily able-bodied.

D. "Suffering Disability": Redemptive Pastoral Praxis

How then to proceed? In this final section, I emphasize a pastoral praxis that focuses on redeeming the suffering of disability, that ministers *to* those suffering disability, and that engages in ministry *with* people with disabilities. Each is interrelated with the others, supporting a holistic pastoral approach.

What does it mean to talk about the redemptibility of disability, including the suffering of disability?[942] Again, temporarily able-bodied pastoral agents should approach such matters cautiously. However, to take off from the preceding discussion about the "four fences" of suffering disability, the main emphasis ought to lie on the fact that while God should not be thought

---

[941] On these matters, Joni Eareckson Tada and Steve Bundy's *Beyond Suffering: A Christian View on Disability Ministry* (Agoura Hills: Christian Institute on Disability, 2011) is exemplary, coming as it does from a woman with quadriplegia and a father of a child with disability; their historically Reformed and Calvinist theological view is front and center although those who come from outside of that tradition may not be as comforted by these perspectives.

[942] The following extends my prior reflections on redeeming disability: Yong, "Many Tongues, Many Senses: Pentecost, the Body Politic, and the Redemption of Dis/Ability," *PNEUMA: The Journal of the Society for Pentecostal Studies* 31, no. 2 (2009): 167–88.

of as sovereignly ordaining or imposing such suffering, whatever the cause of harm, pain, and tragedy, God can bring about something good. As Jesus indicated in response to the disciples' query about whether the man's blindness resulted from his own sin or that of his parents, there is nothing to be gained by attempting to decide what caused the blindness; instead, our focus should be redemptive, following God's overarching intentions: "that God's works might be revealed in him" (John 9:3). The goal is therefore a reorientation from causality or etiology toward redemption or eschatology.[943] Impairments come about variously—congenitally (through genetic mutations, for instance), incidentally (a fall, a car crash, etc.), as a by-product or casualty of the human condition (e.g., wars or natural disasters)—but salvation is God's business. Christian theology will never be able to provide a fully rational theodicy for those suffering disability, but Christian eschatology can outline the basis for human hope amidst the despair of disability. My suggestion is to focus on the cosmological conditions when talking about causality, but then to shift to the theological hope when attempting nurture and trying to inspire human endurance.[944]

Practically, such an accent on the redemptibility of disability and whatever suffering comes in its trail should also provoke ministry to people with disabilities. Ministry to such and their families should of course not be conducted condescendingly or as if out of duty. People with disabilities and those who care for them are in the best position to identify what their needs are and how best the church or others might be able to assist. The temporarily able-bodied must never presume the form that ministry to those suffering disability should take. Instead, life-giving ministry emerges out of a discerning mutuality between all involved. The model here would be the L'Arche community where core members (people with disabilities) and their

---

[943] One of Stanley Hauerwas's most recent books, *Approaching the End: Eschatological Reflections on Church, Politics, and Life* (Grand Rapids: William B. Eerdmans, 2013; 269 pp.), has two chapters on disability (pp. 176–91 and 222–36), but readers will have to connect the dots between disability and eschatology in this book more on their own as they are not clearly delineated by Hauerwas; cf. also my paper, "Disability, the Human Condition, and the Spirit of the Eschatological Long Run: Toward a Pneumatological Theology of Disability," *Journal of Religion, Disability, and Health* 11, no. 1 (2007): 5–25, for a different approach to theology of disability from an eschatological perspective.

[944] Elsewhere I suggest a similar strategy or reorientation from classical approaches to theodicy and suffering, including the suffering of disability, toward a more performative and practical engagement; see Yong, "Disability and the Love of Wisdom: De-forming, Re-forming, and Per-forming Philosophy of Religion," *Ars Disputandi: The Online Journal for Philosophy of Religion* 9 (2009): 54–71 [www.ArsDisputandi.org/], reprinted in *Disability in Judaism, Christianity and Islam: Sacred Texts, Historical Traditions, and Social Analysis*, ed. Darla Schumm and Michael Stoltzfus (New York: Palgrave Macmillan, 2011), 205–27.

attendants relate to one another as equals, but yet also as different.[945] Even if core members are unable to verbally communicate their needs, attendants take the time to carefully learn about and then discern how appropriate caregiving should unfold.

Two aspects are therefore worthy of highlighting. First, most who suffer disability would welcome ministry; however, such ought to be made available in a discerning manner. Second, effective ministry to those suffering disability emerges from out of a genuine human relationship, even friendship. In other words, authentic ministry to people with disabilities opens up when ministers take the time to get to know and even to befriend people with disabilities, their families, and their caregivers, and certainly less out of professional motivation than out of Christian selflessness.[946]

Out of sustained Christian friendship and relationship, ministry *to* people with disabilities opens up to ministry *with* them; more precisely the "us" of those temporarily able-bodied and "them" of those suffering disability will itself be overcome. Not that the differences will be erased, since that would itself not recognize or affirm the bodily form of disability as also uniquely in the image of God. Rather, the point is that the ministry of the body of Christ includes each member in his or her particularity, vulnerability, and even weakness, bearing the gifts of the Holy Spirit.[947] To talk about disability in terms of vulnerability and weakness risks perpetuating able-bodied and normate assumptions that those living with impairments are less strong. However, this is precisely the apostolic counter to the Corinthian presumption about their own nobility, capacity, and intelligence, which included insistence that the ways of divinity involved the mobilization and utilization not of the self-assured but of those who recognized their limitations as creatures made in the image of God.[948] The point to be made is twofold: first, that people with disabilities, no matter how severe or even profound, ought not to be viewed merely as passive objects of ministry, but can also be welcomed as agents of ministry, even if in some circumstances, how such ministry is carried out will require patience, creativity, innovation,

---

[945] The literature is enormous; a helpful discussion of the reciprocity between core members and attendants is Kevin S. Rymer, *Living L'Arche: Stories of Compassion, Love, and Disability* (Collegeville: Liturgical Press, 2009).

[946] Thus the thrust of Hans Reinder's provocative book, *Receiving the Gift of Friendship: Profound Disability, Theological Anthropology, and Ethics* (Grand Rapids: Eerdmans, 2008).

[947] Yong, "Disability and the Gifts of the Spirit: Pentecost and the Renewal of the Church," *Journal of Pentecostal Theology* 19, no. 1 (Spring 2010): 76–93.

[948] See also Yong, *The Bible, Disability, and the Church*, ch. 4, on St. Paul's notion of weakness as providing the rudiments for the first Christian theology of disability; cf. Yong, "Running the (Special) Race: New (Pauline) Perspectives on Theology of Sport," *Journal of Disability and Religion* 18, no. 2 (2014): 209–25.

and persistence;[949] second, and building from this, it is precisely as ministers to others that those suffering disability realize their being created in the image of God, with the capacity to participate in the mission of God, and this itself is redemptive not only for people with disabilities but for all.[950]

Conclusion

This paper intended to accomplish four related purposes:

1. To interrogate the normate assumption that all disability brings about suffering;
2. To clarify how the suffering of disability oftentimes derives from normate expectations related to and temporarily able-bodied treatments of people with disability;
3. To redirect questions of theodicy regarding suffering disability away from theological causality toward a redemptive praxis; and
4. To enable and empower those suffering disability to receive ministry from and be agents of ministry to others.

The foregoing four sections attempted to respond to these objectives. As one who is temporarily able-bodied, I urge others like me to reconsider how their attitudes and approaches to disability not only might be a cause of but also unintentionally perpetuate the suffering that people with disabilities undergo. Awareness of this normate prejudice will take us some way toward alleviating suffering in the world, especially the suffering endured by people with disabilities.[951]

---

[949] Part II of Mark I. Pinsky, ed., *Amazing Gifts: Stories of Faith, Disability, and Inclusion* (Lanham: Rowman and Littlefield, 2011) provides glimpses of "Ministry by People with Disabilities."

[950] See my article, "Disability from the Margins to the Center: Hospitality and Inclusion in the Church," *Journal of Religion, Disability, and Health* 15, no. 4 (2011): 339–50.

[951] An earlier version of this paper was presented at the Caring Theologically and Thinking Pastorally Conference on Disability, sponsored in part by the Bethesda Institute and Southern Methodist University/Perkins School of Theology, Dallas, Texas, 16 June 2014; thanks to the audience for helpful questions leading to clarification of various aspects of the paper.

24.
What Kind of Response Can Pastoral Theology Give in the Midst of Suffering?

Dr. HyeRan Kim-Cragg
Timothy Eaton Memorial Church Professor of Preaching
Emmanuel College of Victoria University
in the University of Toronto, Canada[952]

Introduction	379
A. Suffering and Sacrifice and the Resurrection	380
B. Is Suffering Attributed To God?	382
C. Ritual Attending to Human Suffering	383
D. Don't Confuse Healing with Cure	386
E. A Few Rituals that Aid Pastoral Care	389
Conclusion	390

Introduction

Suffering is not an easy topic to talk about, even though it is a natural part of life. Suffering is even more difficult to discuss when one asks how to respond to suffering, which is the topic of this chapter. Acknowledging its

---

[952] Kim-Cragg earned her ThD from Emmanuel College, University of Toronto; her MDiv from the Hanshin Graduate School of Theology, Hanshin University, Osan, South Korea; and her BS from Dongduk Women's University, Seoul, South Korea. Prior to Lydia Gruchy Professor of Pastoral Studies, St. Andrew's College, Saskatoon Theological Union. Prior her post at Emmanuel College, she was Lydia Gruchy Professor of Pastoral Studies at St. Andrew's College, Saskatoon Theological Union, Canada. In 2019, she received The Rowntree Scholarship at The United Church of Canada Foundation. She is Dean of Global Institute of Theology, the World Communion of Reformed Churches (WCRC) and Co-Moderator of Theology Reference Group for the WCRC. She is a member of the Presbyterian Church in the Republic of Korea and has authored several books and articles, including *What Does the Bible Say?— A Critical Conversation with Popular Culture in a Biblically Illiterate World* (Eugene: Cascade, 2017; 203 pp.); *An Intercultural Adventure Part II—The Authority and Interpretation of Scripture in The United Church of Canada*, co-authored with Don Schweitzer (Daejeon, South Korea: Daejanggan Publisher, 2016); *2 Thessalonians—Wisdom Commentary*, co-authored with Mary Ann Beavis (Collegeville: Liturgical Press, 2016; 254 pp.); *Hebrews—Wisdom Commentary*, co-authored with Mary Ann Beavis (Collegeville: Liturgical Press, 2015; 336 pp.); *Story and Song—A Postcolonial Interplay between Christian Education and Worship* (New York: Peter Lang, 2012; 180 pp.); *The Encounters—Retelling the Biblical Stories from Migration and Intercultural Perspectives*, co-authored with Eun-Young Choi, translated by Lark Kim (Daejeon, Blacksmith Publisher, 2013; 102 pp.); *An Introduction to The United Church of Canada—Key Texts with Introductions and Commentary*, co-edited with Don Schweitzer (Toronto: United Church of Canada, 2013; 91 pp.); *Interdependence: A Postcolonial Feminist Practical Theology* (Eugene: Pickwick, 2018; 188 pp.); *Mission of Koreans Within It*, coauthor with Don Schweitzer (Daejeon, South Korea: Daejanggan Publisher, 2019); "Unfinished and Unfolding Tasks of Preaching: Interdisciplinary, Intercultural, and Interreligious Approaches in the Postcolonial Context of Migration," *Homiletic: The Journal of the Academy of Homiletics* 44, no. 2 (2019); and "Home, Hospitality, and Preaching: A Need for the Homiletical Engagement of Migration," in *Migration and Religion: Negotiating Sites of Hospitality, Resistance, and Vulnerability*, ed. Andrea Bieler, Isolde Karle, Kim-Cragg, and Ilona Nord (Leipzig: Eva, 2019); and many more. See hyeran.kimcragg@utoronto.ca.

difficulty, we suggest ritual as a way that pastoral theology can be helpful for those who are in the midst of suffering. We examine the various roles of ritual in pastoral responses to human suffering:

- Establishing order amidst chaos and confusion,
- Reaffirming meaning of life,
- Bringing community together for support,
- Enabling to cope with ambivalence, and
- Encountering mystery in the presence of grace and hope.

These are a few of the functions that rituals facilitate.

Since ritual is biblically rooted, we will examine how suffering is understood in the Bible, as a witness of people of faith wrestling with God, who is "preoccupied with human and creational suffering."[953] We also note the crucifixion of Jesus as a symbol of suffering and salvation, and we suggest ways to move beyond suffering understood as sacrifice and focus on the resurrection as the locus of salvation.

In that vein this essay theologically explores the relationship between suffering and sin and the responsibility people have and do not have for suffering in the world. Naming injustice is important to adequately deal with suffering. Human agency of hope and solidarity in seeking justice are stressed as crucial to bring about healing.

A. The Cross as the Symbol of Suffering and Salvation[954]

In Christian doctrine, the crucifixion as the symbol of Jesus' suffering has long been interpreted in sacrificial terms to the point that, for many Christians, the statement that the death of Jesus was not a sacrifice seems nonsensical. It is no secret that crucifixion was a particularly painful, violent, and shameful form of execution suffered by many people in the ancient Roman Empire, including Jesus.

The early Christian fixation on the meaning of the death of Jesus is understandable in view of the traumatic impact of his execution on his disciples. However, even in the N.T., there is an important body of scripture that does not exclusively focus on the death in salvation, but that interprets the resurrection as the locus of salvation. This rings precisely true in Luke-Acts, a two-volume set that takes up about a third of the N.T. canon. As N.T. scholar Mark Alan Powell notes, "Luke finds the basis for salvation to

---

[953] Douglas John Hall, *God and Human Suffering: An Exercise in the Theology of the Cross* (Minneapolis: Augsburg, 1986), 16.

[954] A fuller examination of sin, salvation, suffering and sacrifice, see Mary Ann Beavis and HyeRan Kim-Cragg, *What Does the Bible Say?—A Critical Conversation with Popular Culture in a Biblically Illiterate World* (Eugene: Cascade, 2017), chapters 2 and 10.

be manifest in Jesus' life and in his resurrection/exaltation."[955] In the Lukan writings, the crucifixion is not denied, but it is not given any soteriological significance. For example, in Peter's speech in the temple, he summarizes the arrest and execution of Jesus without explicitly mentioning the crucifixion:

> The God of Abraham, the God of Isaac, and the God of Jacob, the God of our ancestors has glorified his servant Jesus, whom you handed over and rejected in the presence of Pilate, though he had decided to release him. But you rejected the Holy and Righteous One and asked to have a murderer given to you, and you killed the Author of life, whom God raised from the dead. To this we are witnesses. And by faith in his name, his name itself has made this man strong, whom you see and know; and the faith that is through Jesus has given him this perfect health in the presence of all of you. (Acts 3:13–16)

The healing of a lame man that precedes the speech is likewise connected with the resurrection (Acts 3:1–9), and the salvific power of faith in the name of Jesus. There is no emphasis on suffering, sacrifice, or atonement. Throughout Luke-Acts: "Jesus is Messiah and Lord on earth during his life (Luke 2:11), and he is officially installed as Messiah and Lord in heaven by virtue of his resurrection and exaltation (Acts 2:36). As such, he has the right to bestow salvation on whomever he chooses."[956]

In short, we attend to the cross not to glorify suffering but to see its telos (inner aim) that points to life, the abundance of life, which is experienced sometimes only by way of an encounter with the reality of suffering that negates life. Suffering is, thus, an affirmative part of life, rather than the antithesis of life. The suffering of Jesus never condones our suffering or the world's suffering. His suffering neither stops our suffering from happening nor numbs our feeling of suffering. But speaking of a Christology, Jesus' humanity is determined by his suffering. To be more precise, the fact that he suffered just like us substantiates his full humanness and his full divineness—God incarnate. This human condition of suffering by Jesus enables humans and God to be in communion. "Emmanuel," God is suffering with us: God as "co-sufferer" is confessed thanks to Jesus, as Canadian systematic theologian Douglas John Hall contends.[957] The belief that Jesus suffered and that God in Jesus continues to suffer with us, therein, the very sharing enables a healing process. Jesus being "co-sufferer" generates a power of "compassion," even a contagious care that comforts

---

[955] Mark Alan Powell, "Salvation in Luke-Acts," *World and Word* 12, no. 1 (1992): 8.
[956] Powell, "Salvation in Luke-Acts," 9.
[957] Hall, *God and Human Suffering*, 36.

and may even change the lives of the ones who are suffering and the ones who share their sharing.

Hall further articulates this compassion by connecting the meaning of the Hebrew word *hesed,* expressed as a compassionate sufferer, the Holy One "who is not powerless but whose power expresses itself unexpectedly in the weakness of love."[958] The practicing of *hesed,* faithfully, and seriously following the teaching of God in Jesus, leads to "the cost of discipleship" clothed in costly hope rather than cheap grace.[959] This hope is rooted in faith, a faith that enables people to be in solidarity to accompany one another and to face real suffering because they know that God suffers with them. Hall writes, "Paradoxical and even offensive as it may seem, solidarity with its suffering may be a better sign of hope for the world."[960]

B. Is Suffering Attributed to God?

This question can be put another way: Is suffering related to sin? That is, does God chastise human beings for committing sin? Is the suffering from AIDS, for example, God's punishment for homosexual people's sinful act? Do children become sick because their parents are divorced? People who answer "yes" to these questions exemplify a pattern of thought that sees suffering as a result of sin. Sickness is therefore a sign that we need to repent. Or, if it is caused by someone else's sin, there is a legitimate reason to blame others. But, of course, these responses are neither theological nor pastoral.

In the area of disability, American liturgical homiletical theologian Kathy Black provides six theological explanations connecting disability with sin that may result in further suffering rather than healing:

1. Disability is God's punishment for the sin of the disabled person or their parents;
2. Disability is God's test of faith and character;
3. Disability is an opportunity of relationship with God;
4. Disability presents an opportunity for the power of God to be made manifest;
5. Suffering through disability is redemptive; and
6. Disability manifests the mysterious omnipotence of God's will which we cannot know.[961]

---

[958] Hall, 158.

[959] Dietrich Bonhoeffer, *The Cost of Discipleship*, trans. R. H. Fuller (New York: Macmillan, 1959).

[960] Hall, *God and Human Suffering,* 147.

[961] Kathy Black, *A Healing Homiletic: Preaching and Disability* (Nashville: Abingdon, 1994), 23.

Black says that this kind of theology portrays God as a great puppeteer, as if God is in total control of all the sufferings in the world and also causes those sufferings.[962]

German systematic theologian Dorothee Sölle also contests such theology calling it "theological sadism," an approach which is inseparably connected to "Christian masochism."[963] As long as we believe in theological sadism, we fall into Christian masochism. These two terms feed each other. Often apparent in abusive relationships, the perpetuator can be the perpetuator only *when* and *because* the victim allows that to happen. This does not suggest that victims of abuse are allowing themselves to be abused willingly. It rather points to the vicious cycle that causes the victim to be tangled in this situation. Unless God intentionally creates this vicious cycle, human relationships with God should never be abusive.

Therefore, human suffering cannot be fully attributed to God, and the human predicament cannot fully be accounted for as one's own responsibility. If one suffers, it is not necessarily someone's fault. Sölle as a Reformed theologian notes that the Reformation strengthened theological sadism by stressing Christian submission. It is important to be acutely aware that all too often theological sadism and Christian masochism continue to operate in Christian life, and they only produce insensitivity and indifference to suffering and perpetuate the contempt for humanity and creation. It is imperative that we both avoid this trap and find a way to offer comfort in times of suffering.

C. Ritual Attending to Human Suffering

Christians often turn to ritual as a source of comfort and liberation. American pastoral theologian Elaine Ramshaw connects pastoral care and ritual, showing how especially corporate and public ritual cares for individuals, the community, and the world. She laments the unhelpful division between liturgical ritualists and pastoral counsellors and their biased understanding of each other. One is often viewed as distancing and insensitive to the specific needs of the one who is suffering, while the latter is accused of being overly privatized and lacking depths of tradition and corporate memory. One way to mend this division, Ramshaw claims, is through ritual that attends to human suffering with the same intensive focus as pastoral counselling.[964]

---

[962] Black, *Healing Homiletic*, 34.
[963] Dorothee Sölle, *Suffering* (Philadelphia: Fortress, 1975), 9, 22.
[964] Elaine Ramshaw, *Ritual and Pastoral Care* (Minneapolis: Fortress, 1987).

Ramshaw suggests five goals of ritual which are directly related to human suffering:
1. Establish order,
2. Reaffirm meaning,
3. Bond community,
4. Handle ambivalence, and
5. Encounter mystery.[965]

Inevitably, and admittedly as humans, we need to make sense out of suffering. This is especially the case when suffering occurs unexpectedly. Many accidents and natural disasters come without the warning. When unexpected things happen, people panic, and those who are in the midst of suffering experience chaos. "Why and How could this happen" are the questions that quickly rise as we seek to make sense out of suffering. Ritual establishes order, helping people in suffering to make sense by ordering their experience.

However, ritual does not mean that one should deny the reality of chaos. American pastoral theologian Bonnie J. Miller-McLemore suggests that the chaos of care should be redeemed as a site for God's good news.[966] The reality of chaos must be faced with care. Just as ordinary human experiences are sacred, chaos as a part of human experience and human life must be fully embraced as affirmative.

This point is closely related to the second goal of ritual, namely—to reaffirm meaning. Despite their suffering, people know that they are loved by God. They want to affirm that life is precious and worth living, in spite of what they are going through. Ritual helps to affirm this. Even a small and mundane matter is important and can help to engage theological issues of suffering, as feminists have taught us.[967] Grandiose and abstract ideas rarely conjure up much healing, but more often the seemingly insignificant ordinary matters are what reconnect people's spirit with their senses, illuminating profound wisdom for life and healing in suffering.

The third goal of ritual has to do with community and strongly highlights the value of ritual compared to pastoral counselling, which is often done individually in a private setting. While suffering is experienced individually and cannot be fully shared by others, an individual can be communally supported in their suffering through ritual. The suffering of another can

---

[965] Ramshaw, *Ritual and Pastoral Care*, 22.

[966] Bonnie J. Miller-McLemore, *In the Midst of Chaos: Caring for Children as Spiritual Practice* (San Francisco: Jossey-Bass, 2007), xiv.

[967] Joyce Ann Mercer, "Feminist and Womanist Practical Theology," in *Opening the Field of Practical Theology: An Introduction*, ed. Kathleen A. Cahalan and Gordon S. Mikoski (Lanham: Rowman and Littlefield, 2014), 98.

never be completely understood or shared. However, there are elements of suffering that can be understood and shared between individuals or in groups. Those who have lost a child, for example, may find a source of comfort and strength to share in a ritual that acknowledges loss with others who have related experiences of loss. Ritual enables them to bond in community and as a community.

The fourth goal is related to the first goal. When suffering hits people, they are confused; their ordinary lives are interrupted and become convoluted. They feel lost. The questions of "Why" and "How" arise, and then they realize that these questions cannot be easily, certainly, or clearly answered. People begin to realize the ambivalence of life. Ritual helps handle this ambivalence. Such ritual does not provide a sure pathway to get out of confusing and messy reality, yet it acknowledges confusion and suffering, which is a necessary first step to any healing. It creates a safe space to name unresolved emotions, feelings of loss, confusion, anger, uncertainty, even that nebulous anxiety, and more. Once these negative and difficult emotions are let out, people who are in suffering begin to see that there is yet still much to be thankful for. That is when people also start to encounter mystery, something beyond their experience that is yet somehow still in relation to us. Ritual through symbols and silence, listening and singing, help people encounter mystery.

Attention to the presence of suffering, which often leads to an encounter with mystery, affirms that suffering is a part of life. While suffering caused by greed, injustice, and oppression must be challenged to be eradicated, suffering as a part of the human struggle in life must also, on some level, be accepted and recognized. One can neither trivialize it nor be overwhelmed by it. "Life is not given all at once, life must be lived, risked, and achieved."[968] Life is given *in time* as a process. That is why life is often called a *journey*. But this journey has no turning back. We may wish that today was already tomorrow or that we could turn back time or turn back the clock and live in yesterday, but we cannot change the course of time or the fact of our mortality. While one may want to avoid suffering and live in denial, still, suffering and death are a part of life and a certain portion of our destiny.

That is why life-cycle rituals are important. Ritual helps people find meaning as each person goes through different stages of life, marking such crucial steps in life as graduation, marriage, getting the first job, giving birth, all of which are to be celebrated. However, life-cycle rituals become even more important when people go through difficult stages of life,

---

[968] Hall, *God and Human Suffering*, 79.

whether they choose to or not. These stages include, but are not limited to divorce, losing one's job, miscarriage, losing one's parents, losing one's partner, and losing one's children. Crisis stages also include losing parts of one's own body or a function of the body due to accidents, illness, or simply being old (losing hearing or sight or mobility or memory).

American liturgical theologian Karen Westerfield Tucker was at a loss for words when she lost her baby during pregnancy, calling it "a silent tragedy." She became more desperate when she learned that there was no ritual that speaks to her suffering. She searched for her church's worship book (United Methodist) and found out that there was no service for families that had lost a child during pregnancy. In response, not only did she write about the need for ritual as a pastoral response to help with her own suffering, she also helped create rituals for those in her Christian community who had the same life experience.[969] Her loss gave birth to a new liturgy that became a service of hope and healing. In this service from *United Methodist Book of Worship*, scripture passages that describe the loss of a child were chosen. 2 Samuel 12:15–23, for example, points to David's utter despair at the death of his child. In the ritual, the pastor, family, and friends are invited to speak the feelings of their loss. This verbal witness is followed by the ritual of the exchange act of signing faith, hope, and love.[970] In the service of death and resurrection for a stillborn child, a prayer includes speaking the name of the baby who died, as well as the names of the mother who carried the baby in her womb, along with the father and other family members who are mourning. The opening prayer conveys the expressions of the disappointment and the loneliness and the heaviness of heart. The prayer of commendation includes a ritual, a symbolic act of standing near the coffin or urn, and laying hands on it.[971]

D. Don't Confuse Healing with Cure

Healing is not to be confused with cure. Not every disease and illness can be cured. But this does not mean that people cannot be healed. Even when the physical self cannot be restored to its full health or the way it was before, still a measure of wholeness can be achieved. Black helps here: "*Cure*," she writes, "almost always means healing, the opposite is not true; *healing* often

---

[969] Karen Westerfield Tucker, "A Pastoral Response to a Silent Tragedy," *The Christian Ministry* 20, no. 1 (January—February 1989): 11–13. With her initiative, the following rituals were included in the *United Methodist Book of Worship* (Nashville: United Methodist Publishing House, 1992). "A Service of Hope after Loss of Pregnancy" (623–26) and "A Service of Death and Resurrection for a Stillborn Child" (170–71).

[970] United Methodist Book of Worship, "A Service of Hope after Loss of Pregnancy," 625.

[971] *United Methodist Book of Worship*, "A Service of Death and Resurrection for a Stillborn Child," 170–171.

does not mean *cure*."⁹⁷² Such distinction becomes especially critical when a person with a disability is viewed as the one who needs healing as if the cure (being free from that particular disability) is equated with healing. Such a view may cause more suffering and even oppression, because people with a disability are not being able to be accepted by society, as *they are*, Black notes.

Not being able to accept one's self leads to isolation. French philosopher and social critic Simone Weil says that isolation has three dimensions: physical, psychological, and social.⁹⁷³ Healing comes when a person (and the community) begins to recognize and accept the presence of affliction. To recognize one's affliction is a step on the road to healing. The same must happen if a community is to be healthy. Black, resonating with Weil, argues that healing happens "through the loving presence of another person."⁹⁷⁴

Black's following story illustrates of this presence:

> A little girl was late getting home from school. Her mother became more and more worried as the afternoon wore on. When she finally arrived, the mother said, "Where have been?! I've been worried sick!" The little girl responded, "Well, I was almost home, but then I saw Suzie sitting on the curb crying. Her dolly was broken." Her mother, relieved, said, "Oh! So you stopped to help her fix her dolly?" The little girl with the wisdom of the universe said, "No, I sat down on the curb, and I helped Suzie cry."⁹⁷⁵

To recognize the presence of affliction is to fully attend to that state of brokenness in the hurting person. It also recognizes its limit. Suzie's broken doll is not going to be fixed. Similarly, a still-born baby is not going to come back to life—even if we use or create a ritual. It is not the *cure* that the ritual achieves here, even if people who lost their baby so desperately wanted the baby back. The state of brokenness remains. However, through ritual a healing can happen. Ritual aids people to attend to suffering with the support in the loving presence of other people. Healing occurs because the healing presence of God is at work in and through others throughout a heartfelt ritual.

We cannot absolutely control the future or predict the outcome. Our temporality, mortality, and finitude require that we be humble. In order to be truly humble, we must surrender to and accept the limit of our knowing. Suffering reminds us of this limit of knowing. But to surrender to this limit does not mean that we become passive. To surrender is a stage to humility

---

⁹⁷² Black, *Healing Homiletic*, 181. The emphasis is original.

⁹⁷³ Simone Weil, "The Love of God and Affliction," *Waiting for God*, trans. Emman Craufurd, introduction by Leslie A. Fiedler (New York: G. P. Putnam's Sons, 1951), 117.

⁹⁷⁴ Black, *Healing Homiletic*, 182.

⁹⁷⁵ Black, 186.

and in no way identical to passivity or indifference. Instead of passivity or a dreaded indifference, an honest humility recognizes that life is both limited and precious. Because life is precious, humility must be sought out actively by embracing suffering fully, unafraid of the darkness another is experiencing, while knowing that we are not masters of our own fate. Yet, God is present with us no matter how we succeed or fail. We give thanks to God and celebrate this preciousness of life through the act of ritual. Ritual expresses our depths of feeling, knowing and unknowing, while allowing us to encounter and walk through the mystery of it all.

Finally, pastoral theology can respond to human suffering when it offers a robust theology that not simply comforts but also empowers people. This empowerment can be done with more than just words. It can be embodied in action through ritual and still involve critical theological reflections. The key to empowerment is connecting justice and compassion. In other words, without confronting injustice and orienting our thoughts and actions toward a more just world, then healing as the main goal of pastoral theology cannot be achieved. As one critically looks at the systematic historical layers of oppressions, addressing injustice is one concrete way to attend to human suffering.[976]

Injustice can be effectively addressed in the ritual of lament, rituals that faithfully hold and even caress the experience of the oppressed. One of the social ills of western modern culture is the absence of lamentation. People have forgotten how to grieve. This forgetfulness is buttressed by the myth that human beings are capable of basic independence and being in control. "Showing tears is a sign of weakness" is one example, which is in reality a state of forgetfulness, and not desirable or healthy. Many parts of modern society have "made the individual sacrosanct, self-sufficiency as eschatological aim."[977]

To heal this sickness, one must engage in public grief. "Public grief," American counsellor and chaplain William Blaine-Wallace claims, "creates the strongest possibility for more genuine reconciliation between perpetuators of violence ... and their victims."[978] The following testimony after the public hearing of the Truth and Reconciliation Commission in South Africa powerfully makes a point in this regard:

---

[976] Katherine Turpin, "Liberationist Practical Theology," in *Opening the Field of Practical Theology: An Introduction*, ed. Kathleen A. Cahalan and Gordon S. Mikoski (Lanham: Rowman and Littlefield, 2014), 157.

[977] William Blaine-Wallice, "The Politics of Tears: Lamentation as Justice Making," in *Injustice and the Care of Souls: Taking Oppression Seriously in Pastoral Care*, ed. Sheryl A. Kujawa-Holbrook and Karen Brown Montagno (Minneapolis: Fortress, 2009), 185.

[978] Blaine-Wallice, "Politics of Tears," 188.

The world is wept.... The sound of your sobbing is my own weeping; your wet handkerchief my pillow for a past so exhausted it cannot rest—not yet. Speak, weep, look, listen for us all. Oh, people of the silent hidden past, let your stories scatter seeds into our lonely frightened winds. Sow more, until the stillness of this land can soften, can dare to hope, and smile and sing; until the ghosts can dance unshackled, until our lives can know your sorrows and be healed.[979]

Here, Archbishop Tutu teaches us the value of a genuine effort of letting the victims and those in suffering share their pains wholeheartedly, so that their voices are neither silenced nor tokenized. This involves emotional, even irrational and physical acts. This posture is the beginning of healing and empowerment. This is the human agency involved in lamentation, a human state out of which the Spirit cries out.

In order to attend to human suffering as a response to and a goal of pastoral theology, we must pay attention to the voices of the marginalized, value their experiences of oppression as much as their power as agents to change their oppressive conditions for the sake of the well-being of all. Blaine-Wallace suggests that faith communities develop a "wailing-lamentation-solidarity" that can lead to "the faint promise of a new, unorthodox, organic, dependent, fragile community."[980]

E. A Few Rituals that Aid Pastoral Care

Ramshaw offers a few examples of ritual and care for the individual as rites of healing. She emphasizes the psychological and spiritual importance of touching. Jesus often healed people by touching.[981] The ritual of touching becomes especially meaningful and critical when a person is isolated by sickness or stigmatized by illness. She gives the example of the cruel shunning of persons with AIDS due to the irrational and ignorant fear of infection.[982] She also introduces a need for rituals with people who have intellectual disability and psychiatric problems. This need is critical because ritual can involve not only cognitive realms but evoke affective and sensory experiences. People who have difficulty comprehending and conceptualizing abstract thoughts and ideas remind the rest of us that the full meaning of liturgical symbols has been impoverished by our heady, rationalistic, and solemn ways of worshipping. People with cognitive impairment of various kinds may help us both realize what we have lost and recover the enriching liturgical heritage that involves hearts, bodies,

---

[979] Desmond Tutu, *No Future Without Forgiveness* (New York: Random House, 1999), 119.
[980] Blaine-Wallice, "Politics of Tears," 197.
[981] Matthew 8:3, 9:29, 20:34; Mark 7:33; Luke 5:13; and John 9:6.
[982] Ramshaw, *Ritual and Pastoral Care,* 64.

movements, senses as well as silence.⁹⁸³ Ritual with people who are mentally ill or unstable is also important. Ramshaw as a Lutheran invites us to explore Luther's writing for helpful ways that he himself understood mental illness (the obsessive-compulsive mental disorder).⁹⁸⁴ Thus, it is critical to develop rituals that enable those who experience anxiety and unworthiness to reclaim their dignity through God's grace and unconditional love.

One of the United Church of Canada's worship books, *Celebrate God's Presence,* offers various rituals that address cases of crisis and tragedy requiring healing. The broad range of pastoral prayers include:

- Prayers after a difficult childbirth,
- Prayers for couples in distress,
- Prayers when one partner leaves,
- Prayers before and after surgery,
- Prayers when natural disaster threatens, and
- Prayers after one has suffered from a violent crime.⁹⁸⁵

Beyond concern for individuals, Ramshaw also shares rituals for the world. Examples include a ritual of Maundy Thursday foot-washing portrayed in Alan Paton's novel *Ah, But Your Land is Beautiful.*⁹⁸⁶ As the story in the novel goes, a white judge is invited to the black church of his family's housekeeper. As he is washing the housekeeper's feet, his heart is stirred to kiss the servant's feet. This act was not required but became an extravagant outpouring of the heart. It was powerful and even scandalous, given that this story was written during the Apartheid era. Ramshaw introduces this novel to demonstrate the power of ritual that can denounce the structures of injustice, while connecting people yearning for reconciliation. The judge's ritual act, she writes, is spontaneous, intimate, and personal, yet it speaks a volume of "a thousand sermons."⁹⁸⁷

Conclusion

The question of this chapter, "What kind of response can pastoral theology give in the midst of suffering?" has emerged from the bigger questions of "Why must we suffer?" "Should we learn from suffering?" "What is the meaning of suffering?" and "Under what conditions can

---

⁹⁸³ Ramshaw, 78.
⁹⁸⁴ Ramshaw, 84–85.
⁹⁸⁵ Emily R. Brink, *Celebrate God's Presence: A Book of Services for the United Church of Canada* (Etobicoke, Ontario: United Church Publishing House, 2000), 556–565.
⁹⁸⁶ Alan Paton, *Ah, But Your Land is Beautiful* (New York: Penguin Books, 1983).
⁹⁸⁷ Ramshaw, *Ritual and Pastoral Care*, 92.

suffering make us more human?"[988] "What conditions enable people to end suffering?" is as important a question as what created the suffering in the first place. These questions beg a critical examination of the biblical understanding of suffering.

We have also considered conditions under which pastoral theology responds to create a more just and more humane world. These conditions include the cultivation of learning to create the loving presence of another person, while recognizing the other's affliction. We countered the myth of self-sufficiency, while seeking to restore interdependent relationships. To do so, we have suggested creating and participating in ritual as an important pastoral response to suffering. In and through ritual, one's pain can be shared, while creating a safe place to grieve and lament.

---

[988] Sölle, *Suffering*, 1, 5.

Bibliography

Slightly annotated list of combined references from all articles.
See pdf of bibliography here with hyperlinks active:
www.PreciousHeart.net/ti/2016/Bibliography-Pastoral-Care.pdf

Ackermann, Henry F. *He Was Always There, The U.S. Army Chaplain Ministry in the Vietnam Conflict.* Vol. 6 of 7 of history of Army Chaplaincy (see "Army, U.S." for ref. 7 vols.). U.S. Army, 1989.
Adams, Jay E. *The Christian Counselor's Commentary: Acts.* Woodruff: Timeless Texts, 1999.
Adams, Marilyn McCord. *Horrendous Evils and the Goodness of God, Cornell Studies in the Philosophy of Religion.* Ithaca: Cornell University Press, 2000.
Akhtar, Salman. *Comprehensive Dictionary of Psychoanalysis.* London: Karnac Books, 2009; 1,497 pp.
Alster, Bendt. *Wisdom of Ancient Sumer.* Bethesda: SDL-Press 2005; 426 pp.
Albright, W. F., and C. S. Mann. *Matthew: Introduction, Translation, and Notes, The Anchor Bible.* New York: Doubleday, 1971.
Alexander, T. Desmond, and David W. Baker, eds. *Dictionary of the Old Testament: Pentateuch.* Downers Grove: InterVarsity Press, 2003.
Ali, Carroll Watkins. *Survival and Liberation: Pastoral Theology in African American Context.* St. Louis: Chalice, 1999.
American Association of Pastoral Counselors. "About Us," accessed in 2016, www.aapc.org/Default.aspx?ssid=74andNavPTypeId=1157.
———. "Brief History on Pastoral Counseling." Accessed in 2916, www.aapc.org/Default.aspx?ssid=74andNavPTypeId=1158.
———. "Pastoral Counseling Today." Accessed in 2016, www.aapc.org/Default.aspx?ssid=74andNavPTypeId=1159.
American Counseling Association. "ACA Code of Ethics." Accessed in 2014, www.counseling.org/docs/ethics/2014-aca-code-of-ethics.pdf?sfvrsn=4.
———. "Definition of Psychology." Accessed in 2016, www.apa.org/about/.
American Psychological Association. "Ethical Principles of Psychologists and Code of Conduct." Accessed in 2010, www.apa.org/ethics/code/index.aspx.
———. "Marriage and Divorce." Accessed in 2010, www.APA.org/topics/divorce/.
Angel, Andrew. "Inquiring into an Inclusio—On Judgment and Love in Matthew." *Journal of Theological Studies* 60, No. 2 (October 2009): 527–30.
Aquinas, Thomas. *Summa Theologica*, I–II, q. 99 a. 4. In *St. Thomas Aquinas: Summa Theologica.* Translated by Fathers of the English Dominican Province. Allen, TX Christian Classics, 1981.
Arbaugh, George E., Niels Thulstrup, Marie Mikulová Thulstrup, eds. *Kierkegaard and Human Values, Bibliotheca Kierkegaardiana*, Vol. 7. Copenhagen: C. A. Reitzels Boghandel, 1980.
Arén, Gustav. *Evangelical Pioneers in Ethiopia: Origins of the Evangelical Church Mekane Yesus.* Stockholm: EFS Förlaget/Addis Ababa, Evangelical Church Mekane Yesus, 1978.
Army, U.S., Chaplaincy Histories in 7 volumes. *From Its European Antecedents to 1791: The United States Army Chaplaincy.* Vol. 1, by Chaplain Parker C. Thompson, 1978. *Struggling for Recognition: The United States Army Chaplaincy 1791–1865*, Vol. 2, by Chaplain Herman A. Norton, 1977. *Up From Handymen: The United States Army Chaplaincy 1865–1920*, Vol. 3, by Chaplain Earl F. Stover, 1977. *The Best and The Worst of Times: The United States Army Chaplaincy 1920–1945*, Vol. 4, by Chaplain Robert L. Gushwa, 1977. *Confidence in Battle, Inspiration in Peace: The United States Army Chaplaincy 1945–1975*, Vol. 5, by Chaplain Rodger R. Venzke, 1977. *He Was Always There, The U.S. Army Chaplain Ministry in the Vietnam Conflict*, Vol. 6, by Chaplain Henry F. Ackermann, 1989. *Encouraging Faith, Supporting Soldiers: A History of the U.S. Chaplain Corps 1975–1995*, Vol. 7, by Chaplain John W. Brinsfield, 1997.
Arnett, J. J. "Emerging Adulthood: A Theory of Development from the Late Teens Through the Twenties." *American Psychologist* 55, no 5 (May 2000): 469–480. See www.ncbi.nlm.nih.gov/pubmed/10842426.
Association of Clinical Pastoral Education. *The Journal of Pastoral Care and Counseling*, est. 1947. See www.ACPE.edu and http://pcc.sagepub.com. This is a joint publication of Journal of Pastoral Care Publications (www.JPCP.org) and Sage Journals, http://online.sagepub.com. As of June 2015, it is

in its 69th volume, running for 69 years, a massive body of literature on professional pastoral care, mostly in the hospital setting. View all volumes http://pcc.sagepub.com/content/by/year, view *all* volumes and articles to 1968—*phenomenal!*

Association of Professional Chaplains. See www.ProfessionalChaplains.org, and its *Chaplaincy Today: Journal of the Association of Professional Chaplains.*

Astrow, Alan B., A. Wexler, K. Texeira, M. K. He, and D. P. Sulmasy. "Is Failure to Meet Spiritual Needs Associated with Cancer Patients' Perceptions of Quality of Care and Their Satisfaction with Care?" *Journal of Clinical Oncology* 25, No. 36 (December 2007): 5753–5757. See www.ncbi.nlm.nih.gov/pubmed/18089871.

———, M. E. Paulk, M. J. Balboni, A. C. Phelps, E. T. Loggers, A. A. Wright, S. D. Block, E. F. Lewis, J. R. Peteet, H. G. Prigerson. "Provision of Spiritual Care to Patients with Advanced Cancer: Associations with Medical Care and Quality of Life Near Death." *Journal Clinical Oncology* 28, No. 3 (January 2010): 445–452. See www.ncbi.nlm.nih.gov/pubmed/20008625. Note conclusion: "Support of terminally ill patients' spiritual needs by the medical team is associated with greater hospice utilization and, among high religious copers, less aggressive care at EoL. Spiritual care is associated with better patient QoL near death."

———, M. J. Balboni, A. C. Enzinger, K. Gallivan, M. E. Paulk, A. Wright, K. Steinhauser, T. J. VanderWeele, H. G. Prigerson. "Provision of Spiritual Support to Patients with Advanced Cancer by Religious Communities and Associations with Medical Care at the End of Life." *JAMA Internal Medicine* 173, no 12 (June 2013):1109–1117. See www.ncbi.nlm.nih.gov/pubmed/23649656.

———, C. M. Puchalski, and D. P. Sulmasy. "Religion, Spiritual, and Health Care: Social, Ethical, and Practical Considerations." *American Journal of Medicine* 110, No. 4 (March 2001): 283–287. See www.amjmed.com/article/S0002-9343(00)00708-7/fulltext.

———, M. J. Balboni, A. C. Phelps, A. A. Wright, J. R. Peteet, S. D. Block, C. Lathan, T. Vanderweele, and H. G. Prigerson. "Support of Cancer Patients' Spiritual Needs and Associations with Medical Care Costs at the End of Life." *Cancer* 117, No. 23 (May 2011): 5383–91. See www.ncbi.nlm.nih.gov/pmc/articles/pubmed/21563177.

Asue, Daniel Ude. *Bottom Elephants: Catholic Sexual Ethics and Pastoral Practice in Africa: The Challenge of Women Living within Patriarchy & Threatened by HIV-Positive Husbands.* Washington DC: Pacem in Terris Press, 2014; 346 pp.

———. "Catholic Sexual Ethics and Tiv Women: A Case-study of Pastoral Practice in Regards to HIV/AIDS." PhD. Diss. Miami: St. Thomas University, 2012.

———. "Divine Revelation in Africa: Challenges of Intercultural Hermeneutics and Inculturation Theology." *Hekima Review* 49 (January 2014).

———. "Ecumenical Tensions among Nigerian Christians: Lessons from Vatican II." *International Review of Mission* 105, No. 2 (November 2016).

———. "Faith-Based Organizations and the Women's Empowerment Process in Nigeria: An Assessment of the Catholic Women Organization in Tivland." *International Journal of African Catholicism* 6, No. 2 (Winter 2015.).

———. "Evolving an African Christian Feminist Ethics: A Study of Nigerian Women." *International Journal of African Catholicism* 1, No. 2 (Summer 2010).

———. "The Evolution of Christian Feminist Ethics as a Demand for Social Justice." Chapter two in *The Kpim of Feminism: Issues and Women in a Changing World.* Edited by George Uzoma Ukagba, Obioma Des-Obi, Iks J. Nwankwor. Victoria, Canada: Trafford Publishing, 2010; 559 pp.

———. "How Does an African Polygamist Experience Grace in the Catholic Church?—A Hermeneutical Retrieval of Tertullian." *Hekima Review* 48 (May 2013).

———. "Muslim Youths in Search of Identity in Nigeria: The Case of Boko Haram Violence." *International Journal of African Catholicism* 3, No. 1 (Winter 2012).

———. "Remodeling Catechesis in Post Vatican II African Church: A Generation Approach." *Asian Horizons, Dharmaram Journal of Theology* 6, No. 3 (September 2012).

———. "Sexual Violence, Contraceptive Use, and the Principle of Self-Defense in Marriage." *Hekima Review* 50 (May 2014).

Augsburg Confession, 1530. See www.stpls.com/uploads/4/4/8/0/44802893/augsburg-confession.pdf.

Aulén, Gustaf. *Christus Victor: An Historical Study of the Three Main Types of the Idea of Atonement.* Translated by A. G. Hebert. New York: Macmillan, 1961.

Avalos, Hector, Sarah J. Melcher, and Jeremy Schipper, eds., *This Abled Body: Rethinking Disabilities in Biblical Studies.* Atlanta: Society of Biblical Literature, 2007.

Ayanga, Hazel. "Inspired and Gendered: The Hermeneutical Challenge of Teaching Gender in Kenya." In *Men in the Pulpit, Women in the Pew? Addressing Gender Inequality in Africa.* H. Jürgens Hendriks, Elna Mouton, L. D. Hansen, and Elisabet Le Roux. EFSA, Institute for Theological and Interdisciplinary Research. Sun Press, Stellenbosch, 2012.

B., Dick. *The Oxford Group and Alcohols Anonymous: A Design for Living That Works.* Kihei, Maui, HI: Paradise Research Publications, 1998.

Bachmann, Theodore, and Helmut Lehmann, eds. *Luther's Work* Vol. 35. Philadelphia: Muhlenberg Press, 1960.

Bai, Joseph. "One Reality Two Languages: The Relationship between Pastoral Language and Doctrinal Language." No date. Accessed July 23, 2019, at www.Academia.edu/4147144/One_Reality_Two_Languages_The_Relationship_between_Pastoral_Language_and_Doctrinal_Language.

Bailey, Kenneth. *Paul through Mediterranean Eyes: Cultural Studies in 1 Corinthians.* Downers Grove: IVP, 2011.

Balboni, Tracy A., M. E. Paulk, M. J. Balboni, A. C. Phelps, E. T. Loggers, A. A. Wright, S. D. Block, E. F. Lewis, J. R. Peteet, and H. G. Prigerson. "Provision of Spiritual Care to Patients with Advanced Cancer: Associations with Medical Care and Quality of Life Near Death." *Journal of Clinical Oncology* 28, No. 3 (January 2010): 445–452. See www.ncbi.nlm.nih.gov/pubmed/20008625.

———, M. J. Balboni, A. C. Enzinger, K. Gallivan, M. E. Paulk, A. Wright, K. Steinhauser, T. J. VanderWeele, H. G. Prigerson. "Provision of Spiritual Support to Patients with Advanced Cancer by Religious Communities and Associations with Medical Care at the End of Life." *JAMA Internal Medicine* 173, no 12 (June 2013):1109–1117. See www.ncbi.nlm.nih.gov/pubmed/23649656.

———, A. C. Phelps, A. A. Wright, J. R. Peteet, S. D. Block, C. Lathan, T. Vanderweele, and H. G. Prigerson. "Support of Cancer Patients' Spiritual Needs and Associations with Medical Care Costs at the End of Life." *Cancer* 117, No. 23 (May 2011): 5383–91. See www.ncbi.nlm.nih.gov/pmc/articles/pubmed/21563177.

———, M. Balboni, M. E. Paulk, A. Phelps, A. Wright, J. Peteet, S. Block, C. Lathan, T. Vanderweele, and H. Prigerson. "Support of Cancer Patients' Spiritual Needs and Associations with Medical Care Costs at the End of Life." *Cancer* 117, No. 23 (December 2011): 5383–5391. See www.ncbi.nlm.nih.gov/pubmed/11247596.

Balisky, Paul. "Ethiopian Church and Mission in the Context of Violence." In *Mission in the Context of Violence.* Edited by Keith E. Eitel. Pasadena: William Cary Library, 2008.

Baloyi, Magezi Elijah. "Wife Beating Among the Africans as a Challenge to Pastoral Care." *In Die Skriflig / in Luce Verbi* 47, No. 1 (2013). Accessed at www.indieskriflig.org.za/index.php/skriflig/article/view/713/2395. See also, www.researchgate.net/publication/269974549_Wife_beating_amongst_Africans_as_a_challenge_to_pastoral_care.

Barbour, I. G. *Nature, Human Nature, and God.* Minneapolis: Augsburg Fortress, 2002.

Barna Group. "2015 State of Atheism in America." Accessed at www.Barna.com/research/2015-state-of-atheism-in-america.

Barnes, Colin, and Geof Mercer. *Exploring Disability: A Sociological Introduction*, 2nd ed. Cambridge, UK; and Malden, MA: Polity Press, 2010.

Barrett, C. K. *A Commentary on the First Epistle to the Corinthians, Black's New Testament Commentaries.* London: Adam and Charles Black, 1968.

———. *The Gospel According to St John: An Introduction with Commentary and Notes on the Greek Text.* London: SPCK, 1960.

Barrow, J. D., and F. J. Tipler. *The Anthropic Cosmological Principle.* Oxford: Oxford University Press, 1986.

Barter, Jane A. "A Theology of Liberation in Barth's Church Dogmatics IV/3." *Scottish Journal of Theology* 53, No. 2 (May 2000): 154–176.

Barth, Christoph. *Die Errettung vom Tode. Leben und Tod in den Klage- und Dankliedern des Alten Testaments* (1947). New edition by Bernd Janowski. Stuttgart: Kohlhammer, 1997.

Barth, Karl (1886–1968). *Kirchliche Dogmatik, Church Dogmatics.* 4 vols, then into 12 part-volumes 1932–1968, 13 vols. by T & T Clark, 1956-1975. Translated by G. W. Bromiley and T. F. Torrance. Then a full study set with Greek, Hebrew, Latin, and French translated by scholars from

Princeton Theological Seminary in a 31-vol. set by Bloomsbury T & T Clark, 2009, www.Bloomsbury.com/us/church-dogmatics-study-edition-31-vols-9780567022790/. Considered one the greatest masterpieces of theology in the 20th century, and Barth is one the greatest in the history of the church.

———. *Ethics*. Translated by Goeffrey W. Bromiley. New York: Seabury, 1981.

———. *The Church Dogmatics* II/1. Translated by W. B. Johnston, T. H. L. Parker, Harold Knight, and J. L. L. Haire. Edited by G. W. Bromiley and T. F. Torrance. New York: T & T Clark, 1957.

———. *The Church Dogmatics* III/1. Translated by O. Bussey J.W. Edwards, Harold Knight. Edited by G. W. Bromiley and T. F. Torrance. Edinburgh: T & T Clark, 1958.

———. *The Church Dogmatics* III/2. Translated by Geoffrey W. Bromiley Harold Knight, J. K. S. Reid, R. H. Fuller. Edited by Geoffrey W. Bromiley and Thomas F. Torrance. Edinburgh: T & T Clark, 1960.

———. *The Church Dogmatics* III/3. Translated by Geoffrey W. Bromiley and R. J. Ehrlich. Edited by Geoffrey W. Bromiley and Thomas F. Torrance. Edinburgh: T & T Clark, 1960.

———. *The Church Dogmatics* IV/1. Translated by Geoffrey W. Bromiley. Edited by Geoffrey W. Bromiley and Thomas F. Torrance. Endinburgh: T & T Clark, 1956.

———. *The Church Dogmatics* IV/2. Translated by G. W. Bromiley. Edited by G. W. Bromiley and T. F. Torrance. New York: T & T Clark, 1958.

———. *The Church Dogmatics* IV/3.1. Translated by Geoffrey W. Bromiley. Edited by G. W. Bromiley and T. F. Torrance. New York: T & T Clark, 1961.

———. *The Church Dogmatics* IV/3.2. Translated G. W. Bromiley. Edited by G. W. Bromiley and T. F. Torrance. New York: T & T Clark, 1961.

———. *Kirchliche Dogmatik*, II/1. Zürich: Theologischer Verlag, 1980.

———. *Kirchliche Dogmatik*, IV/2. Zürich: Theologischer Verlag, 1980.

———. "The Christian Community and the Civil Community." In *Against the Stream: Shorter Post-War Writings, 1946–1952*. Edited by Ronald Gregor Smith. New York: Philosophical Library, 1954.

———. "Jesus Christ and the Movement for Social Justice (1911)." In *Karl Barth and Radical Politics*. Edited by George Hunsinger. Philadelphia: Westminster, 1976.

———. "Johannes 9, 13 (1938)." In *Karl Barth Gesamtausgabe: Predigten 1935–1952*. Edited by Hartmut Spieker and Hinrich Stoevesandt. Zürich: Theologischer Verlag Zürich, 1996: 115–118.

———. "Poverty." In *Against the Stream: Shorter Post-War Writings, 1946–52*. Edited by Ronald Gregor Smith. New York: Philosophical Library, 1954.

Bartholomew, K., and L. M. Horowitz. "Attachment Styles Among Young Adults: A Test of a Four-category Model." *Journal of Personality and Social Psychology* 61 (1991): 226–244.

Bauckham, Richard, ed. *God Will Be All in All: Eschatology of Jürgen Moltmann*. Edinburgh: T & T Clark Ltd, 1999.

Bauer, D., and M. A. Powell, eds. *Treasures New and Old: Recent Contributions to Matthean Studies*. Atlanta: Scholars Press, 1996.

Baxter, Richard (1615-1691). *The Saints' Everlasting Rest—The Blessed State of the Saints in Their Enjoyment of God in Glory*. London by Rob. White for Thomas Underhil & Francis Tyton, Jan. 15, 1649, Imprimatur, Joseph Caryl, at 856 pages. Scotland, Christian Heritage Publications, 2001; 704 pp. See http://digitalpuritan.net/richard-baxter/ for *all* of Baxter's work, including the full *Saints' Everlasting Rest*.

Baxter, Wayne. *Growing Up to Get Along: Conflict and Unity in Philippians*. Rapid City: Crosslink, 2016; 142 pp.

———. *Israel's Only Shepherd: Matthew's Shepherd Motif and His Social Setting*. London: T & T Clark, 2012; 228 pp.

———. *We've Lost. What Now? Practical Counsel from the Book of Daniel*. Eugene: Wipf & Stock, 2015; 158 pp.

Bayer, Oswald. *Martin Luther's Theology: A Contemporary Interpretation*. Translated Thomas H. Trapp. Grand Rapids: Eerdmans, 2008.

Beale, G. K., and D. A. Carson, eds. *Commentary on the New Testament Use of the Old Testament*. Grand Rapids: Baker Academic, 2007.

Beattie, Tina, and D. Culberston, eds. *Visions and Vocations*. The Catholic Women Speak Network. Mahwah: Paulist Press, 2018.

Beavis, Mary Ann, and HyeRan Kim-Cragg. *What Does the Bible Say?—A Critical Conversation with Popular Culture in a Biblically Illiterate World*. Eugene: Cascade, 2017.

Behe, Michael J. *Darwin's Black Box—the Biochemical Challenge to Evolution.* Simon and Schuster, 1998 [1st 1996]; 307 pp.

———, William A. Dembski, and Stephen C. Meyer. *Science and Evidence for Design in the Universe* (Papers presented at a conference sponsored by the Wethersfield Institute, New York City, September 25, 1999). San Francisco: Ignatius Press, 2000; 234 pp.

Bejoian, Lynne M., Molly Quinn, and Maysaa S. Bazna. "Disability, Agency and Engagement: Three Wisdom Traditions' Call to Be Radically Available." In *Disability and Religious Diversity: Cross-cultural and Interreligious Perspectives.* Edited by Darla Schumm and Michael Stoltzfus. New York: Palgrave Macmillan, 2011: 177–99.

Bell, Richard H. "Salvation from the Wrath to Come: An Exposition of Romans 5:9 and 1 Thessalonians 5:9." *Testamentum Imperium* 1 (2007), www.preciousheart.net/ti/2007/003_07_Bell_Romans_5_1Thess_5.pdf.

Bennema, Cornelis. "Moral Transformation in the Johannine Writings." *In die Skriflig/In Luce Verbi* 51 (January 2017): accessed May 8, 2017, https://doi.org/10.4102/ids.v51i3.2120.

Benner, David G. *Care of Souls: Revisioning Christian Nurture and Counsel.* Grand Rapids: Baker Books, 1998.

———, and P. C. Hill, eds. *Encyclopedia of Psychology and Counseling.* 2nd ed. Grand Rapids: Baker Academic, 1999.

———. *Strategic Pastoral Counseling, a Short-term Structured Model*, 2nd ed. Grand Rapids: Baker Academic, 2003.

Bennett, James V. *I Chose Prison.* New York: Alfred A. Knopf, 1970.

Bethge, Eberhard. *Dietrich Bonhoeffer: A Biography.* Rev. ed. Minneapolis: Fortress Press, 2000.

Biblische Enzyklopädie, see: Dietrich, Walter.

Biklen, Douglas, and Lee Bailey, eds. *Rudely Stamp'd: Imaginal Disability and Prejudice.* Washington, DC: University Press of America, 1981.

Bieler, Andrea, Isolde Karle, HyeRan Kim-Cragg, and Ilona Nord, eds. *Migration and Religion: Negotiating Sites of Hospitality, Resistance, and Vulnerability.* Leipzig: Eva, 2019.

Bird, M. F. "Sin, Sinner." In *Dictionary of Jesus and the Gospels.* Edited by Joel B. Green et al. Downers Grove: InterVarsity Press, 1992.

Black, Kathy. *A Healing Homiletic: Preaching and Disability.* Nashville: Abingdon, 1994.

Blackburn, B. "Ethical Issues in Pastoral Counseling." *Christian Ethics Today* 5, No. 2 (April 1999): 22–26, accessed at http://ChristianEthicsToday.com/PDF/CET_Issue_021.pdf.

Blaine-Wallice, William. "The Politics of Tears: Lamentation as Justice Making." In *Injustice and the Care of Souls: Taking Oppression Seriously in Pastoral Care.* Edited by Sheryl A. Kujawa-Holbrook and Karen Brown. Montagno: Minneapolis: Fortress, 2009.

Blanton-Peale Institute and Counseling Center. "About Us." Accessed 2016 at www.blantonpeale.org/about_us.html.

Bloesch, Donald G. *The Last Things: Resurrection, Judgment, Glory.* Downers Grove: IVP, 2004.

Bloomquist, Karen L., ed. *Theological Practices That Matter.* Minneapolis: Lutheran University Press, 2009.

Blum, T. C., and P. M. Roman. *Cost-effectiveness and Preventive Implications of Employee Assistance Programs.* U.S. Department of Health and Human Services. Rockville, MD: SAMSA, 1995. See www.ncjrs.gov/App/Publications/abstract.aspx?ID=160889.

Boff, Leonardo. *Liberating Grace.* Maryknoll: Orbis, 1979.

Bogdan, Robert, Martin Elks, and James A. Knoll. *Picturing Disability: Beggar, Freak, Citizen, and Other Photographic Rhetoric.* Syracuse: Syracuse University Press, 2012.

Boisen, Anton. *The Exploration of the Inner World: A Study of Mental Disorder and Religious Experience.* Chicago and New York: Willett, Clark, and Co., 1936.

———. *Religion in Crisis and Custom: A Sociological and Psychological Study.* Harper and Brothers, 1955.

Bokedal, Tomas. "Canon/Scripture," in *The Dictionary of the Bible and Ancient Media*, edited by Tom Thatcher, Chris Keith, Raymond F. Person, Jr., Elsie R. Stern, 46–48. London: T & T Clark/Bloomsbury, 2017.

———. "Revelation: What Forms of Authority, and to Whom?" In *T & T Clark Companion to the Theology of Kierkegaard.* Edited by Aaron P. Edwards and David J. Gouwens, 279-298. London: T & T Clark/Bloomsbury, 2019.

Bonar, Horatius. *The Everlasting Righteousness.* Edinburgh: Banner of Truth, 1993; first 1874.

Bonhoeffer, Dietrich (1906-1945). *The Cost of Discipleship*. Translated by R. H. Fuller. New York: Macmillan, 1959.
———. *Creation and Fall: A Theological Interpretation of Genesis 1–3*. New York: Collier Books, 1959.
———. *Creation and Fall Temptation: Two Biblical Studies*. New York: Collier Books, 1959.
———. *Dietrich Bonhoeffer Works*. 17 vols. Minneapolis: Fortress Press, 2009– 2014.
———. *Ethics*. Edited by Eberhard Bethge. New York: Macmillan, 1955.
———. *Letters and Papers from Prison*. New York: Simon and Schuster, Touchstone, 1997; first 1953, after Nazi Gestapo executed him in 1945.
———. *Worldly Preaching: Lectures on Homiletics*. New York: Crossroad Publishing Company, 1991.
Bosch, David J. *Transforming Mission: Paradigm Shifts in Theology of Mission*. American Society of Missiology 20th Anniversary Edition. Maryknoll: Orbis Books, 1991; 20th Anniversary Ed., 2011.
Botterweck, G. Johann, and Helmer Ringgren, eds. *Theologisches Wörterbuch zum Alten Testament*. 8 vols. Stuttgart: Kohlhammer, 1973-1995. See *Theological Dictionary of the Old Testament*. Translated by David E. Green, Douglas W. Stott et al. 15 vols. Grand Rapids: Eerdmans, 1973.
Boulton, Wayne G., Thomas D. Kennedy, and Allen Verhey. *From Christ to the World—Introductory Readings in Christian Ethics*. Grand Rapids: Eerdmans, 1994.
Boyd, Gregory A. *Is God to Blame? Moving Beyond Pat Answers to the Problem of Evil*. Downers Grove: IVP, 2003.
Brandt, Walther I., and Helmut Lehmann, eds. *Luther's Work*. Vol. 45. Philadelphia: Muhlenburg Press, 1962.
Braukämper, Ulrich. *Geschichte Der Hadiya Süd-Äthiopiens: Von D. Anfängen Bis Zur Revolution 1974*. Wiesbaden: Steiner, 1980.
Brazal, Agnes, and Maria Theresa Davila, eds. *Living With(Out) Borders: Catholic Theological Ethics in the World Church and the Migration of Peoples*. Maryknoll: Orbis Books, 2016; 260 pp.
Brink, Emily R. *Celebrate God's Presence: A Book of Services for The United Church of Canada*. Toronto: United Church Publishing House, 2000.
Brinsfield, John W. *Encouraging Faith, Supporting Soldiers: A History of the U.S. Chaplain Corps 1975–1995*, Vol. 7 of 7 of history of Army Chaplaincy (see "Army, U.S." ref. for more). U.S. Army, 1997.
Brown, Colin. *Philosophy and the Christian Faith*. Westmont: IVP, 1969.
Brown, Raymond McAfee. *Unexpected News: Reading the Bible with Third World Eyes*. Philadelphia: Westminster Press, 1984.
Brown, Raymond E., Joseph A. Fitzmyer, and Roland E. Murphy, eds. *The New Jerome Biblical Commentary*. Englewood Cliffs, NJ: Prentice Hall, 1990.
Brown, Roderick. "Corrective Rape in South Africa: A Continuing Plight Despite an International Human Rights Response." *Annual Survey of International and Comparative Law* 18, No. 1 (2012): 45–66. See https://digitalcommons.law.ggu edu/cgi/viewcontent.cgi?article=1157andcontext=annlsurvey.
Brown, S. "Faith, the Poor and the Gentiles: A Tradition-Historical Reflection on Matthew 25:31–46." *Toronto Journal of Theology* 6, No. 2 (September 1990): 174–75. See www.utpjournals.press/doi/pdf/10.3138/tjt.6.2.171.
Bruce, F. F. *The Books and the Parchments*. London: Pickering and Inglis, 1950.
———. *The Epistle to the Galatians: A Commentary on the Greek Text, The New International Greek Testament Commentary*. Grand Rapids: Eerdmans, 1982.
———. *New Testament History*. London: Oliphants, 1969.
Bucher, Lloyd M., with Mark Rascovich. *Bucher: My Story*, New York: Doubleday, 1970; 447 pp.
Brunner, Emil. *The Divine Imperative*. Louisville: Westminster, 1947; New York: Macmillan, 1937; 728 pp.
Brushwyler, L. R., S. C. Fancher, J. C. Geoly, J. R. Matthews, J. R., and M. M. R. Stone. *Pastoral Care vs. Professional Counseling: Discerning the Differences*. Westchester: The Midwest Ministry Development Service, 1999. See http://midwestministrydevelopment.org/pdf/Care-Vs-Counseling.pdf.
Buchanan, G. *Matthew, Mellen Biblical Commentary*. 2 vols. Lewiston: Edwin Mellen Press, 1996–97.
Buchanan, James. *The Doctrine of Justification: An Outline of its History in the Church and of its Exposition from Scripture, Lecture XV Justification; It's Relation to the Work of the Holy Spirit*. Edinburgh: T & T Clark, 1867; Solid Ground Christian Books, 2006. See https://books.google.com/books?id=Px0DAAAAQAAJ.

Büchsel, Friedrich. "κρίνω E. The Concept of Judgment in the New Testament." In *Theological Dictionary of the New Testament*. Vol. 3. Edited by Gerhard Kittel, G. W. Bromiley, and Gerhard Friedrich. Grand Rapids: Eerdmans, 1965.

Budge, E. A. W. *The Egyptian Book of the Dead: The Papyrus of Ani Egyptian Text Transliteration and Translation*. New York: Dover Publications, 1967.

Bujo, B., and J. I. Muya, eds. *African Theology in the 21st Century. The Contribution of the Pioneers*. Vol. 1. Nairobi: Paulines Publications Africa, 2003.

Bujo, B. "Introduction to the Tshibangu-Vanneste Debate." In *African Theology in the 21st Century. The Contribution of the Pioneers*. Vol. 1. Edited by B. Bujo and J. I. Muya. Nairobi: Paulines Publications Africa, 2003.

Bulgakov, Sergius. *The Comforter*. Translated by Boris Jakim. Grand Rapids: Eerdmans, 2004.

Bulkeley, Kelly. *Transforming Dreams: Learning Spiritual Lessons from the Dreams You Never Forget*. New York: John Wiley and Sons, 2000.

Burnett, Richard E., ed. *The Westminster Handbook to Karl Barth*. Louisville: Westminster John Knox Press, 2013.

Burton, Ernest DeWitt. *A Critical and Exegetical Commentary on the Epistle to the Galatians, The International Critical Commentary*. Edinburgh: T & T Clark, 1956.

Byrne, D., and S. K. Murnen. "Maintaining Loving Relationship." In *The Psychology of Love*. Edited by R. J. Sternberg and M. L. Barnes. New Haven: Yale University Press, 1998.

Cahalan, Kathleen A., and Gordon S. Mikoski, eds. *Opening the Field of Practical Theology: An Introduction*. Lanham: Rowman and Littlefield, 2014.

Cameli, Louis J. *Catholic Teaching on Homosexuality*. Notre Dame: Ave Maria Press, 2012.

Campbell, Douglas. *The Deliverance of God: An Apocalyptic Rereading of Justification in Paul*. Grand Rapids: Eerdmans, 2013.

Cappa, S. A. "Role Conflicts in Pastoral Care and Counseling." In *Encyclopedia of Psychology and Counseling*, 2nd ed., edited by D. G. Benner and P. C. Hill. Grand Rapids: Baker Academic, 1999: 833–834.

Carpenter, S., and K. Huffman. *Visualizing Psychology*. 2nd ed. Hoboken: John Wiley and Sons, 2010.

Carson, D. A., Peter T. O'Brien, and Mark A. Seifrid, eds. *Justification and Variegated Nomism*. 2 vols. Tübingen: Mohr Siebeck, 2001 and 2004.

Carson, D. A. "1–3 John." In *Commentary on the New Testament use of the Old Testament*. Edited by G. K. Beale and D. A. Carson, 1063–1067. Grand Rapids: Baker Academic, 2007.

Catechism of the Catholic Church. 2nd ed. Washington, DC: US Conference of Catholic Bishops, 1997.

Chadwick, H. et al. "Christianity." In *Encyclopedia Britannica*. Accessed in 2016, www.britannica.com/topic/Christianity/The-Christian-community-and-the-world#ref927214.

Chambers, O. *The Love of God*. Grand Rapids: Discovery House, 1985.

Chapman, T. W., ed. *A Practical Handbook for Ministry from the Writings of Wayne E. Oates*. Louisville: Westminster/John Knox Press, 1992.

Charlton, James I. *Nothing about Us without Us: Disability Oppression and Empowerment*. Berkeley: University of California Press, 1998.

Chesnut, Glenn F. *Changed by Grace: V.V. Kitchen, the Oxford Group, and A.A.* Lincoln: iUniverse, Inc., 2006.

Chester, Stephen J. *Conversion at Corinth: Perspectives on Conversion in Paul's Theology and the Corinthian Church*. London: T & T Clark, 2003.

Chester, Tim. *Good News to the Poor*. Wheaton: Crossway, 2013.

Chevallier, M. A. "Note à propos de l'éxegèse de Matt 25:31–46." *Revue des Sciences Religieuses* 48 (1974): 398–400.

Chopra, Deepak, ed. *The Love Poems of Rumi* (1207–1273). New York: Harmony Books, 1998.

Christianity Today. "Christian history Gregory the great, servant of the servants of God," *Christianity Today* (no author, n.d.). Accessed at www.ChristianityToday.com/history/people/rulers/gregory-great.html.

Ciampa, Roy E., and Brian S. Rosner. *The First Letter to the Corinthians, The Pillar New Testament Commentary*. Grand Rapids: Eerdmans, 2010.

Clapham, Christopher S. *Transformation and Continuity in Revolutionary Ethiopia*. Cambridge: Cambridge University Press, 1988.

Clark, P. A., M. Drain, and M. P. Malone. "Addressing patients' emotional and spiritual needs." *The Joint Commission Journal on Quality and Patient Safety* 29, No. 12 (December 2003): 659–670. See www.ncbi.nlm.nih.gov/pubmed/14679869.
Clifton, Shane. *Husbands Should Not Break: A Memoir*. Prepub. Copy from Shane.clifton@ac.edu.au.
Clinebell, Howard J. *Basic Types of Pastoral Care and Counselling: Resources for the Ministry of Healing and Growth*. Nashville: Abingdon Press, 1966.
Cloud, H., and J. Townsend. *Boundaries in Dating*. Grand Rapids: Zondervan, 2000.
Cobb, John B., Jr., "The Problem of Evil and the Task of Ministry." In *Encountering Evil: Live Options in Theodicy*. Edited by Stephen T. Davis. Atlanta: John Knox Press, 1981.
Cobb, Mark R., Christina M. Puchalski, and Bruce Rumbold, eds. *The Oxford Textbook of Spirituality in Healthcare*. Oxford: Oxford University Press, 2012; 520 pp.
Cochran, Clarke E. "Life on the Border: A Catholic Perspective." In *Church, State and Public Justice: Five Views* (Clarke E. Cochran, Derek H. Davis, Corwin E. Smidt, Ronald J. Sider, and Philip Wogaman). Edited by P. C. Kemeny. Downers Grove: IVP, 2007.
Cohen, Meredith, and Justine Firnhaber-Baker, eds. *Difference and Identity in Francia and Medieval France*. Farnham, UK: Ashgate, 2010.
Coleman, Craig S. "North Korea Unveils USS Pueblo: American Ship Captured in 1968 Now On Display as Tourist Attraction." *Korea Times* (May 3, 1995).
Coleman, Monica A. *Ain't I a Womanist Too: Third-Wave Womanist Religious Thought*. Minneapolis: Fortress Press, 2013.
Collins, G. R. *The Rebuilding of Psychology: An Integration of Psychology and Christianity*. Wheaton: Tyndale House, 1977.
Cone, J. *Speaking the Truth*. Grand Rapids: Eerdmans, 1986.
Congregation for the Doctrine of the Faith. "Declaration on Certain Problems of Sexual Ethics, Persona Humanae." Accessed December 29, 1975, No. 10. In *Vatican Council II: More Post Conciliar Documents*. Edited by Austin Flannery, O.P. Collegeville, MN: The Liturgical Press, 1982.
Connor, Robert A. "The Truth Will Make You Free." Personal Blog, accessed April 07, 2009, http://robertaconnor.blogspot.com/2009/04/theology-of-incarnation-theology-of.html.
Conradie, E., ed. *Reconciliation: A Guiding Vison for South Africa*. Stellenbosch: Sun Press, 2013.
Constantine, M. G., E. L. Lewis, L. C. Conner, and D. SanchEzek. "Addressing Spiritual and Religious Issues in Counseling African Americans: Implications for Counselor Training and Practice." *Counseling and Values* 45, No. 1 (December 2000): 28–38. See https://onlinelibrary.wiley.com/doi/abs/10.1002/j.2161-007X.2000.tb00180.x.
Conway, Pádraic, and Fáinche Ryan, eds. *Karl Rahner: Theologian for the Twenty-first Century*. New York: Peter Lang, Internationaler Verlag der Wissenschaften, 2010.
Cooper, Tracey, and Dame Tina Lavender. "Women's Perceptions of a Midwife's Role: An Initial Investigation." *British Journal of Midwifery* 21, No. 4 (August 2013): 268. See. www.magonlinelibrary.com/doi/abs/10.12968/bjom.2013.21.4.264.
Cooper-White, Pamela. *Braided Selves: Collected Essays on Multiplicity, God, and Persons*. Eugene: Wipf & Stock, 2011.
———. *Many Voices: Pastoral Psychotherapy in Relational and Theological Perspective*. Minneapolis: Augsburg Press, 2011.
———. *Shared Wisdom: Use of the Self in Pastoral Care and Counseling*. Minneapolis: Fortress Press, 2004.
Cope, Lane. "Matthew XXV: 31–46: 'The Sheep and the Goats' Reinterpreted." *Novum Testamentum* 11, No. 1/2 (January–April 1969): 32–44.
Corey, Gerald. *Theory and Practice of Counseling and Psychotherapy*. Pacific Grove: Brooks/Cole, Cengage Learning, 2013 and 2009.
Council of Trent, *Decree on Justification* (1545–1563).
Council of Trent, *Doctrine on the Sacrament of Penance* (1545–1563).
Craig, William Lane. *The Cosmological Argument from Plato to Leibniz*. New York: Macmillan, 1980; 305 pp.
———. *Divine Foreknowledge and Human Freedom—The Coherence of Theism, Omniscience*. Leiden: Brill, 1990; 360 pp.
———. *The Kalam Cosmological Argument*. New York: Macmillan, 1979
———. *The Only Wise God—The Compatibility of Divine Foreknowledge and Human Freedom*. Eugene: Wipf and Stock, 2000 (1st 1987); 157 pp.

———, ed. *Philosophy of Religion—a Reader and Guide*. New Brunswick: Rutgers University Press, 2002; 634 pp.
———. *The Problem of Divine Foreknowledge and Future Contingents from Aristotle to Suarez*. Leiden: Brill, 1997; 298 pp.
———, and Quentin Smith. *Theism, Atheism, and Big Bang Cosmology*. Oxford: Clarendon Press, 1995.
———. *Time and Eternity—Exploring God's Relationship to Time*. Wheaton: Crossway, 2001; 272 pp.
Cohen, Arthur A., and Marvin Halverson, eds. *A Handbook of Christian Theology*. Nashville: Abingdon Press, 1972 & 1980, 1st 1958.
Crislip, Andrew T. *From Monastery to Hospital: Christian Monasticism and the Transformation of Health Care in Late Antiquity*. Ann Arbor: University of Michigan Press, 2005.
Cunningham, L., M. Frassetto, M.D. Knowles, J. L. McKenzie, J. J. Pelikan, and F. C. Oakley. "Roman Catholicism." In *Encyclopedia Britannica*. Accessed in 2016, www.britannica.com/topic/Roman-Catholicism/The-age-of-Reformation-and-Counter-Reformation.
Curlin, F. A., C. J. Roach, R. Gorawara-Bhat, J. D. Lantos, and M. H. Chin. "How Are Religion and Spirituality Related to Health? A Study of Physicians' Perspectives." *Southern Medical Journal* 98, No. 8 (August 2005): 761–766. See www.ncbi.nlm.nih.gov/pubmed/16144169.
Curtis, W. H. Personal communication to Tinsely and Prentice, October 28, 2016.
Cusanus, Nicolaus, *De docta ignorancia* (*On learned ignorance/on scientific ignorance*). Kues, Germany: 1440.

Dahm, Albert. *Der Gerichtsgedanke in der Versöhnungslehre Karl Barths*, Vol. XLVII, Konfessionskundliche und Kontroverstheologische Studien. Paderborn: Verlag Bonifatius-Druckerei, 1983.
Darwall, Stephen. *Deontology*. Hoboken: Blackwell, 2003.
Davies, Oliver. *The Theology of Compassion: Metaphysics of Difference and the Renewal of Tradition*. Cambridge, 2001; Grand Rapids: Eerdmans, 2003.
Davies, W. D., and Dale C. Allison. *The Gospel According to Saint Matthew: A Critical and Exegetical Commentary*, 3 Vols. *The International Critical Commentary*. Edinburgh: T & T Clark, 1988.
Davis, Lennard J., ed. *The Disability Studies Reader*. 2nd ed. New York: Routledge, 2006.
Davis, Stephen T., ed. *Encountering Evil: Live Options in Theodicy*. Atlanta: John Knox Press, 1981.
———, Daniel Kendall, and Gerald O'Collins, eds. *The Trinity: An Interdisciplinary Symposium on the Trinity*. New York: Oxford University Press, 2002.
Davison, Richard J., and Anne Harrington, eds. *Vision of Compassion: Western Scientists and Tibetan Buddhists Examine Human Nature*. Oxford: Oxford University Press, 2001.
Dietrich, Walter, and Wolfgang Stegemann, eds. *Biblische Enzyklopädie*. Stuttgart: Kohlhammer Verlag, 1996ss (12 vols. planned, 9 done; 5 translated into English).
De Gruchy, John W. *Liberating Reformed Theology: A South African Contribution to an Ecumenical Debate*. Grand Rapids: Eerdmans, 1990.
De Lubac, Henri. *A Brief Catechesis on Nature and Grace*. Translated by Brother Richard Arnandez, F.S.C. San Francisco: Ignatius Press, 1984.
Dembski, William A., and Michael Ruse, eds. *Debating Design: from Darwin to DNA*. Cambridge: Cambridge University Press, 2004.
———. *The Design Inference—Eliminating Chance through Small Probabilities*. Cambridge: Cambridge University Press, 1998.
———. *No Free Lunch—Why Specified Complexity Cannot be Purchased without Intelligence*. Lanham: Rowman and Littlefield, 2002.
Demos, E. Virginia, ed. *Exploring Affect: The Selected Writings of Silvan S. Tomkin*. New York: Cambridge University Press, 1995.
Denzinger, Heinrich, original ed., and most recent ed. was Peter Hünermann. *Enchiridion Symbolorum: A Compendium of Creeds, Definitions and Declarations of the Catholic Church*. San Francisco, CA: St. Ignatius Press, 2012; 1,450 pp. See www.Ignatius.com/Enchiridion-Symbolorum-P543.aspx.
Deressa, Samuel Yonas. *Cultural Ethics and Inter-Religious Coexistence and the Ethiopian Context: The Case of Karrayyu Oromo*. Addis Ababa, Ethiopia: Makane Yesus Seminary, 2011; 92 pp.
———. *The Life, Works, and Witness of Tsehay Tolessa and Gudina Tumsa, the Ethiopian Bonhoeffer*. Minneapolis: Fortress Press, 2017; 299 pp.
———, ed. *Revisiting the History, Theology, and Leadership Practice of the Ethiopian Evangelical Church Mekane Yesus (Journal of Gudina Tumsa Theological Forum)*. Minneapolis: Lutheran University Press, 2016; 174 pp.

———. *Emerging Theological Praxis*. Minneapolis: Lutheran University Press, 2012.
Dick B., *The Oxford Group and Alcohols Anonymous: A Design for Living That Works*. Kihei, Maui: Paradise Research Publications, 1998.
Dickson, David (1583–1663), and James Durham (1622–1658). *Sum of Saving Knowledge: or, A Brief Sum of Christian Doctrine*. Edinburgh: Jonstone, Hunter, 1872; first 1650.
Dillistone, F. W. "Redemption." In *Westminster Dictionary of Christian Theology*. Edited by A. Richardson and J. Bowden, 487–488. Philadelphia: Westminster Press, 1983.
Ditmanson, Harold. *Grace in Experience and Theology*. Minneapolis: Augsburg, 1977.
Dodd, C. H. *Gospel and Law: The Relation of Faith and Ethics in Early Christianity*. Cambridge: Cambridge University Press, 1951.
Dominic Prümmer, *Handbook of Moral Theology*. Translated by J. G. Nolan. New York: P. J. Kennedy and Sons, 1957.
Donahue, John R. "The 'Parable' of the Sheep and the Goats: A Challenge to Christian Ethics." *Theological Studies* 47 (February 1986): 3–31.
Donham, Donald L. *Marxist Modern: An Ethnographic History of the Ethiopian Revolution*. Berkeley: University of California Press, 1999.
Donnelly, John Patrick, ed. *Peter Martyr Vermigli: Life, Letters, and Sermons*. The Peter Martyr Library. Vol. 5. Kirksville: Thomas Jefferson University Press, 1999.
Doolittle, B. R., A. C. Justice, and D. A. Fiellin. "Religion, Spirituality, and HIV Clinical Outcomes: A Systematic Review of the Literature." *AIDS Behavior* 22, No. 6 (June 2016): 1792–1801. See www.ncbi.nlm.nih.gov/pubmed/28004218.
Dreher, Rod. "I'm Still Not Going Back to the Catholic Church." *TIME* (September 23, 2013). Accessed at http://ideas.time.com/2013/09/29/im-still-not-going-back-to-the-catholic-church/.
Dreyer, J. S., and J. H. C. Pieterse. "Religious in Public Sphere: What Can Public Theology Learn from Habermas' Latest Work?" *HTS Theological Studies* 66, no.1 (2010). See https://hts.org.za/index.php/hts/article/view/798.
Drum, W. "Pastoral Theology." *The Catholic Encyclopedia*. New York: Robert Appleton Company, 1912. See www.newadvent.org/cathen/14611a.htm.
Drummond, R. J., and K. D. Jones. *Assessment Procedures for Counselors and Helping Professionals*, 7th ed. Upper Saddle River, NJ: Pearson Education, 2010.
Duffy, Stephen. *The Dynamics of Grace: Perspectives in Theological Anthropology*. Michael Glazier, 1993; Eugene: Wipf & Stock, 2007.
Dunkle, Kristin L., Rachel K. Jewkes, Heather C. Brown, Glenda E. Gray, James A. McIntryre, and Siobán D. Harlow. "Gender-based Violence, Relationship Power, and Risks of HIV Infection in Women Attending Antennal Clinics in South Africa." *Lancet* 363, No. 9419 (May 1, 2004): 1415–1421. See www.ncbi.nlm.nih.gov/pubmed/15121402.

Edgar, Thomas R. "Lethargic or Dead in 1 Thessalonians 5:10?" *Chafer Theological Seminary Journal* 6, No. 4 (October 2000). Revised version of his article, "The Meaning of 'Sleep' in 1 Thessalonians 5:10." *Journal of the Evangelical Society* 22, No. 4 (December 1979): 345–49.
Edwards, David L., and John Stott. *Evangelical Essentials: A Liberal—Evangelical Dialogue*. Downers Grove: IVP, 1988.
Edwards, James R. *The Gospel According to Mark*. Grand Rapids: Eerdmans, 2001.
Edwards, Jonathan. *Charity and Its Fruits: Christian Love as Manifested in the Heart and Life*. Scotland: Banner of Truth Trust, 2000; 1st 1852.
Edwards, Mark J., ed. *Ancient Christian Commentary on Scripture: New Testament VIII, Galatians, Ephesians, Philippians*. Downers Grove: IVP, 1999.
Edwards, Aaron P., and David J. Gouwens, eds. *T & T Clark Companion to the Theology of Kierkegaard*. London: T & T Clark/Bloomsbury, 2019.
Egan, Gerard. *Encounter: Group Processes for Interpersonal Growth*. Belmont: Brooks/Cole, 1970.
———. *The Skilled Helper: A Problem-management Approach to Helping*, 10th ed. Cengage Learning, 2013; 1st 1980.
Ehman, J. W., B. B. Ott, T. H. Short, R. C. Ciampa, and J. Hansen-Flaschen. "Do Patients Want Physicians to Inquire about Their Spiritual or Religious Beliefs if They Become Gravely Ill?" *Archives of Internal Medicine* 159, No. 15 (August 1999): 1803–1806. See www.ncbi.nlm.nih.gov/pubmed/10448785.
Eide, Oyvind M. *Revolution and Religion in Ethiopia: The Growth and Persecution of the Mekane Yesus Church, 1974–85*. Oxford: J. Currey, 2000.

Eisen, Ute E., and Christl M. Maier, eds. *Erhard S. Gerstenberger: Die Hebraeische Bibel als Buch der Befreiunjg.* Ausgewaehlte Aufsaetze. 2012; 718p; openaccess@bibsys.uni-giessen.de, published by Justus-Liebig-Universitat, Giessen, Germany, online by article, http://geb.uni-giessen.de/geb/volltexte/2012/8601/; wholly in a single pdf, http://geb.uni-giessen.de/geb/volltexte/2012/8601/pdf/Gerstenberger-Hebraeische-Bibel.pdf.

Eisenberg, Nancy, and Janet Strayer. *Empathy and Its Development.* New York: Cambridge University Press, 1987.

Eisenberg, Nancy. "Empathy-Related Emotional Responses, Altruism, and Their Socialization." Chap. 7, in *Vision of Compassion: Western Scientists and Tibetan Buddhists Examine Human Nature.* Edited by Richard J. Davison and Anne Harrington. New York: Oxford University Press, 2001.

Eitel, Keith E., ed. *Mission in the Context of Violence.* Pasadena: William Cary Library, 2008.

Ellis, Stephen, and Gerrie Ter Haar. "Religion and Politics: Taking African Epistemologies Seriously." *The Journal of Modern African Studies* 45, No. 3 (September 2007): 385-401.

Encyclopædia Britannica. Premium Service, 2004: s.v., "deontological ethics" and "teleological ethics."

Erickson, Millard J. *Basic Guide to Eschatology.* Grand Rapids: Baker, 1998; 200 pp.

———. *Contemporary Options in Eschatology: A Study of the Millennium.* Grand Rapids: Baker, 1977.

———. *Introducing Christian Doctrine.* Grand Rapids: Baker, 1992.

Erikson, Erik. *Childhood and Society.* New York: W. W. Norton, 1950; Erikson afterthoughts, 1985.

———. *Insight and Responsibility: Lectures on the Ethical Implications of Psychoanalytic Insight.* New York: W. W. Norton, 1964.

———, and Joan M. Erikson. *The Life Cycle Completed: Extended Version.* New York: W. W. Norton, 1998.

Ernecoff, N. C., F. A. Curlin, P. Buddadhumaruk, and D. B.White. "Health Care Professionals' Responses to Religious or Spiritual Statements by Surrogate Decision Makers During Goals-of-Care Discussions." *JAMA Internal Medicine* 175, No. 10 (October 2015): 1662–1669. See www.ncbi.nlm.nih.gov/pubmed/26322823.

Eshete, Tibebe. *The Evangelical Movement in Ethiopia: Resistance and Resilience.* Waco: Baylor University Press, 2009.

Evans, Keith A. *Essential Chaplain Skill Sets: Discovering Effective Ways to Provide Excellent Spiritual Care.* Grand Rapids: WestBow Press, 2017. See www.ChaplainSkillSets.com.

Fast, Mary. "A Theodicy of the Cross: Where is God in the Suffering of Disability?" PhD diss. Virginia Beach: Regent University School of Divinity, 2015.

Fastiggi, Robert L., and Steven Boguslawski, eds. *Called to Holiness and Communion: Vatican II on the Church.* Scranton: University of Scranton Press, 2009; 300 pp.

———. *Catholic Sexual Morality.* Eugene: Wipf and Stock, 2018; 236 pp.

———, and Judith Marie Gentle. *De Maria Numquam Satis—The Significance of the Catholic Doctrines on the Blessed Virgin Mary for All People.* Lanham: University Press of America, 2009; 204 pp.

———, co-editor with Jane F. Adolphe and Michael A. Vacca. *Equality and Non-discrimination: Catholic Roots and Current Challenges.* Eugene: Pickwick Publications, 2019; 246 pp.

———. Ludwig Ott. *Fundamentals of Catholic Dogma.* Translator and reviser. London: Baronius Press, 2018; 568 pp.

———, and José Pereira. *The Mystical Theology of the Catholic Reformation—An Overview of Baroque Spirituality.* Lanham: University Press of America, 2006; 309 pp.

———. *The Natural Theology of Yves de Paris.* Atlanta: Scholars Press, 1991.

———. *The Sacrament of Reconciliation: An Anthropological and Scriptural Understanding.* Chicago/Mundelein: Hillenbrand Books, 2017; 176 pp.

———, Jane Adolphe, and Michael Vacca. *St. Paul, the Natural Law, and Contemporary Legal Theory.* Lanham: Lexington Books, 2012; 254 pp.

———, and Michael O'Neil. *Virgin, Mother, Queen: Encountering Mary in Time and Tradition.* Notre Dame: Ave Maria Press, 2019; 192 pp.

———. *What the Church Teaches about Sex—God's Plan for Human Happiness.* Huntington: Our Sunday Visitor Press, 2009; 174 pp.

Fathers of the English Dominican Province, trans. *St. Thomas Aquinas: Summa Theologica.* Allen: Christian Classics, 1981.

Fay, Brian. *Contemporary Philosophy of Social Science: A Multicultural Approach.* Malden: Blackwell Publishers, 1997.

Federal Democratic Republic of Ethiopia Constitution. Ratified by the National Constituent Assembly, December 8, 1994.
Fee, Gordon D. *The First Epistle to the Corinthians, Revised Edition, The New International Commentary on the New Testament.* Grand Rapids: Eerdmans, 2014.
———. *Paul, the Spirit, and the People of God.* Grand Rapids: Baker Academic, 1996.
Feinberg, John S. *No One Like Him: The Doctrine of God.* Wheaton: Crossway, 2005; 879 pp.
Feller, Bryan. *A Business Care for Corporate Chaplaincy.* Los Angeles: Chaplains Inc., 2011. See www.yumpu.com/en/document/view/4730933/a-business-case-for-corporate-chaplaincy-chaplains-inc.
Fenelon, Francois. *Christian Perfection.* Translated by Mildred Whitney Stillman. New York: Harper and Bros., 1947.
Ferguson, Sinclair B. *Children of the Living God.* Carlisle: Banner of Truth Trust, 1989.
———. *A Heart for God.* Carlisle: Banner of Truth Trust, 1987.
Fettke, Steven M. *God's Empowered People: A Pentecostal Theology of the Laity.* Eugene: Wipf & Stock, 2011.
Fiorenza, Francis Schüssler, and John P. Galvin, eds. *Systematic Theology Roman Catholic Perspectives.* Minneapolis: Fortress Press, 1991.
Fiorenza, Francis Schüssler. "Systematic Theology: Task and Methods." In *Systematic Theology Roman Catholic Perspectives*, vol. 1. Edited by Schüssler Fiorenza and John P. Galvin. Minneapolis: Fortress Press, 1991: 1–88.
Fischer, Robert, and Helmut Lehmann, eds. *Luther's Work.* Vol. 37. Philadelphia: Muhlenberg Press, 1961.
Fisher, Anthony. Archbishop of Sidney. "HIV and Condoms within Marriage." *Communio* 36, No. 2 (Summer 2009): 329–359. Access at www.communio-icr.com/files/Fisher36-2.pdf.
Fitzmyer, Joseph A. *First Corinthians: A New Translation with Introduction and Commentary, The Anchor Yale Bible.* New Haven: Yale University Press, 2008.
Flannelly, Kevin J., LindaLEmanuel, GeorgeFHandzo, KathleenGalek, NavaRSilton, and MelissaCarlson. "A National Study of Chaplaincy Services and End of Life Outcomes." *BMC Palliative Care* 11, No. 10 (July 2012): 1. Access www.researchgate.net/publication/228099405_A_national_study_of_chaplaincy_services_and_end-of-life_outcomes.
Flannery, Austin, ed. *Vatican Council II: More Post Conciliar Documents.* Collegeville: The Liturgical Press, 1982.
Fleischer, Doris Zames, and Freida Zames. *The Disability Rights Movement: From Charity to Confrontation.* Philadelphia: Temple University Press, 2001.
Fletcher, Susan K. "Religion and Life Meaning: Differentiating Between Religious Beliefs and Religious Community in Constructing Life Meaning." *Journal of Aging Studies* 18, No. 2 (May 2004): 171–185. See www.ScienceDirect.com/science/article/abs/pii/S0890406504000064.
Frame, John M. *The Doctrine of God: A Theology of Lordship.* Phillipsburg: P & R, 2002; 896 pp.
Frankl, Viktor. *Man's Search for Meaning—An Introduction to Logotherapy.* Boston: Beacon Press, 2006; 1st 1946.
Freedman, David Noel, ed. *The Anchor Bible Dictionary.* Vol. 5. New York: Doubleday, 1992.
———. *Divine Commitment and Human Obligation.* Vol. 1. *Selected Writings of David Noel Freedman.* Grand Rapids: Eerdmans, 1997.
———. "Divine Commitment and Human Obligation: The Covenant Theme." *Interpretation: A Journal of Bible and Theology, Union Seminary Magazine* 18, No. 4 (October 1, 1964): 419–431.See https://journals.sagepub.com/doi/abs/10.1177/002096436401800403.
Frend, W. H. C. *Martyrdom and Persecution in the Early Church.* Oxford: Blackwell, 1965.
Freud, Sigmund. *Standard Edition of the Complete Psychological Works of Sigmund Freud.* 24 vols. Translated and edited by J. Strachey. London: Hogarth Press, 1962.
———. "Civilization and Its Discontents." In *Standard Edition of the Complete Psychological Works of Sigmund Freud.* Translated and edited by J. Strachey. London: Hogarth Press, 1962.
Fretheim, Terence. *The Suffering of God.* Philadelphia: Fortress 1984.
Fruchtenbaum, Arnold G. *The Messianic Jewish Epistles: Hebrews; James; 1 and 2 Peter; Jude.* San Antonio: Ariel Ministries, 2005.

Gallup. "Most Americans Still Believe in God." *Gallup*, June 29, 2016, accessed May 30, 2017, www.Gallup.com; cf. PewForum. "U.S. Public Becoming Less Religious," November 3, 2015, www.PewForum.org, accessed May 30, 2017.

Garland, David E. *1 Corinthians, Baker Exegetical Commentary of the New Testament.* Grand Rapids: Baker Academics, 2003.
Gebissa, Eziekel, and Fekadu Gurmessa. *Evangelical Faith Movement in Ethiopia: Origins and Establishment of the Ethiopian Evangelical Church.* Minneapolis: Lutheran University Press, 2009.
Geisler, Norman L. *Ethics—Alternatives and Issues.* Grand Rapids: Zondervan, 1982, through 13 prints from 1971–82.
———. *Christian Ethics—Options and Issues.* Grand Rapids: Baker Book House, 1989. Revision of his *Ethics—Alternatives and Issues.*
———. "Biblical Absolutes and Moral Conflicts," *Bibliotheca Sacra* (July 1974): 219–228.
Gelso, Charles J., and Jeffrey Alan Hayes, eds. *Countertransference and the Therapist Inner Experience: Perils and Possibilities.* Mahwah: Lawrence Erlbaum Associates, Inc., 2007.
Gemechu, Olana. *A Church under Challenge: The Socio-Economic and Political Involvement of the Ethiopian Evangelical Church Mekane Yesus.*" Berlin University, 2006; Rita, Latvia: Lambert Academic Publishing, 2013.
Gennrich, Daniela et al. *Pietermaritzburg Agency for Christian Social Action (PACSA) Research Report: Churches and HIV/AIDS: Exploring how local churches are integrating HIV/AIDS in the life and ministries of the church and how those most directly affected experience these.* Pietermaritzburg: PACSA, 2004.
Gentry, Peter J. "'The Glory of God': The Character of God's Being and Way in the World: Some Reflections on a Key Biblical Theology Theme." *Southern Baptist Theological Journal* 20, No. 1 (2016): 149–161; see http://equip.sbts.edu/wp-content/uploads/2016/08/SBJT-20.1-Gentry-Gods-Being-Way.pdf.
George, Sam, ed. *Diaspora Christianities: Global Scattering and Gathering of South Asian Christians.* Minneapolis: Fortress Press, 2019; 200 pp.
Gerhard, Johann. *On Sin and Free Choice: Theological Commonplaces.* St. Louis: Concordia Publishing House, 2014.
Gerkin, Charles V. *Living Human Document: Re-Visioning Pastoral Counseling in a Hermeneutical Move.* Nashville: Abingdon Press, 1984.
Gerstenberger, Erhard S. *Der bittende Mensch.* Neukirchen-Vluyn: Neukirchener Verlag 1980, reprint: Eugene: Wipf & Stock, 2009; 206 pp.
———. *Psalms 1—with an Introduction to Cultic Poetry.* Grand Rapids: Eerdmans, 1988; 260 pp.
———. *Psalms 2 and Lamentations.* Grand Rapids: Eerdmans, 2001; 566 pp.
———. *Suffering.* Nashville: Abingdon, 1980; 172 pp.
———. *Theologies in the Old Testament.* Minneapolis: Augsburg Books, 2002; 372 pp.
———. *Woman and Man.* Nashville: Abingdon Press, 1981; 252 pp.
———. *Yahweh—The Patriarch: Ancient Images of God and Feminist Theology.* Translated by Frederick J. Gaiser. Minneapolis: Fortress Press, 1996; 168 pp.
———. See his bibliography here: http://geb.uni-giessen.de/geb/volltexte/2012/8838/pdf/Gerstenberger_Bibliographie.pdf or www.PreciousHeart.net/ti/Gerstenberger-Bibliography.pdf. Also see Ute E. Eisen and Christl M. Maier, eds. *Erhard S. Gerstenberger: Die Hebraeische Bibel als Buch der Befreiunjg,* which translates into English after his name into "*The Hebrew Bible—a Book which Liberates*" (Ausgewaehlte Aufsaetze, 2012; 718p; openaccess@bibsys.uni-giessen.de): published by Justus-Liebig-Universitat, Giessen, Germany, online every article, http://geb.uni-giessen.de/geb/volltexte/2012/8601/, or the whole in a large 87MB pdf, http://geb.uni-giessen.de/geb/volltexte/2012/8601/pdf/Gerstenberger-Hebraeische-Bibel.pdf.
Getz, Hildy G., Ginger Kirk, and Lisa G. Driscoll. "Clergy and Counselors Collaborating Toward New Perspectives." *Counseling and Values* 44, No. 1 (October 1999): 40–54. See https://onlinelibrary.wiley.com/doi/abs/10.1002/j.2161-007X.1999.tb00151.x.
Gidada, Negaso, and Donald Crummey. *The Introduction and Expansion of Orthodox Christianity in Qēlēm Awraja, Western Wällaga, from About 1886 to 1941.* Addis Ababa: Addis Ababa University, 1972.
Gilkes, Patrick. *The Dying Lion: Feudalism and Modernization in Ethiopia.* New York: St. Martin's Press, 1975.
Gladding, S.T., and D. W. Newsome. *Clinical Mental Health Counseling in Community and Agency Settings.* 3rd ed. Upper Saddle River: Merrill/Prentice-Hall, 2010.
Glaser, Ida, and Hannah Kay. *Thinking Biblically About Islam: Genesis, Transfiguration, Transformation.* Carlisle: Langham Global Library, 2016.

Geher, Glenn, and Scott Barry Kaufman. *Mating Intelligence Unleashed: The Role of the Mind in Sex, Dating, and Love*. New York: Oxford University Press, 2013.
Global Consultation on the Ecumenical Response to the Challenge of HIV/AIDS in Nairobi, Kenya (25–28 November 2001).
Godet, Frederic Louis. *Commentary on John's Gospel*. Grand Rapids: Kregel Publications, 1978.
Goldstein, Arnold P., and Gerald Y. Michaels. *Empathy: Development, Training, and Consequences*. Mahwah: L. Erlbaum Associates, 1985.
Goold, William, ed. *Works of John Owen*. Vol. 6. Edinburgh: Banner of Truth, 1967 (repr. 1827).
Gordon, Tom, Ewan Kelly, and David Mitchell Radcliffe. *Spiritual Care for Healthcare Professionals: Reflecting on Clinical Practice*. London: Radcliffe Publishing, 2011.
Graham, Elaine L. *Transforming Practice: Pastoral Theology in an Age of Uncertainty*, Eugene: Wipf & Stock, 1996.
———. "Pastoral Theology in an Age of Uncertainty." *HTS Teologiese Studies/Theological Studies* 62, No. 3 (2006). Retrieved from www.hts.org.za/index.php/HTS. Reprint of chapter two of Graham's book, *Transforming Practice* (1996): 38–55.
Grant, A., and D. A. Hughes, eds. *Transforming the World?* United Kingdom: Apollos, 2009.
Grant, J. "Poverty, Womanist Theology and the Ministry of the Church." In *Standing with the Poor*. Edited by P. P. Parker. Cleveland: Pilgrims Press, 1992.
Gray, S. *The Least of My Brothers: Matthew 25:31–46: A History of Interpretation*. SBLDS 114. Atlanta: Scholars Press, 1989.
Grebe, Matthias. *After Brexit? The Church of England, the European Churches and the Future of European Unity*. Leipzig: Evangelische Verlagsanstalt, 2019; 160 pp.
———. *Election, Atonement, and the Holy Spirit—Through and Beyond Barth's Interpretation of Scripture*. Foreword by David F. Ford. Princeton Theological Monograph Series. Eugene: Wipf and Stock, 2014; 312 pp.
———. *Polyphonie der Theologie: Verantwortung und Widerstand in Kirche und Politik*. Stuttgart: Kohlhammer, 2019; 522 pp.
———. "Revelation as Salvation A Comparison of Revelation in Barth and Tillich" and "Jürgen Moltmann." In *Paul Tillich et Karl Barth: Antagonismes et accords théologiques*, edited by Mireille Hébert and Anne Marie Reijnen. Zürich: LIT Verlag, 2016; 231 pp..
———. "The Problem of Evil." In *The T & T Clark Companion to the Atonement*, edited by Adam J. Johnson. London: T & T Clark, 2017.
———. "Jesus Christ: Victim or Victor? Revisiting Galatians 3:13 in conversation with Karl Barth and Scripture." *Communio Viatorum: A Theological Journal* 57, No. 3 (2015).
———, Will Adam, and Jeremy Worthen. "The Church of England and European Ecumenism: Making our Unity Visible." In Grebe's *After Brexit? The Church of England, the European Churches and the Future of European Unity* (2019).
Green, Clifford J., and Marshall D. Johnson, eds. *Dietrich Bonhoeffer Works*, Vol. 9, *Young Bonhoeffer 1918–1927*. Minneapolis: Fortress Press, 2002.
———, ed. *Ethics, Dietrich Bonhoeffer Works*. Vol. 6. Minneapolis: Fortress Press, 2009.
———. "Editor's Introduction to the English Edition." In *Dietrich Bonhoeffer Works*, Vol. 1, *Sanctorum Communio: A Theological Study of the Sociology of the Church*. Minneapolis: Fortress Press, 2009.
Green, Joel B., Scot McKnight, and I. Howard Marshall, eds. *Dictionary of Jesus and the Gospels*. Downers Grove: InterVarsity Press, 1992.
Green, J. B. "Kingdom of God/Heaven." In *Dictionary of Jesus and the Gospels*. Edited by Joel B. Green, Scot McKnight, and I. Howard Marshall. Downers Grove: InterVarsity Press, 1992.
Gregersen, Niels Henrik, Bo Holm, Ted Peters, and Peter Widmann, authors and editors. *The Gift of Grace: The Future of Lutheran Theology*. Minneapolis: Fortress Press, 2004.
Gregg, Robert C. *Shared Stories, Rival Tellings: Early Encounters of Jews, Christians, and Muslims*. Oxford: Oxford University Press, 2015.
Gregory I the Great (590–604 A.D.). *The Book of Pastoral Rule*. Translated by George E. Demacopoulos. New York: St. Vladimir's Seminary, 1994. Accessed at www.documenta catholicaomnia.eu/01p/0590-0604,_SS_Gregorius_I_Magnus,_Regulae_Pastoralis_Liber_[Schaff]_EN.pdf.
Greider, Kathleen J., Gloria A. Johnson, and Kristen J. Leslie. "Three Decades of Women Writing for Our Lives." In *Feminist and Womanist Pastoral Theology*. Edited by Bonnie J. Miller-McLemore and Brita L. Gill-Austern. Nashville: Abingdon Press, 1999.

Grenz, S. J. *A Primer on Postmodernism*. Grand Rapids: Eerdmans, 1996.
Grimm, Harold J., and Helmut Lehmann, eds. *Luther's Work*. Vol. 31. Philadelphia: Muhlenberg, 1957.
Gritsch, Eric, and Robert Jenson. *Lutheranism: The Theological Movement and Its Confessional Writings*. Philadelphia: Fortress Press, 1976.
Groce, Nora Ellen. *From Charity to Disability Rights: Global Initiatives of Rehabilitation International, 1922–2002*. New York: Rehabilitation International, 2002.
Grosheide, F. W. *Commentary on the First Epistle to the Corinthians: The English Text with Introduction, Exposition and Notes*. The New International Commentary on the New Testament. Grand Rapids: Eerdmans, 1953.
Grudem, Wayne. *Systematic Theology: An Introduction to Biblical Doctrine*. Grand Rapids: Zondervan, 1994.
Guillory, William A. *Spirituality in the Workplace: A Guide for Adapting to the Chaotically Changing Workplace*. Salt Lake City: Innovations International, 1997.
Gunda, M. R. *Silent No Longer! Narratives of Engagement between LGBTI Groups and the Churches in Southern Africa*. Johannesburg: Other Foundation, 2017.
Gundry, R. *Matthew: A Commentary on His Handbook for a Mixed Church Under Persecution*. 2nd ed. Grand Rapids: Eerdmans, 1994.
Gunton, Colin E. *The Actuality of Atonement: A Study of Metaphor, Rationality and the Christian Tradition*. Grand Rapids: Eerdmans, 1989.
———. *Becoming and Being*. SCM Press, 2001; Eugene: Wipf & Stock, 2011.
Gurmessa, Fakadu. *Evangelical Faith Movement in Ethiopia: Origins and Establishment of the Ethiopian Evangelical Church Mekane Yesus*. Translated by Ezekiel Gebissa. Minneapolis: Lutheran University Press, 2009.
Gushwa, Robert L. *The Best and The Worst of Times: The United States Army Chaplaincy 1920–1945*, Vol. 4 of 7 of history of Army Chaplaincy (see "Army, U.S." ref. for more). U.S. Army, 1977.
Gustafson, J. *The Church as Moral Decision-Maker*. Philadelphia: Pilgrims Press, 1970.
Gutiérrez, G. "The task and content of Liberation Theology." In *Cambridge Companion to Liberation Theology*. Edited by Christopher Rowland, 19–38. Cambridge: Cambridge University Press, 2007.

Hadebe, Nontando Margaret. "Commodification, Decolonisation and Theological Education in Africa: Renewed Challenges for African Theologians." *HTS Teologiese Studies/Theological Studies* 73, No. 3 (2017), https://doi.org/10.4102/hts.v73i3.4550.
———. "The Cry of the Earth Is the Cry of Women: Ecofeminisms in Critical Dialogue with Laudato Si." *Grace and Truth* 42, No. 2 (2017).
———. "HIV and AIDS in Southern Africa Gender Inequality and Human Rights: A Prophetic Trinitarian Anthropology." Chapter 19 in *Dignity, Freedom and Grace: Christian Perspective on HIV, AIDS and Human Rights*, Gilliam Paterson and Callie Long. Geneva: WCC, 2016; 168 pp. See www.StAugustine.ac.za and noehadebe@gmail.com.
———. "Moving in Circles. A Sankofa-Kairos Theology of Inclusivity and Accountability Rooted in Trinitarian Theology as a Resource for Restoring the Liberation Legacy of the Circle of Concerned African Women Theologians." *Verbum et Ecclesia* 37, No. 2 (2016), see http://dx.doi.org/10.4102/ve.v37i2.1573.
———. "Not in Our Name without Us: The Intervention of Catholic Women Speak at the Synod of Bishops on the Family: A Case Study of a Global Resistance Movement by Catholic Women." *HTS Teologiese Studies/Theological Studies* 72, No. 1 (2016), see https://hts.org.za/index.php/hts/article/view/3481/8877.
———. "Whose Life Matters? Violence Against Lesbians and the Politis of Life in the Church." In *Visions and Vocations*, edited by Tina Beattie and D. Culberston D. The Catholic Women Speak Network. Mahwah: Paulist Press, 2018.
———. "Toward an Ubuntu Trinitarian Prophetic Theology: A Social Critique of Blindness to the Other." In *Living With(Out) Borders: Catholic Theological Ethics in the World Church and the Migration of Peoples*, edited by Agnes Brazal and Maria Theresa Davila. Maryknoll: Orbis, 2016.
Hagner, Donald A. *Matthew 1–13*, Volume 33A. *Word Biblical Commentary*. Dallas: Word Book, 1993.
Hahn, J., and Blass, T. "Dating Partner Preferences: A Function of Similarity of Love Styles." *Journal of Social Behavior and Personality* 12 (1997): 595–610.
Hall, Douglas John. *God and Human Suffering: An Exercise in the Theology of the Cross*. Minneapolis: Augsburg, 1986.

Haller, Beth A. *Representing Disability in an Ableist World: Papers on Mass Media.* Louisville: The Advocado Press, 2010.

———. "Pity as Oppression in the Jerry Lewis Telethon." In chap. 7 of her *Representing Disability in an Ableist World: Papers on Mass Media.* Louisville: The Advocado Press, 2010.

Halsall, Paul. "Medieval Sourcebook: Bede: Gregory the Great." Fordham University, 1998. Accessed at https://sourcebooks.fordham.edu/source/bede-greggrea.asp.

Halverson, Marvin, and Arthur A. Cohen, eds. *A Handbook of Christian Theology.* Nashville: Abingdon Press, 1972 & 1980, 1st 1958.

Hankin, Harriet. *The New Workforce: Five Sweeping Trends That Will Shape your Company's Future.* New York: American Management Association, 2004.

Hare, D. *The Theme of Jewish Persecution of Christians in the Gospel According to St. Matthew.* Society for New Testament Studies Monograph Series, vol. 6. Cambridge: Cambridge University Press, 1967, 2005.

Harold, Godfrey. *The Apostolic and Prophetic Reformation: A Critical Study.* Rita, Latvia: Lambert Academic Publishing, 2017; 117 pp.

———. "Affirmative Action as an Approach to Economic Restitution in Post-Apartheid South Africa: a Reading of Luke 19:1-10." *The South African Baptist Journal of Theology* 25 (2015): 25-43.

———. "The Christian and Suffering: A Philosophical Question and a Pastoral Response." *Midwestern Theological Journal* 4, No. 2 (2006): 93-100.

———. "An Evangelical Response to Post-modernism." *The South African Baptist Theological Journal* 16 (2008): 61-65.

———. Managing editor. *South African Baptist Journal of Theology.*

———. "The Story of the Indian Church in South Africa." In *Diaspora Christianities: Global Scattering and Gathering of South Asian Christians.* Edited by Sam George. Minneapolis: Fortress Press, 2019; 200 pp.

Hartenstein, Friedhelm. "Ein zorniger und gewalttätiger Gott?" *Verkündigung und Forschung* 58, (2013): 110-127.

Hartsock, C. "Life, Eternal Life." In *Dictionary of Jesus and the Gospels,* edited by Joel B. Green, Scot McKnight, and I. Howard Marshall. Downers Grove: IVP, 1992.

Hauerwas, Stanley. *Approaching the End: Eschatological Reflections on Church, Politics, and Life.* Grand Rapids: Eerdmans, 2013; 269 pp.

———. *Character and the Christian Life: A Study in Theological Ethics.* San Antonio: Trinity University Press, 1985; 240 pp.

———. *Matthew, SCM Theological Commentary on the Bible.* London: SCM Press, 2006.

———. "The Sermon." In his *Matthew, SCM Theological Commentary on the Bible.* London: SCM Press, 2006.

———. *The Peaceable Kingdom—A Primer in Christian Ethics.* 2nd ed. London: SCM Press, 1984.

———. "Jesus: The Presence of the Peaceable Kingdom." In his *Peaceable Kingdom* (1984).

———. *Suffering Presence: Theological Reflections on Medicine, the Mentally Handicapped, and the Church.* Notre Dame: University of Notre Dame Press, 1986; 240 pp.

Hawking, Stephen. *A Brief History of Time.* New York: Bantam, 1988; 226 pp.

Hawthorne, Gerald F., Ralph P. Martin, and Daniel G. Reid, eds. *Dictionary of Paul and His Letters.* Downers Grove: IVP, 1993.

Hays, Richard B. *The Moral Vision of the New Testament: Community, Cross, New Creation, A Contemporary Introduction to New Testament Ethics.* New York: Harper One, 1996.

Health Care Chaplaincy. *PlainViews: Translating Knowledge and Skills into Effective Chaplaincy and Pallative Care.* See www.HealthCareChaplaincy.org.

Hébert, Mireille, and Anne Marie Reijnen, eds. *Paul Tillich et Karl Barth: Antagonismes et accords théologiques.* Zürich: LIT Verlag, 2016; 231 pp.

Heessel, Nils P. *Babylonisch-assyrische Diagnostik.* Münster: Ugarit-Verlag, 2000.

Heitink, Gerben. *Practical Theology: History, Theory, Action Domains.* Grand Rapids: Eerdmans, 1999.

Hendrick, Clyde, Susan S. Hendrick, and Amy Dicke. "The Love Attitudes Scale: Short Form." *Journal of Personal and Social Relationships* 15, No. 2 (April 1998): 147–159. See https://journals.sagepub.com/doi/10.1177/0265407598152001.

Hendrick, Susan S., Amy Dicke, and Clyde Hendrick. "The Relationship Assessment Scale," *Journal of Personal and Social Relationships* 15, No. 1 (February 1998): 137–142. See https://journals.sagepub.com/doi/10.1177/0265407598151009.

Hendriks, H. Jürgens, Elna Mouton, L. D. Hansen, and Elisabet Le Roux. *Men in the Pulpit, Women in the Pew? Addressing Gender Inequality in Africa.* EFSA, Institute for Theological and Interdisciplinary Research. Stellenbosch, South Africa: Sun Press, 2012.

Henry, Carl F. H. *Christian Personal Ethics.* Grand Rapids: Baker, 1977; 1st 1957; 615 pp.

Heym, Stephan. *Hostages.* New York: G. P. Putnam's Sons, 1942.

Hieb, Nathan D. *Christ Crucified in a Suffering World: The Unity of Atonement and Liberation.* Minneapolis: Fortress, 2013; 240 pp.

Hill, MarKeva Gwendolyn. *Womanism Against Socially-Constructed Matriarchal Images: A Theoretical Model Toward a Therapeutic Goal.* New York: Palgrave MacMillan, 2012.

Hiltner, Seward. *Pastoral Counseling.* Nashville: Abingdon Press, 1949.

———. *Preface to Pastoral Theology: Ministry and Theory of Shepherding.* Nashville: Abingdon, 1958.

———. "Pastoral Care and Counseling." *The Journal of Religious Thought* 13, No. 2 (1956): 111–122. Retrieved from www.howard.edu/academics/publications.

Hittenberger, Jeff. "Receiving God's Gift of a Person with Special Needs: Amos Yong's Theology of Disability." In *The Theology of Amos Yong and the New Face of Pentecostal Scholarship: Passion for the Spirit*, edited by Wolfgang Vondey and Martin W. Mittelstadt. Global Pentecostal and Charismatic Studies 14. Leiden and Boston: Brill, 2013: 141–59.

Holifield, E. Brooks. *A History of Pastoral Care in America: From Salvation to Self-Realization.* Eugene: Wipf & Stock, 2005.

Holmes, Kristin E. "23rd Psalm Holds Answers to Many of Life's Questions." *The Riverside Press-Enterprise* (Oct. 25, 2005): B12.

Homant, Robert J. "Ten Years After: A Follow-up of Therapy Effectiveness." *Journal of Offender Counseling, Services and Rehabilitation* 10 (Spring 1986): 51–57.

Hong, Howard V., and Edna H. Hong, eds. *Kierkegaard, Philosophical Fragments.* Princeton: Princeton University, 1985.

———, eds. *Kierkegaard Writings, Practice in Christianity.* Princeton: Princeton University, 1991.

Horst, Johannes. "μακροθυμία B. The Theological Significance of the Terms in the Old Testament (LXX) and Later Judaism." In *Theological Dictionary of the New Testament* (TDNT), Vol. 4., edited by Gerhard Kittel, G. W. Bromiley, and Gerhard Friedrich. Grand Rapids: Eerdmans, 1964.

Howard, J. K. "Christ Our Passover: A Study of the Passover-Exodus Theme in 1 Corinthians." *The Evangelical Quarterly* (1969): 97–108. See https://biblicalstudies.org.uk/pdf/eq/1969-2_097.pdf.

Hsu, Albert Y. *Grieving a Suicide: A Loved One's Search for Comfort, Answers and Hope.* Urbana, IL: InterVarsity Press, 2002.

Human Rights Watch. "Such a Brutal Crackdown: Killing and Arrest in Response to Ethiopia's Oromo Protests." See www.hrw.org/report/2016/06/16/such-brutal-crackdown/killings-and-arrests-response-ethiopias-oromo-protests, accessed 11/02/2016.

Hünermann, Peter (most recent editor), and Heinrich Denzinger (original editor). *Enchiridion Symbolorum: A Compendium of Creeds, Definitions and Declarations of the Catholic Church.* San Francisco: St. Ignatius Press, 2012; 1,450 pp. See www.Ignatius.com/Enchiridion-Symbolorum-P543.aspx.

Hunsinger, George. *Christ Crucified in a Suffering World: The Unity of Atonement and Liberation.* Minneapolis: Fortress, 2013.

———. *Disruptive Grace: Studies in the Theology of Karl Barth.* Grand Rapids: Eerdmans, 2000.

———. *Evangelical, Catholic, and Reformed: Doctrinal Essays on Barth and Other Themes.* Grand Rapids: Eerdmans, 2015.

———, ed. *Karl Barth and Radical Politics.* Philadelphia: Westminster, 1976.

———. *How to Read Karl Barth: The Shape of His Theology.* New York: Oxford University, 1991.

———. "Barth on Jesus, Lord of Time (Hebrews 13:8)." In Hunsinger's *Evangelical, Catholic, and Reformed: Doctrinal Essays on Barth and Other Themes.* Grand Rapids: Eerdmans, 2015.

———. "Karl Barth's Christology: Its Basic Chalcedonian Character." In Hunsinger's *Disruptive Grace: Studies in the Theology of Karl Barth.* Grand Rapids: Eerdmans, 2000: 131–132.

———. "The Politics of the Nonviolent God: Reflections on René Girard and Karl Barth." In Hunsinger's *Disruptive Grace: Studies in the Theology of Karl Barth.* Grand Rapids: Eerdmans, 2000.

———. "The Sinner and the Victim." In *T & T Clark Companion to the Doctrine of Sin.* Edited by Keith L. Johnson and David Lauber, 433–450. New York: T & T Clark, 2016.

———. "A Tale of Two Simultaneities: Justification and Sanctification in Luther, Calvin, and Barth." In Hunsinger's *Evangelical, Catholic, and Reformed: Doctrinal Essays on Barth and Other Themes*. Grand Rapids: Eerdmans, 2015: 189–215.

Hunter, R. J. "Spiritual Counsel: An Art in Transition." *The Christian Century* (Oct. 17, 2001), Accessed at www.ChristianCentury.org/article//spiritual-counsel.

Huntington, Samuel. "Political Development in Ethiopia: A Peasant-Based Dominant-Party Democracy." In the Report to USAID/Ethiopia on Consultations with the Constitutional Commission, 1993.

Isasi-Diaz, Ada, Maria. "The Task of Hispanic Women's Liberation theology – *Mujeristas:* Who We Are and What We Are About." In *Feminist Theology from the Third World A Reader*. Edited by Ursula King, 88–102. Maryknoll: Orbis Press, 1994.

Jackman, David. *The Message of John's Letters. The Bible Speaks Today*. Leicester: IVP, 1992.

Jackson, Leslie C., and Beverly Greene, eds. *Psychotherapy with African American Women: Innovations in Psychodynamic Perspective and Practice*. New York: The Gilford Press, 2000.

Jackson, Maury, and Horace Crogman. "Shepherding Public Discourse Practices: Homiletic Form Aligned to the Logic Operative in Racial Rhetoric and Public Theological Discourse for Secular Liberal Democracies." *Cultural and Religious Studies* 4, No. 9 (September 2016): 2328–2177.

Jackson, Maury. "Answering the Call for a Sacred Conversation on Race." *Spectrum Magazine* 36, No. 3 (Summer 2008): 42–50.

———. "Causality Principle as the Framework to Contextualize Time in Modern Physics." *International Journal of Humanities and Social Science Invention* 5, No. 6 (June 2016): 1–22.

———. "The Heresy Tertullian Overlooked: On Prescription against the Apologist's Use of Rhetoric." *Spes Christiana* 22–23 (2011–2012): 15–30.

———. "Moral Education and the Adventist Print Media." *Adventist Today* 22, No. 4 (Fall 2014): 12–17.

———. "Sketching an Adventist Vision for Global Mission." *Adventist Today* 20, No. 2 (March–April 2012): 16–19.

———. "When Anger Heals: A Christian Response to the Global Healthcare Debate." *Adventist Today* 21, No. 1 (Winter 2013): 4–9.

Jacobs, Jonathan D. "The Ineffable, Inconceivable, and Incomprehensible God: Fundamentality and Apophatic Theology." In *Oxford Studies in Philosophy of Religion*, vol. 6, ch. 7. Edited by Jonathan Kvanvig. Oxford University Press, 2015. Accessed at www.MarcSandersFoundation.org/wp-content/uploads/Jacobs-Phil-Fundamentality-and-Apophatic-Theology.pdf.

Janowski, Bernd. *Ein Gott, der straft und tötet*? Neukirchen-Vluyn: Neukirchener Verlagsgesellschaft, 2013.

Jantzen, Grace M. "Feminists, Philosophers, and Mystics." *Hypatia: A Feminist Philosophy of Religion* 9, No. 4 (Autumn 1994): 186–20.

Jenson, Robert. "Triune Grace." In *The Gift of Grace: The Future of Lutheran Theology*. Edited by Niels Henrik Gregersen, Ted Peters, Bo Holm, Peter Widmann. Minneapolis: Fortress Press, 2005.

Johnson, Adam J., ed. *The T & T Clark Companion to the Atonement*. London: T & T Clark, 2017.

Johnson, Byron R., and David B. Larson. *The InnerChange Freedom Initiative: A Preliminary Evaluation of a Faith-Based Prison Program*. International Center for the Integration of Health and Spirituality (CRRUCS Report), 2003.

Johnson, Byron R. *More God, Less Crime*. West Conshohocken: Templeton Press, 2011.

Johnson, Johnny Ramirez, Carlos Fayard, Carlos Garberoglio, and Clara Jorge RamirEzek. "Is Faith an Emotion? Faith as a Meaning-Making Affective Process: An Example from Breast Cancer Patients." *American Behavioral Scientist* 45, No. 12 (August 2002): 1839–53. See https://journals.sagepub.com/doi/abs/10.1177/0002764202045012006.

Johnson, Keith L., and David Lauber, eds. *T & T Clark Companion to the Doctrine of Sin*. New York: T & T Clark, 2016.

Johnston, Kyle. "Introduction to Pastoral Care and Biblical Counseling." Accessed 2016, https://jubilee.org.za/lesson/read-notes-kyle-johnston-introduction-pastoral-care-biblical-counseling/.

Jones, Major J. *Christian Ethics for Black Theology: Politics of Liberation*. Nashville: Abingdon, 1974.

Kabue, Samuel, Esther Mombo, Joseph Galgalo, and C. B. Peter, eds. *Disability, Society, and Theology: Voices from Africa*. Limuru, Kenya: Zapf Chancery, 2011.

Kaiser, Walter C., Jr. *Hard sayings of the Old Testament*. Downers Grove: IVP, 1988.

———. *Mission in the Old Testament: Israel as a Light to the Nations.* Grand Rapids: Baker, 2000.
Kanyoro, Musimbi R. A. *Introducing Feminist Cultural Hermeneutics. An African Perspective (Introductions in Feminist Theology 9).* Sheffield: Sheffield Academic Press, 2002.
Karp, David. *Speaking of Sadness: Depression, Disconnection, and the Meaning of Illness.* Oxford: Oxford University Press, 1996.
Kasper, Cardinal Walter. *Mercy: the Essence of the Gospel and the Key to Christian Life.* Mahwah, NJ: Paulist Press, 2014.
Kaufman, Gershen. *The Psychology of Shame: Theory and Treatment of Shame-Based Syndromes,* 2nd ed. New York: Springer, 1996.
Kazaku, Peter. *Orthodoxy and Psychoanalysis: Dirge or Polychronion to the Centuries-Old Tradition?* New York: Peter Lang, 2013; 147 pp., from his 2004 master thesis on "Thermos, Thermos" below for the Theological School of Balamand University, Lebanon.
Keener, Craig S. *A Commentary on the Gospel of Matthew.* Grand Rapids: Eerdmans, 1999.
Kelcourse, Felicity Brock. "Pastoral Counseling in the Life of the Church." *Encounter* 63, No. 1/2 (2002): 137-146.
Keller. T. *Generous Justice.* London: Hodder and Stoughton, 2010.
Kelly, Geffrey B., and John D Godsey, eds. *Discipleship, in Dietrich Bonhoeffer Works* (DBW), vol. 4. Minneapolis: Fortress Press, 2003.
Kemeny, P. C., ed. *Church, State and Public Justice: Five Views* (Clarke E. Coshran, Derek H. Davis, Corwin E. Smidt, Ronald J. Sider, and Philip Wogaman). Downers Grove: IVP, 2007.
Khosa-Nkatine, Hundzukani Portia. *Developing a More Inclusive Liturgy Praxis for the Evangelical Presbyterian Church in South Africa* (Rita, Latvia: Lambert Academic Publishing, 2017; 160 pp.). See https://repository.up.ac.za/bitstream/handle/2263/46075/Khosa_Development_2015.pdf
Kiboi, John Michael. *Assurance of Salvation: Towards a Cumulative Case Argument.* Latvia, European Union: Scholars' Press, 2018; 210 pp.
———. *The Tripartite Office of Christ in the Light of Worgoondet: Towards a Sabaot Christology of Inculturation.* Nairobi: CUEA Press, 2017; 249 pp.
———. "Inter-Religious Conflicts in 21st Century: Dialectical-Scepticism as a Panacea." *African Ecclesial Review* (March/June 2017);
———. "From a Post-Colonial Hermeneutic of Suspicion to a Dialectical Theology of Instantaneous and Progressive Divine Revelation." *African Christian Studies* 31, No. 4 (December 2015): 24–53.
———. "Towards a Theodicy of Divine Impotence as a Solution to the Problem of Evil." *African Christian Studies* 33, No. 2 (June 2017).
Killen, Patricia O'Connell, and John de Beer. *The Art of Theological Reflection.* New York: Crossroad, 1994.
Kim-Cragg, HyeRan, and Eun-Young Choi. *The Encounters—Re-telling the Biblical Stories from Migration and Intercultural Perspectives.* Translated by Lark Kim. Daejeon, South Korea: Blacksmith Publisher, 2013; 102 pp.
———, and Mary Ann Beavis. *Hebrews—Wisdom Commentary.* Collegeville: Liturgical Press, 2015.
———. *Interdependence: A Postcolonial Feminist Practical Theology.* Eugene: Pickwick, 2018.
———, and Don Schweitzer. *An Intercultural Adventure Part II—The Authority and Interpretation of Scripture in The United Church of Canada.* Daejeon, South Korea: Blacksmith Publisher, 2016.
———, and Don Schweitzer, eds. *An Introduction to the United Church of Canada—Key Texts with Introductions and Commentary.* Daejeon, South Korea: Blacksmith Publisher, 2014.
———, and Don Schweitzer. *Mission of Koreans Within It.* Daejeon, South Korea: Daejanggan Publisher, 2019.
———. *Story and Song—A Postcolonial Interplay between Christian Education and Worship.* New York: Peter Lang, 2012; 180 pp.
———. *2 Thessalonians—Wisdom Commentary,* co-authored with Mary Ann Beavis. Collegeville: Liturgical Press, 2016; 254 pp.
———. *What Does the Bible Say?—A Critical Conversation with Popular Culture in a Biblically Illiterate World.* Eugene: Cascade, 2017; 203 pp.
———. "Home, Hospitality, and Preaching: A Need for the Homiletical Engagement of Migration," in Andrea Bieler, Isolde Karle, Kim-Cragg, and Ilona Nord, eds., *Migration and Religion: Negotiating Sites of Hospitality, Resistance, and Vulnerability.* Leipzig: Eva, 2019.
———. "Unfinished and Unfolding Tasks of Preaching: Interdisciplinary, Intercultural, and Interreligious Approaches in the Postcolonial Context of Migration." *Homiletic: The Journal of the Academy of Homiletics* 44, No. 2 (2019).

King, D. E., and B. Dushwick. "Beliefs and Attitudes of Hospital Inpatients about Faith Healing and Prayer." *Journal of Family Practice* 39, No. 4 (October 1994): 349–352. See www.ncbi.nlm.nih.gov/pubmed/7931113.

Kirk, Forrest L. *Chaplains as Doctors of the Soul: Navigating Between the Sacred and Secular while Negotiating a Functional and Ontological Ministry Identity.* PhD diss., New Orleans Baptist Theological Seminary. Proquest, Umi Dissertation Publishing, 2011. Cf., an article abridgement of his diss., http://baptistcenter.net/journals/JBTM_9-1_Spring_2012.pdf.

Kirwan, W. T. *Biblical Concepts for Christian Counseling.* Grand Rapids: Baker, 1984.

Kitamori, Kazoh. *Theology of the Pain of God.* Eugene: Wipf & Stock, 2005 (1st pub. 1946, Japan; John Knox Press, 1965).

Kittel, Gerhard (1888–1948), and Gerhard Friedrich, eds. *Theological Dictionary of the New Testament.* 10 vols. Translated by Geoffrey W. Bromiley. Grand Rapids: Eerdmans, 1964–76 (1st German, Stuttgart: W. Kohlhammer, 1932).

Koch, Klaus. "Gibt es ein Vergeltungsdogma im Alten Testament?" *Zeitschrift für Theologie und Kirche* 52 (1955): 1-42.

Koenig, Harold G. "MSJAMA: Religion, Spirituality, and Medicine: Application to Clinical Practice." *JAMA* 284, No. 3 (October 4, 2000): 1708. See https://jamanetwork.com/journals/jama/fullarticle/1843381.

———, Dana King, and Verna Benner Carson. *Handbook of Religion and Health.* 2nd ed. New York: Oxford University Press, 2012; 1,192 pp.

Koester, H. ed. *Hermeneia: A Critical and Historical Commentary on the Bible.* Minneapolis: Fortress, 2005.

Kohut, Heinz. *How Does Analysis Cure?* Chicago, IL: University of Chicago Press, 1971.

———. *The Restoration of Self.* New York: International Universities Press, 1977.

Kolb, Robert, Tomothy J. Wengert, and Charles P. Arand, eds. *The Book of Concord: The Confessions of the Evangelical Lutheran Church.* Minneapolis: Fortress, 2000.

———. "The Bible in the Reformation and Protestant Orthodoxy." In *The Enduring Authority of the Christian Scriptures.* Edited by D. A. Carson, 100–01. Grand Rapids: Eerdmans, 2016.

Kosnik, Anthony, William Carroll, Agnes Cunningham, Ronald Modras, and James Schulte. *Human Sexuality: New Directions in American Catholic Thought.* New York: Paulist Press, 1977.

Köstenberger, Andreas. *A Theology of John's Gospel and Letters: The Word, the Christ, the Son of God.* Grand Rapids: Zondervan, 2009.

Krötke, Wolf. "Sin and Nothingness in the Theology of Karl Barth." In *Studies in Reformed Theology and History*, Vol. 10, edited by David Willis-Watkins. Translated by Philip G. Ziegler and Christina-Maria Bammel. Princeton: Princeton Theological Seminary, 2005.

Kübler-Ross, Elisabeth. *On Death and Dying.* New York: Macmillan, 1969.

Kujawa-Holbrook, Sheryl A., and Karen Brown Montagno, eds. *Injustice and the Care of Souls: Taking Oppression Seriously in Pastoral Care.* Minneapolis: Fortress, 2009.

Küng, Hans. *The Church.* Great Britain: Search Press, 1981.

Kurian, George Thomas, and Mark A. Lamport, eds. *Encyclopedia of Christianity in the United States.* Lanham: Rowman & Littlefield Publishers, 2016; 2,664 pp.

Kushner, Rabbi Harold S. *When Bad Things Happen to Good People.* New York: Schocken Books, 1981; 20th Anniversary Ed., 2001.

Kvanvig, Jonathan, ed. *Oxford Studies in Philosophy of Religion.* 8 vols. Oxford University Press, 2007–17.

Kwazulu Natal Church AIDS Network (KZNCAN). *Churches and HIV/AIDS A Research on KwaZulu-Natal Christian Council (KZNCC)* Pietermaritzburg: KZNCC, 2005.

Kwazulu-Natal Church AIDS Network (KZNCAN). *Perspective, Introductions in Feminist Theology 9.* Sheffield: Sheffield Academic Press, 2005.

Labberton, Mark. *The Dangerous Act of Loving Your Neighbour: Seeing Others Through the Eyes of Jesus.* Downers Grove: IVP, 2010.

LaGioia, Rock M. "Anticipating Christ's Return." *Bulletin for Intercultural Studies of Grace Theological Seminary* 12 (December 2013).

———. "Blackwood, Andrew Watterson," "Chapman, John Wilbur," "Chappell, Clovis Gilham," "Jefferson, Charles Edward," "Jowett, John Henry," "Lee, Robert Greene," "McClain, Alva J.," "McGee, John Vernon," "Marshall, Peter," "Robinson, Haddon W.," and "Talbot, Louis

Thomson" in *Encyclopedia of Christianity in the United States*, edited by George Thomas Kurian and Mark A. Lamport (Lanham: Rowman & Littlefield Publishers, 2016).
———. "Victory Over Trials and Temptations." In *Selah: Pause and Think* (Grace Publishing House, 2013). See lagioir@grace.edu and www.Grace.edu/academics/seminary/faculty/lagioia.
Larebo, Haile M. "The Ethiopian Orthodox Church and Politics in the Twentieth Century: Part I." *Northeast African Studies: Incorporating Ethiopianist Notes Northeast African Studies* 10, No. 3 (1987): 1–17.
———. "The Orthodox Church and the State in the Ethiopian Revolution." *Religion in Communist Lands* 14, No. 2 (1986): 148–159.
Larson, Jeffery H. *Should We Stay Together?: A Scientifically Proven Method for Evaluating Your Relationship and Improving its Chances for Long-Term Success.* New York: Jossey-Bass, 2000.
Lartey, Emmanuel Y. *In Living Color. An Intercultural Approach to Pastoral Care and Counseling*, 2nd ed. London: Jessica Kingsley Publishers, 1997.
———. *Pastoral Theology in an Intercultural World.* Eugene: Wipf & Stock Publishers, 2006.
Lauber, David. *Barth on the Descent into Hell: God, Atonement and the Christian Life.* Aldershot: Ashgate, 2004.
Lee, Courtland C., ed. *Multicultural Issues in Counseling: New Approaches to Diversity*, 3rd ed. Alexandria: American Counseling Association, 2006; 5th ed., Somerset: John Wiley, 2018.
Lee, J. A. "A Typology of Styles of Loving." *Personality and Social Psychology Bulletin* 3, No. 2 (1977): 173–182. See https://psycnet.apa.org/record/1978-03439-001.
———. "Love-styles." In *The Psychology of Love.* Edited by R. J. Sternberg and M. L. Barnes. New Haven, CT: Yale University Press, 1988: 38–67.
Lee, Valerie. *Granny Midwives and Black Women Writers: Double-Dutched Readings.* New York: Routledge, 1996.
Legesse, Asmarom. *Oromo Democracy: An Indigenous African Political System.* Lawrenceville: Red Sea Press, 2000.
Leibniz, Gottfried Wilhelm. A *Theodicy: Essays on the Goodness of God the Freedom of Man and the Origin of Evil.* CreateSpace Independent Publishing Platform, 2015, 1st 2005.
Leslie-Toogood, A., and E. Gill, eds. *Advising Student-athletes: A Collaborative Approach to Success.* Manhattan, KS: NACADA, National Academic Advising Association, 2008.
Lester, Andrew D. *Hope in Pastoral Care and Counseling.* Louisville: Westminister/John Knox, 1995.
Lester, Paul Martin, and Susan Dente Ross. *Images that Injure: Pictorial Stereotypes in the Media.* Westport: Praeger, 2003.
Levine, Donald. *Greater Ethiopia: The Evolution of a Multiethnic Society.* Chicago: University of Chicago Press, 1974.
Lewis, C. S. (1898–1963). *The Four Loves.* New York: Harcourt, Brace and Company, 1960.
———. *The Great Divorce: A Fantastic Bus Ride from Hell to Heaven—a Round Trip for Some, but Not for Others.* New York: Collier, Macmillan, 1946.
———. *A Grief Observed.* New York: Harper and Row, 1961.
———. *The Inspirational Writings of C. S. Lewis.* New York: Inspirational Press, 1994; World Publishing, 1996. Four books in one: *Surprised by Joy, Reflections on the Psalms, The Four Loves, The Business of Heaven.*
———. *Miracles.* London and Glasgow: Collins/Fontana, 1947, rev. 1960.
———. "Reflections on the Psalms." In *The Inspirational Writings of C. S. Lewis.* New York: Inspirational Press, 1994.
Lewis, David J. *Word and Work of David J. Lewis.* Cincinnati, OH: M. W. Knapp, 1900. See https://books.google.com/books?id=_VFDAAAAYAAJ.
Lienhard, Joseph T. "*Ousia* and *Hypostasis*: The Cappadocian Settlement and the Theology of 'One Hypostasis.'" In *The Trinity: An Interdisciplinary Symposium on the Trinity.* Edited by Stephen T. Davis, Daniel Kendall, and Gerald O'Collins, 99–122. New York: Oxford University Press, 2002.
Lieu, Judith M. *The Theology of the Johannine Epistles.* Cambridge: Cambridge University Press, 1991.
———. "What Was from the Beginning: Scripture and Tradition in the Johannine Epistles." *New Testament Studies* 39, No. 3 (July 1993): 458–477. See www.cambridge.org/core/journals/new-testament-studies/article/what-was-from-the-beginning-scripture-and-tradition-in-the-johannine-epistles1/6E384EFC728DC60F6B0393236BDDFBC4.
———. *I, II and III John: A Commentary.* Louisville: Westminster John Knox Press, 2008.
Lillback, Peter. *The Binding of God: Calvin's Role in the Development of Covenant Theology.* Grand Rapids: Baker Academic, 2001.

———, Charles Colson, Wayne Grudem, and Philip Ryken. *Biblical Perspectives on Business Ethics: How the Christian Worldview has Shaped Our Economic Foundations.* Basking Ridge, NJ: Center for Christian Business Ethics Today, 2012.

———. *George Washington's Sacred Fire.* Bryn Mawr: Providence Forum Press, 2006; 1,208 pp.

———, and Richard B. Gaffin. *Thy Word Is Still Truth: Essential Writings on the Doctrine of Scripture from the Reformation of Today.* Phillipsburg: P and R, 2013; 1,440 pp.

Lim, Russell F. *Clinical Manual of Cultural Psychiatry.* 2nd ed. Arlington, TX: American Psychiatric Publishing, 2015.

Linda E. Thomas, ed. *Living Stones in the Household of God. The Legacy and Future of Black Theology.* Minneapolis: Fortress press, 2004.

Lipton, D., R. Martinson, and J. Wilks. *The Effectiveness of Correctional Treatment: A Survey of Treatment Evaluation Studies.* New York: Praeger, 1975.

Livingston, James C., Francis Schussler Fiorenza, Sarah Coakley, James H. Evans Jr. *Modern Christian Thought: The Twentieth Century*, vol. 2 (Minneapolis: Fortress, 2006).

Longchar, A. Wati. "Sin, Suffering, and Disability in God's World." In *Disability, Society, and Theology: Voices from Africa.* Edited by Samuel Kabue, Esther Mombo, Joseph Galgalo, and C. B. Peter. Limuru, Kenya: Zapf Chancery, 2011: 47–58.

Longenecker, Richard N. *Galatians*, vol. 41, *Word Biblical Commentary*. Dallas: Word Book, 1990.

Lührmann, Dieter. *Galatians: A Continental Commentary.* Minneapolis: Fortress Press, 1989.

Lundy, Angela Victoria. "Off the Pillow of Self-pity." In *Amazing Gifts: Stories of Faith, Disability, and Inclusion.* Edited by Mark I. Pinsky, 188–90. Herndon: Alban Institute, 2012.

Luter, A. Boyd, Jr. "Repentance: New Testament." In *The Anchor Bible Dictionary*, vol. 5, edited by David Noel Freedman. New York: Doubleday, 1992.

Luther, Martin (1483–1546). *D. Martin Luthers Werke: Kritische Gesamtausgabe* [*works complete critical edition*], vol. 7. Weimer: Hermann Böhlaus, 1897. Commonly known as the Weimar edition of Luther's works, 121 vols., 1883 to 2009, began in the year of Luther's 400th birthday.

———. "The Blessed Sacrament of the Holy and True Body and Blood of Christ, and the Brotherhoods." In *Luther's Work*, vol. 35, edited by Theodore Bachmann and Helmut Lehmann. Philadelphia: Muhlenberg Press, 1960.

———. "The Bondage of the Will." In *Luther's Work*, vol. 33. Edited by Philip S. Watson and Helmut Lehmann. Philadelphia: Fortress Press, 1972.

———. "The Freedom of a Christian, 1520." In *Luther's Work*, Vol. 31, edited by Harold J. Grimm and Helmut Lehmann. Philadelphia: Muhlenberg Press, 1957.

———. "Temporal Authority: To What Extent It Should Be Obeyed, 1523." in *Luther's Works*, vol. 45, edited by Walther I. Brandt and Helmut Lehmann. Philadelphia: Muhlenburg Press, 1962.

———. "A Treatise on the New Testament, That Is, the Holy Mass, 1520." In *Luther's Work*, vol. 35, edited by Theodore Bachmann and Helmut Lehmann. Philadelphia: Muhlenberg Press, 1960.

———. "Word and Sacrament." In *Luther's Work*, vol. 37, edited by Robert Fischer and Helmut Lehmann. Philadelphia: Muhlenberg press, 1961.

Luz, U. *The Theology of the Gospel of Matthew.* Cambridge: Cambridge University Press, 1995.

———. *Matthew 21–28: A Commentary. Hermeneia: A Critical and Historical Commentary on the Bible.* Translated by J. Crouch. Edited by H. Koester. Minneapolis: Fortress Press, 2005: 290–93.

———. "The Final Judgment (Matt 25:31–46): An Exercise in 'History of Influence' Exegesis." In *Treasures New and Old: Recent Contributions to Matthean Studies.* Edited by D. Bauer and M. A. Powell, 271–310. Atlanta: Scholars Press, 1996.

Lynch, Gordon. "The Relationship between Pastoral Counseling and Pastoral Theology." In *The Blackwell Reader in Pastoral and Practical Theology*, edited by James Woodward and Stephen Pattison. Malden: Blackwell Publishing, Ltd, 2000.

Lynch, Peter. *The Church's Story. A History of Pastoral Care and Vision.* London: Pauline Books, 2005.

MacGregor, Kirk R., and Kevaughn Mattis, eds. *Perspectives on Eternal Security—Biblical, Historical, and Philosophical*, with a foreword by H. Wayne House. Eugene, OR: Wipf & Stock, 2009; compilation of articles from *Testamentum Imperium*, www.PreciousHeart.net/ti.

Macklin, Ruth, and Gaylin Willard, eds., *Mental Retardation and Sterilization: A Problem of Competency and Paternalism.* New York: Plenum Press, 1981.

MacLean, D. Charles, Beth Susi, Nancy Phifer, Linda Schultz, Deborah Bynum, Mark Franco, Andria Klioze, Michael Monroe, Joanne Garrett, and Sam Cykert. "Patient Preference for Physician

Discussion and Practice of Spirituality." *Journal of General Internal Medicine* 18, No. 1 (January 2003): 38–43. See www.ncbi.nlm.nih.gov/pmc/articles/PMC1494799/.

Magister, Sandro. "The Prelate of the Gay Lobby." In *Chiesa* (July 18, 2013). Accessed December 20, 2013, http://chiesa.espresso.repubblica.it/articolo/1350561?eng=y.

Maimela, Simon S., ed. *Culture, Religion and Liberation*. Proceedings of the EATWOT Pan African Theological conference, Harare, Zimbabwe. Pretoria: Penrose Book Printers, January 6–11, 1991.

———. "Religion and Culture: Blessings or Curses?" In *Culture, Religion and Liberation*. Edited by Simon S. Maimela. Proceedings of the EATWOT Pan African Theological conference, Harare, Zimbabwe. Pretoria: Penrose Book Printers, January 6–11, 1991: 1–17.

Maness, Michael G. *Character Counts—Freemasonry USA's National Treasure and Source of Our Founding Fathers' Original Intent*. Bloomington: AuthorHouse, Rev. 2007; 448 pp.

———. *Heart of the Living God—Love, Free Will, Foreknowledge, Heaven*. Bloomington: AuthorHouse, 2004; 728 pp.; www.PreciousHeart.net/foreknowledge.

———. *Heaven—Treasures of Our Everlasting Rest*. Bloomington: AuthorHouse, 2004; 132 pp.; www.PreciousHeart.net/heaven.

———. *How We Saved Texas Prison Chaplaincy 2011—Immeasurable Value of Volunteers and Their Chaplains*. Bloomington: AuthorHouse, 2015; 414 pp.; www.PreciousHeart.net/Saved.

———. *Ocean Devotions—From the Hold of Charles H. Spurgeon*. Bloomington: AuthorHouse, 2008; 440 pp.; www.PreciousHeart.net/ocean.

———. *Queen of Prison Ministry—Story of Gertha Rogers, First Woman to Minister on Texas Death Row*. Foreword by former TDCJ Exec. Dir. Wayne Scott. Bloomington: AuthorHouse, 2008.

———. *When Texas Prison Scams Religion*. Bloomington: AuthorHouse, 2022; 894 pp.; www.PreciousHeart.net/Seminary.

———. *Precious Heart, Broken Heart—Love and the Search for Finality in Divorce*. Bloomington: AuthorHouse, 2003; 192 pp.

———. *Would You Lie to Save a Life?—A Theology on the Ethics of Love*. Bloomington: AuthorHouse, 2007; 432 pp.; www.PreciousHeart.net/love.

———. "A Helping Skills Program at the Gib Lewis State Prison, Woodville, Texas." DMin. Diss. New Orleans Baptist Theological Seminary, 1997; 356 pp.

———, ed., and Kevaughn Mattis, founder. *Testamentum Imperium—An International Theological Journal*. 2005–present. Mattis founded and directed this from its inception, www.PreciousHeart.net/ti.

Maienschein, Jane. and Michael Ruse, eds. *Biology and the Foundation of Ethics.* Cambridge: Cambridge University Press, 1999; 336 pp.

Manetsch, Scott M. *Calvin's Comparing of Pastors: Pastoral Care and the Emerging Reformed Church, 1536–1609*. New York: Oxford University Press, 2013.

Manson, Neil A. *God and Design—The Teleological Argument and Modern Science*. London: Routledge, 2003; 376 pp.

Marguerat, D. *Le Jugement dans l'Evangile de Matthieu*. 2nd ed. Geneva: Labor et Fides, 1996.

Marin, D. B., V. Sharma,E. Sosunov,N. Egorova,R. Goldstein,and G. F. Handzo. "Relationship between Chaplain Visits and Patient Satisfaction." *Journal Health Care Chaplaincy* 21, No. 1 (2015): 14–24. Survey of 8,978 patients, results: "Chaplains' integration into the healthcare team improves patients' satisfaction with their hospital stay." See www.ncbi.nlm.nih.gov/pubmed/25569779.

Marini, Irmo, and Mark A. Stebnicki, eds. *The Psychological and Social Impact of Illness and Disability*, 6th ed. New York: Springer, 2012.

Markakis, John. *National and Class Conflict in the Horn of Africa*. Cambridge: Cambridge University Press, 1987.

Marshall, I. Howard. *The Epistles of John*. Grand Rapids: Eerdmans, 1978.

Martin, Ralph P., and Peter H. Davids, eds., *Dictionary of the Later New Testament and Its Developments*. Downers Grove: IVP, 1997.

Martz, Erin, and Hanoch Livneh, eds., *Coping with Chronic Illness and Disability: Theoretical, Empirical, and Clinical Aspects.* New York: Springer, 2007.

Masamba ma Mpolo, Jean and Nwachuku. *Pastoral Care and Counselling in African Today*. Frankfurt: Peter Lang, 1991.

Massachusetts Catholic Conference, "Emergency Contraception." Public Policy Office, Roman Catholic Church, Massachusetts. Accessed on 2-27-14; www.MaCatholic.org/emergencycontraception/.

Maston, T. B. *The Christian, the Church, and Contemporary Problems*. Waco: Word Books, 1968.

Mattis, Jacqueline S. "Religion and Spirituality in the Meaning-making and Coping Experiences of African American Women: A Qualitative Analysis." *Psychology of Women Quarterly* 26, No. 4 (December 1, 2002): 309–321.

Mattis, Kevaughn, founder, and Michael G. Maness, eds. *Testamentum Imperium—An International Theological Journal.* Mattis founded and directed from inception, www.PreciousHeart.net/ti.

———, and Kirk R. MacGregor, eds. *Perspectives on Eternal Security: Biblical, Historical, and Philosophical,* Foreword by H. Wayne House. Eugene: Wipf and Stock, 2009; 238 pp.

Maul, Stefan M. *Zukunftsbewältigung.* Mainz: Zabern, 1994.

May, William E., *An Introduction to Moral Theology.* 2nd ed. Huntington: Our Sunday Visitor, 2003.

McCord Adams, Marilyn. *Horrendous Evils and the Goodness of God.* Cornell Studies in the Philosophy of Religion. Ithaca: Cornell University Press, 2000.

McCord, Gary, Valerie J. Gilchrist, Steven D. Grossman, Bridget D. King, Kenelm F. McCormick, Allison M. Oprandi, Susan Labuda Schrop, Brian A. Selius, William D. Smucker, David L. Weldy, Melissa Amorn, Melissa A. Carter, Andrew J. Deak, Hebah Hefzy, andMohit Srivastava. "Discussing Spirituality with Patients: a Rational and Ethical Approach." *Annals of Family Medicine* 2, No. 4 (July 2004): 356–361. See www.ncbi.nlm.nih.gov/pmc/articles/PMC1466687/.

McCormack, Bruce L. *For Us and Our Salvation: Incarnation and Atonement in the Reformed Tradition.* In *Studies in Reformed Theology and History.* Edited by David Willis-Watkins. Princeton: Princeton Theological Seminary, 1993.

McCown, L., and V. J. Gin. *Focus on Sport in Ministry.* Marietta: 360° Sports, 2003.

McCrady, Barbara S., and Elizabeth E. Epstein, eds. *Addictions: A Comprehensive Guidebook.* New York: Oxford University Press, 1999.

McDermott, Gerald R. *Can Evangelicals Learn from Non-Christian Religions? Jesus, Revelation and the Religions.* Westmont: InterVarsity Press, 2000; 235 pp.

———, and William A. Fintel, M.D. *Cancer: A Medical and Theological Guide for Patients and Their Families.* Ada: Baker, 2004; 351 pp.

———. *Do Christians, Muslims, and Jews Worship the Same God?: Four Views* Grand Rapids: Zondervan, 2019; 240 pp.

———. *Everyday Glory: The Revelation of God in All of Reality.* Baker Academic, 2018; 224 pp.

———. *Famous Stutterers: Twelve Inspiring People Who Achieved Great Things while Struggling with an Impediment.* Eugene: Cascade, 2016; 121 pp.

———. *Israel Matters: Why Christians Must Think Differently about the People and the Land.* Grand Rapids: Brazos Press, 2017; 192 pp.

———, editor and contributor. *The New Christian Zionism: Fresh Perspectives on Israel and the Land.* Westmont: IVP Academic, 2016; 353 pp.

———, with Ron Story. *The Other Jonathan Edwards: Selected Writings on Society, Love, and Justice.* Amherst: University of Massachusetts Press, 2015; 168 pp.

———, ed. *Oxford Handbook of Evangelical Theology.* Oxford: Oxford University Press, 2010..

———. *Seeing God: Jonathan Edwards and Spiritual Discernment.* Regent College Publishing, 2000.

———, and Michael McClymond. *The Theology of Jonathan Edwards.* Oxford: Oxford University Press, 2012; 784 pp. It won *Christianity Today*'s 2013 award for Top Book in Theology/Ethics. See www.ChristianityToday.com/ct/2013/january-february/2013-book-awards.html.

———, and Harold Netland. *A Trinitarian Theology of Religions: An Evangelical Proposal.* Oxford: Oxford University Press, 2014; 428 pp.

McGinnis, Tracy. "Business Has a Prayer." *Forbes* (June 2006).

McGrath, Alister E. *A Brief History of Heaven.* Hoboken: Wiley-Blackwell, 2003.

McIver, Robert K. "One Hundred-fold Yield-Miraculous or Mundane? Matthew 13:8, 23; Mark 4:8, 20; Luke 8:8." *New Testament Studies* 40, No. 4 (October 1994): 606–608.

McKinnon, Garrett, and Tim Embrey. "2007 Fast Lube Operator of the Year." *National Oil and Lube News* (December 2007).

McKnight, S. "Cain." In *Dictionary of the Old Testament: Pentateuch.* Edited by Desmond Alexander and David Baker, 108–110. Downers Grove: IVP, 2003.

McKnight, Scot. *Embracing Grace: A Gospel for All of Us.* Brewster: Paraclete Press, 2005.

McMinn, M. R. *Psychology, Theology, and Spirituality in Christian Counseling.* Carol Stream: Tyndale House Publishers, 1996.

McNeil, Brenda Salter. *Road Map to Reconciliation: Moving Communities into Unity, Wholeness, and Justice.* Downers Grove: IVP, 2015.

McSherry, Wilfred, and Linda Ross, eds. *Spiritual Assessment in Healthcare Practice*. Keswick, UK: M & K Publishing, 2010.
Melanchthon, Philip. *Loci Communes rerum theologicarum*. Translated by J. A. O. Preus. St. Louis: Concordia Publishing House, 1992; 1st 1543.
Menn, Jonathan. *Biblical Eschatology*. 2nd ed. Eugene: Resource Publications, 2018; 622 pp.
Menz, R. L. *A Pastoral Counselor's Model for Wellness in the Workplace, Psychergonomics*. New York: The Haworth Pastoral Press, 2003.
Mercer, Joyce Ann. "Feminist and Womanist Practical Theology." In *Opening the Field of Practical Theology: An Introduction*. Edited by Kathleen A. Cahalan and Gordon S. Mikoski. Lanham: Rowman and Littlefield, 2014.
Messud, Claire. *The Emperor's Children*. New York: Vintage Books, 2007.
Michaels, J. Ramsey. "Apostolic Hardships and Righteous Gentiles: A Study of Matthew 25:31–46." *Journal of Biblical Literature* 84, No. 1 (March 1965). See www.jstor.org/stable/3264070.
Milbank, John. *Theology and Social Theory: Beyond Secular Reason*. Oxford: Blackwell, 1993.
Miller-McLemore, Bonnie J., and Brita L. Gill-Austern, eds. *Feminist and Womanist Pastoral Theology*. Nashville: Abingdon Press, 1999.
Miller-McLemore, Bonnie J. *In the Midst of Chaos: Caring for Children as Spiritual Practice*. San Francisco: Jossey-Bass, 2007.
Ministry of Agriculture and Settlement. "Ethiopian Measures for Rural Transformation." Addis Ababa, Ethiopia: February 1978.
Moffatt, James. *The First Epistles of Paul to the Corinthians, The Moffatt New Testament Commentary*. London: Hodder and Stoughton, 1938.
———. *Love in the New Testament*. London: Hodder and Stoughton, 1929; New York: R. R. Smith, 1930. An surpassed classic.
Mohr, Sylvia, Pierre-Yves Brandt, Laurence Borras, Christiane Gillieron, and Philippe Huguelet. "Toward an Integration of Spirituality and Religiousness into the Psychosocial Dimension of Schizophrenia." *American Journal of Psychiatry* 163, No. 11 (November 2006): 1952–1959. See www.ncbi.nlm.nih.gov/pubmed/17074947.
Moltmann, Jürgen. *The Coming of God—Christian Eschatology*. Minneapolis: Fortress, 1996; 420 pp.
———. *The Crucified God—the Cross of Christ As the Foundation and Criticism of Christian Theology*. London: SCM, 1973; 513 pp.
———. *Theology of Hope—On the Ground and the Implications of a Christian Eschatology*. London: SCM, 1967; 346 pp.
Morris, Jenny. *Pride against Prejudice: A Personal Politics of Disability*. London: Women's Press, 1991.
Morris, Leon. *Revelation*. Rev. ed. *Tyndale New Testament Commentary*. Grand Rapids: Eerdmans, 1987.
Morris, Sharon. "'Human Dregs at the Bottom of Our National Vats': The Interwar Debate on Sterilization of the Mentally Deficient." In *Social Histories of Disability and Deformity*. Edited by David M. Turner and Kevin Stagg, 142–60. New York/London: Routledge, 2006.
Moulton, James H., (1863–1917). *A Grammar of New Testament Greek*. 5 vols. 2nd ed. Edinburgh: T & T Clark, 1906. Reprint: Edinburgh: T & T Clark, 1993. See vol. 1 at Google Books https://books.google.com/books?id=Be4NAAAAIAA.
Murphy, T. *Pastoral Theology*. Dallas: Primedia eLaunch, 2013.

Naidoo, Marilyn. "The Potential of Spirituality Leadership in the Workplace Spirituality." *Koers: Bulletin for Christian Scholarship* 79, No. 2 (February 2014).
National Association of Social Workers. *Code of Ethics of the National Association of Social Workers*. Accessed 2008, www.SocialWorkers.org/pubs/code/code.asp.
Naudé, Christiaan Frederick Beyers. *The legacy of Beyers Naudé*. Stellenbosch: SUN Press, 2005. Leading Afrikaner anti-apartheid activist, Beyers Naudé, or colloquially as, Oom Bey (Afrikaan for "Uncle Bey").
Neusner, Jacob. *What is Midrash?* Eugene: Wipf & Stock, 1987.
Newberg, Andrew, E. d'Aquili, and V. Rause. *Why God Won't Go Away: Brain Science and the Biology of Belief*. New York: Ballantine, 2001.
Newport, John P. (1917–2000). *Life's Ultimate Questions: A Contemporary Philosophy of Religion*. New York: W Publishing Group/Harper Collins, 1989; 644 pp.; a monumental work.
Niebuhr, H. Richard. *The Responsible Self*. New York: Harper and Row, 1963.

———. "The Meaning of Responsibility." In *From Christ to the World—Introductory Readings in Christian Ethics.* Edited by Wayne G. Boulton, Thomas D. Kennedy, and Allen Verhey. Gand Rapids: Eerdmans, 1994.

Niedecken, Dietmut. *Nameless: Understanding Learning Disability.* Translated by Andrew Weller. New York: Brunner-Routledge, 2003.

Niehaus, Jeffrey J. "Covenant and Narrative, God and Time." *Journal of the Evangelical Theological Society* 53, No. 3 (September 2010): 535–59. See www.etsjets.org/files/JETS-PDFs/53/53-3/Niehaus_JETS_53-3_pp_535-559.pdf.

Norton, Herman A. *Struggling for Recognition: The United States Army Chaplaincy 1791–1865,* Vol. 2 of 7 of history of Army Chaplaincy (see "Army, U.S." ref. for more). U.S. Army, Forest Grove: University Press of the Pacific, 1977.

Nouwen, H. J. M., D. P. McNeil, and D. A. Morison. *Compassion.* USA: Image, 1982.

Nouwen, Henri J. M. *Lifesigns: Intimacy, Fecundity, and Ecstasy in Christian Perspective.* New York: Image Books, 1966.

O'Connell Killen, Patricia, and John de Beer. *The Art of Theological Reflection.* New York: Crossroad, 1994.

O'Connor, Kathleen M. *Lamentations and the Tears of the World.* Maryknoll: Orbis, 2003.

O'Conner, Thomas P. "What Works: Religion as a Correctional Intervention: Part II." *Journal of Community Corrections* 14, No. 2 (Winter 2004–05): 4–26.

O'Tool, Mark P. "The *povres avugles* of the Hôpital des Quinze-Vingts: Disability and Community in Medieval Paris." In *Difference and Identity in Francia and Medieval France.* Edited by Meredith Cohen and Justine Firnhaber-Baker. Farnham, UK: Ashgate, 2010: 157–73.

Oates, W. E. *Pastoral Counseling.* Philadelphia: Westminster Press, 1974.

———. *The Christian Pastor.* 3rd rev. ed. Philadelphia: Westminster Press, 1982.

Oden, Thomas C. *Classical Pastoral Care,* vol. 1. *Becoming a Minister.* Grand Rapids: Baker, 1987.

———. *Kerygma and Counseling: Toward a Covenant Ontology for Secular Psychotherapy.* Philadelphia: Westminster Press, 1966.

———. *Pastoral Theology: Essentials of Ministry.* New York: HarperCollins, 1983.

———. *Transforming Practice: Pastoral Theology in an Age of Uncertainty.* 2nd ed. Eugene: Wipf & Stock, 2002.

Okon, Etim E. "The Universal Declaration of Human Rights: A Philosophical and Ethical Appraisal," *Sophia: African Journal of Philosophy,* 7, No. 2 (April 2005): 114-120. See also, Okon, "The Universal Declaration of Human Rights," *African Pentecost: Journal of Theology, Psychology, and Social Work,* 1, No. 1 (December 2007), 67-82; and Okon, *Religion, Culture and Society* 1, No. 2 (2007): 67-82.
See www.academia.edu/36845674/HUMAN_RIGHT_TO_RELIGIOUS_FREEDOM.

Ogden, K. (n.d.). Seward Hiltner. *Pastoral Counseling, Survey of Major Movements in Pastoral Counseling.* Retrieved from http://pastoralcounseling.weebly.com/seward-hiltner.html.

Oglesby, William B. *Biblical Themes for Pastoral Care.* Nashville: Abingdon Press, 1980.

———. *Referral in Pastoral Counseling.* Nashville: Abingdon Press, 1978.

———. *With Wings as Eagles: Toward Personal Christian Maturity.* Levering: Wyndham Hall, 1988.

Oeming, Manfred and Konrad Schmid. *Job's Journey: Stations of Suffering.* Winona Lake: Eisenbrauns, 2015.

Oliphant, D. G. "Intentional Friendship: A Philosophy of Pastoral Care." PhD diss., University of Western Sydney, 2007. See https://researchdirect.westernsydney.edu.au/islandora/object/uws%3A2377/datastream/PDF/view.

Olson, D. H., and A. K. Olson. *Empowering Couples: Building on Your Strengths.* 2nd ed. Minneapolis: Life Innovations, 2000.

Osmer, Richard R. *Practical Theology: An Introduction.* Grand Rapids: Eerdmans, 2008.

Osterweis, Martin, Arthur Kleinman, and David Mechanic, eds. *Pain and Disability: Clinical, Behavioral, and Public Policy Perspectives.* Washington, DC: National Academy Press, 1987.

Otto, Rudolf. *The Idea of the Holy.* 2nd ed. Translated by John W. Harvey. Oxford, England: Oxford University Press, 1958.

Owen, John (1616–1683). *Of the Mortification of Sin in Believers,* in William Goold, ed., *Works of John Owen.* Vol. 6. Edinburgh: Banner of Truth, 1967; 1st 1827.

———. *A Treatise of the Dominion of Sin and Grace: Wherein Sin's Reign Is Discovered, in Whom It Is and in Whom It Is Not, How the Law Supports It, How Grace Delivers from It by Setting Up Its Dominion in the Heart*. Edinburgh: T. Lumisden and J. Robertson, 1739.

Packer, J. I. *Knowing God*. 20th Anniversary Edition. Downers Grove: IVP, 1993.
Painter, John. *1, 2, and 3 John*. Sacra Pagina. Collegeville: The Liturgical Press, 2002.
Pargament, Kenneth I. *The Psychology of Religion and Coping: Theory, Research Practice*. New York: Guilford Press, 1997.
Park, C. L., C. L. Park, C. M. Aldwin, S. Choun, L. George, D. P. Suresh, and D. Bliss. "Spiritual Peace Predicts 5-Year Morality in Congestive Heart Failure Patients." *Health Psychology* 35, No. 3 (March 2015): 2003-201. See conclusion, "Spiritual peace … were better predictors of mortality risk … than were physical health indicators."
Parker, P. P., ed. *Standing with the Poor*. Cleveland: Pilgrims Press, 1992.
Parsons, Susan Frank, ed. *The Cambridge Companion to Feminist Theology*. Cambridge: Cambridge University Press, 2002.
Pascal, Blaise (1623–62). *Pascal's Pensées*. New York: E. P. Dutton, 1958 (1st in French, incomplete at his death, pub. posthumously 1670).
Pastoral Care Council of the ACT. "Spiritual Care." Accessed online in 2016, http://pastoralcareact.org/pastoral.html. Web site set to expire August 2019. ACT: Australian Capital Territory.
Pastorino, E., and S. Doyle-Portillo. *What Is Psychology?* Belmont, CA: Wadsworth, 2012.
Paterson, Gilliam, and Callie Long, eds. *Dignity, Freedom and Grace: Christian Perspective on HIV, AIDS and Human Rights*. Geneva: WCC, 2016.
Paton, Alan. *Ah, But Your Land is Beautiful*. New York: Penguin Books, 1983.
Patton, John. *Pastoral Care in Context. An Introduction to Pastoral Care*. Louisville: Westminster/John Knox Press, 1993.
Paul Balisky, "Ethiopian Church and Mission in the Context of Violence." In *Mission in the Context of Violence*. Edited by Keith E. Eitel. Pasadena: William Cary Library, 2008.
Pausanias (110–180 A.D.). *Pausanias's Description of Greece*. Vol. 1. Translated and commentary by J. G. Frazer. London: MacMillan and Co. Limited, 1898. Pausanias conducted histories and descriptions of the Athenian topography of the mid-second century.
Pederson, T. (n.d.). *Millennials Believe They Are the Most Narcissistic Generation*. Accessed at http://psychcentral.com/news/2016/03/27/millennials-believe-they-are-the-most-narcissistic-generation/100967.html.
Pelikan, Jaroslav, ed. *Luther's Works*. St. Louis: Concordia, 1958.
Pelka, Fred. *What We Have Done: An Oral History of the Disability Rights Movement*. Amherst/Boston: University of Massachusetts Press, 2012.
Perlin, Michael L. *The Hidden Prejudice: Mental Disability on Trial*. Washington, DC: American Psychological Association, 2000.
Petersen, B. L. *Foundations of Pastoral Care*. Kansas City: Beacon Hill Press, 2007.
Peterson, E. H. *Working the Angles: The Shape of Pastoral Integrity*. Grand Rapids: Eerdmans Publishing Company, 1989.
Pew Forum. "U.S. Public Becoming Less Religious." November 3, 2015, www.PewForum.org, accessed May 30, 2017; cf. Gallup. "Most Americans Still Believe in God." *Gallup*, June 29, 2016, accessed May 30, 2017, www.Gallup.com.
Phan, Peter C. *Being Religious Interreligiously: Asian Perspective on Interfaith Dialogue*. Maryknoll: Orbis, 2015.
———. *The Gift of the Church: A Textbook on Ecclesiology*. Wilmington: Michael Glazier, 2016.
———. *Social Thought: Message of the Fathers of the Church*. Wilmington: Michael Glazier, 1983.
Pillay, Jerry. "An Exploration of the Idea of Economy in Calvin's View of God and the World: Its Implications for Churches in South Africa Today." *Verbum et Ecclesia* 36, no 3, Art. #1474 (2015). See https://repository.up.ac.za/bitstream/handle/2263/50436/Pillay_Exploration_2015.pdf.
Pinnock, Clark H. *Most Moved Mover: A Theology of God's Openness*. Grand Rapids: Baker, 2001.
Pinsky, Mark I., ed. *Amazing Gifts: Stories of Faith, Disability, and Inclusion*. Herndon: Alban Institute, 2012.
Piper, John. "The Meanings of Love in the Bible." Desiring God, January 1, 1975. Accessed at www.DesiringGod.org/articles/the-meanings-of-love-in-the-bible.
Placher, William Carl. *The Domestication of Transcendence: How Modern Thinking about God Went Wrong*. Louisville: Westminster John Knox, 1996.

Plante, Thomas G. "What Do the Spiritual and Religious Traditions Offer the Practicing Psychologist?" *Pastoral Psychology* 56 (January 2008): 429–444. See www.PsychologyToday.com/sites/default/files/attachments/34033/pp2article.pdf.

Plass, Ewald, ed. *What Luther Says*. St. Louis: Concordia, 1959.

Pope Benedict XVI, as Joseph Ratzinger. *Introduction to Christianity*. 2nd Ed. San Francisco: Ignatius, 2004.

———, as Joseph Ratzinger. *Eschatology: Death and Eternal Life*, 2nd Ed. Washington, DC: Catholic University of America Press, 2007; 1st 1988; 307 pp.

———. Cited by the Prelate of Opus Dei, Javier. "Letter from the Prelate." (April 2009): Opus Dei's official website, http://opusdei.org.au/en-au/document/letter-from-the-prelate-april-2009.

Pope Francis, *Misericordiae Vultus*. Bull of Indication of the Extraordinary Jubilee of Mercy. Vatican, 2015.

———. *Laudato Si. On Care For Our Common Home*. Vatican, 2015.

———. *The Name of God Is Mercy: A Conversation with Andrea Tornielli*. Translated by Oonagh Stransky. New York: Random House, 2016.

———. *Amoris Laetitia*. A post-synodal exhortation. Vatican, 2016.

———. *The Joy of Love*. New York: Paulist Press, 2016.

Pope John Paul II. *Dives in Misericordia*. Encyclical. Vatican, 1980.

———. *Familiaris Consortio*. Exhortation. Vatican, 1981.

———. *Reconciliatio et Paenetentia*. Exhortation. Vatican, 1984.

———. *Redemptor Hominis*. His first Encyclical. Vatican, 1979.

Pope John XXIII. *Mater et Magistra*. Encyclical. Vatican, 1961.

Pope Paul VI. *Humanae Vitae*. Encyclical. Vatican, 1968.

Porter, Steven L. "The Gradual Nature of Sanctification: Σάρξ as Habituated, Relational Resistance to the Spirit." *Themelios: An International Journal for Students of Theological and Religious Studies* 39, No. 3 (November 2014): 470–483. See http://tgc-documents.s3.amazonaws.com/themelios/Themelios39.3.pdf and http://themelios.thegospelcoalition.org/article/the-gradual-nature-of-sanctification-as-habituated-relational-resistance-to.

Poschmann, Bernhard. *Penance and the Anointing of the Sick*. Translated by Francis Courtney. New York: Herder and Herder, 1964.

Post, S. G., C. M. Puchalski, and D. B. Larson. "Physicians and Patient Spirituality: Professional Boundaries, Competency, and Ethics." *Annals of Internal Medicine* 132, No. 7 (April 2000): 578–583. See www.ncbi.nlm.nih.gov/pubmed/10744595.

Powell, Mark Alan. "Salvation in Luke-Acts." *World and Word* 12, No. 1 (1992): 5–10. See https://wordandworld.luthersem.edu/content/pdfs/12-1_Luke-Acts/12-1_Powell.pdf.

Power, Paul W., and Arthur E. Dell Orto. *Families Living with Chronic Illness and Disability: Interventions, Challenges, and Opportunities*. New York: Springer, 2004.

Preus, Robert D. *The Theology of Post-Reformation Lutheranism*, Vol 1. *A Study of Theological Prolegomena*. St. Louis: Concordia Publishing House, 1970.

PricewaterhouseCoopers. "Driving the Bottom Line: Improving Retention." Saratoga, Pricewaterhouse Coopers LLP, 2006. See www.shrm.org/hr-today/news/hr-magazine/Documents/saratoga-improving-retention.pdf.

Puchalski, Christiana M., Betty Ferrell, Rose Virani, Shirley Otis-Green, Pamela Baird, Janet Bull, Harvey Chochinov, George Handzo, Holly Nelson-Becker, Maryjo Prince-Paul, Karen Pugliese, and Daniel Sulmasy. "Improving the Quality of Spiritual Care as a Dimension of Palliative Care: the Report of the Consensus Conference," *Journal of Palliative Medicine* 12, No. 10 (October 2009): 885–904. See www.ncbi.nlm.nih.gov/pubmed/19807235.

———, Robert Vitillo, Sharon K. Hull, and Nancy Reller. "Improving the Spiritual Dimension of Whole Person Care: Reaching National and International Consensus." *Journal of Palliative Medicine* 17, No. 6 (2014): 642. See article here, www.ncbi.nlm.nih.gov/pmc/articles/PMC4038982/.

———, and Betty Ferrell. *Making Health Care Whole: Integrating Spirituality into Patient Care*. West Conshocken: Templeton Press, 2010. For Puchalski's PowerPoint of book, https://pdfs.semanticscholar.org/1ea2/4c6af3696f2a8ab40881226af2d9ba5e461f.pdf.

———, and A. L. Romer. "Taking a Spiritual History Allows Clinicians to Understand Patients More Fully." *Journal of Palliative Medicine* 3, No. 1 (Spring 2000): 129–137. See www.ncbi.nlm.nih.gov/pubmed/15859737. Pui-Lan, Kwok. "Feminist Theology as Intercultural Discourse." In *The Cambridge Companion to Feminist Theology*. Edited by Susan Frank Parsons, 23–39. Cambridge: Cambridge University Press, 2002.

Rakestraw, Robert V. "Ethical Choices: A Case for Non-Conflicting Absolutism," 2, No. 2 *Criswell Theological Review* (Spring 1988): 239–267.

Ramirez Johnson, Johnny, C. Fayard, C. Garberoglio, and C. Jorge RamirEzek. "Is Faith an Emotion? Faith as a Meaning-Making Affective Process: An Example from Breast Cancer Patients," *American Behavioral Scientist* 45, No. 12 (August 2002).

Ramshaw, Elaine. *Ritual and Pastoral Care*. Minneapolis: Fortress, 1987.

Ratzinger, Joseph/Pope Benedict XVI. *Eschatology: Death and Eternal Life*, 2nd Ed. Washington, DC: Catholic University of America Press, 2007; 1st 1988; 307 pp.

———. *Introduction to Christianity*. 2nd Ed. San Francisco: Ignatius Press, 2004.

Raymond B. Brown, Joseph A. Fitzmyer, and Roland E. Murphy, eds. *New Jerome Biblical Commentary*. Englewood Cliffs: Prentice Hall, 1990.

Ratzinger, Joseph/Pope Benedict XVI. *Eschatology: Death and Eternal Life*. 2nd ed. Washington, DC: Catholic University of America Press, 2007; 1st 1988.

Razak, Arisika. "Embodying Womanism." In *Ain't I a Womanist Too: Third-Wave Womanist Religious Thought*. Edited by Monica A. Coleman. Minneapolis: Fortress Press, 2013.

Reinder, Hans. *Receiving the Gift of Friendship: Profound Disability, Theological Anthropology, and Ethics*. Grand Rapids: Eerdmans, 2008.

Remen, Rachel Naomi. *My Grandfather's Blessings: Stories of Strength, Refuge, and Belonging*. New York: Riverhead Books, 2000.

Reynolds, N., S. Mrug, L. Britton, K. Guion, K. Wolfe, and H. Gutierr Ezek. "Spiritual Coping Predicts 5-year Health Outcomes in Adolescents with Cystic Fibrosis." *Journal of Cystic Fibrosis* 13, No. 5 (2014): 593–600.

Rice, Richard. *Suffering and the Search for Meaning. Contemporary Responses to the Problem of Pain*. Downers Grove: IVP Academic, 2014.

Richardson, A., and J. Bowden, eds., *Westminster Dictionary of Christian Theology*. Philadelphia: Westminster, 1983.

Richardson, B. L., and L. N. June. "Developing Effective Partnerships in Order to Utilize and Maximize the Resources of the African American Church: Strategies and Tools for Counseling Professionals." In *Multicultural Issues in Counseling: New Approaches to Diversity*, 3rd ed. Edited by Courtland C. Lee, 113–124. Alexandria, VA: American Counseling Association, 2006; 5th ed., Somerset: John Wiley, 2018.

Richter, Horst-Eberhard. *Der Gotteskomplex*. Hamburg: Rowohlt, 1979.

Ritchie, Tony. "A Pentecostal Take on Islamophobia." *Evangelical Interfaith Dialogue*. Evangelicals and Islamophobia: Critical Voices and Constructive Proposals (Fall 2016): 40-41. See article here, https://fullerstudio.fuller.edu/wp-content/uploads/2016/10/Evangelicals-and-Islamophobia-Fall-2016.pdf.

Robertson, E. H. *Dietrich Bonhoeffer*. Richmond: John Knox Press, 1967.

Robinson, John A. T. *The Body: A Study in Pauline Theology*. London: SCM, 1966.

Rogers, Carl (1902–87). *Client-Centered Therapy, Its Current Practice, Implications, and Theory*. Boston: Houghton Mifflin, 1951.

———. *On Becoming a Person*. Boston: Houghton Mifflin, 1961.

———. *Way of Being*. Boston: Houghton Mifflin, 1980.

———. "Empathic: An Unappreciated Way of Being," *The Counseling Psychologist* 5 (1975): 2–10. A classic definition.

Roth, S. John. *The Blind, the Lame, and the Poor: Character Types in Luke-Acts*. Sheffield: Sheffield Academic, 1997.

Rotholz, James M. *Chronic Fatigue Syndrome, Christianity, and Culture: Between God and an Illness*. Binghamton: Haworth, 2002.

Rowdon, H. H., ed. *Church Leaders Handbook*. Milton Keynes: Paternoster, 1969.

Rowland, Christopher, ed. *Cambridge Companion to Liberation Theology* Cambridge: Cambridge University Press, 2007.

Roy, Ranjan. *Social Relations and Chronic Pain*. New York: Kluwer Academic, 2001.

Royle, Anthony. "1 John as Midrash Pesher on Genesis 1–4: Eschatology, Typology, Structure and Early Christian Polemics." Conference paper presented at the British New Testament Society Conference at the University of Manchester, September 6, 2014.

Ruether, Rosemary Radford. "The Emergence of Christian Feminist Theology." In *The Cambridge Companion to Feminist Theology.* Edited by Susan Frank Parsons, 3–22. Cambridge: Cambridge University Press, 2002.
Rumbold, Bruce. *Pastoral Care.* No date. Retrieved from http://pastoralcareact.org/pastoral.html, no longer active. Accessed July 25, 2019, http://www.pastoralcareact.org/what-is-pastoral-care/. From Pastoral Care Council of the ACT. Web site set to expire August 2019. ACT: Australian Capital Territory.
Rumi (1207–1273). *The Love Poems of Rumi.* Edited by Deepak Chopra. New York: Harmony, 1998.
Runesson, Anders. *Divine Wrath and Salvation in Matthew.* Minneapolis: Fortress Press, 2015.
Ruse, Michael, and William A. Dembski, eds. *Debating Design: from Darwin to DNA.* Cambridge University Press, 2004.
Rymer, Kevin S. *Living L'Arche: Stories of Compassion, Love, and Disability.* Collegeville: Liturgical Press, 2009.
Ryrie, Charles Caldwell. *So Great Salvation: What It Means to Believe in Jesus Christ.* Chicago: Moody, 1977.

Saaymann, Willem. "Alternative Community and Antibody: A Dimension of David Bosch as Public Theologian." *Missionalia: Southern African Journal of Mission Studies* 39, No. 1–2 (April 2011): 5–17.
Saguil, Aaron, and Karen Phelps. "The Spiritual Assessment." *American Family Physician* 86, No. 6 (September2012): 546-550. See www.aafp.org/afp/2012/0915/p546.html.
Sanders, J. Oswald. *Heaven: Better by Far—Answers to Questions About the Believer's Final Hope.* Grand Rapids: Discovery House, 1993.
Sankbeil, Harold L. *Sanctification: Christ in Action: Evangelical Challenge and Lutheran Response.* Milwaukee: Northwestern Publishing House, 1989.
Schmidt, Roger, Gene Sager, Gerald Carney, Albert Charles Muller, and Kenneth J. Zanca. *Patterns of Religion.* Belmont: Wadsworth, 1999.
Schnackenburg, Rudolf. *The Gospel According to St John: Commentary on Chapters 5–12.* Vol. 2. New York: The Seabury Press, 1980.
———. *The Gospel According to St John: Commentary on Chapters 13–21.* Vol. 3. New York: Crossroad/Herder, 1983.
Schrage, Wolfgang. *Der erste Brief an die Korinther: 1Kor 6,12–11,16, Evangelisch-Katholischer Kommentar zum Neuen Testament.* Vol. VII/2. Düsseldorf: Benzinger/Neukirchner, 1995.
Schrage, Wolfgang, and Erhard S. Gerstenberger. *Suffering.* Nashville: Abingdon 1980.
Schumm, Darla, and Michael Stoltzfus, eds. *Disability and Religious Diversity: Cross-cultural and Interreligious Perspectives.* New York: Palgrave Macmillan, 2011; 245 pp.
———, eds. *Disability in Judaism, Christianity and Islam: Sacred Texts, Historical Traditions, and Social Analysis.* New York: Palgrave Macmillan, 2011; 261 pp.
Scristoph, Schwobel. "The Quest for an Adequate Theology of Grace and the Future of Lutheran Theology: A Response of Robert W. Jenson." In *The Gift of Grace: The Future of Lutheran Theology.* Edited by Niels Henrik Gregersen, Bo Holm, Ted Peters, and Peter Widmann. Minneapolis: Fortress Press, 2005.
Second London Baptist Confession of 1689. See https://founders.org/library/1689-confession/.
Seed, Caroline G. "The Missional Nature of Divine-human Communion: T.F. Torrance and the Chinese Church." PhD diss. Potchefstroom, ZA: North-West University, 2016.
———. "Monotheism, Messianism and Children of Israel: Reception of the Gospel of John among the Isawa of Northern Nigeria and the Qiang of Western China, 1913-1935." *International Bulletin of Mission Research* (September 2019; first given as a research paper to the 2nd Annual Research Conference of the Presbyterian University of East Africa, 2016.
———. "'Translatability and Non-Translatability,' Bible, Qur'an and Land in northern Nigeria, 1913-1915." A conference paper given at the inaugural conference of The Sanneh Institute, Accra, Ghana, February 26-28, 2020.
Seeley, Karen M. *Cultural Psychotherapy: Working with Culture in the Clinical Encounter.* Lanham: Jason Aronson, 2006.
Seifrid, Mark A. "Judgment." In *Dictionary of the Later New Testament and Its Developments.* Edited by Ralph P. Martin and Peter H. Davids. Downers Grove: IVP, 1997.
Sethi, Sheena, and Martin E. P. Seligman. "Optimism and Fundamentalism." *Psychological Science* 4, No. 4 (July 1993): 256–259. See www.jstor.org/stable/40062552.

———. "The Hope of Fundamentalists." *Psychological Science* 5, No. 1 (January 1994): 58. See https://psycnet.apa.org/record/1994-29394-001.
Shaballa, T. "Entitlement is the key word in racist thinking," accessed at www.rdm.co.za /business/2016/01/12/entitled-is-a-key-word-in-racist-thinking. Viewed 15/01/2016.
Shakespeare, Tom. "The Social Model of Disability." In *The Disability Studies Reader*. 2nd ed. Edited by Lennard J. Davis, 197–204. New York: Routledge, 2006.
Shaver, P., C. Hazan, and D. Bradshaw. "Love as attachment: The integration of three behavioral systems" (1988) in *The Psychology of Love*, edited by Robert Sternberg and Michael L. Barnes, 68–99. New Haven: Yale University Press, 1989.
Shaver, Phillip R., Mario Mikulincer, and Brooke C. Feeney. "What's Love Got To Do with It? Insecurity and Anger in Attachment Relationships." *Virginia Journal of Social Policy and the Law* 16 (January 1, 2009): 491–513.
Sherlock, C. *The Doctrine of Humanity*. Downers Grove: IVP, 1996.
Sherman, A. C., T. V. Merluzzi. J. E. Pustejovsky, C. L. Park, L. George, G. Fitchett, H. S. Jim, A. R. Munoz, S. C. Danhauer, M. A. Snyder, and J. M. Salsman. "A Meta-analytic Review of Religious or Spiritual Involvement and Social Health Among Cancer Patients." *Cancer* 121, No. 21 (2015): 3779–3788. See https://www.ncbi.nlm.nih.gov/pubmed/26258730. "In total,78 independent samples encompassing 14,277 patients were included in the meta-analysis. Social health was significantly associated with overall R/S [Religion and Spirituality]."
Sider, R. J. "The Anabaptist Perspective." In *Church, State and Public Justice: Five Views* (Clarke E. Coshran, Derek H. Davis, Corwin E. Smidt, Ronald J. Sider, and Philip Wogaman). Edited by P. C. Kemeny. Downers Grove: IVP, 2007.
Simpson, Amy. *Troubled Minds: Mental Illness and the Church's Mission*. Downers Grove: IVP, 2013.
Simpson, Gary. "Retrieving Martin Luther's Critical Public Theology of Political Authority for Global Civil Society." In *Theological Practices That Matter*. Edited by Karen L. Bloomquist. Minneapolis: Lutheran University Press, 2009.
Simpson, Michael L. *Permission Evangelism: When to Talk, When to WaLuke* Colorado Springs: Cook Communications Ministries, 2003.
Skrabski, A., M. Koop, S. Rozsa, J. Rethelyi, and R. H. Rahe. "Life Meaning: An Important Correlate of Health in the Hungarian Population." *International Journal of Behavioral Medicine* 12, No. 2 (2005): 78–85. See www.ncbi.nlm.nih.gov/pubmed/15901216.
Smalley, Stephen, *1, 2, 3 John*. Word Biblical Commentary, 51. Waco: Word Books, 1984.
Smith, Aaron, and Monica Anderson. "5 Facts about Online Dating." Pew Center Research. Published online 2-29-16, www.PewResearch.org/fact-tank/2016/02/29/5-facts-about-online-dating/.
Smith, Archie, Jr. *The Relational Self: Ethics and Therapy from a Black Church Perspective*. Nashville: Abingdon, 1982.
Smith, Ebbie C. "The Ten Commandments in Today's Permissive Society: A Principleist Approach." *Southwestern Journal of Theology* 20, No. 1 (Fall 1977): 42–58.
Smith, Margaret Charles, and Linda Janet Holmes. *Listen To Me Good: The Life Story of an Alabama Midwife*. Columbus: Ohio State University Press, 1996.
Smith, Ronald Gregor, ed. *Against the Stream: Shorter Post-War Writings, 1946–1952*. New York: Philosophical Library, 1954.
Smyth, Newman. *Christian Ethics*. New York: Charles Scribner's Sons, 1908.
Sobrino, Jon. *Christ, Christ the Liberator*. Maryknoll: Orbis Books, 2001.
———. *Christology at the Crossroads*. Eugene: Wipf & Stock, 2002.
———. *Jesus, the Liberator*. London: Continuum, 1994.
Søe, N. H. "Anthropology." In *Kierkegaard and Human Values*, Bibliotheca Kierkegaardiana, vol. 7. Edited by George E. Arbaugh, Niels Thulstrup, and Marie Mikulová Thulstrup. Copenhagen: C. A. Reitzels Boghandel, 1980.
Sölle, Dorothee. *Suffering*. Philadelphia: Fortress, 1975.
Soothill, K., S. M. Morris, J. C. Harman, C. Thomas, B. Francis, and M. B. McIllmurray. "Cancer and Faith. Having Faith—Does It Make a Difference among Patients and Their Informal Carers?" *Scandinavian Journal of Caring Sciences* 16, No. 3 (September 2002): 256–263. See www.ncbi.nlm.nih.gov/pubmed/12191037. Of 402 questionnaires, "Not surprisingly, both patients and carers with faith identified a greater need for opportunities for personal prayer, support from people of their own faith and support from a spiritual adviser."
Sorajjakool, Siroj. *When Sickness Heals. The Place of Religious Belief in Healthcare*. Philadelphia/London: Templeton Foundation Press, 2006.

———, Kelvin M. Thompson, Leigh Aveling, and Art Earl. "Chronic Pain, Meaning, and Spirituality: A Qualitative Study of the Healing Process in Relation to the Role of Meaning and Spirituality." *The Journal of Pastoral Care and Counseling* 60, No. 4 (Winter 2006): 369-78. See https://www.ncbi.nlm.nih.gov/pubmed/17265702.

Soulen, R., and L. Woodhead, eds. *God and Human Dignity*. Grand Rapids: Eerdmans, 2006.

Sperry, Len. *Mental Health and Mental Disorders: An Encyclopedia of Conditions, Treatments, and Well-Beings*. Santa Barbara, CA: Greenwood, 2016.

Spieker, Hartmut, and Hinrich Stoevesandt, eds. *Karl Barth Gesamtausgabe: Predigten 1935–1952*. Zürich: Theologischer Verlag Zürich, 1996.

Spriggs, David J., and Eric Sloter. "Counselor-clergy Collaboration in a Church-based CounselingMinistry." *Journal of Psychology and Christianity* 22, No. 4 (Winter 2003): 323–326.

Ståhl, Michael. *Ethiopia, Political Contradictions in Agricultural Development*. Uppsala: Political Science Association in Uppsala, 1974.

Stanley, Charles F. "About Love: Breaking Down the Types of Love in Scriptures." Published January 21, 2015, www.InTouch.org/read/about-love.

Stanton, G. *A Gospel for a New People: Studies in Matthew*. Edinburgh: T & T Clark, 1992.

Steinberg, Robert J. and M. L. Barnes, eds. *The Psychology of Love*. New Haven: Yale University Press, 1988.

Steinberg, Robert J. "A Triangular Theory of Love." *Psychological Review* 93, No. 2 (1986): 119–135. See article here, http://pzacad.pitzer.edu/~dmoore/psych199/1986_sternberg_trianglelove.pdf.

———. "Triangulating Love." In *The Psychology of Love*. Edited by Robert J. Sternberg and M. L. Barnes. New Haven: Yale University Press, 1988.

Steyn, T. H., and M. J. Masango. "The Theology and Praxis of Practical Theology in the Context of the Faculty of Theology," *HTS Teologiese Studies/Theological Studies*, 67, No. 2 (2011): 1–7. See https://hts.org.za/index.php/hts/article/view/956/2095.

Stiker, Henri-Jacques. *A History of Disability*. Translated by William Sayers. Ann Arbor: University of Michigan Press, 1999.

Stott, John R. W. *The Epistles of John*. Tyndale Commentary Series. Grand Rapids: Eerdmans, 1960.

———. *The Message of Acts*. The Bible Speaks Today Series. Downers Grove: InterVarsity Press, 1990.

Stover, Earl F. *Up from Handymen: The United States Army Chaplaincy 1865–1920*, Vol. 3 of 7 of history of Army Chaplaincy (see "Army, U.S." ref. for more). U.S. Army, 1977.

Strachey, J., ed. and trans. *Standard Edition of the Complete Psychological Works of Sigmund Freud*. London: Hogarth Press, 1962.

Strecker, Georg. *The Johannine Epistles. Hermeneia: A Critical and Historical Commentary on the Bible*. Minneapolis: Augsburg Fortress, 1996.

Strobel, Lee. *The Case for a Creator: a Journalist Investigates Scientific Evidence that Points Toward God*. Grand Rapids: Zondervan, 2004; 341 pp.

Susser, Peter, and Peter J. Petesch. *Disability Discrimination and the Workplace*. 2nd ed. Arlington: BNA Books, 2011.

Swarr, Amanda Lock. "Paradoxes of Butchness: Lesbian Masculinities and Sexual Violence in Contemporary South Africa." *Signs Journal of Women in Culture and Society* 37, No. 4 (2012): 962–988. See https://www.jstor.org/stable/10.1086/664476.

Swindoll, Charles R., and Roy B. Zuck, eds. *Understanding Christian Theology*. Nashville: Thomas Nelson, 2003.

Tada, Joni Erickson, and Steve Bundy. *Beyond Suffering: A Christian View on Disability Ministry*. Agoura Hills, CA: Christian Institute on Disability, 2011.

Talbert, Charles H., and Jason A. Whitlark. *Getting "Saved": The Whole Story of Salvation in the New Testament*. Grand Rapids: Eerdmans, 2011.

Targum of Palestine, Commonly Entitled the Targum of Jonathan ben Uzziel on the Book of Genesis. Available from http://targum.info/pj/pjgen1-6.htm, accessed May 9, 2017.

Tertullian (155–240 A.D.). *De paenitentia* "On Repentance." See www.Tertullian.org/anf/anf03/anf03-47.htm.

Tesema, Ta'a. *The Political Economy of Western Central Ethiopia: From the Mid-16th to the Early-20th Centuries*. PhD diss. Michigan State University, 1986.

Thatcher, Tom, Chris Keith, Raymond F. Person, Jr., and Elsie R. Stern, eds. *The Dictionary of the Bible and Ancient Media*. London: Bloomsbury, 2017.

Thatcher, Tom. "Cain the Jew the Antichrist: Collective Memory and the Johannine Ethic of Loving and Hating." In *Rethinking the Ethics of John: "Implicit Ethics" in the Johannine Writings. Contexts and Norms of New Testament Ethics.* Vol III. Edited by Jan G. van der Watt and Ruben Zimmerman. Heidelberg: Mohr Siebeck, 2012.
Theological Dictionary of the Old Testament, see, Botterweck, 1973ss.
Thermos, Vasileios. ed. Founding editor of Greek journal *Psyches Dromoi: Ways of the Soul.*
———. *Psychology in the Service of the Church.* Alhambra: Sebastian Press, 2017.
———. *In Search of the Person: According to Gregory of Palamas.* Alexandria: Alexander Press, 2002.
———. *Sexual Orientation and Gender Identity: Answers and ... People.* Athens: En Plo, 2019. An abridged version of 700-pg book in Greek: *Attraction and Passion: An Interdisciplinary Approach of Homosexuality.* Translated to English from Greek by Vasileios Tsangalos. Alhamba, CA: Sebastion Press, 2019. See https://www.sebastianpress.org/product-p/sp-bk-ps-2019-001.htm.
———. *Thirst for Love and Truth: Encounters of Orthodox Theology and Psychological Science.* Montreal: Alexander, 2010.
———. See above "Kazaku, Peter" for a book on the work of Thermos, *Orthodoxy and Psychoanalysis* (2013).
———. "The Paradox of Mental Health Care and Spirituality: The Culture of Extreme Individualism as a Mediator" was awarded the 2018 prize for the category of "Culture, Care, and Spirituality" by the Jean-Marc Foundation in Switzerland which highlights contributions to the fields of human, social and theological sciences: https://fondationdocteurjmf.ch/wp-content/uploads/2019/03/Prix-Vasileios-Thermos-2017-2018-Anglais.pdf.
Thielicke, Helmut. *Theological Ethics, Volume 1: Foundations.* Edited by William H. Lazareth. Philadelphia: Fortress, 1966.
———. *Theological Ethics, Volume 2: Politics.* Edited by William H. Lazareth. Grand Rapids: William B. Eerdmans, 1979.
Thiselton, Anthony C. *The First Epistle to the Corinthians: A Commentary on the Greek Text, The New International Greek Testament Commentary.* Grands Rapids: Eerdmans, 2000.
Thomas, Carol. *Female Forms: Experiencing and Understanding Disability.* Buckingham/Philadelphia: Open University Press, 1999.
Thomas, John Christopher. *The Devil, Disease and Deliverance: Origins of Illness in New Testament Thought, Journal of Pentecostal Theology Supplemental.* Series 13. Sheffield: Sheffield Academic Press, 1998.
Thomas, Linda E. "Womanist Theology, Epistemology, and a New Anthropological Paradigm." In *Living Stones in the Household of God. The Legacy and Future of Black* Theology, edited by Linda E. Thomas, 37–48. Minneapolis: Fortress, 2004.
Thomas, Linda E., ed. *Living Stones in the Household of God. The Legacy and Future of Black Theology.* Minneapolis: Fortress, 2004.
Thomas, Robert L. *Revelation 1–7: An Exegetical Commentary.* Chicago: Moody Press, 1992.
Thompson, Marianne Meye. *1–3 John. The IVP New Testament Commentary Series.* Leicester: Inter-Varsity Press, 1992.
Thompson, Michael E. W. *Where is the God of Justice? The Old Testament and Suffering.* Eugene: Wipf & Stock, 2011.
Thompson, Parker C. *From Its European Antecedents to 1791: The United States Army Chaplaincy*, Vol. 1 of 7 of history of Army Chaplaincy (see "Army, U.S." ref. for more). U.S. Army, 1978.
Thornton, Sharon G. *Broken Yet Beloved: A Pastoral Theology of the Cross.* Atlanta: Chalice Press, 2002.
Trible, Phyllis. *Texts of Terror: Literary-Feminist Readings of Biblical Narratives.* Minneapolis: Augsburg Fortress, 1984.
Thulstrup, Niels, and Marie Mikulová Thulstrup, eds., *Kierkegaard and Human Values, Bibliotheca Kierkegaardiana*, vol. 7. Copenhagen: C. A. Reitzels Boghandel, 1980.
Thurmond-Malone, Myrna. *Midwifing—A Womanist Approach to Pastoral Counseling.* Eugene: Pickwick, 2019; 182 pp. See https://wipfandstock.com/author/view/detail/id/196440/.
———. "Midwifing: A Womanist Approach to Pastoral Counseling, Investigating the Fractured Self: Slavery, Violence, and the Black Woman." ThD diss. Columbia Theological Seminary, 2015.
———, Alisha Tatem, Brandy McMurry, and Quanika Bynum. *Daughters of the Desert—The Journey Towards Letting Go, Surrendering, and Trusting God.* Scotts Valley: CreateSpace, 2015.
———, Alisha Tatem, Brandy McMurry, and Quanika Bynum. *Selah—Reflections on Sabbath and Self-Care.* Scotts Valley: CreateSpace, 2015.

Thurneysen, Eduard. *Dostoevsky*. Translated by Keith R. Crim. Richmond: John Knox Press, 1964.
Tillich, Paul. *Christianity and the Encounter of the World Religions*. New York: Columbia University Press, 1963.
———. *Christianity and the Problem of Existence*. Washington, DC: Henderson, 1951.
———. *Courage to Be*. New Haven: Yale University Press, 1952.
———. *Dynamics of Faith*. New York: Harper, 1957.
———. *Eternal Now*. New York: Scribner, 1963.
———. *Systematic Theology*. Chicago: University of Chicago Press, 1951.
Tinsley, T. M. "Advising and Counseling High School Student-athletes." In *Advising Student-athletes: A Collaborative Approach to Success*, edited by A. Leslie-Toogood and E. Gill, 139–147. Manhattan: NACADA, National Academic Advising Association, 2008.
———, and Curtis, W. H. "A Counselor and a Pastor's Collaborative Effort to Develop a Culturally Appropriate Counseling Center within a Predominately African-American Church." *The Journal of the Pennsylvania Counseling Association* 10, No. 1 (2009): 33–47.
———. *The Case of Larry Jones*. Unpublished manuscript, c. 2013.
———. "The Church as a Multicultural Sports Team: A Model for Ministry Leadership Development for God's Coaching Staff." D.Min. diss. Dayton: United Theological Seminary, 2016.
Titchkosky, Tanya. "Disability: A Rose by Any Other Name? 'People-First' Language in Canadian Society." *Canadian Review of Sociology and Anthropology* 39, No. 2 (May 2001): 125–40.
Tolo, Arne. *Sidama and Ethiopian: The Emergence [of] the Mekane Yesus Church in Sidama*. Uppsala: Uppsala universitet 1998.
Tomlin, Graham. *Luther and His World: An Introduction*. Downers Grove: IVP, 2002.
Tozer, A. W. *The Dangers of a Shallow Faith: Awakening from Spiritual Lethargy*. Bloomington: Bethany, 2012.
Traill, Robert (1642–1716). *Justification Vindicated*. Carlisle: Banner of Truth Trust, 2002. Original 1692, titled *A Vindication of the Protestant Doctrine Concerning Justification and of its Preachers and Professors from the Unjust Charge of Antinomianism*.
Travis, S. H. "Judgment." In *Dictionary of Paul and His Letters*. Edited by Gerald F. Hawthorne, Ralph P. Martin, and Daniel G. Reid, 517. Downers Grove: InterVarsity Press, 1993.
Travis, Stephen H. *Christ and the Judgement of God: Limits of Divine Retribution in New Testament Thought*. Milton Keynes: Paternoster, 2008.
Tremblay, Joe. "Speaking the People's Language." *Catholic New Agency*. Accessed May 04, 2012, www.CatholicNewsAgency.com/column/speaking-the-peoples-language-2133/.
Trimingham, J. Spencer. *The Christian Church and Missions in Ethiopia (Including Eritrea and the Somalilands)*. London: World Dominion Press, 1951.
Tshaballa, Sim. "'Entitlement' Is the Key Word in Racist Thinking." *Business Life* (January 12, 2016), viewed 5-1-2016 at www.rdm.co.za/business/2016/01/12/entitled-is-a-key-word-in-racist-thinking, only available on subscription.
Tucker, Karen Westerfield. "A Pastoral Response to a Silent Tragedy." *The Christian Ministry* 20, No. 1 (January–February 1989): 11–13. With her initiative, the following rituals were included in the *United Methodist Book of Worship*. "A Service of Hope after Loss of Pregnancy" (pp. 623–26) and "A Service of Death and Resurrection for a Stillborn Child" (pp. 170–71).
Turner, David M., and Kevin Stagg, eds. *Social Histories of Disability and Deformity*. New York/London: Routledge, 2006.
Turner, N. *Syntax*, vol. 3. In J. Moulton, *A Grammar of New Testament Greek*. 5 vols. Edinburgh: T & T Clark, 1963.
Turpin, Katherine. "Liberationist Practical Theology." In *Opening the Field of Practical Theology: An Introduction*. Edited by Kathleen A. Cahalan and Gordon S. Mikoski. Lanham: Rowman and Littlefield, 2014.
Tutu, Desmond. *No Future Without Forgiveness*. New York: Random House, 1999.

Ukagba, George Uzoma, Obioma Des-Obi, Iks J. Nwankwor, eds. *The Kpim of Feminism: Issues and Women in a Changing World*. Victoria, Canada: Trafford Publishing, 2010; 599 pp.
U.S. Army. Chaplaincy Histories, 7 vols., each about 500 pages. *From Its European Antecedents to 1791:The United States Army Chaplaincy* (Vol. 1, by Chaplain Parker C. Thompson., 1978), *Struggling for Recognition: The United States Army Chaplaincy 1791–1865* (Vol. 2, by Chaplain Herman A. Norton, 1977), *Up From Handymen: The United States Army Chaplaincy 1865–1920* (Vol. 3, by Chaplain Earl F. Stover, 1977), *The Best and The Worst of Times: The United States*

  Army Chaplaincy 1920–1945 (Vol. 4, by Chaplain Robert L. Gushwa, 1977), *Confidence in Battle, Inspiration in Peace: The United States Army Chaplaincy 1945–1975* (Vol. 5, by Chaplain Rodger R. Venzke, 1977), *He Was Always There, The U.S. Army Chaplain Ministry in the Vietnam Conflict* (Vol. 6, by Chaplain Henry F. Ackermann, 1989), *Encouraging Faith, Supporting Soldiers: A History of the U.S. Chaplain Corps 1975–1995* (Vol. 7, by Chaplain John W. Brinsfield, 1997).

Ullman, C. "Cognitive and Emotional Antecedents of Religious Conversion." *Journal of Personality and Social Psychology* 43, No. 1 (1982): 182–92. See https://psycnet.apa.org/record/1983-03296-001.

UNAIDS. *Facing the Future Together. United Nations Secretary-General's Task Force on Women, Girls and HIV and AIDS in Southern Africa* (2004). Accessed Jan. 6, 2017, http://womenandaids.unaids.org/regional/docs/Report%20of%20SG%27s%20Task%20Force.pdf.

UNAIDS. *Global AIDS Update 2016.* Accessed April, 29, 2017: www.unaids.org/sites/default/files/media_asset/global-AIDS-update-2016_en.pdf.

United Methodist Book of Worship. Nashville: United Methodist Publishing House, 1992.

Ursula King, ed. *Feminist Theology from the Third World A Reader.* Maryknoll: Orbis Press, 1994.

Utazi, C. M. *The Nature and Subject Matter of Pastoral Theology.* Nairobi, Kenya: Salesian Theological College, 2012.

van der Watt, Jan G., and Ruben Zimmerman, eds. *Rethinking the Ethics of John: "Implicit Ethics" in the Johannine Writings. Contexts and Norms of New Testament Ethics.* Vol III. Heidelberg: Mohr Siebeck, 2012.

van Leeuwen, M. S. *Gender and Grace.* Downers Grove: IVP, 1990.

van Staden, P. J. "The Debate on the Structure of 1 John." *HTS Teologiese Studies/Theological Studies* 47 (April 1991): 487–502.

Vande Kemp, Hendrika. "Helen Flanders Dunbar (1902–1959)." *The Feminist Psychologist* 28, No. 1 (Winter 2001). Accessed www.apadivisions.org/division-35/about/heritage/helen-dunbar-biography.aspx.

VandeCreek, Larry, and Laurel Burton, eds. "Professional Chaplaincy: Its Role and Importance in Healthcare." *The Journal of Pastoral Care* 55, No. 1 (Spring 2001): 81–97. See www.professionalchaplains.org/chaplaincy_importance for this extraordinary and landmark joint statement of the five largest chaplaincy bodies representing 10,000-plus members.

Vatican II, *Dei Verbum.* Vatican II's "Dogmatic Constitution on Divine Revelation." Vatican, November 18, 1965; see www.Vatican.va/archive/hist_councils/ii_vatican_council/documents/vat-ii_const_19651118_dei-verbum_en.html.

Vellem, V. "Rediscovering Reconciliation: A Response to the Call for reconciliation as a Governing Symbol in Post-1994 South Africa." In *Reconciliation: A Guiding Vison for South Africa.* Edited by E. Conradie. Stellenbosch: Sun Press, 2013.

Venzke, Rodger R. *Confidence in Battle, Inspiration in Peace: The United States Army Chaplaincy 1945–1975,* Vol. 5 of 7 of history of Army Chaplaincy (see "Army, U.S." ref. for more). U.S. Army, 1977.

Viviano, Benedict T. "The Gospel According to Matthew." In *The New Jerome Biblical Commentary.* Edited by Raymond B. Brown et al. Englewood Cliffs: Prentice Hall, 1990.

Vlachos, Chris Alex. *The Law and the Knowledge of Good and Evil: The Edenic Background of the Catalytic Operation of the Law in Paul.* Eugene: Wipf & Stock, 2009.

———. "Law, Sin, and Death: An Edenic Triad? An Examination with Reference to 1 Corinthians 15:56." *Journal of the Evangelical Theological Society* 47, No. 2 (June 2004): 277–98. See article here, www.ETSJETS.org/files/JETS-PDFs/47/47-2/47-2-pp277-298_JETS.pdf.

Volf, Miroslav. "The Social Meaning of Reconciliation." *Transformation* 16, No. 1 (1999): 7–12.

———. "When Gospel and Culture Intersect: Notes on the Nature of Christian Difference." *Evangelical Review of Theology* 22, No. 3 (1998): 196–207.

Volf, Miroslav. *A Public Faith: How followers of Christ serve the Common Good.* Grand Rapids: Brazos, 2011.

Vondey, Wolfgang, and Martin W. Mittelstadt, eds. *The Theology of Amos Yong and the New Face of Pentecostal Scholarship: Passion for the Spirit, Global Pentecostal and Charismatic Studies.* Vol. 14. Leiden/Boston: Brill, 2013. See https://brill.com/abstract/title/24131.

Vuola, Elina. *Limits of Liberation. Feminist Theology and the Ethics of Poverty and Reproduction.* London: Sheffield Academic, 2002.

Walker, Alice. *In Search of Our Mothers' Gardens*. New York: Harcourt, 1983.
Wallace, Daniel B. "What Does it Mean to be Justified? A Brief Exposition of Romans 3.21–26." Part 1, https://bible.org/article/what-does-it-mean-be-justified-brief-exposition-romans-321-26-part-1 (2007). "What Does it Mean to be Justified? A Brief Exposition of Romans 3.21–26." Part 2, https://bible.org/article/what-does-it-mean-be-justified-brief-exposition-romans-321-26-part-2 (2007).
Walls, Jerry L., ed. *The Oxford Handbook on Eschatology*. New York/Oxford: Oxford University Press, 2010.
Walther, Carl Ferdinand Wilhelm (1811–1887). *The Proper Distinction Between Law and Gospel*. Translated by William Herman Theodore Dau (1864–1944) from a student's notes of Walther's lectures at Concordia Seminary 9-12-1884 to 11-6-1885. St. Louis: Concordia Publishing House, 1929. Then translated by Herbert J. A. Bouman and edited by August R. Suelflow for Concordia Publishing House, 1981, for vol. 7 in *American Lutheran Classics* series. Walther was a preeminent Lutheran theologian and pastor. When the Lutheran Church-Missouri Synod was founded in 1847, he was its first president. He was also president and theology professor of Concordia Seminary (1850–1887). Some consider this his most important work. See *Concordia Journal* 37, No. 3 (2011) for a list of Walther's work.
Waltke, Bruce C., and Charles Yu. *An Old Testament Theology: An Exegetical, Canonical and Thematic Approach*. Grand Rapids: Zondervan, 2007.
Ware, Bruce A. *God's Lesser Glory: The Diminished God of Open Theism*. Wheaton: Crossway, 2000.
Waters, Larry J., and Roy B. Zuck, eds. *Why, O God? Suffering and Disability in the Bible and the Church*. Wheaton: Crossway, 2011.
Watson, Philip S., and Helmut Lehmann, eds. *Luther's Work*. Vol. 33. Philadelphia: Fortress Press, 1972.
Wax, Trevin. "Beware the Puritan Paralysis." *The Gospel Coalition*. November 20, 2012. See https://blogs.thegospelcoalition.org/trevinwax/2012/11/20/beware-the-puritan-paralysis/.
Webster, John. *Barth's Ethics of Reconciliation*. Cambridge: Cambridge University, 1995.
―――. *Barth's Moral Theology: Human Action in Barth's Thought*. Edinburgh: T & T Clark, 1998.
―――, ed. *The Cambridge Companion to Karl Barth*. New York: Cambridge University Press, 2000.
Wehman, Paul, John Bricout, and John Kregel, "Supported Employment in 2000: Changing the Locus of Control from Agency to Consumer." In *Mental Retardation in the 21st Century*. Edited by Michael L. Wehmeyer and James R. Patton. Austin: Pro-ED, 2000: 115–50.
Wehmeyer, Michael L., and James R. Patton, eds. *Mental Retardation in the 21st Century*. Austin: Pro-ED, 2000.
Weil, Simone (1909–43). *Waiting for God*. Translated by Emman Craufurd. Introduction by Leslie A. Fiedler. New York: G. P. Putnam's Sons, 1951.
―――. "The Love of God and Affliction." In her *Waiting for God*.
Wenham, Gordon J. *Genesis 1–15. Word Biblical Commentary*. Vol. 1. Waco: Word Books, 1987.
Wepener, Cas. "Liturgical 'Reform' in Sub-Saharan Africa: Some Observations on Worship, Language and Culture." *Studia Liturgica* 44, No. 1–2 (September 2014): 82–95. See www.Academia.edu/8416760/Liturgical_inculturation_or_liberation_A_qualitative_exploration_of_major_themes_in_liturgical_reform_in_South_Africa.
―――. "Researching Rituals: On the Use of Participatory Action Research in Liturgical Studies." *Practical Theology in South Africa* 20 (2005): 109–127. See www.Academia.edu/5081647/Researching_Rituals_On_the_use_of_participatory_action_research_in_liturgical_studies.
Werpehowski, William. "Karl Barth and Politics." In *The Cambridge Companion to Karl Barth*. Edited by John Webster. New York: Cambridge University Press, 2000.
West, Gerald O., Kapya Kaoma, and Charlene Van der Walt. *When Faith Does Violence: Re-Imagining Engagement Between Churches And LGBTI Groups On Homophobia in Africa*. Johannesburg: Other Foundation, 2017.
Westerholm, Stephen. *Justification Reconsidered: Rethinking a Pauline Theme*. Grand Rapids: Eerdmans, 2013.
―――. *Perspectives Old and New on Paul: The "Lutheran" Paul and His Critics*. Grand Rapids: Eerdmans, 2004.
Wheatley, Edward. *Stumbling Blocks before the Blind: Medieval Constructions of a Disability*. Ann Arbor: University of Michigan Press, 2010.
White, Michael, and David Epston. *Narrative Means to Therapeutic Ends*. New York: W. W. Norton and Company, 1990.

Williams, Delores. *Sisters in the Wilderness: The Challenge of Womanist God-TaLuke* Maryknoll: Orbis Books, 1993.
Willis, Kimberly. "Persons with Disabilities and the Temporarily Able-Bodied: Becoming the Body of Christ." *Liturgy* 23, No. 2 (February 2008): 1–2. See www.tandfonline.com/doi/abs/10.1080/04580630701870275.
Willis-Watkins, David, ed. *Studies in Reformed Theology and History*, 10 volumes. Princeton: Princeton Theological Seminary, 1993–2005. For list, http://commons.ptsem.edu/?journal-id=srth.
Wimberly, E. *Claiming God, Reclaiming Dignity: African American Pastoral Care*. Nashville: Abingdon, 2003.
Wisløff, Carl. *Jag vet på vem jag tror* ["I Know in Whom I Believe"]: *Orientering i kristen tro*. Göteborg: Kyrkliga förbundets bokförlag, 1992, 1st 1946.
Wittgenstein, Ludwig (1889-1951). *Tractatus Logico-Philosophicus*. Routledge Introduction by Bertrand Russell. New York: Harcourt, Brace; London: K. Paul, Trench, Trubner, 1922. Translated by C. K. Ogden. London/New York: Routledge, 1992. Translated by D. F. Pears and B. F. McGuinness. London/New York: Routledge, 1994, 2001, 2014.
Wolfinger, Nicholas H. "Counterintuitive Trends in the Link between Premarital Sex and Marriage Stability." *Institute for Family Studies*. Published online June 6, 2016, https://family-studies.org/counterintuitive-trends-in-the-link-between-premarital-sex-and-marital-stability/.
Woodward, James, and Stephen Pattison, eds. *The Blackwell Reader in Pastoral and Practical Theology*. Malden: Blackwell Publishing, 2000.
Worden, J. W. *Grief Counseling and Grief Therapy: A Handbook for the Mental Health Practitioner*, 4th ed. New York: Springer Publishing, 2009.
World Council of Churches. *Plan of Action, Nairobi 2001. Global Consultation On The Ecumenical Response To The Challenge of HIV/AIDS* in Nairobi, Kenya, www.wcc-coe.org.
Wright, Nicholas Thomas. *History and Eschatology: Jesus and the Promise of Natural Theology*. Waco: Baylor University Press, 2019; 365 pp.
———. *Jesus and the Victory of God, Christian Origins and the Question of God*. Vol. 2. London: SPCK, 1996.
Wynn, Kerry H. "The Normate Hermeneutic and Interpretations of Disability within the Yahwistic Narratives." In *This Abled Body: Rethinking Disabilities in Biblical Studies*. Edited by Hector Avalos, Sarah J. Melcher, and Jeremy Schipper. Atlanta: Society of Biblical Literature, 2007: 91–101.

Yarbrough, John. *1–3 John. Baker Exegetical Commentary*. Grand Rapids: Baker Academic, 2008.
Yong, Amos. *Beyond the Impasse—Toward a Pneumatological Theology of Religions*. Grand Rapids: Baker Academic, 2003; 207 pp.
———. *The Bible, Disability, and the Church: A New Vision of the People of God*. Grand Rapids: Eerdmans, 2011; 161 pp.
———. *The Cosmic Breath—Spirit and Nature in the Christianity-Buddhism-Science Trialogue, Philosophical Studies in Science and Religion* 4. Leiden: Brill, 2012; 299 pp.
———. *In the Days of Caesar: Pentecostalism and Political Theology—The Cadbury Lectures 2009*. Sacra Doctrina: Christian Theology for a Postmodern Age series. Grand Rapids: Eerdmans, 2010; 397 pp.
———. *The Future of Evangelical Theology—Soundings from the Asian American Diaspora*. Downers Grove: IVP, 2014; 255 pp.
———, Veli-Matti Kärkkäinen, and Kirsteen Kim, eds. *Interdisciplinary and Religio-Cultural Discourses on a Spirit-Filled World—Loosing the Spirits*. New York: Palgrave Macmillan, 2013; 262 pp.
———. *Pneumatology and the Christian-Buddhist Dialogue—Does the Spirit Blow through the Middle Way? Studies in Systematic Theology* 11. Leiden: Brill, 2012; 359 pp.
———, and Jonathan A. Anderson. *Renewing Christian Theology—Systematics for Global Christianity*. Waco: Baylor University Press, 2014; 477 pp. See www.BaylorPress.com/9781602587618/.
———. *Spirit of Love: A Trinitarian Theology of Grace*. Waco: Baylor University Press, 2012; 246 pp.
———. *The Spirit Poured Out on All Flesh—Pentecostalism and the Possibility of Global Theology*. Grand Rapids: Baker Academic, 2005; 320 pp.
———. *The Spirit of Creation—Modern Science and Divine Action in the Pentecostal-Charismatic Imagination, Pentecostal Manifestos* 4. Grand Rapids: Eerdmans, 2011; 252 pp.

———. *Theology and Down Syndrome: Reimagining Disability in Late Modernity.* Waco: Baylor University Press, 2007; 465 pp. See www.BaylorPress.com/9781602580060/.

———. *Who is the Holy Spirit? A Walk with the Apostles.* Brewster, MA: Paraclete Press, 2011; 231 pp.

———. "Disability and the Love of Wisdom: De-forming, Re-forming, and Per-forming Philosophy of Religion." *Ars Disputandi: The Online Journal for Philosophy of Religion* 9, No. 1 (2009): 54–71, www.arsdisputandi.org, reprinted in Darla Schumm and Michael Stoltzfus, eds., *Disability in Judaism, Christianity and Islam: Sacred Texts, Historical Traditions, and Social Analysis* (New York: Palgrave Macmillan, 2011), 205–27. See www.tandfonline.com/doi/abs/10.1080/15665399.2009.10819997.

———. "Disability from the Margins to the Center: Hospitality and Inclusion in the Church." *Journal of Religion, Disability, and Health* 15, No. 4 (November 2011): 339–50. See www.tandfonline.com/doi/abs/10.1080/15228967.2011.620387.

———. "Disability, the Human Condition, and the Spirit of the Eschatological Long Run: Toward a Pneumatological Theology of Disability." *Journal of Religion, Disability, and Health* 11, No. 1 (2007): 5–25, for a different approach to theology of disability from an eschatological perspective. See www.tandfonline.com/doi/abs/10.1300/J095v11n01_02.

———. "Disability and the Gifts of the Spirit: Pentecost and the Renewal of the Church." *Journal of Pentecostal Theology* 19, No. 1 (Spring 2010): 76–93. See www.Academia.edu/7739294/_Disability_and_the_Gifts_of_the_Spirit_Pentecost_and_the_Renewal_of_the_Church_Journal_of_Pentecostal_Theology_19_1_spring_2010_76-93.

———. "Discerning the Spirit(s): A Pentecostal-Charismatic Contribution to Christian Theology of Religions." PhD diss. Boston University, 1999.

———. "Many Tongues, Many Senses: Pentecost, the Body Politic, and the Redemption of Dis/Ability." *PNEUMA: The Journal of the Society for Pentecostal Studies* 31, No. 2 (November 2009): 167–88. See https://brill.com/abstract/journals/pneu/31/2/article-p167_2.xml.

———. "Running the (Special) Race: New (Pauline) Perspectives on Theology of Sport." *Journal of Disability and Religion* 18, No. 2 (May 2014): 209–25.

———. See Wolfgang Vondey and Martin W. Mittelstadt, eds. *The Theology of Amos Yong and the New Face of Pentecostal Scholarship: Passion for the Spirit. Global Pentecostal and Charismatic Studies.* Vol. 14. Leiden: Brill, 2013; 306 pp. See https://brill.com/abstract/title/24131.

Zuck, Roy B., eds., *Understanding Christian Theology.* Nashville: Thomas Nelson, 2003.

Indices

Persons Referenced 431
Scriptures & Semi-sacred 436
General 439

PERSONS REFERENCED

Aaron, 99
Abel, 55, 56, 57, 58, 59, 60, 61, 62, 63, 64, 65, 67, 68, 69, 70, 71
Abraham, 218, 222, 381
Adam, 33, 62, 86, 154, 205, 274, 302, 337, 338
Adam and Eve, 241
Adam, Will, 91
Adams, Marilyn McCord, 296, 297
Adolphe, Jane F., 149
Akhtar, Salman, 186
Albright, W. F., 95
Alexander, Clayton, 259
Alexander, T. Desmond, 63, 108
Ali, Carroll Watkins, 189
Allison, Dale C., 93, 94, 163, 164, 165, 166
Alster. Bendt, 309
Anderson, Jonathan A., 361
Anderson, Monica, 212
Aquinas, Thomas, 109, 121, 152, 153, 158
Arand, Charles P., 77, 81
Arbaugh, George E., 87
Arén, Gustav, 271
Arnandez, Richard, 144
Arnett, Jeffery, 208
Asue, Daniel Ude, 133, 137, 146
Augustine, 8, 128, 129, 153, 262, 335
Aulén, Gustaf, 345
Avalos, Hector, 362
Aveling, Art, 296
Aveling, Leigh, 296
Ayanga, Hazel, 129

Bachmann, Theodore, 276, 277
Bacon, Jehuda, 313
Bai, Joseph, 134
Bailey, Kenneth, 58
Bailey, Lee, 365
Baker, David W., 63, 108
Balisky, Paul, 266
Baloyi, M. Elijah, 196
Baloyi, Magezi Elijah, 202
Bammel, Christina-Maria, 350

Barbarick, Clifford A., 223
Barbour, I. G., 29
Barnes, Colin, 363
Barrett, C. K., 98, 102, 108
Barrow, J. D., 238
Barth, Karl, 91, 100, 217, 240, 258, 304, 339, 340, 341, 342, 343, 344, 345, 346, 347, 348, 349, 350, 351, 352, 353, 354, 355, 356, 357, 358
Bartholomew, K., 208
Basee, Nadia Murad, 313
Bashar, Lamija Aji, 313
Basil, Saint, the Great, 8
Bass, Dorothy, 254
Bauckham, Richard, 119, 123, 124, 125
Bauer, D., 163
Baxter, Richard, 234, 241
Baxter, Wayne, 161, 162
Bayer, Oswald, 86
Bazna, Maysaa S., 366
Beale, G. K., 57
Beattie, Tina, 41
Beavis, Mary Ann, 379, 380
Beckett, Robert Grainger, Prize, 55
Behe, Michael J., 238
Bejoian, Lynne M., 366
Bell, Richard H., 227, 228
ben Uzziel, Jonathan, 61
Benedict XVI, 140, 141
Bennema, Cornelis, 68, 69
Benner, D. G., 30, 31, 34, 35
Bentham, Jeremy, 238
Bethge, Eberhard, 234, 297
Bieler, Andrea, 379
Biklen, Douglas, 365
Bildad, 307
Bird, M. F., 106, 107, 111
Black, Adam, 98
Black, Charles, 98
Black, Kathy, 382, 383, 386, 387
Blackburn, B., 19, 22, 25, 35, 36
Blackwood, Andrew Watterson, 172

Blaine-Wallice, William, 388, 389
Bland, Fireman Howard, 242
Bland, Howard, 233, 241
Blass, T., 207, 210, 211
Bloesch, Donald G, 114, 120, 121, 122, 126, 127, 129
Bloomquist, Karen L., 280
Blumhardt, Christoph, 119
Boesack, Allan, 253
Boff, Leonardo, 279
Bogdan, Robert, 364
Boguslawski, Steven, 149
Boisen, Anton T., 25
Bokedal, Tomas, 73, 74, 81
Bonar, Horatius, 74
Bonhoeffer, Dietrich, 94, 95, 96, 106, 234, 259, 265, 297, 313, 317, 318, 319, 320, 321, 322, 323, 324, 325, 326, 327, 328, 329, 330, 331, 332, 333, 334, 335, 336, 337, 338, 382
Bosch, David J., 253
Botterweck, G. Johannes, 302
Boulton, Wayne G., 238
Boyd, Gregory A., 372
Bradshaw, D., 207
Brandt, Walther I., 280
Braukämper, Ulrich, 267
Bricout, John, 367
Brink, Emily R., 390
Bromiley, Goeffrey W., , 105, 106, 240, 341, 342, 343, 344, 352
Brooks, Christine, 284
Brown, Colin, 239
Brown, R. M., 261
Brown, Raymond, 57, 157
Brown, Roderick, 52
Brown, S., 163, 167, 168
Bruce, F. F., 104
Brunner, Emil, 240, 257
Brushwyler, L. R., 22, 35, 36
Buchanan, G., 164
Buchanan, James, 224, 225
Büchsel, Friedrich, 106

Budge, E. A. W., 165
Bujo, B., 46
Bulgakov, Sergius, 110
Bulkeley, Kelly, 286
Bundy, Steve, 374
Burdette, Matthew, 318, 321
Burnett, Richard E., 217
Bursey, Ernest, 284
Burton, Ernest De Witt, 103, 104, 109
Burton, Laurel, 232
Bussey, O., 352
Bynum, Quanika, 181
Byrne, D., 212

Cahalan, Kathleen, 384
Cahalan, Kathleen A., 388
Cain, 55, 56, 57, 58, 59, 60, 61, 62, 63, 64, 65, 67, 68, 69, 70, 71, 218
Cairns, David, 238
Caliandro, Arthur, 24
Calvin, John, 109, 129, 223, 300, 340, 354, 358
Cameli, Louis J., 138
Campbell, Douglas, 225
Cappa, S. A., 36, 37
Carpenter, S., 23, 24
Carr, Mark F., 284
Carroll, B. H., 253
Carson, D. A., 57, 74, 76
Cassian, John, 155
Chadwick, H., 20, 22
Chambers, Oswald, 204, 209
Chapman, John Wilbur, 172
Chapman, T. W., 27
Chappell, Clovis Gilham, 172
Chesnut, Glenn F., 183
Chester, Stephen J., 97
Chester, Tim, 261
Chevallier, M. A., 170
Choi, Eun-Young, 379
Chopra, Deepak, 287
Chrysostom, Saint John, 8
Chung, Stephanie, 203
Chung, Walter, 203
Ciampa, Roy E., 98, 99, 101, 108, 109
Clapham, Christopher, 268

431

Clifton, Shane, 368
Climacus, 87
Climacus, Saint John, of Sinai, 8
Clinebell, Howard J., 47
Cloud, H., 211
Coakley, Sarah, 141
Cobb, John B., 319, 320, 323
Cochran, Clarke E., 257
Cohen, Arthur A., 238
Cohen, Meredith, 364
Coleman, Craig S., 233
Coleman, Monica A., 190
Collins, G. R., 16
Cone, James, 255, 258
Conner, L. C., 38
Connor, Robert A., 139, 140
Conradie, Ernest, 259
Constantine, M. G., 38
Conway, Pádraic, 217
Cooper, Tracey, 189
Cooper-White, Pamela, 194
Cope, Lane, 164, 165, 168
Corey, Gerald, 294
Costin-Stelian, Dana, 284
Court, J., 164
Courtney, Francis, 158
Covenant of Grace, 79
Craig, William Lane, 238
Craufurd, Emman, 387
Crim, Keith R., 127
Crislip, Andrew T., 364
Crogman, Horace, 335
Crouch, J., 162
Crummey, Donald, 272
Culberston, D., 41
Cunningham, L., 18
Curtis, W. H., 16, 37, 38
Cusanus, Nicolaus, 300

Dahm, Albert, 342, 351
Daramola, Pastor, 196
Darwall, Stephen, 238
Dau, W. H. T., 75
David, King, 386
Davids, Peter H., 99
Davies, Oliver, 260
Davies, W. D., 93, 94, 163, 164, 165, 166
Davis, Lennard J., 369
Davis, Stephen T., 140, 320, 321, 323
de Beer, John, 287
de Gruchy, John W., 258
de Lubac, Henri, 143, 144
Dembski, William A., 238
Demos, E. Virginia, 192
Denzinger, Heinrich, 149, 156
Deressa, Samuel Yonas, xii, 265
Des-Obi, Obioma, 133
Dick B., 183
Dicke, Amy, 208

Dickson, David, 79
Dillistone, F. W., 206
Ditmanson, Harold, 278
Dodd, C. H., 91, 92, 103
Donahue, John R., 164, 167, 169, 170
Donham, Donald L., 268, 269, 272
Donnelly, John Patrick, 174
Doré, Gustave, 232
Doyle-Portillo, S., 15, 16, 24
Dreher, Rod, 142, 143
Dreyer, J. S., 198, 199, 201
Driscoll, L. G., 38
Drum, W., 17, 18, 19
Drummond, R. J., 32
Duffy, Stephen, 274, 275
Duke, Will, 233
Dunbar, Helen Flanders, 25
Durham, James, 79
Dykstra, Craig, 254

Earl, Art, 296
Ebbinghaus, Hermann, 15
Edgar, Thomas R., 228
Edwards, Aaron P., 73
Edwards, David L., 122, 123
Edwards, J. W., 352
Edwards, James R., 227
Edwards, Jonathan, 183, 231
Edwards, Mark J., 118
Ehrlich, R. J., 343
Eide, Oyvind M., 266, 267, 269, 273
Eisen, Ute E., 299
Eitel, Keith E., 266
Elihu, 307, 308
Eliphaz, 307
Elks, Martin, 364
Ellis, Stephen, 198
Emperor Menelik II of Showa, 266, 267, 271, 272
Epstein, Elizabeth E., 187
Epstein, Michael, 183, 184
Erickson, Millard J., 205, 234, 241, 255
Erikson, Erik, 294
Erikson, Joan M., 294
Eshete, Tibebe, 272
Euripides, 255
Evans, James H., 141
Eve, 29, 33, 60, 61, 62, 86, 126, 154, 205, 218, 302
Eve, Adam and, 241
Exenophon, 255

Fabry, Heinz-Josef, 302
Fancher, S. C., 22
Fast, Mary, 368
Fastiggi, Robert, xii, 149, 153
Fay, Brian, 326, 327

Fayard, Carlos, 295
Fee, Gordon D., 97, 98, 108, 110, 223
Feeney, Brooke C., 207
Feinberg, John S., 239
Fenelon, Francois, 121
Ferguson, S. B., 204
Ferguson, Sinclair B., 206
Ferreras, Marlene, 319
Fettke, Steven M., 373
Fiedler, Leslie A., 387
Fintel, William A., ix
Fiorenza, Francis Schussler, 141
Fiorenza, Schüssler, 43
Firnhaber-Baker, Justine, 364
Fischer, Jean-Marc, 2
Fischer, Robert, 274
Fisher, Anthony, 137
Fitzmyer, Joseph A., 109
Flannery, Austin, 154
Fleischer, Doris Zames, 366
Ford, David F., 91
Frame, John M., 239, 258
Francis, Pope, 42, 47, 133, 141, 142, 143, 146, 150, 151, 158, 159
Frankl, Viktor, 252
Freedman, David Noel, 155, 222
Freud, Sigmund, 16, 293, 294
Friedrich, Gerhard, 105, 106
Fruchtenbaum, Arnold G., 172
Fryback, Patricia B., 289
Fulgentius, Fabius Planciades, 118
Fuller, R. H., 352, 382
Funke, Daniel, 73, 74

Gaiser, Frederick J., 299
Galgalo, Joseph, 373
Gandhi, Mahatma, 215, 313
Garberoglio, Carlos, 295
Garland, David E., 97, 109
Gebissa, Ezekiel, 271
Geher, Glenn, 204
Geiger, Michaela, 299
Geisler, Norman L., 231, 235, 236, 244
Gelso, Charles J., 186, 187
Gemechu, Olana, 280
Gennrich, Daniela, 50
Gentle, Judith Marie, 149
Gentry, Peter J., 220
Geoly, J. C., 22
George, Sam, 253
Gerald R. McDermott, iii
Gerhard, Johann, 83, 84
Gerstenberger, Erhard S., 299, 303
Getz, H. G., 38
Gidada, Negaso, 272

Gilkes, Patrick, 267
Gin, V. J., 34
Gladding, S. T., 23
Glaser, Ida, 60, 62
Godet, Frederic Louis, 177
Godsey, John D., 94
Goebbels, Joseph, 314
Goering, Hermann, 314
Gouwens, David J., 73
Graham, E., 15, 20, 22, 26, 27
Grant, J., 262
Gray, S., 162
Grebe, Matthias, 91, 100, 101
Green, Clifford J., 96, 106, 330
Green, Joel B., 93, 94
Greene, Beverly, 187
Gregersen, Niels Henrik, 274
Gregg, Robert C., 61
Gregory I the Great, 21
Gregory the Great, 20, 21, 155
Grenz, S. J., 38
Grieder, Kathleen J., 48
Grimm, Harold J., 275
Gritsch, Eric, 276
Groce, Nora Ellen, 366
Grosheide, F. W., 108
Gruchy, Lydia, 379
Grudem, Wayne, 176
Gunda, M. R., 46
Gundry, 167
Gunton, Colin E., 342, 349
Gurmessa, Fakadu, 271
Gutiérrez, G., 44

Hadebe, Nontando, 41
Hafemann, Scott J., 223
Hagner, Donald A., 94
Hahn, J., 207, 210, 211
Hailemariam, Mengistu, 269
Haire, J. L. M., 341
Hall, Douglas John, 380, 381, 382, 385
Haller, Beth A., 370
Halsall, P., 21
Halverson, Marvin, 238
Hansen, L. D., 129
Hare, Douglas R. A., 167
Harold, Godfrey, xii, 253
Hartsock, C., 94
Harvey, John W., 217
Hauerwas, Stanley, 92, 93, 94, 95, 96, 103, 106, 109, 356, 367, 368, 375
Hawking, Stephen, 249
Hawthorne, Gerald F., 102
Hayes, Jeffrey Alan, 186, 187
Hays, Richard B., 106
Hazan, C., 207
Hebert, A. G., 345

Hébert, Mireille, 91
Hendrick, Clyde, 208
Hendrick, Susan S., 208
Hendriks, H. Jurgens, 129
Henry, Carl F. H., 240
Herodotus, 255
Heessel, Nils P., 303
Heitink, G., 38
Heym, Stephan, 315
Hieb, Nathan D., 339
Hill, MarKeva Gwendolyn, 187, 188
Hiltner, Seward, 15, 23, 24, 25, 321
Hitler, Adolf, 234, 314
Hittenberger, Jeff, 373
Hobbes, Thomas, 238
Holbrook, Hal, 233
Holmes, Kristin E., 292, 293
Holmes, Linda, 190
Holmes, Linda Janet, 190
Hong, Edna H., 87, 88
Hong, Howard V., 87, 88
Horowitz, K. M., 208
Horst, Johannes, 105
House, H. Wayne, 215
Howard, J. K., 98
Hsu, Albert Y., 292
Huffman, K., 23, 24
Hünermann, Peter, 149, 156
Hunsinger, George, 340, 345, 351, 354, 357, 358
Hunter, R. J., 35
Huntington, Samuel, 149, 153, 270

Isaac, 381
Isaiah, 329
Isasi-Diaz, Ada, 45
Ishmael, 218

Jackman, David, 66, 68
Jackson, Leslie C., 187
Jackson, Maury, 317, 335
Jacob, 381
Jacobs, Jonathan D., 217
James, William, 23
Jantzen, Grace M., 42
Jefferson, Charles Edward, 172
Jenson, Robert, 274, 275, 276
Job, 300, 306, 307, 308, 310, 311, 312, 373
John the Baptist, 155
Johnson, Adam J., 91
Johnson, Gloria A., 48
Johnson, Johnny Ramirez, 295, 296
Johnson, Keith L., 351
Johnson, Marshall D., 106
Johnston, K., 21, 23, 24, 27, 33, 37
Johnston, W. B., 36, 341
Jonah, 116

Jones, K. D., 32
Jones, Larry, 28
Jowett, John Henry, 172
Joyce, James, 150
June, L. N., 37, 38

Kabue, Samuel, 373
Kaiser, Walter C., 60
Kant, Immanuel, 238, 257, 285
Kanyoro, Kanyoro, 45
Kanyoro, Musimbi, 45
Kaoma, Kapya, 52
Kärkkäinen, Veli-Matti, 361
Karle, Isolde, 379
Karp, David, 295
Kasper, Walter, 221
Kaufman, Gershen, 185
Kaufman, Scott Barry, 204
Kay, Hannah, 60
Kazaku, Peter, 2
Keener, Craig S., 100
Keith, Chris, 73
Kelcourse, Felicity Brock, 199, 201
Kell, James F., 233
Keller, William S., 25
Kelly, Annie, 51
Kelly, Geffrey B., 94
Kendall, Daniel, 140
Kennedy, Thomas D., 238
Khosa-Nkatine, Hundzukani Portia, 195
Kiboi, John Michael, 113, 130, 131
Kierkegaard, Søren, 82, 86, 87, 88
Kigali Anglican Theological College, 55
Killen, Patricia O'Connell, 287
Kim, Kirsteen, 361
Kim, Lark, 379
Kim-Cragg, HyeRan, 379, 380
Kirk, G., 38
Kirwan, W. T., 205
Kitchen, V. V., 183
Kittel, Gerhard, 105, 106
Klein, Melanie, 294
Kleinman, Arthur, 368
Klepper, Jochen, 314
Knight, Harold, 341, 352
Knoll, James A., 364
Koester, H., 162
Kohut, Heinz, 184, 188
Kolb, Robert, 74, 81, 88
Kosnik, Anthony, 152
Köstenberger, Andreas, 58, 63
Kolb, Robert, 74, 81, 88
Kregel, John, 367
Krötke, Wolf, 350
Kubler-Ross, Elisabeth, 32, 290

Kujawa-Holbrook, Sheryl A., 388
Kung, Hans, 255
Kurian, George Thomas, 172
Kushner, Harold S., 292

LaGioia, Rock M., 172
Lamberton, Henry, 284
Lamech, 60
Lamport, Mark A., 172
Larebo, Haile M., 272
Larson, Jeffery H., 212
Lartey, Emmanuel Y., 47, 335, 336
Lauber, David, 351
Lavender, Dame Tina, 189
Lazareth, William H., 243
Le Roux, Elisabet, 129
Lee, Alan, 207
Lee, J. A., 210, 212
Lee, Robert Greene, 172
Lee, Valerie, 189, 190, 191
Legesse, Asmarom, 268
Lehmann, Helmut, 274, 275, 276, 277, 280
Leibniz, Gottfried Wilhelm, 322, 326
Leslie, Kristen J., 48
Lester, Andrew D., 22
Lester, Paul Martin, 364
Levine, Donald, 272
Lewis, C. S., 206, 209, 241
Lewis, David J., 204
Lewis, E. L., 38
Lienhard, Joseph T., 140
Lieu, Judith M., 57, 69
Livingston, James C., 139, 141
Livneh, Hanoch, 368
Long, Callie, 41
Longchar, A. Wati, 373
Longenecker, Richard N., 97, 103, 104, 109
Lührmann, Dieter, 118
Lundy, Angela Victoria, 370
Luter, A. Boyd Luter, 155
Luther, Martin, 76, 77, 83, 85, 86, 87, 88, 126, 266, 273, 274, 275, 276, 277, 278, 279, 280, 297, 313, 340, 358, 390
Luz, Ulrich, 96, 161, 162, 163, 164, 167
Lynch, Gordon, 320
Lynch, Peter, 47

MacGregor, Kirk R., 215
Machiavelli, Niccolò, 238
Macklin, Ruth Macklin, 366
Magister, Sandro, 150
Maier, Christl M., 299
Maimela, Simon D., 45
Mampolo, Masamba ma, 47

Manasseh, 84
Mandela, Nelson, 313
Maness, Michael G., iii, xi, xiii, 231, 241
Manetsch, Scott M., 201
Maienschein, Jane, 238
Mann, C. S., 95
Manson, Neil A., 238
Marginean, Ioan, 284
Marguerat, D., 161
Marini, Irmo, 369
Markakis, John, 269
Marshall, I. Howard, 65, 66, 69, 93, 223
Marshall, Peter, 172
Martens, E. A., 108
Martin, Michael W., 223
Martin, Ralph P., 99, 102
Martz, Erin, 368
Masango, M. J., 196
Maslow, Abraham, 23
Maston, T. B., 237
Matthews, J. R., 22
Mattis, Kevaughn, iii, xiii, 215
Maul, Stefan M., 303
May, William E., 153
McClain, Alva J., 172
McClymond, Michael, ix
McCormack, Bruce L., 350
McCown, L., 34
McCrady, Barbara S., 187
McDermott, Gerald R., ix, x
McGee, John Vernon, 172
McGrath, Alister E., 241
McGuinness, B. F., 286
McIver, R. K., 227
McKnight, S., 63
McKnight, Scot, 93, 276
McMinn, M. R., 22, 24, 26, 30, 32, 33
McMurry, Brandy, 181
McNeil, Brenda Salter, 258, 259, 260
Mechanic, David, 368
Melanchthon, Philip, 82, 83, 85
Melcher, Sarah J., 362
Menelik II, Emperor, of Showa, 266, 267, 271, 272
Menninger, Karl, 23
Menz, R. L., 25, 26, 33
Mercer, Goef, 363
Messud, Claire, 321
Meyers, B., 261
Michaels, J. Ramsey, 168
Mikoski, Gordon S., 384, 388
Mikulincer, Mario, 207
Milbank, John, 332, 334, 335
Mill, John Stuart, 238
Miller-McLemore, Bonnie J., 384

Mittelstadt, Martin W., 373
Moffatt, James, 97, 100, 109, 234
Moltmann, Jürgen, 91, 119, 123, 124, 125, 234
Mombo, Esther, 373
Montagno, Karen Brown, 388
Morris, Jenny, 370
Morris, Leon, 175
Morris, Sharon, 366
Morrison, D. A., 260
Moses, 93, 98, 99, 103, 219, 220, 221, 225, 260, 337, 372
Moulton, J., 166
Mouton, Elna, 129
Murnen, S. K., 212
Murphy, T., 16, 17, 18, 19, 20, 35

Naidoo, Marilyn, 196, 197, 199
Nam, Julius J., 284
Naudé, Beyers, 253
Netland, Harold, ix
Neusner, Jacob, 57
Newport, John P., 235, 239
Newsome, D. W., 23
Niebuhr, H. Richard, 238
Niebuhr, Reinhold, 123
Niedecken, Dietmut, 369
Niehaus, Jeffrey J., 221
Nietzsche, Friedrich, 238
Nolan, J. G., 154
Nord, Ilona, 379
Nouwen, Henri, 209, 260, 291, 292
Nwankwor, Iks J., 133

O'Collins, Gerald, 140
O'Neil, Michael, 149
O'Tool, Mark P., 364
Oates, W. E., 23, 24, 26, 27
O'Brien, Peter T., 76
Oden, T. C., 15, 16, 19, 20, 21
Oden, Thomas C., 319, 335
Oden. T. C., 17
Ogden, C. K., 24, 286
Okon, Etim E., 196
Olmstead, W. G., 102
Olson, A. K., 212
Olson, D. H., 212
Origen, 118
Oromo, Karrayyu, 265
Orto, Arthur E. Dell, 368
Osmer, Richard R., 200
Osterweis, Martin, 368
Ott, Ludwig, 149
Otto, Rudolf, 217
Owen, John, 77

Painter, John, 64, 67, 68
Palamas, Saint Gregory, 8
Parker, T. H. L., 341

Pascal, Blaise, 287
Pastorino, E., 15, 16, 24
Paterson, Gilliam, 41
Paton, Alan, 390
Pattison, Stephen, 320
Patton, James R., 367
Patton, John, 47, 48
Paul, Pope John Paul II, 138, 142, 143, 144
Peale, Norman Vincent, 25
Pears, D. F., 286
Peck, M. Scott, 23
Preda, Marian, 284
Pedersen, T., 213
Pelikan, Jaroslav, 126
Pelka, Fred, 365
Pereira, José, 149
Perlin, Michael L., 364
Person, Raymond F., 73
Peter, C. B., 373
Petersen, B. L., 20
Peterson, Eugene, 35
Petesch, Peter J., 365
Philo of Alexandria, 61
Pieterse, J. H. C., 198, 199, 201
Pilate, 381
Pillay, Jerry, 254
Pimentel, Richard, xii
Pinnock, Clark H., 239
Pinsky, Mark I., 370, 377
Piper, John, 206
Placher, William Carl, 217
Plante, Thomas G., 16
Plass, Ewald, 126
Plato, 238
Pope Benedict XVI, 141, 234
Pope Francis, 42, 47, 133, 141, 142, 143, 146, 150, 151, 158, 159
Pope Gregory I, 20
Pope John Paul II, 144
Pope John XXIII, 47
Pope Paul VI, 137
Porter, Steven L., 229
Poschmann, Bernhard, 158
Powell, Mark Alan, 163, 381
Power, Paul W., 368
Prentice, Joan, 13
Preus, J. A. O., 82
Preus, Robert D., 74
Prümmer, Dominic, 154, 155
Puchalski, C. M., 32
Pui-Lan, Kowk, 45
Pythagoras, 249

Quinn, Molly, 366

Rahab, the harlot, 237
Rahner, Karl, 217
Ramirez, Clara Ramirez, 295

Ramshaw, Elaine, 383, 384, 389, 390
Rakestraw, Robert V., 231, 235, 236, 244
Rascovich, Mark, 233
Ratzinger, Joseph, 234
Ratzlaff, David, 216
Razak, Arisika, 190
Reid, Daniel G., 102
Reid, J. K. S., 352
Reijnen, Anne Marie, 91
Reinder, Hans, 376
Reinert, Bonita R., 289
Reitzels, C. A., 87
Remen, Rachel Naomi, 291
Rhoads, Ross, 235
Ricca, Battista, 150
Rice, Richard, 291, 292, 293, 322
Richardson, B. L., 37, 38
Richie, Tony, 218
Richter, Horst Eberhard, 315
Ringgren, Helmer, 302
Ritchie, Tony, 218
Robertson, E. H., 331, 332
Robinson, Haddon W., 172
Robinson, John A. T., 101
Rogers, Gertha, 231
Romer, A. L., 32
Root, Andrew, 68, 181, 185, 258
Rosner, Brian S., 98, 99, 101, 108, 109
Ross, Susan Dente, 364
Ross, W. D., 238
Roth, S. John, 366
Rotholz, James M., 369
Rowden, H. H., 20
Roy, Ranjan, 369
Royle, Anthony, 57
Ruether, Rosemary Radford, 144
Rumbold, H. H., 21
Rumi, 287
Runesson, Anders, 161
Ruse, Michael, 238
Russell, Bertrand, 286
Ryan, Fáinche, 217
Rymer, Kevin S., 376
Ryrie, Charles Caldwell, 228

Saint Basil the Great, 8
Saint Gregory, 8
Saint Gregory Palamas, 8
Saint John Chrysostom, 8
Saint John Climacus of Sinai, 8
Sanchez, D., 38
Sanders, J. Oswald, 241
Sanford University, ix, x
Sankbeil, Harold L., 77
Sayers, William, 366
Scamparini, Ilze, 150
Schipper, Jeremy, 362

Schleiermacher, Friedrich, 336, 337, 342
Schmidt, Roger, 289
Schnackenburg, Rudolf, 100, 101, 107
Schrage, Wolfgang, 101
Schumm, Darla, 366, 375
Schweitzer, Don, 379
Scristoph, Schwobel, 274
Seed, Caroline G., 55, 56
Seifrid, Mark A., 76, 99
Selassie I, Haile, 267, 268, 272
Seth, 60
Shabala, T., 256
Shakespeare, Tom, 369
Shaver, P., 207
Shaver, Phillip R., 207
Sherlock, C., 205, 206
Sider, R. J., 256
Sidgwick, Henry, 238
Simelane, Eudy, 51
Simpson, Amy, 364
Simpson, Gary, 280
Sloter, E., 38
Smalley, Stephen, 70
Smith, Aaron, 212
Smith, Archie, 185
Smith, Ebbie C., 235, 237, 240
Smith, Margaret Charles, 190
Smith, Quentin, 238
Smith, Ronald Gregor, 351, 355
Smyth, Newman, 240
Søe, N. H., 87
Sölle, Dorothee, 383, 390
Sorajjakool, Siroj, 284, 285, 287, 289, 290, 296
Soskice, Janet M., 220, 221
Spencer, Herbert, 238
Sperry, Len, 182, 183, 184
Spiegel, John, 186
Spieker, Hartmut, 351
Spriggs, J. D., 38
St. Gregory the Great, 20, 155
St. John Cassian, 155
Stagg, Kevin, 366
Ståhl, Michael, 267
Stanley, Charles, 206
Stanley, Charles F., 210
Stanton, G., 164, 167
Stebnicki, Mark A., 369
Steinberg, Robert, 207
Steinberg, Robert J., 212
Stephen Ministries, 113
Stern, Elsie R., 73
Steyn, T. H., 196
Stiker, Henri-Jacques, 366
Stillman, Mildred Whitney, 121
Stoevesandt, Hinrich, 351
Stoltzfus, Michael, 366, 375

Stone, B., 260
Stone, M. M. R., 22
Story, Ron, ix
Stott, J. R. W., 64, 69, 70
Stott, John, 122, 123
Stransky, Oonagh, 151, 158
Strecker, Georg, 70
Strong, Augustus, 62, 66
Stumpf, Samuel Enoch, 238
Susser, Peter, 365
Swarr, Amanda L., 52
Swindoll, Charles R., 176
Swinton, John, 254

Tada, Joni Eareckson, 374
Talbert, Charles H., 223
Talbot, Louis Thomson, 172
Tatem, Alisha, 181
Ter Haar, Gerrie, 198
Tertullian, 156, 317
Tesema, Ta'a, 268
Thatcher, Tom, 56, 58, 73
Thermos, Vasileios, xii, 2
Thielicke, Helmut, 243
Thiselton, Anthony C., 101, 109, 110
Thomas, Carol, 363
Thomas, John Christopher, 373
Thomas, Linda, 44
Thomas, Robert L., 175
Thompson, Kelvin, 296
Thompson, Marianne Meye, 69, 70
Thornton, Sharon G., 319
Thucydides, 255
Thulstrup, Marie Mikulová, 87
Thulstrup, Niels, 87

Thurmond-Malone, Myrna, xii, 181, 188
Thurneysen, Eduard, 127
Tillich, Paul, 29, 91, 119, 234
Tinsley, T. M.,
Tinsley, Taunya Marie, 13, 28, 33, 34, 37, 38
Tipler, F. J., 238
Titchkosky, Tanya, 366
Tolo, Arne, 267
Tomkin, Silvan S., 192
Tomlin, Graham, 77
Tornielli, Andrea, 151, 158
Torrance, T. F., 56, 225, 341, 342, 343, 344, 352
Townsend, J., 211
Tozer, A. W., 173
Traill, Robert, 77
Trapp, Thomas H., 86
Travis, Stephen H., 102, 104, 110
Tremblay, Joe, 134, 147
Trimingham, J. Spencer, 269
Tucker, Karen Westerfield, 386
Turner, David M., 366
Turner, N., 166
Turpin, Katherine, 388
Tutu, Desmond, 253, 389

Ukagba, George Uzoma, 133
Ulanov, Ann, 284
Ullman, Chana., 289
Utazi, C. M., 14, 15, 17, 18, 19, 20
Uzziah, King, 176

Vacca, Michael, 149
Vacca, Michael A., 149
Van der Walt, Charlene, 52
Van der Watt, Jan G., 56
Van Leeuwen, M. S., 205
Van Staden, P. J., 58, 59
Vande Kemp, H., 25
VandeCreek, Larry, 232
Vellem, Vuyani, 259
Verhey, Allen, 238
Vermigli, Peter Martyr, 174
Viviano, Benedict T., 157
Vlachos, Chris, 219
Vlachos, Chris Alex, 219
Volf, Miroslav, 218, 254, 259, 262
von Soosten, Joachim, 318
Vondey, Wolfgang, 373
Vuola, Elina, 45

Walker, Alice, 188
Wallace, Daniel B., 226
Walls, Jerry L., 117, 241
Walther, C. F. W., 75, 79, 86
Waltke, Bruce, 61
Ware, Bruce A., 239
Watson, Philip S., 280
Wax, Trevin, 223, 224
Weber, Max, 289
Webster, John, 352, 354
Wehman, Paul, 367
Wehmeyer, Michael L., 367
Weller, Andrew, 369
Wengert, Timothy J., 81
Wengert, Timothy J., 77
Wenham, Gordon J., 60, 62
Wepener, Cas, 196, 197
Werpehowski, William, 352

Wesley, John, 183
West, Gerald O., 52
Westerholm, Stephen, 76, 81
Wheatley, Edward, 364
White, Michael, 183, 184
White, Pamela Cooper, 294, 295
Whitlark, Jason A., 223
Willard, Dallas, 22
Willard, Gaylin, 366
Williams, Delores, 188
Willis, David, 350
Willis, Kimberly, 362
Willis-Watkins, David, 351
Wimberly, Edward, 183
Wimberly, Edward P., 47
Wisløff, Carl Fredrik, 82, 84, 85, 86
Wittgenstein, Ludwig, 286
Wolfinger, Nicholas H., 211
Woodward, James, 320
Worden, J. W., 33
Worthen, Jeremy, 91
Wright, "N.T." Nicholas Thomas, , 76, 107, 234
Wynn, Kerry H., 362

Yarbrough, John, 61, 67, 68
Yong, Amos, xii, 234, 361, 373, 374, 375, 376

Yousafzai, Malala, 313
Zacchaeus, 256
Zames, Freida, 366
Zamfir, Cataline, 284
Ziegler, Philip G., 350
Zimmerman, Ruban, 56
Zuck, Roy B., 176, 362

SCRIPTURES & SEMI-SACRED

* Gen. 1   = Genesis 1:1 on page 130
** Gen. 2, 143 = Genesis chapter 2 on page 143
*** 15–20, 229 = and Genesis chapter 2, verses 15–20 on page 205

Gen 1
  1, 130
  26–31, 204
  27, 60
  31, 60
Gen 2, 130, 131
  4, 26, 60
  15–20, 205
  18–24, 204
  19, 58, 60
  23–24, 205
  25, 205
Gen 3, 205, 302
  1–6, 3
  7–10, 205
  8–13, 4
  9, 86
  11–15, 58
  11–16, 205
  12, 58, 63
  15, 60
  24, 218
Gen 4, 58, 71
  1–16, 56, 57, 60
  1, 60
  4, 62
  7, 62
  8–12, 60
  9, 63, 86
  10, 61, 63
  14, 218
  16, 58
  19–21, 58
Gen 1–4, 57, 60
Gen 11
  1–9, 302
Gen 19, 46
Gen 21
  10, 218
  14, 218
  8–12, 61
Gen 25
  6, 218
Gen 32
  22–32, 289

Exod 3
  11–12, 305
  14, 219, 220
Exod 4
  10–13, 305
  11, 372
Exod 18 and 19, 98
Exod 19
  21–24, 312
Exod 19–24, 221
Exod 32
  27–29, 99
  32, 337
Exod 32–34, 221
Exod 33, 219, 260
  12–21, 221
  13, 220
  18, 220
  19, 220
  2, 218
  20, 220
  22, 220
  23, 220
Exod 34
  6, 104, 105, 314

Lev 16, 101
  10, 218
  15–19, 312
  7–26, 4
Lev. 18
  5, 85
  22, 152
Lev 20, 46
  13, 108
Lev 21
  16–24, 314
Lev 25
  25–55, 303

Num 16
  31–32, 99
Num 22–24, 303

Deut 1, 98
Deut 4
  15–20, 312
  16, 300
Deut 5
  22–27, 312
Deut 12
  31, 108
Deut 14
  3, 108
Deut 22
  5, 108
  9–10, 152
Deut 25
  13–16, 108
Deut 27
  15, 108
Deut 30
  17, 153

Deut 32
  22, 115
  39–42, 315
Deut 33
  27, 218

Josh 2
  19, 302

Judg 5, 315
Judg 6
  11–17, 305
Judg 9
  24, 302
Judg 15
  1–8, 302
Judg 16
  28–30, 302
Judg 17
  2, 302

1 Sam 1
  16, 302
1 Sam 28
  7, 303

2 Sam 4
  4, 372
2 Sam 11–12, 302
2 Sam 12
  1–13, 4
  15–23, 386
2 Sam 24
  10–17, 302

1 Kgs 14
  1–3, 303
1 Kgs 2
  32–33, 302

2 Kgs 4
  18–24, 303
  30–35, 303

1 Chron. 16
  34, 116

Job 1–2, 306, 307
Job 2
  5, 312
Job 3
  2–26, 307
  3–12, 306
Job 4
  17, 308
Job 4–5, 307
Job 5
  17, 308
Job 8
  3–4, 308
Job 10
  2, 307
  6–7, 307
Job 11
  4–5, 308
Job 15
  4–5, 308

Job 19
  17–18, 307
  6, 307
  9–14, 307
Job 22
  5, 308
Job 23
  12, 308
Job 25
  4, 308
Job 28, 306
Job 29–31, 306, 308
Job 32–37, 306, 307
Job 3–27, 306, 307
Job 33
  12, 308
  12–28, 308
Job 34
  10–12, 308
Job 38
  9, 306
Job 42
  10–17, 306
  1–6, 308
  5–6, 308
  7, 308

Ps 6
  6, 304
Ps 10
  10–11, 304
Ps 11
  5, 315
Ps 14, 309
Ps 18
  16–50, 315
Ps 22, 303, 310
  1, 302
  1–2, 304
  2, 304
Ps 23, 20
Pss 30–40, 303
Pss 9–10, 304
Ps 24, 315
Ps 25
  10, 121
  7, 84
Ps 31, 303, 310
Ps 32, 84
Ps 34
  21–22, 115
Ps 35, 303, 310
Ps 38, 303, 304
  17, 304
Ps 39, 309
Ps 41, 304
Ps 44, 305, 315
Ps 45
  8, 315

Ps 51, 303
  1, 84
  4, 144
Ps 55, 303
Ps 59, 303
  14, 304
  6, 304
Ps 69, 303, 310
  21, 304
Ps 73, 309
Ps 78
  52–53, 20
Ps 88, 304
  13–18, 305
  2, 304
  3–9, 305
  9-12, 305
Ps 89, 305, 315
Ps 90, 309
Ps 91, 304
Ps 94, 309
  1–3, 315
Ps 102, 303
Ps 103
  8, 104, 314
Ps 110, 310
Ps 111
  4, 314
Ps 113, 315
Ps 118, 310
Ps 119
  104, 315
Ps 136
  1–26, 116
Ps 137, 305
Ps 139, 130
  1–6, 300
  6, 300
  7–12, 121, 312
  13–16, 213
  14, 245
  21, 315
Ps 145
  8, 314

Prov 3
  5–6, 212
Prov 22
  2, 301
Prov 25
  21–22, 126

Eccl 1
  12–18, 302, 309
Eccl 2
  1–11, 309
  18–23, 302
Eccl 3
  16–22, 302

1–8, 302	Isa 60	Hos 11	Matt 5, 97		10, 167
9–22, 309	11, 127	1–11, 179	3, 94		10–14, 312
Eccl 4	Isa 60–62, 311	Hos 2	7, 31		12–14, 166
1–4, 302	Isa 61	1–3, 306	9–11, 97		14, 167
Eccl 5	2, 100	Joel 1	10, 94		15, 166
1–12, 309	Isa 65	1–2	17, 103		18, 156
Eccl 6	17–25, 311	11, 115	18, 240		20, 167
1–6, 309	Isa 66, 162	Joel 2	21–26, 162		23–35, 4
Eccl 7	24, 114	1–11, 162	22–24, 166		26, 91
1–14, 309	Jer 1		22–47, 166		Matt 19
16–21, 309	4–10, 305	Amos 1	32, 153		9, 153
23–29, 309	Jer 2, 306	3–2	43–38, 69		29, 166
Eccl 9	Jer 11	16, 303	Matt 5–7, 153		Matt 20
1–2, 309	6, 305	Amos 2	Matt 6		24, 166
9, 309	18–12	4–8, 306	10, 134		Matt 21
11–16, 309	19, 305	Amos 5	14–15, 161		43, 164
Eccl 10	Jer 15	18–20, 306	33, 31		Matt 22
1–4, 309	10–21, 305	Amos 8	38, 31		24–25, 166
8–20, 309	11, 305	1–3, 306	Matt 7		53, 218
Eccl 11	18, 305	Amos 9	1–6, 162		Matt 22.13, 218
1–6, 309	Jer 17	11–15, 306	3–5, 166		Matt 23
	14–18, 305		12, 96		8, 166
Song of Sol. 1	Jer 18	Jonah 1	21, 226		13, 96
1–4, 206	19, 305	3, 305	Matt 8		39, 164
	19–23, 305, 315	Jonah 3	3, 389		44, 218
Isa 6	Jer 20	10, 116	12, 96, 218		Matt 24
1–8, 179	7, 305	4, 116	Matt 9		9, 164
2, 177	7–18, 305	Jonah 4	29, 389		14, 163
3, 177	8–9, 305	2, 116	35, x		1–41, 162
4, 177	10, 305	Jonah 5	36, ix		16–20, 163
5, 177, 305	14–18, 306	1–4, 116	Matt 7		30, 162
6–7, 177	Jer 31		3, 295		35, 118
8, 178	3, 298	Mic 7	Matt 10, 18		Matt 25, 101, 108,
10, 177	31–35, 103	18, 119	2, 166		118
Isa 5, 116	33–34, 229		5–6, 163		1–13, 164
1–7, 306	40, 229	Zeph 1	18, 164		14–30, 164
Isa 9, 311	Jer 46–51, 303	3, 162	21, 166		30, 218
Isa 11, 311		Zeph 3	23, 163, 164		31–46, 162, 163,
Isa 24–27, 311	Lam 1, 306	17, 209	42, 167		164, 165,
Isa 38	Lam 1–5, 303	Zeph 7	Matt 11		167, 169,
21, 303	Lam 2, 306	2–7, 306	11, 166		170, 261
Isa 40	Lam 3	Zeph 8	21, 329		32, 163, 164
6–8, 302	22, 119	19, 306	Matt 12		35–36, 22
21–24, 302	Lam 4, 306	Zeph 9	35–37, 168		40, 166
Isa 42	22, 306	9, 310	46–48, 166		41–46, 153
1–9, 310	Lam 5	Zeph 11	49–50, 166		46, 115
6, 225	7, 306	13, 310	Matt 13		Matt 27
Isa 43	8–18, 306	Zeph 12	8, 227		2, 164
25–26, 116	19, 306	10, 310	23, 227		11–27, 164
Isa 46	20, 306	Zeph 12–14, 311	24–30, 102		Matt 28
9–11, 321	21–22, 306	Zeph 13	24–30, 227		1–10, 310
Isa 49		7, 310	41, 96		14, 164
1–7, 310	Ezek 1		41–42, 74		18–20, 164
2, 121	26, 300	Mal 4, 162	55, 166		19, 163
8, 225	Ezek 18		Matt 13 & 25, 102		
Isa 50	23, 76, 81	Matt 1	Matt 14		
4–11, 310	32, 76	1, 165	3, 166		Mark 1
Isa 52	Ezek 33	2, 166	Matt 16		4, 155
13–53	11, 81	Matt 2	19, 156		15, 155
12, 310		6, 164	24, 256		Mark 4
Isa 53	Dan 7	Matt 4	Matt 17		8, 227
1–12, 310	13, 310	12–15, 163	1, 166		30-32, 52
6, 84		17, 93	Matt 18, 110		Mark 6
10–11, 310	Hos 1	18, 166	2–4, 95		1–13, 18
Isa 58	6–8, 306	23, 93	3 5, 166		12, 155
7, 165			6, 167		

Mark 8	17, 81, 100	7, 81	1 Cor 1	
34, 106	18, 101, 115	8, 81	3–5, 339	Gal 2
Mark 9	19, 87	10, 81	30, 77	19, 85
43, 115	John 5	Rom 3	1 Cor 10	Gal 3, 165
Mark 10	22–27, 100	11, 87	13, 370	1, 85
2–12, 153	38–40, 30	20, 85	1 Cor 11	2, 86
42–45, 106	39, 218	20–26, 81	1, 103	10, 83
44, 279	John 8	21, 85	1 Cor 12	12, 85
Mark 12	7, 249	21–26, 80, 226	12–31, 310	13, 81, 91
29–31, 262	15, 100	21–31, 86	1 Cor 13, 234	24, 85, 88
Mark 13, 311	34, 84	22, 226	9, 300	28, 256
31, 118	John 9	23, 205, 226	13, 159	Gal 5
Mark 16	2, 372	23–25, 310	1 Cor 15	1, 98, 101
1–8, 310	3, 372, 375	Rom 4, 165	22–26, 336	6, 229
Mark 2	6, 389	7, 81	24, 336	13–18, 227
5, 153, 156	John. 12	15, 85	28, 122	15, 218
7, 156	48, 101	25, 84	35–58, 311	18–23, 219
Mark 20	John. 5	Rom 5	55, 125	19, 211
34, 389	22, 100, 102	1, 81, 347	56, 219	19–21, 74, 97,
	John. 9	8, 141	1 Cor 4	118, 154,
Luke 1	39, 102	10, 82	1, 17, 18	156, 227
50, 143	John 10	15, 273	5, 228	21, 79
77, 84	30, 168	20, 144, 219,	1 Cor 5	22, 223
Luke 5	9, 102	225	7, 109	22–23, 110
13, 389	John 12	Rom 6	1 Cor 6, 46, 75, 96	Gal 6
Luke 6	40–41, 177	3, 99	9, 74	1–2, 227
24–26, 96	42, 100	4, 34	9–10, 78, 79,	2, 103
36, 314	44–45, 168	23, 122	153, 156, 227	7–10, 31
Luke 7	47–48, 121	23, 81, 86, 115	11, 77, 78	7–8, 210
21–26, 162	John 13	Rom 6–7, 219	15–20, 227	
36–50, 229	34–35, 34	Rom 7, 83, 103	18, 211	Eph 1
47, 229	John 14	5, 219	1 Cor 9	4, 208
Luke 8	6, 102, 129	6, 86, 219	21, 103	10, 122
8, 227	9, 168	13, 83		Eph 2
Luke 9	John 15, 99, 102	15, 210	2 Cor 1	8, 85, 86
1–6, 18	1–7, 179	15–25, 5	3, 341	12, ix
Luke 10	3, 102	Rom 8	3–5, 340, 358	Eph 4
28, 85	5, 211	1, 81, 84, 115,	4, 344, 346, 350,	11–12, 20
Luke 12	13, 234	162	352	15, 233
16–21, 3	John 16	3, 81, 108	5, 356, 357	Eph 5
Luke 13	8, 87, 103	6–8, 81	5–6, 310	2, 210
1–5, 303	John 20	9–11, 86	22, 104	3–5, 97, 227
24–30, 162	1–18, 310	13, 77, 79	2 Cor 2	5, 74, 79, 156
Luke 15	22, 86	15–20, 227	15–16, 121	Eph 6
7, 159	22–23, 156, 157	17, 100, 109	2 Cor 3	17, 121
11–31, 208		18, 338	3, 103	
11–32, 312	Acts 2, 86	18–25, 311	2 Cor 4	Phil 2
Luke 16	36, 381	23, 104	13, 223	3, 353
18, 153	Acts 9	30, 77	17, 109	9, 353
19–31, 3	1–2, 167	31–39, 81	2 Cor 5	9–11, 120
Luke 19	Acts 10	39, 81	10, 76, 102, 110	Phil 3
9, 256	43, 86	Rom 9	10–11, 162	20, 234
Luke 21	Acts 15	1, 337	15–17, 34	
33, 118	19–20, 108	22, 104, 105	17, 86	Col 1
Luke 24	Acts 20	Rom 10	18, 82	13, 97
1–12, 310	21, 156	1–10, 218	21, 76, 81, 86,	20, 122
46–47, 155	Acts 3	4, 86, 88	109	Col 2
47, 155	1–9, 381	14, 178	2 Cor 9	9–10, 34
	13–16, 381	17, 178	6, 31	11, 99
John 1	38, 156	Rom 12	8, 31	Col 3
17, 225		2, 240	11, 31	21, 5
29, 153	Rom 1, 46	20, 126	2 Cor 10	
John 3	18, 84	Rom 13, 280	5, 11	1 Thess 4
16, 126, 213	18–3	11, 172	2 Cor 12	13–17, 227
16–17, 162	20, 80, 310		1–10, 179	1 Thess 5
16–18, 118	Rom 2	Rom 14	2 Cor 13	6, 172
16–19, 84	4, 104, 105	10–12, 76	11, 81	9–10, 227

	Heb 12	9, 81	7, 64	10, 329
2 Thess 1	6–11, 227		8, 64, 65, 70	14–2, 180
9, 115	14, 227	1 John 1	8–9, 70	14–22, 179
9–10, 115	23, 100	1, 65, 66	11, 56	15, 175
	Heb 13	1–3, 66	12, 57, 64, 67	16, 175, 329
1 Tim 1, 46	11, 218	1–4, 65	16, 66, 68	17, 175
16, 104, 106	13, 218	2–3, 66	17, 68	18, 175
1 Tim 2		3, 56, 63, 64, 65,	19, 69	19, 176
4, 76	Jas 2	66, 67, 70, 71	1 John 4	Rev 14
1 Tim 4	13, 119	4, 66	2, 67	10–11, 114
12–16, 18	19, 261	5–7, 56	2–3, 64	Rev 16–17, 121
	26, 76	6, 64	3, 56	Rev 19
2 Tim 2	Jas 4	7, 66, 69	5, 64, 68	15, 121
22–25, 18	1–2, 64	8, 70, 76	7, 204	Rev 2, 329
2 Tim 3	Jas 5	8, 10, 64	9, 68, 69	1–7, 179
10, 106	11, 314	9, 56, 77	9–10, 66	3, 173
16, 178	16, 157	10, 76, 141	10, 82	5, 174
16–17, 31		1 John 2	14, 67	12, 121
2 Tim 4	1 Pet 2	2, 82	16, 81	Rev 20
2, 142, 178	9, 97	16, 154	18, 229	11–15, 162
20, 372	1 Pet 3	1 John 15	19, 68	Rev 21
	17–19, 310	16, 56	20, 64	5, 119
Titus 2	20, 104	1 John 2	1 John 5	8, 74, 115, 154
1, 176	20–21, 156	1, 77	1, 67	25, 127, 218
Titus 3	1 Pet 5	1–2, 70	2, 65	27, 74
14, 228	1, 310	2, 56, 64, 65, 66,	21, 65	Rev 22
	1–4, 20	70, 71, 84	6–12, 68	11, 153
Heb 2	8, 172	3, 64	6–9, 66	14, 74
17, 314	9, 310	7–10, 68	10, 65	15, 74, 154
Heb 4		9, 64	13, 56	
12, 121, 350	2 Pet 1	10, 56	14–15, 66	Apoc. 6–22, 311
15, 82	8, 228	12–14, 66	16, 56, 70, 71	5, 61
Heb 9	2 Pet 2	15, 64	16–17, 69, 70,	Wisdom 2
12, 80	20–22, 79, 156	15–17, 68	154	23, 120
23–10	2 Pet 3	18, 67	18, 64, 65	1 QWar Scroll, 162
18, 310	3–9, 162	18–25, 67		1 Enoch 62–63, 164
27, 76	7, 118	19, 63, 65	Jude 1	1 Enoch 100–108,
Heb 10	7–9, 82	20, 67	20–21, 30	162
14, 209	8–9, 84	22, 56	Jude 6, 162	1 Enoch, 164
19, 347	9, 89	22–23, 67		2 Baruch, 164
24–25, 31	15, 104	24–26, 68	Rev 1	4 Ezra, 164, 165
	2 Pet., 125	27, 64, 66	16, 121	
Heb 11		1 John 3	Rev 3, 329	
4, 60, 65, 68	2 Peter 3	4–7, 64	1–6, 179	

439

GENERAL

ἀγοράζειν, 101
ἀθυμία, 5
ἀπαρχήν, 104
ἀρραβών, 104
βασιλείας, 93
διακονία, 355
ἐξιλασμός, 105
εὐαγγέλιον, 93, 96
ἡγιάσθητε, 78
καινὴ κτίσις, 107
κρίμα, 100
Κύριος, 105
μακάριοι, 94
μακροθυμία, 100, 104, 105, 106
μακρόθυμος, 105
μείνατε, 107
ὀργή, 105
πνεῦμα, 103
Πνεύματι Θεοῦ, 103
σάρξ, 103
Σάρξ, 229
τέλος, 103
ὑγιαινούσῃ, 176

4th Ecumenical Council, 9
10th Mountain Division, 133
95 theses, 77

AAPC, 23, 24, 25, 26, 33, 35
Abelites, 58
able-bodied, temporarily, xii, 362, 364, 365, 366, 367, 368, 369, 370, 374, 375, 376, 377
Abrahamic Covenant, 165, 221, 222
acedia, 155
Addis Ababa, Ethiopia, 265
adelphos, 70
adikia, 153
Adonai, 177
Africa's Women's Caucus, 41
African National Congress, 253
agape, 203, 206, 207, 208, 210
aggiornamento, 141
AIDS, 41, 42, 48, 49, 50, 51, 382, 389
American Association of Addictive Medicine, 182
American Association of Pastoral Counselors, 23, 25, 26
American Correctional Chaplaincy Association, 231
American Counseling Association, 24
American Foundation of Religion and Psychiatry, 25
American Psychological Association, 23, 213
Americans with Disabilities Act, 1990, xii
Amhara, 265, 268, 269, 270
Amharanization, 268
androcentrism, 44
Annihilationism, 114, 117, 122, 123, 128, 131

anomia, 153
ANOVA, 208
Antichrists, 56
Anti-Climacus, 87
antinomianism, 244
APA, 23, 24, 35
apocatastasis, 336
Apostles' Creed, 276
Arminian, 223
Army, U.S., 133
Army, U.S., Chaplaincy, 232

Babel, tower of, 302
Bahai, 301
bisexual, 45
Black Angus Steakhouse, 233
Blanton-Peale Institute and Counseling Center, 25
Boko Haram Violence, 133
Brexit, 91
Buddhist/s, 288, 293
Byzantine, 150

Calcedonian Character, 345
Capernaum, 329
care of souls, 18
Caribbean, 44
cataphatic, 371
Catholic Reformation, 18
Chalcedonian doctrine, 9
Chaldean, 150
chiasm, 58
Chorazin, 329
Christian eternal security, 215
cochlear implant, 363
communio peccatorum, 325
communio sanctorum, 276
communion of saints, 276
community of spirit, 333
community-of-the-baptized, 334
community-of-the-cross, 334
concupiscence, threefold, 154
conjurer, sistah, 189
corrective rape, 48, 51
Council of Chalcedon, 140
Council of Constantinople III, 140
Council of Ephesus, 140
Council of Nicaea, 139
Council of Trent, 154, 156, 157, 158
Counter-Reformation, 18
countertransference, 181, 186, 187
CPE, 25
cultural countertransference, 187
cultural transference, 187
culturally-centered theology, 46

dāmīm, 302
Davidic covenant, 221
Day of Atonement, 101
deaf-mute, 373
Decalogue, 88, 98, 153, 240
dehumaninising, 44
deontology, 231, 238, 239
Derg regime, 268, 269

devil, 58, 64, 70, 81, 128, 156, 178, 349, 373, 374
Diaspora Jews, 164
divine impassibility, 342
double-dutched readings, 191
Down Syndrome, 361, 363, 367, 368
durchkreuzen, 356
Dynamic Absolutism, 231, 235, 237, 243

Eastern Orthodox Churches, 156
Eastern Rite Catholics, 150
easy-believism, 223
ecclesia, 297
ecclesia triumphans, 336
Eden, 88, 219
EECMY, 271, 273, 280
ego eimi ho on, 220, 221
ego mechanisms, 4
ekklesia, 48, 57, 255
Elect of God, 267
Election, 128
'ĕmet, 220, 225
Epistemology, 6
epitome of eternal being, 124
Eritrean priests, 271
eros, 206, 207, 208
eschatology, 117
eschaton, 96, 113, 114, 115, 117, 120, 126, 332, 336
Essenes, 255
eternal security, 215
ethics, 17, 24, 27, 35, 49, 65, 96, 98, 109, 162, 169, 223, 353
Ethiopia, 266
Ethiopian Constitution, 269
Ethiopian Orthodox Church (EOC), 266
Eucharist, 158, 276, 277
Evangelical Church Mekane Yesus, 271
Evangelical Theological Society, 235
evil, problem of, 320, 321, 323
exegesis, 7, 163
extra nos, 98, 274

Faranani Facilitation Services, 197
Fathers of the English Dominican Province, 152
FDRE, 269
Federal Democratic Republic of Ethiopia, 269
feminist theology, 44, 45
fertile crescent, 315
FICA Spiritual Assessment, 32
Final Judgment, 161, 162, 163, 164, 165, 166, 167, 168, 169, 170
fomes peccati, 154
Four Noble Truths, 288
fundamentalists, 6, 7, 238

ga'al, 101
găraš, 218

440

Garden of Eden, 4, 60, 126, 241
gay, 45
Gay Lobby, 150
gebbar, 267
Gebere-maheber, 269
gender inequality, 43
generalism, 244
genocide, 45
Global Aids Update, 51
God's perfect plan, 34
Golden Rule, 238, 240, 243, 244, 250
Gospel Project, The, 223

ḥāmās, 302
harmatia, 153
ḥaṭṭā't, 302
Hebrew midwives, 237
Hebrew parallelism, 59
hell, 115, 117, 118, 119, 120, 121, 122, 123, 124, 125, 126, 127, 226, 252
ḥesed, 220, 225, 382
hilasmos, 66
Hitlerist fanatics, 300
HIV, 41, 42, 43, 48, 49, 50, 51, 137, 313
HIV/AIDS, 43, 50
HIV-Positive Husbands, 133
Holy Communion, 276, 277
homo-ousios, 140
homosexuality, 46, 48, 52, 78, 135, 137, 138
horribile dictum, 313
Human Rights Watch, 265
hyperkinetic, 198
hypostasis, 140

I am who I am, 220
Imago Dei, 7, 232, 250, 251, 254, 261, 263, 324
immortality, 238
impassibility, divine, 342
In die Skriflig/In Luce Verbi, 68
in nobis, 98
in persona Christi Capitis., 157
inculturation, 46

Jean-Marc Fischer Foundation, 2
Jeg vet på hvem jeg tror, 84
Jerusalem, 155, 163, 164, 306, 309
Johannesburg, 51

kahal, 255
Kalam Cosmological Argument, 238
kenosis, 353, 354
kenotic love, 260
Kenya, 49
Kingdom of God, 73, 91, 92, 93, 94, 95, 96, 97, 98, 99, 100, 102, 104, 106, 107, 109, 113, 118, 406
Kingdom of Heaven, 91, 93, 94, 96
Kohelet, 300, 309
koinōnia, 56, 57, 63, 64, 65, 67, 68, 69, 70, 71

kurisakos, 255
Kwa Thema, 51
Kwazulu-Natal Church AIDS Network, 50
KZNCAN, 50
L'Arche community, 375
Land Act, 1913, South Africa, 260
Langham Literature, 55
Laodiceans, 175
Last Day, 108
Legality and License, 244
leitmotif, 93
lesbian/s, 45, 51
LGTBIQ, 41, 45, 46, 48, 51, 52
liberation theology, 43
libertinism, 109
Loci Communes rerum theologicarum, 82
logos, 65, 66
Lone Ranger Christianity, x
lovelessness, 29
Love-Styles Theory, 207
ludus, 207, 208, 212

Magisterium, 151
Magnificat, 142
mania, 207, 208
manic defenses, 4
Maronite, 150
Marxist-Leninist, 269
Marxist-Socialist regime, 268
metamelomai, 155
metanoeō, 155
metanoia, 155
mete haymanot, 273
midwifery, 189, 190
midwifing, 181, 188, 192, 193
mikro/teroj, 166
misotheists, 318
Monument to the Victorious Fatherland, 233
Mormons, 301
Mosaic covenant, 221
mujerista, 44, 45

narcissism, 3
narcissistic fantasies, 3
Nazi crimes, 234
Nazi Germany, 234
Nazis, 252
New covenant, 221
Noahic covenant, 221, 222
nomism, 109
Non-being, 123
Non-Conflicting Absolutism, 235
normate, 362
North Korea, 233
Nunciature, 150

Opus Dei, 140
Oromiya, 271
Oromo, 265
Oromo Protests, 265
Oromo slaves, 271
ousia, 140
Ovral, 145

Oxford Group, 183

padah, 101
paradigm shift, 35
parenesis, 164
participatio Christi, 258, 354
particularism, 113, 114, 117, 127, 128, 131
particularist, 118, 128, 130
Passover-Exodus Theme, 98
Pastoral Care Council of the ACT, 2016, 21, 22
patriarchy, 44
Patristic Theology, 8
peccata, 153
peccatorum communio, 325
pentimento, 185
perichoretic unity, 341
phileo, 206
plurality of spirit, 333
polis, 255
porneia, 153
Potong River, 233
povres avugles, 364
POW Medals, 233
pragma, 207, 208
Principleism, 235
Principleist, 235, 237
prison chaplaincy, Texas, 232
pro nobis, 98
problem of evil, 320, 321, 323
protohistorical, 60
protohistory, 56
protology, 325
psychiatry, 27
psychoheresy, 6
Pueblo, 232, 233
Puritan Paralysis, 223
Pyongyang, 233

Qiang, 55
qua fide in nobis, 274
queer, 45

ra'ah, 302
raeša', 302
rape, 43, 51, 52
rape, corrective, 48
redemptibility of disability, 375
Relationship Assessment Scale, 208
Relationship Questionnaire, 208
Robert Grainger Beckett Prize, 55
Roman Catholic Church, 46
Roman Pontiff, 150
Romanian Academy of Science, xii, 284
Royal Man, The, 341
ruach, 130

Sacrament of Penance, 149, 156, 157
Sacred Tradition, 151
Sakharov Prize, 313
ṣālaḥ, 218
sanctorum communio, 325, 333, 337, 338

Sanctorum Communio, 317, 318, 319, 322, 323, 324, 325, 333, 337, 329, 330, 331, 335, 336, 337, 338
Sankofa-Kairos Theology, 41
sapphire, 300
Satan, 60, 61, 63, 65, 71, 118, 223, 234, 250, 312, 371, 373
scapegoating, 4
Scarlet Thread, 251
Second Temple, 162
Second Temple Judaism, 165
See of Rome, 150
self-centeredness, 29
self-scapegoating, 4
sex work, 43
sexism, 44
shaah, 62
Shalom, 88
sheol, 115
shith, 60
simul justus et peccator, 76
Sinai, 219
sistah conjurer, 189
situationism, 244
Sitz im Leben, 303
skotos, 153
Small Window of Time, 241
Sodom, 46
sola fide, 216, 223
sola gratia, 216, 223, 266, 273
Soli Deo Gloria, 229
solo Christos, 216
spirit, community of, 333
spirit, plurality of, 333

spirit, unity of, 333
spiritual warfare, 5
storge, 206, 207, 208
sub-Saharan Africa, 51
synergy, 39
System Legality, 244

taboo themes, 53
teleological/eschatological worldview, 239
Teleological-Deontological Analysis, 246
teleology, 231, 238, 239
temporarily able-bodied, xii, 362, 364, 365, 366, 367, 368, 369, 370, 374, 375, 376, 377
Ten Commandments, 98, 152, 153
Texas Department of Criminal Justice, xi, xii, xiii, 231
Texas prison chaplaincy, 232
theodicy, 91, 113, 292, 308, 311, 312, 319, 320, 321, 322, 323, 324, 338, 375, 377
theosis, 68
theotokos, 140
Tigrians, 270
Time Zone, 241, 242
to'ebah, 302
traditionists, 117
transference, 181, 185, 186, 187, 295
transgender, 45
transgenerationally, 186
Triadological, 6
Triangular Theory of Love, 207

unity of spirit, 333
universalism, 113, 114, 117, 118, 121, 127, 128, 131
universalist, 117, 119, 128
USS *Pueblo*, 233
utilitarianism, 244

Vatican II, 15, 134, 137, 141, 146, 149, 151
vida cotidiana, 45
virgin Jerusalem, 306

womanism, 187, 188, 190
womanist, 41, 44, 181, 187, 188, 190, 384
womanist theology, 44, 181, 188
worldview, teleological/eschatological, 239

Yahweh, 221
yatab, 62
Yesidi women, 313
YHWH, 107

Zealots, 255
zemenawinet, 268
Zophar, 307
Zulu groups, 301

Other Books by Maness

Would You Lie to Save a Life?
A Theology on the Ethics of Love
Love Will Find a Way Home

How We Saved Texas Prison Chaplaincy 2011
Immeasurable Value of Religion, Volunteers and Their Chaplains

Heaven
Treasures of Our Everlasting Rest

When Texas Prison Scams Religion
Stop the Fools' Parade of … Cover Up

Heart of the Living God
Love, Free Will, Foreknowledge, Heaven--
A Theology on the Treasure of Love

Ocean Devotions
From the Hold of Charles H. Spurgeon
Master of Mariner Metaphors

www.PreciousHeart.net

Other Books from *Testamentum Imperium*

Practicality of Grace in Protestant Theology
Foreword by Peter Lillback
President of Westminster
Theological Seminary

Edited by Michael G. Maness &
Kevaughn Mattis

Perspectives on Eternal Security
Biblical, Historical, and Philosophical
Foreword by H. Wayne House
Distinguished Professor of Theology & Law
Faith International University and Seminary

Edited by Kirk R. MacGregor &
Kevaughn Mattis

www.PreciousHeart.net/ti

www.ingramcontent.com/pod-product-compliance
Lightning Source LLC
Chambersburg PA
CBHW071223290426
44108CB00013B/1270